The Family

ADDISON-WESLEY PUBLISHING COMPANY Reading, Massachusetts
Menlo Park, California • London • Amsterdam • Don Mills, Ontario • Sydney

The Family

FUNCTIONS, CONFLICTS, AND SYMBOLS

Peter J. Stein Lehman College, City University of New York

Judith Richman Columbia University

Natalie Hannon Lehman College, City University of New York

ISBN 0-201-07362-5
ABCDEFGHIJ-AL-7987

Preface

OUR GOAL IN THIS BOOK IS TO PRESENT SIGNIFICANT ISSUES in the area of marriage and the family within a context of contemporary sociological theory. In the Introductory Essay, we briefly review the three major theoretical perspectives: the structural-functional, the conflict-Marxian, and the symbolic-interaction perspective. We suggest the aspects of reality these perspectives would lead one to focus on for purposes of explanation and prediction. In the introduction to each chapter, we raise specific questions from the three frameworks which are meant to guide the reader in analyzing the particular articles.

Our selection of articles reflects the view that the paramount issue relative to the family, as well as to the rest of society, is that of inequality. Within the family, differential power is linked to sex status and to age status. Many of the readings focus on problems and conflicts within the family arising out of these inequalities. In addition, a number of alternatives to the traditional nuclear family which have arisen as a challenge to these inequalities are presented. Inequality between families with regard to economic resources, power, and prestige reflects the class and racial positions of families within the societal stratification system. Many of the articles examine these inequalities. In the Introductory Essay, we discuss some of the dimensions of sex, age, class, and racial inequality which have consequences for family functioning.

The book is divided into three parts. Part One offers a macroperspective encompassing the contemporary American family, historical and cross-cultural perspectives, and linkages between family and other institutions and social services. Part Two is a microperspective focusing on the internal development of the family through the life cycle. It includes chapters on courtship, marital dynamics, socialization and parenthood, the later years, and family dissolution. Part Three deals with the family and social change. It includes chapters focusing on alternatives within the nuclear family, alternatives to the nuclear family, and general theoretical analyses on the future of the family.

The work in this book reflects a full partnership among the three editors. The order of authorship reflects the first editor's longer association with the project, while the remaining order is random.

The editors thank Henry Etzkowitz for his critical comments; Lorraine Jordan and Gia Pulliza for their typing, organizational skills, and general support; and Jan Zyniewski, Amy-Beth Snell, Sharon Rodkin, Daphne Joslin, Bob Roher, Lee Heimlich, and Arlene Fergusen for their valued assistance. We warmly thank our editors at Addison-Wesley for their patience and encouragement throughout this project. We also thank the Groves Conference on Sex Roles and the Family which met in Dubrovnik, Yugoslavia, in June of 1975 for bringing us together.

Peter Stein expresses many thanks to Lynda Glennon and Janet Kohen for their encouragement in the development of the book; Roberta Froome and Kathy Roblee Baker for their research aid; and current colleagues in the Department of Sociology at Lehman College and former colleagues at Rutgers University for their support.

Judith Richman expresses appreciation to Maureen Berman, Jennie Kline, Mary Lennon, Irene Bach, her friends in the Social Psychiatry Research Unit and the Psychiatric Epidemiology Training Program at Columbia University, and her parents. This book is for Henry Etzkowitz, with love.

Natalie Hannon thanks Mary Powers, her friends at Fordham University, and her colleagues at Lehman College. And her special gratitude to Peter Hannon.

New York City
January 1977

P.J.S.
J.R.
N.H.

Contents

Introductory Essay

Sociological Perspectives on the Family under Conditions of Inequality

There is the scent of sweet lilacs in the air. The sun is slowly rising to its midday peak as the sounds of organ music spill from the place of worship into the courtyard. Waiting by the side entrance is a tall, handsome young man wearing a tuxedo and a pale blue shirt. Standing by the front entrance is a lovely young woman wearing a long-flowing white gown, holding a bouquet of roses. An older gentleman stands by her side, periodically holding her left hand in a reassuring manner. They are waiting for the right chord that will signal the appropriate time to enter the place of worship, to walk down the aisle, and to take their places at the altar. Parents, relatives, friends, and the clergy are already waiting in their right places. The chord strikes; the bride and her father enter, and in their unique way recreate the beginning of a marital drama that involves several million Americans every year.

MOST, IF NOT ALL, READERS WILL HAVE EXPERIENCED BEING a member or a guest at a similar wedding. We will have witnessed a ceremony which we have learned to regard as important, and one which is defined as important by the social order. As guests, we bring our point of view and perspective on marriage, weddings, and the prospective bride and groom. We might inquire about the ages of the bride and groom, whether a good match has been made, where the couple will honeymoon, and where they intend to live. We might reflect on the location of the wedding, its lavishness, and the number of people attending.

1

SOCIOLOGICAL PERSPECTIVES

Sociologists at the wedding will also notice these things. Additionally, however, they bring a distinctive perspective which enables them to relate the wedding event to the larger societal structure and its cultural context. They are at once observers and interpreters of the social event. They will view the meaning of the event in terms of the society and social group in which it occurs. The sociologists' focus would move away from the specific wedding and the specific people involved to a more general examination of patterns and regularities that are likely to occur, regardless of the individuals who participate in a wedding on any one day. Sociologists would be more interested in the effects of early marriages on the longevity of marriage than in the specific age of a given bride or groom. The sociologist would have greater interest in the reasons men and women give for marrying than in the reasons a specific couple married. Sociologists would be more interested in the influence of religion on marriage and the selection of marriage partners than on the specific religious affiliation of the newly married couple. The sociological perspective directs us to focus on those details that are repetitive and patterned; details that are not unique to a specific situation or specific persons in that situation. As part of this analysis, a sociologist might ask some of the following questions:

1. What are some of the consequences of the wedding event for the bride and groom, their respective families, and the larger groups to which they belong, such as their religious or social class groups?

2. How does the economic system benefit from the creation of a new family unit?

3. What kinds of interaction take place between brides and grooms? What kinds of messages do they communicate to let people know they are in love?

Each question assumes a different set of perspectives for analyzing social reality. Since answers are only as good as the questions asked, we start by suggesting the kinds of questions that might be asked by sociologists using three major sociological frameworks. Although the three preceding questions are all sociological, each is derived from a different perspective. The first question represents a structural-functional approach, the second question represents a conflict approach, and the third question represents a symbolic interaction approach. Each perspective determines the ways in which each sociologist, possessing that perspective, would analyze a social situation.

The Structural-Functional Perspective

The structural-functional perspective is a perspective which is concerned with social order and its persistence in society. In particular, it seeks to

explain how the different subunits of society fit together and are interdependent. The structural-functional model rests on the assumption that
the family and other institutions (the economy, polity, religion, and
education) are all part of the same social system, called society, and that
there is some degree of equity in the exchange of resources and services
between the various institutions composing the system. There is a situation of relative equilibrium.

Functional theorists have varied in their differential emphasis on
societal integration and equilibrium. Some focus primary attention on
institutions and their functions which contribute to societal integration.
Here, the family would be viewed as a consensus-generating institution.
For example, children are reared and socialized within families to accept
the values and goals that are shared by the society, and that help integrate it. Other functional theorists consider not only the positive functions of institutions but also the negative ones, called dysfunctions. They
conceive of society as a series of subunits. Social processes and structures
can have positive consequences for some subgroups, while having
negative ones for other subgroups. Thus, an analysis of the marital roles
in the traditional nuclear family may include the negative consequences,
or dysfunctions, of the housewife/mother role for women. Alice Rossi in
"Transition to Parenthood" (Chapter 6) suggests that the traditional
maternal role is a frustrating and limiting one for women socialized to
have varied interests and expectations. In addition, these women often
transmit these frustrations to their children. Thus, the mother role is
seen to have some negative consequences for both women and children.

Social change occurs through gradual evolution and adaptation rather
than through revolutionary change or systemic conflict. Structurally
induced strains and tensions may lead to alternatives in the traditional
roles. Functional analysts would focus on possible alternative structures
to alleviate these strains. Nevertheless, these alternative structures are
more likely to involve limited modifications rather than basic systemic
changes. For example, women's dissatisfaction with roles in the traditional nuclear family has in part produced the "dual career" family, in
which both the husband and wife work, usually as professionals, and
share housework and child-rearing functions. Sometimes, due to the geographic availability of jobs, spouses must live in separate residences.
This leads to commuter marriages, which are analyzed by Naomi Gerstel
in Chapter 10. Commuter marriages involve modifications of the traditional nuclear family with respect to the woman's role and the geographical
separation of spouses. Yet, the basic dyadic structure is maintained, as is
the occupational structure to which the commuters must adapt.

Other alternatives to the nuclear family that suggest limited rather
than revolutionary change include "open marriage," and "swinging."
Both of these variations, as discussed in Chapter 10, maintain the basic
dyadic relationship, though they broaden involvement in outside relationships.

With respect to the interdependence of social units, institutions are seen as having certain functions, that is, certain consequences, for the larger society. For example, the family historically has performed a number of functions including socialization, procreation, status placement of children, social control, and tension management. These processes have consequences both for family members and for the larger society in which the family exists. Socialization offers an example: while parents introduce social values to their children, they also thereby help to maintain the existing social order relying on such values.

Using a structural-functional perspective a sociologist at the wedding might be concerned with the following questions:

1. What are the consequences of the reception for integrating the family of procreation with the two families of orientation? What are the sources of strain for the different groups involved?

2. What are the functions of the ritual of the wedding ceremony? and for whom?

3. How are the larger societal values reflected in this event?

4. What types of alternative rituals might fulfill the functions of the traditional wedding ceremony?

The Conflict Perspective

In contrast to the structural-functional perspective, the conflict perspective is based on the premise that conflict and coercion are not only endemic to social structures but are also the key explanatory concepts to understand how societies operate. The basis for conflict and coercion in societies is structured social inequality stemming from power and control vested in a privileged elite. Marxist analysis focuses on economic inequality in capitalist societies and on the control of the means of production by the privileged class. The family structure aids in the maintenance of economic control through the intergenerational inheritance of wealth. For example, 19th-century entrepreneurs such as Henry Ford and John D. Rockefeller built up huge family fortunes which they passed on to their children and grandchildren. In addition, the family has traditionally differentiated roles such that one person, the wife, spends a good proportion of her time as consumer of the goods produced by the economy. A large advertising apparatus is directed at encouraging wives to buy specific products for the home. Finally, the family socializes its young males to fit into the economy as part of a compliant labor force, and its young females to become future socializers and consumers.

Another conflict perspective focuses on inequality with respect to authority relationships. Critical theory proponents view authority exercised in the family as directly connected to authority exercised in the workplace. One aspect of socialization in the family involves the learning of obedience to authorities. Thus, children are first taught to do as they are told by their parents, and later extend this to manifesting deference to their future employers.

In contrast to functional analysts, conflict theorists see the basic contradictions in the social system as producing confrontations and revolutionary social change. An example of revolutionary social change with respect to both economic inequality and sexual inequality in the family can be seen in the kibbutz, a form of collective settlement in Israel. Yonina Talmon-Garber, in Chapter 2, discusses the changes in structural arrangements that were instituted in the kibbutz and also gradually modified in subsequent years.

Sexual inequality seems to be inherent in many male-female relationships. Some radical feminists* argue that positive heterosexual love relationships are not possible. Male-female relationships are ridden with conflicts because they are between two unequals. Anne Koedt in "Lesbianism and Feminism" (Chapter 11) sees this conflict as one root of lesbianism, a radical alternative to the nuclear family which replaces totally the heterosexual dyad with a dyad composed of members of the same sex.

Again, focusing on the wedding ceremony, questions the conflict theorist might ask would include:

1. What would happen to a sector of the capitalist economy, namely the marriage industry, an eight million dollars a year business, if the marriage rate declined considerably?

2. What are the contradictions between the wedding ceremony and the needs of the different groups involved?

It should be noted that the structural-functional perspective and the conflict perspective are not mutually exclusive, but often have broad areas of overlap. Both the functionalist and the conflict perspectives deal with the differentiation of society into different social groups with specific needs and interests. These groups are integrated into the society based on interdependencies, a point which is stressed by the structural functionalist perspective; while at the same time conflicting with each other based on contradictory interests, a point stressed by the conflict perspective.

The Symbolic Interaction Perspective

The symbolic interaction perspective essentially focuses on the process by which people interact in face-to-face communication. It is concerned with the meanings of symbols which exist in face-to-face communications

---

*See, for example, Shulamith Firestone, *The Dialectics of Sex*. New York: William Morrow, 1970.

and with how meanings come to be learned and shared within a culture. The perspective can be exemplified by an analysis of family interaction whereby parents call their children by their first names, while children generally call their parents by their titles, Mother and Father, or Mom and Dad. A symbolic interaction theorist might be concerned with how titles are used to symbolize authority relationships between parents and children.

The process by which meanings come to be learned and shared within the context of a specific culture is the process of socialization. While socialization occurs throughout life, the family is the unit in which most persons receive their first and most intensive socializing experiences. Particularly important in the socialization process is the learning of sex roles. In most societies, including ours, boys and girls are trained to behave, think, and feel in different ways, and to learn different things.

In addition to socializing children within the family, marital partners must define and construct the reality of their marriage. Peter Berger and Hansfried Kellner, in "Marriage and the Construction of Reality" (Chapter 5) analyze the process by which marital couples do this through interaction and conversation.

Through socialization, the family becomes the link between the society and the individual. Certain social processes that occur in the larger society are mirrored at the microlevel in the family. For example, the idea of authority and subordination, a major mode of social control in schools, at work, and in other institutions, is first learned in the home. The processes establishing the authority of adults in the family are repeated in other social settings. The family introduces, perpetuates, and reinforces these meanings.

R.D. Laing, in "Mystification, Confusion, and Conflict" (Chapter 6), analyzes the process by which parents sometimes use their authority to define the reality of their children for them. This reality is in accordance with the needs of the parents rather than those of the children. For example, a parent who is tired may say to a child: "I'm sure you feel tired, darling, and want to go to bed now, don't you?"

While observing the wedding, the symbolic interactionist might ask:

1. How and where did the participants in the wedding ceremony come to define the event as a significant one and develop the motivation to participate in it?

2. What is the significance of the seating arrangement at the wedding?

3. How do the different participants define the situation? What are the consequences of those definitions for the participants such as the clergy?

Hence, the perspectives determine the specific questions which the sociologist is interested in asking. They are useful in providing a framework for analyzing social phenomena.

INEQUALITY AND THE FAMILY

A study of the family is meaningful only if it examines not only the behavior within the family itself but also the links between the family and other aspects of society.

One key aspect of all societies is the differentiation of its members into different statuses and groups. These groups not only assume different roles but also assume roles that are unequal in regard to material resources, social prestige, and power. The foundations of inequality and the processes that develop and maintain it vary substantially from one historical period to another, and between societies exhibiting different modes of production and societies held together by different ideologies. Likewise, the groups that bring about challenges to the structures of inequality also vary between societies. However, the prevalence and strength of these groups partially determine the perpetuation or transformation of institutions and of societies.

Many of the issues dealt with in Parts One and Two of this book stem from inequalities within the family, and within the society. Some of the changes in family structure, examined in Part Three and in Chapter 2, "Cross-cultural Perspectives on the Family," have developed as a result of attempts to rectify the existing inequalities.

The structural-functional and conflict perspectives focus on inequality as a major dimension of institutions. The former perspective looks at the positive and negative consequences of different processes for different social groups, while the latter perspective focuses on the contradictions between the needs of various groups and on the conflicts which are expected to arise from these contradictions.

In order to provide a background for analyzing the persistence and alteration of family structures, this section will deal with four main dimensions of inequality relevant to the family: class, sex, race, and age.

Class Inequality

Despite popular myths of widespread wealth and equality of income in the United States, the basic income distribution is about the same now as it was 30 years ago. Extensive poverty accompanies great concentrations of wealth and power. In 1971, the top 20 percent of all families received 41.6 percent of the total aggregate income while the bottom 20 percent received 5.5 percent of the total income.[1] This bottom 20 percent had incomes below the Bureau of Labor Statistics' "lower budget level," which is $6,960 for a family of four.

Careful examination by economists and sociologists of who controls corporate wealth reveals a striking concentration of control. Approximately "one percent of the American adult population owns about 80 percent of all publicly held corporate stock."[2] A few thousand propertied persons and families claim controlling ownership of the corporate world. Of these, most inherited their wealth, and most of their income came from property–capital gains, dividends, and interest.[3]

The impact of income and wealth inequality on families can be traced through an examination of the life chances and life-styles available to families. According to Max Weber, life chances are primarily derived from one's economic resources, whereas life-style has to do with the possession of honor. But in our industrial society, income, wealth, and honor are interrelated in complex ways so that economic factors influence the full range of the human condition. Life chances are regarded as all those things which:

> . . .(1) better-off people can purchase (good education, good medical care, comfortable homes, fine vacations, expert services of all kinds, safe and satisfying occupations) and which poorer people would also purchase if they had the money; (2) these things make life easier, longer, healthier, and more enjoyable; and (3) they are not purchased primarily or mainly for the honor they might also bring.[4]

Life-styles, by contrast, are:

> . . .things to be bought and patterns of conduct to be followed that commend themselves, if at all, chiefly because of the prestige they bring: the 'right' schools, clubs, neighborhoods, suburbs, cars and vacation spots.[5]

When both the use of economic resources (income, wealth) and the search for honor and prestige are involved, the interconnection between these factors cannot be easily separated.

Life chances are closely related to positions on the socioeconomic ladder as defined by occupation, education, and income. In summary, the higher the income, prestige, and socioeconomic standing: (1) the longer one's life; (2) the better the health and medical care received; (3) the better the care for mental problems. Also, the higher the socioeconomic status, the less frequent the serious mental breakdown; the greater the rate of participation in community affairs, and, with that, the greater sense of efficacy and control over one's own destiny; the lower the involvement with detectable criminal deviance, arrest, and imprisonment; the smaller the average number of children per family and the greater control over family size; and the lower the rate of separations, and of families broken by death or desertion.[6] Family life is, therefore, determined largely by the family's class.

Elite families The elite or "privileged strata" include persons with "high degrees of control over flows of rewards and resources, or with special access to those controlling them, and those enjoying freedoms and choices not normally available to all."[7] It constitutes an estimated one to three percent of all American families. The economic security of these families allows them to maintain their important social position through successive generations and their continued hold on privileged access to life chances and life-styles. Wealthy families can afford an elaborate support structure to take care of the details of everyday life. Persons can be hired to cook and prepare meals, to do laundry, and to care for the children. Many of the problems of the division of labor that become issues between spouses in middle class and working class families can be avoided by the wealthy simply by hiring others to do this work.

Wealth becomes a means of social control within the family:

> since the status of all depend on the inherited wealth that is transferable in part through marital arrangements.... The extended family seeks to control mate selection, a process supported partly by the relative isolation of the upper class and partly through the comparatively great rewards it can offer those who go along with its wishes.[8]

Middle-class families Middle-class families with husbands in white collar jobs are characterized by the nuclear family structure with extended kin ties. Upper middle-class families, typically headed by professionals, managers of large companies, and owners of smaller businesses are relatively well off, while lower middle-class families, typically headed by clerical and sales workers, often have difficulty making ends meet.

Although ideologically, most middle-class families posit an egalitarian relationship between husbands and wives, husbands actually have more power, as illustrated in Dair L. Gillespie's "Who Has the Power? The Marital Struggle" (Chapter 5), and Anne-Marie Ambert's "Swinging" (Chapter 10). Wives tend to work more to supplement family income than to pursue careers, although this is changing.

Working-class families Working-class families, those headed by blue collar workers, are typified by contact with extended family networks which provide an important source of support through visits and face-to-face interaction. Traditional roles of husband and wife are still operative, with the husband continuing to be the major breadwinner and head of the household. Thomas Cottle, in "Middle American Marriage," in Chapter 5 illustrates these roles in one working-class family.

The children and the house are primarily the wife's responsibility even though she may be employed full time outside of the home. Children are taught respect and obedience to authorities as discussed by Melvin Kohn in "Social Class and Parent-Child Relationships" (Chapter 7).

Lower-class families S. M. Miller identifies four types of lower-class families.[9] The stable poor constitute regularly employed, low-skilled, and low-salaried stable families; the strained reflect a secure economic pattern, but an unstable family life; the copers represent families having economic difficulties, while keeping their families intact; and the unstable have neither economic nor personal stability. All of these types of families are at or very near the poverty level. Governmental attempts to aid some of these families are examined by Robert Staples' "Public Policy and the Changing Status of Black Families" (Chapter 3).

Competing demands within the family for the inadequate economic resources may result in conflict and tension. Some of this is manifested in desertion, separation, and divorce.

Sex Inequality

Women as a group have experienced additional obstacles to choice and mobility beyond those of social class origin. Social ideology, buttressed by the United States legal and economic system, has placed women in a subordinate position to men.

Sex role ideology following the industrial revolution located women's main role in the home and viewed their gratification as deriving from husband, children, and the homemaker role. In contrast to this ideology, the actual female role has undergone a shift in recent history. A major change in the nature of the American labor force during the 20th century has involved the movement of married women into the labor force. Around 1900, almost all married women—rich and poor alike—stayed at home as full-time wives and mothers. Carl Degler cites a survey of slum districts in five large cities in 1893 which showed that only 5 percent of the wives were employed. In 1940, fewer than 17 percent of all married women in the United States worked. By 1960, 32 percent of all married women worked.[10] In terms of women as a whole, 40 percent of all women over sixteen were in the labor force in 1968.[11] By 1974, 45.7 percent of these women were in the labor force.[12] In addition, the most rapid increase in labor-force participation occurred among mothers of children under six. This group increased its labor-force participation by over 60 percent during the 1960s. By 1968, almost one-third of such mothers worked.

The consequences of this shift in the female role are subject to debate. However, much of the research on sex roles tends to suggest that neither the traditional female role centering on the home, nor the role of employed wife and mother constitute satisfactory options for women. On the one hand, many researchers have documented the sense of powerlessness, monotony, and isolation that many full-time housewives experience as a function of their primary social role. On the other hand, employed women are overburdened by their performance of two full-time roles—the role of worker in the labor force and the role of wife-mother-housekeeper at home. In addition, these women are subject to sex discrimination within the occupational structure.

The traditional female role within the family has been seen to require limited skill, and also to lack social prestige. It thus fails to provide a sense of personal accomplishment for many women. Betty Friedan, from her interviews with upper middle-class American women, concluded:

> Basic decisions as to the upbringing of children, interior decoration, menu planning, budget, education, and recreation do involve intelligence, of course. But as it was put to me by one of the few home-and-family experts who saw the real absurdity of the feminine mystique, most housework, the part that still takes the most time, can be capably handled by an eight-year-old child.[13]

One aspect of the traditional role Friedan was describing involved that of consumer. In the lower social class, scarcity of money makes any satisfaction from this role difficult to attain. In addition, housework has been experienced by both middle-class and working-class women as monotonous, fragmented (involving a series of unconnected tasks), and pressured.[14]

Some sociologists have found that social relations are limited for housewives. Though housewives maintain social ties with relatives and friends, they are bound to the home for at least part of the day, especially when they have young children. Many housewives complain of loneliness and isolation. A key element in the motivation of women to work, next to the need for money, involves the desire to meet and be with other people.[15]

With respect to power or control over decision-making in marriage, a number of studies show that full-time housewives make fewer major decisions in contrast to employed women.[16] Blood and Wolfe tied this power difference to the economic or resource basis for power. "The availability of jobs means that women no longer necessarily depend on a husband (or father) for support."[17]

Employed women tend to have more power in marriages in contrast to that of housewives, but they nevertheless remain subordinate to their husbands. Dair Gillespie, in "Who has the Power? The Marital Struggle" (Chapter 5), discusses the sources of male dominance in marriage. One main source of power consists of men's financial resources and status. Women, in contrast to men, are clearly concentrated in the lower levels of the occupational structure and earn considerably less income than men. A statistical report compiled by Ehrlich *et al.*, (Table I.1) using United States Bureau of the Census data, illustrates the gap between male and female incomes. Additionally, the gap between the incomes of men and women has widened since 1955. By 1973, for every dollar earned by a male worker, a female worker earned 57 cents.

Greater education is another basis for male power. Although a greater number of women are going to college than ever before, the majority of students is still men. Women are still less likely to go to colleges than are men and are less likely to graduate once they are admitted to college.

Another basis for male dominance over women—employed and housewives alike—is rooted in the legal system of the United States. Lenore

**Table I.1 The median annual
income of full-time workers***

	Women	Men	W/M ratio
1955	$2,719	$4,252	0.64
1960	3,293	5,417	0.61
1965	3,823	6,375	0.60
1970	5,403	9,104	0.59
1973	6,488	11,468	0.57

*The Bureau of the Census defines a full-time worker as a person who
worked 35 hours or more a week for 50–52 weeks.
(From Howard J. Ehrlich *et al., Women and men: a socioeconomic factbook.*
Baltimore: Research Group One, 1975.)

Weitzman, in "To Love, Honor, and Obey?" (Chapter 3), surveys the dimensions of male dominance which are based on law, such as the husband's legal right to determine the family's residence and the definition of the husband as the head of the household.

In addition to having less power in marriage than men, employed women experience physical strain from competing demands of work and family. In a comparison of paid and nonpaid work of men and women, Michael Young and Peter Willmott found that in their British sample, housewives spent the least number of hours working, while full-time employed women spent the greatest numbers of hours working.[18]

In addition to physical strains, there are social-psychological strains relating to contradictory normative expectations in regard to family versus work demands, or "sociological ambivalence." Cynthia Epstein has suggested that men are more shielded from this type of conflict due to a societal hierarchy of values which postulate that work is supposed to come first for men.[19] This conflict particularly characterizes professional level occupations which require greater involvement, in time, at least. Willmott and Young found that the professional women in their sample were more involved in their work, but at the same time experienced more guilt about neglecting their families.[20]

Alternatives to the traditional nuclear family, found in Part III of this book, have been embraced by women seeking to alter the traditional balance of power between the sexes. Some of these alternatives maintain the basic family structure (see Naomi Gerstel's discussion of "Commuter Marriages" in Chapter 10) while other alternatives replace the family structure (see Ann Koedt's discussion of lesbianism and Peter Stein's discussion of singlehood in Chapter 11). In addition, other societies have consciously altered social structures and ideology to promote the equality between the sexes (see Yonina Talmon-Garber's discussion of the kibbutz in Israel and Ruth Sidel's discussion of China in Chapter 2).

Racial Inequality

Minorities, like women, have suffered particular barriers to choice and mobility due to societal discrimination. Racial and ethnic discrimination has served to limit their educational achievement, to exclude them from higher prestige occupations, to channel them into lower paying jobs, and to keep their level of unemployment high.

In this essay we limit our discussion of these factors by focusing on one major racial group, black Americans. Alphonso Pinkney, in "The Black Family" (Chapter 1), traces the impact of economic and social conditions on the organization and experiences of black families in the United States. Robert Staples, in "Public Policy and the Changing Status of Black Families" (Chapter 3), examines the impact of governmental policies and their ineffectiveness in trying to strengthen the structure of the black family. Both sociologists view the development of black families as a result of the historical interaction of blacks and whites. Pinkney notes that "with few exceptions, the distinctive features of black life in the United States today stem from the historical, social, and economic forces encountered...in North America (and black institutions) are a reflection of life in a racist society."

One way racism (and sexism) operates is through discrimination in employment. Data from the Census Bureau indicate that the income gap between black and white families continues, and in some respects the gap has increased. The median income for white families in 1972 was $11,550, while the median income for black families was $6860, or about 59 percent of the median income for white families. The jobless rate for blacks, after a brief improvement in the late 1960s, has returned to its historic two to one ratio.

The only group making gains in the direction of income equality are younger, well-educated black families. These young black families (with husbands under 35 years of age), in which both husband and wife work, had a median income of $11,800 in 1971, compared with $11,206 for similar white families. However, such families account for only ten percent of all black families. The other 90 percent of black families continue to bear the brunt of income inequality. Moreover, as Harrington Bryce notes:

> ...the rate of high school completion is 50 percent higher among white males than among black; the rate of college completion among males under 35 is four times higher among whites than blacks.... Unemployment among black teen-agers is over 35 percent. The percentage of housing with inadequate plumbing occupied by blacks remained about 30 percent during the sixties, despite economic gains. Black life expectancy (at age 25) is six years less than white; the black infant mortality rate far exceeds the white.[21]

Many of these statistics reflect the disproportionate number of poor families who are black. Andrew Billingsley suggests that black Americans form an ethnic subsociety with a class structure of its own. This class structure developed out of an interplay of historical, economic, and social forces.

By combining education, occupation, and residence with income, Billingsley offers a portrait of the social position of black families.[22] About 10 percent of black families are upper class, leading comfortable lives headed by highly successful professionals and/or business executives. Two distinct upper-class groups exist. The first is composed of "old families" with long histories of privilege, achievement, and social status. These families tend to be headed by doctors, judges, businessmen, and high government officials who reached the top over several generations. The second group, the "new upper class," consists of families headed by men who were upwardly mobile in one generation, whose parents and grandparents were not well off. Their achievement and success is based on their own ability and social support. These families have good incomes and can afford comfortable housing, entertainment, travel, and college education for their children.

Billingsley divides the black middle class into three distinct groups—upper, solid, and precarious middle class—distinguished by educational, income, and occupational achievement, by family life-style, and by the stability of their middle-class status. Family life tends to be stable, egalitarian, and achievement-oriented. Relative to white middle-class families, these families have lower incomes and less job security. Wives are more likely to work in the labor force.

There are also three lower-class groups. The men in the working non-poor hold steady jobs in the unionized, industrial sector, and are employed as factory workers, truck drivers, and other semiskilled occupations. The second and largest group are the working poor families whose heads work in unskilled and service occupations as janitors, porters, domestic workers, etc., but who do not earn enough money to raise their families out of poverty. They have little job security, and thus during the economic recession of the 1970s they were the first to lose their jobs. Though both husband and wife often work, their salaries are so low that they cannot improve their economic situation.

The last group, the nonworking poor, or the underclass, constitutes about 10 to 15 percent of all black families, yet receives most attention in the literature and in the public press. It consists of adults with little education, few marketable skills, and sporadic work histories. They are largely dependent upon support by relatives, friends, and public welfare. Family disorganization and sheer survival are problems facing this group of families.

More recently, Robert Hill, Research Director of the National Urban League, documented the strength of black families. Prominent characteristics of black families which are functional for their stability and survival include strong kinship bonds, strong work orientation, adaptable family roles, strong achievement orientation, and strong religious orientation. These factors reflect the strengths that help black families survive in our society.[23]

Age Inequality

Age, like class, sex, and race, is a basis of stratification within societies. Age strata differentiate groups of people in terms of their access to wealth, power, and prestige. Movement through the age structure is curvilinear in its relationship to power and wealth, in that the middle-aged have the greatest amount of power and wealth, while the young and the old are relatively powerless and tend to have little prestige and wealth. Neither the young nor the old are considered to be economically productive members of the society. They tend to be perceived as incompetent, and are treated accordingly.[24] For example, society's attitudes toward sexuality in the old and the young are alike. Neither group is supposed to be concerned with sexual behavior and, when they are, the behavior or concern is considered to be deviant and tends to be negatively sanctioned.

The powerlessness of the young is exemplified by their position in the family, and is engendered by the dependency, both financial and emotional, of children on their parents. Parents have the ability to use coercive methods to bring about desired attitudes and behaviors in their children. Melvin Kohn, in "Social Class and Parent-Child Relationships" (Chapter 7), shows how these methods are differentiated by class. Working-class parents are more likely to use physical punishment, while middle-class parents are likely to use emotional withdrawal to discipline their children.

The process of mystification discussed by R.D. Laing in "Mystification, Confusion and Conflict" (Chapter 6), further demonstrates the power of parents over children. Mystification is the process whereby one individual, usually a parent, defines the reality for another individual to meet his or her own needs and, in so doing, negates the needs of the other individual, usually a child.

With more sons and daughters pursuing higher education, their dependency on parents may continue until they are into their twenties. Even with older offspring, as suggested by Stein's "Singlehood: An Alternative to Marriage" (Chapter 11), parents may continue to exert power by influencing their children's mate selection. J. Richard Udry's study of counselors' files indicates the power of parents in determining their children's schools and social club memberships, which in turn influence who the children's friends and dates will be.[25]

Parents' power decreases as the children grow older and become economically independent and productive adults themselves. At this time, the parents, who may be entering old age, are beginning to lose power and prestige, both within the family and the larger society. With the exception of older members of the elite class and some elder politicians and businessmen who retain high power and prestige, most aged Americans have few important roles to play in our society.

Old age is the only stage of the life cycle in which people experience structural losses rather than gains:

> The major life tasks are basically finished, responsibility declines, and dependency may increase. There is severe alienation from central roles through widowhood and retirement; a loss of rewards from drastic declines in income, which is reduced by more than 50 percent after retirement....[26]

The elderly receive less than their proportionate share of economic rewards. Hence, a major problem for many of the aged is a lack of economic resources:

> Some seven million older people, more than one-third of the over-sixty-five population, are impoverished and must depend on someone else—their families or government—for income assistance.[27]

Although as a group, the elderly may be discriminated against in our society, research has shown that the elderly are not isolated. Only five percent of the population over 65 are institutionalized in the society.[28] Ethel Shanas, in "Family Kin Networks and Aging in Cross-Cultural Perspectives" (Chapter 8), presents evidence that the aged have frequent contact with their adult children. Other research by Paul Reiss, Leopold Rosenmayer, and Marvin Sussman tend to confirm Shanas' findings.[29] However, from these studies, we cannot assume that the elderly are important members of the kin network. As Irving Rosow points out:

> Because there is considerable intergenerational contact, we tend to conclude that this necessarily signifies emotional warmth and closeness between the actors...we should be careful about confusing the fact of association with its meaning to the participants.[30]

One way in which the elderly may become part of meaningful social networks is through communal living. Arlie Hochschild, in "Communal Life Styles for the Old" (Chapter 11), discusses the roles the elderly hold in an old-age community. The aged in this community become social-siblings so that they are not dependent on their kin networks for intimate communication. Age inequality is difficult to overcome since the two powerless groups, the young and the aged, have different interests. While the young people have hopes for the future, when they will have more power, many of the elderly have a feeling of hopelessness. These differing perspectives limit the motivation of these two groups to attempt to alter age inequality.

ORGANIZATION OF THE BOOK

This introductory essay has presented the reader with three theoretical perspectives for the study of the family under conditions of social inequality. Four major dimensions of social inequality—class, sex, race, and age were examined. Many of the articles in the book speak to the issues raised in this essay. Within each chapter, readers are guided to examine the articles from each of the three theoretical perspectives.

The articles in Part One, "The Family in Society: A Macroperspective," examine the family as a social unit within the context of the larger social system, in contemporary America, other time periods, and other cultures. Links between families and various social services round out the articles in Part One.

Articles in Part Two, "Within the Family: A Microperspective," examine social processes within the family, beginning with preparation for marriage through courtship, marital interaction, parenting, socialization, the later years of marriage, and the dissolution of marriages.

The articles in Part Three, "Social Change and the Nuclear Family," focus on variations within nuclear families, alternatives to the nuclear family, and the implication of social change for the family's future.

NOTES

1. Judah Matras, *Social inequality, stratification and mobility*. Englewood Cliffs, N.J.: Prentice-Hall, 1975, p. 25.

2. Charles Anderson, *Toward a new sociology*. Homewood, Ill.: Dorsey Press, 1974, p. 87.

3. *Ibid.*, p. 87.

4. Melvin Tumin, *Patterns of society*. Boston: Little, Brown, 1973, p. 104.

5. *Ibid.*, p. 104.

6. *Ibid.*, p. 104.

7. Judah Matras, p. 137.

8. David Schulz, *The changing family*. Englewood Cliffs, N.J.: Prentice-Hall, 1976, p. 35.

9. S. M. Miller, The American lower classes. *Soc. Res.* 31, 1964: 1–22.

10. Carl Degler, Revolution without ideology: the changing place of women in America. In Robert Jay Lifton (ed.), *The woman in America*. Boston: Beacon Press, 1964, pp. 193–210.

11. Eli Ginzberg, Introduction. In Robert Smuts, *Women and work in America*. New York: Schocken, 1971.

12. United States Department of Labor, *Handbook of labor statistics 1975*. Washington, D.C., p. 30.

13. Betty Friedan, *The feminine mystique*. New York: Dell, 1963.

14. Ann Oakley, *The sociology of housework*. New York: Pantheon, 1974.

15. See Ann Oakley, and Michael Young and Peter Willmot, *The symmetrical family*. New York: Pantheon, 1973.

16. See, for example, Robert Blood and Donald Wolfe, *Husbands and wives*. New York: The Free Press, 1960; Lois Wladis Hoffman, Parental relationships and the division of household tasks, in Lois Hoffman and Ivan Nye, *The employed mother in America*. Chicago: Rand McNally, 1963; David Heer, Dominance and the working wife. In Hoffman and Nye.

17. Blood and Wolfe.

18. Young and Willmott.

19. Cynthia Fuchs Epstein, *Woman's place*. Berkeley: University of California Press, 1971.

20. Young and Willmott.

21. As quoted in Tom Wicker, Up the ladder, but how fast? *New York Times*, July 22, 1973, Section 4, p. 13.

22. Andrew Billingsley, *Black families in white America*. Englewood Cliffs, N.J.: Prentice-Hall, 1968, p. 7.

23. Robert Hill, *The strengths of black families*. New York: Emerson Hall, 1972.

24. Anne Foner, Age in society. *American Behavioral Scientist* **19**, 1975: 144–165.

25. J. Richard Udry. *The social context of marriage*. Philadelphia: J. B. Lippincott, 1974.

26. Irving Rosow, *Socialization to old age*. Berkeley: University of California Press, 1974, p. 23.

27. Claire Townsend, *Old age: the last segregation*. New York: Bantam Books, 1970, p. 15.

28. Commission on Population Growth, *Population and the American future*. New York: New American Library, 1972, p. 100.

29. Paul Reiss, The extended kinship system: correlates of and attitudes on frequency of interaction, *Journal of Marriage and the Family* (November, 1962): 333–339; Leopold Rosenmayer, Family relations of the elderly, *Journal of Marriage and the Family* (November, 1968): 673–680; Marvin Sussman, Relationships of adult children with their parents in the United States, in Ethel Shanas and Gordon Streib (eds.), *Social structure and the family*. Englewood Cliffs, N.J.: Prentice-Hall, 1965, pp. 62–92.

30. Irving Rosow, Intergenerational relationships: problems and proposals. In Shanas and Streib, p. 375.

Part One

The Family in Society: A Macro-perspective

Chapter 1
Contemporary and Historical Perspectives

THIS CHAPTER PRESENTS AN ANALYSIS OF the contemporary American family, and its historical antecedents. The modal American family is based on the principle of monogamy and fits the modified nuclear family structure. The family is composed of one man paired with one woman and their possible offspring. Other kinship members generally maintain separate residences, but exchange resources and other forms of support. The nuclear family is the basic primary group in the society. As a primary group, it is concerned with the emotional needs and personality development of its members. The family serves other societal institutions by socializing individuals to fulfill necessary institutional roles, such as economic, political, and military ones. For example, the family is the key motivating force behind the performance of children in schools and workers in the labor force. In addition, the family is involved in the concentration and perpetuation of wealth and private property. It is also the main unit of consumption of goods and services.

The readings in this section analyze different family structures and functions, and identify sources of stability and conflict. William Goode presents a description of the American kinship structure with respect to its major dimensions: dating, courtship, mating, and relationships between husbands and wives. Contemporary American family functioning is contrasted to family functioning in other historical periods and in other cultures. For example, Goode shows how the structural closeness between husband and wife in American society engenders strain to a greater degree than in Hindu families, where contact between spouses is more limited. Another source of strain in America is engendered by the vague role obligations of husbands and wives. At the same time, Goode suggests that larger societal values promote basic adjustment between husbands and wives. Individuals are socialized to believe in monogamy and to avoid divorce.

Natalie Sokoloff, utilizing a Marxist framework, relates the low position of women in contemporary society to the structure and needs of the capitalist economy. While men serve as the producers of goods in the labor force, women function as consumers of goods and reproducers of the labor force. Since women's work in the home is not financially remunerated, they lose both prestige and the capacity to negotiate on their own in the labor market. They are also excluded from most of the sources of decision-making and power in the larger society.

Al Pinkney analyzes the black family within the context of historical and contemporary racial discrimination in American society. He focuses particularly on the material conditions that are experienced by black families to a much greater degree than white families: low family income, inferior housing, and fewer material resources within their homes. In addition, Pinkney deals with the inadequacies of statistics such as the ones used to show black family disorganization: rates of illegitimacy and percentage of female-headed households. Pinkney suggests that the differences that exist between black and white families are a function of social class differences. When black families achieve middle-class status, their patterns become similar to those of white middle-class families.

Barbara Laslett, viewing the family in historical perspective, points to one important trend in family development: the increase in family privacy. She deals with both structural and normative supports for privacy. These include: decreases in family size; the disappearance of family servants, apprentices, and boarders; the decline in religious influence over family norms; and changes in architectural design and household amenities. She suggests that the greater variability in current family forms can partly be explained by the decreased social control exercised over the family by the public domain.

Eleanor Leacock presents the history of the family as proposed by Friedrich Engels. Engels viewed the family as going through three stages which correspond to what Engels defined as the stages in the development of society. These stages are group marriage in hunting-gathering societies, pairing marriage in horticultural societies, and monogamy in class societies. The family changes as the society changes and, in particular, as the economic structure of that society changes. Leacock links the emergence of capitalism to the decreased status of women in the family and in the society.

The three major sociological frameworks suggest a number of questions concerning the contemporary American family and its historical antecedents. Utilizing a structural-functional perspective, readers might ask the following questions: How do American values, particularly the values concerned with emotional fulfillment, happiness, monogamy, and equality, relate to marital functioning? How do they contribute to marital satisfaction or dissatisfaction? What is the function of homogamy in American society? How does the normative support for privacy, in American families, influence role behavior, household composition, and the use of space?

From a conflict perspective, the reader might ask: How is inequality in the larger American society reflected in (1) inequality within the family and (2) inequality between families? How does the family perpetuate inequality in the larger society? What is the particular role of the capitalist economy in creating and/or reinforcing sexual inequality? How does sexual inequality within the American family compare to sexual inequality within families in other societies, particularly noncapitalist societies?

Since these articles are macrosociological, they cannot specifically be looked at from a symbolic interaction perspective. However, the ideas from these articles offer a starting point for asking questions such as: How are individuals' definition of their roles in the family derived from the larger society? How are the roles learned in the family congruent or dissonant to roles in other institutions?

The Contemporary American Family

WILLIAM J. GOODE

AMERICAN KINSHIP STRUCTURE

MORE THAN 200 MILLION PEOPLE IN THE United States live under such a wide variety of family arrangements that it is impossible to characterize them all by a simple formula. Most do follow similar patterns, however, and we can describe them in a general way by noting how at many points they differ from other family systems of the world.

First, of course, the American system is technically monogamous. It has sometimes been called "serial monogamy," since every year several hundred thousand people divorce and soon remarry, and of course a small percentage of these people may have a succession of spouses over their lifetimes. Nevertheless, the structure of daily marital living is very different from a system in which one man is married to several wives (polygyny) or the much rarer system in which one woman is married to two or more husbands (polyandry), since life with a single spouse is much more intense. In point of fact, in most polygamous systems the ordinary person is usually married to only one spouse; even when marriage to two or more wives is approved, only the powerful and well-to-do have the resources to achieve that blissful state. It should also be kept in mind that in such great civilizations as India, China, Japan, and those Western European countries where monogamy has been the legal norm, the aristocratic and the rich have been able to indulge their wish to enjoy mistresses and concubines without fear of punishment. On the other hand, in all these societies the rules against a woman's enjoying the same privilege have always been very strict.

The American family system is also based on the independent family unit, in which a married couple and their children are expected to live physically separated from their kin and from their parents. In most instances, even older parents prefer to live alone if they have the financial means to do so.

Here again our system differs from that of many other societies, such as China, Japan, India, and Arabic Islam, in which a couple might continue to reside for years in either a joint household or under some other kind of shared economic arrangement. To be sure, this kind of living arrangement was always more common among the upper classes, who could more easily afford to take care of a young dependent couple. In most societies a young man has not been able to afford a marriage until he achieved economic independence. Formerly this independence came with owning land; now it comes with holding a job. Nevertheless, in most societies the ideal, if not the universal, practice was one large family unit in which several family units were linked closely together.

Because of the American emphasis upon the independence of the family unit, the age at which people marry in the United States has been somewhat higher than in Eastern countries, though lower than in most European countries. The average age of American males at marriage is approximately twenty-two years of age; that of females is approximately twenty. Thus the majority of American women marry when they are still in their late teens. As noted earlier, the average marital age in the United States was higher fifty years ago. At present, most young women work for a while before they marry. Men who marry young typically have jobs that pay low wages, but they are not as economically dependent upon their parents as rural people were a hundred years ago, when owning land was necessary for making a living.

Pages 13–28 from *The contemporary American family* by William J. Goode. Copyright © 1971 by The New York Times Company. Reprinted by permission of the New Viewpoints division of Franklin Watts, Inc.

In the last two decades a slightly new pattern has emerged, which might be considered the spread of an *older* upper-class pattern: middle-class youngsters have married increasingly earlier but remained economically dependent on their parents. In practice this has meant that young men and women who are in college are permitted to marry, but still continue to receive all or most of their income from their parents. Socially, this pattern overlaps with a deviant arrangement, in which a young middle-class couple lives together with the tacit approval and financial support of their parents, who may or may not hope that the two will ultimately legitimate their union by formal marriage.

Although the American system is still patronymic, since the name of the family line comes from the male side, it is neither a patrilineal nor matrilineal society but a *bilateral* one in which kinship is equally traced through both male and female parents. All of the major civilizations that we know of have been patrilineal, in that the lineage is traced primarily through the male line. Modern research, however, clearly reveals that in all major civilizations at least the informal links with the female side have often counted very heavily.

Patrilineal societies are also likely to give far more authority to the male and, in some societies, to the eldest living male ancestor. In the American system the husband does indeed have more authority than the wife, especially in major decisions, but not only do many women manage to achieve considerable influence in all family relations, but the modern movement in favor of liberating women continues to press for still greater decision-making power for wives.

This marks a difference from most other major societies in the past, and of course represents a substantial departure from America's own historical pattern. For years in the United States wives were not permitted to make contracts on their own. If they possessed real estate when they entered the marriage, the husband could legally use that real estate in order to earn money on his own. It was extremely difficult for a woman to leave her own home without being charged with "abandoning her domicile." She could not gain custody of her children, since children belonged to the husband's line. She could not sue. Along with these and many other legal disabilities, the near impossibility of earning an adequate salary by herself meant that the wife ultimately had to obey the authority of her husband, if he chose to exercise it.

The American kinship system has also been one of equal inheritance, as contrasted with those traditional social systems in which all of the family estate went to a single male heir (as in upper-class England and Japan) or in which the males shared equally (as in China), or in which the male received a larger share than the female children (as in Arabic Islam). In the United States the allocation of an inheritance is largely a problem of the more affluent social strata, and indeed our social patterns place less and less importance on the notion of "building an estate for the children."

Although equal inheritance is the legal norm, in fact there are many informal rules which alter this arrangement. If the family owns a business it is likely that a son, not a daughter, will enter it. If there are two sons, it is likely that the son who enters the business will inherit it, with some financial provision being made for the other son. Sons are likely to receive loans or gifts of money, while daughters are more likely to be left trust funds which give them much less autonomy in financial matters.

The American kinship system is also characterized by "free courtship," which in the adolescent phase of dating to some degree resembles the Polynesian societies in its emphasis upon romance. Perhaps the only European societies that come close to it are the Scandinavian ones, though parental influence in the ultimate choice of the spouse may be greater in those countries than in America. In practice, as is well known, our system permits rather early dating, great freedom of physical movement, privacy, and almost no chaperonage whatsoever. In America, too, there is no sharp line between dating and courtship; the social assumption is that people who go together are merely dating unless they announce that they are serious about their future plans.

The informal assumption of our courtship system is that people date one another on the basis of personal attraction. Yet many researchers have shown the extent to which people are actually participating in a kind of limited "marriage market," in which one excludes most of the population and accepts only people with characteristics very similar to one's own. The element of choice in dating is wider than in marriage, but most people never date across broad caste, religious, class, or age lines. Both parents and peer groups support these restrictions, by cajoling, threats of social ostracism, refusals of invitations, and financial inducements. Thus, technically, anyone may marry almost anyone else who is not barred by incest rules, but in fact informal family patterns confine most people within a fairly narrow pool of eligible dating or marriage partners who share a similar background. Moreover, when people do cross these lines successfully, for the most part they do so only when they have already lost some of the traits that are associated with their particular caste, ethnic group, or class. Thus, for example, a girl from the lower class who has gone to college may well have lost most of the social traits of her own class, and have acquired those of the middle class. Similarly, those who cross religious lines are likely to be less intense in their devotion to the religion in which they were reared, and to move in social circles where religion is not considered very important.

Most family systems of the great civilizations have (or have had) either a dowry system or a bride-price system, but the American kinship pattern has dropped this sort of marriage gift. In Western countries the dowry has been fairly standard, and in Europe it is not uncommon even today in some upper-middle-class circles. When it was in full operation, a family with many daughters might be unable to marry all of them off to husbands of the appropriate class, because such husbands would expect an adequate amount of money, and there might not be enough to divide among all the daughters. A family with sons was of course in a more fortunate position. Under some dowry systems, the money actually went to the elders or to the family estate rather than to the husband himself.

Note, however, that both the dowry and the bride-price system ultimately depend upon a high degree of stability in the marriage itself. When elders have no assurance that the marriage they are

helping to arrange and pay for will continue for any length of time, they are less likely to be willing to make substantial cash investments in it. In any event, over the past century such arrangements have come to be viewed as degrading, for they suggest that the woman is worthless in herself and is valuable only for the money she brings in.

It could be argued that in fact the American family system does operate under a dowry arrangement, though it is not a legal requirement and is never spoken of as a dowry. It is, however, clear that not only are there strong pressures on the part of both parents to contribute as much money and goods to the young couple as possible, but the bride's family is clearly expected to contribute far more than the groom's. Supposedly, the side with the most money contributes most, but this rule is tempered by the social pressure on the bride's parents to contribute more. Not only are they expected to pay for the wedding and reception, which may be elaborate and expensive, but they are expected in addition to come up with other sums and gifts beyond those expected of the groom's parents.

As with the traditional Japanese and Arabic Islamic family, the American system exhibits a high rate of instability. For technical reasons it is difficult to calculate the rate of this instability with any exactitude. Nevertheless, various estimates suggest that approximately one-fourth of all American marriages end in divorce. The divorce figure is certainly lower in rural areas than in urban areas, lower among Catholics than among Protestants, lower among whites than among blacks.

America's high marital instability has in turn meant a high "turnover"—that is, most of those who become divorced or who lose their spouses through death are likely to remarry. As a consequence, the dating and courtship system is not confined to the young, as it traditionally was in European and earlier American society. Other industrial nations are experiencing rapid increases in their divorce rate, but theirs are not as high as that of the United States. Over the past fifty years the social disapproval of divorce in America has dropped substantially, men can obtain most of the services their wives provide by simply buying them (laundry, housekeeping, and so forth), and wives in turn can support themselves by getting jobs on their own. In very few circles these days would a man or woman be ostracized for seeking a divorce.

Crucial to any account of marriage in contemporary America is the great emphasis that Americans place upon individual happiness. Since the supposed purpose of marriage is "happiness through love," and since any relationship of this kind is not likely to continue to yield the same intense feeling year after year, far more is expected of marriage than it can possibly produce. In fact, most American marriages carry too heavy an emotional burden. In this context, divorce serves as an escape valve for all the tensions of a highly intimate, emotionally overloaded relationship from which far too much has been expected.

Another difference between the American kinship system and that of most great civilizations of the past has to do with the position our system accords the elderly. In traditional societies the eldest male has been viewed as head of the family, a figure endowed with great authority and paid enormous deference. In some societies he was thought to be in touch with the spirits of the dead, to control magic, and to be the possessor of considerable wisdom. In the older societies, where most technical procedures and problems might be relatively simple and similar from one decade to another, very likely the older men did in fact have much useful knowledge.

While American society does not withdraw respect from older people, as is obvious to anyone who looks at the age distributions of powerful or esteemed politicians, judges, or corporate executives, nevertheless age itself commands little deference. In the American kinship system the position of the elderly is ambiguous. Few obligations or responsibilities are prescribed by age. The grandfather of sixty may, if he wishes, move to another state, take up water skiing, go to nightclubs, adopt the newest fashions, or even decide to start a new career without much social disapproval. He may also, if he wishes, play a much more traditionally grandfatherly role, again without much criticism. This arrangement has advantages as well as disadvantages. The older kinsman has in effect earned very little credit. Certainly he cannot rest upon his laurels. If he wishes to keep his kin network alive and

active, he will have to take the initiative and continue to contribute to the ongoing flow of affection, services, and funds that characterize family life. He cannot expect his kinsmen to flock around him, as they might once have done to a revered elder. On the other hand, the older kinsman now can shake off some of his traditional responsibilities if he does not wish to maintain them, and can start an almost entirely new life without expecting more than mild joshing or a comment or two about "acting his age."

MATING, DATING, AND COURTSHIP

Moving from this broad perspective to a closer view of the American courtship system, its dynamics become clearer. All courtship systems are "marriage markets," but the American version differs from others in the extent to which each individual tries to sell his own wares and carry out his or her own negotiations. In many traditional societies, by contrast, elder kinsmen made these arrangements for younger people.

In America everyone is permitted to marry as early or as late as he chooses. If he chooses early, his marriage may well fall short of his ideal expectations. This would be especially likely if he is upwardly mobile, for a marriage with someone of his own class origin might prove embarrassing once he had moved up into a higher class. If a man marries late, the marriage market will have been severely narrowed, and his ideal spouse may have already married. If a man desires to marry a pretty, rich, talented woman, he is certainly permitted to make the attempt; but if he has no equivalent gifts to offer, he is likely to be rejected. In order to avoid that risk, he may instead court a young woman whose qualities are worth much less in the market than his own. Although kinsmen and friends will usually offer some advice about his choice, there are no official "go-betweens," or matchmakers, whose responsibility it is to investigate the prospective bride or groom so as to prevent foolish errors of judgment.

Several processes in the American "free-courtship" system can be distinguished. One is the ordinary market process of supply and demand. Some people ask for more than they can get on the market, and others ask less, but in general brides and grooms are likely to be roughly similar in their traits and assets. A girl who is physically attractive can marry a young man who is less handsome but upwardly mobile. A young man in a higher social class is most likely to marry a woman from his own class, but he may go outside his class to choose someone who has money or beauty. An older man is most likely to marry a woman younger than himself (but still in an older age bracket); but if he is rich or influential, he has a good chance of marrying a much younger woman who is very attractive. In general, marital choices are homogamous: like marry like, and discrepancies are likely to be balanced off.

However, underlying all marital choices is a set of preferences, or values, which tend toward homogamy. Everyone is socialized to value certain traits, and thus a man (and his kinsmen and friends who influence his choices) sees others as more or less attractive to the extent to which they possess these traits. The talented young assistant professor of economics may seem very attractive to his female students, but he may appear pretentious, unmanly, and boring to a lower-class woman. People who have been reared mainly within one ethnic or religious group are not only less likely to meet and date outsiders; they are also less likely to enjoy being in an intimate situation with them. Thus the apparently "free" American system of individual courtship presses toward homogamy.

None of this is meant to deny the importance of love. Indeed, until recently, when their own courtship systems became closer to our own, European social commentators often ridiculed Americans for allowing love so large a role in marital choice. The theme of love has for decades pervaded American movies, popular music, literature, and advertising, and is one of the commonest topics of gossip. Perhaps no other major nation ever gave so prominent a position to love; specifically, only Americans have assumed it to be necessary (if not altogether sufficient) for marriage.

By contrast, in some societies love is viewed as a threat to the orderly processes of mate choice, since the choice of a mate is carried out by elder kinsmen, and so strong an attraction between a young man and woman might well thwart those negotiations. In these societies love is rather to be isolated or curbed, either by marrying young people off very early or by controlling access to jobs or land so as to prevent free choice. In still other societies love is not viewed as an aberration or a threat; instead, it is thought acceptable as long as it does not interfere unduly with the marriage arrangements made by kinsmen. This can usually be accomplished by seeing to it that only young men and women who belong to the appropriate class or kinship line have any opportunity of meeting, and hence of falling in love with one another. Our own society, of course, permits love a very large role in marital choice, though the extent to which the likelihood of falling in love is constricted by social and economic factors is great.

Some social analysts have argued that love motivates young people, who after all do not know each other very well, to adjust to one another's foibles and idiosyncracies in the early stages of marriage. It also motivates them to leave their parents and establish their own home. This is especially important in that in our system few people have much stake in maintaining the marriage—at least as compared with people living in those systems in which a large kin network may actually have an economic investment in the marriage. Many couples are disappointed when the high excitement of courtship diminishes, leaving them with a drab and rather humdrum existence. Marital counselors and others point out that if the relationship between men and women is pervaded by love before marriage, it is difficult to tell married people afterwards that it is of secondary importance. In any event love will continue to be of central significance to the American marriage far into the future.

HUSBANDS AND WIVES

A famous actress once protested that what's wrong with getting married is that after the honeymoon husbands always want to go home with their wives. This objection to the day-to-day boredom of marital adjustment is found in many barbed comments from social philosophers, whether professors or cab drivers. On the other hand, every study of marital adjustment reveals that a large majority of husbands and wives claim that they are either "happy" or "very happy" in their marriages. Since the American marriage system encourages maximum closeness between husbands and wives, the opportunities for disagreement are also maximized. How then do they adjust to one another's different behavior in the various areas of married life, such as the division of labor, power and authority, sex, attitudes toward work, and children?

In the traditional Hindu marriage—to look once again at other cultures—a young girl is married in her early teens to an older man and goes to live with her husband's family before the union is finally consummated. Thus she has few resources with which to resist their authority, and is either forced or persuaded to learn the ways to please her husband and his kin. Relieving these pressures somewhat was the custom of fairly long visits to her own relatives, who assured her that her duty was to adjust. In the old Chinese kinship system, the young woman also lost the potential support of her own kin since she moved to the village or area where her husband's family lived, and, like the Hindu girl, she was given no options: divorce was nearly impossible, and she found herself surrounded by older and more powerful people who in any dispute were likely to side with her husband. In addition, both systems prescribed certain tasks that were appropriate to males and females. The young husband had his own duties, and these were clearly separate from those of his wife. If each carried out his or her own traditional duties, then there could be little conflict. The amount of daily contact between the young husband and wife was reduced to a minimum. The young wife cooperated with her female relatives and the young husband carried out male tasks with his male relatives. In these ways the importance of the husband-wife bond was reduced.

In most such traditional kinship systems, again in contrast to our own, the notion of "love and happiness" was simply not the aim of married life at all. The officially supported aims of marriage were continuing the family line, honoring ancestors, contributing to the economic well-being of the larger kin unit, or living a harmonious life according to established religious precepts. By setting a much lower standard of emotional attachment between husband and wife, and by emphasizing specific duties and tasks, such systems made it possible for most people to reconcile themselves to the humdrum qualities of daily married life.

The advantage of such a system is that it prescribes actions, rather than a loving emotion. We can *will* conformity to the former, but not the latter. It is also easier to fulfill marital obligations if both husband and wife agree on what those obligations are, but the American system is probably less clear than almost any other in its specification of what each partner in a marriage is supposed to do. There is thus a wider area of action in which conflict is at least potential: each couple must work out for themselves just who is responsible for what. There are husbands who refuse to help at any household task and others who are willing to share in all of these tasks, from cooking to redecorating the home.

It may be objected that the two great areas of "earning a living" and "taking care of the children" are clear role obligations that are divided by sex. Indeed, it is true that it would be difficult to find many homes in which the wife goes out to earn a living, while the husband stays at home to care for the house and children. Yet if a group of men and women were asked individually to write down a fairly complete list of all the tasks in a marriage, designating which ought to be carried out by the husband and which by the wife, it would soon become apparent that even in a fairly homogeneous group, disagreement is likely to be very large and full of tension. Even in a household where both husband and wife know what in general the other expects, both may also harbor considerable resentments about the way these jobs are allocated.

Husbands and wives, of course, begin the adjustment of such differences as early as their first date together and may continue the process throughout their marriage. From their very first meetings, young men and women inform each other by subtle or not so subtle cues or even full-blown philosophical discussions of how they feel about what husbands and wives ought to do, in areas ranging from sexual relations to how many children a couple should have. Although each may be trying to impress the other, or to present his or her best self, the other is generally able to penetrate these disguises to a considerable extent—certainly to the point where it can be ascertained whether the other's views are traditional or radical, egalitarian or patriarchal, flexible or rigid. By the time they have actually begun their married life together, most of the larger issues have at least been confronted in one way or another, if not actually settled.

No matter how intimate their exploration of each other was before marriage, most couples experience the first year of marriage as a set of discoveries. Some of these are delightful, while others create chagrin and dismay. Like all great alterations in status, the change from single to married life holds surprises that few can anticipate. Some men can be effective and masterful in the dating situation, but once married expect to be fully taken care of by their wives. Some young women seem soft and yielding before their marriages, but these traits often turn out to conceal ruthless ambition and a deep need to dominate. On the other hand, some husbands and wives, once the anxieties and tensions of courtship and early marriage are over, enjoy the relaxation of building a home together and the security of an emotional solidarity in which each takes real pleasure in pleasing the other.

Most couples at least strive to make a go of marriage, and most do stay married until the union is broken by death. If few attain the ecstatic bliss portrayed in TV commercials and popular romances, most do manage to work out a tolerable situation. Husbands and wives learn what will anger or soothe the other, what the other can or will not do, and adjusts his or her actions to these realities of the relationship in so far as possible.

The general form of that adjustment is determined by the values brought to bear by the larger society. We are socialized to believe in monogamy and to avoid divorce if possible; we live as couples in independent households; we have two or three children; we give more authority in large decisions to the husband and expect him to earn most or all of the family income; we expect the wife to manage the household and the children; and so on.

Within each class, ethnic group, neighborhood, or social circle still other values and expectations create pressures toward more specific adjustmental patterns: wives with younger children should not hold full-time jobs unless the economic need is great; young parents should keep in close contact with their parents if possible; to maintain their social standing, husbands and wives should encourage and press their children to go to church or synagogue; it may be permissible for the husband to neglect his wife because he works late hours; and so on. Needless to say, in many circles one or more of these items would be rejected.

Husbands and wives also work out still more detailed adjustments of their own, from the choice of friendship and kinship visits, to sexual and other expectations. Moreover, they may (in private or public) simply ignore some of the directives of the larger society. Couples may agree on these personal adjustments from the beginning, or grow into them gradually, but most are the slow result of many trials, tentative probings, disagreements, errors, and successes.

If two people are to adjust, both must yield somewhat, but it is obvious that who yields in which areas is determined by who has the most resources and who has the greatest will to win. The husband or wife who has a lesser stake in the union will care less whether his or her spouse is displeased, and thus have a greater chance of imposing his or her will. The wife whose husband loves her more than she loves him is more likely to have her whims obeyed. Husbands who enjoy fighting will win more often, at least as long as the marriage lasts. Wives with an independent income are in a better position to act autonomously and to gain their ends. It is not surprising, then, to learn that wives make more adjustments in marriage than do husbands, since their resources are less. Lower-class wives enjoy more influence than do wives closer to the upper social strata, since the discrepancy between their earnings and those of their husbands is less. Women who work full time enjoy a stronger voice in family decisions than those who do not. Husbands who are better educated than their wives have more influence than those with less education.

Such factors continue to affect husband-wife relations throughout the life cycle of the family, and vary according to the area of family life. Other things being equal, wives are listened to more in the realms of children's religious education than in choosing family friends; decisions about small purchases than large ones; about where to spend vacations than whether to move elsewhere for a better job opportunity.

Social change has also transformed the areas in which personal adjustments between spouses can or must be made. The American economic and legal systems have given new options to wives, for example: independent ownership and management of property, custody of the children, graduate education, higher-level occupations, and so forth, thus creating new areas for adjustments as well as potential conflicts. A century ago, husbands and wives had almost no chance of getting a divorce, and thus felt a greater need to make a go of the only marriage they were ever likely to have. New choices expand opportunities for both spouses, but also create new problems of getting along together.

An example is the area of sexual relations. Until well after World War I, it is likely that, although sex relations were not satisfying to a high percentage of husbands and wives, the problem of adjustment was minimal. More husbands than wives felt that sexual intercourse was too rare. For a high percentage of wives—the figure varies from one sample to another—possibly as much as one half, the pleasure of orgasm was not a typical experience. As a holdover from the Victorian period, husbands were not greatly concerned with their wives' enjoyment, and many would still have argued at that time that a real lady should tolerate sex but not exult in it. Husbands were not, however, so likely as wives to be satisfied with a marriage in which the degree of sexual pleasure was low, since women expected less of sex, and other areas of family life counted for more in their eyes. In any case, neither husbands nor wives typically felt sex a problem they had to solve. More accurately it might rather be called a burden which many had to live with. Some wives or husbands went to physicians, and others hoped that time and patience might remedy matters, but in general husbands and wives felt that little could be done about sexual difficulties.

Now this situation has changed radically. The pill and other effective contraceptives have largely removed the fear of pregnancy that so often tainted sexual relations in the past. Hundreds of books explain to anyone who can read how to improve their sexual technique. Much of this information trickles from the upper middle class down, and it is explained and disseminated by the mass media, including films. Of their sex lives, wives and husbands are told frequently that they can and should "do something about it." Young people experiment with sex in order to gain pleasure and sexual competence before settling down to married life. It is safe to say that at the present time a far higher percentage of husbands and wives actually derive pleasure from sex than ever before; yet a far higher percentage of married people also feel frustrated by the need to solve sexual problems that in marriages of fifty years ago would have demanded no special effort because they were not thought capable of solution. Beyond question, far more husbands and wives now expect more pleasure from sex, and may well be disappointed when, as so frequently happens, sex turns out to be no substitute for the need for adjustment in other areas of family living.

The Economic Position
of Women in the Family

NATALIE J. SOKOLOFF

THE RELATIONSHIP BETWEEN (1) THE ECO-
nomic structure of a society, (2) the structure of the
family, (3) woman's position in the family, and (4)
woman's relationship to the larger society—both
economic and noneconomic—is rarely dealt with in
an integrated manner. Most analysts talk only
about one of these aspects. Marx and Engels
pointed to the interrelationship between the larger
economic structure of society, the family, and the
fate of women: both in the family and in the labor
force (Engels 1902).

According to Marx and Engels, the family is a
historically changing product of the changing material conditions of the society in which it is located.
Once property relations change, family relations
will change. With the advent of private property, female subordination to men became institutionalized. In the course of time, propertied men secured
exclusive sexual rights over women, thereby ensuring the orderly inheritance of their properties to
their heirs.

While many people have faulted Marx and
Engels for their understanding of the developmental sequence of the family and the origins of patriarchy, and rightfully so, it is certainly true that capitalism created a set of conditions conducive to the
maintenance of women in low status positions. (See
Grabiner and Cooper 1973, pp. 3–14; Gough 1972,
pp. 107–118.) The industrial revolution, intense concentration of wealth, the capitalist mode of production, and more recent conglomerate mergers have
had a great impact on the family, woman's position
in it, and the relation of both to the larger society.
There is no need to invoke capitalism as *the cause* of
the nuclear family, monogamy, patriarchy, or the
inferior position of women. But capitalism is associated with certain changes that have occurred in
the nuclear family. First, capitalism helped to
change the *quality* of family life—to be more individual, personalized, emotional, psychological, and
isolated; and second, it has helped to change the na-

ture of the relationship between the family and the
labor force by *separating* work from the home
(Chapman 1973).

HOW CAPITALISM AFFECTS
THE ROLE OF WOMEN
IN THE HOME

(A) The Economic Function
of the Family:
Use-Value vs. Exchange Value

In the precapitalist and much of capitalist society,
married women rarely worked outside the home (except as domestics); but then again, neither did men.
That is, in a noncommodity oriented society, the
family or household was the basic unit of production; and production was primarily for the purpose
of use by the household. Productive property was
widely disbursed among numerous individual
owners, in the tradition of an agricultural way of life
and the "frontier" in the United States. The rise of
machine-run factories and the concentration of productive property in the hands of a few in the 19th
century (Zaretsky 1973, pp. 1–108) led to profound
changes: more complex stratification; the separation of work from home; the wide-scale production
of commodities for exchange rather than for direct
use; the individual worker rather than the whole
family as the economically *productive* unit in society; the transfer of goods that were produced in the
home to factory production. This resulted in the
loss of economic status and increased economic dependency of wives on their husbands; the specialized roles of production of goods for the husband

A revised version of a paper presented at the 69th
annual meeting of the American Sociological Association, August 1974, Montreal, Canada. Copyright
© 1975 Natalie J. Sokoloff.

and consumption of goods and services for the wife; the development of separate, and quite unequal, shares of responsibility for husbands and wives instead of the previously joint participation in economic functions: hers in the *private* and emotional world of the home; his in the *social* world of work—from which he could retreat once he got home.

In interpreting the economic and social implications of the change for the role of woman, Margaret Benston (1972, pp. 119-128) shows how women's work in the home had only *use-value* and *not exchange value*, in a commodity-oriented society, thus undermining women's position. Separation of work from home meant the removal of goods formerly produced by women and their families from the home into the factories. The home and woman's position in it lost its *economic productive* function and the prestige linked to the processing and production of these goods. These products were now made in the factories—*for which she had to pay*! The family remains an economic unit only in the sense that it is the focus of concentration and perpetuation of wealth, private property, access to resources, and means of consumption.

Moreover, while the labor she performs with regard to housekeeping and childrearing are absolutely necessary and of *use* to the society, they are not remunerated in the way in which value is measured in a commodity-oriented society: with money. Therefore, she cannot *exchange* her labor for a wage, which will have a value in an exchange relationship in the commodity market. As she is left without access to important resources outside the family, the woman becomes totally economically dependent on her husband. In short, not only does she lose some of her prestige, she loses any capacity to negotiate in the market on her own.

(B) The Family as the Personal Arena Becomes Woman's Specialized Role

As capitalism advances, the woman is "put on a pedestal," given emotional, psychological, and moral responsibility for her husband and children, and is told that her "natural" function is tied to being a wife, mother, and homemaker. Religion supported this ideology through the Protestant notion of "the calling" (Zaretsky 1973); psychology supported it through a faulty understanding of biology and middle-class urban industrial ideology of Freud (1933; also Sherfey 1966; Marmore 1968). However, while women's status is heightened in the personal arena of the home, it is diminished in the labor market. According to Marx, the latter is more crucial in terms of decision making, power, and control in the larger society. At the turn of the 20th century, the ideal woman's role became exemplified by the wives and daughters of entrepreneurs and merchant capitalists of the northeastern United States. An elaborate mythology about "natural" female uselessness, helplessness, frivolity, illogicality, and powerlessness developed. The idleness of upperclass women became expressed as gentility, delicacy, frailty, and a symbol validating status through conspicuous leisure (Veblen 1953). Women, described by some at the turn of the 20th century as "children of a larger growth," were protected from harsh capitalism by a kindly paternalism. However, the elite ideal was hardly possible for the masses.

The roles that men and women play become increasingly specialized: men in the social-instrumental world, women in the expressive-emotional world (Parsons 1954, pp. 177-198). The privatization of the individual nuclear family becomes greater as does the focus on the individual worth of each family member. The interest in personality and emotional development, the focus on childhood and adolescence as periods of special attention, the emphasis on the psychological interior of the individual and the family, and the increasing awareness of sexuality are all associated with the emergence of personal life as a distinct sphere (Zaretsky 1973). Moreover, as labor outside the home becomes more and more alienating, the emotional security of the home becomes increasingly desirable as a refuge from "dehumanizing capitalism." One might say that the theme of alienation expressed by Marx comes through not only in terms of the worker's alienation from the means of production in a capitalist society, but also in terms of the alienation of the family and woman's role in it from the world of work.

(C) The Economic Function of the Family: Consumption

The increasing importance of the individual home and every member in it, the privacy and isolation from kin, the full-time attention of women being devoted to home and family, all fed right into the expanding markets of goods and services becoming available in a mass society. As mass production took hold of the American economy in the 20th century, *mass consumption* became an absolute necessity. Women were to play an important part in this activity.

One of the major functions of the family, and of the full-time housewife in particular, became the consumption of goods and services being produced by her husband and other workers in the labor market. No productive value was assigned to this behavior by women: it was consumption. The family, i.e., women and children, we are told in our introductory sociology textbooks, became a consumption unit and a liability to men, rather than a productive unit as in our agricultural past when the whole family participated in production (Bergers 1972, Ch. 5). It was precisely through consumerism, according to Zaretsky, that the capitalist class could reconcile the masses with the rise of corporate capitalism: the personalization of experience associated with the separation of work and home is extended in a passive way—through purchasing and consuming.

Full-time housewives have both more time and more needs for perpetual consumptive behavior than people caught inside factories and offices all day long: shopping for groceries, clothes for herself, the children and perhaps her husband; beauty aids; and "shopping around" for large household items which is time consuming, even if she does not purchase them without her husband being there, too. In fact, women make 75 percent of all purchases. And, as one advertiser suggested:

> Nothing makes markets like marriage. There's new business in setting up a house, and future business in raising a family. All together it's big business, appliances, and house furnishings to stepped-up insurance and bigger cars. (Salzman-Webb 1971, p. 11)

In addition to the "necessary" goods—food, clothing, and shelter—Veblen reminds us that people engage in "conspicuous consumption"—the expenditure in excess of what is needed for physical comfort in order to gain and hold the esteem of others. This is only possible when your wealth and power is put in evidence "for esteem is awarded only on evidence" (Veblen 1899, p. 42).

Consumer goods eat up more and more of disposable income. The 1960s saw a sharp rise in household and clothing consumption (Salzman-Webb 1971, pp. 11-17). In 1970 it was predicted that consumers would spend more than $36 billion for fashions alone, a 40 percent increase from 1966. Ironically, it was estimated that in 1966 more than $20 billion was spent for advertising. In an advanced capitalist society it appears that the necessity to spend one-fourth or one-third of a war budget (the Vietnam war cost about $60–80 billion in the late 1960s per year) to persuade people to buy is supported by the kind of privatized, separate, personalized, isolated nuclear family. With smaller sized families, parents are convinced they can now offer their children more individual attention, and are encouraged to offer them more and more individualized goods and services.

Advertisers play on women's insecurities in order to sell them commodities. Purchasing goods may be interpreted as the individual's only outlet for "freedom of choice" (Zaretsky 1973). And finally, as Betty Friedan (1973, p. 197) explains in the *Feminine Mystique*, the really important role of the American housewife is:

> ...*to buy more things* for the house.... Somehow, somewhere, someone must have figured out that women will buy more things if they are kept in the underused, nameless-yearning, energy-to-get-rid-of-state of being housewives.

She goes on to explain that with the end of World War II, business had to make consumer sales take the place of war contracts. In so doing, they needed housewives in the home, not busy at work. Moreover, they were faced with the problem of trying to sell women expensive new labor-saving gadgets and appliances for the home that still "give American women that 'feeling of achievement,' and yet keep housework their main purpose in life" (Friedan 1973, p. 201). The problem was to constantly counter and channel back into the home and family all that educational, psychological, emotional, and personal growth that women were experiencing . Why? Because the upkeep of each privatized home is most profitable to capitalism. It reinforces the separation of "man's place" in the social world of work and "woman's place" of "primary" importance with her home and family. This holds true even when the woman works in the labor force.

(D) The Economic Function of the Family: Production, Reproduction, and Ideology

According to Lise Vogel (1973, pp. 9–50), consumption carried out by women which keeps the economy going is in fact economically necessary labor, which is obscured, along with the rest of women's work in the home, by the fact that it occurs outside the world where surplus value is produced. Several independent estimates between 1918 and 1968 agree that if women were to be paid the value of their services as housewives, they would earn about one-fourth of the gross national product (Kreps 1971, pp. 67–68).

> Marx rarely acknowledged that individual consumption is a social process operating through a relatively stable social form, the family. Although it is true that under capitalism the family has been stripped of its former full participation in social production and can to some extent be said to live "outside the process of production," it is also clear that "individual consumption" is a social process involving labor and intense interaction with the world of capitalist commodities. (Vogel 1973, pp. 31, 32)

In addition, this intense interaction is of utmost importance. As Weir and Wilson (1973, pp. 80–94) point out: women reproduce the conditions of capitalist production by two means: *first* by *reproducing labor power* itself. This means that women engage in human reproduction as well as *material reproduction* of labor power. By *human* reproduction, it is meant that (1) women reproduce the children that will be needed in the society—some as workers paid in the labor force, and some as workers unpaid in the home, and (2) women use their husband's (and increasingly, their own) wages for the *material* reproduction of labor power—buying food, clothes, shelter, etc., and processing and maintaining them.

The *second* means by which women reproduce the conditions of capitalist production is by *reproducing the relations of production* (1) through the care and socialization of children "to ensure subjection to the ruling ideology or consent to its practice," and (2) through disciplining her husband "ensuring his continued ideological subjection by explicitly emphasizing her own and the children's dependence on his continuing wage" (Weir-Wilson 1973, p. 85). Within each social class it can be assumed the children are "properly" socialized according to the needs of the larger capitalist society itself (Pearlin and Kohn 1966, pp. 466–479). If it were not necessary to socialize children from the different social classes differently, it would be one less reason for maintaining the ideology that each child must be socialized by his or her very own parent(s). This would no longer be necessary.

In short, the separation of work and home means: (1) women become important consumers in our society; (2) they labor in the home each day making it possible to free men to work outside the home; (3) they reproduce and socialize their children; (4) during which they reinforce the ideology—in each home—that, in essence, that is the way it should be. And the way it "should be" is tied very much to the social class of which the family is a part, as it is incorporated into the larger social class system of the American capitalist economy. Finally, despite the separation of work and home, "the enduring tendency is for more and more ordinary women to be both 'workers' and 'homemakers,' that is, to participate in both wage labor and the process of the maintenance and reproduction of labor-power" (Vogel 1973, p. 34). In so doing, they take on two full-time jobs—which not only is something men do not have to do, but ironically is a disadvantage to them in the labor market.

CONCLUSIONS

Many feminists argue for a *restructuring of the family* itself so that housework and children are not exclusively women's jobs. The danger of focusing only on the ballot, equal education, equal jobs, and equal pay has been that women usually end up with two jobs, leaving all her traditional tasks at home intact for her. This problem not only persists for the contemporary American working wife and mother, but also has been one of the continuing problems in socialist countries (Rowbotham 1972; Haavio-Manilla 1972, pp. 93–110).

Housework and child care are lumped together because they occur in the isolated, privatized home in the urban-industrial capitalist society. However, suggests Rowbotham (1973, p. 122), they should not be so correlated with one another. Housework is drudgery. Perhaps it is best reduced by mechanizing, socializing, and sharing where necessary, as much of it as possible. Caring for small children, on the other hand, is important and absorbing work; but it does not mean one person has to do it all, or all the time. All available research evidence indicates children need good physical care, warm intimate relationships with others, a certain minimum continuity and stability in people caring for them, verbal and nonverbal stimulation. No one has ever found these needs were best satisfied by mothers rather than fathers, females rather than males, or adults rather than—after a certain very young age—younger, same aged, or older children (Oakley 1972, p. 194). The nuclear family itself is frequently said to need reshaping. However, it is not so much the structure of the family that is a problem, but rather its isolation. Some types of cooperative living and sharing of goods, tasks, living space, child care, and financial responsibilities must occur. It is a more efficient means of existence; eliminates the need for each household to purchase the same goods; allows women's time in the home to be freed; increases the availability of time and money for everyone to engage in more useful productive labor in the community; allows men to participate in child care directly while it frees them from total financial responsibility of their families; and reduces the authoritarian and possessive nature of parent-child relationships in the family. However, while socialization of housework and child care may well create new jobs, depending on the methods used to solve these problems, it is important to caution against creating sex-segregated jobs in these new areas.

Most importantly, in order for true equality between the sexes to exist, men and women must engage in the same types of work—in and outside the home. Even in socialist societies, where women have moved into many previously all male jobs, sex-segregated "women's jobs" still persist, e.g., preschool teachers and nurses. Moreover, women still tend to have a major responsibility for child-rearing and housework even though they may work full time. Specialization on the basis of sex hardly appears to be an efficient criteria in modern societies (Oakley 1972, p. 204).

In order for women to be emancipated, this analysis leads us to conclude that women must have control not only over their productive abilities but also over their reproductive functions. One of the basic demands of women's groups today is for low cost or free contraceptive and abortion services which are both safe and readily available. Moreover, male domination of obstetrical and gynecological medical services has frequently been the object of criticism. At present, women are three-fourths of the medical workers in America, but only 7 percent of the doctors, and an even smaller percentage of gynecologists and obstetricians (Reverby 1972, p. 15). Further, some feminists argue, only when women have control over their bodies will forced sterilization and coercive methods of population control cease.

One danger here is that, with the increasing freedom in sexual thought and behavior in our society, women may be more exploited than ever before if sex is used within the context of the old morality: as sexual exploitation and permission to consume more and more (Rowbotham 1973, p. 113).

Finally, while some segments of the women's movement have called for the abolition of patriarchy, others have argued for the redistribution of societal wealth (as was expressed on worldwide level at the 1975 International Women's Year Conference recently in Mexico City) as conditions for the development of equality between men and women.

The ideology of male supremacy and the material concentration of wealth are both long-term and deeply embedded aspects of contemporary American society. They reinforce, and are reinforced by, each and every interlocking institution in our society. The goal for equality of men and women in America will require action at all levels of the society. What has been suggested in this analysis is that the elimination of sexism in the economy must begin with the analysis of women's roles not only in the labor force, but simultaneously in the family.

BIBLIOGRAPHY

ANDERSON, CHARLES, 1974, *The political economy of social class.* Englewood Cliffs, N.J.: Prentice-Hall.

BENDER, MARILYN, 1974, More women advancing into key business posts. *New York Times,* January 20.

BENSTON, MARGARET, 1972, The political economy of women's liberation. In Nona Glazer-Malbin and Helen Youngelson Waehrer, (eds.), *Woman in a man-made world: a socioeconomic handbook.* Chicago: Rand McNally.

BERGER, PETER, AND BRIGITTE, 1972, *Sociology: a biographical approach.* New York: Basic Books.

BLAU, FRANCINE D., 1975, Women in the labor force: an overview. In Jo Freeman (ed.), *Women: a feminist perspective.* Palo Alto: Mayfield, pp. 211–226.

CHAPMAN, PAUL, 1973, Clusters: life-style alternatives for families and single people. Unpublished paper, April 1.

D'ANDRADE, ROY, 1966, Sex differences and cultural institutions. In Eleanor E. Maccoby (ed.), *The development of sex differences.* Stanford: Stanford University Press, pp. 173–203.

DE CROW, KAREN, 1972, Dick and Jane as victims: sex stereotyping in children's readers. By Women on Words and Images. Princeton, New Jersey.

————, 1971, *The young women's guide to liberation.* New York: Bobbs-Merrill.

DIXON, MARLENE, 1972, Why women's liberation—2? In Roberta Salper (ed.), *Female liberation: history and current politics.* New York: Knopf, pp. 184–199.

EHRLICH, HOWARD J., NATALIE J. SOKOLOFF, FRED L. PINCUS, AND CAROL EHRLICH, 1975, Women and men: a socioeconomic factbook. *Research Group One* 13.

————, undated, Selected differences in the life chances of black and white in the United States. *Research Group One* 17.

ENGELS, FRIEDRICH, 1902, *Origin of the family, private property, and the state.* Chicago: Charles H. Kerr.

EPSTEIN, CYNTHIA FUCHS, 1971, *Woman's place.* Berkeley: University of California Press.

FLINT, JERRY, 1971, Job bias against women easing under pressure. *New York Times,* January 31.

FRIEDAN, BETTY, 1973, *The feminine mystique.* New York: Dell.

FREUD, SIGMUND, 1933, *New introductory lectures on psychoanalysis.* New York: W.W. Norton.

GLAZER-MALBIN, NONA, AND HELEN YOUNGELSON WAEHRER (eds.), 1972, *Woman in a man-made world: a socioeconomic handbook.* Chicago: Rand McNally.

GORDON, ANN D., MARI JO BUHLE, AND NANCY E. SCHRAM, 1973, Women in American society: an historical contribution. *Radical America* 5:1–69.

GOUGH, KATHLEEN, 1972, An anthropologist looks at Engels. In Nona Glazer-Malbin and Helen Youngelson Waehrer (eds.), *Woman in a man-made world: a socioeconomic handbook.* Chicago: Rand McNally.

GRABINER, V. ENGQUIST, AND L. B. COOPER, 1973, Toward a theoretical orientation for understanding sexism. *Insurgent Sociologist* 4 (Fall).

GROSS, EDWARD, 1971, Plus ca change...?: the sexual structure of occupations over time. In Athena Theodore (ed.), *Professional woman.* Cambridge: Schenkman, pp. 39–51.

HAAVIO-MANILLA, ELINA, 1972, Sex-role attitudes in Finland, 1966–1970. *Journal of Social Issues* 28.

HARRINGTON, MICHAEL, 1970, *Socialism.* New York: Bantam Books.

KREPS, JUANITA, 1971, *Sex in the marketplace: American women at work.* Baltimore: Johns Hopkins Press.

LEAVITT, RUBY, 1971, Women in other cultures. In Vivian Gornick and Barbara K. Moran (eds.), *Woman in sexist society: studies in power and powerlessness.* New York: New American Library, pp. 393–429.

MARMOR, JUDD, 1968, Changing patterns of femininity: psychoanalytic implications. In Salo Rosenbaum and Ian Alger (eds.), *The marriage relationship.* New York: Basic Books, Chapter 3.

MITCHELL, JULIET, 1972, Women: the longest revolution. In Nona Glazer-Malbin and Helen Youngelson Waehrer (eds.), *Woman in a man-made world: a socioeconomic handbook.* Chicago: Rand McNally, pp. 45–52.

OAKLEY, ANN, 1972, *Sex, gender, and society.* New York: Harper & Row.

PARSONS, TALCOTT, 1954, The kinship system of the contemporary United States. In Talcott Parsons (ed.), *Essays in sociological theory*. New York: Free Press.

PEARLIN, LEONARD T., AND MELVIN KOHN, 1966, Social class, occupation and parental values: a cross-national study. *American Sociological Review* 31 (August).

QUICK, PADDY, 1972, Women's work. *Review of Radical Political Economics* 4 (July): 2-19.

REVERBY, SUSAN, 1972, Health: women's work. *Health PAC Bulletin* 40 (April): 15-20.

ROBY, PAMELA, 1972, Women and American higher education. *Annals of the American Academy of Political and Social Science* 404 (November): 118-139.

ROSENTHAL, JACK, 1973, Two-thirds of job gains in '60s made by women. *New York Times*, February 12.

————, 1972, For women, a decade of widening horizons. *New York Times*, April 10.

ROWBOTHAM, SHEILA, 1973, *Woman's consciousness, man's world*. Great Britain: Pelican.

————, 1972, *Women, resistance and revolution: a history of women and revolution in the modern world*. New York: Vintage Books.

SALZMAN-WEBB, MARILYN, 1971, Woman as secretary, sexpot, spender, sow, civic actor, sickie. In Michele Hoffnung Garskof (ed.), *Roles women play: readings toward women's liberation*. Monterey, Calif.: Brooks/Cole, pp. 7-24.

SEIFER, NANCY, 1973, *Absent from the majority: working-class women in America*. New York: American Jewish Committee.

SHERFEY, MARY JANE, 1966, *The nature and evolution of female sexuality*. New York: Random House.

TARVIS, CAROL, 1972, Woman and man. *Psychology Today* 5 (March): 57-64, 82-85.

THEODORE, ATHENA, 1971, The professional woman: trends and prospects. In Athena Theodore (ed.), *The professional woman*. Cambridge: Schenkman, pp. 1-38.

TREY, JOAN ELLEN, 1972, Woman in the war economy. *Review of Radical Political Economics* 4 (July): 40-57.

UNITED STATES DEPARTMENT OF COMMERCE, *The social and economic status of the black population in the United States*, 1971. Current Population Reports, Series 1-23, No. 42.

UNITED STATES DEPARTMENT OF LABOR, 1972, Working wives: their contribution to family income. In Nona Glazer-Malbin and Helen Youngelson Waehrer (eds.), *Woman in a man-made world: a socioeconomic handbook*. Chicago: Rand-McNally, pp. 194-197.

UNITED STATES DEPARTMENT OF LABOR, WOMEN'S BUREAU, 1969, *Facts about women's absenteeism and labor turnover*. Washington, D.C., August.

VEBLEN, THORSTEIN, 1953, *The theory of the leisure class, 1899, 1912*. New York: Mentor.

VOGEL, LISE, 1973, The earthy family. *Radical America* 7 (July-October).

WALDMAN, ELIZABETH, 1972, Changes in the labor force activity of women. In Nona Glazer-Malbin and Helen Youngelson Waehrer (eds.), *Woman in a man-made world: a socioeconomic handbook*. Chicago: Rand McNally, pp. 30-38.

WEIR, ANGELA, AND ELISABETH WILSON, 1973, Women's labor, women's discontent. *Radical America* 7 (July-October).

WHALEN, EILEEN, 1973, Working women, up from under. *By, for, and about Women* 1: 31-35.

WINKLER, ILENE, undated, Women workers: the forgotten third of the working class. An International Socialists Publication, mimeo.

WORK IN AMERICA, 1973, Report of a Special Task Force to the Secretary of Health, Education, and Welfare, prepared by W. E. Upjohn Institute for Employment Research. Cambridge: MIT Press.

YORBURG, BETTY, 1974, *Sexual identity: sex roles and social change*. New York: Wiley.

ZARETSKY, ELI, 1973b, Capitalism, the family and personal life, Part I. *Socialist Revolution* 3 (January-April): 69-125.

————, 1973a, Capitalism, the family and personal life, Part II. *Socialist Revolution* 3 (May-June): 19-70.

The Black Family

ALPHONSO PINKNEY

THE FAMILY

THE ORGANIZATION AND BEHAVIORAL patterns of the black family in the United States result mainly from economic and social conditions which blacks have encountered. Few survivals of the original African family system remain. From the breakup of the African family during slavery to the overwhelming urbanization of black people in the 1970s, family life has been in a constant process of change, adapting to economic and social forces emanating from the larger society.

Developmental Processes

The family system which developed among black people during slavery was one with few of the characteristics that were normal to the white American family of the time. The very nature of slavery as an economic institution, as well as the attitudes which led to the institutionalization of Afro-American slavery, militated against black family stability. Associations between male and female slaves were frequently for the sole purpose of satisfying sexual desires. Slaveholders could, and often did, mate their slaves to produce additional property. Male slaves were frequently used as stallions; in such cases, no bonds of affection were likely to develop between them and female slaves. Furthermore, since slaves were the property of slaveholders, any family relationships which might develop could be, and frequently were, dissolved through the sale of one of the parties. Any offspring to such a union usually remained with the mother, while the father continued his sexual exploits on a new plantation.

Slave mothers frequently were affectionate and devoted to their offspring, but both the separation of the father and the presence of the slaveholder as a promiscuous role model led to the matricentric family, a development which has to some extent persisted to the present time. Children rarely saw their fathers, and mothers assumed responsibility for parental affection and care. When separated from her children, the slave mother often visited them at night. The mother, then, was the dominant and important figure in the black slave family.

Because of the precariousness of their status—economically, socially, and legally—and because of their slave heritage, with its disregard for stable family life, blacks who were free before the Civil War were unable to develop stable family relations.[1] Family disorganization, including sexual promiscuity, was widespread. However, many of the mulatto children born to black women were kept by their mothers and accorded care despite severe hardships. Among the more economically secure free blacks, family relations attained a high degree of stability. Many of the prosperous mulattoes patterned their families after the middle- and upper-class white families.

The Civil War and emancipation had a disrupting effect on whatever degree of stability slave families had achieved. Marriage as a formal and legal relationship between males and females was not allowed to become a part of the mores among most slaves. However, during slavery some stable families of husband, wife, and children did develop. With the complete uprooting of the social order in the South, family instability was but one element in the widespread social disorganization found among the ex-slaves. In the exodus from the plantations and in the general aimless wandering which accompanied freedom, many black mothers left their children behind. Yet many others refused to depart from their children, and reports testify to the sacrifices which many of them made to keep their children.[2]

Promiscuous sexual relations and frequent changing of partners became the rule among ex-slaves, especially among those who experienced difficulties adjusting in an era largely characterized by anomie. Religious leaders, state legislatures, military authorities, the Freedmen's Bureau, missionary schools, and the mass media all joined the effort to impose institutional marriage and family norms on the freedmen.[3] These efforts succeeded in

Alphonso Pinkney, *Black Americans*, © 1975, pp. 98–109. Reprinted by permission of Prentice-Hall, Englewood Cliffs, New Jersey.

some cases, but in others official monogamous marriage and stable family relations required a difficult form of self-discipline. Nevertheless, by end of the Reconstruction, blacks had come to accept many of the family patterns of the larger society.

The restoration of white supremacy in the South following the Reconstruction imposed economic and social hardships on the black people. It became virtually impossible for the black man to assume a position of dominance or of equality with the black female. Economic exploitation, unemployment, and social subordination of black males in the larger society served to render them ineffectual as husbands and fathers. The appearance of Jim Crow laws toward the end of the 19th century further humiliated the black male; to a great extent these laws were geared toward keeping him "in his place" (i.e., away from the white female). Furthermore, with the widespread urbanization of the blacks after 1900, family life was again disrupted. The social norms which made for family stability in the rural South were without force in the urban slums. Among the lower-income blacks, social disorganization was manifested in broken families, and children born out of wedlock. On the other hand, a growing middle class among urban blacks is characterized by stable family relations and rigid adherence to the norms governing white middle-class families.

The Family in the 1970s: Demographic Characteristics

As of March 1973 there were approximately 5,265,000 black families in the United States. Of these families 61.4 percent were husband-wife families, 34.6 percent were headed by females with no husband present, and 4 percent were headed by males with no wife present.[4] Three out of every five black families were composed of both husband and wife. Of the 48,477,000 white families in the country at the same time, 87.8 percent were husband-wife families, 9.6 percent were headed by females, and 2.5 percent were headed by males. For black families the proportion with both husband and wife present has steadily decreased in recent years. In 1968, 67.9 percent of all black families were husband-wife families, in 1973 61.4 were, representing a

decline of 6.5 percent in five years. Compared to white female heads of families, black women are more likely to have their marriages disrupted through separation (35 percent vs. 15 percent), but white women are more likely to resort to divorce. In 1972, only 16 percent of black women household heads were divorced, compared with 27 percent for white women. Given the economics of divorce, blacks are forced to resort to separation. Also, black women who are heads of families are less likely than white women to be widowed (27 percent for blacks, 43 percent for whites), as a result of the longer life expectancy among white women.

Black families are larger than white families. The average size of the American family in 1971 was 3.6 persons.[5] For black families it was 4.2 persons and for white families it was 3.5 persons. Thirteen percent of all black families contained children under 18 years of age, compared with only three percent for white families. Furthermore, black families are more likely to include other relatives and unrelated individuals than are white families. That is, black families more closely approach the extended family pattern than do white families, and are more likely to be augmented by unrelated individuals.[6] While the vast majority of black families (approximately two-thirds) are nuclear families of husband, wife, and children, nearly one-fourth are extended families, and one-tenth are augmented families.

In some cases black families are made up of two or more nuclear families in the same household. This extended family arrangement is called a subfamily. In 1970, six percent of all black families were subfamilies, compared with only two percent for white families.[7] Although black families are larger, they earn significantly less than do white families. In 1972 the median income for black families was $6864, or 59 percent of the $11,549 median income for white families. This difference in family income existed despite the greater proportion of working wives in black families than in white families. Some 55 percent of black wives worked, compared with 44 percent of white wives.

Regionally, black families in the United States are about evenly divided between the southern and nonsouthern states, but within these regions some differences occur. Few black families outside the South (approximately three percent) live on farms, whereas in the South about ten percent live on farms. The black family is larger in the South than outside that region, and contains more dependent children.

Black families are less likely than white families to own their own homes. In 1970, for example, 42 percent of all black families owned their homes; 65.4 percent of white families were homeowners.[8] Black home ownership is greatest in the South (46.9 percent), followed by the North Central region (42 percent), and the West (40 percent). In the Northeast it is lowest (28.6 percent).

Because black families earn less than white families, they are required to spend a larger percentage of their earnings for basic expenses—food, shelter, and clothing. While black and white families spend approximately the same proportions of their incomes for food, blacks are forced to spend proportionally more for shelter (including fuel, light, refrigeration, and water) and for clothing. Furthermore, black families live in more congested housing than white families. In 1970, 14 percent of all black families occupied housing units in which there was an average of 1.5 persons per room (defined "seriously overcrowded" by the U.S. Department of Commerce), while three percent of white females lived under these conditions. Whether they own or rent their places of residence, black families are more likely than white families to live in housing units lacking some or all plumbing facilities.[9] Seventeen percent of all black families lived in housing lacking complete plumbing facilities, compared with five percent of white families. In short, black families are required to pay a greater portion of their incomes than white families for inferior housing.

In an affluent society like the United States certain household appliances and equipment are taken for granted by the vast majority of citizens. But, as is true in every other area, blacks lag behind whites in this regard. In 1970, nearly three-fourths of all white households (74 percent) contained washing machines and dryers for clothes, while one-half of black households (51 percent) contained washing machines and only 12 percent contained clothes dryers.[10] Few blacks (three percent) had dishwashers, while nearly one-half of white families (49 percent) had this appliance. A similar pattern holds

for air conditioning (18 percent for blacks, 39 percent for whites). Virtually all American households contain at least one television set, but eight percent of black households do not, compared with four percent of white households. Finally, while only slightly more than one-half of black households (57 percent) had automobiles available in 1970, more than four-fifths of white households (85 percent) did and more than one-third had the use of two or more automobiles.

Family Stability

The economic and social conditions under which black Americans have been forced to live have adversely affected their family lives. The legacy of slavery, widespread poverty, racial segregation and discrimination, and rapid urbanization have led to what has been characterized as "family disorganization" among blacks. This is usually said to characterize lower-class black families, for their life-style often differs from that of middle-class white families. Some evidence indicates that when black people achieve middle-class status, family stability becomes even more important than it is among the white middle class.[11] But a majority of black people are found in the lowest socioeconomic status positions in the society.

Perhaps no institution in the black community has been more distorted and misunderstood than the black family. As late as March 1965, the Office of Policy Planning and Research of the Department of Labor issued a controversial report, compiled by Daniel P. Moynihan, Assistant Secretary of Labor, entitled *The Negro family: the case for national action.* In this report Moynihan declared: "At the heart of the deterioration of the fabric of Negro society is the deterioration of the Negro family. It is the fundamental source of weakness of the Negro community at the present time."[12] Such a charge was supported by the following allegations: (1) "Nearly a quarter of urban Negro marriages are dissolved," (2) "Nearly one-quarter of Negro births are now illegitimate," (3) "Almost one-fourth of Negro families are headed by females," and (4) "The breakdown of the Negro family has led to a startling increase in welfare dependency." Since its publication this report has been criticized by black civil rights leaders and social scientists.[13] There are many criticisms to be made of Moynihan's formulation as well as his assumption that American blacks are themselves to blame for conditions forced on them by the society. In June 1965, President Lyndon Johnson announced in a commencement address at Howard University that he would convene in the fall "a White House conference of scholars, and experts, and outstanding Negro leaders—men of both races—and officials of government at every level. This White House conference's theme and title will be 'To Fulfill These Rights.' " That the so-called breakdown of the black family, which Moynihan (who assisted in drafting the speech) had characterized as a "tangle of pathology," would be the theme of the conference was clear from the President's comments in the speech: "The family is the cornerstone of our society. . . . When the family collapses it is the children that are usually damaged. When this happens on a massive scale the community itself is crippled."[14] Angered by the age-old American tactic of "blaming the victim," black civil rights leaders and educators forced the scaling down of the White House conference to a planning meeting for a larger one to be held the following spring. When the conference finally met, those in attendance seized the opportunity to criticize what had become known as the Moynihan Report.

It cannot be denied that the black family has shown an amazing ability to achieve and maintain a remarkable degree of stability in spite of the overwhelming odds of white racist oppression. If the black family somehow managed to survive the brutality of slavery, the total disruption of the post-Civil War years, and the degradation of institutionalized white supremacy, it is likely that in an era of increasing black pride it is stronger than ever.

Examination of Moynihan's indicators of black family "deterioration" quickly explains the anger expressed by black leaders. If the high rate of dissolution of marriages among urban blacks indicates black family breakdown, then the urban American white family is also breaking down. The marriage rate among Americans in 1971 was approximately 10.6 per 1000 population, and the divorce rate was 3.7 per 1000 population.[15] While black families are more likely to be dissolved through separation, the divorce rate is not significantly higher for blacks

than for whites. But these data hardly tell the whole story. In many black families the husband and father technically leaves the household so that the wife and mother can become eligible for public assistance.[16] These marriages are then recorded as dissolved. Thus the family can supplement its meager income.

The question of children born out of wedlock has concerned almost all scholars who write about the black family. In 1967 it was estimated that nine percent of all live births in the United States were out of wedlock births. The rate for blacks is said to be seven times that of whites.[17] These data are questionable. White out of wedlock births frequently occur in private hospitals in which the mother is attended by sympathetic physicians. Most black babies are born in public hospitals where they are more likely to be recorded as "illegitimate." These different circumstances are likely to lead to significant differentials in reporting.

Childbirth outside of marriage is invariably seen by Americans as a function of moral laxity. Although one of the norms of the society prohibits sexual intercourse prior to marriage, a report of the Department of Health, Education, and Welfare estimates that one-third of all firstborn children in the United States between 1964 and 1968 were conceived out of wedlock.[18] In most cases marriages were hastily arranged before the birth but the marriage partners had still violated the social taboo on premarital sexual intercourse. With such high figures it is clear that the proportion of blacks involved could have been responsible for only a fraction of these premarital pregnancies. Furthermore, studies show that a high proportion of black children who are born out of wedlock are "legitimized" by the subsequent marriage of the natural parents.[19] In other words, cultural variation operates to impel white parents to "legitimize" the prospective offspring before birth, while among blacks it is more likely to happen after birth.

Furthermore, black unwed expectant mothers are less likely than whites to terminate pregnancy through abortion. When abortion was illegal in the United States, it was estimated that nearly two million such operations were performed yearly, and that white women accounted for approximately 90 percent of them. The stigma attached to children born out of wedlock has never been as pervasive among blacks as among whites.[20] Bernard concluded after summarizing studies of premarital pregnancies that while black women do not reject the societal taboo on premarital pregnancies, out of wedlock birth among blacks is "not accepted—let alone welcomed," even in low-income families. For many it is a traumatic experience.[21] Once the baby is born it is likely to be seen as having a right to live in the family and the community without being stigmatized. Such babies are usually kept within the mother's family, while in white families they are more likely to be offered for adoption.

Moynihan's third indicator of black family "deterioration" is the high proportion of black families headed by females. According to the Bureau of the Census, in 1973 more than one-third of all black families (34.6 percent) were headed by females, in contrast to about one-tenth of white families (9.6 percent).[22] In order to survive in a hostile atmosphere black families have historically been forced to develop a network of informal arrangements. One of these is the quasi-extended family pattern characteristic of many of the world's people. Black families are frequently headed by females because such societal pressures as employment discrimination against black men make it difficult for them to support their families. When the black husband leaves the family, the children are frequently left in a household in which there are many adults—aunts, uncles, and grandparents. (Such an atmosphere might be said to be more wholesome than the small isolated nuclear family.)

The effects of so-called family disorganization on the personalities of children have been the subject of many studies.[23] Children from homes in which the father is absent are said to seek immediate gratification far more than children with the fathers present in the home. This inability to defer gratification has been alleged to be correlated with immature, neurotic, and criminal behavior. Furthermore, such children are reported to experience difficulty in distinguishing sex roles, a condition which supposedly manifests itself in femininity among males, in delayed marriage or divorce, and in pseudomasculine toughness. Finally, it has been suggested that families without fathers are more likely to produce schizophrenic children than families in which the father is present.

Many of these studies employ dubious methodology or draw unwarranted conclusions from the data. For example, one study said that children from homes in which the father was absent tended to seek more immediate gratification than those from homes in which the father was present; conclusions were based on whether the children chose to receive a small candy bar immediately or a large bar a week later. Those from father-absent families were more likely to choose the small candy bar rather than wait, while those from families in which the father was present were more inclined to wait for the larger candy bar.[24] Whether this represents an accurate measure of the ability to delay gratification is open to question, as is the assertion that such behavior is an important factor in criminal, immature, and neurotic behavior. Another study maintained that black males from lower-class, father-absent homes scored higher on measures of femininity than white males from comparable class backgrounds but from father-present families. This conclusion was arrived at because black men were more likely than whites to agree with such statements as "I would like to be a singer."[25] Clearly this method of reaching conclusions says more about those administering the test and interpreting the results than about the subjects.

In still another study, the researcher matched 21 adult black males whose fathers had been absent during early childhood with 21 black men who possessed similar social characteristics but whose fathers were present during their early childhoods. When asked whether they felt they had been victims of discrimination, 48 percent of those from father-absent families in childhood responded affirmatively, compared with 29 percent whose fathers were present during childhood.[26] The interpretation given to this finding is that adult males from father-absent families during childhood are more inclined to feel that they had been "victimized" during childhood than their counterparts from father-present families. It seems that these data were misinterpreted—any adult black male who does not know that he has been a victim of discrimination at some point in his life is clearly living in a fantasy world.

If the so-called breakdown of the black family has led to an increase in welfare dependency, as Moynihan maintains, it says more about American racism than about black people. At the time of the report the government of the United States was beginning the expensive military buildup in Indochina, one of its many wars of agression which cost the taxpayers $1000 billion between 1946 and 1969, a sum far in excess of that spent on social welfare programs. Furthermore, in 1969, 90 percent of all black families receiving Aid to Families with Dependent Children (AFDC) were those in which the father was absent, compared with 73 percent of all white recipients. On the other hand, in black families with the father present only 11 percent received AFDC, in contrast to 24 percent for white families with the father present.[27]

It would be a mistake to minimize the problems faced by black families in the United States, for there are many. However, from the break-up of the African family during slavery to the overwhelming urbanization of blacks in the 20th century, the black family has demonstrated an amazing degree of resilience, adapting to the social and economic forces emanating from the larger society. The black family is a complex social institution, and its members must not be blamed for the problems imposed by the larger society.

Patterns of Family Life

In many ways black family life in the United States differs from white family life. It is often maintained that in the black family dominance is vested in the female, while in white families dominance is vested in the male or is shared by the husband and wife. In the vast majority of black families, as in white families, dominance is shared between the mother and the father (egalitarian pattern) or is vested in the father (patriarchal pattern).[28] Although about one-third of all black families are headed by females, they represent a minority. These are the poorest families in the society; as soon as blacks achieve middle-class status, their family patterns become similar to those of economically comparable white families. Consequently, the major differences in patterns of family life between blacks and whites result from economic factors.

One of the chief societal functions of the family is the socialization of offspring. In the case of black parents this role becomes more difficult, for theirs is not simply a task of instilling skills, knowledge,

attitudes, and values; they must also socialize their offspring into the peculiar status of being black in a racist society. Child-rearing practices constitute crucial aspects of the socialization process. In the 1940s Davis and Havighurst conducted a study of racial and class differences in child-rearing practices. They reported that few differences existed when black and white families occupied similar social class positions.[29] Subsequent studies report findings inconsistent with these.[30] One similar study, however, reports that black mothers are less likely to expose themselves to child-rearing literature than are white mothers, regardless of social class position, but that black mothers who are so exposed express more favorable attitudes toward child-rearing than do white mothers.[31] Although contradictory findings are reported, considerable evidence indicates that middle-class black parents are more like middle-class white parents in their child-rearing practices than they are like lower-class black parents.

In an effort to counteract the proliferation of books characterizing the black family as pathological, several black social scientists have published studies which attempt to present the black family as an institution characterized by both strengths and weaknesses.[32] In general, these studies posit that an examination of the strengths of black families is a necessary antidote to past and present preoccupation with their weaknesses. Historically the black family has been presented in American scholarship as a "matriarchal" institution so unstable that it is responsible for many of the problems faced by blacks in the United States.

Robert Hill has enumerated some of the strengths of black families.[33] He sees certain characteristics of black families that contribute to their survival, development, and stability: strong kinship bonds, strong work orientation, adaptability of family roles, strong achievement orientation, and strong religious orientation. In black families, kinship relations are strong, minors and the elderly are absorbed in the family, and informal adoption is relatively commonplace. Contrary to popular stereotypes, black families place a strong emphasis on work, as is evidenced by the number of families with two or more wage earners. When blacks refuse to work it is because they are relegated to the lowest paid jobs.

Although most black families are two parent families in which decision making is shared, it is often necessary for each member of the family to temporarily assume the roles of others, as when both parents work or when a key member is absent for some unexpected reason. Another of the strengths of black families is their high achievement orientation, even among the poor. Indeed, black parents maintain higher aspirations for their children than do white parents, and black youth have higher educational and occupational aspirations than their white counterparts.[34] Finally, a strong religious orientation has served as a survival mechanism for black families throughout a long and difficult history.

Any social institution in a society with as many contradictions, inconsistencies, and prejudices as exist in the United States is likely to face problems. And the black family has its share of these problems. In a period of rapid social change, as is characteristic of American society, much can be learned from the black family, an institution which has maintained a high degree of stability through a long series of crises.

NOTES

1. See E. Franklin Frazier, *The Negro family in the United States*. Chicago: The University of Chicago Press, 1966, especially Chap. 10.

2. See, e.g., *ibid.*, Chap. 5.

3. Jessie Bernard, *Marriage and the family among Negroes*. Englewood Cliffs, N.J.: Prentice-Hall, 1966, pp. 10–13.

4. United States Bureau of the Census, *The social and economic status of the black population in the United States, 1972.* Washington, D.C.: Government Printing Office, 1973, p. 68.

5. United States Bureau of the Census, *Statistical abstract*, p. 39.

6. See Andrew Billingsley, *Black families in white America.* Englewood Cliffs, N.J.: Prentice-Hall, 1968, pp. 16–21.

7. Robert B. Hill, *The strengths of black families.* New York: Emerson Hall Publishers, 1972, p. 42.

8. United States Bureau of the Census, *Statistical abstract*, p. 687.

9. United States Bureau of the Census, *The social and economic status of the black population in the United States, 1971.* Washington, D.C.: Government Printing Office, 1972, pp. 94–96.

10. *Ibid.*, p. 97.

11. See E. Franklin Frazier, *Black bourgeoisie.* Glencoe, Ill.: Free Press, 1957, pp. 82–83.

12. United States Department of Labor, *The Negro family: the case for national action.* Washington, D.C.: Government Printing Office, 1965, p. 5.

13. Many of the criticisms have been reprinted in Lee Rainwater and William Yancey (eds.), *The Moynihan report and the politics of controversy.* Cambridge, Mass.: M.I.T. Press, 1967.

14. Remarks of the President at Howard University, June 4, 1965, in *ibid.*, p. 130.

15. United States Bureau of the Census, *Statistical abstract*, p. 63.

16. See C. Eric Lincoln, The absent father haunts the Negro family. *New York Times Magazine*, November 28, 1966, p. 60.

17. United States Bureau of the Census, *Statistical abstract*, p. 51.

18. The *New York Times*, April 8, 1970, p. 1.

19. Adelaide Hill and Frederick Jaffe, Negro fertility and family size preferences: implications for programming of health and social services. In Talcott Parsons and Kenneth Clark (eds.), *The Negro American.* Boston: Houghton Mifflin, 1966, pp. 210–213.

20. See Joyce Ladner, *Tomorrow's tomorrow: the black woman.* New York: Doubleday, 1971, pp. 220–225.

21. Bernard, pp. 50–55.

22. United States Bureau of the Census. *Social and economic status*, p. 68.

23. For a review of such studies, see Thomas F. Pettigrew, *A profile of the Negro American.* Princeton, N.J.: Van Nostrand, 1964, pp. 15–24.

24. W. Mischel, "Father-absence and delay of gratification: crosscultural comparisons. *Journal of Abnormal and Social Psychology* **63** (1961): 116–124.

25. Pettigrew, p. 19.

26. *Ibid.*, p. 20.

27. Robert Hill, p. 49.

28. See Russell Middleton and Snell Putney, Dominance in decisions in the family: race and class differences, *American Journal of Sociology* **65** (May 1960): 605–609. However in a study of black and white families in the Detroit, Michigan area and in southeastern Michigan it is reported that, whereas the majority of white families are egalitarian (54 percent), the largest percentage of black families are dominated by the wife. The husband was found to be dominant in 19

percent of the black families; the wife was dominant in 44 percent; and 38 percent were egalitarian. See Robert A. Blood, Jr., and Donald M. Wolfe, *Husbands and wives.* Glencoe, Ill.: Free Press, 1960, pp. 34–36.

29. Allison Davis and Robert J. Havighurst, Social class and color differences in child rearing. *American Sociological Review* 11 (December 1946): 698–710.

30. See, e.g., Martha S. White, Social class, child-rearing practices, and child behavior. *American Sociological Review* 22 (December 1957): 704–712.

31. Zena S. Blau, Exposure to child-rearing experts: a structural interpretation. *American Journal of Sociology* 69 (May 1964): 596–608.

32. See, e.g., Andrew Billingsley, *Black families in white America*; Robert Hill, *The strengths of black families*; Joyce Ladner, *Tomorrow's tomorrow*; Robert Staples (ed.), *The black family: essays and studies*, Belmont, Calif.: Wadsworth Publishing Co., 1971; Charles V. Willie (ed.), *The family life of black people.* Columbus, Ohio: Charles E. Merrill, 1970.

The Family as a Public and Private Institution: An Historical Perspective

BARBARA LASLETT

THIS PAPER ATTEMPTS TO SPECIFY SOME of the ways in which the modern family in the United States differs from its historical predecessor through a distinction between the public and private character of social institutions. Access to institutions and events that are considered private is more limited—both structurally and normatively—than is access to more public acts and activities. One consequence of this more limited access is that there is greater control over the audience of potential observers within private than within public institutions. To the extent that behavior is influenced by accountability to others, privacy is likely to reduce social control and publicness to increase it. If structural mechanisms which inhibit social control over the enactment of family roles have been reduced in the modern American family, then there is reason to expect greater variability in these behaviors in the more contemporary period than was true in the past.

The specific hypothesis being investigated here is that the private family—that is, an institution characterized by relatively limited access and greater control over the observability of behavior—is a modern development which has occurred only within this century in the United States.[1] This development, it will be argued, is one consequence of the separation of work and family activities, historically associated with industrialization in the west and with the changing characteristics of the family setting which have followed from this differentiation. The role of norms in this process of change will also be explored.[2]

The main focus of this analysis is on the context in which family activities occur. An attempt will be made to describe the "audience" of family behavior, i.e., the people who comprise the actual or potential observers of family life, and the demographic, spatial, and normative mechanisms which permit and prohibit observation as they have varied over historical time. If one is willing to accept the general sociological assumption that individuals are responsive to their surroundings, of which persons who share a given physical space with them are a part, then different consequences are likely to occur, both in the family as an institution as well as in the quality and character of the behavior which occurs within the family, when the interactional context varies.

Within the sociological literature, there have been three major themes in discussions of the family across time: (1) the development of the isolated nuclear family in the more recent period compared to an extended family structure in the past (part of what William Goode 1963 has called "the classical family of Western nostalgia"); (2) the growth of the companionship compared to the traditional or institutional family (see Burgess and Locke 1953); and (3) the loss of functions by the family in the modern period compared to the past (see Ogburn and Nimkoff 1955). Each of these views relates changes in the family to the development of an urban, industrial, and highly mobile society, and thus dates its formation as following these developments.

Some historians (see for instance, Aries 1962; O'Neill 1967; Laslett 1969, 1971; Lockridge 1966; Demos 1968, 1970; and Greven 1966, 1970) have, in contrast, argued that certain aspects of the modern family structure predate industrialization. To the extent that "modern" is defined in terms of nuclear or conjugal family structure, there are good demographic reasons to believe that the nuclear family form was predominant before the advent of industrialization, at least in western Europe and America, since in societies which have late marriage ages and low life expectancy, only a small proportion of households are likely to exhibit an extended structure at any one point in time. (Berkner (1972, p. 405), in an analysis of 651 peasant households in one Austrian manor in 1763, found that when the age of the male head of the household was 18 through 27, 60 percent of the families were extended, while when the age of the male household head was 58 through 90, 15 percent of the families were extended.)

Historians who have emphasized the importance of ideology in the development of the modern family also dispute whether its development was prior to or post industrialization. O'Neill (1967, p. 5) argues, as does Aries (1962), that the development of the modern family is related to "the discovery of the child," i.e., to the conception of the "child" as a social category separate from adults, requiring spe-

cial concern and attention. O'Neill says (1967, p. 17):

> The emergence of the modern family has had very little to do with the industrial revolution, which it predated, but instead has been substantially influenced by ideology.

Goode (1963, p. 19) suggests that:

> The ideology of the conjugal family is likely to enter the society through some spokesman *before* the material conditions for its existence are present, but the ideology does prepare individuals for adjustment to the demands of the new society.

Thus, ideology cannot be used as evidence for the actual existence of the family form which it describes. Furthermore, despite Goode's contention, the material and structural conditions which actually develop do not necessarily produce the kind of family for which the ideology has prepared the individual. Consequences of changed structural conditions, which were unanticipated by the ideology, may lead to a disjunction between expectations and reality, rather than have a preparatory effect.

PRIVACY AND FAMILY ROLE BEHAVIOR

Privacy, in this analysis, then, refers to the structural mechanisms which prohibit or permit observability in the enactment of family roles. The hypothesis being investigated here will be supported if the institution of the family can be shown to exhibit greater privacy, i.e., that people's activities in their family roles are observable to fewer and less varied others, and if the institution of the family has greater control over the character of that observation in the more recent period of American history than was the case in the past.

One of the structural changes which has been associated with industrialization has been the separation of home and work activities. The consequences of this differentiation are extremely varied, but one result for the family may be seen in terms of the potential audience of behavior in different roles.

When the family was economically productive as a unit, the setting of activities which engaged work and family roles were often the same. For instance, Riis (1968, p. 182), describing conditions in the tenements of New York, in the last decade of the 19th century, reports:

> ...we found in such an apartment five persons making cigars, including the mother. Two children were ill with diphtheria. Both parents attended to the children; they would syringe the nose of each child and without washing their hands, return to their cigars.

Aries (1962, p. 383), describing 17th-century life in France, at least among the professional classes, says:

> There were no professional premises, either for the judge or the merchant or the banker or the businessman. Everything was done in the same room where he lived with his family.

These examples illustrate structural conditions which would permit a heterogenous audience and relatively low control over one's observability in the enactment of family roles.

Merton (1957) makes the general point in his discussion of the role set. Although various members of one's role set may have differing views about appropriate and desirable behavior on the part of the status occupant, spatial and temporal separation of interactions with different others can reduce potential conflict between their expectations. When such spatial differentiation occurs, the individual, in the enactment of family roles, is less accountable to varied others, since observability of behavior is reduced. Thus social control over family behavior declines when privacy is increased. It should be noted, though, that the audience of family behavior also affects the sources of social encouragement and reward for the maintenance of normative behavior within the family.

Privacy permits variability based on individual preference and predilection which public accountability might tend to discourage. But the very structural conditions which may limit the sources of social control can also affect the availability and character of social support.[3] In statistical terms,

this might lead one to expect that a distribution descriptive of some behavior or attitude related to the family would show greater deviation from the mean under conditions of privacy and greater concentration around the mean under conditions of publicness.[4]

PRIVACY AND HOUSEHOLD COMPOSITION

Different structural mechanisms are likely to affect the audience of family behavior composed of persons who are members of the household compared to those who are not. Although one's observability will vary, even within the household, by the amount and usage of space (the number of rooms and the behavior which is designated as appropriate to them, the design of rooms and the means of access to them, etc., some of which will be discussed in a later section), there is likely to be less control over the observability of behavior by persons who share a household than by those who do not. Therefore, household composition is relevant to an analysis of the audience of behavior in family roles. This section will look at the ways in which household composition has changed over the period of American history as a means of answering questions about the composition and character of the audience of family behavior within the household.

As already mentioned, recent research has shown that the dominant structure of the family in the preindustrial household, both in England and in the American colonies, was nuclear. (Parish and Schwartz (1972, p. 170) conclude from their analysis of household complexity in 19th-century France "that nuclear families existed over most of northern France, if not most of Europe, before industrialization.") Laslett (1971), for preindustrial England, and Demos (1970), Greven (1970), and Lockridge (1966) for colonial New England, all describe the predominantly nuclear character of the household. While demographic factors (particularly the link between age of marriage and expectation of life) are likely to account, in part, for this structure in England (see Laslett 1971, pp. 94–97), these purely demographic factors are less likely to explain such a structure in the early American setting. Marriage ages, particularly for women (see Greven 1970, p. 290; Demos 1970, p. 193) were younger in the American colonies than in England at a similar time, but of greater importance for family structure was that life expectancy appears to have been higher in the New World than in the Old. (Laslett (1971) discusses mortality in 17th-century England, and Greven (1970), Demos (1970), Farber (1972a), and Vinovskis (1971) discuss mortality in the early American period. Vinovskis (1972) discusses some of the problems of working with mortality data before 1860, of making comparative statements based on them, and some of the sources of variation associated with differential mortality.)

The changed demographic conditions of the American colonies, compared with the England from which many of them had come, has led John Murrin (1972, p. 238) to suggest that:

> ...New England might have been responsible for a simple but tremendously important invention, at least in terms of scale—grandparents—who became numerous enough by the 1660s to raise serious problems in a paternalistic social environment.

Yet the solution of this problem does not seem, to any great extent, to have been the proliferation of trigenerational households. Thus the potential audience of family behavior resident within the household in the colonial period was not often expanded to include grandparents or other kin, despite changes in the demographic capability of doing so.

Beyond the early colonial experience, the available evidence continues to support the conclusion that an extended kinship structure was in no way characteristic of a large proportion of American households. Pryor (1972), in a study of Rhode Island family structure, found that in 1875, 82 percent of families were nuclear. (In 1960, 85 percent of Rhode Island households were nuclear.) Bloomberg et al. (1971), in an analysis of southern Michigan families, show that in 1880, 7.1 percent of rural households, 9.0 percent of village and town households, and 6.6 percent of Detroit households included parents of the household head.

In terms of the evidence now available, then, it seems legitimate to conclude that that part of the potential audience of family behavior which is made up of household residents does not, for the overwhelming majority of American families, include fewer grandparents or other kindred in the present than it did in the past. Thus, while the extended versus nuclear character of family structure cannot be used to support the hypothesized change of the family from a more public to a more private institution, other changes in family structure and household composition do provide such evidence. One part of this evidence relates to the structure of the household kindred group and the other relates to the nonkindred residents within the household.

One major change that has occurred in the household kindred group of American families is a decrease in the number of children born per family (see Coale and Zelnik 1963, p. 36). The audience of family behavior has been the focus of this analysis because of its potential for social control over and support for the normative enactment of family roles. While young children are meaningful members of any family, and concern over their well-being may determine many activities of family members, they are not likely to be seen as the repositories of socially approved behavior. Their membership in the audience of family behavior is less likely to provide a source of control, support, or companionship for their parents than might the presence of adult children or other adult observers.[5]

The number of children born will affect the age structure, and thereby the composition, of the household kin group, as Table 1 indicates. If children are likely to serve as meaningful sources of social control and support only when they are adults (or quasi-adults), then the larger family is likely to have such persons in its midst for a longer period of the family cycle than will smaller families, and therefore experience less privacy. Privacy is increased in smaller families by the effect which fewer children have on the age distribution of potential audience members.

Although children may not serve as mechanisms of normative social control or support during their childhood, as adults they are likely to be particularly important members of the household audi-

Table 1 Hypothetical age distribution of children in two- and five-child families (assuming no child mortality and a constant two-year birth interval*)

Age distribution of children in		Age distribution of children in		Age distribution of children in	
Two-child family	Five-child family	Two-child family	Five-child family	Two-child family	Five-child family
under 1	under 1	5	5	10	10
2	2	7	7	12	12
	4		9		14
	6		11		16
	8		13		18

*Birth intervals are, in fact, parity-specific, with longer intervals between each succeeding birth. The assumption of a constant two-year birth interval leads to a conservative estimate of the age distribution of children in large families, which would tend to strengthen the argument presented in the text.

ence to their parents.[6] Beresford and Rivlin's (1966) analysis shows that the proportion of grown children (in the age group 15 to 24)—both male and female—who were likely to be living in their parents' households declined markedly from 1940 to 1960. Although these changes have been occurring since the latter part of the 19th century,[7] Beresford and Rivlin (1966, p. 248) say:

A dramatic change did occur between 1885 and 1960 in household relationships of young adults in Massachusetts, but most of the change seems to have taken place since 1940.

This removal of young adults from the households of their parents has the result not only of increasing the privacy from familial sources available to the young adults themselves, but also of increasing the privacy of the households which they have left, since their departure has decreased the observability of their parents' behavior. Thus, privacy at both older and younger ages is increased by the removal of young adults from their parental households. The finding that this change has occurred most markedly in the middle of the 20th century is partial confirmation of the hypothesis that the development of the private family is a phenomenon which has taken place in the 20th century.

(Katz (1972a, 1972b) has shown, in some very interesting work on Hamilton, Ontario, that a large proportion of young men and women in the 19th century (between the ages of 12 and 20) experienced a period of semidependency, during which they lived as boarders and servants in other people's homes. When young adults move into the households of others, privacy will be affected in a different way than when they establish homes of their own. It is this latter phenomenon to which Beresford and Rivlin are referring.)

While variations in the audience of family behavior within the household is partly related to changes in the kindred group, there have also been marked changes in the nonkin group resident within the household which has affected the audience of family behavior within the home. In the distant as well as the recent past, categories of persons other than kin have had legitimate and normal access to the household as resident members of it. Such persons were likely to include servants, boarders and lodgers, apprentices, and the children who were received into the household as part of the practice of "putting out" children. The presence of these persons, as resident members of the household, is likely to have affected the degree of privacy which was available within it. Their presence lessened the degree to which family members could control observation of their behavior in the enactment of their family roles, and their removal increased that control.[8]

Demos, in describing the practice of "putting out children" in Plymouth Colony, says (1970, p. 72):

> There was little formal schooling anywhere in the old Colony until the last quarter of the [17th] century, and the practice of placing children out may have constituted a functional equivalent for at least some of its young people.

Morgan, on the other hand, suggests (1944, pp. 76, 77) that:

> Puritan children were frequently brought up in other families than their own, even when there was no apparent educational advantage involved.... Puritan parents did not trust themselves with their own children, they were afraid of spoiling them by too great affection.

Whichever explanation is correct (or if both of them are), the practice of "putting out children" and apprenticeship was widespread in the past.[9]

Neither apprenticeship, the "putting out" system, nor service was restricted to a single class, although the conditions and terms of the contract varied by social class. (See, among others, Morgan 1944, p. 132; Farber 1972a, pp. 50–52; Demos 1970, p. 73; Katz 1972a, 1972b, for some examples of the relationship between social class and residence in others' households.) While the association of these practices to the stratification system is not wholly clear, their effect on the family is. Although, as Laslett (1971) describes the relationship of apprentices and Demos (1970) and Aries (1962) describe the relationship of servants to the heads of the households in which they lived, as similar to family members, differences also existed (see Farber 1972a, p. 50), and the presence of such persons within the household restricted domestic privacy. Hecht (1956) discusses the constraint on privacy which servants imposed on household members in 18th-century England. Gilman (1910, p. 42) discusses the same issue in relation to turn-of-the-century homes in the United States when she says:

> With servants living in our home by day and night, confronted with our strange customs and new ideas, having our family affairs always before them, and having nothing else in their occupation to offset this interest, we find in this arrangement of life a condition as far removed from privacy as could be imagined.

The practice of "putting out children" and apprenticeship, the varied social characteristics of the servant class, and widespread use of servants throughout many sectors of the social hierarchy indicate that the public-private distinction is not associated with a single social class only.

The tasks which were performed by servants, as well as by other nonkindred within the household, included many activities other than the domestic chores which we tend to associate with servants today, especially those related to the demands of an agricultural and domestic economy. In return, the master or head of the household was responsible for the moral and educational, as well as the physical, well-being of the persons within his domain. (See, among others, Aries 1962; Demos 1970; Morgan 1944; Farber 1972a.) But the guardian and/or educational role which was associated with the presence of nonkin within the household changed rather early in the American experience. Farber (1972a, p. 49) says:

> By the end of the 18th century, the apprentice system, stripped of its role of socializing youths and controlling deviants, had become somewhat rationalized.

Douglas (1921), in a discussion of the history of American apprenticeship, also dates the beginning of this decline with the end of the 18th and the beginning of the 19th century, i.e., with the development of the factory system of production, although he indicates that the timing of this change varied by industry and area of the country. Douglas (1921, p. 55) says:

> His [the apprentice's] home had formerly been at his master's. He had lived and worked familiarly with him, receiving his board and clothing in return for his services. Now, with the growth of industry, the master could no longer house

all of his apprentices. He had to let them find their own shelter, and commute their former benefits into cash allowance.... In brief, master and apprentice had stood in the relation of father and son; they now stood in the relation of employer and employee.

The growth of the factory system and of machine production, therefore, removed a nonkin segment of the household population who had once been included as quasi-family members.[10]

While the decline of apprenticeship may have reduced the proportion of nonkin residents within the household, an alternate source was to be found among boarders and lodgers, particularly in the growing urban centers. Modell (1972) provides a detailed analysis of patterns of boarding and lodging, particularly in the late 19th and early 20th centuries. Lodging was more frequent for men than for women, was almost as common among American-born as foreign-headed households, and, although less common among affluent compared to poorer families, was not restricted to the poor only.

Modell's analysis of household composition among working-class families indicates the importance of life cycle factors for the practice of taking in boarders. Among childless couples, 15.9 percent took in boarders, while in families in which the father was 45 years or older and had no child less than four years old living at home, 41.2 percent took in boarders. An even larger percentage of this latter group (54.7 percent) was found to include boarders among the poorest, when economic factors were taken into account. Thus, a sizeable proportion of families were likely to have boarders in their midst at some points in their lives.

The decline of boarding as a widespread practice did not occur until well into the 20th century. Modell (1972) says:

> Extensive if imperfectly representative data on working-class families collected in industrial areas by the Commissioner of Labor in 1903 found that about 22 percent of the native-born and 25 percent of foreign-headed families had some income from boarders and lodgers in the previous years.... By 1930, the proportion of all United States families in urban areas who

kept a lodger was 11.4 percent, a figure perhaps somewhat inflated by the depression which apparently continued to keep the figure as high as 9.0 percent in 1940.... Prosperity, changes in housing, availability, and changed tastes reduced the urbanized-areas figure to 3.0 percent in 1960.

While apprentices and other people's children may have declined as sources of nonkindred household members early in the 19th century, and servants decreased steadily as industrialization grew, boarders seem to have replaced these other groups as nonkin household residents. It is not until well into the middle of the present century that household composition became restricted to the nuclear kin group.

PRIVACY AND THE USAGE OF SPACE

The analysis of the audience of family behavior, so far, has concentrated on family activities and interactions within the household. Yet the house does not provide the only site for family activities, and the privacy associated with the enactment of family roles can be measured in at least two spatial contexts, one within the house and the other outside of it. Parks, streets, churches, ball parks, camp sites, etc., are also places where the family group may be seen together. Therefore, the usage and availability of space, both in- and outside the household, is relevant to a consideration of the ways in which spatial characteristics will affect the visibility of family behavior. (Smith, 1971, discusses ways in which household space is likely to affect family interactions.)

Demos's (1970, pp. 24–51) description of some of the residences in Plymouth Colony—a small house of few rooms, with limited sources of heating—exemplifies conditions in which spatial limitations contributed to a lack of privacy within the household. Furthermore, the absence of what Hall (1969, pp. 103–107) refers to as "fixed-feature space" as a characteristic of room organization in the past—even when crowding was less of a problem than in the colonial cottage—also contributed to a lack of privacy in the enactment of family roles. Flaherty (1972, pp. 25–84) argues that privacy was not only valued but attainable in the New England colonies, but his descriptions, too, support the view that crowding existed within the household and privacy was difficult to attain.

Changes in architectural styles and practices are also likely to have had considerable effect on within-family interaction, although further study is necessary to elaborate on the nature of these changes. Flaherty (1972, p. 40), discussing the design of 18th-century American homes, says:

> . . . the absence of hallways . . . remained a basic flaw in the floor plan of the central-chimney house. Movement from one part of the house to another required passage through adjacent rooms.

The development of the central hallway, with rooms opening onto it, permitted a degree of within-family privacy not previously available. Frank Lloyd Wright's development of the open floor plan, where only bedrooms were separated from the free and open access of all other parts of the house (see Wright, 1954) also had a great effect on family interactions within the house. But Wright's modern innovation occurred when household composition (according to the evidence presented in the preceding section) was more likely to be composed of nuclear family members only, contributing to different consequences in the "open plan" colonial house or cottage compared to the modern suburban house.

Handlin (forthcoming) claims that the development of the single-family detached house as an ideal setting of American domestic life took place at the beginning of the 19th century and has had great influence on the work of architects and designers in the field of domestic design. The increasing population density and visibility which accompanied the change from rural to urban living from the mid-19th century onward may have motivated a search for privacy within the home which had been less necessary (and less available) in an earlier period. Lynd and Lynd (1929, p. 26) describe changes in the usage of space in Middletown in the following way:

> In the eighties, with their ample yards, porches were not urgently needed. Towards 1900, as smaller yards were driving the family closer to the house, people began to hear of porches . . . and the era of porch furniture began. Already, however, business class homes are leading the way in a reversion to porchless designs with glassed-in sun parlor and sleeping porch. . . . The trend is apparently to divert the money formerly put into front porches to sleeping porches, glassed-in dens, and other more private and more often used parts of the house.

Evidence that privacy continues as a 20th-century ideal for home design can be found in a recent analysis of the urban environment in which Michelson (1970, p. 101) discusses "the ultimate desirability of single-family housing in today's technology."

Several discussions of the family in the past have emphasized the out-of-doors settings of family interactions. A report in the *Architectural Record* (1892, p. 56) describing middle-class apartment living in New York at the end of the 19th century, remarks on "the tendency of many tenants to make parlors of, and hold receptions on, the stoops." McLaughlin (1971) describes similar patterns among first-generation Italians in Buffalo, New York, at the beginning of the 20th century, and it is precisely the decline in such patterns which Jane Jacobs (1961) discusses in her analysis of contemporary American cities. Sennett (1970) describes the importance of parks for the social life of upper-class families in Chicago in the early part of the 19th century. If and when family social life takes place in the open, the possibility of observability is increased: the number of observers is likely to be greater and there will be less control over who those observers are in such a setting.[11]

Evidence still remains to be collected to support the claim that the spatial characteristics of the setting in which family interactions occur in the more recent period of American history has contributed to less public scrutiny of the enactment of family roles than was true in the past. There are several reasons, though, to believe that further work will uncover such evidence.

The involvement of the federal government (through VA and FHA loan programs) and private banks and insurance companies in financing the construction of dwelling units is likely to have contributed to a decrease in room overcrowding. These same factors are likely to have contributed to the realization of the single-family detached home ideal in this century to a greater extent than was true of any earlier period in American history.

Changes in the amenities available within the home—those associated with comfort (central heating, indoor plumbing, air conditioning, etc.) as well as those associated with entertainment (radio, television, and phonographs)—are likely to have decreased the proportion of family activities which take place outside the home, where control over visibility is limited, and to have increased the proportion of such activities which take place within the home, where control over visibility is increased.

Each of these factors provides a background for hypothesizing that further research into architectural and housing data will provide supporting evidence for the thesis that the private family is a 20th-century development.

PRIVACY AND NORMS

The previous sections of this analysis have considered some of the structural and material conditions which have affected the context of family role behavior in the past and in the present. This section will discuss changes in the norms which are likely to have had an impact on behavior within these changing contexts.

Morgan (1944) describes the importance of religion for family relationships and behavior among the Puritans in 17th-century New England. Not only did religion specify the correct relationships between family members—their duties and responsibilities to each other—but it also made it a sacred duty of members of the church to see that these edicts were fulfilled. Laws were enacted to ensure that proper behavior within families took place, and punishments were meted out to those who defaulted.

The quality of family relationships was also subject to legal control. Demos (1970, p. 93) says:

It was not enough that married persons should simply live together on a regular basis; their relationships must be relatively peaceful and harmonious.

And courts had jurisdiction to punish offenders who deviated from "peaceful and harmonious" behavior. According to Morgan (1944, pp. 39–40):

The government was not satisfied with mere cohabitation but insisted that it be peaceful. Husbands and wives were forbidden by law to strike each other, and the courts enforced the provisions on numerous occasions.

Husbands and wives were fined for using "ill words" to each other or "railing" at each other or "striking and kicking."

Thus, the norms regulating family relationships in the earliest period of American history were heavily influenced by religion, and were enforced through law via the scrutiny of others who were empowered by those same religious beliefs to mind their neighbors' business. (Demos (1970, pp. 49–51) has suggested that the anger which crowded living conditions generated in Plymouth Colony was unconsciously displaced onto neighbors through a "chronic hostility" toward them. Such a dynamic may have been reinforced by the sense that neighbors acted as constant watchdogs over an institution that Flaherty (1972, p. 45) claims was "the primary place where colonists sought privacy.") The same norms which specified what family behavior should be also specified that others had the right to hold one accountable for its proper enactment. Thus, public accountability was built into the system of norms surrounding the performance of family roles.

Handlin (forthcoming) claims that the 19th century saw major changes in American domestic life. Horace Bushnell, "an influential minister, living in Hartford, Connecticut, but with a national audience through his published sermons," referred to these changes as a "transition from mother and daughter power to water and steam power." Mothers and daughters were being released from some of the drudgery which had characterized housekeeping in the past. Some greater freedom of choice was becoming available in the public world of work through the changing demands of an industrialized economy. The growing place of women in public life—through club, consumer, and reform groups—also provided alternatives in the realm of public activity for the mothers and daughters whose energies were being somewhat released by technological advance. But the ideology which accompanied the structural changes in family life into the 20th century emphasized the traditional place of women in their family roles, which were enacted in settings that were increasingly private. In my view, an important aspect of this ideology for the modern family can be traced through the development of what was later to become an organized, institutional effort to "professionalize" domestic activities—i.e., through the growth of the home economics movement in the United States.

The home economics movement, whose history can be traced back to the efforts of 19th-century women's clubs and other organizations (see Baldwin 1949; Bevier 1924) was formally organized in 1899 at the first Lake Placid Conference on Home Economics, and was replaced in 1908–09 by the still ongoing American Home Economics Association. The story of the development of home economics as a subject of interest and attention in America cannot be told here in any detail. Its relevance to this analysis is in terms of the norms about family life which it exhibited, the mechanisms by which these norms were circulated and the ways in which they interacted with the changing structural bases of family life at the beginning of the twentieth century.[12]

Although varied ideas were expressed by early members of the home economics movement, two seem particularly important: (1) the belief that family roles were not instinctual or natural, but were to be learned; and (2) that skills must be taught and learned, not in the home, but in the schools, from specially trained personnel. The emphasis was on the need for scientific management, efficiency, and economy within the home and on the role of the school in producing these desired ends. (An interesting account of the background to these concerns within the field of education can be found in Cremin (1961).)

The argument was put in various ways in the *Proceedings* of the early annual conferences, in the *Journal of Home Economics* (which began publication in 1909), and in other writings. Some examples follow:

A woman does not keep house by inspiration as formerly thought. She keeps house 'well' only by application of intelligence and technical training. Neither does a woman take care of her children by inspiration. (Lake Placid Conference 1902, p. 50)

Many think that home economics is an instinct, the same that leads young birds to nest building, and that no special training is required. The man that undertakes any business goes through some form of apprenticeship and becomes familiar with all the details of management, but to the majority of women housekeeping is a combination of accidental forces.

...So we are working toward a more systematic method of carrying on home work. Women and girls should have special education and training in this subject.... (Lake Placid Conference 1907, p. 84)

The principles of health, sanitation, and nutrition had to be taught. They were neither instinctual nor could the home, through maternal teaching or example, be expected to provide the technical knowledge which proper housekeeping required.

To choose the food for a family and to prepare it properly are feats the successful accomplishment of which require a technical training.... She [the homemaker] can not afford to disregard this increasing knowledge of the dependence of health on food, she can not afford to deprive her family, her children, of any aid that science can give to equip them in the most efficient manner for the stress and strain of life. (Lake Placid Conference 1904, pp. 42–43)

The new knowledge and skills had to be made available to middle-class families experiencing the decline in available servants, to immigrant peasant women who were ignorant of modern housekeeping techniques and who could not, therefore, pass these skills on to their daughters, and to working girls whose labor force participation had deprived them of the opportunity of learning at home the old skills, if not the new.

The answer to the problem was clear—education. Julia Lathrop, first head of the Children's

Bureau (founded in 1912), said, in a speech to a class reunion at Vassar College (Addams 1935, pp. 40–41):

> ...the present status of the education of women demands a new specialization to be signaled by the creation of centers of study and research in the service of family life....It is no less than a revolution which is implied. Its aim is to give the work of the woman head of a household the status of a profession.

Isabel Bevier, one of the most active early members of the home economics movement and President of the American Home Economics Association in 1911 and 1912, wrote (1924, p. 161):

> The original Lake Placid group had distinguished itself by putting emphasis upon the educational phase of the question and, from the first, there had been committees commissioned to find ways and means so to develop the subject-matter that it would find favor with public school boards and makers of college curricula.

And their efforts met with considerable success, from the federal government, which provided funding for home economics education (see Douglas 1924, p. 294; Cremin 1961, p. 56; Bevier 1924, pp. 172–178) and from colleges, universities, and public school systems which, for a while at least, steadily increased their offerings and training facilities in the field of home economics. (See Bevier 1924, pp. 142–143.)

The concerns and ideology of the home economics movement were also disseminated through other channels than the schools. The General Federation of Women's Clubs, with a membership of 800,000 women in 1907 and affiliates in 47 states (see Lake Placid Conference 1907, p. 98) was also interested and active in this work. Mrs. C. S. Buell, President of the State Federation of Clubs in Madison, Wisconsin, said to the Ninth Lake Placid Conference (1907, pp. 97–98):

> ...we of the Federated women's clubs may be of aid in bringing to the active homemaker the results of your studies....We appeal to you for your best thought and effort, pledging you our loyal support and earnest endeavor to make your purposes as far-reaching as possible.

The home economics movement, then, can be seen as developing a modern ideology for the American family in general and for the woman in it in particular. The goal of scientific home management and efficiency, and the use of educational institutions to achieve this end through the training of girls to be modern homemakers, emphasized traditional views of women's place in the home and reinforced the sanctity and privacy of the individual family. Not only was there the old will, reinforced by a scientific ideology, but there was also the way, provided by the new structural characteristics of the family described in earlier sections. The privacy which the New England colonists had valued so highly more than two centuries earlier was finally attainable.

CONCLUSION

The argument made here is that an attempt to understand changes in the American family may fruitfully be pursued by attention to variations in the family as a public and private institution. When it is common practice for family life to occur elsewhere than within the confines of the domestic establishment, such as in parks or on front stoops, when it is common for nondomestic activities—such as political and economic—to be pursued within the domestic context, when it is common for nonfamily members—such as servants, apprentices, and boarders—to constitute part of the household, then the family can be described as having a public character.

Structural and normative support for privacy within the family is, I would suggest, a more accurate description of the 20th-century family than it was of its historical predecessor, despite the potential for much variation in publicness and privacy along other lines. A setting in which most of the interactions of family members take place in the home and those activities defined as appropriate to the home are related primarily to domestic and familial activities, there is greater control over the composition of the audience of family behavior, and thus a greater degree of privacy.

To the extent that family privacy has increased, then, it is also likely that there has been a decrease in social control over and social support for a traditional definition of the performance of family roles. The consequences of this development (as well as the truth of the claim itself) remain to be studied and discussed further. One theme in current considerations of the family is about the viability and future of the nuclear family form. (See, for instance, Gordon 1972, pp. 1–22; Skolnick and Skolnick 1971, pp. 1–32.) These discussions often point to the strains of nuclear family living which have led to experimentation with alternative family styles, such as communal living, group marriages, and single-parent families. If social control declines as privacy increases, then there may be structural reasons for believing that the current variability in the styles of American family life will continue.[13] The point should be made, though, that an increase

of alternate family living styles does not necessarily herald the death of the nuclear family, but rather a variability in which several types of family organization will exist simultaneously.

One further observation may be appropriate. Goode's (1963) analysis of changing family patterns throughout the world led him to conclude that the conjugal family unit will become predominant as the structural and ideological features associated with the western experience of industrialization occur elsewhere. This analysis, which focuses on privacy, rather than on nuclearity per se, suggests that the change in family patterns which Goode sees in the future of newly industrializing nations may be an historical phase within each culture, and not necessarily a permanent development. If the analysis presented here, of the American case, has any predictive value, it is in suggesting that change will continue to occur beyond the development of the conjugal family.

NOTES

1. This statement should not be taken as an assertion that privacy as a general phenomenon has increased in the United States. The hypothesis relates to privacy in the enactment of family roles only.

2. Any essay-length presentation which discusses changes in the family over the whole of American history is bound to commit errors of oversimplification. While on a general level I believe the changes described here to be accurate, there are likely to be deviations from them along local, temporal, socio-economic, and ethnic lines. Socioeconomic and ethnic variation in family structure and behavior has attracted considerable sociological attention, although an analysis of variations in privacy by social class or ethnicity still remains to be done. The absence of attention to these variables in the analysis presented here in no way signifies their lack of importance.

3. The presence or absence of social support for and social control over the enactment of family roles may provide some insight into the impact of feminist movements in the United States on traditional definitions of appropriate female behavior in their family roles. The growth of a private family not only means that the sources of social control over women's behavior in their familial roles has declined, but that the sources of social support and satisfaction for the enactment of traditionally defined family behavior for women has also been reduced.

4. A further consequence, suggested in personal communication by Bonacich (stemming from his experimental work on Prisoner Dilemma problems; see, for instance, Bonacich, 1972) is that under conditions of privacy, the adherence to normative precepts is likely to depend on whether norms have been internalized by the individual, since external pressures to conformity are reduced.

5. While young children may not act as sources of social control and support for their parents, changes in the number of children are likely to have marked effects on the children themselves, since siblings are important sources of socialization for each other. Demos discusses some of the consequences of changes in the size, and therefore the age structure of the sibling group, for the development of children (1970, p. 69; 1972).

6. When a child becomes an adult is, at least in part, a social question, and there has been considerable variation in the timing of this transition. Aries (1962), Demos (1970), Demos and Demos (1971), and Hunt (1970) discuss this point in relation to western European and early American families.

7. The authors present a detailed comparison of Massachusetts household relationships in 1885 and 1960, as well as 1940 through 1960 comparison for the whole of the United States. Pryor's (1972) analysis of Rhode Island households in 1875 and 1960 indicates

a growth of one-person households within that state, which would confirm Beresford and Rivlin's general finding.

8. Any overall discussion of changes in American household composition that neglects the effects of slavery is certainly incomplete. Greven's (1972) analysis of household composition in South Carolina discusses this issue to some extent. While the presence of slaves will not be discussed here, their existence is likely to have had effects not wholly dissimilar to the presence of other nonkindred household residents in terms of privacy by providing potential members for the audience of family behavior.

9. This argument may appear specious in that, having argued that larger families lead to less privacy, I now claim that children were not at home, but were reducing privacy in someone else's home. It is likely that social class, and other sources of differentiation in the society, led to the privacy of many families being affected by the number and circulation of children.

10. The growth of schools is relevant to a discussion of the dispersion of those activities which were once located in the home. Some relevant material may be found in Bailyn (1960) and Cremin (1970) for the colonial period. Cremin (1951, 1961) discusses educational thought and institutions through the middle of the twentieth century.

11. Some constraints on observability, particularly in this case, those associated with residential segregation by class, would nevertheless continue to operate.

12. The relevant historical context must be kept in mind. These events occurred at a period in which young women and children continued to be a source of factory labor, when the availability of domestic servants was sharply declining, when problems of health, sanitation, overcrowded housing, immigration, and poverty in the rapidly growing urban centers were attracting the attention of many social and political reformers.

13. A continuation and extension of such variability, though, assumes that external forces will not impose greater conformity. Farber's (1972b) analysis of recent changes in law relating to the family and privacy suggests that legal restrictions in "the interests of the state" may provide a basis for limiting privacy and variation. The authority of the state, therefore, may attempt to impose restrictions on family life in the modern period in a manner familiar in colonial New England. That such legal restrictions, though, may have different consequences for different social class groupings in the society, again indicates the importance of that variable in understanding the process and change being discussed.

REFERENCES

ADDAMS, JANE. *My friend, Julia Lathrop.* New York: Macmillan, 1935.

Architectural Record 1 (July-September 1892): 55–64.

ARIES, PHILIPPE. *Centuries of childhood: a social history of family life.* New York: Knopf, 1962.

BAILYN, BERNARD. *Education in the forming of American society.* Chapel Hill: University of North Carolina Press, 1960.

BALDWIN, KETURAH E. *The AHEA saga.* Washington, D.C.: American Home Economics Association, 1949.

BERESFORD, JOHN C., AND ALICE M. RIVLIN. Privacy, poverty, and old age. *Demography* 3 (1966): 247–258.

BERKNER, LUTZ K. The stem family and the developmental cycle of the peasant household: an eighteenth-century Austrian example. *American Historical Review* 77 (April 1972): 398–418.

BEVIER, ISABEL. *Home economics in education.* Philadelphia: Lippincott, 1924.

BLOOMBERG, SUSAN E., MARY FRANK FOX, ROBERT M. WARNER, AND SAM BASS WARNER, JR. A census probe into nineteenth-century family history: Southern Michigan, 1850–1880. *Journal of Social History* 5 (Fall 1971): 26–45.

BONACICH, PHILLIP. Norms and cohesion as adaptive responses to potential conflict: an experimental study. *Sociometry* 35 (September 1972): 357–375.

BURGESS, ERNEST W., AND HARVEY J. LOCKE. *The family: from institution to companionship.* New York: American Book Company, 1953.

CLARK, EUPHEMIA. A campaign for home making. *Journal of Home Economics* 1 (April 1909): 167–170.

COALE, ANSLEY J., AND MELVIN ZELNIK. *New estimates of fertility and population in the United States.* Princeton: Princeton University Press, 1963.

CREMIN, LAWRENCE A. *The American common school.* New York: Teachers College, Columbia University, 1951.

————. *The transformation of the school: progressivism in American education.* New York: Knopf, 1961.

————. *American education: the colonial experience, 1607–1783.* New York: Harper & Row, 1970.

DEMOS, JOHN. Families in colonial Bristol, R.I. *William and Mary Quarterly* 25 (January 1968): 40–57.

————. *A little commonwealth.* New York: Oxford, 1970.

————. Demography and psychology in the historical study of family life: a personal report. In Peter

Laslett (ed.), *Household and family in past time*, pp. 561-569. Cambridge: Cambridge University Press, 1972.

_____, AND VIRGINIA DEMOS. Adolescence in historical perspective. In Bert N. Adams and Thomas Weirath (eds.), *Readings on the sociology of the family*, pp. 30-40. Chicago: Markham, 1971.

DOUGLAS, PAUL H. *American apprenticeship and industrial education.* Studies in History, Economics and Public Law XCV. New York: Columbia University, 1921.

FARBER, BERNARD. *Guardians of virtue: Salem families in 1800.* New York: Basic Books, 1972.

_____. Historical trends in American family law. Paper read at a National Conference on the Family Social Structure and Social Change, April 27-29, 1972. Clark University, Worcester, Mass.

FLAHERTY, DAVID H. *Privacy in colonial New England.* Charlottesville: University Press of Virginia, 1972.

GILMAN, CHARLOTTE PERKINS. *The home: its work and influence.* New York: Charlton, 1910.

GOODE, WILLIAM J. *World revolution and family patterns.* New York: Free Press, 1963.

GORDON, MICHAEL, (ed.) *The nuclear family in crisis: the search for an alternative.* New York: Harper & Row, 1972.

GREVEN, PHILIP. Family structure in 17th-century Andover. *William and Mary Quarterly 23* (April 1966): 234-256.

_____. *Four generations: population, land, and family in colonial Andover, Massachusetts.* New York: Cornell University Press, 1970.

_____. The average size of families and households in the province of Massachusetts in 1764 and in the United States in 1790: an overview. In Peter Laslett (ed.), *Household and family in past time*, pp. 545-560. Cambridge: Cambridge University Press, 1972.

HALL, EDWARD T. *The hidden dimension.* New York: Anchor Books, 1969.

HANDLIN, DAVID P. The detached house in the age of the object and beyond. Chapter of a forthcoming book, *New dimensions in housing.*

HECHT, J. JEAN. *The domestic servant class in eighteenth-century England.* London: Routledge and Kegan Paul, 1956.

HUNT, DAVID. *Parents and children in history: the psychology of family life in early modern France.* New York: Basic Books, 1970.

JACOBS, JANE. *The death and life of great American cities.* New York: Vintage Books, 1961.

KATZ, MICHAEL B. Four propositions about social and family structures in preindustrial society. A paper

prepared for the Comparative Social Mobility Conference, Institute of Advanced Study, Princeton, New Jersey, June 15-17, 1972.

_____. Growing-up in the nineteenth-century. Working Paper #31. Canadian Social History Project, 1972.

Lake Placid Conference on Home Economics. *Proceedings of the fourth annual conference.* Lake Placid, New York, 1902.

_____. *Proceedings of the ninth annual conference.* Lake Placid, New York, 1907.

LASLETT, PETER. Size and structure of the household in England over three centuries. *Population Studies 23* (July 1969): 199-223.

_____. *The world we have lost.* (2nd ed.) London: University Paperbacks, 1971.

LOCKRIDGE, KENNETH A. The population of Dedham, Massachusetts, 1636-1736. *Economic History Review 19* (1966): 318-344.

LYND, ROBERT S., AND HELEN MERRELL LYND. *Middletown.* New York: Harcourt Brace, 1929.

MCLAUGHLIN, VIRGINIA YANS. Working-class immigrant families: first generation Italians in Buffalo, New York. Paper delivered before the Organization of American Historians, April 1971.

MERTON, ROBERT K. The role set: problems in sociological theory. *British Journal of Sociology 7* (June 1959).

MICHELSON, WILLIAM. *Man and his urban environment: a sociological approach.* Reading, Mass.: Addison-Wesley, 1970.

MODELL, JOHN. Strangers in the family: boarding and lodging in industrial America. Paper read at a National Conference on the Family, Social Structure and Social Change, April 27-29, 1972. Clark University, Worcester, Massachusetts.

MORGAN, EDMUND S. *The Puritan family.* New York: Harper, 1944.

MURRIN, JOHN. Review essay. History and Theory. *Studies in the Philosophy of History 2*, 1972.

OGBURN, W.F., AND M. F. NIMKOFF. *Technology and the changing family.* Boston: Houghton Mifflin, 1955.

O'NEILL, WILLIAM L. *Divorce in the progressive era.* New Haven: Yale University Press, 1967.

PARISH, WILLIAM L., AND MOSHE SCHWARTZ. Household complexity in nineteenth century France." *American Sociological Review 37* (April 1972): 154-173.

PRYOR, EDWARD T., JR. Rhode Island family structure: 1887-1960. In Peter Laslett (ed.), *Household and family in past time*, pp. 571-589. Cambridge: Cambridge University Press, 1972.

RIIS, JACOB. *Jacob Riis revisited: poverty and the slum in another era.* Edited with an introduction by

Francesco Cordasco. New York: Doubleday, Anchor, 1968.

SENNETT, RICHARD. *Families against the city: middle-class homes of industrial Chicago, 1872-1890.* Cambridge, Mass.: Harvard University Press, 1970.

SKOLNICK, ARLENE S., AND JEROME H. SKOLNICK (eds.) *Family in transition: rethinking marriage, sexuality, child rearing, and family organization.* Boston: Little, Brown, 1971.

SMITH, DOROTHY E. Household space and family organiza-

tion. *Pacific Sociological Review* **14** (January 1971): 53-78.

VINOVSKIS, MARIS A. American historical demography: a review essay. *Historical Methods Newsletter* **4** (September 1971): 141-148.

_____. Morality rates and trends in Massachusetts before 1860. *Journal of Economic History* **32** (March 1972): 184-213.

WRIGHT, FRANK LLOYD. *The natural house.* New York: Horizon Press, 1954.

On Engels' Origin of the Family, Private Property and the State[1]

INTRODUCTION

ELEANOR BURKE LEACOCK

IN THE *ORIGIN OF THE FAMILY, PRIVATE Property and the State*, Engels outlines the successive social and economic forms which underlay the broad sweep of early human history, as mankind gained increasing mastery over the sources of subsistence. The book was written after Marx's death, but was drawn from Marx's as well as Engels' own notes. It was based on the work, *Ancient Society*, which appeared in 1877 and was written by the anthropologist Lewis Henry Morgan, who, as Engels wrote in 1884, "in his own way... discovered afresh in America the materialistic conception of history discovered by Marx 40 years ago." The contribution Marx and Engels made to Morgan's work was to sharpen its theoretical implications, particularly with regard to the emergence of classes and the state. Although Engels' book was written well before most of the now available material on primitive and early urban society had been amassed, the fundamentals of his outline for history have remained valid. Moreover, many issues raised by Morgan's and then Engels' work are still the subjects of lively debate among anthropologists, while the theoretical implications of these issues are still matters of concern to Marxist scholars generally.

Morgan described the evolution of society in some 560 pages. Engels' book is far shorter, summarizing Morgan's material and focusing sharply on the major differences between primitive society and "civilization" with its fully developed classes and political organization. The questions Engels deals with pertain to three major topics: (1) developmental stages in mankind's history, (2) the nature of primitive society with regard to property, rank, family forms and descent systems, and (3) the emergence of commodity production, economically based classes and the state. A fourth subject of importance to contemporary anthropological research and but briefly referred to by Engels involves primate social organization and its relevance for an insight into early man.

THE EMERGENCE OF MONOGAMY AND THE SUBJUGATION OF WOMEN

The pages in which Engels discusses early marriage forms are the most difficult in *Origin*, partly because kinship terminologies and practices are

Reprinted by permission of the author and International Publishers.

complicated and unfamiliar to the Western reader, and partly because confusions about biological and social forces obscure the significant parts of his discussion. However, Engels' fundamental theme is clear. He writes:

> "We...have three principal forms of marriage which correspond broadly to the three principal stages of human development: for the period of savagery, group marriage; for barbarism, pairing marriage; for civilization, monogamy..."

Monogamy arises from a transitional stage of polygyny, "when men have female slaves at their command;" coupled with male supremacy, it is "supplemented by adultery and prostitution," and is from the beginning monogamy for the women only. Marriage was frankly polygynous throughout classical times, and covertly so thereafter.

The significant characteristic of monogamous marriage was its transformation of the nuclear family into the basic economic unit of society, within which a woman and her children became dependent upon an individual man. Arising in conjunction with exploitative class relations, this transformation resulted in the oppression of women that has persisted to the present day. As corollary to, or symptomatic of this transformation, the reckoning of descent was changed from "mother right" (matrilineality) to "father right."

In the field of anthropology, it is the last proposition, that matrilineality was prior to patrilineality in the history of mankind, which has received most attention. The rest of Engels' discussion has been virtually ignored, and it is unfortunate testimony to the status of women both within and without the field that detailed studies of women's status and role in primitive societies are so rare. Nonetheless, there is sufficient evidence at hand to support in its broad outlines Engels' argument that the position of women relative to men deteriorated with the advent of class society, as well as data to fill in many particulars of his thesis. Above all, however, there is crying need for further analysis of existing materials and for the collection of new data.

Let us first examine the point that marriage is essentially different in hunting-gathering ("savage") and horticultural ("barbarian") societies on the one hand, and class society ("civilization") on the other, and that there is a further distinction between the freer "group marriage" or hunter-gatherers and its successor, "pairing marriage." The term "group marriage" unfortunately conjures up an unrealistic image of mass weddings that are nowhere to be found. In fact, however, Engels' actual analysis of "group marriage" as it obtained in Australia concurs with what has come to be called "loose monogamy" in anthropological writings. "All that the superficial observer sees in group marriage," Engels pointed out, "is a loose form of monogamous marriage, here and there polygyny, and occasional infidelities." Through the "mass marriage of an entire section of men...with an equally widely distributed section of women...the Australian aborigine, wandering hundreds of miles from his home...often finds in every camp and every tribe women who give themselves to him without resistance and without resentment." On a day-to-day basis, marriage takes the form of a "a loose pairing" among partners whose marriageability is defined at birth by their membership in one or another so-called marriage class.

The Australian "marriage classes" are today conceived to be part of a system whereby various categories of kin are named so that a person can readily define his relationships within any group with whom he comes into contact.[2] The system is far more elaborate than anything found among other hunter-gatherers, but nonetheless, all of them share common features of family life. Divorce is typically easy and at the desire of either partner, although it is not particularly common. Death more frequently seems to break up the marriage relationship; close and warm pairing relationships are the rule. These are not based, however, on any assumption of sexual exclusiveness for either partner among most hunter-gatherers about whom we have information. Perhaps it is because they were first contacted by whalers instead of missionaries that we have so much data on this point for the Eskimo. According to custom, it is hospitable for an unattached Eskimo woman, or else the host's wife, to sleep with a visitor. The practice has at times been referred to as evidence of the low status of women where it obtains—an ethnocentric reading which presumes that a woman does not (since she should not) enjoy sex play with any but her "real" husband and which refuses to recognize that variety in sex relations is entertaining to women (where not circumscribed by all manner of taboos) as well as to men (a moralistic assumption from which Engels himself was not wholly free).

"Pairing marriage" is more hedged around with restrictions. Engels wrote: "the decisive considerations are the new ties of kinship which are to give the young pair a stronger position in the gens and tribe." Parents take a hand in the choice of marriage partners, and marriages are cemented through an exchange of goods—cattle, foods, or luxury items—between the relatives of the bride and those of the groom. The kin of the young partners now have a vested interest in the permanence of the marriage. Engels wrote, that although "still terminable at the desire of either partner...among many tribes...public opinion has gradually developed against such separations. When differences arise between husband and wife, the gens relatives of both partners act as mediators, and only if these efforts prove fruitless does a separation take place."

There is no lack of data on what Morgan called the "pairing family." It is intimately related to the clan organization of agricultural peoples, whereby communal relations in the production and distribution of goods are maintained in what have become relatively large and stable groups. Hunting-gathering bands of some 25 to 40 or so people can operate almost anarchistically, but with the development of agriculture more complex institutions are needed for ordering interpersonal relationships in villages of several hundred and more. Virtually everyone still stands in the same direct relation to production; at most a healer or priest-chief may receive gifts enough to release him or her from some agricultural and other labors. Therefore, economic, political, and social relations remain united; ties of kinship formalized as "gentes" or the term more commonly used today, "clans," form the framework of community life. With clan organization, kin are counted on one side only—you belong either to your mother's or your father's clan, not to both, and you marry "out" (clans are normally "exogamous").

The two practices, unilineality and exogamy, enable discrete groups to last over generations (which is difficult with "bilaterality" and overlapping lines of kinship), while at the same time the groups become linked through a network of marriage ties.[3]

The nuclear family of parents and children was embedded in the clan and village structures through a network of reciprocal relations.[4] Parties of relatives worked together in the fields and on the hunt, and exchanged foodstuffs and manufactured goods on the many occasions that called for festivity, such as at births, baptisms, puberty rites, marriages, deaths, and seasonal and religious ceremonies. The acceptance by the clan and village community, as formally represented by its respected elders, of the ultimate responsibility for the welfare of any member, was so totally taken for granted that it went unstated. On a day-to-day basis, however, it was the immediate lineage of grandparent, parent, and children, with spouses, that functioned as a working unit.

The significant point for women's status is that the household was communal and the division of labor between the sexes reciprocal; the economy did not involve the dependence of the wife and children on the husband. All major food supplies, large game and produce from the fields, were shared among a group of families. These families lived together in large dwellings among most village agriculturalists, and in hunting-gathering societies either shared large tepees or other such shelters in adverse climates, or might simply group together in separate wickiups or lean-tos in tropical or desert areas. The children in a real sense belonged to the group as a whole; an orphaned child suffered a personal loss, but was never without a family. Women did not have to put up with personal injuries from men in outbursts of violent anger for fear of economic privation for themselves or their children. By comparison with more "advanced" societies where wife-beating became accepted, even to the point of death, a mistreated wife could call on her relatives for redress or leave if it was not forthcoming. Nor can "household management" be construed as it would be today. Whether a "public" industry or not, "managing the household" as the "task entrusted to the women" might be viewed dubiously as hardly very satisfactory. However, in primitive communal society, the distinction did not exist between a public world of men's work and a private world of women's household service. The large collective household *was* the community, and within it both sexes worked to produce the goods necessary for livelihood. Goods were as yet directly produced and consumed; they had not become transformed into "commodities" for exchange, the transformation upon which the exploitation of man by man, and the special oppression of women, was built.

In fact, women usually furnished a large share—often the major share—of the food. Many hunter-gatherers depended on the vegetable foods gathered by women as the staples to be augmented by meat (the Bushmen of the Kalahari Desert are a case in point), and in horticultural societies women, as the former gatherers of vegetable foods and in all likelihood, therefore, responsible for the domestication of crops, generally did most of the farming. Since in primitive communal society decisions were made by those who would be carrying them out, the participation of women in a major share of socially necessary labor did not reduce them to virtual slavery, as is the case in class society, but accorded them decision-making powers commensurate with their contribution.

There has been little understanding of this point in anthropological literature. Instead, the fact that men typically made decisions about hunting and warfare in primitive society is used to support the argument that they were the "rulers" in the Western sense. Men did indeed acquire power under the conditions of colonial rule within which the lifeways of hitherto primitive peoples have been recorded. Nonetheless, the literature again and again reveals the autonomy of women and their role in decision making; albeit such data are as often as not sloughed off with supposedly humorous innuendos about "henpecked husbands" or the like, rather than treated seriously as illustrative of social structure and dynamics.

Unfortunately, the debate over women's status in primitive society has largely ignored the actual role of women in primitive society in favor of an almost exclusive focus on descent systems. The growing body of literature on the world's cultures in the latter 19th century showed the clans of horticultural peoples to be commonly matrilineal, and that women often participated formally in the making of "political" decisions. Morgan had described the power the elder women among the Iroquois held in the nomination and possible deposition of the sachems, and the importance of "queen mothers" in Africa had been described. There, a woman and her brother (or son or nephew) often shared chiefly or royal responsibilities somewhat analogous to those of a Department of the Interior and Department of State respectively. And the magnificent army of perhaps 5000 volunteer women soldiers of Dahomey were the legendary Amazons incarnate. All of this caught the imagination of theoreticians in so male-dominated and property-conscious a culture as was Victorian society,[5] and scholars spoke of patriarchal society as historically preceded by the "matriarchy," where rule by women was based on the indisputability of legitimacy reckoned in the female line.

It soon became clear that matriarchy, in the sense of power held by women over men comparable to that later held by men over women, had never existed. However, questions about the significance that matrilineal descent held for the status of women in primitive society remained. It is impossible to review here the twists and turns of subsequent argument over the universal priority of matrilineal descent. Suffice it to say that it is clear that matrilineal systems give way to patrilineal systems with the development of exploitative class relations. In many cases a patrilineal (or patrilocal) system can be shown to have been matrilineal (or matrilocal), but in other cases ethnohistorical data sufficient for definitive proof are lacking. Hence statistical studies of descent and its correlates have yielded conflicting interpretations.[6]

A standard contemporary formulation, at least in the United States, is that horticultural societies were generally structured around matrilineally related groups since women were responsible for the major share of the farming, but that hunting societies were male-centered in their structure due to the importance of the men as hunters. The fact that the produce gathered by the women in many such societies was as important a source of food, or more so, than the produce of the hunt, led Service, in a recent formulation of this position (1966, pp.

37–38) to point out that hunting required a close collaboration that is not important in most gathering activities. To Service, it was the need for the "delicate coordination of several people" that led to the practice whereby closely related men stayed together as the core of a hunting band while women married into other bands. The case is, however, that some hunter-gatherers are matrilineal, and others have been so in the recent past. My own field work among the Naskapi hunters of the Labrador Peninsula showed that patrilineal-patrilocal ties were strengthened at the expense of matrilineal-matrilocal ties after European contact, under the influence of missionaries, government agents, and especially the fur trade (Leacock, 1955, 1969). Despite the arduousness of hunting in the northern woods and tundra, there was no suggestion whatever that men had to grow up together to work well as a unit. Instead it was the norm for men in the past to marry away from the band of their youth.

In a recent study Martin also questions the "patrilocal band" as the primordial type of social organization. On the basis of reviewing descent and residence patterns, interband relations, and the recent histories of 33 predominantly matrilocal South American hunting-gathering peoples, she points out that there is greater cohesiveness with matrilocal rather than patrilocal organization. With matrilocal residence the men, who are responsible for defense and hence offense, are dispersed among related bands rather than forming localized clusters (1969, pp. 256–57).

Works that deal directly with the role of women in primitive society are few and far between, and much of what has been done pertains to personality rather than socioeconomic structure. Margaret Mead's early exposition of contrasting sex-role definitions in three primitive societies is a case in point (1950). Interestingly enough, Mead contradicts her own argument for the cultural definition of sex role by her later position which, in conformity with widely accepted Freudian thought, argues for a universal active-passive dichotomy differentiating male from female roles (1955). By contrast there is an early book by Mason, *Women's Share in Primitive Culture*, and the book, *The Mothers*, by Briffault, a surgeon, novelist, and amateur anthropologist. These draw together scattered ethnographic references to (1) women's role in decision-making and the administration of tribal affairs; (2) their importance as inventors of techniques for food production and the manufacture of baskets, leather goods, woven materials, etc.; and (3) their part in ritual and religious life. Impressive though the record of women's part in society appears, however, the data are lifted out of context and seem to be contradicted by the vast majority of extant ethnographic materials, for these seldom assess the impact of colonialism on the peoples described and generally focus on the activities and affairs of men. (The latter is not solely a problem of masculine bias, but also due to the greater ease of communicating with men who are far more commonly thrown into contact with Europeans and speak a European language.)

An unusually detailed study of women among a hunting-gathering people is afforded by Kaberry's work on the original inhabitants of Northwest Australia (1939). It is commonly stated that women's status is low among these people, as evidenced by their exclusion from the important ceremonies of the men and from participation in political affairs. Kaberry points out that the men in turn are kept out of the secret rituals held by the women; and that while warfare and the holding of formal meetings are the sole responsibility of the men, intragroup problems are handled by older women along with older men. Women are restricted as to whom they marry; but so are men, and young people are free to have premarital affairs which either sex may initiate. In daily life, these Australian women emerge as autonomous participants in the affairs of their people, acting with assurance upon their rights and responsibilities, a view reinforced by a newly published study of Tiwi women by Jane Goodale (1971).

Similarly, biographical materials on Eskimo women contradict common assumptions about their subservient role, even in spite of its deterioration in recent times. The biography of Anauta (Washburne and Anauta 1940), an Eskimo woman of Baffin Land who migrated to the United States with her children after the death of her husband, reveals her independence of action and strong sense of personal autonomy. Short biographies of Nunivak Island Eskimo women, one of them a shaman (a person who can communicate with the supernatural powers, usually for healing and/or divination), likewise indicate considerable freedom of choice and leeway for women to take the initiative in the running of their own lives (Lantis 1960).

The position of women among the Naskapi hunting people of the Labrador Peninsula was stronger in the past than it is today. Seventeenth-century Jesuit missionaries writing of their experiences state that "the women have great power here" and that "the choice of plans, of undertakings, of journeys, of winterings, lies in nearly every instance in the hands of the housewife" (Thwaites, 1906: Vol. 5, p. 181; Vol. 68, p. 93). A Jesuit scolds a man for not being "the master," telling him "in France women do not rule their husbands" (Vol. 5, p. 181). To make the women obey their husbands became one of the concerns of the missionaries, particularly in relation to the sexual freedom that obtained: "I told him that it was not honorable for a woman to love anyone else except her husband, and that, this evil being among them (women's sexual freedom) he himself was not sure that his son, who was there present, was his son." The Naskapi's reply is telling: "Thou hast no sense. You French people love only your own children; but we love all the children of our tribe" (Vol. 6, p. 255).

Women are no longer shamans, as they could be in the past, nor do they commonly hunt, nor join the men in the sweat bath, nor hold their own formal councils in case of emergency (Vol. 2, p. 77; Vol. 6, p. 191; Vol. 7, pp. 61, 175; Vol. 14, p. 183). However, traditions of individual autonomy, mutual support, and collective responsibility for the children still leave their mark on Naskapi life despite great changes. One of many incidents I observed must suffice to indicate what can lie behind the stereotyped ascription in monographic accounts of such people: the men hunt; the women gather berries and care for the children. For the greater part of one day a man sat patiently, lovingly crooning over his sickly and fretful infant of but a few weeks old. His wife was busy. Though worried for the baby's health, he appeared in no way inept or harassed by his responsibility, nor did he call on another woman around the camp for help. His unself-conscious assurance and patience set him quite apart from latter-day readers of Dr. Spock. This was his task while his wife tanned a caribou skin, a skilled and arduous job that demanded her complete attention. The men knew how to cook and tend the babies when called upon to do so, but did not really know how to tan leather.

There is a real need for studies that reconstruct from extant materials on primitive communal and transitional societies something of women's functioning before the development of the male dominance that accompanied European economic and colonial exploitation. For example, how were goods distributed in horticultural societies where garden produce still lay in the women's domain? How did older women function in the settling of disputes, a role often referred to but little documented? What were the paths of influence women held in relation to the men's sphere of war and the hunt? Conversely, what was the role of men in socializing young children? A recent analysis by Mintz (1971) of the entrepreneurial role played by Yoruba women traders exemplifies how published data can be used to begin answering such questions.

An interesting subject for reassessment is the mystique that surrounds the hunt and, in comparison, that surrounding childbirth. A common formulation of status among hunter-gatherers overlooks the latter and stresses the importance and excitement of the hunt. Albeit the primary staple foods may be the vegetable products supplied by the women, they afford no prestige, it is pointed out, so that while not precisely subservient women are still of lower status than men. However, women's power of child-bearing has been a focus for awe and even fear as long ago as the Upper Paleolithic, judging from the fertility figurines that date from that period. This point is easy to overlook, for the ability to bear children has led in our society not to respect but to women's oppressed status. Similarly, the mystique surrounding menstruation is underestimated. Attitudes of mystery and danger for men are interpreted in terms of our cultural judgment as "uncleanliness." Indeed, the semantic twists on this subject would be amusing to analyze. Women are spoken of as "isolated" in "menstrual huts" so that the men will not be contaminated. Where men's houses exist, however, they are written about respectfully; here the exclusion of women betokens men's high status. Doubtless this congeries of attitudes was first held by missionaries and traders, and from them subject peoples learned appropriate attitudes to express to whites.

However, a recent study by Hogbin (1970) on the religion of a New Guinea people reveals another side to the picture. Intriguingly titled "The Island of Menstruating Men," the study describes a practice also found among other peoples in this part of the world whereby the men simulate the phenomenon of menstruation. Blood is drawn from the penis (or some other part of the body among other groups) and men go through the ritual cycle of menstruation, retreating from the ordinary round of daily affairs, observing various taboos, then re-entering, cleansed and renewed.

In some ways it is the ultimate alienation in our society that the ability to give birth has been transformed into a liability. The reason is not simply that, since women bear children, they are more limited in their movements and activities. As the foregoing discussion indicates, this was not a handicap even under the limited technology of hunting-gathering life; it certainly has no relevance today. Nor did women's low status simply follow their declining importance in food production when men moved into agriculture; nor automatically follow the growth in importance of domestic animals, the province of the men, although herding did relate to lowered status for women. However, what was basic was that these transitions occurred in the context of developing exploitative relations whereby communal ownership was being undermined, the communal kin group broken up, and the individual family separated out as an isolated and vulnerable unit, economically responsible for the maintenance of its members and for the rearing of the new generation. The subjugation of the female sex was based on the transformation of their socially necessary labor into a private service through the separation of the family from the clan. It was in this context that women's domestic and other work came to be performed under conditions of virtual slavery.

The separation of the family from the clan and the institution of monogamous marriage were the social expressions of developing private property;

so-called monogamy afforded the means through which property could be individually inherited. And private property for some meant no property for others, or the emerging of differing relations to production on the part of different social groups. The core of Engels' formulation lies in the intimate connection between the emergence of the family as an economic unit dominated by the male and this development of classes.

> The distinction of rich and poor appears beside that of freemen and slaves—with the new division of labor, a new cleavage of society into classes....The transition to full private property is gradually accomplished, parallel with the transition of the pairing marriage into monogamy. The single family is becoming the economic unit of society.

Engels outlines for early Greece the way in which the division of labor and development of commodity production enabled new wealth in the form of slaves and herds to be accumulated by single individuals, thereby leading to a conflict between the family and the gens. Since men owned the "instruments of labor" (having largely displaced women in the fields, it is important to note, following the decline of hunting as an important activity), conflict between family and gens took the form of a conflict between the opposing principles of father right and mother right.

> As wealth increased it made the man's position in the family more important than the woman's, and...created an impulse to exploit this strengthened position in order to overthrow, in favor of his children, the traditional order of inheritance.

Therefore, the formation of family as the economic unit of society was affirmed by the overthrow of mother right, the "*world historical defeat of the female sex*" (italics Engels').

Far more empirical documentation than Engels offers is needed to clarify the process of women's subjugation, both in relation to the initial rise of class societies in the Old and New Worlds, and to the secondary diffusion of commodity production and class divisions that accompanied European expansion and colonial domination. Essentially

Engels offers a paradigm, posing a sharp contrast between women's status in primitive communal society and in classical Greece and Rome. He then touches on Medieval Europe and jumps to industrialization. The many changes within the great span of history covered and the variations from place to place need analysis and, even more important, so do the variations in women's position in different classes: slave, free worker, peasant, serf, burgher, aristocrat.

Engels focuses on the emergence of the upper-class family as an instrument for the concentration of individual wealth. He does not clearly define the lower-class family as affording an important buttress for class society by making the individual acutely vulnerable to exploitation and control. The separation of the ordinary laborer from the communal security of the gens meant the worker was responsible as an individual not only for his own maintenance but also that of his wife and children. This to a large measure insured not only his labor, but also his docility; it rendered him—as he is to this day—fearful of fighting against the extremities of exploitation as endangering not only to himself but also his wife and his dependent children. With wonderful wit and satire, and warm sympathy, Engels deals with the conjugal relations produced by monogamy, but largely in relation to the bourgeois family. He writes of the proletarian wife who moves into public industry under conditions of great difficulty for herself and her children, but does not elaborate on the enormous ambivalence the individual family creates in the working-class man and his wife as a result of their isolation.

The dehumanization of conjugal relationships, caught as men and women are in a network of fear and confusion; the brutalization and petty dominance of the man; the anger and bitterness of the woman; the nature of marriage, all too often as a constant battle—all this is only too well known. Despite the fact that the pre-class societies which have been studied have already been undercut by European and American colonization, a quality of respectful ease, warmth, and assurance in interpersonal relations, including those between husband and wife, often persists as evidence that the tensions associated with conjugal relations in our society are based in our social structure, not in the natures of women and men.

NOTES

1. This selection from Eleanor Burke Leacock's extensive essay on Engels' book deals with only one part of his work which analyzes the role of women in the monogamous family.

2. A description of kinship among the Arunta of Australia can be found in Service, 1963. These systems become unusually elaborate in parts of Australia, although somewhat comparable elaborations are to be found in nearby Melanesian tribes.

3. The social basis for incest taboos and exogamous marriage are discussed in White 1949: Chapter 11; Slater 1959; Aberle et al. 1963; and in Washburn and Lancaster, "The Evolution of Hunting," in Lee and DeVore 1968: especially 302. The ties of kinship and exogamous marriage were already practices in hunting-gathering societies, although they were more formally defined among the settled gatherers and fishermen than among nomadic hunters. This raises the question whether they were generally more well defined in early human society and lost under the harsh conditions endured by the Indians and Eskimo of the north and other hunters pushed into marginal areas. In any case, with agricultural society, they become highly defined and elaborated upon with endless variations from group to group. The Soviet anthropologist, Julia Averkieva, has suggested to me that in her view clan organization was primeval, and that its elaborate definition occurred when it was already beginning to decay. For further discussion of hunting-band organization, see Leacock 1969.

4. These have seldom been described better than by one of the founders of the "functionalist" school of anthropology, Bronislaw Malinowski, in his writings on the Trobriand Islanders of Melanesia. Try, for example, his very readable *Crime and Custom in Savage Society*, 1926.

5. Although one cannot help but note that the very age was named after a woman. This fact points to the priority of class considerations over sex in the socialization of women when it came to royalty. Princesses were, first of all, potential rulers. Thus we have the anomaly that in the history of Europe the only public area in which individual women were in every way the equal of men, both to the general view and in their own behavior and abilities, was that

associated most deeply with stereotypes of masculinity—the area of leadership, power, and decision making.

6. An early study by Hobhouse *et al.* (1965) found the matrilineal-matrilocal principle to be more common among "lower hunters" than the patrilineal-patrilocal principle. A later study of Murdock's finds that "simpler cultures tend to be matrilineal, more advanced ones patrilineal," although "the patrilineate coexists too frequently with the absence of traits...(of more complex culture) and the matrilineate with their presence, to be consistent with the theory of universal matrilineal priority" (1937), p. 467). In a later work, Murdock writes: "While matrilineal societies appear, on the average, to be somewhat more archaic in culture than patrilineal societies the difference is relatively slight, the overlap is very great, and the disparity may well reflect principally the preponderant influence exerted throughout the world in recent centuries by the bilateral and patri-

lineal peoples of the Eurasiatic continent" (1949, p. 186). Using Murdock's figures, but without reference to Murdock's early study that involved a relatively sophisticated statistical analysis, Aberle comments on the greater patrilineality among hunter-gatherers than matrilineality, although bilaterality far exceeds them both (Schneider and Gough, 1961). Two distinctions between Murdock's figures and those of Hobhouse *et al.* must be noted. First, one of Murdock's criteria for selection of his sample was that each major rule of descent should be represented for each culture area, a factor he took into account in his own analysis, but which does not seem to have been considered by Aberle. The second consideration involves the passage of time. For the people with whom I am most familiar, the Naskapi, Hobhouse *et al.* use a 17th-century Jesuit account that showed them to be matrilineal-matrilocal in orientation; Murdock uses 20th-century accounts that describe them as bilateral and bilocal with a paternal emphasis.

REFERENCES

GOODALE, JANE C., 1971. *Tiwi wives, a study of the women of Melville Island, North Australia.* Seattle: University of Washington Press.

HOGBIN, IAN, 1970. *The island of menstruating men.* San Francisco: Chandler Publishing Co.

KABERRY, PHYLLIS M., 1939. *Aboriginal woman, sacred and profane.* London: Routledge and Sons, Ltd.

LANTIS, MARGARET, 1960. *Eskimo childhood and interpersonal relationships, Nunivak biographies and genealogies.* Seattle: University of Washington Press.

LEACOCK, ELEANOR, 1954. *The Montagnais "hunting territory" and the fur trade.* Memoir 78, The American Anthropological Association.

————, 1955. Matrilocality in a simple hunting economy (Montagnais-Naskapi). *Southwestern Journal of Anthropology* 11, 1.

————, 1958a. Introduction to "Social stratification and evolutionary theory: a symposium." *Ethno-history* 5, 3.

————, 1958b. Status among the Montagnais-Naskapi of Labrador. *Ethnohistory* 5, 3.

————, 1964. North American Indian society and psychology in historical perspective. *Proceedings of the Seventh International Congress of the Anthropological and Ethnological Sciences,* Moscow.

————, 1969. The Montagnais-Naskapi band. Band Societies, David Damas (ed.), *National Museums of Canada Contributions to Anthropology,* Bulletin 228, Ottawa.

MARTIN, KAY M., 1969. South American foragers: a case study in cultural devolution. *American Anthropologist* 71.

MASON, OTIS TUFTON, 1898. *Women's share in primitive culture.* New York: D. Appleton and Co.

MEAD, MARGARET (ed.), 1937. *Cooperation and competition among primitive peoples.* New York: McGraw-Hill.

MEAD, MARGARET, 1950. *Sex and temperament in three primitive societies.* New York: New American Library.

————, 1955. *Male and female, a study of the sexes in a changing world.* New York: New American Library.

MINTZ, SIDNEY W., 1971. Men, women, and trade. *Comparative Studies in History and Society* 13, 3.

MORGAN, LEWIS HENRY, 1876. Montezuma's dinner. *North American Review* 122. (Reprint A-251 in Bobbs-Merrill Reprint Series in the Social Sciences.)

————, 1963. *Ancient society,* Eleanor Burke Leacock (ed.). New York: World Publishing Company.

SERVICE, ELMAN R., 1962. *Primitive social organization: an evolutionary perspective.* New York: Random House.

————, 1963. *Profiles in ethnology.* New York: Harper and Brothers.

————, 1966. *The hunters.* Englewood Cliffs, N.J.: Prentice-Hall.

THWAITES, R.G., (ed.), 1906. *The Jesuit relations and allied documents.* 71 vols. Cleveland: The Burrows Brothers Co.

WASHBURNE, HELUIZ CHANDLER, 1959. *Land of the good shadows, the life story of Anauta, an Eskimo woman.* New York: Knopf.

Chapter 2
Cross-cultural Perspectives

GEORGE MURDOCK (1949), IN A SUMMARY of cross-cultural studies, postulated that the nuclear family was universal and that it performed four functions that were needed by every society. These functions were (1) socialization, (2) economic cooperation, (3) reproduction, and (4) sexual relations. Murdock assumed that these functions were necessary for the survival of society, and that they had to be performed within the nuclear family.[1]

Talcott Parsons, in the 1950s, further theorized that the family was isolated from other primary groups and universally differentiated within the family along sexual lines, with the economic function being performed by men, and the socialization and reproduction functions performed by women. Parsons argued that the family was a small group which had certain properties found by Robert Bales to be characteristic of small groups in general. One person always assumed the role of instrumental or task-oriented leader, while another person assumed the role of socio-emotional leader concerned with holding the group together. Parsons suggested, given this universal role differentiation in small groups, that women were best suited for the socio-emotional role due to their biological connection with child-bearing.[2]

In the period since these two classic analyses were written, studies of various cultures have suggested that the nuclear family, as defined by Murdock, may not be universal, and that its functions may be carried out by structures other than the nuclear family. Works in the United States by

Marvin Sussman[3] and Eugene Litwak[4] have shown that not only the nuclear family but also other primary groups such as extended kin, friends and neighbors are involved in fulfilling certain functions, such as exchanging material resources and other forms of support. In addition, it has been shown that the family has not always and does not have to be differentiated into instrumental and socio-emotional roles. Individuals in a family can perform a variety of roles at different times.[5]

The preceding discussion of the variety of primary group structures that can carry out necessary social functions, and of the different individuals in the family that can perform different roles, suggest the possibility of many types of family forms. Certain societies such as the People's Republic of China or subcultures within a society such as the kibbutzim in Israel have consciously altered existing family structures in radical ways, in order to fulfill social goals. One of these goals has been the equality between the sexes. Another goal has been that of economic equality.

The readings in this section illustrate some of the variations in family structure and functioning that occur in different societies. The article by Evelyn Stevens deals with the middle-class extended family in the context of Latin American culture. The middle-class family structure in Latin America in contrast to the other family structures analyzed in this chapter most closely fits the classic sex role pattern described by Parsons. Roles are clearly differentiated in the family with the husband involved in economic support of the family, and the wife fulfilling reproduction and socialization functions. The ideology that supports this role differentiation in Latin America is analyzed by Stevens. She deals with male "machismo," the cult of virility, and female "marianismo," the veneration of and belief in women's moral and spiritual superiority to men. Stevens places this role differentiation and value system within the class and racial structure of traditional, agrarian Latin American society. She suggests that structural changes associated with the process of industrialization may alter the traditional family structure and the position of women in it.

Yonina Talmon-Garber deals with three different family types within Israel: the kibbutz, the moshav, and the isolated immigrant families. The kibbutz was founded on the basis of socialist and feminist principles. Communities were created in which the economic and child-rearing functions were removed from each nuclear family and fulfilled collectively. Women were freed from their traditional family roles centering on domestic activities and child care. Talmon-Garber traces the transition in the kibbutz from the early communal and feminist ideologies to a gradual strengthening of the nuclear family ties, and an increase in sex role differentiation. In the moshav, the traditional nuclear family structure was maintained. However, families joined together to cooperate in economic activities. Talmon-Garber shows how kinship ties became a basis for the creation of cooperative units. In contrast to the kibbutz and moshav, other immigrants remained in more isolated nuclear families.

Ruth Sidel illustrates the implementation of the commitment to sex equality in the People's Republic of China. She describes the nurseries set up in factories and other workplaces where mothers can leave their infants and young children while they work. Sidel deals with the ideology in China

which validates the transference of part of the child-rearing and socialization function from the family to nurseries as legitimate and beneficial to societal needs.

These three articles dealing with family structures cross-culturally illustrate the variations in existing structures and the varying degrees to which the functions dealt with by Murdock are fulfilled by the nuclear family, extended kinship, communal organizations, and other institutions. Utilizing a structural-functional perspective, the reader might assess the consequences for men and women of participating in different societal family structures. To what degree is the traditional female role in Latin America different from the female role in Israel and in the People's Republic of China? What other institutional arrangements might be enacted in Israel and China to achieve total equality between the sexes? Readers might also assess the consequences for children of growing up in different societal contexts. For example, how do opportunities and resources given to children and the individuals who influence them vary in the different cultures considered?

From a conflict perspective, readers might consider contradictions within the different family structures in their class and social contexts arising from the needs of different family members. What is the cost to Latin American women in the servant class of accepting and internalizing their roles in contrast to that of middle-class Latin American women? How was sex-role change brought about in China in contrast to the forces for future change in Latin America as discussed by Stevens?

A symbolic interactionist might compare the process of sex role socialization in Latin America with that found in the various Israeli family forms and in China. How do the boys and girls in each of these societies come to define their appropriate sex roles?

NOTES

1. George Murdock, *Social structure.* New York: Macmillan, 1949.

2. Talcott Parsons and Robert Bales, *Family, socialization and interaction.* Glencoe: Free Press, 1955.

3. Marvin Sussman, Relationships of adult children with their parents in the United States. In Ethel Shanas and Gorden Streib (eds.), *Social structure and the family: generational relations.* Englewood Cliffs, N.J.: Prentice-Hall, 1965.

4. Some of the studies include Eugene Litwak, Occupational mobility and extended family cohesion, *American Sociological Review*, 25, 1960, pp. 9–21; Eugene Litwak and Ivan Szelenyi, Primary group structure and their functions: kin neighbors and friends, *American Sociological Review* **34** 4, (August), 1969.

5. Eugene Litwak and Josefina Figueira, Technological innovation and ideal forms of family structure in an industrial democratic society. In Reuben Hill and Renée Fox (eds.), *Families in east and west.* Paris:Mouton, 1970.

The Prospects for a Women's Liberation Movement in Latin America*

EVELYN P. STEVENS

WHEN THE ANGLO–AMERICAN WOMEN'S liberation leader, Gloria Steinem, visited Puerto Rico in 1971, she adressed the Women's Press Club, an organization which owes its origins to the fact that the previously existing Press Club had refused to admit women members. After Ms. Steinem finished her talk, the president of the club, Angela Luisa Torregrosa (viuda de Corcova Chirino) replied to the guest speaker's remarks by stating that there was no need for a women's liberation movement in Puerto Rico, because the female citizens of the island commonwealth were already liberated (San Juan *Star*, March 2, 1971).

In spite of—or perhaps because of—the apparent paradox revealed by the incident, it may be appropriate to inquire in what sense Ms.[1] Torregrosa may have felt justified in rejecting the Northern woman's missionary efforts. In a broader sense, we might find it instructive to examine the nature of female–male relationships in Latin America in an effort to discover the bases of stability as well as the possible sources of change.

Our search for answers might begin by rephrasing the question. We might ask, for example,

under what conditions the demand for women's liberation has arisen in some societies, and how these conditions differ from those existing in other societies in which the movement has not yet become a major force. Even prior to this inquiry, however, there is a need to understand the political meaning of women's demand for equality.

Since the end of World War II, but especially in the decade recently ended, the questions which have engaged the energies of activists have focused on the expansion of political participation to include all sectors of the population. Hitherto neglected groups (e.g., blacks, "ethnic" whites, students, indigents) have become conscious—or have been exhorted to become conscious—of their right to share in the decision-making function at *all* levels of policy choices. The activists saw this not as a new revolution but rather as the completion of the democratic revolution begun in the 18th century, which was frustrated in the 19th century in France by the triumph of the bourgeois, reduced in Britain to issues of electoral reform, and detoured in the United States by Alexander Hamilton's defense of the businessman.

*Based on research conducted in 1972.

Like their Russian predecessors, the Narod-naya Volya of the 1860s, the European and American populist leaders of the post-World War II era have in the main been young, relatively affluent, and university-educated. Young women have been a significant proportion of the total force; they have marched, sung, sat in, and picketed together with their male classmates. But even at the beginning, sex-based differential participation could be observed. In the 1964–65 student uprising in Berkeley, it is true that some women were included in early strategy sessions, and some women were allowed to speak from the steps of Sproul Hall over the male-controlled public address system. But it soon became apparent that Marx's dictum, "From each according to his [sic] abilities. . . ." meant that women made and distributed the coffee and sandwiches that sustained the strikers, women typed the manifestos (". . . because we men don't know how to type . . ."), and women applauded as men issued the thundering proclamations of the Free Speech Movement. Once again, women became aware that they had been relegated to the role of "ladies' auxiliary to the human race" (see, for example, Seese).

At the same time that young women were being reminded of their "proper place," their mothers' generation was discovering that their "place" was disappearing from the structure of neo-industrial society. The stage of technological development presently attained in the North Atlantic nations has brought about important changes in the organization of the nuclear family, resulting, in turn, in the functional superfluity of the classic stereotype of mother and housewife. As is often the case, structural changes have been rapidly reflected in decreased prestige accorded to role occupants, while redefinition of the roles themselves has proceeded with glacial slowness. Finding themselves ground between tradition and the slow but nevertheless perceptible forward thrust of social change, middle-class white women in Europe and America have been experiencing the existential agony of losing their identity as child-producers, cradle-rockers, and supplementary wage-earners.

Neo-industrial society is consumption-oriented rather than production-oriented (Galbraith 1967; Riesman et al. 1953). The work ethos, so important as the initial impetus of maximum economic growth, is becoming an embarrassing impediment to the full utilization of available technology. As a result of the cybernation revolution, millions of unskilled, semiskilled, and even professional workers have become displaced persons, no longer needed to turn the wheels of industry. Each year additional sectors of the population are affected by the phenomenon; it will not be long before large groups of middle-class men, heretofore secure in the belief that they were performing indispensable functions, will join the ranks of the unemployed, underemployed, or prematurely retired persons who have suddenly been deprived of their existential raison d'être.

Because life expectancy during the past century has far outpaced reproductive usefulness, middle-aged middle-class women who had outlived their childbearing functions were the first group to face the existential problem, at precisely the historical juncture when the existential movement and the secularization of established religions snatched the possibility of religious consolation away from them. But now a much younger group of women is being affected. Preferring to face the problem and to seek remedial action rather than spend the second half of their lives in frustrated quietude, educated young women have become the vanguard of the women's liberation movement. This is the group who were "liberated" by the first effects of consumer-oriented value patterns; liberated from having to start bearing children at age 16 to 20 to contribute them to the labor force. Thus they are now free and almost obliged to consume an education. But as the market for productive functions is dwindling in neo-industrial society, women have nothing to do with their education after they get it.

In the face of these developments two powerful motivations can be deduced for the opposition presented to the women's liberation movement by certain sectors of society. The first of these is the familiar phenomenon of culture lag: many European and North American nations are now consumer societies with a hang-over producer ethos. A redefinition of roles requires psychic adjustments so painful that it produces intense hostility toward the perceived cause of discomfort.

There is, however, an even more important motivation: the competition for scarce goods. At a time when countless operations by humans have been rendered obsolete, men are scrambling to accommodate themselves to the new economic conditions and are competing—often desperately—for the available jobs in a dwindling labor market. But more than money, these men are competing in an effort to find existential salvation. They see the proponents of women's liberation as trying to shoulder them all the sooner into functional superfluity in order to save themselves.

But what has this to do with the prospects for a women's liberation movement in Latin America? If the above discussion of the phenomenon in the North Atlantic nations has any explanatory value, a comparison with the conditions existing in the other area may enable us to assess the possibility of similar developments.

As a result of the previous analysis, it was seen that the demand for equality has come principally from white, middle-class, educated women. It might be assumed as an operating hypothesis that if a movement toward equality of the sexes were to occur in Latin America, its articulation would arise from women of parallel socioeconomic and racial characteristics. The following observations should be understood, therefore, as applying to educated middle-class *mestizo* women in countries whose population is composed of more than one racial group (e.g., Mexico, Peru, Ecuador, Brazil) or simply to educated middle-class women in countries whose population is principally of European background, e.g., Chile, Argentina, Uruguay (for discussions of correlation between race and class, see, for example, Mörner 1967; Hoetink 1967; Wagley 1952; Pitt-Rivers 1965; and Freyre 1956).

At the outset, an important distinction should be made between the North Atlantic and the Latin American culture areas. In the former, relations between the sexes are largely secular in nature, while those of the latter are suffused with sacred significance. In this sense, the religious antecedents of Latin American sex attitudes and behavior can be traced historically throughout most of the Mediterranean area (Mediterranean contributions to Latin American attitudes toward female-male relationships are described in Stevens 1972).

The *machismo-marianismo* pattern of attitudes and behavior is a major variant of the universal functional requirement of a division of labor. The main characteristics of this pattern can be observed throughout the mestizo sector of Latin American society, subject to certain variations associated with socioeconomic status and degree of modernization.

The pattern provides a rationale for the division of labor along sex lines by offering a ready-made set of ideal characteristics for the members of each sex. A definition of each of the pair of terms used above is indispensable because there is a dynamic interplay between the two elements of the pattern.

Machismo designates a way of orienting which can most succinctly be described as the cult of virility, the chief characteristics of which are exaggerated aggressiveness and intransigence in male-to-male interpersonal relationships and arrogance and sexual aggression in male-to-female relationships (for a fuller discussion of this phenomenon, see Stevens 1965). *Marianismo* is a term which I have coined but which I hope will be adopted in future discussions of the subject, because it both reflects the present complex psychic content and connotes the historical development of the pattern. *Marianismo* is the cult of female spiritual superiority which teaches that women are semidevine, morally superior to, and spiritually stronger than men.

Both *marianismo* and *machismo* are New World phenomena with roots in Mediterranean cultures, but the fully developed syndrome occurs only in Latin America. It is important here to distinguish between *marianismo* as a secular pattern and *marianism*, a word sometimes used to designate a movement within the Roman Catholic Church which has as its object the speical veneration of the figure of the Virgin Mary (Laurentin 1965). It would be interesting to speculate about which of the two phenomena—if either of them—is the independent variable, but that would be the subject of another project, by another investigator. What seems evident, however, is that marianism or mariology, as it is called by theologians, has provided a central figure and a convenient set of assumptions around which the practitioners of *marianismo* have erected a secular pattern of beliefs and practices related to the position of women in society.

There is a fairly unbroken line of descent from Mediterranean—especially Spanish—religious beliefs to those of the mestizo population of the New World. The cult of the Virgin of Guadalupe, patron saint of Mexico and of all Latin America, was initiated in 1531, about a decade after Cortes' conquest of Mexico (de la Maza 1953). Observers agree that mestizo communities exhibit the characteristics of the marianismo attitudes and that Indian communities do not.

We have already mentioned the attitudinal triad: the belief in the semidivinity, moral superiority, and spiritual strength of women. How are these beliefs manifested in behavior? In brief, spiritual strength is shown by abnegation, i.e., humility (the basically arrogant "holier-than-thou" or "humbler-than-thou" behavior) and sacrifice. Patience with the "sinfulness" of the less-perfect men is another manifestation. Respect for the sacredness of the mother figure is also an important feature (note for example that the "fighting words" regarded as the most insulting everywhere in Latin America are those which allude to one's mother). Submissiveness to the demands of men is a corollary of the often amused, sometimes resigned, tolerance which regards men as spoiled little boys whose whims must be humored. Sadness is the obverse of this tolerance, springing from a conviction that the road to heaven is much longer and more difficult for men than for women, and even impossible to traverse successfully without the intercession of the women in behalf of the men.

The description offered above applied to the ideal portrayed in both classic and vulgar literature and in the popular media of communication, e.g., radio, television, and cinema (Reyes Nevares 1971). Many women devote their whole lives to trying to approximate this ideal. Many others, however, deviate from the ideal to a greater or lesser degree in their actual behavior. To mention a few areas of nonconformity, we might specify sexual behavior (see Portugal 1970 for the contrast between actual behavior and the ideal of premarital chastity), educational and professional accomplishments, and male–female social relationships. Latin American women, although undoubtedly under strong pressures to conform to the ideal, can avail themselves of a number of options, and many intelligent and energetic women do so.

The myth of Latin American male dominance is just that: a myth. Latin American women have contributed to the perpetuation of the myth because it preserves inviolate a way of life which offers many advantages for them. In fact, the pattern persists because it has compensations for members of both sexes. The division of labor based on an arbitrary but universally respected assignment of attributes is not demonstrably dysfunctional according to any logical criteria which are free of ethnocentric bias.

If male dominance is a myth, it follows that female passivity is also a mistaken notion. Women are not passive anywhere in the world; they simply have different styles for pursuing their objectives than do men, and they often choose to maximize different values.

The social framework within which these values are maximized is an important variable affecting the Latin American style of action. Most interpersonal communication takes place in the setting of the extended family, where the prescriptive norms for authority–deference relationships are much more clearly spelled out than in the nuclear families of more highly industrialized societies. This is due to the abundance of models for each ideal role that are available as didactic resources in the socialization process. Thus a female child learns what will be expected of her as an adult by observing and listening to her mother, aunts, godmother, and grandmothers. She will learn that all family members must cater to her father's whims, and that she is less important than the least of her brothers. But she will also observe the enormous veneration with which her father treats his own mother and the respect bordering on religious awe accorded to her mother by her brothers (Diaz-Guerrero, 1955). "For a child to strike his mother, even to lift his hand against her, is a foul sacriligious act" (Lloyd Rogler, personal communication to author, 1971).

On the other hand, it does not take much intelligence for a growing girl to observe and imitate the techniques by which the female members of the family manipulate the males in order to attain their own objectives (Diaz, 1967). In this uneven struggle for domination, the outcome of which is seldom in doubt, men are almost always the losers and women's most valued resource is the carefully tended legend of their martyrdom.

For a Latin American woman, earthly approximation to sainthood is contingent upon achievement of motherhood, while numerous offspring afford visible proof of virility for men who are in constant need of reassurance on that score. Thus the emotional needs of both men and women are nurtured by the practice of multiple procreation. But for a woman to give birth to many children is not enough; maximum enjoyment of the prerogatives of motherhood depends upon the homage rendered by a large number of *adult* offspring. Thus the fullest rewards are reaped only by older women. "I may be unfaithful to my wife; I may even occasionally beat my mistress, but under no circumstances would I ever be disrespectful to my dear mother," stated a 60-year-old Puerto Rican businessman in an interview.

Because behavioral norms require that men spend most of their time away from home, male children absorb many of their notions about the proper relationship between the sexes from the female members of the family. As a boy spends very little time in the company of his father, the model for his own future behavior is constructed from women's descriptions. Even when he emerges from the family atmosphere to attend school, he finds little information of a contradictory nature because the members of his peer group have been socialized in a similar manner. So pervasive is the myth of male dominance and martyred female submissiveness that Latin Americans accept it unquestioningly as a datum, in spite of the fact that they continually encounter examples of behavior too numerous to be dismissed as statistically unimportant deviations from the norm.

Whatever flexibility exists in behavioral norms is weighed in favor of women. While men are simply not allowed to occupy roles which call for dependent behavior, there are no hard and fast strictures against women's active and even aggressive participation in economic and political affairs. But when women do choose such a course, they frequently adopt a style calculated to reassure possible critics as to their respect for stereotypes. Thus, campaign literature in Mexico calls attention to a woman candidate's numerous children, and her devotion to her home and her husband, even though her actual personality may be quite at variance with this idealized picutre. In Puerto Rico, Felisa Rincón de Gautier occupied the post of city manager of San Juan for more that 20 years. Although childless, she stressed a maternal attitude toward her political adherents and adopted the costume traditionally reserved for venerable grandmothers: a full black dirndl topped by a loose white *broderie anglaise* overblouse.

Now that we have examined the characteristics of the *machismo–marianismo* pattern in the setting of the extended family, it is possible to view the Latin American variant of male–female relationships as contributing to the maintenance of the existing social system. But this system in turn operates within the context of economic conditions peculiar to the entire region, and it is these conditions which we must now examine for further clues to stability or change.

While the capitalist economies of the North Atlantic nations have been rapidly approaching the stage of neo-industrialism, with its consequent emphasis on consumption, the capitalist economies of Latin American nations are still oriented toward accelerated productivity through industrialization. Expanded agricultural production, which could be promoted through rationalization of techniques, would complicate the problems of the economic policymakers at this time by increasing the already widespread rural unemployment and underemployment through the use of capital-intensive methods (e.g., mechanization) rather than the existing labor-intensive methods.

A number of conditions associated with the status quo have relieved the economic planners of the necessity of dealing at this time with this potential complication. The most important of these conditions is the marginality to macroeconomic and macropolitical processes of large sectors of society which, taken together, comprise the majority of

Latin America's total population (Lambert 1963; Gonzalez Casanova 1970). Expanded participation of these groups in the benefits of growth would constitute a process of economic and political development (Labastida 1966).

In many Latin American nations certain characteristics of some sectors of the marginal population facilitate continued discrimination. The traditional culture of Indian groups, for example, places a very low value on the operation of a market economy and emphasizes instead those activities which favor zero economic growth combined with some version of equitable distribution of available goods. Some members of these groups, it is true, have been willing to trade those values for more modern attitudes, and have broken their ties with their villages, moving into and integrating with the largely urbanized mestizo community that holds modern value orientations. In Lerner's terms (1958), these cultural migrants are termed "transitional *men*" (sic; italics mine). In the process of making the transition, they become a major component of the lowest stratum of modern economic organization, constituting a reserve of low-paid labor, as unskilled manual workers and domestic servants. Because of their lack of education and residual attitudes, awareness of relative deprivation has been slow to develop among members of this group and governments have largely failed to implement publicly articulated policies favoring their fuller economic and political integration.

In the mestizo countries that continue to constitute the object of our examination in this essay, the next largest group of marginal individuals is made up of mestizo women. At the outset it should be emphasized that their relative deprivation, in both the economic and the political sense, places them in a much more privileged stratum than that of either the Indians or the "transitional" individuals. Many of them are equipped with attitudes and skills that are indispensable to continued economic growth, and when they become active, their share of the available goods is much higher than that of the other two marginal groups. Thus by contrast with those groups, their marginality may be masked.

In fact, mestizo women have used their relatively privileged position vis-à-vis the transitional group to exploit the latter and to increase their own share of benefits. Middle-class mestizo women in particular have utilized the abundance of low-paid domestic servants to support a style of life that has long since disappeared, except at the highest economic level, in the neo-industrial nations of the North Atlantic area. They enjoy a leisure and freedom which almost entitles them to be described as the "beautiful people" of the underdeveloped world. The monotonous and demeaning aspects of household work have been unknown to them, as have been the burdens and restrictions of child care.

To individuals socialized under the conditions prevailing in industrialized countries, the atmosphere of the extended family, with its intricate network of obligations, its limited contact with outsiders, and its lack of privacy, seems to negate the value of the individual. Among its many compensations, however, is the umbrella-like shelter which relieves the individual of the task of building a network of personal relations. The family sustains, nourishes, and protects while at the same time it demands a lion's share of time and energy. In this sense, it "liberates" the individual from seeking satisfactions outside the home.

Although mestizo men spend much more time outside the home than do mestizo women, their range of sociable activity is almost as narrow as that of the women. This apparent paradox is intelligible if it is recalled that much of the men's extrafamilial activity is devoted to the feverish cultivation of a reputation for sexual prowess, usually by exploitation of women who belong to the same transitional group that is being exploited as domestic servants by mestizo females. While this is social activity of a sort, it can hardly be described as sociable. Thus the men must conform to the sociable expectations of the extended family in addition to the time they spend at work and at illicit "play."

Mestizo women are under no similar obligation to distribute their time and energy among so many claims. When they pursue intellectual interests or professional careers they do so without being subject to the economic duress imposed on men and they have often found fewer obstacles and fewer conflicting claims on their loyalties than women in more "advanced" countries. In fact, however, the rising chorus of complaints from some middle-class Latin American women about the relative scarcity of domestic help can be taken as a rough measure of incipient industrialization. This is so because domestic servants constitute a large pool of readily available labor for new urban-based manufacturing enterprises and the service industries associated with them. As "transitional" people, servants manifest attitudes which render them more readily trainable than the traditionals of the rural Indian communities. The transitionals, too, are eager to increase their small share of benefits from the market economy and so are willing to exchange their miserably paid semislavery of domestic labor for the slightly less miserable wages accruing from long hours of industrial labor. By comparison with the situation in the highly industrialized nations, the complaints of middle-class Latin American women seem premature. The author is familiar with the case of a Puerto Rican woman who persuaded her husband to transfer her and their children to a luxury hotel suite when her staff of household servants was temporarily reduced to three from the customary five.

Under such circumstances, we might ask whether the objective condition of middle-class women in Latin America is appropriate for the rapid growth of a women's liberation movement there. It would seem not. But what of subjective awareness of relative deprivation, i.e., a manifest desire to share the privileges envisioned as presently monopolized by middle-class mestizo men? Occasionally a lone voice is raised, like the one which recently declared that Latin American society is "repressive and *machista*" (Portugal 1970). Curiously enough, such explicit statements by women, implying a desire to change the existing situation, are rather rare. They should not be confused with the constant chorus of lamentations about the unredeemed wickedness of men and the saintly martyrdom of women which we have seen as part of the *marianismo* behavioral pattern.

From a practical viewpoint, typical *marianismo* complaints serve to reinforce a sense of inherent

worthlessness in middle-class mestizo men—a conviction which has already been inculcated in them by the early socialization processes described above. Even more rare, however, is the insight expressed by one male that the real victims of the assumption of female superiority are the men (Adolph 1970). From the point of view of a female researcher familiar with the context of Latin American culture, it is interesting to note that most Anglo-American male investigators readily accept the postulates of *machismo–marianismo* (e.g., Lewis 1959.)

It is possible that in the near future a demand for equality will be raised by some Latin American women, but it is incumbent on the social analyst to assess the breadth and depth of such a demand. The possibility should be kept in mind that a phenomenon of this nature may owe its origin to the demonstration effect of the women's liberation movement in the neo-industrialized nations. Other recent phenomena such as the spread of "hippie" behavior and the craze for "rock" music in Mexico have been seen by some native observers as essentially imitative (Monsivais 1971).

Under what circumstances, then, might we expect to see a genuine surge of women's liberation activity, of significant dimensions in Latin America? As the extended family shrinks toward nuclear dimensions (a phenomenon that seems to accompany industrialization everywhere), women may find themselves deprived of the milieu in which *marianismo* has flourished. As personal isolation sets in, women will be deprived of the mother-goddess models traditionally furnished by the older generation of women in the family (mothers, mothers-in-law, godmothers, grandmothers, and widowed female relatives) and in turn these young women will find their sphere of influence greatly reduced. There may also be fewer dependent minors (as the birthrate drops—another accompaniment of industrialization) whom they can socialize into the values of *marianismo*.

Industrialization everywhere in the world has been accompanied by a reduction in and finally virtual disappearance of household servants. This change would make it impractical to maintain large households swarming with otiose women. Dispersal of the family will deprive the "lady of the house" of her last line of defense—the built-in baby-sitter. In turn, reduction of family size will undermine the economic rationale for keeping a staff of servants. The result will be that the wife will be forced to absorb the functions formerly distributed among several different female role occupants. At that point she will be nearer to her sisters in the North Atlantic industrialized nations than have been her female ancestors during the previous 300 years, i.e., free to share the hard work with men without sharing in the making of policy choices (Schuster 1971). The ideally portrayed Latin American women is in for a bad time of it as industrialization erodes her semisacred position and reduces her to the position of unpaid domestic servant.

But this state of affairs does not seem to be imminent. As long as the Indian sector of the population remains marginal to the processes of modernization and industrialization, this group of women and men will provide an apparently unlimited source of laundresses, cooks, charwomen, nursemaids, gardeners, and chauffeurs for middle-class mestizo households.

It may be instructive to recall that women in the new-industrial nations are virtually the only remaining group of any significant proportions that has not yet benefited from a widespread change in attitudes. Formal-legal recognition of their demands has been sporadic and incomplete; real implementation is still years away. The subjective awareness now exists; the active demand for basic change has been formulated, but with respect to irreversible achievements, the women's liberation movement lags approximately two decades behind the achievements of the black liberation movement in the United States. It may, in fact, be a long time before women's liberation becomes a reality anywhere in the world. The neo-industrial nations may find their capacity to expand participation taxed to the full for the present and the immediate future by the insistent, sometimes violent, demands of racial and ethnic minorities.

Change in social structure often lags behind change in economic structure, giving rise to an echo of Hamlet's classic complaint that "the time is out of joint." We have seen that the time is indeed out of joint in the North Atlantic nations and that this disjuncture has been associated with the upsurge of a new awareness and new movements. In Latin America, the time is just beginning to get slightly out of joint; the process has a long course to run—if, indeed, it does continue—before the objective conditions are ripe for full equality of the sexes. A necessary prior condition, it would seem, would be the achievement of equality by the presently exploited indigenous population. As long as millions of "transitionals" are available to hew wood, draw water, scrub floors, and care for the babies of middle-class mestizo society, women of the latter group are unlikely to become uncomfortable enough to demand and achieve widespread change.

We must also consider the political implications of such changes. Under the current arrangement of *marianismo–machismo*, women achieve their objectives largely as individuals working within the framework of the extended family, operating upon the male members of the family who become, as it were, the instruments of female policy. The sum of the achievements of all the private policy choices of women does not, however, constitute political action. It remains a cultural variable related to the *style* of political action in Latin America (Stevens 1965).

Not even when women are accorded full use of the franchise at every level of government (local, regional, national) can it be said that their use of the vote constitutes a political variable distinguishable from the male exercise of this right. This would only be so if it could be demonstrated that the policy choices effected after the achievement of women's suffrage have been qualitatively different from those made before that achievement—and then only if all other variables were held constant. I know of no case where this can be demonstrated in Latin America.

It is only when women enter the political arena as a group, pressing for policy choices directly related to their interests (e.g., the Equal Rights Amendment), or to some peculiarly female interpretation of the public interest, that we can speak of female political action.

Is this an ethnocentric approach to politics, implying a pluralistic view? I think not. What it does mean is that achievement of at least some of the preferred policies of special groups in society may be a necessary prelude to the acceptance of those groups as full partners in all aspects of the political process. Where this "interest group" stage is skipped entirely, as in some socialist political systems, we often find striking underrepresentation of members of certain social groups (e.g., women) at any but the lowest levels of political action (Patai 1967, p. 406; Purcell 1971). Conversely, we can sometimes observe the gross overrepresentation of certain groups in such societies, e.g., the predominance of Russian nationals in positions of power in the USSR.

It is precisely this insistence on *meaningful* participation in the political process which distinguishes the current populist movements in many industrialized countries from the formal–legal arguments traditionally employed to demonstrate the equality of all adult citizens. In many political systems the first task of populist leaders has been to educate members of minority groups so that they understand the gap between real participation and formal–legal assurances of adequate representation. These attempts at consciousness-raising seem somewhat beside the point when we examine the conditions in Latin American. It would be unsound

to view Latin American women as dupes of a male-dominated power-elite. That they are fully conscious of their role and have demonstrated a preference for individual action is, I think, clearly reflected in the phenomenon of *marianismo*.

A word of caution, suggested by the prudent reservation voiced in the foregoing paragraphs, may be appropriate here. Just as there is no need to assume that economic change in Latin America is predestined to pass through the same stages that have been observed in the North Atlantic nations, so it would be ethnocentric to anticipate that a women's liberation movement is the only kind of change which can take place in the relations between the sexes. As Silvert (1970, p. 6) has observed, the interesting questions in the comparative study of politics are ". . . not the biological or geographical frontiers that define our being at any given historical moment, but rather the ways in which individuals and societies have chosen their variations on the common themes of humanity." It is from this viewpoint that we might speculate on the possible future approaches of Latin American societies to the questions raised in this essay. Such an analytic effort, however, must await another opportunity.

NOTE

1. Philology note: Many Spanish-speaking groups have used semantic detours around the matter of a woman's marital status, e.g., the familiar term *seña,* which can mean either *señora* or *señorita;* the respectful term *Doña* couples with a woman's given name, accorded to older women of high social status; the use of the term *señorita* (Spain, Mexico) to address all women, regardless of age or marital status.

REFERENCES

ADOLPH, JOSE B., 1970, La emancipación masculina en Lima. Mundo Nuevo 46 (April): 39–41.

DE LA MAZA, FRANCISCO, 1953, *El guadalupanismo mexicano.* Mexico: Porrúa y Obregón.

DIAZ, MAY NORDQUIST, 1967, Tonala: a Mexican peasant town in transition. Berkeley: University of California Press.

DIAZ-GUERRERO,ROGELIO, 1955, Neurosis and the Mexican family structure. *American Journal of Psychiatry* 112 (December): 411–417.

FREYRE, GILBERTO, 1956, *The masters and the slaves* (2nd ed. rev.) New York: Knopf.

GALBRAITH, JOHN KENNETH, 1967, *The new industrial state.* Boston: Houghton Mifflin.

GONZALEZ CASANOVA, PABLO, 1970, *Democracy in Mexico.* New York: Oxford University Press.

HOETINK, H., 1967, *The two variants in Caribbean race relations.* New York: Oxford University Press.

LABASTIDA, HORACIO, 1966, Programación social. In Escuela Nacional de Economía (ed.), *Bases para la planeación economica y social de México.* Mexico: Universidad Nacional Autónoma de Mexico, Siglo XXI Editores, pp. 177-198.

LAMBERT, JACQUES, 1963, *Amérique Latine, structures*

sociales et institutions politiques. Paris: Presses Universitaires de France.

LAURENTIN, RENÉ, 1965, *The question of Mary.* New York: Holt, Rinehart and Winston.

LERNER, DANIEL, 1958, *The passing of traditional society.* Glencoe: Free Press.

LEWIS, OSCAR, 1959, *Five families.* New York: Basic Books.

MONSIVAIS, CARLOS, 1970, *Dias de guardar.* Mexico: Biblioteca Era.

MÖRNER, MAGNUS, 1967, *Race mixture in the history of Latin America.* Boston: Little, Brown.

PATAI, RAPHAEL, 1967, *Women in the modern world.* New York: Free Press.

PITT-RIVERS, JULIAN, 1965, Who is an Indian? *Encounter* 25 (September): 41–49.

PORTUGAL, ANA MARIA, 1970, La peruana, 'tapada' sin manto? *Mundo Nuevo* 46 (April): 20–27.

PURCELL, SUSAN KAUFMAN, 1971, Modernizing women for a modern society: the Cuban case. Paper delivered at the 1971 meeting of the Latin American Studies Association, Austin, Texas.

REYES NEVARES, SALVADOR, 1970, El machismo en Mexico. *Mundo Nuevo* 46 (April): 14–19.

RIESMAN, DAVID, NATHAN GLAZER, AND REUEL DENNEY, 1953, *The lonely crowd.* Garden City N.Y.: Doubleday.

SCHUSTER, A., 1971, Women's role in the Soviet Union: ideology and reality. *Russian Review* 30 (July): 260–267.

SEESE, LINDA, 1969, You've come a long way, baby. *Motive* 29 (April): 68–71.

SILVERT, KALMAN, 1970, *Man's [sic!] Power.* New York: Viking Press.

STEVENS, EVELYN P., 1965, Mexican machismo: politics and value orientations. *Western Political Quarterly* 18 (December): 848–857.

_____ 1973, Marianismo: the other face of machismo in Latin America. In Ann Pescatello (ed.), *Female and male in Latin America.* Pittsburgh: University of Pittsburgh Press.

WAGLEY, CHARLES, 1963, *Race and class in rural Brazil.* New York: Columbia University Press.

Family vs. Community: Patterns of Divided Loyalties in Israel

YONINA TALMON-GARBER

INTRODUCTION

THE PURPOSE OF THIS PAPER IS AN analysis of the impact of radical and rapid social change on patterns of family organization and on the relationship between the family and the community. We shall be dealing here with three of the types of family found in Israel: (a) the family in collective settlements (kibbutzim); (b) the family in cooperative settlements (moshavim) settled by immigrants from Islamic countries; and (c) the family among European refugees in urban centres. We shall focus our analysis on these cases because they represent three analytically distinct modes of inter-action between the family and the community. In the kibbutzim the community reigns supreme and the family is subordinated to it. The traditional family in the moshavim is kinship centred—the elementary family is subordinated to wider kinship groupings which mediate between it and the community. The isolated refugee family in urban centres is cut off from kin and estranged from the community.

Reprinted by permission of Unesco from the *International Social Science Journal* 14, 3, © Unesco 1962.

THE FAMILY
IN COLLECTIVE SETTLEMENTS

The main features of collective settlements or kibbutzim[1] are: common ownership of property, except for a few personal belongings, and communal organization of production and consumption. Members' needs are provided for by communal institutions on an equalitarian basis. All income goes into the common treasury; each member gets only a very small annual allowance for personal expenses. The community is run as a single economic unit and as one household. It is governed by a general assembly, which meets as a rule once a week, by a secretariat and by various committees. The kibbutzim are an outgrowth of the revolutionary phase of Jewish immigration to Israel. The ideological urge to migrate to the new country and establish kibbutzim in it has not affected either whole communities or whole kinship groups—it cut through and disrupted kinship ties. Most immigrants during this phase were young and unattached. They came to the country unaccompanied by parents or relatives, having discarded their former way of life and their former social setting. The disposition to establish cohesive communities and relegate the family to a secondary position is closely connected with this process of dissociation from former ties. The cohesion of the new primary relations, developed in the youth movements and later on in the kibbutzim, replaced the discarded family ties.

Examination of the first stages[2] of the Collective Movement and the first phases of the development of each kibbutz reveals that there is a certain basic incompatibility between intense collective identification and family solidarity. The members of the kibbutz agree voluntarily to subordinate their personal interests to the attainment of communal goals and to seek self-expression only through service to their community. The conception of an all-absorbing task dominates their life and defines every aspect of it. The devotion to the realization of communal ideals takes precedence over kinship obligations. The intimate person-to-person relations, the intense togetherness, the unity which permeates all contacts, become more significant than family loyalties. The intense collective identification counteracts any tendency to renew contacts with relatives outside the kibbutzim. Relatives who are not members are by definition outsiders, almost strangers. It is felt that external ties should not be allowed to interfere with internal unity. The formation of families of procreation in the kibbutzim introduces a new source of conflict, in this case an internal conflict. Deep attachment to the family may weaken the primary group characteristics of the kibbutz and disrupt its unity. The families may tend to become competing foci of intensive emotional involvement and to infringe upon devotion to the community.

From its inception the Collective Movement has realized the danger inherent in external contacts and conflicting loyalties and set out to counteract centrifugal tendencies by a redefinition of the position of the family. The kibbutzim curtailed family obligations and attachments and took over most of its functions. They have evolved many ingenious devices in order to prevent the consolidation of the family as a distinct and independent unit. Delegation of functions to the kibbutz is the most important aspect of the "collectivization" of the family during the first phases of the movement. Husband and wife are allotted independent jobs. There is a strict ban on assigning members of the same family to the same place of work. Division of labour in the occupational sphere is based on a denial of sex differentiation. Women participated to a considerable extent in hard productive labour as well as in defence activities. All meals are taken in the common dining hall. Members' needs are provided by communal institutions. Families look after their own rooms but have few other household responsibilities. Thus each mate works in one branch or another and receives his share of the goods and services distributed by the kibbutz. Interaction between the sexes in the economic sphere occurs on the level of the community as a whole and not directly between mates. There is during this stage a far-reaching limitation of functions of the family in the sphere of replacement and socialization as well. The birthrate in the kibbutzim was for a long time below the level of replacement. The kibbutzim ensured their continuity and growth not so much by natural increase but by means of recruitment of volunteers from external sources.³ The physical care and rearing of the children were basically the responsibility of the kibbutz and not so much of their parents. In most kibbutzim children live apart from their parents. From their birth on they sleep, eat, and later study in special children's houses. Each age group leads its own life and has its autonomous arrangements. Children meet their parents and siblings in off-hours and spend the afternoons and early evenings with them. On Saturdays and holidays they stay with their parents most of the time. In most kibbutzim parents put their young children to bed every night. There are thus frequent and intensive relations between parents and children. The main socializing agencies are, however, the peer age group and the specialized nurses, instructors, and teachers. The age group is a substitute for the sibling group. It duplicates the structure of the community and mediates between children and adults. Basically the children belong to the community as a whole. The core of internal family activities which looms so large in other types of family has thus diminished considerably. The family has almost ceased to be an autonomous unit from this point of view of division of labour.

Another important aspect of the process was the change in internal family relations. The union between spouses did not require the sanction of the marriage ceremony. A couple who maintained a stable relationship for some time and decided to establish a family applied for a room and started to live together without any formalities or celebrations. The wedding was usually deferred until the birth of children and was performed in order to legitimize them in accordance with the law of the land. Execution of family tasks was based on the tenet of equality of the sexes and husband and wife were in many respects interchangeable. Both conjugal and parent–children relationships were exceedingly nonauthoritarian. The dominant pattern of family interaction during this stage is comradeship on equal terms.

A fairly strong antifamilistic bias is clearly manifested in patterns of informal social relations and leisure-time activities. Members spent most of their free time together. They met every evening in the communal dining hall, in the reading room or on the central lawn and spent their time in committee work and heated discussions. Spontaneous community singing and folk-dancing were the main recreational activities. Public opinion discouraged constant joint appearance of the couple in public. Husband and wife who stuck together and were often seen in each other's company were viewed with ridicule. Each member of the family was likely to have friends of his own. There was little regard for the family relationships in work allocation. Husband and wife were often assigned to jobs with different timetables and consequently did not see much of each other. There was very little coordination of vacations and holidays. Even the weekly day off of husband and wife often fell on different days. There was hardly any family entertainment or family visiting. Members of the family functioned independently and were pulled in different directions.⁴

It should be noted that while the kibbutzim limited the functions of the family drastically and emphasized the collective aspect, they did not abolish the family altogether.⁵ Even during the earliest phases when the antifamilistic trend was at its strongest the family remained a distinct unit. While premarital sexual relations were permitted, there was a clear-cut distinction between casual sexual experimentation, love affairs, and the more durable and publicly sanctioned unions. By asking for a room of their own, the couple made public their wish to have permanent relations and eventually have children. Residence in a common bedroom-living room allocated by the kibbutz conferred legitimacy on the couple. While children did not actually share a common domicile with their parents, they visited their parents' room every day, and it was their home by reference. The family did not relinquish its communal functions completely either. Parents contributed to the economic support of their children indirectly by working jointly rather than separately. Similarly, though educators were the designated representatives of the kibbutz rather than of the parents, the parents exercised a direct and continuous influence on the trained personnel in charge of their children. Since children's institutions were not segregated from the community either ecologically or socially, parents were able to supervise closely the way their children were raised there. They exercised considerable direct influence on their children during the time they spent together every day.[6] While interaction of members of the family with each other was in many cases less frequent than interaction with outsiders, internal ties were more continuous, more meaningful, and more intense. The emotional ties that bound husband and wife and parents and children were much more intimate and more exclusive than their ties with other members of the community. The family combined physical and emotional intimacy and supplied its members' needs for close personal contacts which were partly independent of their position in the community. By providing unconditional love and loyalty, it insulated its members from communal pressures and enhanced their security.

The extreme limitation of familial functions and relations was most pronounced in the initial phases of the development of the Collective Movement. It is still to be found, though in a less extreme form, in newly established collectives. The transition from undifferentiated and extremely cohesive communities to a more differentiated and less cohesive ones entails a considerable enhancement of the position of the family. The original homogeneity of the initial stage is disrupted by division of labour and by the establishment and growth of families. The community is further differentiated by the crystallization of various groups of settlers that join the core of founders in each community at different stages of its development. The collectives become more tolerant towards differentiation and subdivision and the family is assigned a place among other subgroups.

The appearance of the second generation is of crucial importance in this context because children are the main focus of segregated family life in the kibbutzim. Marriage does not entail a redefinition of roles and a new division of labour and does not cause a clearly perceptible cleavage between the couple and the rest of the community. The birth of children makes manifest the partial independence of the family. There emerges a core of specific family duties and the continuity of the family is no longer dependent only on the vicissitudes of the love relationship between the spouses. It becomes more safely anchored in their common attachment to their children and their joint responsibilities to them. The birth of children affects the family in yet another way. The appearance of the second genera-

tion introduces a gradual shift of emphasis from disruption of intergeneration ties to continuity. Children are expected to settle in the kibbutzim founded by their parents and continue their lifework there. The family of orientation is no longer an external and alien influence. Parents and children are members of the same kibbutz. They live in close proximity and share, at least to some extent, the same ideals. Identification with one's family may thus reinforce identification with the collective.

The shift of emphasis from discontinuity to continuity in more differentiated and less cohesive collectives is expressed in a partial "emancipation" of the family. The family regains some of its lost functions in the sphere of housekeeping. Most families will have their afternoon tea at home with their children. In some of the kibbutzim families will often eat their evening meal at home too. Most families do it only occasionally, as a special treat for their children, while some eat at home regularly almost every evening. Couples spend a considerable part of their personal allowances on their flats. The housing policy of the kibbutzim has changed considerably. While the houses built during the first phases of the movement were barrack-like and the dwelling unit consisted of only one room, the typical dwelling unit now consists of a semidetached flat containing one or two rooms, kitchenette, and private sanitary facilities. The flat serves in many cases as an important symbol of the togetherness of the family and a physical manifestation of its separateness. Members usually tend their flat with care and have a strong desire to make it as neat and as pleasant as possible.

There is a considerable increase of the family's functions in the sphere of reproduction and socialization. Examination of demographic data indicates a considerable increase in fertility in the kibbutzim. The dwindling of external recruitment sources and the difficulties experienced by the kibbutzim in absorption of new immigrants have greatly enhanced the importance of natural increase. Emphasis has shifted from recruitment of volunteers from outside to expansion from within. The family is now called upon to help the kibbutz to ensure its continuity and growth. Parents tend to take a more active part in the socialization of their children. There is much closer cooperation between nurses, instructors, teachers, and parents. Parents help in looking after their young children. They take turns in watching them at night and nurse them when they are ill. They help in the preparation of festivals arranged for the children and attend most of them. There is considerably more parental supervision of the children's behaviour, their choice of friends and their reading habits. Parents try to influence their children's choice of future occupations and insist on their right to be consulted on this matter. Some of the kibbutzim have introduced a more radical reorganization. Children in these kibbutzim no longer sleep in the children's houses. They stay with their age groups during the day but return home every afternoon. Duties of child care and socialization have thus partly reverted to the family.

The line dividing internal family activities and external activities has shifted considerably in all spheres except for the occupational sphere. There is considerable pressure to reduce the number of hours that women work in communal enterprises, but only small concessions have been made in this sphere—mothers of babies get more time off from work now and aging women start to work part time earlier than the men. The kibbutzim put the main emphasis on the occupational role and it has remained the major focus of activity for both men and women. Yet even in this sphere we witness considerable modifications. There is now a fairly clear-cut sex-role differentiation in work organization. Women are mainly concentrated in occupations more closely allied to traditional housekeeping such as cooking, laundry service, nursing, and teaching.[7]

Modification in patterns of internal family relationships is yet another aspect of the process of change. Marriage normally now precedes the establishment of a family. Most couples attach considerable importance to the wedding celebration and want it to be a memorable event. There are many signs of the emergence of a fairly fixed albeit flexible and fluctuating internal division of labour. Husbands help in households duties, but in most families women do most of the work and it is mainly their responsibility. The husband is regarded as the wife's assistant or temporary stand-in but not as a co-worker on equal terms. There is considerable cooperation and interchangeability in the relationship to the children, yet in spite of a considerable blurring of differences between the father role and the mother role, there are some signs of differentiation. The mother is as a rule more concerned with the bodily well-being of the children and takes care of them while they are at home. She has usually more contact with the children's institutions and the school and supervises the upbringing of her children there. There are indications that while the wife has more say in routine matters it is the husband who usually decides on matters of principle.

The tendency towards a more familistic pattern may also be discerned in the subtle transformation of informal relations and leisure-time activities. Free time spent in public has diminished considerably. Members are not as eager as they used to be to participate in public discussions or attend public meetings. Spontaneous dancing and community singing sessions are rare. Members tend to retire to their rooms and to stay at home most of the time. Husband and wife will spend most of their free time together. They usually sit near each other during evening meals and on all public occasions. There is a far better coordination of work schedules as well as of vacations and holidays. Families get special consideration in this respect and are able to spend their free time together. Entertaining and visiting are becoming joint family affairs. It is now considered impolite to invite only one of the spouses. Friends who are not congenial to both husband and wife are gradually dropped. Many families regularly celebrate birthdays and wedding anniversaries and attach considerable importance to such family affairs.

In the sphere of parent–children relations we witness an interesting "dialectical" process. The extreme limitation of the functions of the family in the sphere of maintenance and socialization of its children has not led to disruption of family solidarity. Paradoxically, the curtailment of obligations reinforced rather than weakened the parent–children relationship and enhanced the importance of the emotional ties between them. It is mainly within the family that both parents and children have intimate relations unpatterned by their positions in the community and that they are free from routine duties. The child's position outside the family is prescribed only to a small extent. He has to compete with his age peers for a position in his group and for the approval of the adults in charge of it. All children in the same age group have the same claim to attention. It is only in the family that they get love and care which they do not have to share with many others. Insofar as the family has ceased to be the prime socializing agency, it avoids to some extent the inevitable ambivalence towards the agents of socialization. Parents do not have to play the two-sided role of ministering to the children's needs for care and security on the one hand and of thwarting their wishes in various ways on the other. Parents do not carry the main responsibility for disciplining their children and can afford to be permissive. Examination of our material indicates the overall importance of parent–children relationships. The children have come very often to occupy the emotional centre of the parents' life. They have become a major preoccupation with most mothers. Young children are deeply dependent and very often overdependent on their parents. The children eventually outgrow this dependence. They become attached to their age mates and drift away to a certain extent from their parents. Parents resent this partial estrangement and will often blame it on the usurpation of communal institutions. Many feel bereaved of function and crave for closer contacts with their children. It is this process which is at the root of recent reorganizations.[8] Parents now emphasize the unity of the family and encourage closer contacts between all its members. Older children are often entrusted with the care of younger ones and there is a considerable amount of interaction between siblings.

Another outstanding feature of the process of change is the gradual development and renewal of wider kinship ties. As long as the generational structure of the kibbutz remained truncated, most members did not have any kin besides members of their own elementary family living with them in the same community. A gradual process of change sets in when the children of the founders establish families and the kibbutz develops into a full-scale three-generational structure. The kibbutzim have in addition accepted social responsibility for aging or sick parents[9] and transfer many of them to their chil-

dren in the kibbutz. Old parents live either in separate blocks of dwellings or in little semidetached flats adjoining those of their children. Relatives who live in the same community maintain close contacts through frequent visiting and mutual help. There are many indices of the emergence of cohesive kinship groupings. Relatives tend very often to cluster and form united blocks which have a considerable influence on communal affairs. Wider kinship ties serve also as connecting links with the outside world. Members tend to renew their contacts with relatives who live outside the kibbutz. They will stay with their relatives when they go to town and will invite them to visit them. They accept personal presents from kin and reciprocate by sending farm produce from time to time. The wider kinship category is amorphous and ill defined, but there is quite a strong moral obligation to maintain amicable relations with kin. Kinship ties have thus broken through the self-imposed isolation of the kibbutzim from outside contacts.

It should be stressed that in spite of the considerable change in the position of the family the kibbutzim still remain basically nonfamilistic. The shift from intergenerational discontinuity to continuity attentuates the tension between the family and the kibbutz but the basic rivalry is still operative. Insofar as the family accepts the primacy of collective considerations it may become a valuable ally. Inasmuch as it resents a subordinate position and disputes the authority of collective institutions it is still a potential source of conflict and competition.[10] The kibbutzim make far-reaching demands on their members. The proper functioning of the kibbutz depends on the wholehearted identification of members with its aims and ideals. The collectives cannot afford to allow the family to become an independent and self-sufficient unit lest it undermine the primacy of collective considerations. They still fear that if the family is given a free hand it will become the main focus of primary relations and kinship ties will become preponderant over the ties between co-members.

The violent antifamilism of the revolutionary phase has abated but all traces of it have not disappeared completely. It is superseded by a moderate collectivism which regards the family as a useful though dangerous ally. The kibbutzim control and limit the family and employ it for the attainment of collective goals.

THE TRADITIONAL FAMILY IN COOPERATIVE SETTLEMENTS[11]

The effect of immigration and a new type of community life on the relations between the elementary family and the wider kinship group can be best studied by examination of traditional or semitraditional families in cooperative settlements. We shall deal here mainly with North African Jews who arrived in Israel after the establishment of the State, as there is more reliable and up-to-date information on this group than on any of the others. Moreover, they provide us with the best and clearest example of the transformation taking place in such groups.

Jews in North Africa, before the French occupation, were able to maintain the continuity of their traditional social and cultural structure. In the main, they formed small communities, composed of large patriarchal families of three or four generations. The father directed his married and unmarried sons in work tasks and maintained discipline within a joint residence unit. Kinsmen, in particular patrilineal kin, formed friendship and visiting groups and joined together in cases of conflict and crisis. Males customarily held dominant positions and female roles were limited to home and family. The synagogue was an important place of male gathering. Allegiance to Jewish ritual and observance centred around the synagogue and the religious schools.

This traditional structure remained more or less intact in the villages and small towns but it has changed considerably in the big urban centres. The French influence and mass migration to the big new cities have greatly undermined this traditional structure. Rapid migration very often splintered the kinship group since kin dispersed throughout different communities. Young men could now enter new occupations and become independent. Upon marriage they tended to sever their close ties with their families of orientation and establish independent households. Secularization estranged the younger generation from the older one and weakened the allegiance to traditional kinship obligations. In urban sectors of North Africa the traditional structure was undergoing rapid change. There were many manifestations of severe strain in both the nuclear and the extended families. The larger kinship groupings suffered most and were rapidly disintegrating.

Immigration to Israel affected both the traditional and semitraditional sectors. Immigrants from North Africa had, on the whole, a positive identification with Israel but this identification was a traditional one and differed greatly from the secular-national identification which was dominant in the absorbing society. In the traditional sector immigration was motivated mainly by a deep sense of Jewish solidarity and vague messianic striving. In the transitional sector the main factor was a search for security and economic advancement. Immigrants from both sectors had little disposition to change. They came to Israel hoping to be able to continue their way of life undisturbed and unmolested. The adherence to preexisting patterns of life affected the composition of immigration. Immigration took place in many cases in preexisting group clusters. Families, neighborhoods, inhabitants of local areas and even whole communities immigrated together.

Part of the North African immigrants were directed by the settling agency to cooperative settlements. The cooperative settlement or moshav[12] is based on a semi-independent family working on its family farm. The principles underlying the cooperation of these family units are: public ownership of land and machinery, equality as to size of farm and basic investment, ban on hired labour, mutual aid and cooperative marketing and purchasing. The cooperative settlement is governed by democratic procedures. Long-term policy is determined at periodic village meetings while daily affairs are entrusted to elected officers, committees and hired experts and professionals. The cooperative settlements combine a familistic division of labour with mechanized and intensive farming and with centralized and specialized management of cooperative institutions. They emphasize both autonomy and interdependence. The cooperative settlements which were founded during the pre-State period were formed by volunteer pioneering groups who sought to realize both personal and national ideals. The post-State moshavim are administered communities planned and managed to a large extent by governmental and semigovernmental agencies. State planners, guided by defence considerations and by a desire to disperse the Israeli population, ordered the construction of 274 cooperative settlements and directed new immigrants to these villages. While some communities become progressively autonomous, many others remain dependent on outside agencies.

The settling agency regarded the traditional kinship-centred social organization of the immigrants as inimical to the development of a modern cooperative village. The planners did not take into consideration the former group composition of the settlers and intentionally disregarded their former attachments and loyalties. The social composition of each village was during the initial phase a matter of organizational decision based on administrative considerations. Kinship groups were dispersed. With the exception of a few relatives and former friends, all the original settlers in the villages were unrelated. Most of the settlers had never met each other before their immigration. Strangers became neighbours and had to cooperate with each other in many vital matters.

It is significant that the traditional kinship structure soon reasserted itself and the composition of most settlements has changed rapidly. Settlers sought out their relatives and encouraged them to settle in the same village. Other settlers left the village and joined their relatives in some other settlement. Kinsmen tended to seek one another out and cluster together. After a considerable reshuffle and change of population, most villages have emerged with two or three major kinship groups. There remains in the villages only a number of smaller kinship groups or of unrelated nuclear (elementary) families. These families try to attach themselves to one of the strong kinship clusters by concluding marriages with them. Some legitimize the connexion with a kinship cluster by fabricating fictitious kinship ties with it. Even purely political allegiances are legitimized in terms of kinship obligations. Kinsmen assist and support each other. In spite of the fact that the moshav economy is based on the nuclear family and each nuclear family has a

separate household, a separate farm, and a separate account, there is intense cooperation between members of the same kinship group. Kinship units are also intervisiting and recreational groups. The nuclear families are subordinated to the kinship groups and the villages have all become kinship dominated.[13]

Reunion of kinsmen occurred more easily and rapidly in traditional families who had maintained their wider kinship ties and had arrived in the country in groups of families and neighbourhood units. However, this process occurred in the semi-traditional sectors too. Even relatives who had already been separated in North Africa and had not seen each other for years sought each other out and revived the dormant kinship ties between them. In the unfamiliar and unstructured social setting, kinship ties regained their lost significance and served as a major basis for spontaneous reorganization.[14] As a result of this process, the villages which were at their inception artificial amalgams of unrelated families became communities based on kinship where most elementary families were embedded and controlled by the larger kinship groupings.

Not only was the kinship reconstituted but it also began to assume new functions. The kinship unit has a political significance. Village politics revolve about control of communitywide institutions, and, preeminently, control of the central committee. Controlling the central committee involves not only prestige but organizational and financial advantages as well. With control so advantageous, the kin groups become rival factions, each struggling with the other for power. Since membership in the central committee is based upon democratic election, the relative size and internal composition of the kinship units had a direct bearing on their position in the village. The "political history" of each village involves a continuous struggle between the kinship groups, which jockey for control by offering various promises to other families or groups of families. Political allegiances are formed and re-formed, always with the bigger kinship groups at the centre. Politics serve to reinforce the ties between kin. Kinship and the kin group have assumed new, essentially political functions. The relative size of the kinship clusters is of utmost importance in the political struggle yet there are many indications that internal cohesion of the kinship unit is in some cases more important than mere size. It seems that closely knit clusters which unite close relatives are more stable and more powerful than clusters based on more distant and more vague kinship affiliations. Paradoxically, radical modernization has strengthened and revived the kinship dominated traditional order.[15]

The strengthening and reconstitution of the kinship unit has helped the immigrants to adapt to the new settling. The kinship group is a strong cooperative unit. Cooperation within it is legitimized by traditional norms and obligations. It extends to all its members economic assistance and political backing. It creates a basic field of security and continuity. The kinship group mediates between the elementary families and the community and in this way links the old traditional order to the new one. Adaptability to the new setting was found to be highly correlated with kinship solidarity.

Yet the growing dominance of the kinship group is fraught with grave danger to the village community. The strong particularistic loyalty to the kinship groups very often destroys the loyalty to the village as a whole. Election of village officers and voting on community issues tend to follow kinship lines. Decisions are not based on any objective criteria. Village officers and committee members function as representatives of their kinship unit and are not much concerned about the interests of the village as a whole. They discriminate, without compunction, against members who are not their relatives and see to it that their kinship unit and its allies get as much of the available facilities and rewards as possible. The nepotism of officeholders breeds inefficiency and suspicion. It engenders, in addition, bitter feuds. The villages are often divided into hostile factions which conduct a constant fight against each other. These factions very often reach a deadlock and the management of cooperative institutions on the village level is immobilized for many months. It sometimes becomes necessary to transfer one of the warring factions to another village in order to put an end to a feud which threatens to destroy the village. The solidarity of the kinship group develops at the expense of the solidarity of the village community.

The Settling Agency was faced with a dilemma. Since radical modernization has strengthened rather than weakened the traditional order, there is now a growing tendency to come to terms with it and initiate gradual and selective change. The planners have come to realize that the kinship groups are vitally important units in the absorption of traditional immigrants and should not be disrupted or suppressed. They therefore accept the kinship groups and only try to restrict them to internal activities by limiting their influence on central cooperative institutions. In some of the villages, there is a growing tendency to replace officeholders by hired experts who are unrelated to any kinship unit in the village. They are not involved in the village feuds and are better trained. Consequently, they are more objective and far more efficient. Management is thus partly dissociated from the relations between the kinship units. Cooperative institutions can continue to function even in cases of severe tension. A certain loosening of the cooperative structure has a beneficial effect in this respect too. Dependence on central institutions enhances the importance of political control of the central committee. Restriction of cooperation to a more limited sphere narrows the area of tension and of competition and diminishes the intensity of conflict. In many cases it has become necessary to enhance the control by external agencies and postpone the initiation of full local self-government until the village becomes an ongoing concern and the settlers have gained some experience in the techniques of communal self-management.

In the long run the future of the villages described here depends on the second generation.[16] The children of the immigrants go to school and join the army. They temporarily leave their village and learn new skills. Their general outlook and their basic value orientation change considerably. In many cases, they develop an aversion to the traditional way of life and tend to ignore, scoff at, or openly rebel against it. They feel that their parents are hopelessly dated and out of place and reject them. Conflict between parents and children has a particularly corrosive effect on the traditional order. Reverence for elders and respect of parents are core elements in the traditional value system.

The young generation does not have an acknowledged right to independence and insubordination engenders bitter strife. Since moral precepts and social obligations are to a large extent directly rooted in acceptance of parental authority, deprecation of parents often leads to serious loss of orientation. In many cases, the impinging influences undermine the traditional values and loyalties without replacing them effectively with new ones, thus causing confusion and alienation. The hope of an effective and continuous change lies in a system of education and training which orients young people to new values but does not breed estrangement between generations. The second generation is able to transform the traditional order and adapt it to the new social setting only when it retains its basic loyalty to the kinship unit and respects its values.

THE ISOLATED REFUGEE FAMILY IN URBAN CENTRES[17]

This type of family is prevalent mainly among immigrants who came to the country after the second World War from countries which were formerly under German occupation. The methodological extermination of Jews in these countries annihilated whole communities. In many flourishing Jewish centres only a few managed to escape and very few families remained intact. Immigrants of this type were uprooted and isolated. They arrived in the country with few or no relatives. Their former social setting was completely and irrevocably destroyed. They had all undergone severe hardships and most of them spent long periods of compulsory collective living in prison camps.

Most immigrants of the type described here were not members of Zionist movements. They had received no preparatory ideological indoctrination and had not undergone vocational training. They were thus unprepared for the difficult conditions of settlement in the new country. Many of them remembered their shattered prewar past with nostalgic yearning and tended to idealize it. Consequently, they had little disposition to change and found it difficult to adapt themselves to the new setting. They usually had a diffuse positive attitude towards Israel but no strong identification with its aims and values. These immigrants were concerned with their personal problems. They hoped to regain and better their lost status. Their experience of camp life had instilled in them a deep yearning for privacy and undisturbed personal development. This concentration on personal aspirations ran counter to the ideological and collectivist orientations of the absorbing society.

Another important factor which affected the relationship between the immigrants and the absorbing society was the bureaucratization of absorption. The mass immigration was handled by various bureaucratic agencies and not by primary groups of old-timers. During the initial phase of settlement the immigrants had little contact with old-timers and little opportunity to take the initiative in solving their problems in their own way. They had only a hazy and insufficient knowledge of the aims and norms of the bureaucratic bodies which competed and cooperated in the process of their absorption. They had great difficulty in finding their way in the maze of rules and regulations and resented the impersonal way in which their personal problems were dealt with. They felt confused and alienated.

These immigrants were thus cut off from the community.[18] Their contacts with the institutional framework tended to be formal and specific. As we have already mentioned, they had few relatives and hardly any former friends. The newly acquired contacts with neighbours and work associates revolved around limited interests. In addition, these contacts were of short duration and had not had time to grow into meaningful and mutually binding ties. Consequently, all the wider contacts of immigrants of this type were partial, shallow, and devoid of any deep personal meaning.

The reaction of the immigrants to their alienation and isolation is a wholehearted and very intense attachment to their elementary family.[19] Since external ties have little significance, the immigrants developed a compensatory involvement with internal family relationships. The family withdraws to its small and isolated private world. The immigrants seek solace and security in the spontaneous and warm intimacy of their family. They defend the independence of their family life in opposition to the constant demands of the absorbing society. In their family they are their own masters and need not constantly accommodate themselves to these demands. They try to insulate the family against outside influences and continue to cultivate their former patterns of life.[20]

The occupational role gains its meaning only in conjunction with the family. Life revolves about the home and the place of work, but the real centre of gravity is the home. The occupational role is secondary and derivative and has no meaning in its own right. Instrumental relations developed during work are very often devoid of any expressive significance. The real life goal is the unity, well-being, and economic advancement of the family. The immigrants work indefatigably and persistently as long as it benefits their family, but are unconcerned with purely occupational problems and uninterested in the wider implications of their work.

Isolated families develop only a few significant contacts outside the inner circle of the family. Their informal relations and leisure-time activities are family centred. They refrain from joining voluntary associations and societies. They have a deep distrust of the authorities at any level and hold political parties in cynical contempt. They have no contacts and no identification with established *élites* of any kind. They keep aloof from any political or social activities and are apathetic to the goals of society as a whole.[21]

The crisis of war, mass extermination, and immigration has greatly reinforced the internal solidarity and unity of the nuclear family, but this heightened cohesiveness has developed at the expense of solidarity in wider social groupings. It very often prevents the development of a more comprehensive involvement and identification. It blocks efforts of resocialization since it enables the family to adapt to the new social setting with a bare minimum of conscious reorientation to new goals. The family is able to cling to its initial expectations and role–images, even when these images are incompatible with the new social setting. The isolated family protects the uprooted individual and supports him. It creates a basic field of security and continuity. However, as long as the family remains cut off from the realities of life in the new country and as long as

it is related to the wider framework of institutions, associations, and primary groups, it may become a fool's paradise, jealousy guarding its fictitious independence against the outside world.

Eventually the self-imposed isolation of this type of family adversely affects its unity. External relations impinge on its internal relations in the form of parents–children conflict. The children gradually adopt the values of the absorbing society. They soon realize that their parents cannot guide them in their efforts to adapt themselves to the new setting and to find their proper place in it. They are torn between gratitude to their parents and disappointment. They develop an ambivalent attitude towards their family and treat it with a mixture of frustrated love and violent hatred. The conflict between parents and children hits the isolated family very hard and destroys its precarious unity and stability. Isolation of the family is thus inimical to its own solidarity as well as to the cohesion of the community.

The main problem which confronts the isolated family from a dynamic point of view is the gradual widening of its horizon of participation and identification beyond its limited confines. Local authorities and community centres have tried to cope with these problems by conducting periodic campaigns among members of isolated families, calling on them to participate in voluntary activities, recruiting them to various associations, and nominating them to committees. These efforts of recruiting meet with some success only when concentrated in spheres directly adjoining the family. The best example of such successful extension of spheres of activity of parents' committees in school. "Isolated" parents have the well-being and advancement of their children very much at heart. The children are in fact their main life goal. It is therefore comparatively easy to draw them into voluntary participation in a committee which controls and promotes the local school. By serving on this committee they are able to wield some influence on the education of their children and at the same time gain a better understanding of the norms and aims of the school. They are also better able to understand the problems of their children. They get much closer to their children and at the same time narrow the gap which separates them from the absorbing society. The school may serve as a major link between the isolated family and the wider social setting.

Reorganization of the occupational sphere often serves a similar purpose. Occupational advancement has a direct bearing on the family. It is possible to arouse the interests of the family in the activities of trade unions and professional associations to a certain degree. Organizations dealing with practical issues on the local level may also serve as a starting point for extension of participation. Interest in general ideological and political problems is much more difficult to awaken and most members of isolated families remain politically uncommitted and passive. At first, participation is limited to practical matters which directly concern the family. Gradually, however, the new members of committees regain confidence in themselves and in their fellow members. They learn to take the initiative and plan ahead and accumulate practical experience in dealing with their problems. Since the committees operate on a local basis and involve face-to-face contacts they provide opportunities for getting to know neighbours and making friends. The social environment becomes less menacing, less alien, less confusing, and therefore much more manageable.[22] In many cases, such limited participation becomes a steppingstone to wider participation and to more comprehensive identification.

CONCLUSION

It was our purpose to examine the impact of radical change on family solidarity and on the position of the family in the community. We have seen that the processes of change entailed in immigration have had a disruptive effect on family cohesion in the case of the kibbutzim, yet they have greatly enhanced the solidarity and independence of the family in the other two case studies. Internal relations within the elementary family or within the kinship group have become the main source of material assistance and emotional support in these cases. Immigration confronts the family with new problems of adjustment and increases its need for aid. Yet at the same time it cuts it off from its former sources of external support. The family is forced to rely on its internal resources and resort to mutual aid. The absence of competing foci of identification acts in the same way. Inasmuch as members of the family or the kinship unit have fewer comprehensive and significant external ties and loyalties, they tend to turn inwards. Intensified co-operation among kin develops also as a compensatory and countervailing mechanism. Intimate face-to-face relations between relatives come to mean so much during the first phases of adjustment because they mitigate the anonymity and the insecurity incurred by immigration. By partly segregating its members, the family protects them from overpowering external pressures and enables them to maintain a partial autonomy. Radical change enhances the importance of familial continuity.

Examination of our case indicates that the elementary family, the kinship unit, and the community are in a sense competing foci of identification. Intense involvement with the collective develops at the expense of the solidarity of the family and the kinship unit. The heightened cohesion of the reconstituted traditional kinship group encroaches on the independence of the elementary family and is also inimical to cohesion at the level of community organization. There is an inverse correlation between the intense commitment to the elementary family of the refugees and solidarity in wider social groupings.[23] It should be stressed, however, that while a very intense and comprehensive commitment to any of these units may interfere with and threaten the loyalty to the two others, they are by no means inherently mutually exclusive and incompatible. In the kibbutzim we witness a transition from intense rivalry to controlled coexistence and coordination. Insofar as the family accepts the primacy of collective considerations, it may become a valuable ally and identification with it may reinforce the identification with the kibbutz. A similar transition may be discerned in the moshavim. Limitation of the functions of the kinship clusters coupled with a concomitant modification of communal organization brings about better coordination and mutual reinforcement rather than opposition. In the case of the refugees we found that participation in voluntary associations serves as a steppingstone to more comprehensive identification. Yet it consolidates the solidarity of the elementary family.

The family in the kibbutzim and the family among refugees in urban centres develop in opposite directions. In the "collectivized" family we witnessed a partial disengagement and emancipation of the family from the collective. In the "isolated" family we found a process of reengagement and reorientation of the family towards the community. The main problem of the kibbutzim from a dynamic point of view is how to allow the family units more privacy and more independence without harming the cohesion of the community. The main problem

that confronts communities containing a considerable number of "isolated" families is how to preserve the internal solidarity of the elementary families and at the same time find ways and means of extending the range of their participation and identification. The main problem which confronts the moshavim dealt with here is how to preserve the unity and solidarity of the kinship group and at the same time limit its influence on overall village management. These communities are trying now to introduce a gradual transformation of the traditional kinship-dominated structure by combining continuity and change.

NOTES

1. See M. Spiro, *Venture in Utopia*, 1956.

2. For a similar process, see R. Schlesinger, *The family in USSR*, 1949; L.A. Coser, Some aspects of Soviet family policy, *American Journal of Sociology* 56, 5, 1953; K. Geiger, Changing political attitudes in a totalitarian society, *World Politics* 8 1956; N.S. Timasheff, The attempt to abolish the family in Russia, in D. W. Bell and E. T. Vogel (eds.), *A modern introduction to the family*, 1960.

3. See Y. Talmon-Garber, Social structure and family size, *Human Relations* 12, 2, 1959.

4. For a fuller analysis of the process described here, see Y. Talmon-Garber, The family in collective settlements, *Transactions of the World Congress of Sociology*, 1957.

5. See M. Spiro, Is the family universal? The Israeli case, in Bell and Vogel (eds.), *op. cit.*, pp. 55–64.

6. See M. Spiro, *Children of the kibbutz*, 1958; see also R. Bar-Yoseph, The patterns of early socialization in the collective settlements in Israel, *Human Relations* 7, 4, 1959, pp. 345–360; E. E. Irvine, Observations in the aims and methods on child-rearing in communal settlements in Israel, 5, 3, 1952, pp. 247–275; A. I. Rabin, Infants and children under conditions of intermittent mothering, *Am. J. of Orthopsychiatry* 28, 3, 1958.

7. For a more detailed analysis of the emergence of sex-role differentiation, see Y. Talmon-Garber, *Sex-role differentiation in an equalitarian society*, 1959, mimeographed.

8. See Y. Talmon-Garber, The family and collective education in the kibbutz. *Niv-Hekvutsah* 8, 1, pp. 2–52 (in Hebrew). See also H. Faigin, Social behaviour of young children in the kibbutz, *Journal of Abn. Soc. Psych.* 56, 1, 1958; A. I. Rabin, Attitudes of kibbutz children to parents and family, *Am. J. of Orthopsychiatry* 29, 1, 1959.

9. See Y. Talmon-Garber, Aging in a planned society, *Am. J. of Soc.* 68, 3, 1961, pp. 286–296.

10. On the problems caused by the increased influence of the family on the occupational placement of its children, see Y. Talmon-Garber, Occupational placement of the second generation in collective settlements, *Megamoth* 8, 1957, pp. 369 ff. (in Hebrew). See also M. Sarell, Continuity and change—the second generation in collective settlements, *Megamoth* 11, 1961, pp. 2–23 (in Hebrew).

11. Analysis in this section is based on S. N. Eisenstadt, *Absorption of immigrants*, 1954; C. Frankenstein, *Between past and future*, 1956; A. Weingrod, Change and continuity in a Moroccan immigrant village, *Middle East Journal*, 1960, and *Administered communities*, 1961, mimeographed; D. Weintraub and M. Lissak, *The absorption of North African immigrants in agricultural settlements in Israel*, 1959, mimeographed; M. Coles, Patterns of cultural adaptation of immigrants from the Atlas Mountains, *Megamoth* 7, 1956, pp. 345–376 (in Hebrew); O. Shapira, *Social factors and economic development*, 1961, mimeographed (in Hebrew). In addition, we have used extensively reports and memoranda prepared by the sociologists attached to the Settlement Agency. Of special interest are the reports by M. Minkowitz, R. Rahat, and O. Shapira.

12. On the structure of the pre-State moshavim, see Y. Talmon-Garber, Differentiation in cooperative settlements. *Br. J. of Soc.* 3, 4, 1952.

13. We have very little material on internal sex-role differentiation and authority structure of the elementary family and cannot therefore deal with it here.

14. We have no systematic research on North African immigrants in urban centres. There are, however, many indications that even in an urban setting there is a strong tendency to revitalization of kinship ties

and spatial coalescence. Kinsmen serve as important communication outposts and provide the immigrants with badly needed information on jobs, houses and community facilities. They are potential sources of aid and often provide the newcomers with a considerable amount of economic and social support. On the interrelation between migration and kinship ties, see E. Litwak, Geographical mobility and family cohesion. *American Sociological Review* 25, 3, 1960, pp. 385-394.

15. It should be noted that we have completely disregarded internal cleavages based on heterogeneity of country of origin. Some of the moshavim discussed here have a mixed population and even in relatively homogeneous moshavim there are factions based on community of origin. A full analysis of this problem would take us too far afield and we have therefore refrained from dealing with it here.

16. See E. P. Hutchinson, *Immigrants and their children*, 1957; also I. Child, *Italians and Americans*, 1949, and D. Handlin, *The uprooted*, 1954. For analysis of parent-children relationship among oriental immigrants in Israel, see A. Simon, "Parents and children among immigrants from Islamic countries," *Megamoth*, 1957, pp. 41-55 (in Hebrew), and S. N. Eisenstadt and J. Ben David, "Intergeneration tensions in Israel," *International Social Science Bulletin*, 1956, pp. 59-75. It should be noted that in some ethnic groups the process of change is much smoother and gradual. See E. Katz and A. Zlotzower, Ethnic continuity in an Israeli town, *Human Relations* 14, 4, 1961, pp. 293-309.

17. Isolated families were found mainly in urban centres. It should be stressed, however, that they were found in rural settlements too. A fuller analysis of isolated families will be found in S.N. Eisenstadt, *Absorption of immigrants*, 1954. Additional material was obtained from a more recent ecological study of new urban centres in development areas conducted by Professor Eisenstadt and Mr. E. Cohen. I would like to express my gratitude to Mr. E. Cohen, Mrs. L. Shamgar, and Mrs. H. Adoni for placing their material at my disposal and for their useful comments.

18. It should be noted that cities and towns are not communities in the same sense as the kibbutz and the moshav. The kibbutz and the moshav are closely-knit and cohesive communities which contain the families living in them and mediate between them and the wider social system. The social environment of urban families is best considered not as the local community in which they live but rather as a comparatively loosely knit network of actual social relations which they maintain regardless of whether these relations are confined to the local community or go beyond its boundaries. Yet since we are dealing here mainly with small and medium urban centres in which there is a certain degree of local cohesion and where most significant relationships are confined to the local community, analysis of development of solidarity on the local level is not unwarranted. See E. Bott, *Families and social networks*, Chapters 3 and 4.

19. On a similar development in families of refugees in Germany, see H. Schlesky, *Wandlungen der deutschen Familie in der Gegenwart*, 1954.

20. We have very little material on internal sex-role differentiation in these families and cannot therefore test E. Bott's hypothesis on the relation between loosely knit networks and cooperation in execution of familial tasks. Our data seem to indicate, however, that the tendency to develop a more joint role relationship is often blocked by a strong defensive attitude towards former patterns of behaviour. These patterns are often ritualized and resist both external and internal pressures towards change.

21. Since the term "isolated" is often used to describe the position of ordinary families in urban centres, it should be stressed that we do not employ it here in this sense. The urban family is differentiated as a distinct and to some extent autonomous social group but it is not isolated. We use the term "isolated" to describe the refugee family because, unlike the "normal" urban family, it is not embedded in a sustaining network of external relationships and in many cases is at first virtually cut off from relatives, neighbours, friends and colleagues. See E. Bott, *op. cit.*

22. See E. Litwak, Voluntary associations and neighborhood cohesion. *Am. Soc. Rev.* 26, 2, 1961, pp. 258-271.

23. For an analysis which views the elementary family and the kinship group as competing foci of identification, see M. Gluckman, *Custom and conflict in Africa*, 1955. See also E. Bott, *op. cit.*

Multiple Mothering in China

RUTH SIDEL

For the ego, for the personality to develop, the infant needs to experience satisfaction and challenge at his own pace. But nowhere has it been demonstrated that for survival, or mental health the satisfactions, challenges, and frustrations must all originate in the same person.

Bruno Bettelheim
The children of the dream

THE PEKING HANDICRAFT FACTORY IS comprised of one large five-story building and a sprawling set of workshops built around an open courtyard. When we visited this factory, we wandered from workshop to workshop with our interpreter, Dr. Hsu, the secretary general of the Chinese Medical Association, Mr. Hsu, and others in our party and watched women using extraordinarily fine brushes to paint intricate pictures on the inside of bottles about three-inches high. We also saw vases being fashioned by the elaborate process of cloisonné. In another workshop, men and women sitting on wooden stools were painting Chinese red designs on black lacquer tables and cabinets; in a corner, the master designer was teaching an apprentice new designs for the furniture. They smiled as we watched them but continued with their work. We saw jade and ivory being carved so delicately that we felt we had to tiptoe around the room lest we jar a worker's elbow. We watched as traditional pictures were painted on long strips of bamboo in lovely, muted colors.

Before 1949, we were told, this was all done by individuals working alone, with no guarantee that they could make a living from their artistry. After Liberation, the workers were collected together in one place and in 1952 formed cooperatives. The factory we visited was established in 1958 and the workers are entitled to all the benefits enjoyed by other factory workers. Everything in the factory is hand-crafted; the goods are made for sale to foreigners in China or for export.

One of the advantages for women working in the factory is that they can bring their newborn babies to the factory's nursing room when they return to work after maternity leave. The nursing room is upstairs on the fourth floor of the large building here. When we visited late one afternoon, there were twenty-seven babies in the nursing room and four adults caring for them. This visit to the nursing room was spontaneous, as were many of our visits to other nurseries and kindergartens. As we were being shown around the handicrafts factory, we had asked if it had a nursery or a kindergarten. When our hosts explained that they had a nursing room in addition to a nursery-kindergarten combination, I asked to see the nursing room; a member of the revolutionary committee, an interpreter, and I went upstairs to visit right then. In much the same way, we met the worker-doctor in one of the workshops; my husband spotted a worker-doctor's medical bag, asked to whom it belonged, and therein began an hour-long conversation with the worker-doctor, who turned out to be a charming and knowledgeable person.

The four adults in the nursing room—dressed in white coats and called "Auntie" by the children—lost none of their aplomb when I was shown in, asked many questions, peered down at the very cute sleeping babies, taking notes all the while. The babies in this nursing room ranged from fifty-six days to a year and a half. Most of the children seemed to be under eight months, though there were a few babies about one year old in playpens at the front of the room. The aunties corroborated that most mothers breast-feed their babies and come in twice during the day to do this; if the babies need more to eat, the aunties supplement with a bottle.

There were few toys in evidence, but the children who were awake were two to a playpen and two to a bamboo carriage, so they had each other for company. Some of the babies slept in cribs and some in carriages. When I asked what was done when the babies cried, I was told that they cannot be picked up, as there are too many; instead, the aunties wheel them back and forth in the carriages. Occasionally, however, they do pick one of the children up. The rather dark, dismal-looking room, painted as many of these rooms are, green from the floor to about halfway and white the rest of the way to the ceiling, was in direct contrast to the very pretty, multicolored clothes, supplied by the parents, that the children were wearing. The colorful quilts which covered each baby were also provided by the parents.

I wondered how the aunties were chosen. They told me that they were chosen from among the workers in the factory who are the "most responsible and the most patient." They have no special training.

Noticing the cement floor, nearly every square inch of which was covered with cribs, playpens, and carriages, I wondered if, as the children get older, they have an opportunity to walk around the nursing room. We were told that either they walk in a walker or the mother takes the child outside at lunchtime for a walk, but they do not walk on the floor, because it is "dirty." I had heard other aunties show the same concern over dirt and restrict children's mobility because of it. Here, as in other nurseries, they take the children's fingers out of their mouths because "their fingers are dirty." The children do not cry when their fingers are taken out of their mouths. And we saw no evidence of the use of pacifiers.

I took this opportunity, as I did several other times during our trip, to collect developmental data on very young children:

Developmental data

Attends nursing room	56 days
Begins solid foods	5 months (if teeth)
Sits alone	6 months
Alternatively, may begin solid foods	7 months
Crawls	8 months
Stands alone	10–12 months
Begins to walk	1 year
Walks steadily	1½ years
Weaned to cup	1½ years
Begins to feed self with spoon	1½ years
Feeds self more steadily	2 years
Toilet-training	12–18 months
Speaks simple words	1½ years
Speaks sentences	1½–2 years
Eats with short chopsticks	3½ years

The developmental data are a composite of conversations with several people involved in child-rearing; there was nearly always consensus on the ages of the various developmental stages. It is interesting to note that, according to ancient custom, the Chinese say a child is one year old at birth and celebrate a collective birthday (so much that they do is collective!) every year on New Year's Day. Thus, a child who is born in October becomes two years old on New Year's Day, which in 1972 was February 15, and adds a year every subsequent New Year. This form of reckoning ages began with the Chinese lunar calendar during the reign of Huang Ti around 2697 B.C. but was replaced by the Western calendar on January 1, 1912, by the Sun Yat-sen government. Today nearly everyone, and certainly people working in the field of child care, uses the Western system of calculating age, but if one sees a small infant and is told he is a year old, one had better ask further.

Asking about motor development first, we were told that babies generally sit alone at about six months, crawl at around eight months, stand alone at from ten to twelve months, begin to walk at about one year, and walk more steadily by one and a half. Since I had been told by a Canadian living in

China that Chinese children develop far more slowly than Western children and that Chinese mothers were aghast at the quick development of Western children, I made a point of asking at what age Chinese children walked. I was told everywhere that they generally walked at around one year; occasionally a little later. I corroborated this by noticing young children who seemed to be beginning to walk and asking their ages; invariably, they were around a year old. Interestingly, the motor development of Chinese children and of American children occurs at strikingly similar ages. However, the Chinese data are anecdotal and therefore the age estimates might be younger than if the data were systematically gathered.

Solid foods—noodles and porridge—are introduced at five months if the baby has a few teeth; if his teeth do not come in until later, he will start on solids at seven months. By a year and a half, too, the child can feed himself with a spoon, but it isn't until he is two that he can hold the bowl more steadily and feed himself with greater ease. All the children we saw eating were using small metal bowls and spoons, not chopsticks; when they are three and a half, they use a shorter version of chopsticks.

Toilet-training is collective and is begun at a year or a year and a half. From infancy until he is about eighteen months old, the baby wears diapers with a plastic covering, particularly at night. The most common sight, however, is the child with pants that open in the back—so he can squat to urinate or defecate when he needs to. And occasionally we saw small children do just this in the streets of Peking. Children wear open pants from the time they first wear trousers at around three months until they are from two and a half to three years old. Myrdal reports children wearing open pants in Liu Ling Village until they are six years old. Between twelve and eighteen months, the teachers begin toilet-training the children in the nursing rooms. After breakfast the children sit on white enamel potties and all have their bowel movements together! In another nursing room we visited, we were told that the children all sit on potties after lunch as well. Chinese children are expected to be trained by the age of eighteen months, but if they are not, the teachers in the nursery to which they go at a year and a half will help them. I did not have the feeling that toilet-training was an area of particular difficulty; adults were matter-of-fact when I talked with them about it and seemed to feel it was all fairly routine.

Children begin to speak simple words at between a year and a year and a half. In the nursing room of the Shanghai Machine Tool Plant, a factory famous for training workers to be engineers and technicians, there is a separate room for children twelve to eighteen months old. Half of the room was a sort of playpen in which the children could roam freely and play with toys, small dolls, paper flowers, a ball or two, that were more plentiful than in most other nursing rooms or nurseries. The teacher was in this play area with the children, and when we arrived, unannounced, she got them to sing to the accompaniment of an accordion. Clearly, these children were already speaking and singing. They also all walked. We were told at this nursing room that children begin to walk at ten months.

In the nursing room of the machine tool factory, fourteen adults were caring for sixty children, an astonishing ratio of one adult to every four children. This was the highest ratio of adults to children that we saw anywhere. This factory nursing room also had more varied equipment—individual playpens, rocking horses, toys, decorations on the walls and ceilings—but the structure of the rooms was similar to others; the floors and walls were cement, the rooms were generally dark, but with warm, smiling adults. The teachers were either junior or senior middle-school graduates with some knowledge of educational work. In addition to their training in education, they were given instruction in medical care by the factory's health center, so they could handle the "minor complaints" of the children.

As we have seen, children from a very young age receive multiple mothering—from the mother, while she is nursing, from the time the workday ends until it begins again the next day, and on her day off; from the several "aunties" in the nursing room, for they all care for all the children; and quite possibly from a grandmother who may live with the family. Bettleheim discusses the process whereby the infant must internalize both the satisfying and the frustrating aspects of mothering and points up the difficulties for the infant when the mothering figures are radically different from one another. As Bettleheim states with particular reference to the "collective upbringing" of the kibbutz in Israel, however, the adjustment to multiple mothering is made far easier for the infant when one strong central value system is held in common by the mother-figures.[1] This, as we have discussed in the previous chapter, is the case in China today. Everyone we met seemed to hold similar values and to practice child-rearing in remarkably similar ways. This similarity was particularly striking to us as we are so accustomed to seeing a diversity of child-rearing patterns in the United States—from breast-feeding to bottle-feeding with a "propped" bottle; from constant use of a pacifier, sometimes until two or three years of age, to a forbidding of any extra sucking, pacifier or thumb; from toilet-training at ten months to training at three years; from the creation of a "child-proof" environment in which the child can wander freely to one in which a harness is used to control his every movement. Thus, China may be at one extreme of cohesiveness and American child-rearing at another extreme of diversity.

Another way of looking at "multiple mothering" or "shared mothering" is that infants can thrive physically and emotionally if the mother-surrogates are constant, warm, and giving. Babies in China are not subjected to serial mothering; we were repeatedly told that aunties and teachers rarely leave their jobs. The children show none of the lethargy or other intellectual, emotional, or physical problems of institutionalized children. Quite the opposite!

Not only are the mother-surrogates warm and loving, but so are the parents and grandparents. A word here might be helpful on the interaction between adults and children in general. During our wanderings in the cities and communes, we must have seen hundreds of adults with small children strolling along the streets looking at the National Day lights at night, walking through parks enjoying the sunshine and the brilliant red flowers set out for the holiday, hurrying to catch a bus to get to work, or shopping in large department stores or in small sidewalk shops. A few children who appeared to be less than a year old were pushed along the sidewalks in bamboo strollers, sometimes two strollers attached, with a baby in each of them. A more frequent sight, however, was mothers or fathers carrying babies asleep in their arms or strapped on their backs. Babies older than a year are likely to be carried in the parent's arms in a sitting position. The toddler most often walks between two adults, perhaps mother and father or parent and grandparent. The child's hand is held while he walks along or crosses the street; we rarely saw a child under seven or eight walking without some physical contact between adult and child.

And the children are remarkably well-behaved. Out of the several hundred children that we saw, we might have seen three or four misbehave. They were surely on their best behavior when Americans were visiting their kindergartens, but this cannot account for the calm, relatively quiet, obedient, small-adult air of the children who were simply walking along the street. There just does not seem to be a battle going on between children and adults in the way that we know it. However, we were happy to see young boys doing cartwheels in Peking's Tien An Men Square!

We never saw an adult become angry with a child while we were in China. We saw a few children cry, we even saw a few children misbehave, but this never occasioned anger in an adult. The adult spoke quietly to the child, patting him to reassure him, and indicating with a word or pressure of the hand or arm the direction his behavior or his body should take. Discipline was a combination of gentle admonition and encouragement: a pat on the shoulder and a smile combined to alter the behavior. In Peking, for example, we saw a small boy being carried on his mother's back pounding on her; the grandmother, who was walking beside them, gently patted his head and spoke to him quietly; he soon stopped. Coming out of a department store in Peking, we saw a girl perhaps five years old having what seemed to us to be a temper tantrum; her grandfather simply held her in his arms, standing in back of her as she stood on the sidewalk crying. The last we saw, her crying had subsided.

We have asked some Chinese-American students about the remarkably good behavior of Chinese children. In public, children are likely to be good, we were told, and parents would consider it a loss of face if they had to become angry in public. However, the students we spoke to all admitted to having been spanked in the privacy of their homes. We, of course, could not observe Chinese parents in their homes, except as visitors, which is a different thing.

Many people have asked us what has happened to the Chinese family since Liberation. Although the economic basis for the extended family has been eliminated by land reform, the family is still an important part of Chinese life and three generations frequently live together. The husband's mother has lost much of her former power, but the grandparents' role in child-rearing continues to be important. Before Liberation, the family was the individual's primary reference point, the central group he interacted with, the medium through which he learned about birth, death, religion, planting, and harvesting. Ideas were handed down within a family, scarcely questioned; and the individual's primary allegiance was to his family. Today the individual in China has multiple allegiances: to his family, his work, his Mao Tse-tung study group, his party branch, his local revolutionary committee, his city or commune, a set of ideas, and to China itself.

He is actively involved in groups on many levels. If he lives in the city, he may belong to groups at the factory and in the building or neighborhood where he lives; if he lives on a commune, he may be involved at the team, brigade, or commune level. This may be visualized as the individual being inside several circles which overlap and intersect to form a complex pattern. While the family still seems strong, other relationships are also important and many other influences now come to bear on the individual's thinking.

As the individual enters into multiple relationships all through his life, so does the infant start with multiple mothering in the nursing room, a beginning of the process of educating the new human being the Chinese are trying to fashion.

NOTE

1. Bruno Bettelheim, *The children of the dream.* New York: Avon, 1970, pp. 211-216.

Chapter 3

Public Policy, Social Services and the Family

C. WRIGHT MILLS[1] HAS SOUGHT TO IDENtify the crucial difference between "personal troubles" and "public issues":

> While "*troubles* occur within the character of the individual and within the range of his immediate relations with others, . . . *issues* have to do with matters that transcend these local environments of the individual [to] the organization of many such milieux into the institutions of an historical society as a whole."

Issues are public matters in which certain shared values are threatened. Issues often involve crises in institutional arrangements, and the interrelationships between institutions. If only one person out of tens of thousands is unemployed we would want to know about his personality and his habits to understand why he is out of work. When 10 to 15 percent of the population is unemployed, we would want to examine the economic and social situations giving rise to such a development. It then becomes a public issue, one that needs to be dealt with by social institutions and public policy.

The differences between personal troubles and public issues are complex. Individuals and families have limited control over public policies which have direct effect on their lives. The economic system and bureaucratic structures create the social conditions to which families must adjust in order to survive. The solution to many troubles would thus involve institutional change, rather than changes in individuals or the internal dynamics of families. However, personal troubles have come to be defined as problems of individuals which should be solved by themselves or their families. Basic social services attempt to help them solve these "personal troubles."

Basic social services are referred to as "income multipliers," since their availability offers families and individuals a standard of living not available merely on their own income. Social services include education, medical services, housing, transportation, legal services, child-care facilities, environmental protection, welfare services, and recreational facilities. These services are generally regarded as essential for an adequate standard of living and they are most often financed and provided by the federal, state, and local governments. Where services are inadequate, incomplete, or unavailable, the standard of living for families declines. Since many of these services require a strong community tax base, poorer communities with poorer families tend to offer fewer and lower quality social services. This condition presents a primary contradiction in American society: poor families most in need of social services are least likely to get them and when they do, the services are often of substandard quality.

The availability of social services for various families reflect public policy which in turn reflect the predominant values of a society. Katherine Ellis and Rosalind Petchesky examine the availability of child-care facilities as a public policy which has been influenced by the ideological and economic values of American capitalism. The authors point up the historical correlation between the demand for an inexpensive reserve labor force made up of women, who receive lower wages than men, and the increased provision of publicly supported day-care centers. Thus, the government and private corporations were willing to support day care for women in the low-paying sectors (clerical, service, and certain manufacturing jobs) of the economy, while there has been no general movement to make child-care facilities available to middle-class women who might then be able to compete for and fill better paying jobs and careers. Thus, public policy developed to support parental authority and parental involvement for middle-class families while offering day-care services as a bonus for the children of welfare mothers who register to work or to be trained. Day-care programs which are helpful for corporate capitalism during periods of economic expansion receive public support, while others that might lead to economic equality are rejected.

Even when social services are available, they are often inadequate. Robert Staples focuses on the needs of black families for improved social services. He suggests that inadequate social services for black families stem from the society's racism and generally negative attitudes toward all poor people. Staples recommends specific public policy changes including a guaranteed annual income, community-controlled child-care centers, and comprehensive child development programs.

Public policy is partly an outgrowth of the legal structure of the society. The family is shaped by the prevailing laws dealing with marriage, the roles of husbands, wives and children, the division of responsibilities within marriage, and the dissolution of marriages. Leonore Weitzman examines the state-imposed "unwritten" contract of legal marriage. She discusses the main components of the traditional marriage contract which

(1) recognizes the husband as head of the house-

hold; (2) holds the husband responsible for support; (3) holds the wife responsible for domestic services; and (4) holds the wife responsible for child care.

Weitzman then focuses on the legal restrictions on alternative family forms, and some recent changes that may provide legal protection for these variant family forms.

The last article in the chapter focuses on a social service that is primarily provided by the private sector. Elaine Pivnick Eisenman examines the needs for family therapy and the various approaches available. Families are seen as closed systems in which members interact in a growth-restraining manner. The goal of family therapy is to enable the family to realize and develop its potential for openness and growth.

The three perspectives suggest a number of questions. Using the structural-functional perspective, the reader might focus on the relationship between families as units and the quality and availability of social services. What functions, traditionally performed by the family, are supported or hindered by the available social services? How is the family's ability to provide a socialization setting influenced by its location in the social system of stratification? How are cultural norms reflected in social policies aimed at variant family forms? How does family therapy treat the family as a system? How do such family systems maintain themselves and what changes are sought by the family therapist in their functioning?

From a conflict perspective readers might identify the contradictions between the needs of the family and the demands of the larger society. How do Ellis and Petchesky identify the corporate interest in child care and how does the corporate order and its ideological interests reflect social policies toward child care? How can social change be effected with respect to public policies toward families, such as the black family?

The symbolic interaction framework might lead us to ask questions about family interactions which lead to the mental illness of family members. What sorts of communications lead to family interactions that require family therapy? What sorts of roles can be identified in "schizophrenogenic" families? How does a family member become a scapegoat? What interactional changes are sought in families by family therapists? With respect to the law, how do the roles of husband and wife come to be defined by the state through its legal system?

NOTE

1. C. Wright Mills, *The sociological imagination.* New York: Oxford University Press, 1956.

Children of the Corporate Dream: An Analysis of Day Care as a Political Issue under Capitalism

INTRODUCTION

KATHERINE ELLIS AND ROSALIND PETCHESKY

THE AUTHORS OF THE FOLLOWING ARTIcle were involved in a year-long struggle to establish a community-based, parent- and teacher-controlled child-care center on the upper west side of Manhattan. It was this involvement that first alerted us to the ambiguities of the child-care issue for the women's movement and for the larger revolutionary movement in this country. Child care, like other "social welfare" issues, is a demand that is, in human terms, unmistakably urgent and, in political and economic terms, easily co-optable. Its urgency, however, should not lead us to overlook its potential as a means for capitalist socialization of children and a source of commercial profit. This article is an attempt to think critically about the long-range implications of child-care politics in capitalist society, their relation to the ideologies supporting women's oppression, and their place in a revolutionary politics.

I. THE ECONOMIC AND IDEOLOGICAL CONTRADICTIONS OF CHILD CARE

The current interest in child care on the part of politicians and businessmen is but one symptom of the increasingly evident fact that women as a cheap reserve labor force are once again in demand, even exceeding their importance in the World War II economy. Far from being a marginal category women now constitute 38 percent of the entire work force and close to 60 percent of all service workers. Since 1947 women's employment has grown much faster than men's: men's jobs have increased by 6.8 million and women's by 12.5 million.[1] The expanding, labor-intensive areas of the economy are precisely those clerical and service jobs that have traditionally been "women's work." Moreover, one-third of women workers, many of them heads of households, have children under six years of age. Given these trends in demand for women's labor, it is no surprise that liberal congressmen, federal administrators and corporate employers and investors are becoming vocal advocates of child care, working under the assumption that the combination of publicly funded day care and rock-bottom wages can be passed off as a cheap, profitable substitute for full-scale (male) employment at a decent wage.

This is not to deny that there are other important motives, besides the economic ones, for liberal

Reprinted by permission from *Social Revolution* 2, 6, 1972.

support of day-care programs. Most important among these (more so, probably, than a concern for "women's rights") is the kind of thinking that also underlay Project Head Start: alarm arising from the claims of psychologists that early childhood is decisive in the development of future patterns of learning, work, and authority relations. The defeated Comprehensive Child Development Act, for example—sponsored by a bipartisan group of liberal senators—was motivated by the desire to extend the socializing functions of public education to children during "the first few years of life."[2] At the same time, however, the demand for day care on a large scale threatens the nuclear family structure and the traditional ideology of "woman's place," which has been its mainstay. The politics of day care thus brings into focus certain fundamental contradictions in the structures and legitimations used by welfare state capitalism in the sphere of "reproduction."

Historically, the correlation between a high utilization of the female "labor reserve" and an increased provision of public or work-related day-care services is hardly new. The demand for female employees during World War II resulted in the Lanham Act, under which federal funds were distributed through the Department of Labor to the states to provide day care for the children of women workers in defense industries.[3] Hundreds of thousands of children were cared for under this program, and women who participated in it were considered "good mothers" and "patriotic citizens." But with the return of women to "their place" after the war, child-care facilities were abruptly closed down, illustrating the view still persisting in Nixon's child-care policy: broad programs are at best a necessary evil appropriate to crisis conditions and are not a universal right.

Since the mid-sixties, the pressure to employ women has again been accompanied by a significant upsurge of government and corporate programs to establish child-care centers. But both employment trends and day-care programs treat women and children differently depending on their economic position. That is to say, the demand for women's labor continues to grow primarily in low-paying clerical and service sectors, as well as in the manufacturing industries historically associated with "women's work" (e.g., textiles, clothing, food and electrical equipment). Correspondingly, the companies that have set up their own day-care programs belong primarily to these industries.[4] In addition, the Work Incentive Program (WIN) and Nixon's pending Family Assistance Plan use public day-care services to help channel welfare recipients (mainly ADC mothers) into the lowest-level public employee jobs. In other words, day care is *a crucial adjunct to a large-scale tracking program for poor and underpaid women.*

Just as there is no general move in the established system to bring all women into the work force, much less into jobs that have been the traditional (and higher paying) preserves of men, neither is there any intention on the part of the capitalist power structure to recognize the legitimacy of day care as a demand for everyone. It is widely assumed that "middle-class" women[5] are by definition good mothers, and that their role as buttresses of the decaying legitimacy and authority of the family is more crucial than ever. Nixon, while touting the virtues of day care for the poor in his Family Assistance Program, strenuously vetoed the Comprehensive Child Development Act because of its "family-weakening implications":

> Good public policy requires that we enhance rather than diminish both parental authority and parental involvement with children—particularly in those decisive early years when social attitudes and a conscience are formed and religious and moral principles are first inculcated.... For the Federal Government to plunge headlong financially into supporting child development would commit the vast moral authority of the National Government to the side of communal approaches to child rearing over against the family centered approach.[6]

This "headlong plunge" would have provided public or publicly aided child care services for preschool children of *all* working mothers and single parents. Nixon's policy, on the other hand, is to reinforce the bourgeois ideology of the family among most working people, while applying a very different standard to the poor. Thus his veto speech contrasts sharply with the "work incentive" provisions of his welfare reform bill (H.R. 1),[7] a bill that would offer day-care services as a "bonus" for the children of mothers on welfare who register for work or training.

These provisions, as well as recent New York State legislation that forces people to accept low-paying, servile jobs to pay for their welfare grants, have been sharply condemned by welfare and civil liberties organizations as clear attempts to exploit poor people and create a cheap labor pool. The creation of such a labor pool not only threatens to take away the jobs of unionized workers, replacing them with people forced to work at well below the minimum wage; it also will drive wages down generally.

What is important to note here is that the overwhelming percentage of those who, under present circumstances, would be recruited into this labor pool under the Family Assistance Plan are poor women with children. Of the 5.6 million (or over one in ten) families in the United States headed by women, 3.4 million have incomes below the poverty line, and according to official sources these figures are increasing at a geometric rate.[8] While H.R. 1 ostensibly makes registration for work or training voluntary for women with children under the age of six (or under the age of three after 1974), the House Ways and Means Committee, which reported out the bill, makes it clear that the administration expects the child-care provisions to serve as a lure to bring most of these women into the WIN program and thus take them off welfare.[9] In order to rationalize this obvious inconsistency with the official family ideology and the bill's alleged purpose of "reducing the rate of family breakup" (the root of so many "problems" in the ghetto), the committee argues that

> by and large, the child of a family eligible under these [child-care] programs will benefit from the contribution of quality child care and the example of an adult in the family taking financial responsibility for him. Nor should it be forgotten that the mother who takes the training or gets a job will have more money available to improve the family's circumstances and more adequately provide for the children.[10]

In other words, the capitalist work ethic is here being applied to women on welfare, with the expressed aim of expanding domestic markets and socializing children into the discipline of wage-labor. The ambiguous character of such a program is the source of its particular danger, for under different circumstances an opportunity for women to work could be positive. Industrial day-care centers have behind them the same double-edged ideology, as illustrated by a proposal made by KLH to set up a plant-based day-care center with the help of government funds:

> The child will have as a model a working parent, rather than welfare support. Moreover, he will gain a familiarity with the world of work, and feel at home there, through the school's association with men who work. The relation of the school to the adult world can give a context to the education offered.

Indeed it can! Moreover, the KLH proposal is quite specific in linking the socializing aim of day care with the profitability of an increase in the pool of cheap labor:

> In times of high unemployment, it is important for the government to encourage programs for developing human resources to prevent children from being transformed into unproductive citizens by the deadening effects of poverty. In times of manpower shortages, it is valuable to government that employment be offered to a wider group of workers, including some mothers on welfare. This could help prevent competition for workers that pushes up wage rates, promotes inflation and causes production bottlenecks.[11]

It is important to remember, too, that conditions of chronic unemployment in one sector and "manpower shortages" in another may exist side by side, as they do at present, due to uneven development within the economy. Even in periods of male unemployment cheap female labor reserve is a permanent benefit to some corporate interests.

Needless to say, child-care programs cannot "liberate" anyone so long as they are tied to enforced work requirements, and so long as monotonous, low-paid labor is seen as an acceptable way of eliminating poverty. Yet this is the explicit philosophy behind federal support of child care, whether the funds are earmarked for city and state use or for corporations like KLH, whose proposal asserts enthusiastically that day care

> prevents poverty by enabling people to work. Even beginning unskilled workers at KLH might be "the poor" if defined by a $3000 income, but it is important to remember that they are not the poor because they are employed.

Behind this formulation lies the function, essential to the reproduction of labor power under capitalism, of *work as a form of social discipline*, through which values such as obedience, thrift, and respect for authority can be inculcated and reinforced. Children raised in ghetto homes, suffering from "the deadening effects of poverty," are found by their teachers to reject the values of obedience and willingness to do meaningless work that are so necessary to a smoothly running school and a smoothly running (capitalist) economy. Perhaps the reason for the "failure" of Head Start was its inability to provide "the relation of the school to the adult world" that a work-related day-care center offers, whether it be attached directly to the plant or to the government qua wage-slave broker.

One very important point about the child-care provisions of Nixon's bill (H.R. 1) is that they would take jurisdiction out of the hands of HEW, the agency traditionally responsible for and experienced in welfare and child-care programs, and place it directly under the Secretary of Labor. What this means, in effect, is that the two programs, enforced work and child care, are linked together within the same agency without any outside review procedures. Thus the state, as boss, controls the child-care programs attached to work in a manner exactly analogous to the corporations who set up day-care facilities for their workers. This arrangement makes it all the easier to use child-care benefits to make women accept the work requirement. It also creates one more outlet for underpaid female labor, namely the day-care centers themselves, which are bound to be custodial at best, due to the low ($600 to 800 per child) annual allocation and the lack of authorization for parent and community involvement.

Above all, the enforced submission of poor (primarily black) women to the capitalist work ethic represents just another racist double standard laid on women to oppress and divide them. For while the majority of women are told that their place is still in the home, where their children need them, poor black and other Third World women are told that they are "unqualified" to take care of their own children, who will be better off having before them the example of a "responsible" wage earner. Working-class women (i.e., the millions of women employed in offices, stores, and factories throughout the country) are left in the most contradictory situation of all, being expected to uphold both ideologies at once.[12]

This ideological contradiction as a reflection —and also a *reinforcer*—of class differences among women is far from new. During the late 19th and early 20th centuries, when American capitalism was "taking off" and women were beginning to participate in substantial numbers in the work force, a similar split prevailed. Thus, while immigrant and black women and their daughters were ushered en masse into factories and domestic jobs, their upper- and middle-class counterparts were taught "the conviction of polite society that a gentlewoman's place was in the home."[13]

In fact, the conflicting dogmas of "work" and "family" represent the two dominant ideologies that have served to pacify and discipline the work force throughout the history of modern capitalism. Until now they have been held in a delicate balance, supported at bottom by a sexist division of labor. As long as it could be made to appear that women's entry into the labor force was either a temporary expedient or a necessary evil, then the old ideology about "woman's place" could be securely maintained. But when the demand for more and more women workers in some sectors gives the lie to the myth of women's marginality in the work force, then the contradiction in the prevailing ideology begins to be exposed.

Nevertheless it is not enough simply to point out the relationship between the uneven development of contemporary capitalism's labor needs, on the one hand, and its ideological contradictions on the other. A great deal of additional research concerning women's position in the work force is needed to determine where such labor requirements are *real* (in the bourgeois economic sense) and where they are merely pseudorequirements, or *make-work*, deliberately imposed to reinforce the capitalist work ethic. One example of the latter case, it seems to us, is Rockefeller's new "Incentives for Independence" program, or the recent United States Senate Finance Committee proposal to force all "employable" welfare recipients to hire themselves out, through the states, as domestics and janitors. This emphasis on the absolute value of work seems particularly relevant at a time when the welfare system has completely undermined the family for masses of poor people, and yet bourgeois ideology has come up with no alternative other than the old "work" and "family" ethics to enforce social discipline.

In fact, we see day-care programs limited to the poor as a possible attempt to provide such an alternative. On the one hand, day care seems to offer a means of buttressing the capitalist work ethic at a time when it is in serious trouble. On the other hand, it threatens the bourgeois idea of the family that has traditionally been a principal support of capitalism and capitalist ideology. Thus the issue poses a serious contradiction for the system and its ruling interests. From their perspective, if the demand for day-care services could be contained among the poor—hence creating a potential cheap labor reserve—it might serve as a supplementary pacification device for those who now have the most to gain in any revolutionary struggle. From a very different perspective, however, if child-care centers were to come under the real control of their clients and workers, they would lose their character as either paycheck bonuses or doles and might thus become less co-optable as instruments for maintaining large-scale dependency and containing radical change.

II. CORPORATE INTERESTS IN CHILD CARE

The constant need for capitalism to find new outlets for the absorption of surplus has led not only to militarism and the search for new markets abroad, but also to the extension of investment at home beyond the industrial sector and into the seemingly nonprofit area of social services. The pioneering work done by Health PAC in exposing how this development has overtaken the field of health care has been fully documented in its monthly bulletins, as well as in Barbara and John Ehrenreich's *The American health empire: power, profits and politics*.[14] Their research vividly describes how the health care delivery system has expanded its original profit-making base of doctors, hospitals and drugs into a vast empire encompassing chains of private hospitals, nursing homes, fancy computerized equipment, hospital supplies, health insurance, construction, real estate, and an array of superfluous and costly drugs, fat research grants, and slick advertising campaigns. Above all, most of the health care empire is underwritten by government subsidies (i.e., the taxes of low and lower-middle-income people) particularly through the Medicare programs. Only a small fraction of the money invested is returned to the people in the form of actual improvements in the quality and scope of health care delivery.

This empire has been allowed to grow virtually unchecked because it is supported by an increasingly potent weapon of capitalist ideology: the authority of the "expert." This, coupled with an increasing reliance on the part of the "experts" on mystifying technology, has given the medical empire builders unlimited opportunities for profit. A similar situation is beginning to emerge in the area of early childhood education, and businessmen are already moving in to meet the "needs" of parents who, frightened lest they fail their children but uncertain as to what to do, are an easy target for a burgeoning market of educational gimmicks. As the crisis of confidence in the public school system increases, and as educators and psychologists place more and more emphasis on the first five years as the key to success in later life, we will witness the growth of an "empire" of purveyors of high IQs similar to that of the purveyors of health. And, as happened in the health empire, the field of early childhood education appears to be already opening up a vast arena for exploitation by a "partnership" of government and corporate profit-seekers.[15]

Up to now, what federal funding there has been for day care has been channeled primarily through the public sector, through state and local departments of social services and through work incentive and job-training programs like WIN and CAP.[16] The problem with these arrangements is that, given the growing fiscal crisis of the cities and the consequent haggling over funds between city and state government, it is becoming harder and harder for cities to get from the state budgets the 25 percent necessary to pull in federal matching funds. Thus in New York City, for example, where only about ten percent of the day-care need is being met, and where waiting lists are more than double the actual enrollment, an allocated five million dollars went unspent in 1969.[17] It is therefore easy to see why, at a conference entitled "Profit Possibilities in Day Care" held in New York in June 1970, representatives from OEO voiced impatience with state and city bureaucracies, as well as with community groups, and were eagerly turning to the private interests who set up the conference and who seemed ready to give the government a better return on its money.

Private investment in day care takes two forms: centers located at a factory such as the KLH center referred to earlier, and private centers, often marketed on a franchise basis. In both cases, the long-range advantages of social discipline that we have mentioned are not the only benefits reaped from day care by the corporations. The KLH proposal, which was offered for sale and used as a model by other companies, made the point that on-site day care would reduce employee turnover (at an estimated saving to the company of $2000 per employee) and absenteeism, improve worker–employer relations, and upgrade the performance of workers through a reduction of "family-related anxiety." And while the KLH plan itself did not succeed,[18] other companies have found that a day-care center operated by the company carries all these benefits while increasing the company's ability "to attract more steady and dependable workers" and showing at the same time "an increase in productivity of employees who are using the services."[19] For those companies located in areas with a high concentration of female heads of households (in other words, where plants have been located deliberately to exploit cheap female labor, such as textile mills in the rural South), day-care services have been set up as "a necessary service" in order to recruit women workers. Perhaps most significant, however, day care has been found to provide a "fringe benefit" that could be traded off for unpaid overtime, "shift rotation," and the demand for promotion.

Finally, day care has been conceived by corporations as one more way in which to socialize and pacify their workers (and particularly their women workers) by implanting in their minds the image of the company as a benevolent protector. Marx's idea of the factory as a socializing force that would give rise to working-class solidarity is parodied in the KLH proposal, a typical example of corporate thinking on the subject of employer–employee relations:

> In a sense, a factory is a community. Workers spontaneously form committees for various activities related and unrelated to their jobs, and become involved in group activities that are initiated at work, such as sports and parties. They attend one another's weddings and funerals, and celebrate birthdays constantly. The gifts they exchange are elaborate, and indicate the importance to them of their relationships with their fellow workers. They identify with the work situation in a way that some of them are not likely to do in their urban neighborhoods.

What the proponents of this idyllic and highly propagandistic picture of factory life do not go on to describe is the infinite subtlety with which employers make use of this "social life" to mask competition between workers and between groups of workers, and to secure at the same time the hearts and minds of their employees.

The failure of the KLH program has made other corporations cautious about the profitability of day care as a "fringe benefit." Thus the greatest interest in profit possibilities for private investors exists where day care is the "product" being sold. At this writing, 22 companies are in the business of setting up franchise day-care centers using the cost-cutting principles of Colonel Sanders and Ronald McDonald. These companies are aiming their wares at a middle-class market that can afford to pay $20 to $40 a week for child care. According to the *New York Times*, some of these franchisers are already collecting federal or state funds, or are courting federal agencies for additional support.[20] As a spokesman for one of the companies put it, "When the government is ready to pay for it, we will be set up to provide it."

This means that when some version of the Nixon Family Assistance Plan goes into effect for those mothers of preschool children who will be channeled into the work force under the plan, the franchisers will be set up to provide day care that will yield a profit to private investors, while government funds subsidize a steady clientele of mothers who are being forced into the labor pool. Still better, H.R. 1's child-care provisions enable the federal government, through the Department of Labor, to contract for the services of the private, profit-making day-care industry, just as it does now with the defense and aerospace industries.

We should expect, therefore, to see an increased partnership between business and government, of the sort that is well advanced in the health empire, that is, with private expenditures underwritten by government subsidization and encouraged by government contracts. Indeed, it would seem that this "partnership" is already the dominant pattern in the financing of social welfare programs, even while the media are transmitting the message that "the private sector" is dipping into its own pockets ("because we care") to lend a hand in alleviating "social ills." What this ideology of "partnership" conceals is the characteristic way in which neoliberal governments operate on the home front: underwriting corporate investments and risks with public revenues, and at the same time delegating policymaking and administrative authority to the same special interests that reap high profits from the programs underwritten.

But corporate expectations of handsome profits from day care are not solely contingent upon the prospect of government aid. In a series of articles in *Barron's* (July 5 and 19, and August 9 and 16, 1971) Richard Elliot celebrates the potential of day-care centers not only as sources of profit themselves (regardless of what the federal government does) but also as test centers for a whole battery of educational hardware that companies can develop while at the same time creating their own markets for their products:

Seldom in the annals of American education has opportunity seemed to beckon venture capital quite the way it does these days in the preschool field. Ironically, the confluence of pressures now shaping the social scene —women's liberation, welfare's staggering toll, the incontrovertible evidence of why Johnny can't read—is behind this powerful thrust. Private enterprise hasn't taken long to discover that a vast and virtually untapped market—hitherto suspicious of the profit motive—stands ready to support the massive development, under businesslike management, of well-conceived, quality-controlled centers for the care and teaching of small children. Mothers of America, indeed, are all but crying out for it.[21]

Besides listing a startling number of privately owned and operated day-care centers expected to "go public" during the next year, Elliot finds that investors anticipate a total profit in child care for American business of "up to a potential of 7.5 billion dollars a year." The tally of profit margins among proprietary day-care operations already in full swing is in the range of 20 to 30 percent. And many of these concerns are in the process of rapid expansion both vertically and horizontally, on the one hand diversifying into related fields such as the manufacture of educational equipment and toys that we mentioned earlier, and on the other hand acquiring or developing chains of similar centers across the country.

How are these high profits being achieved? Through the same methods capitalists have always used to rip off surplus value: low wages, speed-up, and automation. For not only does private enterprise have the advantage of the latest in "day-care market research," but "once it proves successful an educational curriculum, like a blueprint, can be used over again, each time at a lower prorated cost." That is to say that day care, like any other commodity, can be mass-produced, canned, and marketed. The most important element, however, in the private operator's strategy for making day care pay off is what Elliot refers to as "control of personnel costs," or "holding the line on payroll." This, of course, is just a euphemistic way of talking about rock-bottom wages and teacher-pupil ratios "ranging from 1:8 to 1:15" (education's version of speed-up) in a field which is "unencumbered by civil service, organized labor, or outmoded teaching methods."

This evidence suggests that we need to revise our thinking about the traditional division between government and private spending, insofar as some areas of government spending that used to be non-competitive for private investment are now becoming lucrative terrain for capitalist ventures. The health business is matched by drug "rehabilitation," teaching machines, and corporate-controlled day care—all new areas which serve as direct sources for corporate exploitation and profit.

III. CHILD CARE AS PART OF A REVOLUTIONARY STRATEGY

The analysis above raises the obvious questions: why, if day-care programs are helpful and even indispensable to corporate capitalism and the state, are they at the same time a necessary part of any revolutionary strategy for women and all oppressed people? and how may their blatantly exploitative and co-optative aspects be combated?

The welfare pacification process has within it the seeds of its own destruction. It operates, in a way strikingly analogous to the factory system described by Marx, through increasingly centralized, socialized mass institutions which concentrate formerly isolated individuals together, thus creating the material conditions in which a collective consciousness may emerge. This can be seen happening daily in urban renewal areas, in public and mental health clinics, in schools and prisons, and in welfare and "child development" agencies—institutions that are assuming many of the functions previously performed by the family. The most oppressed elements in urban society, finding themselves literally massed around these dehumanizing institutions, are now becoming aware of their common oppression and their collective power. They are beginning to make demands that ultimately cannot be met by the capitalist system.

Women, in the materially and sexually determined roles allocated to them by capitalist society, form the vanguard of struggles around community (as opposed to industrial or penal) institutions. Women comprise the great majority of welfare recipients and endure, in their family roles, the prime responsibility for the health and socialization of children. For although the state has taken over the education function that once belonged to the family, the sexist dynamics of capitalist society determine, all the same, that mothers remain the main link between the family and the schools. A strategic understanding of this situation is sufficient to defeat the notion that all women "as women," or in their family roles, are unorganizable. For in their family roles, masses of state-dependent women, at least, are becoming less and less isolated and privatized.

But 32 million women also work outside the home; and, as Engels pointed out, a prerequisite to the liberation of women (and all people) is the admission of women into the work force on an independent footing—equal, that is, to men in terms both of type of work and amount of compensation. It goes without saying that equality in any genuine sense is impossible within the constraints of capitalist production. But "equality" in a liberal sense seems to us a necessary precondition for women to share fully in the process of changing inherently unequal, hierarchical working conditions through the transformation of the production system itself. So long as the mythology of "women's work" prevails —that housework is not "real work" and that most women who work do so for "extras" or "pin money"—a socialist revolution in which masses of women participate seems to us unlikely. As Juliet Mitchell writes:

> Women are brought up to think of themselves primarily as mothers and wives; yet finding themselves despite this nevertheless out at work, it is this family identification that determines their relationship to their job and their companions. . . .
>
> Because the economic role of women is obscured (its cheapness obscures it) women workers do not have the *preconditions of class consciousness*. Their exploitation is invisible behind an ideology that masks the fact that they work at all—their work appears inessential.[22]

A crucial part of creating the conditions both for more women to enter independently into the work force and for women's working-class consciousness to develop is clearly the provision of free public child-care facilities. Yet there is nothing particularly revolutionary about day care in itself. In order for it to become integrated into a revolutionary movement, day care, like any other social welfare program, must be disarmed as a pacification tool in the service of the corporate ruling class and transformed into an instrument of revolution. Generally, this means mass education about the limits of social welfare programs as presently operating and attempts to wrest control over their operation from the hands of corporate bosses and state bureaucracies. Specifically, it suggests several points about day care.

First, in order to avoid the co-optation of day-care demands we must make these demands consistently on behalf of all women and children and must strongly oppose any attempts to divert such demands for purposes of creating a cheap labor pool of poor women. The demand for free universal child care must thus be made in conjunction with the demand for "equal work and equal pay." Otherwise, women will continue to be paid less then men, with part of the difference made up to women in day-care "fringe benefits."

Second, the extent to which private day-care profiteers presently rely on low wages and speed-up to guarantee profits in the child-care "industry" clearly indicates that unionization of child-care workers is a trend we should support. (The question of which union, and whether to agitate for radical caucuses or a focus on women's issues within those unions organizing day-care workers, is a separate problem.) It would be a mistake for community people involved in day care to regard unionization per se as a threat to their own power. On the other hand, day-care workers must avoid letting unions become instruments for the further suppression of the genuine interests of parents and children.

We do not suggest, however, that a strategy of "community control" be adopted at the expense of worker control. Workers' control over the processes and means of production is as important in education (institutions for the production of ideology and the reproduction of labor power) as in any sector of the economy. On the other hand, community struggles are precisely how women—particularly poor, Third World women—are beginning to have a sense of their collective power and to develop skills in leading movements in which people are defining their own needs as clients and consumers. A solution to this dilemma, it seems to us, must be worked out in revolutionary practice.

Until women have achieved both working-class status and working-class consciousness, a child care strategy in which either "worker control" or "client control" is pushed exclusively, or which works on either one of these bases without confronting racism and sexism, is a strategy that is bound to be co-opted. In day-care centers, governing structures must be developed in which parent participation and worker control are not played off against one another, but which replace strife within the ranks of the oppressed with a growing recognition of, and power against, the real enemy.

In the last analysis, however, whether or not day-care programs move beyond these strictly defensive measures to become part of a movement for socialist revolution in the United States will depend, first, upon the creation of such a movement and, second, upon the ways in which the *content* of child-care programs becomes consciously translated in terms of the goals of that movement. Even under prerevolutionary conditions, child-care struggles may become important as a means of raising consciousness about the traditional family and its reinforcement of sex-role stereotypes; about the socializing functions of educational institutions at all levels of capitalist society; and about the possibility of freer, more social child-rearing alternatives. In this regard, we envisage day-care centers which (1) actively support the restructuring of men's work to allow their participation in child-care struggles and programs; (2) attempt to establish cooperative, nonhierarchical relationships among staff (e.g., through abolishing ranks and pay scales); and (3) give priority to the socialization of children in terms of cooperative, nonauthoritarian, anti-racist, and antisexist values.

NOTES

1. Women's Bureau, United States Department of Labor, *1969 Handbook on women workers* (1969), pp. 9–15; Women's Bureau, United States Department of Labor, *Underutilization of women workers* (1970).

2. Press release, Senator Walter Mondale (Democrat–Minnesota), April 1971.

3. Women's Bureau, United States Department of Labor, *Day-care services: industry's involvement* (1971), p. 3.

4. *Ibid.*, pp. 8–9.

5. See "Note on Class and Women," p. 110.

6. *New York Times*, 10 December 1971, p. 20.

7. This bill was defeated in October 1972.

8. Robert L. Stern, The economic status of families headed by women, *Monthly Labor Review*, December, 1970; *Handbook on women workers*, p. 130.

9. United States of Representatives, Report No. 92–231, Social Security Amendments of 1971, Report of the Committee on Ways and Means on H.R.1, 26 May 1971, p. 163.

10. *Ibid*. Emphasis added.

11. KLH Child Development Center, *A proposal to establish a work-related child development center*. Cambridge, Mass.; May 1967. (KLH produces phonographs.)

12. See "Note on Class and Women," below.

13. Robert W. Smuts, *Women and work in America*. New York, 1971, p. 48.

14. The Health Policy Advisory Center is a New York group doing research and political education on America's health industry for the national radical health movement. The Ehrenreichs' book was published as a Vintage paperback in 1971.

15. See Ann Cook and Herbert Mack, The discovery center hustle, *Social Policy*, (September–October) 1970.

16. Vicki Breitbart, Day care, who cares? In *Notes on child care*, edited by the Child Care Collective of the New York Women's Union. See also Vicki Breitbart and Beverly Leman, Why child care? In *Up from Under* 1, 3 (January–February, 1971), pp. 10–14.

17. *New York Times*, 14 February 1970.

18. The KLH center met resistance from employees who were unwilling to transport their children from their neighborhoods, which were often a considerable distance from the workplace. The center is now operated as a nonprofit service for residents of neighborhoods near the KLH plant.

19. *Day-care services: industry's involvement*, pp. 13, 17.

20. *New York Times,* 27 December 1969.

21. *Barron's*, 5 July 1970, p.3.

22. Juliet Mitchell, *Women's estate*. New York, 1971, p. 139. Emphasis added.

NOTE ON CLASS AND WOMEN

The attempt to define the class position of various groups of women—and men as well—under advanced capitalism poses certain analytical problems. We are aware of these problems but can only begin to suggest an approach to them within the limits of a paper on day care. First, we agree it is important to expose the sexism often inherent in definitions of women primarily in terms of the men they relate to (husbands, fathers, etc.) rather than in terms of the work that women themselves do in both production and "reproduction." Yet there are also very real ways in which many women's class position and consciousness is still *conditioned* by the class situation of the men on whom they depend, both affecting the reality of women's lives and resulting in serious divisions among women.

Second, while in the broadest structural sense it is understood that we define "class" in terms of relationship to the means of production, there are nevertheless complex differences—not merely of status, but also of values, culture, and economic possibilities—that make it meaningful to speak of a "middle class." By that we generally mean, not so much the large segments of rapidly proletarianized "white collar" and service workers included by bourgeois sociologists, but rather the managerial, professional, and technocratic/scientific groups who benefit directly from a system of exploitation even though they do not actually "own" it. Women may belong to this class through their own direct participation, through family background, or through marriage. The most important problem, as we see it, is how to develop working-class consciousness among women who are objectively working class (as proletarianized clerical, service, and factory workers) but continue to be defined and to define themselves primarily in terms of their family roles and circumstances.

Public Policy and the Changing Status of Black Families*

ROBERT STAPLES

ACCORDING TO BELL AND VOGEL (1968), THE family contributes its loyalty to the government in exchange for leadership which will provide direct and indirect benefits for the nuclear family. While there is little doubt that black families have been loyal to the political state in America, it appears that they have derived few reciprocal benefits in return. Although the political system has the power to affect many of the conditions influencing black family life, it has failed to intervene in the service of the black population and, in fact, has been more of a negative force in shaping the conditions under which black families must live. As Billingsley (1968, 177) has stated, "no subsystem has been more oppressive of the Negro people or holds greater promise for their development."

Historically, we find that state, local, and federal governmental bodies have pursued policies that have contributed to the victimization of black families. Under slavery, marriages between slaves were not legal since the slave could make no contract. The government did nothing to ensure stable marriages among the slave population or to prevent the arbitrary separation of slave couples by their owners. Moreover, the National Government was committed to the institution of slavery, a practice which was most inimical to black family life (Frazier 1939).

Although this fact may not seem relevant today, it illustrates the federal government's default in protecting the integrity of the slave family. This failure to intervene and its impact is most clearly demonstrated when compared to the laws passed in many South American countries that possessed slaves. While the slave states in North America had slave codes that required slaves to submit to their masters and other white men at all times, the South American governments passed laws that provided for the physical protection and integrity of the slaves, as it did for free citizens

(Elkins, 1968). Because the United States government was not as benign, slavery was a more oppressive institution which has left us with a legacy of racial inequality in all spheres of American life—a past that had significant repercussions in the area of black family life.

In more recent years, some state governments have passed laws which impose middle-class values on lower-income families, many of which are black. Various state legislatures have passed laws designed to reduce or eliminate welfare benefits to women who have given birth to a child out-of-wedlock. A few states have even attempted to pass laws sterilizing women on welfare who have had more than one "illegitimate" child. All these attempts have failed, as the laws were subsequently invalidated by the courts.

While the welfare system may be viewed as a positive governmental action in assisting families who are economically deprived, it has often served to tear low-income families asunder. The Aid to Families with Dependent Children (AFDC) program was designed to economically maintain children whose father was absent from the home. Hence, it was available, until recently, only to those families where the husband/father was not present in the home. A family in need of assistance due to the male breadwinner's unemployment could not receive help unless he "deserted" the family. Many lower-class black males have been forced to abandon their wives and children in order to satisfy this restrictive governmental welfare policy.

When the federal government finally decided to develop a program to strengthen black family life, the attempt was made in a very curious way. It

*A revised version of a paper presented to the National Council on Family Relations Annual Meeting, Portland, Oregon, November 1972. Copyright © 1973 by the National Council on Family Relations. Reprinted by permission.

began with a report by Daniel Moynihan (1965) who was then an Assistant Secretary of Labor. According to Rainwater and Yancey (1967), Moynihan wanted to have the black problem redefined by focusing on the instability of the black family. As an index of black family deterioration, he used the census reports which revealed that blacks had more female-headed households, illegitimate children, and divorces than white families. While these characteristics were applicable to only a minority of black families, Moynihan generalized their effect and influence to the entire black population.

Since the validity of the Moynihan Report has been dealt with extensively elsewhere (Staples 1971), our concern here is with the role of the government in formulating a policy for strengthening black family life. First, we might question the political strategy involved in issuing such a report on the black family at that particular time or at any time. The Moynihan Study was published at a time when blacks had defined their problem as deriving from institutionalized white racism. The effect of the Moynihan Report was to redefine the problem as emanating from weaknesses in the black family, which was the main factor in the alleged deterioration of black society. In other words, blacks were largely reponsible for their condition, not the legacy of slavery or subsequent racist practices in American life.

Moreover, the national action that Moynihan spoke of was not delineated in the report. At a later time, he did recommend social services and noted that a policy of benign neglect had not been too detrimental. Moreover, he is generally credited with being the creator of one government policy designed to affect the family life of low-income Americans. This policy proposed the creation of a Family Assistance Program, which was designed to correct the inadequacies of the AFDC system by substituting workfare for welfare. At this time the proposal has not yet been acted on by Congress.

The Family Assistance Program ostensibly was designed to aid families who are not eligible for welfare benefits under the present welfare system. However, the additional benefits seem to be secondary to the strong work requirements contained in the present bill. In fact, the purpose of the plan is to force several million black welfare mothers to work—mostly at wretchedly paid, menial jobs. This purpose is unmasked by the fact that economic benefits under the proposed plan would actually be lower than those presently given in most state controlled AFDC programs (Axinn and Levin 1972).

In a recent study of welfare families, Goodwin (1972) noted that the results of the FAP may be just the opposite of those intended. The past history of work programs have conclusively demonstrated that few of the welfare mothers will find work at all, and those who do are in jobs no better than domestic service. These low-paying jobs will not provide a sufficient income for women to support their families without continued governmental aid. Moreover, being confined to ill-paid jobs that do not enable them to support their families may reinforce the same psychological orientation which presently characterize low-income families and discourage them from further work activity.

This emphasis on mandatory work requirements is based on the false stereotypes of the poor as lacking the incentive to work because of the economic security provided them by public assistance programs. Yet, Goodwin (1972) found that the poor have just as strong a work ethic as the middle class. In fact, poor black youth who have grown up in welfare families have a more positive attitude toward the desirability and necessity of work than the children of the white middle class. Furthermore, black women on welfare see getting a job as far more important than middle-class white women for whom work has little relevance to their upward mobility. However, securing employment for these black women really depends on the availability of meaningful, decent-paying jobs, not on a training program.

It can reasonably be stated that the federal government's efforts to promote black family solidarity have been misguided and ineffective. The purpose of this article is to review the changing status of black families and its implications for a meaningful public policy to strengthen black family life. In describing the contemporary condition of black families, we will not attempt to deal with the larger sociological factors responsible for current black family patterns. Our intent is to point out the changes that are taking place and the public policy that would be relevant to future trends among black families.

EDUCATION, EMPLOYMENT, AND INCOME

Among the principal variables that undergird family life are education, employment, and income. Looking at the 1970 census, we find some absolute progress in certain areas for black families, little change in their status vis-à-vis white families, and the general problems of poverty and unemployment unchanged overall for many black families. In education, for example, the proportion of blacks graduating from high school increased slightly. Nevertheless, blacks were still more likely than whites to be high school dropouts. The median number of school years completed by black Americans over 24 years of age was 10.0 in contrast to 12.1 for white Americans (United States Bureau of the Census 1971).

There are two important aspects of the education situation to consider in assessing its relevance to blacks. First, black women tend to be slightly more educated than black men at all levels. In the past decade, the educational level of white men increased to reach the average of white women, while black men continued to lag behind black women (United States Bureau of the Census 1971). Hence, an increase in the educational level of the black population will not automatically mean a rise in income or employment opportunities. The fact that much of that increase in education belongs to black women reduces the mobility level for blacks because black women, even educated ones, tend to be concentrated in lower-paying jobs than black men. Another significant factor is the sexual discrimination that women in our society face in the labor force (Pressman 1970).

The second important aspect of education is that it does not have the same utility for blacks as it does for whites. While the yearly incomes of black college graduates and whites who have completed only elementary school are no longer the same, the equal educational achievements of blacks and whites still are not reflected in income levels. The 1970 census reveals that blacks are still paid less for comparable work than whites. While white male professional, managerial, and kindred workers earned $11,108, blacks in the same occupational category only earned $7659. Among craftsmen, foremen, and kindred workers the white median was

$8305, the black median was $5921. Similar, but smaller, black-white discrepancies appear in other occupational categories (United States Bureau of the Census 1971). These figures lend substances to the Jencks et al. (1972) argument that education alone will not equalize the income distribution of blacks and whites. In fact, the relative income gap between blacks and whites increases with education. While both blacks and whites incur difficulties due to a low level of education, college educated whites face fewer barriers to their career aspirations. In computing the estimated lifetime income of blacks as a percentage of white estimated lifetime income at three educational levels, Siegel (1965) found that the black elementary school graduate would earn 64 percent of his white counterpart's lifetime income, but the black college graduate's lifetime earnings would be only 50 percent of his white peer's lifetime income. Hence, highly educated blacks suffer the brunt of income discrimination more intensely than those with less education.

During the past decade, the median family income for blacks increased at a faster rate than the median for the population as a whole. Yet, black family income is still only 60 percent of white family income. The median income for white families in 1970 was $9961, for black families only $6067. Even these figures are misleading because they do not show that black family incomes must be used to support more family members and that their family income is more often derived from the employment of both the husband and wife. Also, according to the Labor Department, the majority of black families do not earn the $7000 a year needed to maintain themselves at a nonpoor intermediate standard of living (United States Bureau of the Census 1971).

Furthermore, about a third of the nation's black population is still living in official poverty. About a fourth of them are receiving public assistance. The comparable figures for whites were ten and four percent. Almost half of these black families living in poverty are headed by females. About 41 percent of all black children are members of these families, who exist on an income of less than $3700 a year. Only ten percent of white children live in households that are officially defined as poor (United States Bureau of the Census 1971).

The unemployment rate for blacks in 1971 was at its highest level since 1961. Overall, 9.9 percent of blacks were officially unemployed compared to 5.4 percent for whites. In the years 1969–1971, black unemployment increased from 5.8 to 8.7. Furthermore, this increase in unemployment during that three-year period was highest among married black men who were the primary breadwinners in their household. Just as significant is the unemployment rate of black women who were heads of families and in the labor force. About ten percent of that group was unemployed as compared to six percent of white women. The highest unemployment rates in this country are among black female teenagers in low-income areas of central cities. Their unemployment rate is about 36.1 percent and has risen as high as 50 percent (United States Bureau of the Census 1971).

What the recent census figures indicate is that the decade of the sixties saw little significant change in the socioeconomic status of black families. An increase in educational achievements has produced little in economic benefits for most blacks. Based on the rate of progress in integrating blacks in the labor force in the past decade, it will take 9.3 years to equalize the participation of blacks in low-paying office and clerical jobs and a period of 90 years before black professionals approximate the proportion of blacks in the population (Purcell and Cavanagh 1972).

CHANGING PATTERNS OF BLACK FAMILY LIFE

Recent years have brought about significant changes in the marital and family patterns of many Americans. We have witnessed an era of greater sexual permissiveness, alternate family life-styles, increased divorce rates, and reductions in the fertility rate. Some of these changes have also occurred among black families and have implications for any public policy developed to strengthen black family life.

The sexual revolution has arrived, and blacks are very much a part of it (Staples 1972). By the age of 19, over half of the black females in a recent study had engaged in intercourse. While the proportion of comparable white females was only 23.4 percent, they were engaging in premarital coitus more often and with a larger number of sexual partners. However, a larger number of sexually active black females were not using reliable contraceptives, and 41 percent had been, or were, pregnant (Zelnik and Kantner 1972).

One result of this increased premarital sexual activity among blacks is the large number of black children born out of wedlock. Almost 184 of every 1000 black births were illegitimate in the year 1968. However, this rate was lower for blacks than in the most recent earlier periods. The racial differences in illegitimacy rates also narrowed in the last 20 years (United States Bureau of the Census 1971). One reason for the decline is the easier accessibility to safe, low-cost abortions. Nationwide, black women received 24 percent of all legal abortions performed in hospitals (Population Council 1971). In all probability, the black birthrate will continue to decrease as contraception and abortion readily become available.

When blacks choose to get married, the same economic and cultural forces that are undermining marital stability in the general population are operative. In the last decade, the annual divorce rate has risen 75 percent. For white women under the age of 30, the chances are nearly one in three that their marriage will end in divorce. Among black women, their chances are one in two. In 1971, 20 percent of ever married black women were separated or divorced compared to six percent of similar white women. The divorce rate of middle-class blacks is lower, since the more money that a family makes and the higher their educational achievements, the greater are their chances for a "stable" marriage (United States Bureau of the Census 1971).

A combination of the aforementioned factors has increased the proportion of black households headed by females. The percentage of female-headed families among blacks increased eight percent in the last decade, from 22 percent to 30 percent. A third of these female household heads worked and had a median income of only $4396 in 1971. The proportion of black children living with both parents declined in the last decade, and currently only 64 percent of children in black families are residing with both parents. It is apparently the increasing pressures of discrimination, urban living, and poverty that cause black fathers to leave their homes or never marry. At the upper-income level of $15,000 and over, the percentage of black families headed by a man is similar to that for white families (United States Bureau of the Census 1971).

The fertility rate of black women is hardly a factor in the increase of female-headed households among blacks. Between 1961 and 1968, the total birthrate for black women decreased sharply. The fertility rate of black women (3.13 child per black women) is still higher than the 2.37 birthrate for white women. However, the average number of total births expected by young black wives (2.6) and young white wives (2.4) are very similar. As more black women acquire middle-class status or access to birth control and abortion, we can expect racial differentials in fertility to narrow (United States Bureau of the Census 1971). The birthrate of college educated black women is actually lower than their white counterparts (Kiser and Frank 1967).

This statistical picture of marital and family patterns among blacks indicates a continued trend toward attenuated nuclear families caused by the general changes in the society and the effects of the disadvantaged economic position of large numbers of black people. An enlightened public policy will address itself to the needs of those families, rather than attempting to mold black families into idealized middle-class models, which no longer mean much, even for the white middle-class. What is needed is a government policy that is devoid of middle-class puritanism, the Protestant ethic, and male-chauvinist concepts about family leadership. In the concluding section, we will spell out the elements of such a public policy.

A PUBLIC POLICY FOR BLACK FAMILIES

The following elements of a public policy for black families is a combination of the author's ideas and other recommendations by various black groups concerned with certain problems of the black family.

In most proposals to strengthen black family life, it is common to assert that providing meaningful, gainful employment to black males is necessary in order to ensure that they will remain with, and support, their families. While this is of concern here, it will not be accorded the highest priority. Although unemployment and low income are key factors in black family disorganization, there are other cultural and social forces which threaten the continued existence of the black nuclear family. Among them are weaknesses in the institution of marriage itself, which make it less than a viable solidarity medium for either blacks or whites. The demographic nature of the black community will also insure the existence of large numbers of female-headed households among them. Since there are approximately one million more black females than males, there is less opportunity for many black women to establish a monogamic nuclear family. Although part of this sex-role differential is due to underenumeration of black males in the census, there is a shortage of more than a million black males available to black women for marriage because of the higher male rates of mortality, incarceration, homosexuality, and intermarriage.

Our focus will be on efforts needed to assist families which may be headed by women. These should include decisive and speedy government action to remove all arbitrary sex-role barriers in obtaining employment and providing opportunities for job mobility for women. Those women in low-income categories should be given subsidized training for jobs which pay decent salaries and are not restricted only to men. Since the economy is not really geared to provide jobs to prepared and willing workers, we would recommend a guaranteed income of $6000 to a family with at least one parent and three children.

While the above figure has been criticized as being too high and not politically feasible, it seems a reasonable amount in light of the Labor Department's admission that an annual income of $7000 is required to maintain a family of four at the nonpoor but low standard of living in urban areas. This will also free women of their dependency on men to maintain a decent standard of living. Women will be able to enter marriage out of desire, rather than economic need. Although this may not slow down the rising tide of dissolved marriages, it does give women a greater life choice.

To facilitate the entrance of women into the labor force, we also recommend community-controlled 24-hour child-care centers. The Bureau of Labor Statistics show that a larger proportion of black women are employed full-time than white women. This is particularly true of the 16–24 year age group, who are most likely to have very young children with no child-care facilities they can afford in which to leave them. These child-care services should be provided on a sliding fee scale, based on income, by the government. They will serve a dual function by freeing women from the responsibilities of child care and providing employment for women and men who work in the child-care centers.

Closely related to the concept of child-care centers is the need for the government's commitment to a national comprehensive program of child development. This would provide for the establishment of a national system of child development centers and programs which would provide comprehensive health service, education, recreation, and cultural enrichment for preschool children (Billingsley 1972).

To further protect black children, we need to reconsider the traditional methods of child placement. Since caring for other's children on a temporary basis is a time-honored practice in the black community, there is no reason why the family who accepts a child on a permanent basis should not be subsidized by the government to do so. The idea of subsidized adoption should become a part of public policy and would deal with the paradoxical situation of mothers who do not want to rear their children and families who want them, but cannot afford them. We should also get some community input into foster care arrangements.

For black women who do not wish to bear children, there should be available safe, free contraceptives or abortion. However, these services should be organized into a community-controlled comprehensive health program and center. This will demonstrate that white society is not only concerned about preventing black children from entering the world, but wants to safeguard the health of the mothers and provide decent health care to those black children that are born.

Also, any governmental policy to help black families should recognize the desire of blacks to control their own community and destiny. Thus, the initial formulation of such a public policy should include a major input from the black community. Programs imposed by white people on black families are no longer acceptable or desirable if we wish to establish a policy which will begin to promote the conditions necessary for a strong black family structure.

In concluding, we might note that public policy has not favored any family which is poor or uneducated, but the black family has been singled out and discriminated against in employment, housing, education, health, and other services which require special remediation. Although public policy was not designed to disadvantage any particular group, its ineffectiveness has been felt most significantly in the area of lower-income black family life. This special need of black families, however, should not distract from the necessity of a major governmental effort on behalf of all families. Work training means nothing unless there is a commitment to provide jobs for all willing to work. And, the provision of jobs will mean little to black families unless there is a concomitant elimination of racial discrimination in employment and promotional opportunities.

REFERENCES

AXINN, JUNE, AND HERMAN LEVIN. Optimizing social policy for families. *The Family Coordinator* 21, 163–170, 1972.

BERRY, MARY. *Black resistance—white law: a history of constitutional racism in America.* New York: Appleton-Century-Crofts, 1971.

BILLINGSLEY, ANDREW. *Black families in white America.* Englewood Cliffs, N.J.: Prentice-Hall, 1968.

BILLINGSLEY, ANDREW. *Children of the storm.* New York: Harcourt Brace Jovanovich, 1972.

ELKINS, STANLEY. *Slavery: A problem in American institu-*

tional and intellectual life. Chicago: University of Chicago Press, 1968.

FRAZIER, E. FRANKLIN. *The Negro family in the United States.* Chicago: University of Chicago Press, 1939.

GOODWIN, LEONARD. *Do the poor want to work? A social-psychological study of work orientations.* Washington: Brookins, 1972.

JENCKS, CHRISTOPHER, *et al. Inequality: A reassessment of the effect of family and schooling in America.* New York: Basic Books, 1972.

KISER, CLYDE, AND MYRNA FRANK. Factors associated with the low fertility of nonwhite women of college attainment. *Milbank Memorial Fund Quarterly,* October: 425–429, 1967.

Population council report on abortions by age and race. Washington: U.S. Government Printing Office, 1972.

PRESSMAN, SONIA. Job discrimination and the black woman. *The Crisis,* March: 103–108, 1970.

PURCELL, THEODORE, AND GERALD CAVANAGH. *Blacks in the industrial world.* New York: The Free Press, 1972.

RAINWATER, LEE, AND WILLIAM YANCEY. *The Moynihan report and the politics of controversy.* Cambridge, Mass.: The M.I.T. Press, 1967.

SIEGEL, PAUL M. On the cost of being Negro. *Sociological Inquiry* 35, 52–55, 1965.

STAPLES, ROBERT. Towards a sociology of the black family: a theoretical and methodological assessment. *Journal of Marriage and the Family* 33, 19–38, 1971.

———. The sexuality of black women. *Sexual Behavior* 2, 4–14, 1972.

United States Bureau of the Census, Department of Commerce. *The social and economic status of the black population in the United States,* Series P.23, No. 42, 1971.

ZELNIK, MELVIN, AND JOHN KANTNER. Sexuality, contraception, and pregnancy among young unwed females in the United States. A paper prepared for the Commission on Population Growth and the American Future, May 1972.

To Love, Honor, and Obey? Traditional Legal Marriage and Alternative Family Forms*

LENORE J. WEITZMAN

THE MARRIAGE CONTRACT IS UNLIKE most contracts: its provisions are unwritten, its penalties are unspecified, and the terms of the contract are typically unknown to the "contracting" parties. One wonders how many men and women entering marriage today would freely agree to the provisions of the marriage contract if they had the chance to read it and to consider the rights and obligations to which they were committing themselves. However, no state gives them the opportunity to read the terms of their marriage contract, nor does any state ask them if they are willing to assume the duties, rights, and obligations it specifies. It is simply assumed that everyone who gets married will want to (or will have to) abide by the state-imposed "unwritten" contract known as legal marriage.

The first section of this article will examine the terms of this unwritten marriage contract, and thus the basic rights and obligations embodied in the legal structure of marriage. The second section will explore the ways in which the legal structure of marriage serves to restrict and limit alternative family forms. Finally, recent legal developments and prospects for change will be examined.

Underlying each section is a challenge to the present legal structure of marriage. It will be shown that the law is sex-based and anachronistic; it serves to enforce a rigidity and specificity which denies legality to the diversity of family forms in the United States today.

TRADITIONAL LEGAL MARRIAGE: STATE-IMPOSED INEQUALITY AND RIGIDITY

In the common law of England the husband and wife merged into a single legal identity, that of the husband. Under this common law doctrine, called coverture, a married woman was a "femme couverte," a legal nonperson (Blackstone 1765). She gave up control of her real property to her husband and lost the ownership of her chattels to him as well. She could neither make a contract nor be sued in her own name. If she worked, her husband was entitled to her wages, and if she and her husband were to separate, her husband would invariably gain custody of the children. Even her criminal acts, if done in her husband's presence, were assumed to be committed under his command, and her husband was held responsible for them (Clark 1968, p. 223).

*I am especially indebted to William J. Goode, Herma Hill Kay, and Carol Bruch for comments on an earlier draft. This work was partially supported by NIMH Grant #MH-24216, NSF Grant #GI-39218, and The Center for the Study of Law and Society, University of California, Berkeley. The material in the first section of this article is excerpted from the more lengthy analysis in Lenore J. Weitzman's Legal regulation of marriage: tradition and change, *California Law Review.* July–September, 1974, **62**, (4), © 1975 by Lenore J. Weitzman. Reprinted with permission.

Most of these legal barriers to property were removed by the passage of Married Women's Property Acts in the 19th century (Kanowitz 1969). But today, one hundred years later, the basic legal obligation between husbands and wives remain bound by English common law. Although private practices within marriage may not always conform to the traditional marriage contract, it is clear that the present marriage contract—the legal contract embodied in both statutory and case law—continues to enforce the common law obligations of husbands and wives.

The four essential provisions of the traditional marriage contract are those which: (1) recognize the husband as head of the household; (2) hold the husband responsible for support; (3) hold the wife responsible for domestic services; and (4) hold the wife responsible for child care.

The Husband Is Head of the Family

Today, when a woman marries, she still loses her independent identity: she assumes her husband's name, his residence, and his status—socially and economically.

The married woman's loss of an independent identity is clearly symbolized by the loss of her name. Women who try to retain their maiden names may have difficulty voting, obtaining a driver's license, running for office, and securing credit (Brown *et al.* 1971). In some states a woman with children is forced to retain her husband's name even after they divorce. As recently as 1972, the United States Supreme Court upheld an Alabama law requiring a married woman to use her husband's surname on her driver's license (*Forbush v. Wallace*).

Although many women may want to assume their husband's name upon marriage, a coerced change of name, as Professor Kay has noted, is "resented by the woman who wishes to retain her birth name in order to establish a continuity of identity throughout her life" (Kay 1974, p. 125). A career woman in public or professional life may suffer a real loss of recognition when she marries and adopts her husband's name, and a greater loss if she marries more than once.

Recently several states have adopted a more progressive attitude, and have held that a married woman may choose any name she wishes (*Stuart v. Board of Supervisors of Elections* 1972). However, in other states a married woman who does not want to assume her husband's surname may still have to contend with laws and administrative regulations which restrict her freedom to do so.

A second indication that the married woman takes her husband's identity is provided by her traditional assumption of his domicile upon marriage (Clark 1968). The location of a person's domicile affects a broad range of legal rights and duties, including the place where he or she may vote, run for public office, serve on juries, receive free or lowered tuition at a state school, be liable for taxes, sue for divorce, register a car, and have his or her estate administered (Brown *et al.* 1971). Although the privilege of choosing one's own legal domicile is accorded to all other adults, the married woman may find herself severely disadvantaged because she has no choice in the matter. For example, a woman who is, and always has been, a state resident, and therefore receives free tuition at the state university, may suddenly be charged out-of-state tuition if she marries a male student whose legal domicile is in another state.

A more severe hardship may result from these domicile rules. In most states, if a woman refuses to accept her husband's choice of domicile, she is considered to have deserted him. Desertion is not only grounds for divorce, but in the great majority of states which still use grounds for divorce, a woman found guilty of abandonment would be "at fault" in the divorce action and could be deprived of property and her right to seek alimony. In other states married women may be subjected to unfavorable tax consequences or lose the privilege of running for public office in their home state (Kay 1974). In some states a women cannot retain her own domicile for the purposes of voting, and in others she cannot do so for the purpose of paying taxes. As of 1971, only three states in the United States—Alaska, Arkansas, and Wisconsin—permitted a woman to have a separate domicile from her husband for all legal purposes (Brown *et al.* 1971). As Professor Kanowitz has observed, "the practical function of the domicile rule is to deprive wives of certain

governmental benefits they would otherwise have"
(Kanowitz 1969, p. 52).

The rule that "the husband may choose any reasonable place or mode of living and the wife must conform" appears to be based on the assumption that the husband is solely responsible for the support of the family. As the court stated in *Carlson v. Carlson* (1953, p. 256):

> The general rule by the great weight of authority is that the wife must adopt the residence of the husband....There are sound reasons for this rule. The law imposes upon the husband the burden and obligation to support, maintenance and care of the family and almost of necessity he must have the choice of the situs of the home. There can be no decision by majority rule as to where the home shall be maintained....One domicile for the family home is still an essential in our way of life.

These domicile rules, and the principles upon which they are based, are anachronistic in our mobile industrialized society where the decision of when and where to move is not made by the husband alone and is not based solely on his career. Yet if he chooses to, the husband can enforce his legal right to establish the marital domicile, and his wife must conform with his decision or face the legal consequences. The law thus refuses to recognize a wife's equal interest in the location of the marital domicile and thereby denies her equal protection of the law. Further, for the growing minority of two-career families, the domicile rules may raise tax, employment, and other legal problems for the woman who commutes to a job in another state or who lives apart from her husband for substantial periods of time.

In addition to the law of domicile and surname, administrative regulations regarding unemployment insurance, social security benefits, federal survivors and disability insurance, and public assistance recognize the husband as head of the household with his wife's identity subordinate to his (Walker 1971).

Other regulations, such as those governing consumer credit, are derived from legal principles but have acquired an authority of their own. For example, the restrictions that a married woman faces in obtaining credit are a direct outgrowth of the traditional marriage contract. At common law, the husband gained control of his wife's property upon marriage and therefore assumed responsibility for her debts as well as her support (Clark 1968). Today, however, despite the fact that married women earn money, hold property, and acquire debts in their own names, in most cases they are still required to apply for and obtain credit in their husband's names—and they need their husband's explicit permission to do so (NOW 1973). A married woman's independent right to seek bank loans, home mortgages, federal housing loans, department store charge accounts, and credit cards in her own name is thus severely circumscribed by the prevailing assumption that her husband is the head of the household (Brown 1973). The result in this area, as in many others, is a series of social customs and regulations which surround and enlarge the husband's strictly "legal" rights as head of the household and consequently further diminish those of his wife.

The Husband Is Responsible for Support

The traditional marriage contract assumes a strict division of labor within the family. The financial aspects of family life are delegated to the husband; he is responsible for support. Professor Homer Clark, who characterizes the laws on spousal obligations as extraordinarily conservative, summarizes them as follows:

> Specifically, the courts say that the husband has a duty to support his wife, that she has a duty to render services in the home, and that these duties are reciprocal.... The husband is to provide the family with food, clothing, shelter and as many of the amenities of life as he can manage, either (in earlier days) by the management of his estates or (more recently) by working for wages or a salary. The wife is to be mistress of the household, maintaining the home with the resources furnished by the husband, and caring for the children. A reading of

contemporary judicial opinions leaves the impression that these roles have not changed over the last two hundred years, in spite of the changes in the legal position of the married woman carried through in the 19th century and in her social and economic position in this century (Clark 1968, p. 181).

All states, even those with community property systems, place the primary obligation of family support upon the husband: he is to provide necessities for both his wife and his children (Kay 1974). In contrast, a wife is *never* held responsible for the support of her husband in two-thirds of the states, and in the remaining minority of states, a wife is held responsible for her husband's support only if he has become incapacitated or a public charge (Kay 1974; Clark 1968). The wife's obligation for the support of her children is similarly circumscribed, requiring her to contribute to child support only if her husband is unwilling or unable to do so (Clark 1968).

Because the courts have held the traditional view of the husband bearing the total responsibility for the family's financial support, husbands and wives are not allowed to make private contracts that would alter or limit the husband's responsibility.

One effect of placing the primary support obligation on men is to further reinforce the husband's position as head of the household and, more specifically, his authority over family finances. While the husband's obligation for support does not alone bestow upon him the mixed blessings of financial authority and financial responsibility, most of his financial power stems directly from this obligation. For example, in most states, because the husband has the primary responsibility for family support, he has the power to manage and control family income and property.[1] In some states, again because of his responsibility for support, his permission is necessary before his wife can open a business or trade in commodities (Kanowitz 1959, p. 57). The penumbra of financial powers that flow from the husband's assumed position as master of the family treasury now embraces newly emerging areas such as pensions, insurance, social security, and dependency allowances, as well as the more traditional areas of income and real property.

This increase in the husband's financial authority feeds a vicious cycle in which the advantages given to husbands enhance their financial skills, while the restrictions imposed on wives reduce theirs. Thus if married women were not less financially competent than their husbands initially, the financial restrictions imposed on them would certainly have the effect of making them so; it is more difficult for a married woman to develop financial competence when the force of social and legal restrictions serve to keep her financially dependent on men and prohibit her from gaining the very experience she needs.

When the law continues to assume that husbands must be held responsible for the financial support of the family, it must also continue to make the parallel assumption that wives are economically incapacitated and economically dependent. Yet it is obvious that such automatic assumptions about the dependency of wives are outmoded and unnecessary.

Married women now constitute 60 percent of the female labor force (United States Department of Labor 1971) and their wages are of vital importance to their families (Suelze 1970). Today, when 43 percent of all married women are in the labor force, social reality strongly contradicts the legal assumption that the husband alone should (and does) support his family.

The law diverges from social reality in a second respect. In practice, the spousal support obligations of the husband are rarely enforced, because the courts have been reluctant to interfere with an ongoing marriage. In the leading case in this area, *McGuire v. McGuire* (1953), the wife complained that her husband had not given her any money and not provided her with clothes for the previous three years. Although he was a man of substantial means, her husband had also refused to purchase furniture and other household necessities (beyond the groceries, which he paid for by check). The court, however, refused to consider the wife's complaint because the parties were still living together and the court did not want to "intrude" on the marital relationship. In the language of the court:

The living standards of a family are a matter of concern to the household, and not for the courts to determine, even though the husband's attitude toward his wife, according to his wealth and circumstances, leaves little to be said in his behalf. As long as the home is maintained and the parties are living as husband and wife it may be said that the husband is legally supporting his wife and the purpose of the marriage relation is being carried out. Public policy requires such a holding (*McGuire v. McGuire*, 1953, p. 342).

If a wife does not receive the court's assistance in obtaining support during her marriage, then it becomes meaningless to speak of the husband's legal obligation to support his wife. The Citizens' Advisory Council on the Status of Women (1972, p. 8) aptly describes the present situation: "a married woman living with her husband can, in practice, get only what he chooses to give her." The law's promise of support is thus a hollow guarantee—one that affords a married woman no more protection than her husband will willingly grant.

Women do not fare much better after divorce, although the husband's theoretical responsibility for support continues with his obligation to provide alimony for his former wife (Clark 1968).

The guarantee of alimony is based on the continuing assumption that women, like children, are incapable of supporting themselves. Alimony was originally awarded by the English ecclesiastical courts which gave only divorce *a mensa et thoro* (from bed and board), authorizing the husband and wife to live apart but not freeing them from the marital bond (Vernier and Hurlbut 1939). An alimony award under these circumstances was an enforcement of the husband's continuing duty to support his wife. Since the husband retained control over his wife's property, and employment opportunities for women were lacking, alimony alone provided a woman's essential means of support.

The survival of alimony today, despite recent changes in women's status and labor force participation, reflects the continued legal assumption of the wife's dependency on her husband (and perhaps the law's cognizance of the realistically poor employment opportunities for a middle-aged woman who has devoted her productive years to full-time housework and child care). Because the law encourages a woman to give up her independent earning potential in favor of her marriage, the provision for alimony is based on the assumption that women have done just this—and are, as a result, incapable of independent financial survival.

Yet if a woman relies on the law's promise that her husband will continue to support her, she will find her expectations thwarted. Even though most states continue to hold the husband theoretically liable for alimony, in fact, alimony is actually awarded in less than 15 percent of the all divorce cases (Nagel and Weitzman 1971). Since alimony is a tax deduction for the man, and child support is not, the husband is likely to want to label some of his child support as alimony. Thus, *true* alimony may be given in even fewer cases. Widespread noncompliance with alimony awards, coupled with minimal enforcement efforts further reduce the percentage of women who actually receive alimony (Nagel and Weitzman 1971). Although the myth of "alimony drones" persists, it should be emphasized that for over 85 percent of divorced women, alimony is just that—a myth, a theoretical right which is rarely realized.

Although alimony awards are already rare,[2] it has been widely assumed that grants of alimony will decline further in the future, as the occupational status and earnings of women improve. However, if legal marriage were viewed as a contractual partnership, like a business partnership, it would not be unreasonable to provide compensation for a spouse who contributes, as the housewife does, to building the family's wealth and property (Weitzman 1974, pp. 185–186, ff. 82). Thus it could be argued that many wives have a right to alimony—or to some monetary reimbursement after divorce—irrespective of their financial needs. If a wife has contributed to her husband's employability and helped to advance his career, as most married women have, she should be considered his economic partner with a financial investment in his earnings.

Traditionally the law has assumed that family property is limited to items of real and personal property. However, in a mobile urban society the spouses' earning powers have become the major assets of most families. Thus a modern conception of marital property might well be broadened to include the "earning power" of the marital partners. The recognition of earning power as marital property would legitimately compensate a non-income earning spouse for contributing to the other's education, employability, and job success. In families with a single income, the single career is often actually a "two-person career," or the product of a cooperative effort by the partnership (Papanek 1973), and both partners should have a future share in it.

The Wife Is Responsible for Domestic Services

In legal marriage the man exchanges financial support for his wife's service as companion, housewife, and mother. A man can legally expect the following services from his wife:

> She has a duty to be his helpmate, to love and care for him in such a role, to afford him her society and her person, to protect and care for him in sickness, and to labor faithfully to advance his interest. [*Citations omitted.*] Likewise, she must perform her household and domestic duties...without compensation therefor. A husband is entitled to the benefit of his wife's industry and economy (*Rucci v. Rucci* 1962, p. 221).

The husband's rights to the services of his wife have been most clearly articulated in suits for loss of consortium. In addition to housework and child care the husband's rights of consortium include love, affection, companionship, society, and sexual relations from his wife (Brown *et al.* 1971).

The woman's obligations as wife, housewife, and mother are so basic to the legal conception of family roles that one can view a large body of case law which supposedly deals with many other issues

as really a single social sanction for ensuring that women are not sidetracked from their domestic duties. For example, the Supreme Court decisions over the women's roles show a remarkably consistent pattern of insistence on a woman's domestic obligations above all else.

Beginning in 1873, in *Bradwell v. Illinois*, the Supreme Court upheld an Illinois State court decision denying a married woman the right to practice law.[3] Writing of the paramount destiny of women to be wives and mothers, Justice Bradley's concurring opinion states:

> Man is, or should be, woman's protector and defender. The natural and proper timidity and delicacy which belongs to the female sex evidently unfits it for many of the occupations of civil life. The constitution of the family organization, which is founded in the divine ordinance, as well as in the nature of things, indicates the domestic sphere as that which properly belongs to the domain and functions of womanhood. The paramount destiny and mission of women are to fulfill the noble and benign offices of wife and mother. This is the law of the creator (*Bradwell v. Illinois* 1873, pp. 130, 147).

Later Supreme Court justifications for women's domestic roles became more sophisticated, shifting from a reliance on the "law of the creator" to that of "sociological truth." In *Muller v. Oregon* (1908), which upheld an Oregon law limiting female employees to ten hours of work a day, the Brandeis brief introduced a vast amount of sociological data to support differential treatment of women because of their social roles as wives and mothers. The court, ruling in Brandeis's favor, also based their opinion on these sociological "givens":

> That woman's physical structure and the performance of maternal functions place her at a disadvantage in the struggle for subsistence is obvious. This is especially true when the burdens of motherhood are upon her...as healthy mothers are essential to vigorous offspring, the physical well-being of woman becomes an object of public interest and care in order to pre-

serve the strength and vigor of the race (*Muller v. Oregon* 1908, pp. 412, 421–422).

Thus *Muller* established a precedent for future legal decisions by holding that special legislation for women could be justified if it supported their roles as wives and mothers. Although at the time of *Muller* minimum hour laws were considered a benefit for women, the same reasoning has been used to women's detriment. Most notably, the courts have used this rationale in employment cases to uphold the exclusion of women from specific occupations, such as bartending; in job classifications, such as restricting jobs requiring weight lifting and overtime work; and in periods of employment, such as the regulation of women's work just before and just after childbirth.

There is, of course, a growing constitutional challenge to such laws, both in the present attempt to obtain ratification of the Equal Rights Amendment and in the court's recent decisions based on equal protection rules (e.g., *Alexander v. Louisiana* 1972, *dicta*). But although the long-established pattern of differential treatment for married women is changing (*Frontiero v. Richardson* 1973; *Cleveland Board of Education v. LaFleur* 1974) it is not consistent, and the Supreme Court is still willing to allow differential treatment of married women in some cases. (See, for example, *Kahn v. Shevin* 1974, in which the Supreme Court upheld a Florida law applying differential tax exemptions to widows and widowers.) Thus, without the Equal Rights Amendment, the law may continue to enforce the traditional sex-based marital obligations and may continue to hold the wife responsible for domestic services.

Because the courts have always considered a wife's domestic services to be owed to her husband, they have traditionally refused to honor contracts whereby a husband has agreed to pay his wife for them. Even when husband and wife have agreed that her work was different from and in addition to domestic services, such as working in her husband's business, or doing farm labor, the courts have voided contracts which obligated her husband to pay her (*Youngberg v. Holstrom* 1961; *Frame v. Frame* 1931; *Ladden v. Ladden* 1960). (For recent developments in the legality of such contracts, see Weitzman 1974.)

When the law assumes that a wife "owes" her domestic services to her husband, the law undermines the value and importance of the wife's labor in building the family wealth and property, both during the marriage and at the time of dissolution. When a woman's labor is "seen as a service she owes her husband rather than as a job deserving the dignity of economic return" (Kay 1974, p. 142) the contribution and value of the housewife is greatly underestimated. Although there is "much rhetoric about the value of homemaking and child rearing," the law does little to ensure that these tasks are accorded "status, dignity, and security" (Citizens' Advisory Council 1974, p. 6).

The National Organization for Women has urged that housework be treated as a bona fide occupation with compensation and fringe benefits (NOW 1971). Using estimates of the value of housework (such as the computation used by Galbraith that the average housewife's yearly services are worth $13,654 (Galbraith 1973; Walker and Gauger 1973), feminists have suggested paying the housewife for her work to lessen her dependency status.

The current dependency of housewives and the undervaluation of housework could also be reduced if women were covered as independent workers under social security. Clearly housewives do work, even though they do not receive monetary compensation for their work. Yet today's housewife does not have an independent right to benefits from her husband's social security (although her work at home clearly contributes to family support) until she has been married to him for twenty years. Without independent coverage a wife cannot provide for her retirement or old age as an independent person. If, instead, the wife's contribution to the family were recognized as work, she would be independently entitled to insurance based on her homemaking and child-care services.

Recognition of the housewife's contribution to the marriage may be even more important at the time of divorce. In many states, the woman discovers that her contribution to the family wealth and property is ignored upon dissolution because her "husband's" property is not subject to equitable distribution upon divorce. Although marriage is considered a partnership in theory, when the partnership profits are divided, the woman's contribution is devalued in all but the eight community property states. Foster and Freed argue that "the shocking unfairness" of the "obsolete and archaic marital property laws of many states" is illustrated by the New York case of *Wirth v. Wirth* (1971):

> Both husband and wife were employed and for 22 years of their marriage, their earnings were pooled. She also raised two children. In 1956 it was agreed between them that the husband would start a "crash" savings program and that family expenses would be met out of her income and his would be used for investments. According to the wife, the husband said that the program was "for our latter days" and "for the two of us." All the investments were taken in the husband's name and none was held by joint ownership.
>
> Upon divorce it was held that she had no interest whatsoever in the assets they had accumulated as a nest egg for both of them, and that although she might be entitled to alimony (after some forty years of marriage), he got to keep all of the investments. The decision makes a fetish of how title is held and ignores the tradition of equity courts in effecting justice (Foster and Freed 1974, pp. 174–175).

A recent report by the Citizens' Advisory Council on the Status of Women (1974) urges a careful evaluation of the economic effects of divorce laws to insure that the homemakers' contribution to the marital property is not ignored. They have specifically urged states adopting no-fault divorce laws to change their laws on the division of property, alimony, child support, and enforcement so that the law explicitly recognizes the contribution of the homemaker.

It is ironic that the law seems to punish a woman who has devoted herself to being a mother and wife while at the same time encouraging all women to remain housewives. The law thus puts women in a double bind: the legal structure of marriage seems to provide incentives and rewards for women to remain in domestic roles, but it also penalizes them if their marriages dissolve. Since a woman cannot ensure the survival of her marriage, and since with no-fault divorce she may have no choice about its dissolution, the marriage may be dissolved and she may be punished through no fault or intention of her own.

The Wife Is Responsible for Child Care

The fourth provision of the state-imposed marriage contract places almost total responsibility for child care, both during marriage and after dissolution, upon the wife. The woman's role as mother remains at the very core of our legal conceptions of her place in society; it is a basic source of stereotype, the "most stubborn and intractable bastion of discrimination" (brief for appellees in *Geduldig v. Aiello* 1974, p. 41).

Although women have been given great deference because they are mothers, they have also faced many exclusions because of their mothering roles, as noted above. As recently as 1971, in an important decision against sex discrimination in employment (*Phillips v. Martin Marietta*), the Supreme Court left open the possibility of special exclusions of mothers with preschool children. And in 1974 the Supreme Court allowed the State of California to exclude pregnancy-related disabilities from its normal health plan (*Geduldig v. Aiello* 1974). This clearly differential treatment for women was allowed in violation of EEOC regulations.

The continued legal assumption that the woman is the natural and proper caretaker of the young is most clearly reflected in child custody dispositions. Women continue to be awarded custody of their children in over 90 percent of divorce cases (Goode 1965). Although most divorcing women want custody of their children, the extreme deference for the mother as custodian may have the social effect of further reinforcing the woman's social roles as housewife and mother, and in many cases of reinforcing her dependency on her husband for support.

The practice of automatically giving the mother custody of the children may have two other detrimental effects. First, it may not take sufficient, if any, account of the needs of the children and the qualifications of the parents involved. Second, in practice, it has the ultimate effect of causing the mother to bear the greater, if not the total, financial burden of child support.

The current preference for the mother in custody cases is so pronounced that fathers may be denied an equal right to custody because the presumption of a mother's fitness is so hard to overcome. Fathers who would be better custodians face an uphill battle in most courts, and many are discouraged from trying. Children may also suffer when their interests are ignored or undermined by this *a priori* custody assumption.

Further, it is not clear that the mother benefits from the presumption in her favor. Because it is assumed that all mothers will want custody of their children, there is a strong legal and social pressure for women to assume this role without thinking about it and without considering its consequences. Since custody awards to the mother are so routine, the woman who admits that she would prefer not to have her children is viewed suspiciously and made to feel deviant and guilty. She may therefore be coerced into a role which is harmful to both her and her children.

This legal deference to mothers may have been appropriate when our country was young, needed population growth, and wanted to encourage women to have many children. But today our population needs, and more importantly the needs and desires of many women, have changed. Until recently, women would seldom express a dislike for child care or their feelings of being trapped into forced mothering. Today, however, the availability of reliable contraceptives, changing population pressures, and expanding labor force opportunities offer them a real choice. The law should allow women who do not want to be full-time mothers to choose this option.

Once again, the law seems to be based on stereotyped assumptions about the proper roles of men and women. Women who may not want to be full-time mothers are coerced into it, and fathers who want custody are prevented by the legal priorities given to women. Certainly public policy would be better served by eliminating these rigid role prescriptions and increasing the options available to both sexes.

When the mother is awarded custody, she is expected to perform child-care services without pay. The father's obligation is limited to direct financial support for the child. Even the Uniform Marriage and Divorce Act, which represents the enlightened vanguard in family law, makes no provision for the custodial parent to be compensated for his or her labor in taking care of the children.

The father, as the noncustodial parent, is typically ordered to pay child support. However, most fathers do not support their children as ordered (Nagel and Weitzman 1971, p. 190). Indeed 62 percent fail to comply fully with the court-ordered payments in the first year after the order, and 42 percent do not make even a single payment (Eckhardt 1968). By the tenth year, 79 percent of the fathers are in total noncompliance. Yet, despite the alarmingly high rate of noncompliance, legal action against nonpaying fathers is rarely taken (Eckhardt 1968).

These data indicate that the practical effect of making the mother the children's custodian is to make her primarily responsible for her children's support. When her former husband refuses to support his children, she, as their custodian, is left to bear the responsibility alone.

Just as it is unfair to place the total burden of support on men, so it is unfair to assume that women should have exclusive responsibility for household services and minor children. Both prescribed roles are based on sex stereotypes, and both compel an unnecessary rigidity and specificity; it is highly questionable whether the law should serve to enforce outmoded sex roles in an increasingly egalitarian society.

LEGAL BARRIERS TO ALTERNATIVE FAMILY FORMS

The legal system's narrow and rigid conception of a family and its imposition of legal responsibilities on the basis of sex serves to restrict and constrain alternative families. By exercising their monopolistic control over access to marital status, states have been able to impose their own definition of a family on all those who seek legal recognition for their relationship. Traditionally the states have limited this definition of appropriate marriage partners to monogamous heterosexual unions, thus precluding homosexual and group marriages. States have also restricted alternative family forms by enforcing the narrowly prescribed roles of husbands and wives examined above. Each of these barriers to alternative family forms will be discussed briefly below.

The Restriction of Limited Access: Homosexual and Group Marriages

The Judeo-Christian ideal embodied in law is one of a monogamous heterosexual union, that is, two single individuals of the opposite sex. The assumption of a heterosexual two-person marriage is so basic that it is rare to find legislation which explicitly excludes homosexual or group marriages. However, in recent years, in response to challenges by those who wished to alter either the number or sex of the partners, the courts have affirmed the legal system's limited conception of "a marriage" and "a family" and have explicitly withheld legal recognition from these alternative family forms.

The issue of homosexual marriages was first raised in the courts in *Baker v. Nelson* (1971), a case in which a male homosexual couple applied for a marriage license in Minnesota. In challenging the state's restrictions on homosexual marriages, they argued that the right to marry without regard to the sex of the parties is a fundamental right of all persons. Further, they contended that restricting marriages to couples of the opposite sex was irrational and an invidious means of discrimination. The court disagreed, however, and affirmed the traditional position that marriage "is the state of union between two persons of the opposite sex" (*Baker v. Nelson* 1971, p. 311). A Kentucky court has followed *Baker* by sustaining the denial of a marriage license to two women (Kay 1971, p. 201).

The denial of a marriage license may impose burdens on a homosexual couple beyond the loss of formal legitimacy for their relationship. Persons who are legally married receive concrete economic advantages in filing income tax returns; in obtaining social security, disability, unemployment, and pension benefits; in securing mortgages, homes, apartments, and insurance; in receiving loans and credit as a family; in adopting or obtaining custody of their children; and in gaining the property and tax benefits of inheritence laws.

As Del Martin and Phyllis Lyon have explained, homosexual couples may want to contract a legal marriage for a variety of reasons:

For some, marriage means a religious sacrament and commitment. For others it may also take on a legal significance in terms of community property, the filing of joint income tax returns, and inheritance rights. Recognition of a lesbian union might also serve to validate the couples who wished to take on the legal responsibility of adopting homeless, unwanted children. It would also simplify insurance problems, making the couple eligible for family policies, for family rates on airlines travel and for that matter, for "couple" entry to entertainment functions, too (Martin and Lyon 1972, p. 103).

It is unlikely, however, that the courts will soon recognize homosexuals who want to legitimize their relationships. The *Baker* court said it was not persuaded by the petitioners' contentions, nor did it find any support for them in previous Supreme Court decisions. In fact, the court simply dismissed the issues by affirming that "the institution of marriage as a union of man and woman is as old as the book of Genesis" (*Baker* 1971).

Although the courts remain reluctant to legitimate homosexual marriages, more are now willing to allow homosexual parents to retain custody of their children (Basile 1974). The recent lesbian mother cases indicate some progress from the well publicized *Nadler* decision in which the trial court held a lesbian mother unfit as a matter of law (*Nadler v. Superior Court* 1967).

In 1972, several trial courts awarded custody to women in an acknowledged lesbian relationship provided that the mothers did not live with their lovers (*Isaacson v. Isaacson* 1972; *M. v. M.* 1972). But in 1973 and 1974, two appellate courts overturned orders that lesbian mothers must live separate and apart, holding that a homosexual relationship does not render a home unfit for children (*People v. Brown* 1973; *Schuster v. Schuster* 1974). Homosexual fathers' rights to both custody and visitation have also been upheld (*A. v. A.* 1973).

New possibilities for legal recognition of homosexual unions are discussed in the final section of this article on de facto families.

Traditionally, individuals living in communes and group marriages have also been excluded from the benefits and legal protections accorded to families. Most states have statutory prohibitions against bigamy, and there is a long history of Supreme Court decisions prohibiting plural marriage. "There has never been a time in any State of the Union when polygamy has not been an offense against society, cognizable by the civil courts and punishable with more or less severity" (*Reynolds v. United States* 1878). As recently as 1946 (*Cleveland v. United States*), a fundamentalist Mormon was convicted of violating the Mann Act because he transported a woman across a state line for a plural marriage ceremony and subsequent co-habitation.

Plural marriage and communal families suffer from many of the same legal restrictions that homosexual unions face: they are excluded from the economic advantages in filing joint income tax returns; from family benefits under social security, disability, and health insurance programs; from property and tax benefits of inheritance laws; and they may lose custody of their children.

In recent years communal families have had difficulties with health, food stamp, and housing regulations (e.g., *Moreno v. United States Department of Agriculture* 1973). In *Palo Alto Tenants Union v. Morgan* (1970), and *Village of Belle Terre v. Boraas* (1974), two communities successfully excluded groups living together as a family from "single family residential neighborhoods." In Palo Alto, the group specifically asserted that they were living together as a family, "treating themselves and treated by others as a family unit." In both cases the groups contended that the zoning restrictions violated their constitutional rights to privacy and freedom of association. But while the courts recognized the strongly held value of protection for the traditional family relationship, they were unwilling to attach the same status to the voluntary family. Their reasoning is instructive as it reiterates the traditional legal position:

> The traditional family is an institution reinforced by biological and legal ties which are difficult, or impossible, to sunder. It plays a role in educating and nourishing the young which, far from being "voluntary," is often compulsory. Finally, it has been a means for uncounted millenia of satisfying the deepest emotional and physical needs of human beings. A zoning law which divided or totally excluded traditional families would indeed be "suspect."

The communal living groups represented by plaintiffs share few of the above characteristics. They are voluntary, with fluctuating memberships who have no legal obligations of support or cohabitation. They are in no way subject to the State's vast body of domestic relations law. They do not have the biological links which characterize most families. Emotional ties between commune members may exist, but this is not true of members of many groups. Plaintiffs are unquestionably sincere in seeking to devise and test new life-styles, but the communes they have formed are legally indistinguishable from such traditional living groups as religious communities and residence clubs. The right to form such groups may be constitutionally protected, but the right to insist that these groups live under the same roof, in any part of the city they choose, is not (*Palo Alto Tenants Union v. Morgan* 1970).

The Restriction of Prescribed Marital Roles: Egalitarian Family Patterns and Individual Contracts

In the past 200 years there have been profound transformations in our society which have impelled corresponding changes in the nature and functions of the family. While the productive and economic functions of the family have declined, the family's role as the major source of psychological and social support for its individual members has increased. Sharing, companionship, and emotional solace in the marital bond have become primary for most couples in our society—and many feel that these needs can only be fulfilled in a more egalitarian family.

The traditional marriage contract, with its rigidly prescribed roles for husbands and wives, is seen as inconsistent with the more egalitarian family pattern in which authority is increasingly shared and decisions are made jointly by husband and wife. Today it is typical for husbands and wives to talk over family problems. Financial matters such as budgeting, purchasing, and saving are now more often decided jointly. Similarly, decisions concerning the family residence, such as when and where to move, are no longer made by the husband alone nor are they based solely on his career.

The assumption that the husband is head of the family, with his wife's identity subordinate to his, is also being challenged by the increased number of women who are retaining their maiden names and their independent social and financial identity. Many married women are deciding that they may be better off in the long run if they keep their own names and maintain their driver's licenses, diplomas, tax records, and credit cards in their maiden names.

The spousal obligations of the traditional contract, which hold the husband primarily responsible for family support and the wife responsible for domestic chores, are similarly challenged by changing social reality. The 60 percent of married women in the labor force are sharing the responsibility for family support and an increasing number of married men are sharing domestic responsibilities. Many couples are alternating and interchanging the traditional household roles, with men playing a greater role in cooking, shopping, and cleaning, and women assuming more responsibility for family budgets, working in the garden, and fixing things around the house. There is a growing acceptance of the idea that when a woman returns to the labor force, and thus shares the responsibility of supporting the family, the husband in turn must share equal responsibility for the household.

Finally, parenthood is coming to be defined more and more as the joint enterprise of both husband and wife, not only because women are insisting that men share some of the load, but because many young professional men themselves no longer accept as their fate the compulsive male careerism characteristic of the 1950s (Skolnick 1974).

Despite these social changes, males and females who try to alter the traditional contract, by private agreement or by writing their own contracts, face continued legal barriers. Although postnuptial and prenuptial agreements between husbands and wives have become widely accepted in law, they have been severely restricted because the courts will not enforce contracts which alter the "essential" elements of the marital relationship.

Two aspects of the traditional marriage relationship have been considered "essential obligations": the husband's duty to support the wife, and the wife's duty to serve the husband. When spouses try to change these essential obligations the courts refuse to uphold these contracts. For example, husbands and wives cannot agree to alter or limit the husband's obligation to support his wife. The contract is considered void as being in violation of public policy. Even in cases where the wife is independently wealthy and has no wish for financial support from the husband, the courts have deemed the husband responsible. The law's position on this subject is absolute: "A husband may not be absolved from his duty to support his wife, nor can this duty be qualified or limited. The husband's duty as a matter of policy is an obligation imposed by law and cannot be contracted away" (Grant 1962, p. 160).

Similarly, the courts will not allow husbands and wives to contract for the husband to pay the wife for her domestic services. The contract is held void for lack of consideration, since a party cannot contract to perform that which she or he is already legally bound to do (*American Jurisprudence* 1968, p. 322). As recently as 1961 the Iowa Supreme Court held that a wife's performance of "the usual duties of a farm wife, such as raising poultry, at times hogs, and a big garden" did not constitute consideration in an alleged oral contract between husband and wife to make mutual wills, stating that it was "well settled that a husband's agreement to pay for services within the scope of the marital relation is without consideration and contrary to public policy" (*Youngberg v. Holstrom* 1961, p. 815). As this case shows, the wife's duty to her husband is often found to extend beyond the performance of basic household tasks.

The designation of the sex-stereotyped duties of the marital contract as "essential obligations of marriage" is being increasingly challenged and would clearly be in violation of the proposed Equal Rights Amendment (Weitzman 1975). In addition, there is a growing interest in marriage contracts and the possibilities such contracts provide for structuring and legitimating egalitarian family forms and alternative life-style unions. Although only a few of these new-style contracts have been tested in the courts in very recent years, the courts are beginning to change and it can be hoped that these contracts, if properly written, will receive increased legal recognition in the near future (Weitzman 1974). The change, in large part, is a result of the new legal trends discussed in the next section of this article.

RECENT DEVELOPMENTS: RECOGNITION OF THE DE FACTO FAMILY

Unmarried couples have traditionally been in a position structurally akin to homosexuals, communards, and those writing their own marriage contracts in seeking the same rights and benefits as those who are legally married—filing joint income tax returns, receiving social security and other governmental benefits as a spouse, and having their children recognized and treated as legitimate children.

In general, the law seems to be moving in the direction of according them this recognition and legitimization, as the legal distinction between married and unmarried couples, between wed and unwed parents, and between legitimate and illegitimate children is becoming increasingly irrelevant. Five recent Supreme Court decisions are indicative.

In *Stanley v. Illinois* (1972), the court upheld the rights of an unwed father to obtain custody of his illegitimate children. In *Levy v. Louisiana* (1968), it upheld the right of an illegitimate child to recover for the wrongful death of its mother. In *Weber v. Aetna Casualty* (1972), the court recognized the right of dependent, unacknowledged, illegitimate children to recover for the death of their father, under Louisiana's workmen's compensation law, on an equal footing with his dependent legitimate children.[4] In *Davis v. Richardson* (1972), the Supreme Court upheld a challenge to a provision of the Social Security Act which discriminated against illegitimate children in the payment of benefits on the death of a wage-earning parent. And finally, in *Gomez v. Perez* (1973), it held that fathers are responsible for the support of their illegitimate as well as their legitimate children.

In less than a decade, in this series of cases, the Supreme Court has taken the position that unwed parents and illegitimate children should not be penalized because of the lack of a legal marriage between the man and woman—thus extending many of the rights of legitimacy to illegitimate children, and some of the benefits of marriage to unwed adults. Several very recent state court decisions have gone even further in attempting to extend the benefits of marriage to an unmarried wife.

Before discussing these cases, however, it is important to distinguish between persons who are living together but are intentionally unmarried (legally termed a "meretricious" relationship) from persons who mistakenly, but in good faith, believe themselves married (legally termed "putative" spouses). When one or both parties are putative spouses and mistakenly believe they are married, the law has traditionally protected them and allowed them to receive many of the incidents of a valid marriage. For example, the Uniform Marriage and Divorce Act provides that any person who has cohabited with another person, in the good faith belief that they were married, may acquire the rights of a legal spouse, including the right to property, maintenance, and support. Most of the putative spouse cases involve women who have been deliberately misled or taken advantage of by men, and the doctrine affords these unmarried women many of the rights of a legal wife (Kay 1974).

Unlike the putative spouse, the meretricious spouse has received no protection in the past. The rule has been that a meretricious spouse who willfully lives in a sinful relationship acquires no property rights. If a meretricious spouse has contributed funds toward a joint investment, she has been allowed to recover her property interest under the general equitable doctrines in law, such as implied partnership and constructive trust. However, in the past these principles have been applied only to situations in which the woman made a financial investment. In the past, if a woman contributed only her services (as a housewife and a mother), the courts held that she, as a meretricious spouse, was not entitled to recover an interest in the resulting property.

In 1972, in a break from this long-standing tradition of no recovery for meretricious spouse, the

Supreme Court of Washington held that a meretricious ranch "wife" could recover a partnership interest on the basis of her contributions to the ranch labor and decision making (*Estate of Thornton*). In *Thornton* the woman bore and raised four children in a family relationship and worked hard raising cattle and managing the ranch for over sixteen years. The court held that her efforts significantly contributed to the success of the business venture, and found a prima facie case of implied partnership. On the basis of this implied partnership she was allowed to recover her share of the ranch upon Thornton's death. This case is significant because it is the first to apply the principles of an implied business partnership to an intimate relationship.

Moving even further from tradition, the California courts have allowed meretricious spouses to recover for their housework and child-care services even in the absence of a business venture or a business relationship between the parties. In 1973, in *In re Marriage of Cary,* a California appellate court held that a meretricious spouse should have the same property interest as a putative spouse.

The principal trial issue in the *Cary* case was the question of Janet Forbe's rights in the property acquired with Paul Cary's earnings. Because California is a community property state, each spouse has an equal right to the property acquired during the marriage, including the parties' income. Thus, if the Carys were legally married, Janet would have been entitled to half the property acquired with Paul's earnings. Similarly, if Janet were a putative spouse, the property would have been treated as community property and divided in substantially the same manner. However, the relationship between the parties in the *Cary* case was clearly a meretricious relationship, one in which Janet would traditionally be without rights. The record shows that "both knew they were not married; they had talked several times about a wedding ceremony, but somehow they never got around to it" (*In re Cary* 1973, p. 348). Yet Janet Forbes took the name of Janet Cary and lived with Paul Cary for eight years. They filed joint income tax returns and she bore and raised their four children. Janet also performed the usual domestic

services of a wife and mother. The *Cary* court considered their relationship that of a family because they appeared to have a "family relationship, with cohabitation and mutual recognition and assumption of the usual rights, duties, and obligations attending marriage" (*In re Cary* 1973, p. 353). In deciding to overlook the parties' unmarried state, the court reasoned that with no-fault divorce, the courts were mandated to dissolve *family* relationships *without* respect to *fault* or *guilt*. It therefore ignored the guilt of both parties in maintaining their illegitimate union, and proceeded to divide their property equally.

A further vindication of the property rights of meretricious spouses occurred most recently, in 1975, in *Estate of Atherley.* *Altherley* explicitly follows *Cary*, and quotes from *Cary* in awarding a meretricious spouse one-half of the property upon her "husband's" death. However, *Atherley* extends the *Cary* doctrine to families without children and goes beyond even the possibilities of assuming a common-law marriage, because the husband in *Atherley* remained legally married to another woman.[5] In addition, the opinion in *Atherley* clearly acknowledges the previous sex-based discrimination against the housewife:

> This result receives implicit support from more recent changes in California statutes. Pre-Cary case law did not consider meretricious spousal services, such as cooking and housekeeping, valuable contributions to the acquisition of assets. This discriminates against the woman, since very often the man is the sole contributor of monies and property of value. Thus one spouse was favored solely due to the typical sex-based division of labor within the family unit...It would be inconsistent with this policy to allow a meretricious husband, or those who talk through him, advantage over a meretricious wife simply because in our present stage of social development the husband is usually the breadwinner (*In re Estate of Atherley* 1975, pp. 769–770, n. 11).

These recent cases have done more than extend the rights of unmarried women; their new doctrines will also help the married women to establish the value of her services. This will be especially useful to married women in noncommunity property states, where the woman is not guaranteed any fixed share of her husband's property upon divorce. Married women in these states may be able to apply the doctrine of implied partnership, used in *Thornton*, or of constructive trust, used in the most recent Washington case of *Omer* (1974). They may also be better able to secure the more generally available equitable remedies of the law: the implied-in-fact contract, where actions show that persons living together intended to share financial assets; the implied-in-law contract, where a person may recover the value of services rendered; and unjust enrichment, the doctrine whereby one person may not unjustly enrich himself or herself at another's expense (Bruch 1975).

It is important to note, however, that each of the cases discussed above involves a "traditional type" of relationship, and each deals with a potential benefit sought by one of the partners. There are, however, many unwed couples who have intentionally remained unmarried because they want an alternative type of relationship, and many of them would consider the rights and obligations of legal marriage a burden rather than a benefit.

Thus, in contrast to those unwed couples who want to be treated as if they were married, there are many unwed individuals who have intentionally avoided legal marriage. These couples do not want the state to interfere with or regulate their relationship, and they do not want the state to legislate their marital roles. Despite their wishes, however, some unwed couples have been surprised to find themselves defined as a "legal family" and thus subject to the legal obligations imposed on spouses and parents. For example, in some states, two college students who live together in a family-like relationship may discover that when their relationship dissolves the male may be legally obligated to support the female. In other states, they may discover that the courts can dispose of the property and income that each has acquired while living together, as the *Cary* court did.[6] This is one of several practical legal questions that the *Cary* decision leaves unanswered: how can people who live together find out whether their rights and property may be affected by their relationship?

If the state can unilaterally define personal relationships, individuals who wish to avoid marriage (and to thus avoid state control of their intimate relations) may be left without alternatives. The traditional marriage contract is already coercive insofar as it dictates prescribed roles and obligations to the spouses. Today, at least some people believe they have the option of rejecting it. If *Cary* and *Atherley* are extended, people who want to live together according to an alternative arrangement may find these options foreclosed.

In summary, the extension of the "benefits" of marital status can cut both ways: while it may provide critical rights to some unwed partners and illegitimate children, it may also impose unwanted regulation and burdens on others. Further, it may have unanticipated negative consequences for individuals who are trying to establish alternative personal and family life-styles. Individuals who want to live together without a permanent commitment, and those who want to establish an egalitarian relationship, may be thwarted by the state's imposition of its conception of marital rights and obligations.

Given the increasing diversity of family forms, and the growing trend towards experimentation and innovation in personal relationships, what is needed is a legal system with increased flexibility and a tolerance for the diversity of individually structured relationships. While the *Cary* doctrine provides the long-needed protection for unwed housewives (and, by extension, married ones too), it may create other inequities by imposing obligations and roles on those who want to live in alternative families. It would seem that the equitable remedies suggested by the line of *Cary*-type cases (such as implied partnership and implied contract), could provide for the vindication of property rights in traditional relationships, but still allow for alternative arrangements and innovations by agreement of the parties.

CONCLUSION

The state-imposed marriage contract assumes a limited, sex-based, traditional family form: the union of a single man and woman who commit themselves to each other for life. The psychological tyranny in this model is that it allows no individual choice in the degree of commitment and involvement in a relationship. Yet in our rapidly changing society, not all people want the same degree of intensity in their personal relationships: some want it in individual relationships, at specific times, but not necessarily in a marriage relationship at all times. Further, a single family form cannot fit the needs of all individuals in a society as diverse as ours. But those who could provide the present legal model with the flexibility and adaptability it needs—homosexuals, communards, unwed couples, and those who are trying to reorder their family relationships through personal contracts—have been precluded from legal marriage.

The legitimacy and relevancy of legal marriage would be greatly improved if the law permitted alternative family arrangements and judged them by the traditional legal standards developed in equity and contract law—instead of the outmoded family law.

Although the states have traditionally had autonomy over rules and laws governing marital status, certainly the time for change has come. Supreme Court decisions in *Griswald* (1965) and *Loving* (1967) may provide the basis for this change in holding that "traditional state control of marriage has to give way to current notions of individual liberty and the right of privacy" (Foster 1968). Further, the Equal Rights Amendment to the United States Constitution would require that the sex-based disabilities imposed by the marriage contract be removed. Hopefully, the law will soon begin to change in accord with these new standards, and in the future family law will allow, rather than thwart, a diversity of alternative family forms.

NOTES

1. In half of the community property states he is given this power by law. In common-law property states it is de facto power.

2. Preliminary data from our research on the impact of the California no-fault divorce law indicate that alimony awards are based primarily on the husband's income and are confined to middle-class families. See also Foster and Freed, 1973.

3. Almost twenty years before this question was raised in court, Elizabeth Cady Stanton wrote to Susan B. Anthony: "I feel, as never before, that this whole question of women's rights turns on the pivot of the marriage relation, and, mark my word, sooner or later, it will be the topic of discussion" (A. Rossi 1973).

4. The court did draw a very fine distinction between these cases and *Labine v. Vincent* (a 1971 case decided between *Levy* and *Weber)* in which the court upheld as reasonable a state intestate succession statute which permitted illegitimate children to inherit only to the exclusion of the state. In *Labine,* the court noted that the father could leave property by will, or legitimize the child, and the state rule was therefore not an unsurmountable bar to the illegitimate child's inheritance.

5. Only thirteen states currently recognize common-law marriage. Most require that both persons *intend* to enter a common-law marriage, cohabit, and hold themselves out as husband and wife (*Massey* and *Warner* 1974). If either person is married there can never be a valid common-law marriage; thus the *Cary-Atherley* doctrine goes much further than common-law marriage.

6. The Berkeley Co-Op now offers a course in preventive legal care for couples in living-together arrangements (so that they may learn to avoid the unwanted effects of the present law). See Massey and Warner (1974) and King (1975), two books of legal advice for unmarried cohabitants.

REFERENCES

A. v. A., 514 P. 2d 358 (Ore. Ct. App. 1973).

Alexander v. Louisiana, 405 U.S. 625 (1972) dicta.

Baker v. Nelson, 191 N.W. 2d 185, MN, (1971).

American Jurisprudence, Second series, 1968, 41.

BASILE, R. A. Lesbian mothers. *Women's Rights Law Reporter* 2, 2, 1974.

BLACKSTONE, WILLIAM. *Commentaries* 1, 1765.

Bradwell v. Illinois, 83 U.S. 130 (1873).

BROWN, BARBARA, THOMAS EMERSON, GAIL FALK, AND ANN FREEDMAN. The Equal Rights Amendment. *Yale Law Journal* 80, 940, 1971.

BROWN, DAVID IRA. The discredited American woman: sex discrimination in consumer credit. *University of California Davis Law Review* 6: 61–82, 1973.

BRUCH, CAROL. Rights of meretricious spouses. Paper presented at the Women and the Law Conference, Palo Alto, March, 1975.

Carlson v. Carlson, 75 Ariz. 308, 256 P. 2d 249 (1953).

In re marriage of Paul A. and Janet E. Cary, 34 C.A. 3d 345, 109 *Cal. Reporter:* 862 (1973).

Citizens Advisory Council on the Status of Women. *The equal rights amendment and child support laws.* Washington, D.C., United States Government Printing Office, 1972.

Citizens Advisory Council on the Status of Women. *Recognition of economic contribution of homemakers and protection of children in divorce law and practice.* Washington, D.C., United States Government Printing Office, 1974.

CLARK, HOMER. *The law of domestic relations.* St. Paul: West Publishing Co., 1968.

Cleveland v. United States, 329 United States 14, 24 (1946).

Cleveland Board of Education v. La Fleur, 414 U.S. 632 (1974).

Davis v. Richardson, 409 United States 1069 (1972).

ECKHARDT, KENNETH. Deviance, visibility, and legal action: the duty to support. *Social Problems* 15: 470, 1968.

Estate of Atherley, 44 Cal. App. 3d 758 (1975).

Estate of Thornton, 88 Wash. 2d 72 (1972).

Forbush v. Wallace, 405 United States 970 (1972).

FOSTER, HENRY. Marriage: a basic civil right of man. *Fordham Law Review* 37: 51, 1968.

————, AND DORIS JONAS FREED. Economic effects of divorce. *Family Law Quarterly* 7: 275, 1973.

————. Marital property reform in New York: partnership of co-equals? *Family Law Quarterly* 8: 169–170, 1974.

Frame v. Frame, 120 Tex. 61, 36 S.W. 2d 152 (1931).

Frontiero v. Richardson, 411 U.S. 677 (1973).

GALBRAITH, JOHN K. The economics of the American housewife. *The Atlantic,* August, p. 78, 1973.

Geduldig v. Aiello, 94 S. Ct. 2485 (1974).

Gomez v. Perez, 409 U.S. 535 (1973).

GOODE, WILLIAM J. *Women in divorce.* New York: Free Press, 1965.

GRANT, ISABELLA. Marital contracts before and during marriage. In *California family lawyer,* Berkeley: Continuing Education of the Bar, 151–160, 1962.

Griswold v. Connecticut, 381 United States 479 (1965).

Holstrom v. Youngberg, 252 Iowa 815, 108 N.W. 2d 498 (1961).

Isaacson v. Isaacson, No.D-36867, Wash. Sup. Ct., Kings City, Dec. 22, 1972.

Kahn v. Shevin 94 S. Ct. 1734 (1974).

KAY, HERMA H. *Sex-based discrimination in family law.* St. Paul: West Publishing Company, 1974.

KANOWITZ, LEO. *Women and the law: the unfinished revolution.* Albuquerque: University of New Mexico Press, 1969.

KING, MORGAN D. *Cohabitation handbook: living together and the law.* Berkeley: Ten Speed Press, 1975.

Ladden v. Ladden, 59 N.J. Super. 502, 158A. 2d 189 (1960).

Lebine v. Vincent, 401 United States 532 (1971).

Levy v. Louisiana, 391 United States 68 (1968).

Loving v. Virginia, 388 United States 1 (1967).

M. v. M., No. 240665, Calif. Sup. Ct., Santa Clara City, June 8, 1972.

MARTIN, DEL, AND PHYLLIS LYON. *Lesbian/woman.* San Francisco: Glide Publications, 1972.

MASSEY, CARMEN, AND RALPH WARNER. *Sex, living together, and the law.* Berkeley: Nolo Press, 1974.

McGuire v. McGuire, 175 Neb. 226, 59 N.W. 2d, p. 336, 352 (1953).

Moreno v. United States Department of Agriculture, 413 U.S. 528 (1973).

Muller v. Oregon, 208 United States 412 (1908).

Nadler v. Superior Court, 225 Cal. App. 2d 523 (1967).

NAGEL, STUART, AND LENORE WEITZMAN. Women as litigants. *Hastings Law Journal* 23: 189–191, 1971.

The National Organization for Women. *Women and credit.* Chicago: N.O.W., 1973.

The National Organization for Women, Task Force on Marriage and the Family. *Suggested guidelines in studying and comments on the uniform marriage and divorce act.* Chicago: N.O.W., 1971.

Omer v. Omer, 11 Wash. App. 386 (1974).

Palo Alto Tenants' Union v. Morgan, 321 F. Supp. 908, N.D. Cal. (1970).

PAPANEK, HANNA P. Men, women; and work: reflections on the two-person career. *American Journal of Sociology* 78: 90–110, 1973.

People v. Brown, 49 Mich. App. 358 (1973).

Phillips v. Martin Marietta. 400 United States 542 (1971).

Reynolds v. U.S., 98 United States 145 (1878).

ROSSI, ALICE. *The feminist papers: from Adams to De Beauvoir.* New York: Columbia University Press, 1973.

Rucci v. Rucci. 23 Conn. Sup. 221, 181 A. 2d 125, Super. Ct. (1962).

Schuster v. Schuster, No. D-36868, Wash, Super. Ct. Sept. 3, 1974.

SKOLNICK, ARLENE. *The intimate environment.* Boston: Little, Brown, 1973.

Stanley v. Illinois, 405 U.S. 645 (1972).

Strauder v. West Virginia, 100 United States 303 (1880).

Stuart v. Board of Supervisors of Elections, 226 Md. 440 (1972).

SUELZE, MARY JEAN. Women in labor. *Transaction.* 8: 50 1970.

United States Department of Labor. *Women workers today.* 1971.

VERNIER, CHESTER G., AND JOHN B. HURLBUT. The historical background of alimony law and its present statutory structure. *Law and Contemporary Problems* 6: 197, 1939.

Villiage of Belle Terre v. Boraas, 94 S. Ct. 1536 (1974).

WALKER, COLQUITT. Sex discrimination in government benefit programs. *Hastings Law Journal* 23: 281, 1971.

WALKER, ALICE, AND WILLIAM GAUGER. *The dollar value of household work.* Ithaca, NY: State College of Human Ecology, 1973.

Weber v. Aetna Cas. and Sur. C., 405 United States 164 (1972).

WEITZMAN, LENORE J. Legal regulation of marriage: tradition and change. *California Law Review* 62: 1169–1288, 1974.

————. Legal equality in marriage: The ERA's mandate for change. Article for Equal Rights Amendment, 1975.

Wirth v. Wirth, 38 App. Div. 2d 611, 326 N.Y.S. 2d 308 (1971).

Youngberg v. Holstrom, 252 Iowa 815, 108 N.W. 2d 498 (1961).

The Origins and Practice of Family Therapy

ELAINE PIVNICK EISENMAN

There were Two Little Bears Who lived in a Wood,
And One of them was Bad and the Other was Good.
Good Bear learnt his Twice Times One
But Bad Bear left all his buttons Undone.
. . .And then quite suddenly (just like Us),
One got better and the Other got Wuss
Good Bear muddled his Twice Times One
But Bad Bear never left his buttons undone.
. . .I think there's a moral, though I don't know what.
But if One gets better as the Other gets Wuss,
These Two Little Bears are just like Us. . . .

A. A. Milne

THIS PERCEPTIVE OBSERVATION ABOVE provides an excellent illustration of the dynamic equilibrium which exists between the members of a family unit. Recent studies of family interaction indicate that it is the reciprocal relationships of the family members which determine individual behaviors. Behavioral change or role alteration in one member will lead to a parallel change in another member; often, as the member who is identified as mentally ill begins to get better, another member will begin to become ill. In such a fashion, the homeostatic balance of the family system is maintained. The adage, "mental illness is when nobody else can stand you," is given meaning when the family is viewed as a living system which, like all living systems, strives to maintain homeostasis. This balance, which in disturbed families is especially fragile, is disrupted when one member's behavior deviates from his or her accepted and expected pattern of behavior without a reciprocal change in another member. When this disruption occurs, the system's regulatory mechanisms must correct the imbalance or the system is in danger of extinction. The functional structure of disturbed families includes ample mechanisms for such contingencies (Framo 1965).

For the purpose of this paper, the term "disturbed families" refers to those families at the extreme end of a continuum beginning with healthy families. In reality, the distance between these two types of families is not as rigid and distinct as one might imagine. There are elements of shared and overlapped behavioral characteristics between both groups; healthy families are not totally healthy nor are disturbed families totally disturbed. The distinction, however, lies in the primary mode of functioning over time. Healthy families are growth-oriented and, as such, are open to change. The relationships between the family members as well as between the family unit and the world is open and fosters free exchange of ideas and concepts. The family is able to cope with conflicts and minor crises and resolve them without the possibility of complete extinction. Role relationships are flexible and complementary and conducive to and supportive of individual growth and strivings toward autonomy and independence. There is a sense of enjoyment and pleasure from relationships between the family members, and the desire for closeness is sought rather than imposed.

Over the past half-century, the development of theories which suggested the role of the family in the development of mental illness have resulted in the initiation of a treatment technique known as family therapy. In order to best understand the practice and rationale for the differing models of this technique, it is first necessary to become familiar with the roots and development of the concept of the disturbed family. This paper will present a broad overview of the major theoretical contributions to the current conception of the family as well as a discussion of the incorporation of these theories into the general framework of the practice of family therapy. **NB:** The reader should recognize that this discussion is necessarily limited, and does not purport to do more than skim the surface of the major concepts in this ever-widening field. The reader is referred to original sources for more indepth discussion of these concepts.

THE CONCEPT OF THE DISTURBED FAMILY

Prior to the formal recognition of the role of the patient's family in the development of mental illness, specifically psychosis, the illness was generally considered to be caused by intrapsychic processes. The problem was the patient's, and the patient's alone; the family of such a person was to be pitied for the heartbreak caused by a mentally ill offspring. Slowly, over the past half-century, clinicians and researchers have recognized that mental illness does not simply occur within an individual without that individual being affected as well as affecting other individuals in his or her immediate environment. Certain characteristics were noticed as common to the great majority of schizophrenic patients as well as characteristics common to their families. Studies were published which indicated that schizophrenic patients who were hospitalized and then sent home to their families regressed more quickly than patients who were sent to boarding houses. Other studies indicated social and cultural differences in the rate of schizophrenia. In regard to these and many comparable findings, the question then arose as to why, if schizophrenia was primarily an intrapsychic phenomenon, such findings could occur.

The initial goals in the studies of the families of schizophrenics were to quantify family characteristics into diagnostic criteria. Yet such a goal was also related to the widely accepted belief that despite the unusual characteristics that the families of schizophrenics might display, their child, the patient, was the only member who was truly disturbed. It is now known that the child's disturbance is but a reflection and symptom of the family's disturbance.

SCHIZOPHRENOGENIC MOTHERS

The path to the present recognition of the family as a system in which if one member is disturbed, all members are disturbed to varying degrees, was a winding but sure path. Through the progression of theories, each family member was held singularly accountable for one member's illness, until the structure of the system as a total interactional unit was awarded collective accountability. The initial focus, after the patient, was on the mother. The earliest studies indicated that schizophrenic patients had mothers who were extremely harsh, domineering, rejecting, yet insecure; the task of parenting the child was totally in the mother's hands. Such a woman was termed schizophrenogenic because it was assumed that she alone was responsible for the genesis of the child's mental illness. In contrast, the father was passive, disinterested, and inadequate in his paternal role (Fromm-Reichman 1948).

EMOTIONAL DIVORCE

The next consideration in the development of the characteristics of the family members was the relationship between the marital pair. An understanding of their relationship was viewed as critical as the governance of the total family is usually dependent upon the parents. In addition, the parents are the earliest source of role identification and socialization. The relationship between the parents of schizophrenic patients was found to be virtually nonexistent. The husband and wife were both inadequate, emotionally immature individuals who were totally isolated from each other in an "emotional divorce" (Bowen 1960). Their marriage represented the joining together of two individuals with severe personality deficits who formed the second generation of a three-generational line necessary for the development of schizophrenia.

This line began with the couple's parents. Both sets of parents were functional yet suffered from moderate developmental gaps which were then intensified in their children. Due to inadequate parenting, neither child was able to master the primary maturational tasks, and the marriage of these grown-up children brought together two adults with serious emotional and maturational impairments. One spouse, usually the mother, overcompensates for her inadequacy by becoming domineering, while her spouse, unable to compete, retreats and intensifies his inadequacy. Neither spouse is able to meet the others needs as their emotional resources are depleted. When their child is born, this child represents the answer to the mother's loneliness and despair. At last she has someone to meet her needs and fulfill her desires; someone who will not disappoint her as her husband has done. Thus, the mother-child relationship becomes paramount in the family. This relationship is based on the mother's projection of her inadequacies onto the child, and then mothering the (perceived) helpless child. Through the symbiosis which develops, the mother's needs are met as are the child's dependency needs (Bowen 1960).

THE FATHER'S ROLE

The father, however passive he may ostensibly appear to be, is not blameless. The failure of this model, in which the mother totally dominates the family, is that it ignores the father's failure to rescue the child from the mother's psychic entrapment. It would appear logical that the father would attempt such a rescue unless he, too, possessed significant pathology to render him unable to provide the positive nurturance necessary for such a rescue. Not surprisingly, the father's role was found to be equal in emotional destructiveness to the mother's. The primary difference lies in the mode of destruction. Early studies (Lidz and Fleck et al. 1965) identified five different types of fathers involved in the development of schizophrenic children. A common thread between all five groups was the absence of a mature and reality-bound self-identity. These men were developmentally incapable of providing positive male role models for their children, just as they were incapable of forming a strong marital relationship with their wives.

SKEWED AND SCHISMATIC RELATIONSHIPS

The relationship between these spouses can be categorized as either "skewed" or "schismatic" (Lidz and Fleck *et al.* 1965). Male schizophrenics are found most frequently in skewed families, while female schizophrenics are found most often in schismatic families. The skewed family can be described as one in which there is no overt conflict, since the most disturbed spouse, usually the mother, dominates the household. Her passive, inadequate mate makes no attempt to intercede. Their schizophrenic child is symbiotically bound to the mother with the requisite blurring of ego boundaries. For the male child, this bonding prevents separation and development of male role identification with the father. A primary result is confusion over sexual and role identity as well as an inability to individuate from the mother.

In contrast, the schismatic family presents as one in which open conflict is the rule. The spouses are separated by their own pathology and, through their mutual mistrust, constantly undercut each other, fostering family divisiveness. Their child, usually female, represents very different needs for each parent. Because the mother is usually unable to accept her own identity, she cannot accept that of her daughter; the child is a threat, resulting in the mother's noninvolvement and emotional aloofness. For the father, the daughter is seen as a source of bolstering his fragile male identity and low self-esteem; thus he acts seductively to his daughter while simultaneously disparaging all women, especially his wife with whom he cannot compete. The daughter then is unable to incorporate a positive and realistic female identity, nor is she able to see herself as other than her father's girlfriend or wife-substitute.

Contrary to prior belief, the other siblings do not grow up unscathed. Preliminary research findings indicate a high degree of personality constriction (Singer, cited in Lidz *et al.* 1971). For the most part, the most seriously disturbed siblings are those of the same sex as the schizophrenic sibling; opposite sex siblings, while limited in various developmental and emotional levels of functioning, appear to escape from the major devastation. Variables which appear to determine the selection of the schizophrenic child include birth position, sex, degree of parental conflict, functional level of each parent at time of child's birth, and prebirth expectations of the parents (Lidz *et al.* 1971).

PATHOLOGIC NEED COMPLEMENTARITY

The requisite of reciprocal relationships in such disturbed families can further be seen through the concept of pathologic need complementarity (Boszormenyi-Nagy 1965). This concept describes the mechanism by which members of the family exist to fill the needs of each other. Each member has a very specific and carefully defined role within the unit and with each other, yet the relationships are not truly reciprocal as no allowance for personal growth is made. Autonomy is not acknowledged, and messages which might lead to differentiation and the meeting of individual needs are selectively disregarded. The schizophrenic child exists in order to fill the holes of the parents deficits; his or her values, beliefs, and identity are totally dependent upon their needs. This situation is almost as if the parental needs were analogized to a board with holes of varying shapes, and the family members were pegs made out of clay. The shape of the peg would then be determined by the shape of the hole into which it was placed. Through such careful fit, there is a deep experience of relatedness among family members, although the relatedness is of a regressive and stagnating nature.

CONFLICT

Despite this close fit, conflict, both internal and external, can occur. For all families, conflict is essential to growth, for it necessitates the continual negotiation and renegotiation of values, beliefs, and goals. One way of exploring conflict, which has special relevance for disturbed families, predicts four possible outcomes (Ackerman 1961). In the first outcome, the conflict is correctly perceived, and an early and rational solution is found. The next outcome would be one in which the conflict is correctly perceived, but it must be contained as its solution is presently unavailable. The third outcome relates to disturbed families, for the conflict is not correctly perceived due to distortion. Because of this distortion, the conflict is inadequately contained for a solution is impossible; irrational acting-out behavior then results. In the final outcome, the family is unable to cope with the failure to adequately control the conflict, and the cumulative effect of repeated failure results in the progressive deterioration of the family.

It is this ability to cope and thus to control conflict which determines whether a family unit is able to grow. A primary failure in the ability to control conflict leads to a requisite increase in anxiety and a reluctance and inability to meet new challenges. Because such a family is then threatened by the unknown, they close themselves off from new experiences which in turn results in their becoming increasingly rigid and stereotypic in their behaviors, and growth is impossible. Through this closing off, the balance of family functions becomes distorted, resulting in a rigidification of some functions with a disproportionate focus of attention on some members over others. Often, this beleaguered family will break into "warring factions" with each side competing for dominance. Through this process, one member becomes the symbolic representation of all that is wrong with the family. Surface unity is regained when a suitable "scapegoat" is designated, and the family can be satisfied with the belief that all would be well if it were not for that one person. (Ackerman 1961)

The attempts of the disturbed family to handle conflict can take different forms. As noted earlier, in growth-oriented, functional families members can express dissatisfaction or anger and can question values and beliefs for a shared set of values is assumed rather than enforced. The sense of shared values can be termed "alignment," while the expression of dissatisfaction can be termed "splits." These experience states vary in degree of intensity between all family members and are not mutually exclusive; there is no sense of total agreement versus total disagreement. (Wynne 1961)

PSEUDO-MUTUALITY

In disturbed families, however, such acceptance of a duality of feeling states is not possible. There can be no questioning of goals, for the fragile balance of the relationships would be endangered, and the resultant conflict could not be adequately contained. These families exist as if a "rubber fence" surrounds them; the structure of the family unit may appear to be open to the influences of the environ-

ment but, in reality, the member who ventures out too far is bounced back into the accepted perimeter. The mechanisms of "pseudo-mutuality" and "pseudo-hostility" describe this process of keeping the unit under control and preventing the members from experiencing conflict or threat (Wynne 1961).

In a family which utilizes the mechanism of "pseudo-mutuality," exploration of the relationships is halted through the blurring or obscuring of the underlying splits. The level and depth of the experience is fixed by a vigilantly enforced surface alignment which prevents the recognition of the implicit threat of greater distance or of greater intimacy.

This mechanism of imposed superficial togetherness can be illustrated by the following example. Every Sunday the Jones family joins together for a large Sunday dinner because "happy families want to eat together on Sundays" and they are a happy family. In actuality, however, Mrs. Jones hates to cook, Mr. Jones would rather watch the ball games on TV, and the children would prefer to go to the movies or spend the time with their friends. Yet, in order to preserve their image as a happy family they are compelled to eat together; no member may voice the desire to do otherwise, for to do so would be to question the happiness of the family unit. Therefore, each member will continue to attend these dinners, while suppressing their anger at being there. Interestingly, the desires of the members are complementary, but they will never know this, as they cannot explore below the surface alignment; the possibility of discovering differences or true similarities is too threatening.

A second mechanism, yet one which achieves the same result, is "pseudo-hostility." Through this mechanism, threat is prevented through a surface split. Here, the confrontation is superficially intense and noisy but the true source of anxiety is effectively covered over. In this way, energy release is achieved, and the family can believe that they have dealt with the issue!

Through the behavioral manifestations of pseudo-hostility, the family will often be seen as constantly bickering over seemingly trivial matters. Inconsequential events assume major import, while major issues are covered over and ignored. All family members are involved in this constant state of argumentativeness. An example of this mechanism would be when a child is extremely late in coming home, and his parents are unable to locate him; they are frantic, but unable to admit to their concern over his safety. Instead, they focus on his disobedience and carelessness. When· he finally arrives home, he is yelled at because he is late, his clothes are dirty, and the dinner is cold. The true source of anxiety, his welfare, is not and cannot be discussed, as the threat of intimacy is too great.

Through the use of these dynamically similar mechanisms, the family's boundaries remained fixed and growth resistant, while the overt anxiety level as well as the ability to deal with stress and threat is diminished.

DOUBLE-BIND THEORY

Within this framework of rigidity, certain distinctive patterns of interaction were discerned. The "double-bind" (Bateson, Haley, Jackson, and Weakland 1968) describes the interactional situation which occurs, preventing the schizophrenic child from learning the correct conceptual skills necessary for true and logical communication. In a double-bind situation the person is literally caught in a "damned if you do, damned if you don't" situation in which he or she cannot win. An example of the communication involved in such a situation might be the mother who serves her son two types of pastry, brownies and cookies. When he finishes them both, he tells her that they were both delicious, and she insists that he have more to eat. He refuses, but finally relents and asks for another brownie; her response is "What's the matter? You didn't like my cookies?!"

There are five requirements for a true double-bind situation to occur. They include (1) at least two people involved in (2) a repeated experience. Also essential is the context of learning as punishment avoidance rather than as reward seeking; this is considered to be (3) the "primary negative injunction", for the person is told either "Do not do so and so, or I will punish you" or "If you do so and so, I will punish you." Next, (4) the "secondary injunction" conflicts with the first on a more abstract level and is enforced by punishment or by signals which threaten survival. This injunction is communicated through nonverbal as well as verbal com-

mands. Here the message is to negate the reality such as "Do not see this as punishment" although it is clearly punishment. The conflict is intensified when one parent sabotages the injunctions of the other parent. Last, (5) a "tertiary injunction" prohibits escape through threat of punishment or promises of love. As the child develops in an environment filled with these conflictual messages, the double-bind situation is totally incorporated to the extent that all communications are ultimately treated as if they too were double-binds. This person then develops a system of metacommunication, or communications about communications. (Bateson *et al.* 1968, pp. 35–36) A simplistic example of a metacommunication might be when one person greets another person who he has not seen in a long time with "Hello, how have things been going for you since I last saw you?" While he is saying this, however, he is continuing to walk by this person. The metacommunication is his disinterest which conflicts with his primary communication of words of concern. In a family situation this communication can be exemplified by a woman who wants to go out to dinner instead of making dinner at home. Instead of asking her husband if he would like to go out to dinner also, or of telling him that she would like to go out to dinner, she begins the day by complaining of a headache and of feeling weak and tired. Throughout the day she develops her presentation of her inability to do tasks around the house, so that when her husband arrives home she is almost totally afunctional. When he does not suggest that they go out to dinner, she becomes furious at him and retreats to her room; he does not know what is wrong, and also retreats. They eat separately, each preparing a separate dinner. Here the metacommunication is her wish to be taken care of by being taken out to dinner. Because this wish is never put into the form of a primary communication, it is not interpreted correctly by the husband. The primary communication is her sudden exhaustion of seemingly unknown origin.

MYSTIFICATION

Also involved in the process of distortion of communication is the act of mystification (Laing 1965). In this process, too, interactions and perceptions are distorted as well as actual issues being blurred.

This blurring occurs when one person mystifies another person by the substitution of false conceptions for true ones. As this process is covert and insidious, the person being mystified does not actually recognize his or her own confusion for he or she may not experience intrapsychic conflict over the issues being altered and obscured; the actual issues may not be recognized. Like the double-bind, this process is one which must constantly be repeated until the patterning is complete. An example of the communication style utilized in this process would be a family in which the parents are always arguing. They do not, however, argue in front of the children, preferring to argue "behind closed doors." One day the daughter says, "You and Daddy woke me up last night when you were yelling at each other. What have you been fighting about so much lately?" The mother replies, "What are you talking about? You didn't hear us arguing because we don't argue. You are imagining it. Daddy and I have a happy marriage and happily married people don't argue." In this situation there is a clash between two people's perceptions as well as the daughter being placed in the position of being obligated not to pursue the issue further for to do so would be to question the happiness of her parents' marriage. When this type of situation is constantly replicated, the daughter would become mystified over her perceptions.

SUMMARY

The preceding discussion has presented the major theories of the disturbed family's structure and interactions. The picture which emerges is that of a virtually closed system in which the schizophrenic child serves a critical homeostatic function. The other members of this system are equally important in the maintenance of homeostasis, as they aid in preventing destruction of the system when conflict and threat impinge on its integrity. Their reciprocal relationships, however, are not truly reciprocal for only very limited types of growth are tolerated and permitted. No personal autonomy or individuation can be allowed since the threat of the potential loss of the members to outside forces is too great. Again, disturbed families and healthy families are on opposite ends of a continuum; there are comparable behavioral elements in both groups. The pri-

mary difference between the two extremes is the pattern of behavior over time. In disturbed families the destructive, growth-retardive behaviors are constantly repeated, while in healthy families they are the exception, since feelings of concern and intimacy as well as of anger can be expressed and worked through successfully.

DEVELOPMENT OF FAMILY THERAPY

Family therapy developed in response to the need for new treatment options which could begin to take into account the research on the dynamics of the disturbed family, as well as to collect more data on the family. If one was to accept the concept that a "sick" person indicated a "sick" family or at the very least a family which suffered a major disturbance in its patterns of interaction, one could not hope to achieve change in an individual who returned daily to this same family without including the family in the change process.

> Family therapy offered family members the opportunity to express warded-off feelings which had heretofore been expressed indirectly or symbolically, often in hurting ways. The actual physical presence of the family members within the therapeutic milieu in which co-therapists made explicit that which had been implicit, facilitated emotional exchanges; the family members were all helped to say things to each other which they had never been able to say before (Boszormenyi-Nagy and Framo 1965).

Thus, family therapy treats the family, not simply a member of the family. The family is viewed as a system which functions collectively through its reciprocal relationships and interpersonal and interdynamic motivations, and singularly through the individual member's intrapsychic conflicts. These multilevel forces are then acted out in the present. In this way, the goal of family therapy is not to save or extricate the identified patient, but rather to open up the family system to a recognition of their potential for growth both as a unit and individually. Also, through family therapy, the family is helped to recognize their affection for one another and to learn new methods of interacting which reflect this caring. Finally, and perhaps most importantly, the family is helped to accept the patient as an integral part of the family, and to acknowledge that his pain is also their pain; similarly they are helped to recognize their culpability in his illness.

SIX THERAPEUTIC FRAMEWORKS

Quite possibly, there are as many ways of practicing family therapy as there are family therapists. At present there are six major therapeutic frameworks. In the first framework, the family is not viewed as the basic unit of treatment, but rather as a reference point; here there are three possibilities: each member has his or her own therapist; each member sees the same therapist individually; one member has a therapist who periodically sees all the other members. This framework, however, is not considered by many clinicians to be "true" family therapy. Next, in dyadic or joint therapy, the therapist sees two family members; marital or couple therapy would most usually be considered in this model, but any two members could constitute the dyad.

Third, conjoint or family group therapy is based upon the application of small-group theory to the functional family group, and focuses on helping the family solve their day-to-day problems in living together (Satir 1964, Bell 1975). A fourth framework, multiple family groups, brings together several families in an attempt to introduce social validation and peer support into the family process (Laquer 1973). Fifth, multiple impact therapy (MIT) provides an intense, highly consolidated therapeutic encounter in which a team of therapists works with the family group over a total three-day period (MacGregor 1971). The sixth framework, which builds on systems theory, is network therapy in which a team of therapists go to the home and assemble all those people who are of significance to the family; this includes neighbors, friends, family, and community representatives. Here, the social network is helped to become the legitimate support system for the family (Speck 1973). Conjoint therapy is the most widely utilized framework for family-centered treatment.

PLACE OF TREATMENT

Just as the framework for the type of practice differs, the place of treatment differs between therapists. Family therapy can really be 'done' anywhere that there is a willing family. While the majority of clinicians use the office as the locus of treatment, treatment can also be undertaken in the home or in the hospital ward as when entire families have been admitted to the hospital for treatment (Bowen 1971). Although many clinicians believe that seeing the family in the home provides too many distractions for both the family and the therapist, the home visit as a means of collecting more objective data is considered extremely valuable. Home visits not only provide the answers to the questions of how space is allocated and utilized, where people sleep as well as where they interact, but also home visits afford the opportunity to observe the family's interactions in their own environment. There is often a great difference in the quality of these interactions outside the artificiality of the neutral office setting. One of the most effective times to observe the process of family interaction is during mealtime, and it is believed that this data is also critical for understanding the family's mode of functioning (Ackerman 1958).

FAMILY ATTENDANCE

In addition to the location for treatment, the question of attendance is also important. Again, there is no one universally accepted answer. Depending on the therapist's theoretical base for practice, the family group can consist of simply the nuclear family or of as many extended family members as the family views as significant to the family's daily living; the family's pets may also be included. Some therapists include all children regardless of age, while other therapists include only older children believing that younger children are unable to truly contribute to the therapy, and provide too many distractions. The extreme number of attenders is found in network therapy where upwards of 35 persons are involved.

TREATMENT TEAM

Similarly, the number of therapists involved in the treatment process varies among therapists. There is a continuing debate over the optimum number of therapists involved. For the most part, in conjoint therapy, one therapist is considered to be the most effective. Having more than one therapist is believed to introduce the probability of the family's division into separate groups, one attached to each therapist, resulting in competition between the groups as well as between the therapists. Also, the problem of diffusion of content between the two therapists is a drawback. This diffusion, specifically of anger, however, can also be considered as a positive outcome of using two co-therapists. The proponents of using more than one therapist believe that more realistic assessment is possible as each therapist can provide ongoing validation of process and role for his or her co-therapist. Also, two therapists working together can provide role models for the family, especially if the therapists are of opposite sexes. **NB**: The cost and availability of family therapists varies according to the area of the country and, often, proximity to family therapy teaching institutes. When two co-therapists practice as a team their fee is not necessarily twice that of one therapist.

THERAPISTS' ROLES

In actuality, the decisions regarding number of therapists, definition of the family unit to be treated, and location for treatment, is based upon both the theoretical orientation and the therapeutic bias of the therapist. Haley (1970) succinctly outlines the choices shaped by these determinants. They include not only the treatment components mentioned above but also the criteria for diagnostic assessment, the definition of therapeutic goals (whether limited to symptom resolution or to effecting change in the family relationship), orientation to conflicting theories of behavior and of therapeutic processes, and the social, cultural, and political biases. He notes further, it "is not surprising that, given these many choices, family therapists tend to polarize and specialize: They intervene on selected aspects of the family phenomenon. And, as might be expected, in the final analysis each does what he likes to do and what he does best" (Haley 1970, p. 445).

This is not to imply that the techniques and practice of family therapy are either capricious or arbitrary. For the most part, the therapist's primary roles are to serve as both a family mediator and family buffer. Depending on the level of therapeutic goals, this role description can expand to include helping the family to interpret and alter their system of communication, to look at their behavior in relation to each other as well as to evaluate their relationships, to expand their perceptions of each other's personality differences and similarities, and to begin to problem solve from a reality base. Thus, therapists' roles may alter from mediator to interpreter to initiator, to problem solver.

CONCLUSION

This discussion has provided a broad overview of the major theoretical contributions for understanding the structure of the disturbed family. The understanding of this structure led to the initiation of a new form of therapeutic treatment, family therapy. Although the early focus of family therapy was primarily on the schizophrenogenic family, the present focus extends to all family groups experiencing difficulty in their interpersonal relationships or day-to-day functioning in society. The practice of family therapy has been important both as a treatment option and as a continuing source of data for further understanding of family dynamics. At present, the three conceptual models for practice are the psychoanalytic model, the psychosocial model, and the general systems model. Each model overlaps, for as yet none is sufficient unto itself. For this reason, just as the boundaries of the healthy family system are always open to change and growth, the practice of family therapy is everchanging and expanding in response to new insights.

REFERENCES

ACKERMAN, NATHAN, *The psychodynamics of family life.* New York: Basic Books, 1958.

_____, The growing edge of family therapy. In Clifford Sager and Helen Singer Kaplan, *Progress in group and family therapy.* New York: Brunner and Mazel, 1972, pp. 440-456.

_____, A dynamic frame for the clinical approach to family conflict. In Nathan Ackerman *et al., Exploring the base for family therapy.* New York: Family Service Association of America, 1961, pp. 52-67.

_____, *Treating the troubled family.* New York: Basic Books, 1966.

_____, Prejudice and scapegoating in the family. In Gerald Zuk and Ivan Boszormenyi-Nagy, *Family therapy and disturbed families.* Palo Alto, Calif.: Science and Behavior Books, 1967, pp. 48-57.

BATESON, GREGORY, DON JACKSON, JAY HALEY, AND JOHN WEAKLAND, Toward a theory of schizophrenia. In Don Jackson (ed.), *Communication, family, and marriage.* Palo Alto, Calif.: Science and Behavior Books, 1968, pp. 31-54.

_____, "A note on the double-bind 1962. In Don Jackson (ed.), *Communication, family, and marriage.* 1, Calif., Science and Behavior Books, 1968, pp. 55-62.

BELL, JOHN E., *Family therapy.* New York: Jason Aronson, 1975.

BOSZORMENYI-NAGY, IVAN, A theory of relationships: experience and transaction. In Ivan Boszormenyi-Nagy and James Framo, *Intensive family therapy.* New York: Harper & Row, 1965, pp. 33-86.

_____, Intensive family therapy as process. In Ivan Boszormenyi-Nagy, Ivan, and James Framo, *Intensive family therapy,* New York, Harper & Row, 1965, pp. 87-142.

_____, Relational modes and méaning. In Gerald Zuk and Ivan Boszormenyi-Nagy, *Family therapy and disturbed families.* Palo Alto, Calif.: Science and Behavior Books, 1967, pp. 58-73.

BOWEN, MURRAY, Family psychotherapy. In John Howells, *Theory and practice of family psychiatry.* New York: Brunner and Mazel, 1971, pp. 843-862.

_____, *A family concept of schizophrenia: the etiology of schizophrenia.* New York: Basic Books, 1960.

FERBER, ANDREW, MARILYN MENDELSOHN, AND AUGUSTUS NAPIER, *The book of family therapy.* Boston: Houghton Mifflin, 1973.

FRAMO, JAMES, Symptoms from a family transactional viewpoint. In Clifford Sager and Helen Singer Kaplan (eds.), *Progress in group and family therapy.* New York: Brunner and Mazel, 1972, pp. 271-308.

_____, Rationale and techniques of intensive family therapy. In Ivan Boszormenyi-Nagy and James Framo, *Intensive family therapy.* New York: Harper & Row, 1965, pp. 143-212.

HALEY, JAY, Whither family therapy? In Jay Haley, *The power tactics of Jesus Christ.* New York: Avon Books, 1969, pp. 99-143.

_____, The art of being schizophrenic. In Jay Haley, *The power tactics of Jesus Christ.* New York: Avon Books, 1969, pp. 147-176.

_____, Family therapy. In Clifford Sager and Helen Singer Kaplan (eds.), *Progress in group and family therapy,* New York: Brunner and Mazel, 1972, pp. 261-270.

HOWELLS, JOHN, Theory and practice of family psychiatry, part I, in John Howells, *Theory and practice of family psychiatry,* New York: Brunner and Mazel, 1971, pp. 3-162.

JACKSON, DON D., (ed.), *Etiology of schizophrenia.* New York: Basic Books, 1960.

_____, The question of family homeostasis. In Don D. Jackson (ed.), *Communication, family, and marriage* 1. Palo Alto, Calif.: Science and Behavior Books, 1968, pp. 1-11.

_____, Family interaction, family homeostasis, and some implications for conjoint family psychotherapy. In Don D. Jackson (ed.), *Therapy, communication, and change* 2. Palo Alto, Calif.: Science and Behavior Books, 1968, pp. 185-203.

_____, Family therapy in the family of the schizophrenic, in Don D. Jackson (ed.), *Therapy, communication, and change* 2. Palo Alto, Calif.: Science and Behavior Books, 1968, pp. 204-221.

_____, and JOHN WEAKLAND, Conjoint family therapy. In Don D. Jackson (ed.), *Therapy, communication, and change* 2. Palo Alto, Calif.: Science and Behavior Books, 1968, pp. 222-248.

_____, AND VIRGINIA SATIR, A review of psychiatric developments in family diagnosis and therapy. In Nathan Ackerman *et al., Exploring the Base for Family Therapy.* New York: Family Service Association of America, 1961, pp. 29-51.

_____, Aspects of conjoint family therapy. In Gerald Zuk and Ivan Boszormenyi-Nagy, *Family therapy and disturbed families.* Palo Alto, Calif.: Science and Behavior Books, 1967, pp. 28-40.

LAING, R. D., Mystification, confusion, and conflict. In Ivan Boszormenyi-Nagy, and James Framo (eds.), *Intensive family therapy.* New York: Harper & Row, 1965, pp. 343-363.

_____, and A. ESTERSON, *Sanity, madness, and the family.* Great Britain: Pelican Books, 1970.

LAQUER, H. P., Multiple family therapy. In Andrew Ferber *et al., The book of family therapy.* Boston: Houghton-Mifflin, 1973, pp. 618-636.

LIDZ, THEODORE et al., Schizophrenic patients and their siblings. In John Howells, *Theory and practice of family psychiatry.* New York: Brunner and Mazel, 1971, pp. 807–818.

———— et al, *Schizophrenics and their families.* New York: International Universities Press, 1965.

MACGREGOR, ROBERT, Multiple impact psychotherapy with families. In John Howells, *Theory and practice of family psychiatry.* New York: Brunner and Mazel, 1971, pp. 890–917.

MILNE, A. A., Twice times. In A. A. Milne, *Now we are six.* New York: E. P. Dutton, 1951.

ROSENBAUM, PETER, *The meaning of madness.* New York: Science House, 1970, Ch. 7.

SATIR, VIRGINIA, Symptomatology: a family production. In John Howells, *Theory and practice of family psychiatry.* New York: Brunner and Mazel, 1971, pp. 663–670.

————, *Conjoint family therapy.* Palo Alto, Calif.: Science and Behavior Books, Inc., 1964.

SPECK, ROSS, Family therapy in the home. In John Howells, *Theory and practice of family psychiatry,* New York: Brunner and Mazel, 1971, pp. 881–917.

————, AND CAROLYN ATTNEAVE, Social network intervention. In Clifford Sager and Helen Singer Kaplan (eds.), *Progress in group and family therapy.* New York: Brunner and Mazel, 1972, pp. 416–439.

————, Network therapy. In Andrew Ferber et al, *The book of family therapy.* Boston: Houghton Mifflin, 1973, pp. 637–665.

WYNNE, LYMAN, The study of intrafamilial alignments and splits in exploratory family therapy. In Nathan Ackerman et al, *Exploring the base for family therapy.* New York: Family Service Association of America, 1961, pp. 95–115.

————, AND MARGARET SINGER, Thought disorders and family relations of schizophrenics. In John Howells, *Theory and practice of family psychiatry.* New York: Brunner and Mazel, 1971, pp. 807–818.

WATZLAWICK, PAUL, A review of the double-bind theory. In Don D. Jackson (ed.), *Communication, family, and marriage* 1. Palo Alto, Calif.: Science and Behavior, 1968, pp. 63–86.

ZUK, GERALD, AND DAVID RUBENSTEIN, A review of concepts in the study and treatment of families of schizophrenics. In Ivan Boszormenyi-Nagy and James Framo (eds.), *Intensive family therapy,* New York: Harper & Row, 1965, pp. 1–31.

Part Two

Within the Family: A Micro–perspective

Chapter 4

Preparation for Marriage– Courtship

FOR FAMILIES TO BE CREATED, A PROCESS must exist to bring future husbands and wives together. This process has a number of dimensions. First, young adults with affect invested in their families of origin must be motivated to transfer some of their involvements and emotions from parents to future spouses. The ideology of romantic love serves this function in contemporary society. This ideology helps channel young adult emotions in the direction of attraction to opposite sex members.

Second, the array of potential future spouses is not composed of societal members at random, but generally consists of members from the same class, ethnic, and racial backgrounds. The implicit rule which attempts to limit potential mates to those of similar social backgrounds is labeled homogamy. Homogamy functions to maintain and perpetuate the differentiation of groups in societies. In traditional societies, parents selected the future spouses of their children by means of arranged marriages. In contemporary industrial societies, parents influence the selection process indirectly: they socialize their children to be attracted to specific types of individuals and place their children in locations where they will meet these individuals—for example, specific schools, neighborhoods, and religious institutions.

Third, the traits desired for the two sexes in the dating process are different and correspond to the roles that they are expected to play as married adults. Males are expected to demonstrate the capa-

city for future occupational and economic achievement, while females are expected to manifest physical attractiveness and emotional support.

Alix Kates Shulman's article describes the dating process in the 1940s and 1950s. She deals with the sports activities of boys that prepared them "for the wins and losses of life" and the interests of girls in clothes, perfume, and makeup that helped them win boys and prepared them for winning and keeping their future husbands. "The War in the Back Seat" was based on a double standard of sexuality that stated that boys had to make sexual conquests to prove their manhood, while girls had to resist sexual advances to remain "nice girls." The quote from the beginning of her article, "In those days, nice girls didn't lead on the dance floor" symbolizes the general position of power that males maintained in the dating situation.

The current dating "market" is analyzed by Judith Richman on the basis of her study of a dating service. She shows that most males and females still desire to date individuals who conform to traditional sex roles. At the same time, a proportion of individuals in the sample supported the Women's Liberation Movement and embraced less differentiated sex roles. She suggests that the traditional "bargaining situation" will not be substantially altered until economic inequality between the sexes in the occupational structure is ended.

The article by Eleanor Macklin describes heterosexual cohabitation among college students, a phenomenon seen as a rejection of the "superficial dating game" described by Shulman and Richman. Here, individuals go beyond the dating symbols of future adult roles by enacting aspects of the actual roles by living together. Macklin deals with the benefits and problems of cohabitation as seen by the participants.

The three sociological perspectives provide frameworks in which to analyze the dating and courtship process. Utilizing a symbolic interaction perspective, the student might consider the ways in which the different aspects of dating help define the identities that the daters will take on as future husbands and wives. How might the process of identity formation involved in Shulman and Richman's dating descriptions differ from the description by Macklin?

From a functional perspective, students might consider the consequences of both traditional, and egalitarian dating patterns for individuals of different class and age groups as well as for men and women. On the basis of Richman's analysis, which groups benefit from the traditional models, and which groups benefit from the egalitarian models?

Utilizing a conflict approach, readers might assess the political significance of the ideology of romantic love. Shulamith Firestone, in "The Dialectic of Sex," has suggested that a healthy love relationship is impossible in a society in which women are economically dependent on men, and relegated to family roles.[1] In terms of a conflict model, how do the articles on dating and courtship illustrate Firestone's statement? What perpetuates inequality in dating relationships? Are there potential sources for change?

Readers might also evaluate the three articles together by considering how dating has evolved from Shulman's description of the 1940s and 50s through Macklin's description of contemporary cohabiters. Has inequality between the sexes increased, decreased, or remained the same?

NOTE

1. Shulamith Firestone, *The Dialectics of Sex*. New York: William Morrow, 1970, pp. 126-145.

The War in the Back Seat

ALIX KATES SHULMAN

In those days, nice girls didn't lead on the dance floor, or...

THE REVIVAL OF THE FORTIES AND FIFties is upon us. That Middle-American time of my youth is gaining its place in our historical imagination. Movies, essays, stories, novels, and the sheer passage of time have already begun transforming that era from banal to exotic. The record is being filled not only with nostalgia but with critical insight, as writing men of wit try to pin down those days. Nevertheless, something crucial is missing, for the reality being recorded about that era is essentially a male reality, the experience a male experience. And until the female side is acknowledged and recorded, the era cannot even begin to emerge in perspective.

Richard Schickel, in a recent essay entitled "Growing Up in the Forties," tries to elicit the factors that shaped Middle-American adolescence. After discussing sports (baseball and football, activities from which the female sex was barred) as "Middle America's only universal metaphor," he goes on to describe with regret those painful scenes in the back seats of parked card where sex was meted out piecemeal. "The curve of a breast briefly explored by two sly fingers making their way ...through some interstice in a girl's clothing," runs his plaintive lament—"Oh, God, was this to be all, forever?" It is a lament endlessly repeated in most of the documents about those times. Gilbert Sorrentino's story "The Moon in Its Flight," Dan Wakefield's *Going All the Way*, Frederick Exley's *A Fan's Notes*, Philip Roth's *When She Was Good*, the screen's recent *Summer of '42, Carnal Knowledge*, and *The Last Picture Show*—however widely they may vary in tone, intent, subtlety, and success, all portray a monolithic male experience in which the War, movies, athletics, and the burden of sex denied emerge as the shaping forces of adolescent life, and girls, when presented at all, are the "problem."

The settings of my memories are frequently the same. Growing up in Ohio in the forties, I too was affected by those irresistible forces. Girls sat in the same movie theaters, attended the same football games, struggled in the back seats of the same parked cars. But the view from the bleachers is very different from the one on the field; and whether we gave in or held out in those parked cars, we had more fearsome concerns than simply making out. We were concerned with survival.

Our experience was no less important, our feelings no less urgent. Yet for some reason, only male versions have been recorded. Well, it certainly won't be the first time we were left out of the chronicles. Even back then it was the boys who delivered the graduation speeches; boys who got their pictures in the paper for football, win or lose; boys who, claiming the American privilege of free speech, spread slanderous things about us to boost their ratings. And the girls? The girls, when we were not simply ignored, were too often driven against our will to some dark lonely street where we were badgered or sweet-talked into going one step further than intended, and afterwards were frightened into silence. Only now are we beginning to speak.

Well, then—what was it like out there in a white middle-class suburban girl's Ohio in the cold decade between 1942 when I turned ten and 1952 when I turned twenty? What were we doing after school while the luckier boys were in varsity practice and the others were fielding high flies bounced off their garages? What were we feeling as we sat captive in our bedrooms waiting for our myriad pin curls to dry, the "Hit Parade" playing in the background? What forces, comparable in magnitude and significance to the War and athletics, shaped our emerging consciousness and thus our destiny? What was it like among the bobby-soxers? In the bleachers? In the passenger seat of those borrowed cars in which boys drove us around and all too soon ruined everything by trying to feel us up?

In the early years of that decade we got together after school in each other's houses to talk about movie stars and play Monopoly, or to dress up in our mothers' clothes, jewelry, high heels, and lipstick, pretending we were seventeen going out on dates. If I couldn't ignore the sounds with which my brother filled up our house—his roar in the winter, his baseball games blasting on the radio in the summer—I tried to drown them out with my records of the Voice, over whom I actually "swooned"—my sexual initiation.

By the middle of the decade, wearing by then my own ruby lipstick, I got together with my friends in larger groups ("clubs," we called them in junior high, finding "sorority" too pretentious, though we gave our clubs Greek letter names), where we practiced for our futures by dancing among ourselves to the latest Big Band releases, leading and following by turns, and sometimes even practiced kissing.

After school I hung around the drugstore sipping nickel pop, or, sitting entranced in a listening booth of the local record store, tried to determine whose version of a recent hit was the best one out. I doodled certain initials on my notebooks, passed compromising notes in study hall, consulted a ouija board about chancy matters, whispered, knitted argyle sox in class for a constantly changing secret someone until the teacher made me stop.

In the evenings when my radio programs were over, my share of the dishes done, my homework finished, my hair set in pin curls for the night, I confided in each of my girl friends on the telephone until my parents exploded. When I was sure nothing more could happen that day, I spilled my surging feelings to my five-year lockup diary, the very form of which led directly into the future. And once in bed, I would not surrender to sleep until the last possible moment, but listened to the radio I kept beside my pillow, memorizing the lyrics of every love song, the inflections of every vocalist, and the arrangements of every instrumental. Living for music and love.

Some of us were happy in love, more of us were sad—but in either case we lived for the next climatic installment of our own true romance, be it a rumor, a look, a word, or an actual date. It might come unexpectedly in a corridor between classes, or by careful design on a weekend—at the Saturday afternoon picture show, at our occasional Saturday night pajama parties, or at our mixers following school basketball or football games. Even if we loved no boy at all, we might fake it or boost a friend's romance in order to have material on which to base a whole new week's conspiracy and something to enter in our tear-smeared diaries. In lean times, we dedicated songs on the air, through the medium of snickering disc jockeys, to unsuspecting boys. ("Our songs," we called them, though we listened alone.)

On Friday nights, boys or no, we attended our club meetings wearing each other's borrowed sweaters over Peter-Pan collared dickies and pleated-all-round skirts in specified combinations (pink and maroon, baby blue and royal, cherry and white for a start), shod in saddle shoes or penny loafers. Brands mattered. Some of us kept our bobby sox up with colorless nail polish, others, ignoring our mothers' warnings about cutting off our blood circulation, kept them up with rubber bands. Sitting on the floor in one another's living rooms (with our hair still in pin curls, to be combed out only moments before the meeting ended and the boys arrived), we planned "affairs"—hayrides, sleighrides, movie parties, turnabout dances—to which we might legitimately invite the boys. Glorious 1944 and 1948: the leap years of my youth.

Oh, those clothes! We tried them on for hours in department stores, we changed our outfits repeatedly before each date. In the only novel I have seen by a woman covering approximately that era,

Patricia Dizenzo's *An American Girl*, some of the most evocative passages are those in which the narrator describes the clothes.

> If I had the money I would have bought a royal blue wool jumper...a maroon skirt to wear with a white sweater, a black and white plaid pleated wool skirt to wear with a long-sleeved red sweater, a black-watch plaid skirt to wear with a white or navy sweater, a gray wool straight skirt to wear with....

And more, more. I remember Teddy Bear coats, the New Look, White Shoulders perfume, pointy Whirlpool bras (not infrequently improved with cotton stuffing), Ipana smiles, eyelash curlers. We had to sharpen our wits and reward our bodies with something, we who never knew the joy of football!

And can there really have been nothing more for us than clothes, dancing, music, boys?

Alas, there really was nothing more. Little else was permitted. Just as the boys practiced tackling and developed game plans to prepare them, as Schickel says, for "the wins and losses of life, especially the former," we prepared for the only thinkable future available to us: marriage. Even the vocational counselors who took over Heights High School two days per semester hinted that the kind of secretarial position we ought to apply for—legal stenographer, dental assistant, executive secretary—should be keyed, respectively, to the kind of husband we hoped to nab; unless we were so unimprovably plain that we needed some more permanent vocation to "fall back on"—in which case, if we were "college caliber," we were urged to train as teachers, librarians, nurses, or dieticians.

In my own brief, sheltered life I had already seen how far one could go as a secretary. Ever ambitious, I had gone from band secretary (handing out the music) to homeroom secretary (handing out homework) to nurse's aid (handing out hall passes) to running for the highest female office in the school: school secretary. When I lost, I ended my secretarial career.

We did sometimes go out for drama, for glee club, for art, for debating, piano, class politics, or even cheerleading (to this day I have yet to hear of a cheerleader scholarship to college); but the life they prepared us for was marriage, for that is the sum of what, for most of us, life consisted. As in later years when men may have positions and families while women have only families, so in high school boys had football and love while we had only love. When we cheered, we cheered the boys; whatever hobby we cultivated, it too led ultimately down the aisle.

By the end of the decade we were openly and frankly discussing the subject, with all its pitfalls and implications. What kind of husband did one want? What kind of wedding? How many children? How many bridesmaids? And trickiest of all—the part that gave us the heebie-jeebies—how in the world to snare one? For it was common knowledge that boys (who, with snowballs in winter and dunkings in summer, gave daily evidence of despising us) sought to avoid, or at least postpone, marriage as eagerly as we sought to achieve it. It was no secret. The entire culture conspired to show that life was a battle of the sexes: *them* against *us*. We knew, of course, that the boys would marry eventually; the question was, Could we get them to marry *us*? As Schickel observes, "It never occurred to us that there was some link between these [pinup] photos and the girls in school or the girls we passed in the streets," and that fact was readily apparent. How get them to notice us without ruining our chances by putting out? Wakefield succinctly captures the predominant male attitude toward marriage, at least as it was expressed by Middle-American boys: "With the talk of marriage his prick had gone soft" (the very talk that held some promise of arousing us). Or, again: "Shit, he wouldn't get married. He was getting laid all over Chi." Such an attitude was simply impossible for a girl. In other places and other years a girl might manage to use sex to *get* a spouse (in *The Last Picture Show*, for example), but never, never to escape from one.

To snag a man. It was for that final, apocalyptic maneuver that I, like my sisters, wound up before the three-way mirror (as limiting as blinders and confining as a cage) practicing batting my eyes like Hedy Lamarr, flashing a smile like Betty Grable, wringing my hands like June Allyson, and night after night, equipped with comb, a glass of water for dipping, rubber-tipped bobby pins and metal clips, and a large triangular hairnet, setting my hair according to the instructions in every new issue of

Seventeen magazine. As it was impossible for us to make our mark upon the world (except, eventually, through offspring), we had nowhere to make it but on ourselves. The mark to make and how to make it was all spelled out for us in every document of female adolescence: if our faces were round, we set our pin curls in one direction, if our jaws were square we set them in another. But no matter how we started out, if we studied the magazines and the movies and each other carefully enough, we could come up with the perfect formula for enhancing our assets.

Back in the early days, I confess, I wanted more. I remember pledging my daily allegiance to our 48-star flag with such ardor that my voice quavered and brought me ridicule. When the War started, I collected old newspapers and flattened tin cans with as much enthusiasm as my brother. And as a young teen-ager, I dreamed of getting a factory job—as much for the daring and glamour of it as for productivity and patriotism. But by that time my parents had only to convince me that, despite Veronica Lake and Rosie the Riveter, nice girls didn't work in factories (even though nice boys did) to induce me to abandon the ambition. Just as nice girls didn't wear too tight skirts, or stockings to school, or their hair upswept.

In fact, the older we got, the longer grew the list of inviting things that nice girls didn't do. (*Nice Girl*?, with Deanna Durbin, was the first adult movie I ever saw. And though I didn't understand it at the time, I accepted the fact that the phrase "nice girl" would always be followed by a question mark.) Nice girls didn't smoke on the street. Nice girls didn't kiss on the first date. Nice girls didn't lead on the dance floor. Nice girls didn't curse (or allow cursing in their presence). Except to ask an opening question about sports, nice girls didn't take the initiative in conversation. Nice girls didn't show they were smart, speak out of turn, laugh at risqué jokes, hang around the football field or the pool hall, go unaccompanied to bowling alleys, dance halls, movies, beaches, skating rinks—anywhere, really, except to two or three specified restaurants. Nice girls didn't wear their heels the wrong height, their sweaters without slips, the wrong kind of bras, their hair the wrong style. Nice girls didn't talk to boys to whom they hadn't been introduced, clinch too long with boys to whom they had, and more important still, talk to girls who weren't nice girls.

With such a list of prohibitions—and plenty more coming up behind—who wouldn't want to light out like Huck and every other red-blooded American boy for the territories? Or at least go off on a weekend tear? But unfortunately, nice girls didn't do that either. Nice girls didn't even stay out after midnight unchaperoned.

And if we did? If, out of some adventurous spirit or sexual desire that managed to survive the poison of our puberty, we did break the rules—what happened then? We risked nothing less than our futures. A few lucky ones (I have met two or three), finding boys they could trust, actually managed to have good sex—a miracle, considering how dangerous a game they played. But for the rest of us, even the possibility of good sex disappeared before the specter of what we might be losing. For we risked losing the one asset that kept us listed on the Big Board in the Marriage Market—"respect"—and getting instead the one that scratched us off— a "reputation." And once that occurred, a girl turned from a nice girl, who at least had the right (as well as the duty) to protest a boy's sexual advances, into a "real girl," against whom anything went. According to conventional wisdom, ridicule was the least she deserved, but even rape, particularly if done in a gang, was forgivable.

The hero of Exley's *A Fan's Notes* relates the circumstances of his sexual initiation:

> My initiation into sex had taken place on the ground behind a billboard sign advertising beer....The girl had received, with neither complaint nor enthusiasm, a good part of Watertown High School's 1945 football team. Afterward I had had to help her up and walk her, while she clung unsteadily to my arm and wept, to her house some distance down the highway.

In Wakefield's novel a slightly different sort of group spirit is shown to operate against the girl with a reputation:

> ...whatever happened to Donna Mae Orlick [?]

Big Quinn hooted and slapped his knee. "Married," he said. "Settled down. Can ya picture it?"

"How'd it happen?" Gunner asked, in the tone of a man inquiring about a great pianist who had lost his fingers.

"Some guy from Terre Haute knocked her up. She had a pie in the oven, and the guy married her."

"Shit," Gunner said, "couldn't he have got three witnesses to testify?"

It was said that if a girl got pregnant and you could get three other guys to testify they had fucked her, too, there was some law that said you didn't have to marry her because she was a loose woman or something....

"Buddy, you talk about three—he could of got three hundred," Big Quinn said. "But the guy was from Terre Haute. He didn't know."

In Philip Roth's *When She Was Good*, the hero, Roy Bassart, speculates about the possibilities of getting into a cheerleader, Ginger Donnelly:

> This fellow named Mufflin...said that his friends over in Winnisaw told him that at a party across the river one night, back in Ginger's freshman year...she had practically taken on the whole Wannisaw football team. The reason nobody knew about it was because the truth was immediately suppressed by the Catholic priest, who threatened to have all those involved thrown in jail for rape if even one of them opened his mouth.
>
> It was a typical Mufflin story, and yet some guys actually believed it—though Roy wasn't one.

In fact, the image of the "real girl" who winds up "taking on the entire team" turns up again and again in male books about Middle America in that era. Whether she existed or not (and in either case, it was certainly not we who created her), she was always there in our consciousness, the terrible threat, the living alternative to being "good." No wonder, then, that my most intense memory of adolescence is that anxious moment in the back seat of the car (one scenario, many actors), after my lipstick has been smeared and my hair irreparably mussed, yet before my "please stop now" has been overruled, turning a promising intimacy into an anxious struggle.

It was the boys who put us in those compromising positions (we never asked to be driven to those dark streets), the boys who decided whether or not they would tell (we always begged them not to), the boys who imposed our dilemmas, knowing perfectly well what would happen to us if they went too far. Then why is it that men writing about the forties and fifties so frequently misunderstand our concern with our reputations? Some of them, like Exley, find it mean and contemptible, some find it silly, dog-in-the-manger, or simply misguided. But few understand it as a survival response; few allow the legitimacy of our fears. To most of them it is simply the unfortunate source of their bad sex. Even in such a generally sympathetic story as Sorrentino's sensitive "The Moon in Its Flight," it is assumed that girls desire sex as much as boys, that it was only social circumstances or blind allegiance to a code that kept us apart.

But the fact is, for many of us who grew up in those days, once we understood the real consequences of indulging in sex, sex became a genuinely horrifying thing, not desirable at all. Even if it could have been practiced with finesse, which under the circumstances was hardly possible, who among us could have abandoned herself to it happily, knowing the consequences? When we said no, when we struggled to get the boys' hands off our breasts, when we crossed our legs in rigid rejection of those ubiquitous probing fingers, it was not because we were blindly, stupidly accepting some code handed down by our mothers. Our concern with virginity was not something we learned, as Schickel suggests, at the movies; not some gleeful conspiracy among us to deny boys their pleasure or some perverse way to titillate. It was hardly a matter of "pleasure" at all. The question of pregnancy quite aside, we learned to ignore our reputations at our peril because of the sanctions that *they* imposed upon *us*—sanctions so damaging to our sexuality that many of us never managed to recover. Like the characters in the Feiffer-Nichols movie *Carnal Knowledge*, boys made it quite clear to us that there were certain kinds of girls they simply would not care to marry. In the cliché of the period, we had "nothing to gain and everything to lose" from submitting—as they had the very opposite. Nor was it a simple double standard we had to contend with; it was an inverse one, whereby, diabolically, we lost to the extent that they won, and vice versa. And worse: for if they lost, if they failed to "score" or even get, as they so blatantly analogized, to "first base," they were always free to try it again next inning. At best they wasted an evening's effort. But if one of us lost, we risked losing for good; once we gave in, we could never again expect our protests to be heeded.

Why did we cling to our reputations? As the fox who failed to catch the hare explained, "I was running for my dinner, but he was running for his life." Perhaps if we had been permitted access to some of life's touted rewards through other routes than sex and marriage; perhaps if the boys had been happy to marry us despite our reputations; perhaps if they had known how to keep their mouths shut or offered us reasonably good sex, we might then have been tempted to relent a little. But instead they offered us battle and frequently contempt. Not even nice girls were safe from it. "Where I had come from," says the narrator of *A Fan's Notes*,

> seducing a "nice" girl was hard work. In the back seat of wintry cars one chewed on lower lips for longer periods of time than starlets cohabit with producers. One moved lower then, leaving a trail of perfumed saliva on ears and necks along the way, coming to plant already swollen lips on wool-sweatered nipples...meeting convulsive, furious hands all the way....Even if one did make it...one didn't dare look down in fear of seeing a half-dressed, broken-bra'ed, bedraggled, pimply, snot-nosed, shivery-assed creature feigning for conscience-inducing sleep, trying not to moan.

On balance, given the circumstances, I think we did well to fight them. When Betty Grable in some old movie of the forties whacked Don Ameche across the face for trying to kiss her, I think she probably had the appropriate impulse for the period.

In a recent issue of *Esquire* with a supplement on the forties and a Petty Girl swinging on the cover there is the statement: "The Forties were—well, *natural*, without pretense or guile."

Without pretense or guile? Boys among themselves, perhaps, where we could not overhear them (*Esquire* should know); in the locker room or the barracks maybe; but between boys and girls, as I recall, it was primarily pretense and guile. In fact, one reason we have such a hard time getting the story straight about those days is that evidently no one ever told the truth. About the thing that mattered most for us, our reputations, there were only lies. Whatever the boys did with the girls, they claimed to have done more; at the very least it was kiss and tell. ("It was really pretty much of a failure," says the narrator of *Going All the Way*, "if you parked with a girl and got only covered-tit, and sometimes when Sonny just got covered-tit he actually lied if anyone asked and said he got bare-tit.") As for us, whatever we did or we didn't, we denied everything all the same.

Without pretense or guile? From *A Fan's Notes:*

If we were lucky . . . we ended in the sack with some long-legged, energetic, none-too-bright airline hostess who afterward wept while we assured her of our undying devotion, even as we plotted how to get rid of the creep.

From *Going All the Way*:

She thought Gunner's name was Ron. That was for safety, so if you ever knocked up one of those broads, they couldn't track you down. That's why Gunner introduced Sonny as "George."

And even the young Catcher in the Rye, Holden Caulfield, Mr. Guileless-Charm himself, whose life was devoted to eschewing the "phony," whose dream spot was a cabin in the woods where "if anybody tried to do anything phony, they couldn't stay"—even Holden confesses to the usual equivocal back-seat-of-the-car hanky-panky:

At first she didn't want to, because she had her lipstick on and all, but I was being seductive as hell and she didn't have any alterna-

tive. . . . Just to show you how crazy I am, when we were coming out of this big clinch, I told her I loved her and all. It was a lie, of course, but the thing is I *meant* it when I said it. I'm crazy. I swear to God I am.

And maybe Roy Bassart meant it too, in Philip Roth's spectacularly accurate parked-car scenes in *When She Was Good* (a book which, though widely hailed as the definitive portrait of the Great American Bitch, seems to recognize, even to understand, the Middle-American girl's plight—and yet still manages to blame her for all the awful consequences):

There [at Passion Paradise] Roy would turn off the lights, flip on the radio, and try with all his might to get her to go all the way.

"Roy, I want to leave now. Really."

"Why?"

"I want to go home, please."

"I sort of love you, you know that."

"Don't say that. You don't. . . ."

In the back he told her how much he could love her. He was pulling at her uniform buttons.

"Everybody says things like that when they want what you want, Roy. Stop. Please stop. I don't want to do this. Honestly. Please."

"But it's the *truth*," he said, and his hand, which had touched down familiarly on her knee, went like a shot up her leg.

"No, *no*—"

"Yes!" he cried triumphantly, *"Please!"* . . .

"Roy—!"

"But I love you. Actually now I do." . . .

[And a little later:] "You say love," Lucy said. "But you don't mean love."

"I get carried away, Lucy. That's not a lie. I get carried away, by the mood. I like music, so it affects me. So that's not a 'lie.' "

Yes, even Richard Schickel, in whose innocence I believe and with whose longings I sympathize—even he will have to admit there was something less than guileless and certainly less than understanding going on in the parked cars where he and his friends hoped that "somehow in our paw-ings, pleadings and arguments we would stumble upon the magic combination of verbal and (shall we say?) subverbal appeals that would loosen the hold that virginity as a concept" had upon girls.

Most of the writers and directors who have been reconstructing the forties and fifties for us have kept a certain distance from their period char-acters; they are clearly moved by something other than nostalgia. Those were not pretty times, and most of the writers who survived them seem to want to expose them. Feiffer's protagonists in *Car-nal Knowledge* are shown to be the same sexual bullies as the boys I remember. The grim adolescent sex scenes in Bogdanovich's *The Last Picture Show*—hands rigidly clapped on thigh or breast without passion, much less tenderness, the very opposite of caresses—are remembered rightly with bitterness. Nevertheless, the girls are still pre-sented neither with sympathy nor understanding. Somehow, when the stories are all over, when the callowness and conformity, elitism and racism of the time and place have been exposed and decried, the girls still come off looking like cock-teasers and ballbusters, or else, in the most cutting insult of the period, "beasts." In all those documents of the time of my youth, whether movie, essay, story, or novel, in those crucial battles in the back row of the movie house or on the floor in the living room or out be-hind the backstop or in the darkened back seat of a parked car—those scenes which are the very essence of pretense and guile—the girls somehow always wind up the culprits, bitchy or ridiculous, damned if they do and damned again if they don't.

It is that scene, with all its variations, that for me stands out as the paradigm of the era, as "Mid-dle America's universal metaphor." Not sports (no, forgive me, boys, not even football, without which, says Exley, life would have been inconceivable); not dancing, though at least that activity was open to both sexes and conformed in important respects to life's larger expectations (Holden Caulfield, the nicest sixteen-year-old boy in America says: "Do you know when a girl's really a terrific dancer?...If I think there isn't anything underneath my hand—no can, no legs, no feet, no *anything*—then the girl's really a terrific dancer"); not yo-yoing, for which Frank Conroy in *Stop-Time* (as well as Abbie Hoffman in *Esquire*) makes such an inspired case. Not the Army, not the movies, not Captain Mid-night or the Shadow. No. But if the Battle of Water-loo, as Wellington claims, was won on the playing fields of Eton; if the fate of Indochina, as Schickel suggests, was set on the scrimmage lines of Whit-tier, California; then the destiny of the female half of Middle America in times gone by was settled in the dirty back seat of some parked car as the male half relentlessly tried to score.

Bargaining for Sex and Status: The Dating Service and Sex-role Change

JUDITH RICHMAN

IT HAS OFTEN BEEN SUGGESTED THAT the mainstream 19th-century feminist movement brought about only limited alterations in the female role because it could not go beyond legal issues—in particular—the quest for female suffrage. In contrast, the current feminist movement has addressed itself to much broader normative and structural issues. Marlene Dixon (1971) has suggested that:

> the most original and creative politics of the current womens' liberation movement has come from a direct confrontation with the issue of marriage and sexuality...from the revolt against dehumanized sexual relationships, against the role of women as sexual commodities....

This paper is concerned with one area of male-female relationships that has been affected by the feminist movement: the differentiation of roles in the institution of dating.

Sociologists of marriage and the family have viewed the process whereby single males and females interact socially with each other and eventually choose mates in Western societies as a bargaining situation. (Goode 1963, 1964; Scanzoni 1972) This bargaining situation, according to Goode, involves certain characteristics which are highly valued, individuals having differential degrees of control in striking the bargains, and certain rules by which the agreements are made. One basic rule Goode explicitly dealt with was that of homogamy: individuals dated and married others from similar class, ethnic, and racial backgrounds. However, he also added, "There is a rough equality in the exchange: a girl of great charm or beauty may be able to move entirely outside the marriage market in which she was born, exchanging her qual-ities for money and prestige" (Goode, 1963). He was implicitly suggesting that the bargaining situation involves one set of attributes that are highly evaluated with respect to males and a different set of attributes that are highly evaluated with respect to females. In another work, Goode clearly illustrated this differential rating of the two sexes. He suggested that when a woman's beauty enables her to marry a man of higher class status, the marriage is viewed as an appropriate exchange. However, if a rich woman marries a man of low-class status because he is handsome, it is deemed highly inappropriate (Goode, 1964).

In *Silent majority*, Westley and Epstein (1969) spelled out the differential attributes that they saw as being highly evaluated for each sex:

> The qualities that boys and girls seek in each other are predictive of those they will seek in marriage. Girls generally boast of the social skills and status characteristics of their dates—their dancing, their cars, and the places they went. Boys boast of the physical appearance, social skills, and cooperativeness of the girls. Later, when they marry, girls are said to make a good marriage when they marry a successful or up-and-coming man, boys when they marry a beautiful girl. To some degree, then, the attributes of a successful marriage (from the girls' viewpoint) can be translated into social status.

Revised version of a paper presented at the Annual Meeting of the New York State Sociological Association, October, 1974. The author would like to thank Naomi Gerstel, Mary Lennon and Peter Stein for comments on an earlier draft. © Judith Richman, 1976.

Goode, and Westley and Epstein have depicted the differential attributes that men and women have traditionally been socialized to desire in each other. However, in recent years the current feminist movement has pushed for sexual equality. In addition, structural changes have occurred in the recent past in the United States involving a large increase in the movement of women, including married women, into the labor force (Degler 1964; Hoffman and Nye 1963). By 1968, more than 40 percent of women sixteen years of age and over were in the labor force (Ginzberg 1971). Thus, the female role has become more similar to that of the male. The question then arises: has the traditional bargaining situation between the sexes been altered or has it remained the same?

To deal with this question, the author did "participant observation" (verbally, by phone) in the operation of a New York City dating service during the fall of 1972. This paper describes and analyzes the set of attributes that women and men viewed as desirable in themselves and in the opposite sex within the context of the dating institution. In addition, it examines the social characteristics of those individuals embracing either traditional or changing sex-role orientations in order to theorize about the process of sex-role change.

THE SAMPLE

To empirically study the existence and degree of differential attributes highly desired currently in males and females, I assumed the role of dating service operator and talked by phone to the men and women that phoned the dating service. These individuals had answered an ad in the *Village Voice* or the *Jewish Press* to "meet somebody on your own wavelength."

In respect to the comparability of this particular sample with the general population, the women in this sample were slightly older, the percentage of Jews was higher, and the sample was almost entirely white. In terms of psychological characteristics, it is difficult to determine the comparability since little research has been done on the psychological characteristics of users of "bureaucratic" modes of access to dating. This group may be some-

what deviant in that the use of a dating service involves a degree of social stigma. However, various sociologists have discussed the general difficulty that singles in large urban environments have in meeting others they desire to interact with on a social basis. Starr and Carns (1972) concluded in their analysis:

First, the popular image of the "swinging singles" spawned and nurtured by the media is clearly false. There is little in the bars to attract these people... they are people coping with the same problems we all face "finding a place to live, searching for satisfaction from their jobs, and seeking friends, dates, and ultimately mates in an environment for which they have been ill-prepared and which does not lend itself to the formation of stable relationships."

Though Starr and Carns were describing the experiences and environment of young college-educated singles in the city, it is conceivable that they might apply to older individuals of different educational backgrounds and to the previously married. Thus, given the structural barriers to social interaction in large cities, psychologically and attitudinally, the users of dating services may not differ radically from a general population. In support of this assumption, a comparison of some of the findings in this study will be made with those of a 1973 national study of Daniel Yankelovich.

METHODOLOGY

When individuals called the dating service, I asked them questions involving the following background characteristics: age, religion, race, educational background, occupation, political orientation, and marital status. I then asked a series of open-ended questions in the following manner: (1) Tell me about yourself: what you are like, your personality, interests, or anything else you consider important about yourself. (2) What age group of men/women would you like to meet? (3) Give me an idea of what you consider to be your ideal date: what qualities in a man/woman are most important to you? and (4) How do you feel about the Women's Liberation Movement as it affects your own relationships? For example, do you think that one person should play a more dominant or aggressive role in a relationship?

The sample of individuals that I spoke to over the phone included 59 persons: 27 females, and 32 males. This sample consisted of all the persons who called the dating service on a Wednesday or Thursday over a four-week period. I gained, in addition, a general summary of the sex-role attributes desired by over 1000 individuals from my informant, the dating service owner.

FINDINGS

1. Female Responses

Of the 27 women, ranging from the age of 17 to 64, with the median age in the mid-30s, over half desired to meet men who had attained high achievement and status in their occupations. Comments were made such as: "he has to be a professional or businessman with a good job," "I prefer a doctor or a lawyer," "makes a nice living," "comfortably situated financially," and "has a good position." Most of these women also mentioned expressive or intellectual qualities and about half mentioned qualities pertaining to physical appearance. The types of expressive qualities were: "good moral character," "good personality," "a sense of humor," "outgoing," "unpretentious," "a comfortable person," "fine character," "sincere," "kind", and "likes himself." The qualities dealing with physical appearance about equally included height-weight and general attractiveness ("good-looking"). Only one female referred to sexuality or sexual characteristics in describing desired traits in males. Intellectual qualities were mentioned in the following way: "bright," "interesting," or "intelligent." The women who failed to mention the criterion of high occupational status stressed the expressive qualities already mentioned or "similar interests." Almost all of the women in the sample desired to meet men who were older than they were. The desired ages extended up to 15 years or older.

In response to the question that involved the self-concepts that the women were bringing into the bargaining situation, 44 percent (12) of the female respondents first labeled themselves on the basis of their physical attributes and generally emphasized

them. Eleven women claimed that they were attractive and one woman said that she did not look her age. The other qualities mentioned by these women were expressive ones such as "understanding," "friendly," "personable," "honest," and "sensitive." The other women also described themselves in terms of their physical attributes and expressive qualities. Only two women mentioned intelligence as a quality descriptive of themselves, with one referring to it in an inverse manner—by labeling herself as "not stupid". Three women referred to their personalities in terms normatively viewed as undesirable. One claimed that she was "hard to get along with, high-strung, and impatient." Another woman stated that she was "uncomfortable among people and socially backwards in some ways." The third woman stated that she has felt "very insecure."

In response to the question concerning the Women's Liberation Movement, 67 percent (18) of the female respondents spoke against the movement or had no opinion of it while the remainder were sympathetic to it. The nine women sympathetic to the Women's Liberation Movement were the women who desired to meet men with certain expressive qualities or similar interests instead of those of high-class statuses. The women favorable to women's liberation also tended to be under 35 years of age, college-educated, and politically to the left. The remainder of the women in the sample (the majority) held more conservative political orientations, were generally older, and more often received solely a high school education. Religion and marital status were not related to attitude toward women's liberation.

The difference in educational attainment between the women expressing traditional attitudes and those expressing feminist attitudes in this sample corresponds to recent findings by Daniel Yankelovich (1974). In his 1973 national sample of youth, he found college women to be much more likely to embrace feminist values than noncollege women.

The findings of my sample were consistent with the general impressions maintained by the dating service owner concerning the attributes the females desired in the males, the female self-concept descriptions, and the female attitudes concerning the Women's Liberation Movement. He was also able to better characterize the women most sympathetic to the Women's Liberation Movement, as he spoke to about 15 women of this persuasion. These women were mainly in their 30s and had at least a college education with many of them holding graduate and professional degrees. They stressed intelligence as one of the major assets they possessed and desired the following attributes in men: "intelligence," "similar interests," and "nonchauvinism". The most striking divergence between the women strongly supporting women's liberation ideology and the remainder of the sample involved the desired ages of their dates. The traditional women generally wanted men older than themselves, ranging from a minimum of several years older to a maximum of 15 years older. In contrast, the feminist-oriented women said one of the following: that age was unimportant, that they wanted men their own age, or that they were willing to go out with younger men.

2. Male Responses

Of the 32 men, aged 19 to 57 (with the median age in the mid-20s), 66 percent (21) of them mentioned and generally emphasized qualities pertaining to physical appearance in respect to the traits they desired in females. The attributes involved (1) general attractiveness, (2) specific references to height, weight, and hair color, and (3) references to sexual attractiveness ("well-proportioned," "well-built"). For nine of these men, references to physical attributes along with a permissive attitude toward sex constituted the entire set of desired attributes in women. The other men who emphasized physical appearance also mentioned a combination of expressive-intellectual (though mostly expressive qualities) similar to those mentioned by the women as being desirable in men. These were qualities such as: "good personality," "easy-going," "sincere," "honest," "creative," and "intelligent." These types of traits were also mentioned by the 35 percent (11) of the males who manifested less interest in the physical appearance of their potential female dates.

The attributes that the males in the sample gave in response to their own self-concepts that they were bringing into the bargaining situation differed from the females' self-concepts in that (1) a smaller percentage of the males emphasized their physical attributes (22 percent of the men as opposed to 44 percent of the women), (2) there was much more emphasis on achieved statuses ("well-educated," "quite well off," "have a good career," "have a good future") and (3) the men generally labeled themselves in more positive terms than did the women (i.e., "extremely extroverted to the point of brashness," "forceful, confident," "overintelligent").

In the area of attitudes toward women's liberation ideology, a slightly smaller percentage of men (28 percent) favored the movement in contrast to women who favored it (33 percent). These males were generally the individuals seeking intellectual and expressive qualities in women rather than focusing chiefly on physical qualities or sexual behavior. Like the females expressing support for the Women's Liberation Movement, they tended to be among the younger individuals in the sample (in their 20s), college-educated, and politically more liberal than the other males in the sample. Religion and marital status were not related to attitudes toward feminism. The males embracing equal sex roles were also similar to the females embracing equal sex roles in their attitudes involving the desired age of their date. Likewise, the attitudes toward desired age of date of the traditionally oriented men were similar to those of the traditionally oriented women. In the same manner that the traditionally oriented women desired men who were older than themselves (in some cases, up to 15 years older), the traditionally oriented men desired women who were younger than themselves (in some cases, up to 20 years younger). In contrast, the men supporting women's liberation ideology, like the women of the same persuasion, said that age was unimportant or desired their dates to be of the same age. One difference between the feminist men and women, however, was that feminist women were willing to date younger men. The feminist men did not express willingness to date older women.

ANALYSIS

On the basis of the self-concepts that the men and women calling the dating service appeared to bring into the bargaining situation, their conceptions of the ideal date they hoped to obtain, and their attitudes concerning women's liberation, what theoretical inferences can be drawn concerning sex roles in this particular New York sample? The responses of the majority of males and females in this sample were consistent with the sociological conceptualization of the traditional bargaining relationship between the sexes. The majority of women consistently cited and placed greatest emphasis on the achieved occupational–economic statuses of men while the majority of men placed greatest emphasis on the ascribed physical qualities of women. At the same time, most of the women who emphasized achieved statuses of men were also concerned with the mens' expressive qualities, whereas for many men, physical qualities alone were considered sufficient in women. Generally, these men and women presented themselves (listed their own attributes) in conformity with the expectations and wishes of the opposite sex. Thus, one might conclude that the traditionally oriented males and females in the sample had internalized and were acting upon the norms governing the trade-off in heterosexual dating relationships of male occupational–economic achievement for female attractiveness–sexuality.

On the basis of this research, it appears that one consequence arising from traditional sex-role orientations is a greater psychological insecurity accompanying the female role (as seen from the male and female "presentations of self"). Two hypotheses might explain this apparent sex difference. First, the women may be more insecure because the male expectations in regard to the female role involve a narrower sphere for possible action and thus involve less possibility for control. This sphere largely centers on ascribed characteristics which provide less freedom for self-development than do desired attributes related to achievement-oriented spheres. Alternatively, male insecurity deriving from different sources (i.e., from having to attain high achievement levels, given the absence of opportunity, ability or both) may not as readily be apparent due to the traditional masculine requirement forcing males to manifest strength and conceal weakness. Support for this hypothesis is suggested in a study by Komarovsky. She found, in her study of Ivy League college males, that 30 percent

of her sample reported intellectual insecurity or strain with their dates. She viewed this strain as deriving from "a socially structured scarcity of resources for role fulfillment" (Komarovsky, 1973).

In order to theorize about the factors influencing individuals to embrace changing sex roles rather than traditional ones, a comparison will be drawn, along various status dimensions, between the two "ideal types" of individuals. First, in regard to social class, the men and women embracing the changing sex roles tended to be better educated and in higher status occupational positions than those embracing traditional roles. I would hypothesize that college educations have facilitated exposure to the Women's Liberation Movement and changing sex-role ideology for both sexes. However, intellectual exposure to new sex-role orientations may be a necessary but not sufficient basis for female sex-role change. In addition, the opportunity to attain a moderately high occupational status is necessary to motivate women to embrace equal sex roles. Scanzoni (1972) suggests that, "Power rests on resources. Husbands, because of their unique relationship to the opportunity structure, tend to have more resources (material status), hence more power than wives." Thus, women with little education and occupational experience (equal to the status level they desire a man to attain) and with little chance to attain it on their own might logically cling to traditional roles as a means for upward mobility, despite exposure to equal sex-role ideology. "It would seem, wrote Scanzoni (1972), "to take more incentive than a job on an assembly line or in a variety store to motivate moderately educated women to press seriously for new marital arrangements." Thus, women must have the assets to obtain economic resources on their own in order to relinquish their economic dependency on men.

In comparing the age differences between those males and females embracing traditional and equal sex roles, it is apparent that those individuals of both sexes in the younger group (under 35) are more susceptible to changing sex-role orientations. In the case of women, the younger age, I would hypothesize, is related to the greater opportunity structure allowing this cohort educational and occupational channels through which they can attain independent economic statuses.

The liberal–left political orientation of the males and females embracing equal sex roles is indicative of the greater orientation to change maintained by individuals to the left of the political spectrum (coupled with the overall emphasis, in current liberal–left ideologies, on change in the direction of "equality" in respect to numerous statuses—race, age, student, etc.).

A final contrast between the individuals embracing traditional and equal sex roles involves the desired age of their dates. Israel and Eliasson (1971) have theorized about the traditional norms allowing men to date women much younger than themselves but restricting women from dating younger men:

> It is characteristic . . . for relations between classes or groups of people with varying degrees of power in the social structure. Thus the factual right of access to sexual partners of one's own choice, or the demand for such rights, is one of the signs of a class of people occupying superior power positions. The same right is usually denied those who factually occupy inferior positions or are perceived as such.

Israel and Eliasson (1971) further show how this traditional power differential is tied to the economic structure of industrial society:

> Men, at least in middle-class occupations or professions, tend to improve their economic position with increasing age whereas women do not. In fact, there may be a reversed trend for women. Therefore, older men in our society have certain actual possibilities to acquire sexual partners, especially since the economic structure and prospects as criteria for male sexual attractiveness are supported by existing norms.

Thus, increasing economic status coupled with traditional sex-role ideology have improved men's sexual bargaining power as their chronological age increases. On the other hand, since women have traditionally bartered their physical attractiveness in the dating exchange, one could infer that, in our youth-oriented society, women have less bargaining power as they increase in age. Israel and Eliasson neglect, however, to deal with the power differentials in the converse situation: younger men in relationship to women of the same age (or older). Given traditional sex roles, younger men wield less power than women their own age in that they have fewer occupational-economic achievement assets to offer to women. At the same time, given traditional sex roles, men wield more power than women in choosing social partners for a much greater proportion of their lives. They are occupationally and economically productive for a greater period of time than women are at the height of their physical attractiveness. I would hypothesize that the greater "oppression" of younger males might contribute toward making them more open to sex-role changes in contrast to older males benefiting from their ability to wield power. The general sample of individuals applying to the dating service, stratified by age, empirically illustrates these male-female power relationships. Since the use of a dating service involves a degree of social stigma (as was quite evident by the hesitations and nervousness of many of the callers), one might speculate that the individuals using it have less recourse to other means of obtaining dates. The larger distribution of younger men and older women calling the dating service may be indicative of their lower bargaining position in traditional dating interaction.

CONCLUSION

This research has empirically examined the degree to which the current dating institution involves a differential bargaining situation between the sexes. The findings show that the classical conceptualization of the bargaining situation remains empirically valid: women exchange physical attractiveness for male economic status. Some consequences of this situation have been analyzed; in particular, the relationship between age and worth on the market. The findings also suggest that a proportion of the population have embraced less differentiated roles. These individuals are of a higher class status and ideologically to the left of the political spectrum.

The findings from this research lead the author to the speculation that the traditional bargaining situation between the sexes will be radically altered only when the economic position of women changes. Despite the increase in women in the labor force,

Summary of Sex-Role Attitudes and Dating Interaction

	Females	
	Traditional attitudes	*Feminist attitudes*
1. Self-identity	Centered around physical attributes and express- ive qualities	Encompassing own achievement, interests, and intelligence in addition to physical and expressive characteristics
2. Identity of desired date	Great emphasis on achievement and social status of potential date, secondarily on expressive–intellectual qualities	Encompassing similar interests, achievements, intelligence and physi- cal and expressive qualities
3. Age difference	Assumption that male will be older	Age unimportant or assumption that date will be the same age
	Males	
	Traditional attitudes	*Feminist attitudes*
1. Self-identity	Centered around achieved status	Encompassing physical and expressive char- acteristics, own achievement, intelli- gence and interests
2. Identity of desired date	Great emphasis on phy- sical characteristics and secondarily on expressive qualities	Encompassing similar interests, achievements, intelligence and phy- sical and expressive qualities
3. Age difference	Assumption that female will be younger	Age unimportant or assumption that date will be same age

most women still seek personal fulfillment mainly from their roles as wives and mothers rather than from their occupational roles. In contrast, work is at the center of the male role (Stoll, 1974). This sex difference may partly persist because women are still concentrated in the lower levels of the occupational structure and earn considerably less than men (Smuts 1971; Epstein 1971; HEW 1973). Thus, when the economy ceases to discriminate between the sexes, we may also see the beginning of a bargaining situation in the dating institution that is not differentiated by sex.

REFERENCES

DEGLER, CARL, Revolution without ideology: the changing place of women in America. In Robert Jay Lifton (ed.), *The woman in America*, Boston: Beacon, 1964, pp. 193–210.

DIXON, MARLENE, Why women's liberation? *Liberation Now*, New York: Dell, 1971.

EPSTEIN, CYNTHIA, *Woman's place*. Berkeley: University of California Press, 1971.

GINZBERG, ELI, "Introduction," to Robert Smuts, *Women and work in America*. New York: Schocken, 1971.

GOODE, WILLIAM J., *The family*. Englewood Cliffs, N.J.: Prentice-Hall, 1964.

————, *World revolution and family patterns*. New York: The Free Press, 1963.

HOFFMAN, LOIS, AND F. IVAN NYE, *The employed mother in America*. Chicago: Rand McNally, 1963.

ISRAEL, JOACHIM, AND ROSMARI ELIASSON, Consumption society, sex roles, and sexual behavior. *Acta Sociologica* 14:1–2, 1971.

KOMAROVSKY, MIRRA, Cultural contradictions and sex roles: the masculine case. In Joan Huber (ed.), *Changing women in a changing society*. Chicago: University of Chicago Press, 1973.

SCANZONI, JOHN, *Sexual bargaining*. Englewood Cliffs, N.J.: Prentice-Hall, 1972.

SMUTS, ROBERT, *Women and work in America*. New York: Schocken, 1971.

STARR, JOYCE, AND DONALD CARNS, Singles in the city. *Society* 9 (February):43–48, 1972.

STOLL, CLARICE STASZ, *Female and male*, Dubuque: William Brown, 1974.

UNITED STATES DEPARTMENT OF HEALTH, EDUCATION AND WELFARE, *Work in America*. Cambridge: M.I.T. Press, 1973.

WESTLEY, A. W., AND N. B. EPSTEIN. *Silent majority*. San Francisco: Jossey, Bass, 1969.

YANKELOVICH, DANIEL, *The new morality*. New York: McGraw-Hill, 1974.

Heterosexual Cohabitation among Unmarried College Students

ELEANOR D. MACKLIN

DURING THE PAST FIVE OR SIX YEARS there have been periodic allusions in the popular press to a developing pattern of cohabitation among unmarried youth (*Newsweek* 1966; *Esquire* 1967; Grant 1968; McWhirter 1968; Schrag 1968; *Time* 1968; Bloch 1969; Karlen 1969; Rollin 1969; Sheehy 1969; *Life* 1970; Coffin 1971), but little attempt has been made to explore this phenomenon in the professional literature. The majority of research has continued to dwell on questions regarding the sexual values and attitudes of college students, documenting their increased willingness to engage in and to approve of premarital sexual relations (Bell and Chaskes 1970; Cannon and Long 1971; Christensen and Gregg 1970; Herr 1970; Kaats and Davis 1970; Mosher and Cross 1971; Luckey and Nass 1972), but providing little information about the changes in living patterns which are simultaneously occurring. Exceptions include a series of published interviews with cohabiting college couples (Ald 1969), an unpublished master's thesis based on interviews with 28 cohabiting student couples at the University of Iowa (Johnson 1969), the unpublished work on "unmarried college liaisons" ("unmalias") by sociologist Robert N. Whitehurst (1969), a study of student and parental attitudes with respect to the university's responsibility in the area of off-campus cohabitation at Michigan State University (Smith and Kimmel 1970), and a call for further research and counseling facilities by emotional health consultant Miriam Berger (1971).

It was because so little was known about the current patterns of cohabitation among college youth that the present study was undertaken. This report summarizes the initial pilot phase of this research. In order to obtain a more complete picture of the various forms which living together might

assume, a fairly inclusive definition of cohabitation was adopted: To share a bedroom for at least four nights per week for at least three consecutive months with someone of the opposite sex. Throughout this paper, this definition of cohabitation will be used.

The objectives of this phase of the research were to gain an estimate of the prevalence of this experience, and an understanding of the nature of the relationship, the reasons for involvement, and the problems and benefits experienced. A series of four-hour semistructured interviews was conducted in April 1971 with fifteen junior and senior female students at Cornell University, Ithaca, N.Y., who had experienced heterosexual cohabitation. In September 1971, a questionnaire based on the interview schedule was given to 104 junior and senior women in a course on adolescent development at Cornell. Of the 86 who responded, 29 had experienced cohabitation. The fifteen interviewees had been involved in a total of 20 such relationships (eleven had experienced one such relationship, three had had two, and one, three). The 29 questionnaire respondents had experienced a total of 35 cohabitation relationships (24 had had one, four had had two, and one had had three).

The following discussion will be based on the information obtained from the combined group of 44 cohabitants. Questionnaire data will serve as the basis for all quantitative reporting, but it should be understood that interview data were generally corroborative.

Reprinted by permission from Heterosexual cohabitation among unmarried college students, by Eleanor D. Macklin, *The Family Coordinator*, October 1972, pp. 463–471.

PREVALENCE

From the present data one can only surmise the frequency with which cohabitation currently occurs at Cornell. Of the 86 junior and senior women who completed the questionnaire,[1] 34 percent had already had such an experience by the beginning of the 1971 fall term. When these 86 students were asked to predict what percentage of Cornell undergraduates probably experience cohabitation prior to graduation, almost three-quarters predicted that 40 percent or more would do so. When asked how many of their close friends had experienced or were experiencing cohabitation, only seven percent said "none," and over 40 percent said "many" or "most."

Of the 57 respondents who had not experienced cohabitation as defined, almost two-thirds checked that they had stayed with someone but not for as long as indicated in the definition. When asked why they had not cohabited, the large majority indicated that it was because they had not yet found an appropriate person. A few checked that it would be unwise for them at present due to the stage of their relationship, their immaturity, the possibility of discovery, or physical impracticality. Only one person said she had not because it would be wrong to do so outside of marriage.

Further clues to the frequency of cohabitation come from the questionnaire pretest which was given to two undergraduate classes in April 1971. Of 150 underclassmen responding, 28 percent indicated having experienced cohabitation. From an upperclass seminar on delinquency taught by the author, 12 of the 20 students volunteered to be interviewed regarding their cohabitation experience. One is led to conclude from all available evidence that cohabitation is a common experience for students on this particular campus and is accepted by many as a "to-be-expected" occurrence.

DESCRIPTION OF THE COHABITATION EXPERIENCE

A wide variety of types of cohabitation experiences were revealed: among them, living with a male roommate in a co-op (with no sexual involvement and with both roommates having other romantic attachments), living in a tent while traveling in Europe, sharing a dormitory or a fraternity room, or sharing a room with another cohabiting couple. However, the most common pattern was for the girl to move into the boy's room (or vice versa) in an apartment or house which he was sharing with several other males (one of whom might also have a girl living in). Graduate student pairs are more likely to live alone in an apartment or a house; freshman couples are more likely to share a dormitory room. Very few couples shared their bedroom with a third person.

In the majority of cases, living quarters had not been obtained initially with living together in mind (although many men arrange to have a single room in order to allow privacy for any potential entertaining). Living arrangements were not usually jointly arranged until the second year of a relationship. However, even then, couples were hesitant to arrange for a single joint living situation, and planning simply involved ensuring that the potential apartment-mates were willing to have a girl share the premises. Practically all girls also maintained a room in the dormitory or sorority or in an apartment with other girls. Most went back once a day for a few hours to visit, get messages or mail, exchange clothes, shower, or study. Maintaining a separate residence precludes having to explain to parents, ensures a place to live if the relationship is not working well, helps maintain contact with female friends, serves as a convenient place to study, and provides often necessary storage space (the boy's room being too small to hold both sets of belongings).

In about half of the relationships, the couple spent seven nights a week together. In the remaining half, the girl returned to her own room one or two nights a week in order to see her friends and to allow him time with his friends. It should be noted at this point that spending the night together, even in the same bed, need not imply a full sexual relationship. Aside from the instance of the nonemotionally involved coed roommates, there were couples who had lived together for more than three months without intercourse because they did not yet feel ready for this experience (these were usually virgin women). The irony of this is the frequency with which the older generation refuses to accept that this could be true, or if it is, insists that the male must be a "queer."

There was a wide range in amount of time spent together. The majority reported being together about 16–17 hours a day on weekdays (5 P.M. to 8 A.M. plus lunch). Most couples shared at least two meals a day, although occasionally dinner was eaten separately because of the inconvenience involved in having an extra person at dinner or because her parents had already paid for her meals on campus and funds were tight. There was practically no instance of total pooling of finances in these relationships, although the couple normally shared food and entertainment expenses. Usually the girl paid her way and maintained her own separate finances, either because the couple could not afford otherwise or as a matter of principle. When there were chores involved, the couple generally did them together (e.g., shopping or laundry), although there was a tendency for the girl to assume responsibility for cooking and cleaning. There was a wide range in the degree to which they shared activities (e.g., classes, study, or hobbies) or spent time with others. The tendency was to share the majority of activities, to have many mutual friends, and to spend much of their time with others as opposed to time only with one another.

WHY STUDENTS LIVE TOGETHER

There are three aspects to the question of why students are now living together: the circumstances existing at the particular institution, the broader societal reasons, and the personal motivations of the specific students.

Changes in dormitory regulations and the slow demise of *in loco parentis* have greatly facilitated the development of the new pattern. If one goes back to earlier issues of the campus newspaper (*Cornell Daily Sun* 1962, 1963, 1964), one notes that in 1962, a graduate student was indefinitely suspended from the university for living with a woman in his apartment, and in 1964, a male student was reprimanded for staying overnight at a local hotel with a nonuniversity female. Sexual morality was considered a legitimate concern of the university faculty and "overnight unchaperoned mixed company" was considered by the faculty council on student conduct to be a violation of sexual morality. (*Cornell Daily Sun* 1962, p. 2)

Today, Cornell students are free to live in much the same way that nonstudents who are living and working in the outside world are free to live: they are likely to be residing in a structure which also houses persons of the opposite sex (many of the dorms are now coed, with men and women segregated by floors, wings or suites, although there is experimentation with men and women living on the same corridor); if they are sophomores or beyond, they are free to elect to live off campus; and they may entertain someone of the opposite sex in their room at any time during the 24-hour day. Official policy still prohibits "continuous residence" with someone of the opposite sex in the dormitory setting, but this is difficult to police.

These changes in curfew and dormitory policy must be seen as a reflection of broader social changes: a change in the status of women which makes it difficult to justify different regulations for men and for women, youth's increasing demand that they no longer be treated as children, a questioning of the rigid sexual mores which have traditionally governed people's lives, a greater willingness to grant individuals the right to select their own life-style, and the increasing availability of contraception and abortion services.

When students are asked to hypothesize why cohabitation has become more common and more open, they mention youth's search for meaningful relations with others and the consequent rejection of the superficial "dating game"; the loneliness of a large university and the emotional satisfaction that comes from having someone to sleep with who cares about you; the widespread questioning of the institution of marriage and the desire to try out a relationship before there is any, if ever, consideration of permanency; the desire on the part of many to postpone commitment until there is some certainty that individual growth will be compatible with growth of the relationship; the fact that young people mature earlier and yet must wait so long until marriage is feasible; and the fact that the university community provides both sanction and feasibility for such a relationship to develop. Given peer group support, ample opportunity, a human need to love and be loved, and a disposition to question the traditional way, it seems only natural that couples should wish to live together if they enjoy being together. One might almost better ask: Why do students choose *not* to live together?

When one asks students why they personally become involved in a cohabitation relationship, one finds a mixture of enjoying being together and expediency (e.g., too far to drive her home at night, easier to stay than to get up and go back at midnight, less expensive, someone else living with one's roommate, or partner was sick and needed someone to care for him). On occasion, curiosity about what it would be like to live with the opposite sex was involved, and sometimes "to test out the relationship" was mentioned, but it was rarely such a purposeful act.

In fact, living together was seldom the result of a considered decision, at least initially. (Cf. Ryder, Kafka, and Olson's concept of "unquestioned beginnings" which they suggest characterize much of courtship in our society.) Most relationships involved a gradual (and sometimes not so gradual) drifting into staying together. The general pattern was to stay over one night; in several weeks, if all was well, to stay for the weekend; in another few weeks to add a week night; in another few weeks, a second week night, and so forth. In half the relationships the couple had begun staying together four or more nights a week by the end of four months of dating.

If and when a decision with conscious deliberation was made, it was usually precipitated by some external force (e.g., need to make plans for the summer or next fall, graduation, unexpected pregnancy, or a necessary housing or room change). Until this time, there was only a mutual, often unspoken, recognition of the desire to be together—a natural progression of the relationship.

NATURE OF THE RELATIONSHIP

When asked to indicate the nature of the relationship at the time they began living together four or more nights per week, about half checked that they "had a strong, affectionate relationship, not dating others" (i.e., "going steady"—although they resisted this term). Another large group indicated that they "had a strong affectionate relationship but were also open to other relationships." Only a few indicated tentative engagement; even fewer stated that they were just "friends." See Table 1.

Table 1 Nature of relationship when couple first started living together for at least four nights per week, as reported by 29 upper-class female students for 35 cohabitation-relationships

Nature of relationship	Number of relationships
Formally engaged	1
Tentatively engaged (contemplating marriage)	3
Strong, affectionate relationship; not dating others ("going steady")	17
Strong, affectionate relationship; open to other dating relationships	12
Friends	1
Other ("met and immediately started living together")	1
Total	35

It is interesting to note that the above is very similar to answers given by all 86 questionnaire respondents when asked what kind of relationship they felt should exist before college-aged students cohabit (see Table 2). One is impressed by the fact that cohabitation is more frequently associated with the "going steady" stage of a relationship than with engagement, even tentative engagement.

The initial commitment to the relationship varied greatly. Some saw it strictly as temporary (e.g., "while traveling," "he was planning to leave Ithaca," or "he was already committed to someone else") and a few, at the other extreme, definitely planned "marriage in the future when it was more convenient." But the vast majority entered it either with a "let's see" attitude (i.e., to test the relationship—to stay together as long as it was mutually satisfying), or—a somewhat more definite commit-

Table 2 Responses of 86 upperclass female students to, "What kind of relationship do you feel should prevail before college-aged students cohabit?"

Nature of relationship	Percent of respondents
Married	4
Formally engaged	—
Tentatively engaged (contemplating marriage)	8
Strong, affectionate relationship; not dating others ("going steady")	60
Strong, affectionate relationship; open to other dating relationships	15
Friends	8
Other (e.g., "anything acceptable to both parties")	5
Total	100%

ment—planned to do all they "could to develop a lasting relationship, but future marriage was not definite."

This raises some question about the label "unmarried marrieds" which has often been applied in the popular literature to unmarried cohabitation. Most of the undergraduate couples did nôt consider themselves married in any sense of the word. Not only did they not consider themselves married, they rarely considered marriage as a viable alternative to their present cohabitation. When asked, "Did you consider the possibility of getting married instead?" a frequent response was "Heavens no!" Marriage might be seen as a possibility for the future, but the distant future. The future seemed too indefinite to plan that far ahead, they needed more time to grow and develop before considering marriage, and it was financially impractical. Moreover, marriage appeared to have some negative connotations for many of these students—it was seen as limiting their freedom and their growth (cf. the period of youth as discussed by Keniston in *Young Radicals*), and they feared falling into the traditional roles they associated with being wives, even though over two-thirds of those interviewed said their parents would consider their own marriage "very successful."

PROBLEMS ENCOUNTERED

As with any real relationship, these were not always blissful. It was encouraging that those interviewed seemed very aware of the problem areas and were able to verbalize about them easily.

Problems could be divided into four major categories: emotional problems, sexual problems, problems with parents, and problems related to the living situation. (In the interviews, no one had experienced problems with the community; thus the question was not included in the questionnaire.)

The major emotional problem (see Table 3) was the tendency to become overinvolved and to feel a subsequent loss of identity, lack of opportunity to participate in other activities or be with friends, and an over-dependency on the relationship. On the basis of the available data, one is tempted to hypothesize that how this issue is dealt with and the success with which it is handled are major determinants of the outcome of the relationship. The problem of how to achieve security without giving up the freedom to be oneself, and how to grow together and yet leave enough space so the individuals can grow also, appears central.

Other problems in this category were feelings of being trapped (should break up but afraid to do so), feelings of being used, jealousy of partner's involvement in other activities or relationships, and lack of feeling of belonging (e.g., "When I expect that he will share his money with me now that my parents have cut me off, he reminds me that we are not married"). It should be recognized, however, that although there were a few who indicated that these problems caused them a great deal of trouble, the majority indicated little or no problem. It is also important to note that more than two-thirds indicated no feelings of guilt, and the remainder indicated only a minimal amount. In the interviews, when guilt was stated to be present, it was usually related to having to conceal the relationship from parents or it occurred in those instances where they knew that the relationship could not last.

Sexual problems were common (see Table 3). Only a few indicated "no problem" in this area. Differing degrees or periods of sexual interest, lack of orgasm, fear of pregnancy, vaginal irritations, feelings of sexual inhibition, and less satisfaction with sex as the relationship deteriorated were the

Table 3 Extent to which emotional, sexual, and living situation problems were experienced in 35 cohabitation relationships as reported by 29 upperclass female students (categories are ordered by number of persons reporting the problem)

Problem area	Number no problem	Indicating some problem	Average rating given by those indicating some problem*
Emotional problems			
Overinvolvement (loss of identity, lack of opportunity to participate in other activities or with friends, over-dependency)	14	21	2.7
Jealousy of partner's involvement in other activities or relationships	14	15	3.1
Feeling of being trapped	18	15	2.9
Feeling of being used	19	13	2.6
Guilt:			
at beginning of relationship	20	9	3.7
during relationship	25	5	3.8
at end of relationship	15	2	4.0
Lack of feeling of "belonging" or of being "at home"	22	9	3.4
Other "will have to separate for a while after his graduation"	—	1	3.0
Sexual problems			
Differing degrees or periods of sexual interest	10	23	3.4
Lack of orgasm	11	21	3.6
Fear of pregnancy	15	15	3.1
Vaginal irritation or discharge after intercourse	17	15	3.4
Discomfort of partner during intercourse	18	10	3.7
Impotence of partner	23	6	3.0
Problems related to living situation			
Lack of privacy	15	17	3.4
Lack of adequate space	19	13	3.0
Did not get along with apartment or housemates	20	6	2.2
Lack of sufficient money	26	6	3.3
Disagreement over use of money, sharing of money, etc.	27	4	3.5

*Respondents were asked to rate each problem from 1 to 5, with 1: great deal of problem, 5: no problem (no other points defined). The last category (5: no problem) has been separated because it may be qualitatively different from the other rating categories. Average ratings are therefore based on ratings from 1 to 4; thus, the lower the average rating, the greater the problem for those experiencing it.

more frequently mentioned problems. However, in spite of problems, over three-fourths of the respondents rated the relationship as sexually satisfying. Practically all used contraception (over 80 percent used either the pill or the diaphragm), with about two-thirds of these having started contraception before or at the time of the first intercourse in the cohabitation relationship.

A major problem area was parents. More than one-fourth indicated that parents had caused "some" or "many" problems: parental disapproval of the boy, fear of discovery, guilt because they were deceiving or hurting their parents, rejection by or ultimatums from parents, and most frequently, sadness at not being able to share this important part of their lives with their parents. Because of fear of disapproval or unpleasant repercussions, more than two-thirds had tried to conceal the relationship from their parents—by not telling them the whole story, by distorting the truth, and by developing often elaborate schemes to prevent discovery. Almost half of the respondents believed their parents to be unaware of their cohabitation, with the remainder divided equally between those who felt they definitely knew, those who thought they probably knew, and those who were unsure. The boy's parents were much more likely to be aware.

Problems related to the living situation were considered minimal. Lack of privacy, lack of adequate space, lack of sufficient funds or disagreement over money, and friction with apartment mates were all mentioned, with lack of space or privacy and tension with others in the living situation the most common. It should be noted that there was practically no problem experienced as a result of the external community, i.e., landlords, local employers, school administration, neighbors, or contemporaries. In fact, the great majority felt their friends strongly approved of and supported their relationship. In cases where this was not true, it was because friends considered this particular relationship rather than the cohabitation per se undesirable.

BENEFITS

It is important that the problems not be seen as outweighing the values of such relationships. More

than half rated their relationship as "very successful," and more than 80 percent checked that it was "both maturing and pleasant." Even in those few cases where the relationship was said to be "painful," they emphasized the personal growth which had occurred, e.g., "I question whether I'd understand myself as well without the hard times." In no case was the experience rated "very unpleasant" or "not at all maturing," and in no case was it considered primarily detrimental to the person involved. In more than 60 percent of the cases, they would do it over again with the same person, even in those relationships which had broken up at the time of the report.

The benefits seen by the participants included a deeper understanding of themselves and of their needs, expectations, and inadequacies; increased knowledge of what is involved in a relationship and of the complexities of living with someone else; clarification of what they wanted in a marriage; increase in emotional maturity and in self-confidence, e.g., "learned not to commit myself too soon," "learned through breaking up how much strength I have," increased ability to understand and relate to others; emotional security and companionship, e.g., "because we have coped with problems and come out topside, I have more faith that we will be able to do so again." The main undercurrent in the data was the many ways in which the experience had fostered growth and maturity. All persons interviewed indicated that they would not consider marriage without having lived with the person first, and all—while hesitant to say what others should do—felt the move toward cohabitation could only be seen as a healthy trend.

OUTCOME OF THE RELATIONSHIP

At the time of the questionnaire, one-third of the relationships had dissolved (having lasted an average of four and one-half months from the time they began staying together four or more nights a week), one-third were married or planning to be married, and another third were still in the process of defining the relationship (either were still living together but not yet contemplating marriage, or were still "going together" but not living together—either because the partner was away or they sought more freedom than they had when living together). A somewhat larger portion of those interviewed had broken their relationship, but this may be due to the fact that the interview was later in the academic year. The 23 relationships which were still in process had existed an average of 13 months, with five having continued for two or two and one-half years.

IMPLICATIONS

1. It appears that cohabitation has become an increasingly common aspect of courtship on the campus studied and one could predict that the trend will proliferate.

Although the phenomenon of unmarried persons living together is obviously not a new one, either in this society or others (Berger 1971), it has certainly not been a common phenomenon among unmarried middle-class youth in the United States until quite recently. Some pass it off by saying it is merely a more open expression of what students have been doing sexually on the sly for years, but this suggests a very narrow interpretation of the present situation. The pattern which is currently evolving appears to be primarily concerned with total relationships and only incidentally with the sexual aspects. It is this concern with getting to know another as a whole person and the emphasis on sharing as openly and as completely as possible with that person, which is probably the major new dimension being added to old courtship patterns.

2. There is some question whether cohabitation as now practiced on the college campus fits the concepts of trial marriage, premarital marriage, companionate marriage, or two-stage marriage which some have sought to apply to it (Berger 1971; Grant 1968; Karlen 1969; LeShan 1971; Mead 1966). Trial marriage, for instance, tends to imply a level of commitment usually associated with the engagement portion of the courtship continuum which is not characteristic of the campus relationships studied. These students do not in general see themselves as consciously testing or even contemplating a potential marriage, at least not initially. Instead, in most cases, living together seems to be a natural component of a strong, affectionate "dating" relationship—a living out of "going steady"—which may grow in time to be something more, but which

in the meantime is to be enjoyed and experienced because it is pleasurable in and of itself.

3. In addition to the question of whether it does in fact lead to healthier marriages or more "fully functioning" persons, there are other intriguing issues. For instance, what is the relationship between commitment to a relationship and identity formation? To what extent must one have developed a strong identity before one can achieve a strong intimate relationship (in Erikson's sense)? What chance is there for a mature, mutual relationship when the individual is still so necessarily focused on his own development? How much commitment to a relationship is necessary for it to have a strong chance of success? Alternately, does early commitment to a relationship hinder identity development? When a person should be at a point of maximum identity development, is it healthy for him to be devoting so much of his energy to the development of a relationship or will this simply accelerate the process? These become very real problems as cohabitation inevitably occurs earlier and becomes increasingly common as a freshman experience.

4. There is a great need to help society adjust to the evolving courtship patterns. Parents in particular tend to see cohabitation as antithetical to all that they consider healthy or moral. They need help if they are to understand and to react without alarm, recrimination, and rejection. Consideration will have to be given to legal implications of the new patterns—some present laws conflict and maybe should be changed, and some new protections for the rights of unmarried participants may be necessary. The professions touched by the new trends are myriad. Bankers, for instance, as they seek to help parents write wills and set up trust funds, and as they themselves seek to administer these trusts, find themselves confronted with having to understand and interpret the new patterns. Students in particular need more realistic preparation, both at home and in school, and more opportunity for relationship and sex counseling, if they are to cope as responsibly and effectively as possible with the increased freedom and the new pressures. The first step, which most of the adult population has not yet taken, is to acknowledge that the changes are actually occurring and to be willing to entertain the hypothesis that they may indeed be an improvement on the traditional patterns.

NOTE

1. Of the 104 junior and senior women in the class, 86 completed the questionnaire. Of these, 58 handed it in on the due date and 28 after a follow-up request. Since the percentage of cohabitants was the same for the initial and the follow-up respondents, it is assumed that the percentage would be similar for the eighteen non-returnees.

REFERENCES

ALD, ROY, *Sex off campus*. New York: Grosset and Dunlap, 1969.

BAUMAN, KARL E., Selected aspects of the contraceptive practices of unmarried university students. *Medical Aspects of Human Sexuality* 5 (August 1971):76-89.

BELL, ROBERT R., AND JAY B. CHASKES, Premarital sexual experience among coeds, 1958 and 1968. *Journal of Marriage and the Family* 32 (1970):81-84.

BERGER, MIRIAM E., Trial marriage: harnessing the trend constructively. *The Family Coordinator* 20 (1971): 38-43.

BLOCH, DONALD, Unwed couples: do they live happily ever after? *Redbook*. April 1969, p. 90.

CANNON, KENNETH L., AND RICHARD LONG, "Premarital sexual behavior in the sixties." *Journal of Marriage and the Family* 33 (1971):36-49.

CHRISTENSEN, HAROLD T., AND CHRISTINA F. GREGG, Changing sex norms in America and Scandinavia. *Journal of Marriage and the Family* 32 (1970):616-627.

COFFIN, PATRICIA, Young unmarrieds: Theresa Pommett and Charles Walsh, college grads living together. *Look*, January 26, 1971, p. 634.

College and University Business. Parents OK strict rules. December 1968, p. 16.

Cornell Daily Sun, October 9, 1962; October 8, 1963; March 6, 1964.

CRIST, TAKEY, The coed as a gynecological patient. Mimeographed. Chapel Hill, N.C.: University of North Carolina, 1970.

DAVIDS, LEO, North American marriage: 1990. *The Futurist*, October 1971, pp. 190-194.

Esquire, Room-mates. September 1967, pp. 94-98.

FELL, JOSEPH P., A psychosocial analysis of sex-policing on campus. *School and Society* 98 (1970):351-354.

FLEMING, THOMAS, AND ALICE FLEMING, What kids still don't know about sex. *Look*, July 28, 1970, p. 59.

GRANT, A., No rings attached: a look at premarital marriage on campus. *Mademoiselle*, April 1968, p. 208.

HALL, ELIZABETH, AND ROBERT A. POTEETE, A conversation with Robert H. Rimmer about Harrad, group marriage, and other loving arrangements. *Psychology Today* 5 (1972):57-82.

HERR, SYLVIA, Research study on behavioral patterns in sex and drug use on college campus. *Adolescence* 5 (Spring 1970):1-16.

HUNT, MORTON, The future of marriage. *Playboy*, August 1971, p. 117.

JOHNSON, MICHAEL P., Courtship and commitment: a study of cohabitation on a university campus. Master's thesis. University of Iowa, 1969.

KAATS, GILBERT R., AND KEITH E. DAVIS, The dynamics of sexual behavior of college students. *Journal of Marriage and the Family* 32 (1970):390-399.

KARLEN, ARNO, The unmarried marrieds on campus. *New York Times Magazine*, January 26, 1969, p. 29.

KENISTON, KENNETH, *Young radicals*. New York: Harcourt, Brace, and World, 1968.

LESHAN, EDA J., *Mates and roommates: new styles in young marriages*. Public Affairs Pamphlets, No. 468. New York: Public Affairs Pamphlets, 1971.

LEVER, JANET, AND PEPPER SCHWARTZ, Men and women at Yale. *Sexual Behavior*, October 1971.

Life, Coed dorms: an intimate campus revolution. November 20, 1970, p. 32.

LUCKEY, ELEANORE B., AND GILBERT D. NASS, Comparison of sexual attitudes in an international sample of college students. *Medical Aspects of Human Sexuality* 6 (1972):66-107.

MALCOLM, ANDREW H., Sex goes to college. *Today's Health,* April 1971, pp. 27-29.

MCWHIRTER, WILLIAM A., The arrangement at college. *Life*, May 31, 1968, p. 56.

MEAD, MARGARET, A continuing dialogue on marriage: why just living together won't work. *Redbook*, April 1968, p. 44.

————, Marriage in two steps. *Redbook*, July 1966, p. 48.

MOSHER, DONALD L., AND HERBERT F. CROSS, Sex-guilt and premarital sexual experiences of college students. *Journal of Consulting and Clinical Psychology* 36 (February 1971):27.

MOSS, J. JOEL, FRANK APOLONIO, AND MARGARET JENSEN, The premarital dyad during the sixties. *Journal of Marriage and the Family* 33 (1971):50-69.

Newsweek. Unstructured relationships: students living together. July 4, 1966, p. 78.

PACKARD, VANCE, *The sexual wilderness*. New York: David McKay, 1968.

PETERS, MURIEL, AND WILLIAM PETERS, How college students feel about love, sex, and marriage. *Good Housekeeping Magazine*, June 1970, p. 85.

REISS, IRA L., The sexual renaissance in America: summary and analysis. *Journal of Social Issues* 22 (April 1966):123-137.

RIMMER, ROBERT H. *The Harrad experiment*. Los Angeles: Sherbourne Press, 1966.

ROCKEFELLER, JOHN D., III., Youth, love, and sex: the new chivalry. *Look*, October 7, 1969, p. 32.

ROLLIN, BETTY, New hang-up for parents: coed living. *Look*, September 23, 1969, p. 22.

RYDER, ROBERT G., JOHN S. KAFKA, AND DAVID H. OLSON, Separating and joining influences in courtship and early marriage." *American Journal of Orthopsychiatry* 41 (April 1971):450-464.

SARREL, PHILIP M., AND LORNA J. SARREL, How we counsel students on sex problems at Yale. *The Osteopathic Physician*, June 1971.

SCHRAG, PETER, Posse at generation gap: implications of the Linda LeClair affair. *Saturday Review*, May 8, 1968, p. 81.

SHEEHY, GAIL, Living together: the stories of four young couples who risk the strains of nonmarriage and why. *Glamour*, February 1, 1969, p. 136.

SMITH, PATRICK B., AND KO KIMMEL, Student-parent reactions to off-campus cohabitation. *Journal of College Student Personnel*, May 1970, pp. 188-193.

Time, Linda, the light housekeeper. April 26, 1968, p. 51.

WHITEHURST, ROBERT, The unmarried on campus. Presented at NCFR Annual Meeting. 1969. Copy available from author, University of Windsor, Windsor, Ontario, Canada.

————, The double standard and male dominance in nonmarital living arrangements: a preliminary statement. Presented at the American Orthopsychiatric Association Meeting, New York, 1969. Copy available from author, University of Windsor, Windsor, Ontario, Canada.

Chapter 5

Marital Dynamics

MARRIAGE IS A SOCIAL ARRANGEMENT IN which the persons involved define their social reality as well as have it defined for them by larger social structures. Both the family one is born into (the family of orientation) and the family one starts with a spouse (the family of procreation) provide crucial experiences and personalized world views for their members. The "world we take for granted" is created for us during the early years of life; it is here that we are first introduced to basic conceptions of what is "natural," "real," and "important" in life. Early childhood experiences infused with strong emotions carry over into adulthood and continue to influence our behavior in adult years. This world view, with some important changes and modifications, becomes the world view we hold as our own through maturation, courtship, marriage, and parenthood, that is, as we go through the family life cycle. Boyd Rollins and Harold Feldman[1] examined the marital satisfaction of about 800 couples at various stages of the family life cycle. Different states of the family life cycle appear to be more closely linked with the marital satisfaction of wives than of husbands. Wives experienced reduced satisfaction during childbearing and the early child-rearing phase, despite cultural myths to the contrary. For husbands, events outside of the family, such as occupational experiences, were most likely to affect their marital satisfaction. It is suggested then that men and women have different meanings for marriage.

Peter Berger and Hansfried Kellner describe the nature of marriage as a new reality constructed by the married couple. One way in which the new marital reality emerges is through ongoing conversations in which the meaning of day-to-day events and interactions is discussed and agreed on. Much of the small talk between married persons helps construct and reinforce their world as their roles take on a firmer, more reliable character. Marriage is tentative, emerging and developing. Marriage develops a new reality—a dialectical one in which the two partners construct the marriage and the marriage acts back on the partners, "welding together their reality." It leads to a life that is more stable because marriage partners "settle down—cognitively, emotionally, and in terms of self-identification." The authors point to the essentially conserving nature of marriage which reinforces "socially predicatable" and "psychologically balanced" actions. Families have much to "conserve"—their marital possessions, their children, their life-style, their property, and their careers.

In contrast to the consensus framework offered by Berger and Kellner, the reality of the Graziano marriage, captured by Thomas Cottle, suggests breaks in the socially constructed reality. The Grazianos exemplify the way family interaction occurs, the way events and persons become defined in marriage, and the importance of conversation in the emergence of shared, and sometimes disagreed upon, realities. Although Theodore and Eleanor Graziano have shared their lives for many years, the interaction reveals some fundamental differences in their views of the world. The Grazianos have a construction of reality which Ted Graziano chooses to violate, and in so doing angers Ellie. The reality must be reconstructed into one which is mutually shared.

Dair Gillespie's article critiques the assumption maintained by a number of sociologists that marriage has become more egalitarian. Gillespie shows that power within the family is determined by control of the available resources. However, competence and control of resources occur in couples not by chance, but is strongly determined by the location of husbands in the world of work, and the continuing discrimination against women in the larger society. In terms of the social construction of reality, Gillespie would suggest that husbands have more power in constructing that reality than do wives.

From a structural functional perspective, students might consider the consequences of marital interaction patterns for individuals of different classes, different ages, and for men and women. How do the occupational roles of men and the reproduction roles of women influence their constructions of reality?

A conflict theorist might ask: How does a critical view of power within the family, such as the analysis offered by Gillespie, affect what Berger and Kellner say about the construction of marriage? Are husbands and wives equal partners in marriage, in its construction and in its development? What are the links between power held outside the marriage and power within the marriage?

From a symbolic interaction perspective, how does conversation and communication mold the reality of marriage? How might the identity formation, within marriage, offered by Berger and Kellner, and Cottle, differ from that suggested by Gillespie? How are marriages constructed at the outset, and how would the construction continue and change over the family life cycle for husbands and wives?

NOTE

1. Boyd Rollins and Harold Feldman 1970. Marital satisfaction over the family life cycle. *Journal of Marriage and the Family* 32: 20-28.

Marriage and the Construction of Reality: An Exercise in the Microsociology of Knowledge

PETER BERGER AND HANSFRIED KELLNER

EVER SINCE DURKHEIM IT HAS BEEN A commonplace of family sociology that marriage serves as a protection against anomie for the individual. Interesting and pragmatically useful though this insight is, it is but the negative side of a phenomenon of much broader significance. If one speaks of *anomic* states, then one ought properly to investigate also the *nomic* processes that, by their absence, lead to the aforementioned states. If,

Reprinted from Peter Berger and Hansfield Kellner, "Marriage and the Construction of Reality," *Diogenes* 46, © 1964, pp. 1-25, by permission of the publisher.

consequently, one finds a negative correlation between marriage and anomie, then one should be led to inquire into the character of marriage as a *nomos*-building instrumentality; that is, of marriage as a social arrangement that creates for the individual the sort of order in which he can experience his life as making sense. It is our intention here to discuss marriage in these terms. While this could evidently be done in a macrosociological perspective, dealing with marriage as a major social institution related to other broad structures of society, our focus will be microsociological, dealing primarily with the social processes affecting the individuals in any specific marriage; although, of course, the larger framework of these processes will have to be understood. In what sense this discussion can be described as microsociology of knowledge will hopefully become clearer in the course of it.[1]

Marriage is obviously only *one* social relationship in which this process of *nomos*-building takes place. It is, therefore, necessary to first look in more general terms at the character of this process. In doing so, we are influenced by three theoretical perspectives—the Weberian perspective on society as a network of meanings, the Meadian perspective on identity as a social phenomenon, and the phenomenological analysis of the social structuring of reality especially as given in the work of Schutz and Merleau-Ponty.[2] Not being convinced, however, that theoretical lucidity is necessarily enhanced by terminological ponderosity, we shall avoid as much as possible the use of the sort of jargon for which both sociologists and phenomenologists have acquired dubious notoriety.

The process that interests us here is the one that constructs, maintains, and modifies a consistent reality that can be meaningfully experienced by individuals. In its essential forms this process is determined by the society in which it occurs. Every society has its specific way of defining and perceiving reality—its world, its universe, its overarching organization of symbols. This is already given in the language that forms the symbolic base of society. Erected over this base, and by means of it, is a system of ready-made typifications, through which the innumerable experiences of reality come to be ordered.[3] These typifications and their order are held in common by the members of society, thus acquiring not only the character of objectivity, but being taken for granted as *the* world *tout court*, the only world that normal men can conceive of.[4] The seemingly objective and taken-for-granted character of the social definitions of reality can be seen most clearly in the case of language itself, but it is important to keep in mind that the latter forms the base and instrumentality of a much larger world-erecting process.

The socially constructed world must be continually mediated to and actualized by the individual, so that it can become and remain indeed *his* world as well. The individual is given by his society certain decisive cornerstones for his everyday experience and conduct. Most importantly, the individual is supplied with specific sets of typifications and criteria of relevance, predefined for him by the society and made available to him for the ordering of his everyday life. This ordering or (in line with our opening considerations) nomic apparatus is biographically cumulative. It begins to be formed in the individual from the earliest stages of socialization on, then keeps on being enlarged and modified by himself throughout his biography.[5] While there are individual biographical differences making for differences in the constitution of this apparatus in specific individuals, there exists in the society an overall consensus on the range of differences deemed to be tolerable. Without such consensus, indeed, society would be impossible as a going concern, since it would then lack the ordering principles by which experience alone can be shared and conduct can be mutually intelligible. This order, by which the individual comes to perceive and define his world, is thus not chosen by him, except perhaps for very small modifications. Rather, it is discovered by him as an external datum, a ready-made world that simply is *there* for him to go ahead and live in, though he modifies it continually in the process of living in it. Nevertheless, this world is in need of validation, perhaps precisely because of an ever-present glimmer of suspicion as to its social manufacture and relativity. This validation, while it must be undertaken by the individual himself, requires ongoing interaction with others who cohabit this same socially constructed world. In a broad sense, *all* of the other coinhabitants of this world serve a validating function. Every morning the newspaper boy validates the widest coodinates

of my world and the mailman bears tangible validation of my own location within these coordinates.
However, some validations are more significant
than others. Every individual requires the ongoing
validation of his world, including crucially the
validation of his identity and place in this world, by
those few who are his truly significant others.[6] Just
as the individual's deprivation of relationship with
his significant others will plunge him into anomie,
so their continued presence will sustain for him that
nomos by which he can feel at home in the world at
least most of the time. Again in a broad sense, all
the actions of the significant others and even their
simple presence serve this sustaining function. In
everyday life, however, the principal method
employed is speech. In this sense, it is proper to
view the individual's relationship with his significant others as an ongoing conversation. As the
latter occurs, it validates over and over again the
fundamental definitions of reality once entered into,
not, of course, so much by explicit articulation, but
precisely by taking the definitions silently for
granted and conversing about all conceivable
matters on this taken-for-granted basis. Through
the same conversation the individual is also made
capable of adjusting to changing and new social
contexts in his biography. In a very fundamental
sense it can be said that one converses one's way
through life.

If one concedes these points, one can now state
a general sociological proposition: the plausibility
and stability of the world, as socially defined, is
dependent upon the strength and continuity of
significant relationships in which conversation
about this world can be continually carried on. Or,
to put it a little differently: the reality of the world
is sustained through conversation with significant
others. This reality, of course, includes not only the
imagery by which fellowmen are viewed, but also includes the way in which one views oneself. The
reality-bestowing force of social relationships depends on the degree of their nearness;[7] that is, on
the degree to which social relationships occur in
face-to-face situations and to which they are
credited with primary significance by the individual. In any empirical situation there now emerge
obvious sociological questions out of these
considerations; namely, questions about the patterns of the world-building relationships, the social

forms taken by the conversation with significant
others. Sociologically, one must ask how these
relationships are *objectively* structured and
distributed, and one will also want to understand
how they are *subjectively* perceived and experienced.

With these preliminary assumptions stated we
can now arrive at our main thesis here. Namely, we
would contend that marriage occupies a privileged
status among the significant validating relationships for adults in our society. Put slightly differently: marriage is a crucial nomic instrumentality in
our society. We would futher argue that the essential social functionality of this institution cannot be
fully understood if this fact is not perceived.

We can now proceed with an ideal-typical
analysis of marriage; that is, seek to abstract the
essential features involved. Marriage in our society
is a *dramatic* act in· which two strangers come
together and redefine themselves. The drama of the
act is internally anticipated and socially legitimated
long before it takes place in the individual's biography, and amplified by means of a pervasive
ideology, the dominant themes of which (romantic
love, sexual fulfillment, self-discovery, and self-
realization through love and sexuality, the nuclear
family as the social site for these processes) can be
found distributed through all strata of the society.
The actualization of these ideologically predefined
expectations in the life of the individual occurs to
the accompaniment of one of the few traditional
rites of passage that are still meaningful to almost
all members of the society. It should be added that,
in using the term "strangers," we do not mean, of
course, that the candidates for the marriage come
from widely discrepant social backgrounds—
indeed, the data indicate that the contrary is the
case. The strangeness rather lies in the fact that,
unlike marriage candidates in many previous
societies, those in ours typically come from
different face-to-face contexts—in the terms used
above, they come from different areas of conversation. They do not have a shared past, although their
pasts have a similar structure. In other words, quite
apart from prevailing patterns of ethnic, religious,
and class endogamy, our society is typically exogamous in terms of nomic relationships. Put
concretely, in our mobile society the significant
conversation of the two partners previous to the

marriage took place in social circles that did not overlap. With the dramatic redefinition of the situation brought about by the marriage, however, all significant conversation for the two new partners is now centered in their relationship with each other—and, in fact, it was precisely with this intention that they entered upon their relationship.

It goes without saying that this character of marriage has its root in much broader structural configurations of our society. The most important of these, for our purposes, is the crystallization of a so-called private sphere of existence, more and more segregated from the immediate controls of the public institutions (especially the economic and political ones), and yet defined and utilized as the main social area for the individual's self-realization.[8] It cannot be our purpose here to inquire into the historical forces that brought forth these phenomena, beyond making the observation that these are closely connected with the industrial revolution and its institutional consequences. The public institutions now confront the individual as an immensely powerful and alien world, incomprehensible in its inner workings, anonymous in its human character. If only through his work in some nook of the economic machinery, the individual must find a way of living in this alien world, come to terms with its power over him, be satisfied with a few conceptual rules of thumb to guide him through a vast reality that otherwise remains opaque to his understanding, and modify its anonymity by whatever *"human relations"* he can work out in his involvement with it. It ought to be emphasized, against some critics of "mass society," that this does not inevitably leave the individual with a sense of profound unhappiness and lostness. It would rather seem that large numbers of people in our society are quite content with a situation in which their public involvements have little subjective importance, regarding work as a not too bad necessity and politics as at best a spectator sport. It is usually only intellectuals with ethical and political commitments who assume that such people must be terribly desperate. The point, however, is that the individual in this situation, no matter whether he is happy or not, will turn elsewhere for the experiences of self-realization that do have importance for him. The private sphere, this interstitial area created (we would think) more or

less haphazardly as a by-product of the social metamorphosis of industrialism, is mainly where he will turn. It is here that the individual will seek power, intelligibility and, quite literally, a name—the apparent power to fashion a world, however Lilliputian, that will reflect his own being: a world that, seemingly having been shaped by himself and thus unlike those other worlds that insist on shaping him, is translucently intelligible to him (or so he thinks); a world in which, consequently, he is *somebody*—perhaps even within its charmed circle, a lord and master. What is more, to a considerable extent these expectations are not unrealistic. The public institutions have no need to control the individual's adventures in the private sphere, as long as they really stay within the latter's circumscribed limits. The private sphere is perceived, not without justification, as an area of individual choice and even autonomy. This fact has important consequences for the shaping of identity in modern society that cannot be pursued here. All that ought to be clear here is the peculiar location of the private sphere within and between the other social structures. In sum, it is above all and, as a rule, only in the private sphere that the individual can take a slice of reality and fashion it into his world. If one is aware of the decisive significance of this capacity and even necessity of men to externalize themselves in reality and to produce for themselves a world in which they can feel at home, then one will hardly be surprised at the great importance which the private sphere has come to have in modern society.[9]

The private sphere includes a variety of social relationships. Among these, however, the relationships of the family occupy a central position and, in fact, serve as a focus for most of the other relationships (such as those with friends, neighbors, fellow members of religious and other voluntary associations). Since, as the ethnologists keep reminding us, the family in our society is of the conjugal type, the central relationship in this whole area is the marital one. It is on the basis of marriage that, for most adults in our society, existence in the private sphere is built up. It will be clear that this is not at all a universal or even cross-culturally wide function of marriage. Rather has marriage in our society taken on a very peculiar character and functionality. It has been pointed out that marriage in contemporary society has lost some of its older functions and taken on new ones instead.[10] This is certainly correct, but we would prefer to state the matter a little differently. Marriage and the family used to be firmly embedded in a matrix of wider community relationships, serving as extensions and particularizations of the latter's social controls. There were few separating barriers between the world of the individual family and the wider community, a fact even to be seen in the physical conditions under which the family lived before the industrial revolution.[11] The same social life pulsated through the house, the street, and the community. In our terms, the family and within it the marital relationship were part and parcel of a considerably larger area of conversation. In our contemporary society, by contrast, each family constitutes its own segregated subworld, with its own controls and its own closed conversation.

This fact requires a much greater effort on the part of the marriage partners. Unlike an earlier situation in which the establishment of the new marriage simply added to the differentiation and complexity of an already existing social world, the marriage partners are now embarked on the often difficult task of constructing for themselves the little world in which they will live. To be sure, the larger society provides them with certain standard instructions as to how they should go about this task, but this does not change the fact that considerable effort of their own is required for its realization. The monogamous character of marriage enforces both the dramatic and the precarious nature of this undertaking. Success or failure hinges on the present idiosyncracies and the fairly unpredictable future development of those idiosyncracies of only two individuals (who, moreover, do not have a shared past)—as Simmel has shown, the most unstable of all possible social relationships.[12] Not surprisingly, the decision to embark on this undertaking has a critical, even cataclysmic connotation in the popular imagination, which is underlined as well as psychologically assuaged by the ceremonialism that surrounds the event.

Every social relationship requires objectivation; that is, requires a process by which subjectively experienced meanings become objective to the individual and in interaction with others become common property and thereby massively objective.[13] The degree of objectivation will depend on the number and the intensity of the social relationships that are its carriers. A relationship that consists of only two individuals called upon to sustain by their own efforts an ongoing social world will have to make up in intensity for the numerical poverty of the arrangement. This, in turn, accentuates the drama and the precariousness. The later addition of children will add to the, as it were, density of objectivation taking place within the nuclear family, thus rendering the latter a good deal less precarious. It remains true that the establishment and maintenance of such a social world makes extremely high demands on the principal participants.

The attempt can now be made to outline the ideal-typical process that takes place as marriage functions as an instrumentality for the social construction of reality. The chief protagonists of the drama are two individuals, each with a biographically accumulated and available stock of experience.[14] As members of a highly mobile society, these individuals have already internalized a degree of readiness to redefine themselves and to modify their stock of experience, thus bringing with them considerable psychological capacity for entering new relationships with others.[15] Also, coming from broadly similar sectors of the larger society (in terms of region, class, ethnic, and religious affiliations), the two individuals will have organized their stock of experience in similar fashion. In other words, the two individuals have internalized the same overall world, including the general definitions and expectations of the marriage relationship itself. Their society has provided them with a taken-for-granted image of marriage and has socialized them into an anticipation of stepping into the taken-for-granted roles of marriage. All the same, these relatively empty projections now have to be actualized, lived through, and filled with experiential content by the protagonists. This will require a dramatic change in their definitions of reality and of themselves.

As of the marriage, most of each partner's actions must now be projected in conjunction with those of the other. Each partner's definitions of reality must be continually correlated with the definitions of the other. The other is present in nearly all horizons of everyday conduct. Furthermore the identity of each now takes on a new character, having to be constantly matched with that of the other, indeed being typically perceived by people at large as being symbiotically conjoined with the identity of the other. In each partner's psychological economy of significant others, the marriage partner becomes the other *par excellence,* the nearest and most decisive coinhabitant of the world. Indeed all other significant relationships have to be almost automatically reperceived and regrouped in accordance with this drastic shift.

In other words, from the beginning of the marriage each partner has new modes in his meaningful experience of the world in general, of other people and of himself. By definition, then, marriage constitutes a nomic rupture. In terms of each partner's biography, the event of marriage initiates a new nomic process. Now, the full implications of this fact are rarely apprehended by the protagonists with any degree of clarity. There rather is to be found the notion that one's world, one's other-relationships and, above all, oneself have remained what they were before—only, of course, that world, others, and self will now be shared with the marriage partner. It should be clear by now that this notion is a grave misapprehension. Just because of this fact, marriage now propels the individual into an unintended and unarticulated development, in the course of which the nomic transformation takes place. What typically *is* apprehended are certain objective and concrete problems arising out of the marriage—such as tensions with in-laws, or with former friends, or religious differences between the partners, as well as immediate tensions between them. These are apprehended as external, situational, and practical difficulties. What is *not* apprehended is the subjective side of these difficulties, namely, the transformation of *nomos* and identity that has occurred and that continues to go on, so that all problems and relationships are experienced in a quite new way, that is, experienced within a new and ever-changing reality.

Take a simple and frequent illustration—the male partner's relationships with male friends before and after the marriage. It is a common observation that such relationships, especially if the extramarital partners are single, rarely survive the marriage, or, if they do, are drastically redefined after it. This is typically the result of neither a deliberate decision by the husband nor deliberate

sabotage by the wife. What rather happens, very simply, is a slow process in which the husband's image of his friend is transformed as he keeps talking about this friend with his wife. Even if no actual talking goes on, the mere presence of the wife forces him to see his friend differently. This need not mean that he adopts a negative image held by the wife. Regardless of what image she holds or is believed by him to hold, it will be different from that held by the husband. This difference will enter into the joint image that now needs to be fabricated in the course of the ongoing conversation between the marriage partners—and, in due course, must act powerfully on the image previously held by the husband. Again, typically, this process is rarely apprehended with any degree of lucidity. The old friend is more likely to fade out of the picture by slow degrees, as new kinds of friends take his place. The process, if commented upon at all within the marital conversation, can always be explained by socially available formulas about "people changing," "friends disappearing," or oneself "having become more mature." This process of conversational liquidation is especially powerful because it is one-sided—the husband typically talks with his wife about his friend, but *not* with his friend about his wife. Thus the friend is deprived of the defense of, as it were, counterdefining the relationship. This dominance of the marital conversation over all others is one of its most important characteristics. It may be mitigated by a certain amount of protective segregation of some nonmarital relationships (say, "Tuesday night out with the boys," or "Saturday lunch with mother"), but even then there are powerful emotional barriers against the sort of conversation (conversation *about* the marital relationship, that is) that would serve by way of counterdefinition.

Marriage thus posits a new reality. The individual's relationship with this new reality, however, is a dialectical one—he acts upon it, in collusion with the marriage partner, and it acts back upon both him and the partner, welding together their reality. Since, as we have argued before, the objectivation that constitutes this reality is precarious, the groups with which the couple associates are called upon to assist in codefining the new reality. The couple is pushed toward groups that strengthen their new definition of themselves and the world, avoids those that weaken this definition. This, in turn, releases the commonly known pressures of group association, again acting upon the marriage partners to change their definitions of the world and of themselves. Thus the new reality is not posited once and for all, but goes on being redefined not only in the marital interaction itself but in the various maritally based group relationships into which the couple enters.

The individual's biography marriage, then, brings about a decisive phase of socialization that can be compared with the phases of childhood and adolescence. This phase has a rather different structure from the earlier ones. There the individual was in the main socialized into already existing patterns. Here he actively collaborates rather than passively accommodates himself. Also in the previous phases of socialization, there was an apprehension of entering into a new world and being changed in the course of this. In marriage there is little apprehension of such a process, but rather the notion that the world has remained the same, with only its emotional and pragmatic connotations having changed. This notion, as we have tried to show, is illusionary.

The reconstruction of the world in marriage occurs principally in the course of conversation, as we have suggested. The implicit problem of this conversation is how to match two individual definitions of reality. By the very logic of the relationship, a common overall definition must be arrived at—otherwise the conversation will become impossible and, ipso facto, the relationship will be endangered. Now, this conversation may be understood as the working away of an ordering and typifying apparatus—if one prefers, an objectivating apparatus. Each partner ongoingly contributes his conceptions of reality, which are then "talked through," usually not once but many times, and in the process become objectivated by the conversational apparatus. The longer this conversation goes on, the more massively real do the objectivations become to the partners. In the marital conversation a world is not only built, but is also kept in a state of repair and ongoingly refurnished. The subjective reality of this world for the two partners is sustained by the same conversation. The nomic instrumentality of marriage is concretized over and over gain, from bed to breakfast table, as the partners carry on the endless conversation that feeds on nearly all they individually or jointly experience. Indeed, it may happen eventually that no experience is fully real unless and until it has been thus "talked through."

This process has a very important result —namely, a hardening or stabilization of the common objectivated reality. It should be easy to see now how this comes about. The objectivations ongoingly performed and internalized by the marriage partners become ever more massively real, as they are confirmed and reconfirmed in the marital conversation. The world that is made up of these objectivations at the same time gains in stability. For example, the images of other people which before or in the earlier stages of the marital conversation may have been rather ambiguous and shifting in the minds of the two partners, now become hardened into definite and stable characterizations. A casual acquaintance, say, may sometimes have appeared as lots of fun and sometimes as quite a bore to the wife before her marriage. Under the influence of the marital conversation, in which this other person is frequently "discussed," she will now come down more firmly on one *or* the other of the two characterizations, or on a reasonable compromise between the two. In any of these three options, though, she will have concocted with her husband a much more stable image of the person in question than she is likely to have had before her marriage, when there may have been no conversational pressure to make a definite option at all. The same process of stabilization may be observed with regard to self-definitions as well. In this way, the wife in our example will not only be pressured to assign stable characterizations to others but also to herself. Previously uninterested politically, she now identifies herself as a liberal. Previously alternating between dimly articulated religious positions, she now declares herself an agnostic. Previously confused and uncertain about her sexual emotions, she now understands herself as an unabashed hedonist in this area. And so on and so forth, with the same reality—and identity—stabilizing process at work on the husband. Both world and self thus take on a firmer, more reliable character for both partners.

Furthermore, it is not only the ongoing experience of the two partners that is constantly shared and passed through the conversational apparatus. The same sharing extends into the past. The two distinct biographies, as subjectively apprehended by the two individuals who have lived through them, are overruled and reinterpreted in the course of their conversation. Sooner or later, they will "tell all"—or, more correctly, they will tell it in such a way that it fits into the self-definitions objectivated in the marital relationship. The couple thus constructs not only present reality but reconstructs past reality as well, fabricating a common memory that integrates the recollections of the two individual pasts.[16] The comic fulfillment of this process may be seen in those cases when one partner "remembers" more clearly what happened in the other's past than the other does—and corrects him accordingly. Similarly, there occurs a sharing of future horizons, which leads not only to stabilization, but inevitably to a narrowing of the future projections of each partner. Before marriage the individual typically plays with quite discrepant daydreams in which his future self is projected.[17] Having now considerably stabilized his self-image, the married individual will have to project the future in accordance with this maritally defined identity. This narrowing of future horizons begins with the obvious external limitations that marriage entails, as, for example, with regard to vocational and career plans. However, it extends also to the more general possibilities of the individual's biography. To return to a previous illustration, the wife, having "found herself" as a liberal, an agnostic and a "sexually healthy" person, ipso facto liquidates the possibilities of becoming an anarchist, a Catholic, or a lesbian. At least until further notice she has decided upon who she is—and, by the same token, on who she will be. The stabilization brought about by marriage thus affects the total reality in which the partners exist. In the most far-reaching sense of the word, the married individual "settles down"—and *must* do so, if the marriage is to be viable, in accordance with its contemporary institutional definition.

It cannot be sufficiently strongly emphasized that this process is typically unapprehended, almost automatic in character. The protagonists of the marriage drama do *not* set out deliberately to re-create their world. Each continues to live in a world that is taken for granted—and keeps its taken-for-granted character even as it is metamorphosed. The new world that the married partners, Prometheuslike, have called into being is perceived by them as the normal world in which they have lived before. Reconstructed present and reinterpreted past are perceived as a continuum, extending forwards into a commonly projected future. The dramatic change that has occurred remains, in bulk, unapprehended and unarticulated. And where it forces itself upon the individual's attention, it is retrojected into the past, explained as having always been there, though perhaps in a hidden way. Typically, the reality that has been "invented" within the marital conversation is subjectively perceived as a "discovery." Thus the partners "discover" themselves and the world, "who they really are," "what they really believe," "how they really feel, and always have felt, about so-and-so." This retrojection of the world being produced all the time by themselves serves to enhance the stability of this world and at the same time to assuage the "existential anxiety" that, probably inevitably, accompanies the perception that nothing but one's narrow shoulders support the universe in which one has chosen to live. If one may put it like this, it is psychologically more tolerable to be Columbus than to be Prometheus.

The use of the term "stabilization" should not detract from the insight into the difficulty and precariousness of this world-building enterprise. Often enough, the new universe collapses *in statu nascendi*. Many more times it continues over a period, swaying perilously back and forth as the two partners try to hold it up, finally to be abandoned as an impossible undertaking. If one conceives of the marital conversation as the principal drama and the two partners as the principal protagonists of the drama, then one can look upon the other individuals involved as the supporting chorus for the central dramatic action. Children, friends, relatives, and casual acquaintances all have their part in reinforcing the tenuous structure of the new reality. It goes without saying that the children form the most important part of this supporting chorus. Their very existence is predicated on the maritally established world. The marital partners themselves are in charge of their socialization *into* this world, which to them has a preexistent and self-evident character. They are taught from the beginning to speak precisely those lines that lend themselves to a supporting chorus, from their first invocations of "Daddy" and "Mummy" on to their adoption of the parents' ordering and typifying apparatus that now defines *their* world as well. The marital conversation is now in the process of becoming a family symposium, with the necessary consequences that its objectivations rapidly gain in density, plausibility and durability.

In sum: The process that we have been inquiring into is, ideal-typically, one in which reality is crystallized, narrowed, and stabilized. Ambivalences are converted into certainties. Typifications of self and of others become settled. Most generally, possibliities become facticities. What is more, this process of transformation remains, most of the time, unapprehended by those who are both its authors and its objects.[18]

We have analyzed in some detail that process that, we contend, entitles us to describe marriage as a nomic instrumentality. It may now be well to turn back once more to the macrosocial context in which this process takes place—a process that, to repeat, is peculiar to our society as far as the institution of marriage is concerned, although it obviously expresses much more general human facts. The narrowing and stabilization of identity is functional in a society that, in its major public institutions, must insist on rigid controls over the individual's conduct. At the same time, the narrow enclave of the nuclear family serves as a macrosocially innocuous "play area," in which the individual can safely exercise his world-building proclivities without upsetting any of the important social, economic, and political apple carts. Barred from expanding himself into the area occupied by those major institutions, he is given plenty of leeway to "discover himself" in his marriage and his family, and, in view of the difficulty of this undertaking, is provided with a number of auxiliary agencies that stand ready to assist him (such as counseling, psychotherapeutic, and religious agencies). The marital adventure can be relied upon to absorb a large amount of energy

that might otherwise be expended more dangerously. The ideological themes of familism, romantic love, sexual expression, maturity, and social adjustment, with the pervasive psychologistic anthropology that underlies them all, function to legitimate this enterprise. Also the narrowing and stabilization of the individual's principal area of conversation within the nuclear family is functional in a society that requires high degrees of both geographical and social mobility. The segregated little world of the family can be easily detached from one milieu and transposed into another without appreciably interfering with the central processes going on in it. Needless to say, we are not suggesting that these functions are deliberately planned or even apprehended by some mythical ruling directorate of the society. Like most social phenomena, whether they be macro- or microscopic, these functions are typically unintended and unarticulated. What is more, the functionality would be impaired if it were too widely apprehended.

We believe that the above theoretical considerations serve to give a new perspective on various empirical facts studied by family sociologists. As we have emphasized a number of times, our considerations are ideal-typical in intention. We have been interested in marriage at a normal age in urban, middle-class, western societies. We cannot discuss here such special problems as marriages or remarriages at a more advanced age, marriage in the remaining rural subcultures, or in ethnic or lower-class minority groups. We feel quite justified in this limitation of scope, however, by the empirical findings that tend toward the view that a global marriage type is emerging in the central strata of modern industrial societies.[19] This type, commonly referred to as the nuclear family, has been analyzed in terms of a shift from the so-called family of orientation to the so-called family (of procreation as the most important reference for the individual).[20] In addition to the well-known socioeconomic reasons for this shift, most of them rooted in the development of industrialism, we would argue that important macrosocial functions pertain to the nomic process within the nuclear family, as we have analyzed it. This functionality of the nuclear family must, furthermore, be seen in conjunction with the familistic ideology that both reflects and reinforces it. A few specific empirical points may suffice to indicate the applicability of our theoretical perspective. To make these we shall use selected American data.

The trend towards marriage at an earlier age has been noted.[21] This has been correctly related to such factors as urban freedom, sexual emancipation, and equalitarian values. We would add the important fact that a child raised in the circumscribed world of the nuclear family is stamped by it in terms of his psychological needs and social expectations. Having to live in the larger society from which the nuclear family is segregated, the adolescent soon feels the need for a "little world" of his own, having been socialized in such a way that only by having such a world to withdraw into can he successfully cope with the anonymous "big world" that confronts him as soon as he steps outside his parental home. In other words, to be "at home" in society entails, *per definitionem*, the construction of a maritally based subworld. The parental home itself facilitates such an early jump into marriage precisely because its controls are very narrow in scope and leave the adolescent to his own nomic devices at an early age. As has been studied in considerable detail, the adolescent peer group functions as a transitional *nomos* between the two family worlds in the individual's biography.[22]

The equalization in the age of the marriage partners has also been noted.[23] This is certainly also to be related to equalitarian values and, concomitantly, to the decline in the "double standard" of sexual morality. Also, however, this fact is very conducive to the common reality-constructing enterprise that we have analyzed. One of the features of the latter, as we have pointed out, is the reconstruction of the two biographies in terms of a cohesive and mutually correlated common memory. This task is evidently facilitated if the two partners are of roughly equal age. Another empirical finding to which our considerations are relevant is the choice of marriage partners within similar socioeconomic backgrounds.[24] Apart from the obvious practical pressures towards such limitations of choice, the latter also insure sufficient similarity in the biographically accumulated stocks of experi-

ence to facilitate the described reality-constructing process. This would also offer additional explanation to the observed tendency to narrow the limitations of marital choice even further, for example in terms of religious background.[25]

There now exists a considerable body of data on the adoption and mutual adjustment of marital roles.[26] Nothing in our considerations detracts from the analyses made of these data by sociologists interested primarily in the processes of group interaction. We would only argue that something more fundamental is involved in this role-taking —namely, the individual's relationship to reality as such. Each role in the marital situation carries with it a universe of discourse, broadly given by cultural definition, but continually reactualized in the ongoing conversation between the marriage partners. Put simply: Marriage involves not only stepping into new roles, but, beyond this, stepping into a new world. The *mutuality* of adjustment may again be related to the rise of marital equalitarianism, in which comparable effort is demanded of both partners.

Most directly related to our considerations are data that pertain to the greater stability of married as against unmarried individuals.[27] Though frequently presented in misleading psychological terms (such as "greater emotional stability," "greater maturity," and so on), these data are sufficiently validated to be used not only by marriage counselors but in the risk calculations of insurance companies. We would contend that our theoretical perspective places these data into a much more intelligible sociological frame of reference, which also happens to be free of the particular value bias with which the psychological terms are loaded. It is, or course, quite true that married people are more stable emotionally (i.e., operating within a more controlled scope of emotional expression), more mature in their views (i.e., inhabiting a firmer and narrower world in conformity with the expectations of society), and more sure of themselves (i.e., having objectivated a more stable and fixated self-definition). *Therefore* they are more liable to be psychologically balanced (i.e., having sealed off much of their "anxiety," and reduced ambivalence as well as openness towards new possibilities of self-definition) and socially predictable (i.e., keeping their conduct well within the socially established safety rules). All of these phenomena are concomitants of the overall fact of having "settled down"—cognitively, emotionally, in terms of self-identification. To speak of these phenomena as indicators of "mental health," let alone of "adjustment to reality," overlooks the decisive fact that reality is socially constructed and that psychological conditions of all sorts are grounded in a social matrix.

We would say, very simply, that the married individual comes to live in a more stable world, from which fact certain psychological consequences can be readily deduced. To bestow some sort of higher ontological status upon these psychological consequences is ipso facto a symptom of the mis- or non-apprehension of the social process that has produced them. Furthermore the compulsion to legitimate the stabilized marital world, be it in psychologistic or in traditional religious terms, is another expression of the precariousness of its construction.[28] This is not the place to pursue any further the ideological processes involved in this. Suffice it to say that contemporary psychology functions to sustain this precarious world by assigning to it the status of "normalcy," a legitimating operation that increasingly links up with the older religious assignment of the status of "sacredness." Both legitimating agencies have established their own rites of passage, validating myths and rituals, and individualized repair services for crisis situations. Whether one legitimates one's maritally constructed reality in terms of "mental health" or of the "sacrament of marriage" is today largely left to free consumer preference, but it is indicative of the crystallization of a new overall universe of discourse that it is increasingly possible to do both at the same time.

Finally, we would point here to the empirical data on divorce.[29] The prevalence and, indeed, increasing prevalence of divorce might at first appear as a counterargument to our theoretical considerations. We would contend that the very opposite is the case, as the data themselves bear out. Typically, individuals in our society do not divorce because marriage has become unimportant to them, but because it has become so important

that they have no tolerance for the less than completely successful marital arrangement they have contracted with the particular individual in question. This is more fully understood when one has grasped the crucial need for the sort of world that only marriage can produce in our society, a world without which the individual is powerfully threatened with anomie in the fullest sense of the word. Also, the frequency of divorce simply reflects the difficulty and demanding character of the whole undertaking. The empirical fact that the great majority of divorced individuals plan to remarry and a good majority of them actually do, at least in America, fully bears out this contention.[30]

The purpose of this article is not polemic, nor do we wish to advocate any particular values concerning marriage. We have sought to debunk the familistic ideology only insofar as it serves to obfuscate a sociological understanding of the phenomenon. Our purpose has rather been twofold. First, we wanted to show that it is possible to develop a sociological theory of marriage that is based on clearly sociological presuppositions, without operating with psychological or psychiatric categories that have dubious value within a sociological frame of reference. We believe that such a sociological theory of marriage is generally useful for a fully conscious awareness of existence in contemporary society and not only for the sociologist. Secondly, we have used the case of marriage for an exercise in the sociology of knowledge, a discipline that we regard as most promising. Hitherto this discipline has been almost exclusively concerned with macro-sociological questions, such as those dealing with the relationship of intellectual history to social processes. We believe that the microsociological focus is equally important for this discipline. The sociology of knowledge must not only be concerned with the great universes of meaning that history offers up for our inspection, but with the many little workshops in which living individuals keep hammering away at the construction and maintenance of these universes. In this way, the sociologist can make an important contribution to the illumination of that everyday world in which we all live and which we help fashion in the course of our biography.

NOTES

1. The present article has come out of a larger project on which the authors have been engaged in collaboration with three colleagues in sociology and philosophy. The project is to produce a systematic treatise that will integrate a number of now separate theoretical standards in the sociology of knowledge.

2. Cf. especially Max Weber, *Wirtschaft und Gesellschaft.* Tuebingen: Mohr, 1956; *Id., Gesammelte Aufsaetze zur Wissenschaftslehre.* Tuebingen: Mohr, 1951; George H. Mead, *Mind, self, and society.* Chicago: University of Chicago Press, 1934; Alfred Schutz, *Der sinnhafte Aufbau der sozialen Welt.* Vienna: Springer, 1960; *Id., Collected Papers,* I. The Hague: Nijhoff, 1962; Maurice Merleau-Ponty, *Phénoménologie de la perception.* Paris: Gallimard, 1945; *Id., La structure du comportement.* Paris: Presses Universitaires de France, 1953.

3. Cf. Schutz, *Aufbau,* pp. 202–220; *Id., Collected papers,* I, pp. 3–27, 283–286.

4. Cf. Schutz, *Collected papers,* I, pp. 207–228.

5. Cf. especially Jean Piaget, *The construction of reality in the child.* New York: Basic Books, 1954.

6. Cf. Mead, *op.cit.,* pp. 135–226.

7. Cf. Schutz, *Aufbau,* pp. 181–195.

8. Cf. Arnold Gehlen, *Die Seels im technischen Zeitalter.* Hamburg: Rowohlt, 1957, pp. 57–69; *Id., Anthropologische Forschung.* Hamburg: Rowohlt, 1961, pp. 69–77, 127–140; Helmut Schelsky, *Soziologie der Sexualitaet.* Hamburg: Rowohlt, 1955, pp. 102–133. Also, cf. Thomas Luckmann, On religion in modern socieity, *Journal for the Scientific Study of Religion* (Spring) 1963: 147–162.

9. In these considerations we have been influenced by certain presuppositions of Marxian anthropology, as well as by the anthropological work of Max Scheler, Helmuth Plessner, and Arnold Gehlen. We are indebted to Thomas Luckmann for the clarification of the social-psychological significance of the private sphere.

10. Cf. Talcott Parsons and Robert Bales, *Family, socialization, and interaction process.* Glencoe, Ill.: Free Press, 1955, pp. 3–34, 353–396.

11. Cf. Philippé Ariés, *Centuries of childhood.* New York: Knopf, 1962, pp. 339–410.

12. Cf. Kurt Wolff (ed.), *The sociology of Georg Simmel.* Glencoe, Ill.: Free Press, 1950, pp. 118–144.

13. Cf. Schutz, *Aufbau,* pp. 29–36, 149–153.

14. Cf. Schutz, *Aufbau,* pp. 186–192, 202–210.

15. David Riesman's well-known concept of "other-direction" would also be applicable here.

16. Cf. Maurice Halbwachs, *Les cadres sociaux de la mémorie.* Paris: Presses Universitares de France, 1952, especially pp. 146–177; Also, cf. Peter Berger, *Invitation to sociology—A humanistic perspective.* Garden City, N.Y.: Doubleday-Anchor, 1963, pp. 54–65.

17. Cf. Schutz, *Collected Papers,* I, pp. 72–73, 79–82.

18. The phenomena here discussed could also be formulated effectively in terms of Marxian categories of reification and false consciousness. Jean-Paul Sartre's recent work, especially *Critique de la raison dialectique,* seeks to integrate these categories within a phenomenological analysis of human conduct. Also, cf. Henri Lefebvre, *Critique de la vie quotidienne.* Paris: l'Arche, 1958–1961.

19. Cf. Renate Mayntz, *Die moderne Familie.* Stuttgart: Enke, 1955; Helmut Schelsky, *Wandlungen der deutschen Familie in der Gegenwart.* Stuttgart: Enke, 1955; Maximilien Sorre (ed.), *Sociologie comparée de la famille contemporaine.* Paris: Centre National de la Recherche Scientifique, 1955; Ruth Anshen (ed.), *The family—its function and destiny.* New York: Harper, 1959; Norman Bell and Ezra Vogel, *A modern introduction to the family.* Glencoe, Ill.: Free Press, 1960.

20. Cf. Talcott Parsons, *Essays in sociological theory.* Glencoe, Ill.: Free Press, 1949, pp. 233–250.

21. In these as well as the following references to empirical studies we naturally make no attempt at comprehensiveness. References are given as representative of much larger body of materials. Cf. Paul Glick, *American families.* New York: Wiley, 1957, p. 54. Also, *cf. Id.,* The family cycle. *American Sociological Review,* April 1947, 164–174. Also, cf. Bureau of the Census, *Statistical abstracts of the United States,* 1956 and 1958; *Current population reports,* Series P–20, No. 96 (November 1959).

22. Cf. David Riesman, *The lonely crowd.* New Haven: Yale University Press, 1953, pp. 29–40; Frederick Elkin, *The child and society.* New York: Random House, 1960, *passim.*

23. Cf. references given above under Note 21.

24. Cf. W. Lloyd Warner and Paul Lunt, *The social life of a modern community.* New Haven: Yale University Press, 1941, pp. 436–440; August Hollingshead, Cultural factors in the selection of marriage mates, *American Sociological Review,* October 1950, 619–627. Also cf. Ernest Burgess and Paul Wallin, Homogamy in social characteristics. *American Journal of Sociology,* September 1943, 109–124.

25. Cf. Gerhard Lenski, *The religious factor.* Garden City, N.Y.: Doubleday, 1961, pp. 48–50.

26. Cf. Leonard Cottrell, Roles in marital adjustment. *Publications of the American Sociological Society*, 1933, 27:107–115; Willard Waller and Reuben Hill, *The family—a dynamic interpretation.* New York: Dryden, 1951, pp. 253–271; Morris Zelditch, Role differentiation in the nuclear family. In Parsons and Bales, *op. cit.*, pp. 307–352. For a general discussion of role interaction in small groups, cf. especially George Homans, *The human group.* New York: Harcourt Brace, 1950.

27. Cf. Waller and Hill, *op. cit.*, pp. 253–271, for an excellent summation of such data.

28. Cf. Dennison Nash and Peter Berger, The family, the child and the religious revival in suburbia. *Journal for the Scientific Study of Religion*, fall 1962, 85–93.

29. Cf. Bureau of the Census, *op. cit.*

30. Cf. Talcott Parsons, Age and sex in the social structure of the United States. *American Sociological Review*, December 1942, 604–616; Paul Glick, First marriages and remarriages. *American Sociological Review*, December 1949, 726–734; William Goode, *After divorce.* Glencoe, Ill.: Free Press, 1956, pp. 269–285.

A Middle-American Marriage

THOMAS J. COTTLE

Theodore and Eleanor Graziano are fictitious names that have been used to hide the identity of a real family. For six years, my research has been devoted to working with families in various Boston communities. One purpose of this work is to describe the daily experience of these families, and the history of their members, as well as my relationship with them. I met the Grazianos quite accidentally five years ago through a young man who worked for Ted Graziano. I soon met Eleanor, their children, and other members of their family.

As a methodological note, I work without tape recorder or prepared questionnaire, believing that both devices constrain interactions already made somewhat unnatural by my presence. In all instances, the families read my manuscripts and grant permission to publish them.

Thomas J. Cottle

I HAD BEEN LATE ARRIVING AT THE Grazianos' house on Poplar Street. Some unexpected traffic, coupled with the uncongenial design of Boston's streets, was enough to put me almost forty-five minutes behind schedule. Theodore Graziano (his friends call him Mushy) had Tuesdays off from work; so the time I could spend with him and his wife Eleanor was precious. Normally, I would interview one of them alone.

For about fifteen years, Ted Graziano has worked for a Boston newspaper. Starting as a stockroom "boy" (he was almost 25 at the time), he had worked his way up to where now, at 39, he was foreman of the shipping operation. Salaries had risen over the past years, bringing his take-home pay to where he could just about get by. The important thing for him was the security, a factor he had mentioned several times when we spoke at his office.

"This is not the time to be sitting on any gamble," he had said. "This is the time when the economy of the country demands that you get yourself a job that looks like it's got to hold out. Doctors, lawyers, judges, they got it best. The workingman, like always, he's going to be the first to get hit. Unemployment starts at the bottom and works its way up. It's like a disease that they can't find a cure for. You know it's out there and you just gotta do the best you can to avoid getting it. Stay warm, eat good food . . . .

"You take a job like this." He waved his right arm about as if to take in the enormous shipping area, partitioned offices, and truck docks. "It's one hell of an operation. I got real responsibility here. You ask any man they got working here and they'll tell you about that responsibility. I tell you, though, in the beginning, ten years ago or so, it was one hell of a challenge. Couple nights there I got so damn excited with the prospect of it all, I could barely go to sleep. Now it's just another job to me.

"Man, there are times I'm working when I think about how nice it would be to be anywhere else. Sitting in the sun, or doing what you're doing. You know, walking around, talking to people. But most of the time I have to take those thoughts and crush 'em up like little paper balls and throw 'em away." He shook his head from side to side, crumpling an imaginary sheet of paper in one of his strong hands. Then he looked back at me. I had no answer for him.

Since our home meetings took place in the kitchen, I entered by the back door as the family members did. Alone in the house while his wife visited her mother, Ted had been sitting in the kitchen reading the newspaper. Eleanor had left us two glasses of milk and a cake covered with tinfoil on the kitchen table.

"Come on, let's eat," Ted said. "I've been dying with hunger waiting for you." He took great pleasure in cutting a slice of cake for me, and laid it gently on a plate. He reached over and placed a fork on the plate, then pushed one of the glasses of milk toward me. When I was taken care of he prepared a piece, considerably smaller, for himself. Ellie, I knew, would decline an invitation to eat with us. Baking this extra item affected their budget; the cake would have to last several days.

"So what do we talk about today, or shouldn't we say anything until Ellie gets here?" Ted asked, his mouth full of cake.

"Talk about anything you like, Ted," I said. "I'm not listening anyway with this cake here."

"Eat it up. There's lots more where it came from. Your wife cooks though, doesn't she?"

"Yes, she does."

"Well then, you aren't hurting too much." He sighed deeply, wiping some crumbs from his chin. "Lots of guys have it pretty bad. I told myself a long time ago, no wife of mine's going to work. Ever! No matter how bad it is, a man provides in his way, a woman in hers. Ellie doesn't need to go cleaning or secretarying, or work at the phone company like all her girlfriends. We'll manage. Eight thousand years and I'll have this house paid off, and when I die she'll be set up. She don't ever have to work if she don't want to. That's the way it's supposed to be. You agree?"

"Well, people have to work it out the way they want," I answered.

"You're not going to tell me you're one of those liberation people are you?" he grinned at me.

"Well, I guess in a way I am. Men and women, it seems to me, have to enhance one another, support each other to be what they want."

"Now that I like. That I'll buy. That's all right. You know, now that you mention it, that's maybe like my biggest gripe. I never did have anyone enhance my life. I can look back at it now, forty years next July, I can't see a person anywhere enhanced me, helped me to get anything."

"You have Ellie," I suggested. His eyes were closed slightly as several thoughts seemed to touch him at once.

"Yeah, I got Ellie, all right. Probably a good thing for me too. But that's not the kind of support I'm talking about. A wife is a wife, she doesn't help you out there." He pointed at the window above the sink. "That's not what I mean."

"Can you talk about it?"

"Let me get the words first." He paused, looking into his glass. "The living day by day that women do is not what helps a man. There's a way a man has to get his whole life together. It's all got to fit somehow, make sense. You know what I mean?" He didn't wait for an answer. "It's got to be set up so that every move you make has some reason in a plan that you have to formulate somewhere along the line. It has to build toward something.''

He looked at me. "You know about these things. You may be richer than I am, I'll bet you are too. And you may have a more interesting job, which I know you do. I even told you once, remember?''

"Yes. In the shop.''

"At the office, right,'' he corrected me.

"Office.''

"But the important thing is that a man knows what it means to arrange for his life. That, no woman knows! That I know for sure.'' A melancholy feeling was taking the place of anger. "There's a kicker in it though, you know?''

"Which is?''

"Which is that a life that asks us to make certain that pasts and presents and futures fit together in some logical way has a price. You know yourself, as time goes on it gets harder and harder to just live each day and get the most out of it. You don't live each day like that when you're a man. What you live is your work at the moment, your plans, what you call your prospects, *and* your regrets, what you should have done. You think about having bits of time back again to work with. You think how nice it would be to see what the future holds, even in a job like mine where I practically know how everything's going to turn out. Still, you'd like to take a little peek. Maybe just to know whether all those connections you're making are really sticking. You follow me?''

"Yes I do,'' I answered.

"So you don't say the hell with what was and what will be. That's the way you think when you go out drinking. At least, that's the way it is for me. I go out and get a little in the bag,'' he started to smile. I smiled too as I saw his face take on, of all things, a look of pride. "That's when my future disappears, my past disappears, and I got once and for all my present moment and nothing else goddammit *to be concerned about!*'' He shouted the words as he straightened up in his chair. "But now, I ask you, how long's a man with any respect gonna run around in the bag? So you come home, and you sleep, and you drink coffee, and you make nice to your wife, and there you are the next day, thinking the same things all over again: how it all fits together, and how you wish you could be young

again, and how great it would be to know what the future's got waiting for you.''

"That's one hell of an analysis,'' I said.

"Well, I don't know as I'd call it an analysis, exactly,'' he said. "You just keep your eye on the future, because the name of the game is that since you don't have much to say about dying, you have to fill in as many of the empty spaces out there as you can. You don't leave things to chance. Ellie always talks to me, when I get in one sort of a huff or another, about God or about fate. 'Things will just happen,' she says all the time. 'Things are just going to happen.' Sure. They are. Lots of things are just going to happen. Like the roof might fall in on our heads, right here in the kitchen. But the odds are against it because *I* fix the roof, because *I* make certain things like that *won't* happen.

"You know what it's like, Tom? It's just like football. There's a good reason why men like football. It's a man's game because it's played out the way men think. First, you got competition. Then you have a game plan. And you stick with it until you have to find a new one. And it's all leading up to something. Something you could practically predict. If you move here, I'll move there. You move here, I'll move there.'' He pushed his fingers against the tabletop, his right hand representing my team, his left hand representing his team.

"I can't say these things to Ellie. Of course, the kids don't want to hear about it. I talk with some of my friends, but not too many of them are as smart as you. I guess you know how little schooling we all have. Our kids, I hope, will be different. I'm starting to sound like the old lady. Hoping instead of arranging.''

"Well,'' I tried to assure him, "there's got to be a place for hope in the plan.''

"Sure,'' he said with resignation. "Of course there's a place for hope. But first you make preparations. Whatever is left over that you can't in any way control for, that falls over into the hope category. I don't need God or prayer, or hope.''

We had been speaking almost an hour when Eleanor Graziano entered the kitchen. She was flushed and out of breath.

"Please, please excuse me. I'm so late. I went over to my mother's for a minute. I didn't even take my coat off, and before you know it an hour's gone." I nodded to her and started to say something about my own lateness. "Did you find the cake?" she asked me.

"Did we," I replied.

"Was it all right?" she asked modestly. I grinned at her.

"Fair. It was fair, Ellie." She laughed and turned her face downward. Ted laughed too.

"A couple of jokesters I got here. Two little boys with no place to go and nothing to do but eat cake and get fat." I couldn't resist: "Oh, you love it and you know it, Mrs. G."

"You I love," she laughed. "Mushy I'm not so sure about." Ted and I laughed again and looked at one another.

"You better be careful, wife, or I'll tell *you* what I've been telling Tom here for the last hour about *you.*"

"Yeah, and what's that?" she asked, removing her boots and throwing them in the back hallway.

"Oh," he started, "about people enhancing one another's lives. Game plans. You know, the usual . . . ." He winked at me.

"Game plans?" she asked. "Football? Football! Is that it?"

"That's it," I said.

"Not quite," Ted said.

"Then what is it?" she wanted to know.

"Sit down, Ellie. You and Tom talk. I'm going to the corner for cigars. When I come back we'll continue with this. It's time for a commercial."

"Commercial? Tom, will you tell me please what he's babbling about?"

"I will."

"Go on then," she said to her husband. "I've got a few things for Tom you don't have to know about."

Ellie moved about the kitchen, peering into cabinets at canned goods and plates: "Can't seem to find . . . don't tell me I forgot to get . . . if I don't make a list when I go to the store I'm dead. Can you beat this? I'm not forty yet and my mother, who's almost seventy, has a brain in better shape than mine."

"I doubt that."

"No, it's true," she protested without looking back. "So what do we speak about today? Are you still asking the same questions?"

"Same questions, I suppose."

"Well, I don't know what else I can tell you. Mushy's the one with all the answers. There's nothing you could ask him that he wouldn't have some answer for. Some man, Mr. Graziano." I watched her lay out supplies and utensils in preparation for making dinner. The counter tops were spotless, the sink empty of dishes and garbage, the faces of the cabinets glistening. It was all quite a change from our first meeting four years ago, on the day actually when the Grazianos had moved from a four-room apartment less than a mile away. Suddenly Ted had gotten it in his head to buy a house. Ellie had argued that they couldn't afford it. But he was driven to buy, and on borrowed money they had managed. They had three bedrooms now, and they "could spread out," as Ellie said, finally admitting to her delight. "The children can stay in the same school, and I'm even closer to my mother. If we can just manage," she sighed, "it will be a blessing, *the* blessing of my whole life."

While Eleanor Chadwick had never known poverty as a child, she also had never imagined that her marriage to Teddy Graziano, "the Mushy man," would ever lead to a home and a kitchen glowing with warmth and pride like this one. Her father had been an elevator operator and starter during the day, a warehouse inspector four nights a week. He had lived his entire life in Boston. His salary allowed his wife and five children to live comfortably enough in a three-story walk-up apartment. A screened-in back porch opened out from the kitchen of that apartment, and on hot summer evenings the family gathered there feeling as cool as one could during a Boston summer.

"That was ever so lovely, just to be together, even when it was so hot you thought you might die." Ellie and I had had a long conversation about her childhood when the Grazianos moved into their new home. We had sat in this same kitchen on cardboard boxes filled with supplies and clothes. "I would love to have those days back again," she had said. "Even before Mushy and all this. Even before. So many, many times, I wish that tomorrow would be the beginning of a change, a sort of change backward. It's not like you might think, that I fear getting older. No, it's just that wonderful feeling of worriless peace, childhood, being a little girl and having those long hours with my father. He was a delight to know. You would have liked him, Tom. 'Course that's not saying too much, since Dad never had an enemy. He got on with everyone. You know, in many ways, he was very much like Mushy. Mushy without the anger. Dad knew he would never be rich, that he'd never achieve anything special or wonderful in his life. He knew lots of rich people too, but I never heard him complain or compare himself with someone else. The world was the way it was and he was big enough to accept it.

"Mushy's the same way up to a point. I'm sure he feels that he's not going anywhere in his life, at his job, I mean, but he's not about to accept any of that. He'll always tell me that if next year's the same as this year, then he's been a failure. There's no other way. That kind of statement I never heard once from my father's mouth. Never once. For me, you see, that's the sign of a good man. If next year's the same as this one, then you thank God. You get down on your knees at night and you thank God that everybody is well, and that you have enough to eat, and a comfortable place to sleep. You know that everything is provided for. But Mushy doesn't want it that way. The comfortable things, of course, he wants. Like, he wanted this house." I remember Ellie looking about at the boxes lying everywhere and seeing in her face a look of, How are we ever going to get set up again? I saw excitement too, a controlled excitement as though one were not supposed to ask for such delicious treasures but could adore them if they came one's way.

"Well, I'm set here for life. I get used to something very quickly and don't ever want to change. You know something, I can feel in my hands the curtains we used to have in the apartment where I lived as a child. And the tables in the living room and the kitchen too. That's how strong my memory is, so that must be how strong my attachment to things is. To people too. It grieves me, it really does, that the good times are gone and by many, sad to say, forgotten. I think Mush is that way. Something good happens, like maybe a party. He lives it as much as anyone. But then, when it's over, that's sort of the end of it. Me, I'm so different from him it's hard to believe we could have gotten along as long as we have. Something important happens, it doesn't matter whether it's good or bad, I hang on to it. It's just like the house. I love this, of course.

But you give me the largest mansion you can find, a palace, and I'll sit in my bedroom, I mean bedrooms," she laughed, "and I'll be thinking of that little apartment I grew up in, the porch and summers, and all the rest of it."

That was part of our conversation almost four years ago. Now, as we waited together in the same kitchen for Ted to return, I knew that we both felt a nostalgia, a longing for something, for the people of four years ago, for the people of our respective childhoods as well.

"You're pretty deep in thought, young man." Ellie surprised me.

"Yeah. I guess I was pretty deep into something there. I was remembering the discussion we had when you first moved. Remember that?"

"Yes." She strained to recover some of those earlier words. "Barely I do. About my childhood and the old place?"

"Yes. And your mother and father," I reminded her.

"Yes. I remember. I wonder what Mushy remembers of those days. I'll bet you very little. He sure likes to lock his past away. He thinks only of the future now. Every night in bed he's got another plan, another dream. Trips, property, real estate. The kids going to college. I have to tell him, 'Mushy, it's 1973, not 1993. Let time pass. You're living in an age that hasn't even been born yet. Give the world a chance to do what it's going to do. Mushy wants it to be 1993, that's fine with me, but he can damn well get there without me. I'll just take my own sweet time about it." She ended by pulling extra hard on the tie of her apron strings.

After sitting a while in silence, I rose from my chair. Through the window above the sink I saw Ted walking through a light rain. Ellie did not see him.

"I know one thing that makes me different from Mushy," she said. "I worry more than he does. I worry about what will happen. I worry there may not be ways to get things done as we want them to. But I don't worry about what I can't see, about what's not here yet. What's more, I believe you must live with a belief in God. Some things only God knows what to do with. Mushy thinks I'm nuts when I say this. So I've stopped saying it in front of him, and, for that matter, in front of the children when he's around. He worries too, but for him it's more that there won't be enough time to finish all the things he's planned to do. As for God, he's about as far from God as I am from…from…I don't know what. The President of the United States." I saw the top of Ted Graziano's head pass under the window.

"Don't you think for one minute I'm telling you little petty businesses in our lives," Ellie continued. "I'm telling you the most important things. We run, you might say, on different clocks. You know, like the East Coast and the West Coast. We're in the same country, speaking the same language most of the time, but we've got clocks inside of us that I'm sure run at different speeds, and in different directions as well." She hesitated again. She had more to say. The back door flew open and Ted entered the kitchen.

"A man with cigars," he began, "is a man halfway to heaven." He slammed the door shut so that the latch chain smacked loudly against the glass pane.

I had turned my body to greet him. Beside me I heard Ellie say quietly: "Two separate clocks, each ticking their own sweet time, each heading off in a direction that would probably confuse the Almighty."

How and when the tension in their conversation grew to the proportions it would that rainy afternoon I cannot recall, or make myself recall. I was part of the tension, for I had asked the questions that aroused so many feelings. And I had split them apart by speaking intimately with each of them. Ellie was seated at the table across from me, Ted stood in the doorway between the dining space and living room, pacing in and out of our vision.

"You know, Ellie," he was saying, his anger rising, "that's probably where it all goes wrong, every time with every man and every woman."

"Where?" she asked. "Where does what go wrong?"

"Look. You and I may come from the same background," he pointed at his wife, "but there are times when we're so different it's almost laughable that we've made it this long."

"Are the kids upstairs?" Ellie questioned.

"Oh, the hell with the kids. Let 'em hear. What the hell's the difference if they hear? What do you want, children who don't know what's going on in their own house?"

"No, I don't." Ellie's voice sounded frightened.

"That's exactly what my parents always did. They tried to keep everything from us as though we didn't know what was going on. Let 'em hear for once."

"You've never been able to understand what my life is made of. I tell you plans, what might happen at work, I tell you my dreams, little that you could care."

"I listen to every one of them."

"Listening isn't enough, goddammit. It's like Tom here. He listens. But it isn't enough. You think my plans are nuts or that I live in the future somehow. Or that I got a lot of pipe dreams."

"I didn't say that."

"You do in your way. Here's a stranger come in this house is more sympathetic to the way I want to carve out my future than the woman I married. That's really a laugh."

"That's not fair, Ted," I said.

"I don't care about fair," he shot back. "We're way beyond talking about what's fair and what's not fair. I tell you things about my life, you don't come back with all the junk I have to hear from her!"

"*Her* is still in this room," Ellie said sharply. "Why don't you speak a little to *her*?"

"I *am* speaking to you. Who the hell you think I'm speaking to? The man in the moon?"

"I thought you might have been speaking to him," she nodded at me.

"When I want to speak with him, I'll speak with him. This is *our* business."

"Hey, maybe I should go," I suggested.

"No sir, you sit right there. You want to know about us, you listen to this part too. You stay around and see the seamy side, too."

"Ted," Ellie broke in, "you're sounding foolish!"

"Oh shut up!" She didn't move. "You stay, Tom. I want you to hear. I work five hard days a week. That newspaper goes under, I'm out a job. I'd like you, Mrs. Know-it-all, to tell me just exactly what I'm supposed to do then. Huh? You got this

philosophy you take every day one at a time? Isn't
that your usual speech?"

"That's my usual speech," Ellie responded with
resignation.

"Yeah. That's it. That's a terrific philosophy.
You know where I'd be with that philosophy running my life? Do you *know*? *Do* you?

"No, I don't, Ted. Where would you be?"

"I'd be with the same job I had when I was
eleven years old. I'd be delivering for that
McCrackle or McCarver or whatever the hell his
name was." Ellie began to smile.

"Mencken," she corrected him.

"Mencken. McCracken. What the hell's the
difference? You don't understand what I'm saying
anyway."

"That's not true," his wife answered him. "I
do."

"Yeah? Then what am I saying?" He looked at
her smugly.

"That if you hadn't had some dream or goal you
wouldn't have gone beyond the life you knew as a
little boy."

"That's exactly right. So what I'd like to learn
from you is, if you understand that, how can you be
so...so...I don't know what, when it comes to listening to me?"

"I try to listen to you." Ellie's voice was kind.

"Maybe you do then. But our worlds are too
different. You can't possibly understand what's in
my head."

"I tell you what I believe in the best ways I
can."

"That the God...you mean that God stuff?"

"Yes," she said firmly. "That God stuff, as you
call it."

"That's where we part. I mean, that's where it
all falls apart."

"Why? Where? What's falling apart, Ted?"

"Us. You, me. The whole thing. It falls apart.
You rely on some set of beliefs that bring nothing."
His anger, which had subsided, rose again. "God
doesn't buy homes. God doesn't pay bills. Men do
that. God don't provide! Love don't provide! You
can go to church...."

"I realize that."

"You can go to church every day of the week,
my friend, but if I don't work, or you don't work,
you don't eat. You ever hear God throwing down

food, or clothes? Or homes? Does your friend God
do *that*?"

"Of course not. That's not why people...."

"You see you're wrong there. I'm sorry to correct you, but that's exactly what all those poor
slobs go there on Sundays for. They march off to
church and give their last pennies to God and beg
Him to give them food or shelter, or whatever the
hell they ask for."

Ted bent over and pointed at her, all the while
keeping his distance. "That's why the poor are
poor!" he yelled at her.

"Ted."

'C'mon, Ted," I joined in.

"Ted nothing," he came back. I made another
gesture to leave. Ted came at me and grabbed my
shoulder, pushing me back in the chair. "You wanna
think of me as a madman, go ahead. But you'll leave
here only when I'm finished."

"C'mon, Ted," I tried again.

"No, *you* listen! Both of you. The reason the
poor stay poor is because of what *you* believe." He
pointed at Ellie.

"You mean *I'm* the cause of people being poor,"
she said sarcastically.

"That's exactly right. *You're* the cause. All this
business of living day by day, of wanting God to
solve problems, of not doing things until they
actually happen, until they actually fall into your
goddamn lap, *you* believe that, and that's why people like you don't get anywhere. People are making
it in this country every day of their lives. You still
have a chance. But this business of laughing at
someone 'cause he plans, or...praying—that's the
end, boy. That's the living end. You hold onto your
childhood, you've never let it go, and we're married
almost twenty years. You see your mother as much
as you see your husband. I'd love to know what in
hell you two can find to talk about every day.
That's something for you to study, Tom." Ellie had
placed her head in her hands. She made no sound.
"But you don't hear me complain about what portion of my salary goes to supporting your mother,
do you?"

"No, I don't hear you complain," Ellie whispered.

"*What'd you say*?" Ted screamed at her. She
lifted her head and answered him loudly: "I said,
'No, I don't hear you complain.'"

"No, I don't complain. I just shell out dough left and right for all those little things you bring her every day because that beautiful saint of a father of yours who loved everybody and everybody loved him, never planned, never dreamed. It ain't enough to be nice."

"Don't you dare speak about my father," Ellie said bitterly, staring at him.

"I'll speak about anyone I damn please. Who the hell's paying for this house anyway?"

"Yeah, well you don't have to speak about the dead."

"I'm not speaking about the dead. I'm speaking about poor people; people who think love and niceness and praying in a church are what matter. It's all a lot of *shit*! Your parents were *full* of shit!"

"Ted!" she screamed at him. "Stop it!"

"And *my* parents were full of shit. None of 'em knew what was going on. They minded their own business and decided if this is what history brought them, then that's the way it had to be. Now you go ahead and look around at their children. Who's doing anything worthwhile? Huh? Who's dreaming about the future and not about the past? Huh? You and your mother cause poverty. You sit together like mentals dreaming of the good old days when your father was alive, and none of you gives a rat's ass that you were poor."

"Ted, please." Across from me, Ellie began to weep. My presence made it more difficult for her.

"Ted," I said, "I'm gonna go."

"You're not going. I'm not done." We looked at Ellie. "Let her cry. She cries all the time. Maybe we should call her mother over and they could have a good cry together about the old days. Maybe we could make an invention and bring back the dead." Ellie was sobbing.

"You're a monster."

"*I'm* the monster. Sure. *I'm* the monster, because I'm a little different from those idiots who run to church. I speak the truth. All you have is yesterday and today. That's *all* women have. Memories, tears, dreams, *Mothers*! You take a look at rich people someday. You know what they're doing?" He continued to pace up and back across the room. "They're planning so many things for their lives they ain't got time to go to church. They got the lives of their kids planned and their kids' kids. Jesus, you talk to some rich guy with his insurance

policies and his trust funds. You ask them if they live day by day. They're an army, the rich. They march on the future and rip it up. They don't wait to see how their kids are turning out. They put 'em in the best schools, like these finishing schools, so's they can make sure the kids will *have* to turn out right."

He stopped, then pointed over his wife's shoulder. "You get windows over kitchen sinks like this one." I looked at him quizzically. "Windows over kitchen sinks," he repeated, nodding his head up and down. "The rich work to make their lives work out. They've got things figured out you wouldn't even be able to dream of. Believe me, I know. They think in enormous blocks of time. They're moving decades, all the time left in this century. It's all big business. That's what their life is based on. Big business. Now, in this shitty little house, which is about the best I'm ever gonna be able to do, this woman here stands in front of a sink looking out the window all day worrying either about the weather, or whether it's daytime or nighttime. That's all women know. If it's daytime you make breakfast, if it's nighttime you make dinner. Bills, plans, what's going to become of us, they couldn't care less. Nighttime, daytime, all they want to know is what's in the cabinets to eat. Women and children. They're one and the same."

"So what do you want of me, Ted? What do you want of me?" Ellie's voice and tears were frightening to Ted. He moved back, disappearing into the dining area. "Okay," she said, "you're a big man, you're doing a great job here in front of us, putting on this big show, probably for Tom. Now, just what is it that you want? Just what do you want me and my mother and *your* children to do? Why don't you answer that instead of carrying on here like a mental case. *You* answer, for once. You want me to work? Is that it? You want the kids to stop going to school and go to work? Here, give me the phone. I'll call up the schools and pull the kids out. That's what you want isn't it? C'mon. C'mon. Here, big guy, gimme the phone. Come on!" She held her open hand out in front of her. "*Here!*" she screamed. Ted walked toward her.

"Stop it, goddammit. The both of you," I heard myself yell.

"I'll give you," Ted was saying, "I'll give you

the phone, across your fresh mouth is where I'll give you the phone."

"Go ahead," Ellie yelled. "You talk so much. Why don't you do something instead of babbling on like this, like some kind of an escapee from a mental hospital."

His mouth closed, he nodded sarcastically. "Escapee from a mental.... This is what I gotta take. Every day of my life. I'm making it possible for four human beings to lead their lives with a little dignity." His voice had quieted somewhat. "Four ungrateful human beings. I don't have a soul to talk to in this house. I see the way people are living. I see the way people are dying, and we're not getting any of it. I can't even afford to get us ground in the cemetery. Has that, Mrs. Big Mouth, ever crossed that brilliant brain of yours? Where, exactly, would you like them to put my corpse when I die if I don't arrange for a plot? Here? Would you like it in the kitchen maybe? Just where do the poor die? You ever think of that?"

"I see the future that you and your mother and all those idiots at church pray to God to take care of for you. I *see* that future. I'm already seventy years old and still working, still lifting Sunday papers, still dragging my ass around that goddamn hole. You're praying, and I'm working to have enough money to buy a place, and a way to get rid of my body which, if you'd really care to know, was dead a long, long time ago."

He glared at the two of us before continuing.

"Let me give you both a bit of a lesson. You," he said, pointing to me, "will have to excuse me if I don't sound like some important professor from M.I.T. A man doesn't die when his heart stops. That's not the only death a man has got to look forward to. There are lots of deaths . . ."

"Like when your parents die?" Ellie quietly interrupted.

"*No!*" he yelled at her. "Wrong again. Those are the deaths that women fall apart with. Men don't die at the sight of death. You talk to soldiers. They fight with guys falling down all around 'em. Women go to cemeteries and fall apart. Men hold women together because they know more about death than women. They know more about death because they work. They work every damn day of their lives and so they know what it is to reach a point where you can't go any further. That's the

death a man knows. The death of effort. You ever hear of the word incapacitated?" he asked his wife.

"Of course I did," Ellie answered.

"Of course I did," he mocked her in baby talk. "Of course you *don't*, you mean. You can't know 'cause women can't know the thought every day of your life something happening and you're not able to work again." He glared at Ellie, asssured that I, a man, would have to agree. "That's death, my friend."

"And women don't know that?" she inquired.

"No, women don't know that. You don't know the feelings of these other deaths until you find yourself in a world where you don't have any choice, and you just stay at it, like it or not, knowing you better damn well stay healthy or a whole group of people are going to fall flat on their faces."

"You're talking through your hat," Ellie started. "How hard do you think it would be for all of us to go to work? We could all make up the difference. Did *you*, Mr. Bright Ideas, ever think of *that*?

"Many, many, many times," Ted replied softly. "Many times I've thought about what it would be like having your wife and children working while you sat around the house, sick or tired or something. That, my friend, is another form of death. That may be the worst death of all. When women work it's a fill-in. They substitute, and brother, when they put in the substitutes it's because the first team either stinks or can't play. Or maybe," he smiled, " 'cause the first team's got a lead they'll never catch. If only it worked that way. If only I could ever get ahead of it, instead of always chasing, chasing, chasing. . . ."

"What are you chasing, chasing, chasing?" Ellie asked, looking up. "What is it that you're always after that you can know all these *special* deaths that no one else seems to know anything about? Huh?"

"I'm chasing life!" he yelled back at her. "I'm chasing the rich and the government and my bosses and taxes and bills. That's what I'm chasing. I'm a drowning man, chasing after a breath. After air. Is that enough for you? I don't take life day by day and sit back and dream about the beautiful past. Anybody does that has already drowned.

"How do you think it works out there? That somebody just *gives* you things? Things come to you because you work your goddamn ass off. And what's more, you can work your ass off every day of your life and end up with this!" He held his hand up making a zero sign with his thumb and index finger. "Zero!" he yelled. "Nothing! You can work just like your father did and end up with nothing!"

"He was a happy man on the day he died."

"The hell he was. You don't know anything about your father. You ask your brother about your father. Ask your mother. She knows. Maybe now that you're a big girl she'll tell you some of the real facts of life. Go ask her when you see her tomorrow. Go now, for Christ's sake, it's been almost an hour since you've seen the old lady. And ask your mother about his drinking."

"Shut up, Ted," Ellie was angered and embarrassed. She looked at me.

"I'm not supposed to be saying anything about that, eh? I'm supposed to keep my mouth shut so Tom can think that everything around us and our beautiful childhoods was perfect? You ask your mother about how many times your father died in his life before the Good Lord took him away. Ask her. She'll tell you. He died every night of his life. Every night he came home to that dump your family lived in, he died. You think it's easy for a man every day to look around at his life and be reminded of what a pitiful failure he is, and always will be? That's the death part, Ellie. And that's the part, reporter, you better write about if you want to understand people like us. It's seeing every day of your life what you got and *knowing*, knowing like your own name, that it ain't never gonna get any better. That's what you live with, and that's what your father had in his mind and in his body every day, and every night. That's why a man drinks. Believe me, I know. You keep it from your children just so long. In this country, there ain't no one who fails and holds his head up. Any man who holds his head up after he loses is just trying to protect himself. No one likes a loser. That's why the rich can't stand us. That's why we moved here. What we had together all those years were *prisons*. They were

advertisements of how much we didn't have. You got any doubts about it, you just turn on the TV and see the way people are living with their new cars and their boats, and with their homes in the country. How many times a day they gotta remind you of that, I'd like to know?"

For the first time, Ellie was nodding assent. I had seen her face show relief moments before when, unthinkingly, Ted had used the phrase, "the Good Lord took him away." Now she was her husband's wife, his woman. The direction of his anguish had shifted, and it was America, the rich, social classes, me, that he attacked and held responsible. No longer was it men against women; it was the poor against the rich, those who can, with a genuine sense of autonomy and possibility underwriting it, achieve with dignity, and those who must sweat out the work, the waiting, and the decisions of bosses for bonuses and a chance to move ahead slightly.

Ted stood, not exactly next to his wife, but closer to her, leaving me, still seated, the third person. For long minutes the three of us were silent. Ellie and I staring at the tabletop, Ted standing near us, motionless. I could feel my eyebrows rising and falling as though something in me wanted to signal the two of them. Ted broke the silence, and turned to me. His voice was even and resolute. "Don't you worry about us. You go ahead and write whatever you feel you should." That was all he said the rest of that afternoon.

Two feelings had come over me, two feelings as distinct as shaking hands with both Grazianos simultaneously. Ted's right hand in my right hand. Ellie's hand in my left hand. I felt first, that I had been as moved by these two people as I had ever been by anyone or anything. But I felt, too, a desire to make all three of us special and unforgettable; famous, I suppose. I was halfway home, driving through an angry rain that made visibility almost impossible, before the one word that swirled in my head finally came to rest. Immortality.

Who Has the Power?
The Marital Struggle

DAIR L. GILLESPIE

*Marriage is the destiny traditionally offered to women by society.
It is still true that most women are married, or have been to be, or
suffer from not being. The celibate [single] woman is to be
explained and defined with reference to marriage whether she is
frustrated, rebellious, or even indifferent in regard to that institution.*

Simone de Beauvoir

THE CHANGING
POWER STRUCTURE

MODERN THEORISTS OF THE FAMILY
agree that the American family has evolved from a
paternalistic to a much more democratic form. Before the Civil War married women had many duties,
few rights. They were not permitted to control their
property, even when it was theirs by inheritance or
dower, or to make a will. To all intents and purposes
they did not own property. The husband had the
right to collect and use the wife's wages, to decide
upon the education and religion of the children, and
to punish his wife if she displeased him. The right to
will children, even unborn, to other guardians was
retained by the husband. In the case of divorce,
when granted at all, the husband had the right to
determine the control of the children. To a married
woman, her husband was her superior, her companion, her master. In every sector of the social arena,
women were in a subordinate position. The church
was one of the most potent forces for maintaining
them in this position. Within the church, women
were segregated from men, were not allowed to
sing, preach, or take public action. There were no
high schools for girls, and no college in the world admitted women. Unpropertied males, slaves, and all
women were not allowed into the political process at
all.

Today, as the textbooks never tire of telling us,
couples are more free to choose partners than
formerly, they are able to separate more easily, the
differences in age and culture between husband and
wife are less marked than formerly, the husband
recognizes more willingly the independence of his
wife's demands, they may share housekeeping and
diversions, and the wife may even work. In fact,
sociologists claim that the modern husband and
wife are so nearly equal in power that marriage
today can be termed "democratic," "equalitarian,"
or "egalitarian."

These changes in the form of marriage are generally attributed to the entrance of women into the
economic structure and to the extension of an equalitarian ideology to cover women. This type of explanation is careful to emphasize socioeconomic conditions of the past and the "rise of women" in the
American economy. However, socioeconomic conditions of the present are no longer examined, for it is
assumed that women have won their rights in all
social arenas, and if they haven't—well, ideology
takes a while to filter down to the masses. New
egalitarian ideals, they tell us, will bring about
further socioeconomic changes and a better position
for women.

In a major research project on the modern
American family, Blood and Wolfe (1960, pp. 29-30)
state:

Reprinted from *Journal of Marriage and the Family*,
August 1971, pp. 445-458, by permission of the
author and the National Council on Family Relations.

Under former historical circumstances, the husband's economic and social role almost automatically gave him preeminence. Under modern conditions, the roles of men and women have changed so much that husbands and wives are potential equals—with the balance of power tipped sometimes one way, sometimes the other. It is no longer possible to assume that just because a man is a man, he is the boss. Once upon a time, the function of culture was to rationalize the predominance of the male sex. Today the function of culture is to develop a philosophy of equal rights under which the saying goes, "May the best man win!"—and the best man is sometimes a woman. The role of culture has shifted from sanctioning a competent sex over an incompetent sex to sanctioning the competent marriage partner over the incompetent one, regardless of sex.

There is good evidence, however, that the balance of power is tipped the same way it always was, and that the best man is very seldom a woman. I am arguing, then, against the *personal* resource theory and am positing that, in fact, this is still a caste/class system rationalizing the preponderance of the male sex.

THE MEASUREMENT OF POWER

Before examining the causes of male dominance in marital power, I would like to examine first how Blood and Wolfe[1] conceive of power and how they measure it (Fig. 1). Operationally, power is restricted to who makes the final decision in each of eight areas, ranging from those traditionally held entirely by the husband to those held entirely by the wife. These eight areas include:

1. What job the husband should take.
2. What car to get.
3. Whether or not to buy life insurance.
4. Where to go on vacation.
5. What house or apartment to take.
6. Whether or not the wife should go to work or quit work.
7. What doctor to have when someone is sick.

8. How much money the family can afford to spend per week on food.

These questions were asked because (a) they are all relatively important, (b) they are questions which nearly all couples have to face, and (c) they range from typically masculine to typically feminine decisions, but affect the family as a whole (1960, pp. 19–20).

This measurement of power leaves much to be desired. Safilios-Rothschild has made probably the most telling criticisms of such studies. She points out that all decisions are given equal weight even though not all decisions have "objectively" the same degree of importance for the entire life of the family. Which job the husband would take (with important consequences in terms of time to be spent away from home, location of job, salary level, amount of leisure available, etc.) and which doctor to call were considered decisions equally affecting the family and the balance of power within the family. Further, some decisions are made less frequently than others; thus, while a decision such as "what food to buy" requires a daily or weekly enactment, a decision such as "what car to buy" is only made every few years. In addition, some decisions are "important" and frequent, others frequent but not "important," others "important" and not frequent, and still others not important and not frequent. Thus, the familial power structure may not be solely determined on the number of areas of decisions that one can appropriate for himself or herself. She also mentioned the multidimensionality of some of the decision-making areas and suggested that it is possible that one spouse decides which make of car to buy and the other specifies color (1969, pp. 297–298).

It seems, then, that the conception and measurement of power is already biased in that it does not expose certain kinds of power which automatically accrue to the husband by virtue of his work; and second, that it takes no account of the differential importance of the eight decisions in the power structure of the marriage. Further, there is good evidence that even if we accepted Blood and Wolfe's measures as being true measures of power, the husband still controls most of the power decisions in the family. I must conclude, then, that the

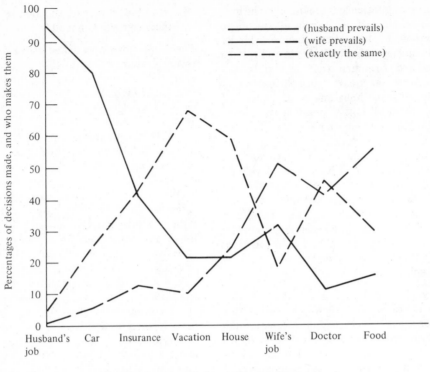

(Husband's mean power. 5 = total power, 0 = no power)

Job	4.86	House	2.94
Car	4.18	Wife's job	2.69
Insurance	3.50	Doctor	2.53
Vacation	3.12	Food	2.26

husband has much more power than he appears to have according to Blood and Wolfe's analysis.

Their discussion of "who decides" is even more convincing that there are power differentials which are being overlooked. For example, they explain (p. 22):

> That the husband should be more involved in his wife's job decisions than she with his is understandable. For one thing, her work is seldom her major preoccupation in life the way it is for a man. Even if she works just as many hours a week, she does not usually make the same lifelong commitment to the world of work. Nor is her pay check indispensable to the family finances (if only because it is smaller). In such ways the choice of whether to work or not is less vital to a woman than to a man.

> In addition, the wife's decisions about working have repercussions on the husband. If his wife goes to work, he will have to help out more around the house. If he is a business executive, he may prefer to have her concentrate her energy on entertaining prospective clients at home. As a small businessman or independent professional, he may need her services in his own enterprise. On the other hand, regardless of his own occupation, he may want her to work in order to help him buy a house or a business or pay for the children's education.

It may be, then, that the work role is so much the responsibility of the husband in marriage that even the wife's work is but an adjunct of his instrumental leadership, leaving this decision in his hands.

In these *justifications* of the division of power, Blood and Wolfe use the device of examining why a husband would want more power in particular areas. The basic assumption is, of course, that he can have it if he wants it. I think a more pertinent question would be not who wants power, since there are always myriad reasons why anyone would want power, but why he is able to get it if he wants it. This question is not even broached.

William Goode in *World revolution and family patterns* (1963, p. 70) comments on this aspect of power and authority:

After evaluating the conflicting comments and data published by Shaffner, Rodnick, Schelski, and Wruzbacher, Baumert comes to the conclusion which seems eminently reasonable, that claims of fundamental equalitarianism in the German family (or in any other European family) are not correct and that an unequivocally equalitarian family is rarely to be found. In the final analysis, only a few family relations are not determined by the male. It is not possible at present to state just how well such a statement could be applied to other countries. In reality, in all countries there are many women who manage to dominate the man, but it seems likely that in most countries, when the husband tries to dominate he can still do this. Even when the husband performs the household chores, his participation means that he gains power—the household becoming a further domain for the exercise of prerogatives for making decisions.

Perhaps the crucial qualitative difference is to be found in the extent to which, in one country or another, the male can still dominate without a definite effort to do so.

In *The family*, Goode calls this "negative authority—the right to prevent others from doing what they want" (1964, p. 75).

I must conclude, then, that the power structure is much more lopsided than Blood and Wolfe lead us

to believe, and that it is the husband who holds this hidden power. Why does the husband have all this power? How does he obtain it? How does he maintain it?

It is assumed that most marriages begin with partners at a somewhat egalitarian level. All evidence points to homogamous marriage, i.e., that the woman's *husband* and *father* occupy similar positions in the soceioeconomic structure. However, regardless of her background, "her future rank is mainly determined by the future job achievement of the man she marries, rather than by the class position of his family,"[2] or hers, needless to say. In discussing differentials in power which emerge in marriage, most social scientists use an individualistic perspective as do Blood and Wolfe in *Husbands and wives*. They remark (p. 37):

The balance of power is, after all, an interpersonal affair, and the wife's own characteristics cannot long be disregarded if we are to understand who makes the decisions. Whenever possible it is desirable to compare the wife and the husband on the same characteristics, for then the comparative resourcefulness and competence of the two partners can be discovered. Once we know which partner has more education, more organizational experience, a higher status background, etc. we will know who tends to make the most decisions.

The major error made by Blood and Wolfe (and others who use this perspective) is in assuming that this control of competence and resources occurs in individual couples by chance rather than being structurally predetermined (in a statistical sense) in favor of the male. To state it more clearly, I am arguing that it is still a caste/class system, rationalizing the preponderance of males. The distribution of power is not an interpersonal affair, but a class affair. Blood and Wolfe continue (p. 29):

Some husbands today are just as powerful as their grandfathers were—but they can no longer take for granted the authority held by older generations of men. No longer is the husband able to exercise power just because he is the "man of the house." Rather, he must prove his right to power, or win power by virtue of his own skills and accomplishments *in competition with his wife*. (Emphasis mine.)

I am arguing that in the competition with his wife, the man has most of the advantages. If we assume that the marriage contract is mutual mobility bet for gaining ascendancy in power, personal autonomy, and self-realization, we will find that the opportunity for winning the bet is very slim for the woman. She is already at a disadvantage when she signs the contract. For further self-realization, for further gains in status and experience as compared with her husband, the cards are already stacked against her, for women are *structurally* deprived of equal opportunities to develop their capacities, resources, and competence in competition with males.

Since theorists of marriage have a quite notable tendency to disregard the psychological, legal, and social blocks put in the way of women as a class when they are discussing power differentials and their sources, I would like to examine some of these differences.

SOURCES OF MARITAL POWER

Socialization

Men and women are differentially socialized. By the time women reach marriageable age, we have already been damaged by the socialization process. We have been systematically trained to accept second best, not to strive, and to accept the "fact" that we are unworthy of more. Naomi Weisstein's "Kinde, küche, kirche as scientific law" states this process clearly:

> How are women characterized in our culture, and in psychology? They are inconsistent, emotionally unstable, lacking in strong conscience or superego, weaker, "nurturant" rather than productive, "intuitive" rather than intelligent, and if they are at all "normal," suited to the home and family. In short, the list adds up to a typical minority group stereotype of inferiority; if they know their place, which is in the home, they are really quite loveable, happy, childlike, loving creatures. In a review of the intellectual differences between little boys and little girls, Eleanor Maccoby has shown that there are no intellectual differences until about

high school, or if there are, girls are slightly ahead of boys. At high school, the achievement of women now measured in terms of productivity and accomplishment, drops off even more rapidly. There are a number of other, nonintellectual tests which show sex differences; I chose the intellectual differences since it is seen clearly that women start becoming inferior. It is no use to talk about women being different but equal; all of the tests I can think of have a "good" outcome and a "bad" outcome. Women usually end up at the "bad" outcome. In light of social expectations about women, what is surprising is not that women end up where society expects they will; what is surprising is that little girls don't get the message that they are supposed to be stupid until high school, and what is even more remarkable is that some women resist this message even after high school, college, and graduate school.

Thus, women begin at a psychological disadvantage when we sign the marriage contract, for we have differential training and expectations.

MARRIAGE: A FREE CONTRACT BETWEEN EQUALS

Sociologists universally fail to discuss legal differences in power when the marriage contract is signed.[3] Marriage is ordinarily considered a contract freely entered into by both partners, and the partners are assumed to stand on common footing of equal rights and duties. Shelia Cronan (1969, pp. 2–4) examined this "free" contract between equals and found a few unlisted terms.

Sex She found that the husband can legally force his wife to have sexual intercourse with him against her will, an act which if committed against any other woman would constitute the crime of rape. By definition, a husband cannot be guilty of raping his own wife, for "the crime (of rape) is ordinarily that of forcing intercourse on someone other than the wife of the person accused" (Gallen 1967, p. 6). Women are well aware of the "right" of the husband to "insist" and the "duty" of the wife to submit to sexual intercourse. The compulsory nature of sex in marriage operates to the advantage of the male, for though the husband theoretically has the duty to have intercourse with his wife, this normally cannot occur against his will. (Both partners are protected in that a marriage can be annulled by either party if the marriage has not been consummated.)

Other marital responsibilities Women believe that we are voluntarily giving our household services, but the courts hold that the husband is legally entitled to his wife's services, and further, that *she cannot be paid for her work*. In *Your marriage and the law*, Pilpel and Zavin (1964, p. 65) state:

> As part of the rights of consortium, the husband is entitled to the services of his wife. If the wife works outside the home for strangers, she is usually entitled to her own earnings. But domestic services or assistances which she gives her husband are generally considered part of her wifely duties. The wife's services and society are so essential a part of what the law considers the husband is entitled to as part of the marriage that it will not recognize any agreement between spouses which provides that the husband is to pay for such services or society.
>
> In a Texas case David promised his wife, Fannie, that he would give her $5000 if she would stay with him while he lived and continue taking care of the house and farm accounts, selling his butter and doing all the other tasks which she had done since their marriage. After David's death, Fannie sued his estate for the money which had been promised her. The court held that the contract was unenforceable since Fannie had agreed to do nothing which she was not already legally and morally bound to do as David's wife.

The legal responsibilities of a wife are to live in the home established by her husband, to perform the domestic chores (cleaning, cooking, washing, etc.) necessary to help maintain that home, and to care for her husband and children (Gallen 1967, p. 4). The husband, in return, is obligated to provide her with basic maintenance which includes "necessities" such as food, clothing, medical care, and a place to live, in accordance with his income. She has no legal right to any part of his cash income, nor any legal voice in spending it ("Know your rights," Women's Bureau, Department of Labor, 1965, p. 1). Were he to employ a live-in servant in place of a wife, he would have to pay the servant a salary, provide her with her own room (as opposed to "bed"), food, and the necessary equipment for doing her job. She would get at least one day a week off and probably would be required to do considerably less work than a wife and would not be required to provide sexual services.

Thus, being a wife is a full-time job for which one is not entitled to pay. (Chase Manhattan Bank estimates a woman's overall workweek at 99.6 hours.) Furthermore, the wife is not entitled to freedom of movement. The husband has the right to decide where the family will live. If he decides to move, his wife is obliged to go with him. If she refuses, he can charge her with desertion. This has been upheld by the courts even in cases where the wife could be required to change her citizenship. In states where desertion is grounds for divorce (47 states plus the District of Columbia), the wife would be the "guilty party" and would therefore be entitled to no monetary settlement (Gallen 1967, p. 6).

A married woman's name Leo Kanowitz in *Women and the law* (1969, p. 41) found that the change in a woman's name upon marriage is not only consistent with social custom; it also appears to be generally required by law.

> The probable effects of this unilateral name change upon the relations between the sexes, though subtle in character, are profound. In a very real sense, the loss of a woman's surname represents the destruction of an important part of her personality and its submersion in that of her husband. . . . This name change is consistent with the characterization of coverture as "the old common-law fiction that the husband and wife are one . . . [which] has worked out in reality to mean that the one is the husband."

The law of support The universal rule is that it is the primary obligation of the husband to provide financial support for the family. Kanowitz (1969, p. 69) explored some of the legal ramifications of this general rule.

> The effects of the basic rule upon the marital relationship itself are complex. In common law

marital property jurisdictions, the husband's legal obligation to support the family is not an unmixed blessing for the wife. That obligation has been cited, for example, as justifying his right to choose the family home. It has no doubt also played an important part in solidifying his legal role as head and master of the family. For in according the husband this position within the family, the law often seems to be applying on a grand scale the modest principle that "he who pays the piper calls the tune." However, even the community property states, in which a wife's services in the home are theoretically viewed as being equal to or exceeding in monetary value the husband's earnings outside of the home, husbands have generally been given the rights to manage and control the community property, along with other superior rights and interests in it.

Thus, it is clear that husbands have access to legal advantages which wives do not have. True, the wife does gain legal protection against capricious action by the male, but in exchange, she becomes his vassal. He is the economic head of the joint household, and hence, represents it in view of society. She takes his name and belongs to his class. She follows where his work calls to determine their place of residence. Their lives are geared to the daily, weekly, annual rhythms of his life. She gives him her person and her private labor, but he wants more.

The "White Man's Burden" In today's "love match," the husband does not merely require an obedient and efficient worker, he wants something more. He wants his wife to love him, that is, to freely choose over and over again to be subjected to the control of the other, to make his welfare the center of her being.[4] This very demand is the crux of what husbands term their "oppression" as Simone de Beauvoir (1968, p. 151) has so clearly observed:

> Her very devotion seems annoying, importunate; it is transformed for the husband into a tyranny from which he tries to escape; and yet he it is who imposes it upon his wife as her supreme, her unique justification. In marrying her, he obliges her to give herself entirely to him; but he does not assume the corresponding obligation, which is to accept this gift and all its consequences.

It is the duplicity of the husband that dooms his wife to a misfortune of which he complains that he is himself the victim. Just as he wants her to be at once warm and cool in bed, he requires her to be wholly his and yet no burden; he wishes her to establish him in a fixed place on earth and to leave him free; to assume the monotonous daily round and not to bore him; to be always at hand and never importunate; he wants to have her all to himself and not to belong to her, to live as one of a couple, and to remain alone. Thus she is betrayed from the day he marries her. Her life through, she measures the extent of that betrayal.

Throughout their lives together, she attempts to wrest back from him some measure of her independence. Surely, it is not entirely an accident that divorce rates are highest at this early phase of the marriage cycle and drop with the birth of children, when women are most dependent upon the husband economically and emotionally.

ECONOMIC SOURCES OF POWER

It is clear that an economic base of power is important in marriage, for the higher the husband on the social scale, the greater his decision making in the family. Using three indices of success in the community, Blood and Wolfe found that all three affected power differentials in the family.

1. The higher the husband's occupational prestige, the greater his voice in marital decisions.

2. Income was an even more sensitive indicator of power than his occupation. The higher the husband's income, the greater his power.

3. The higher the husband's status (based on occupation, income, education, and ethnic background), the more power he had to make decisions.

The major break in power fell between white-collar occupations, the middle-class husbands having much more power than working-class husbands. The increment to power by income was steady. By social status there is a curvilinear relationship to power. The low blue-collar workers had more power than high blue-collar workers, and power for the husband increased again at the low white-collar level and the high white-collar level. Middle-class husbands, then, are generally more powerful than blue-collar husbands, but in the blue-collar marriages, the low blue-collar worker has more power than the high blue-collar worker. I will discuss some of the possible causes of this in the section of education.

These material bases of power were operant despite the fact that middle-class husbands espouse a more egalitarian ideology than do working-class husbands. William Goode (1963, p. 21) commented on this tension between the ideal and the real distributions of power.

> Since at present this philosophy [of equalitarianism in the family] is most strongly held among better educated segments of the population, and among women more than among men, two interesting tensions may be seen: Lower-class men concede fewer rights *ideologically* than their women in fact *obtain,* and the more educated men are more likely to concede *more* rights ideologically than they in fact grant.

He then supplies us with an excellent example of how ideology may be modified to justify the current distribution of power:

> One partial resolution of the latter tension is to be found in the frequent assertion from families of professional men that they should not make demands which would interfere with his *work*: He takes preference as a *professional*, not as a family head or as a male; nevertheless, the precedence is his. By contrast, lower-class men demand deference as *men*, as heads of families.

As we can see, marital power is a function of income to a large extent, and egalitarian philosophies have very little impact on the actual distribution of power. It seems clear that the authority of the male is used as a justification of power where it is useful (working-class), and new justifications will arise as they are useful, as in the case of professional men who demand deference because of their work, thus enabling them to accept the doctrine of equality while at the same time undermining it for their own benefit as males. If this is the effect of that much touted egalitarian ideology which will bring about better conditions for women and racial and ethnic minorities as soon as it filters down to the masses,

it seems we will have a long, long wait for cosmic justice.

Blood and Wolfe claim that this superior power of high-status husbands is not due to coercion, but to the recognition by both partners that the husband is the one eminently qualified to make the decisions in the family. This argument is reminiscent of arguments in labor relations. The labor contract is assumed to be freely entered into by both partners. The power conferred on the one party by the difference in class position—the real economic position of both—is not taken into account. That economic relations compel the worker to surrender even the last semblance of equal rights is of no concern. Coercion (however subtle) based on economic power is still coercion, whether it involves wife-beating or not.

As further evidence that individual competence and resourcefulness (regardless of sex) are not the real issues, we must examine Blood and Wolfe's discussion of the *deviant* case—wife dominance. In these cases, they claim that wives who have superior power acquire it, not because they have access to pragmatic sources of power or because they are more competent than their husbands (heaven forbid!), but by default.

> We will find throughout this study dissatisfaction associated with wife-dominance. This is not, however, simply a reflection of the breaking of social rules. Rather, the circumstances which lead to the wife's dominance involve corresponding inadequacies on the husband's part. An inadequate husband is by definition unable to make a satisfactory marriage partner. So the dominant wife is not exultant over her "victory" but exercises power regretfully by default of her "no good" or incapacitated husband (p. 45).

For Blood and Wolfe, wives can never gain dominance legitimately; it falls in our unhappy laps and is accepted only unwillingly and with much bitterness.

Despite the superior power gained by the husband because of his economic position, there are conditions under which wives do erode that power to some extent. Not surprisingly, the wife's participation in the work force is an important variable. Women who work have more power vis-à-vis their husbands than do nonworking wives, regardless of race or class. The number of years the wife has worked also affects the balance of power—the longer she has worked, the more power she is able to obtain. This, to some extent, explains why blue-collar wives have more power than white-collar wives (in comparison to their husbands), since their participation in the work force is much higher than for the wives of high-status, high-income husbands (Blood and Wolfe 1960, pp. 40–41).

ORGANIZATIONAL PARTICIPATION

Organizational participation, too, is a factor which affects marital decision making as shown by Blood and Wolfe's data. Women with much more organizational participation than their husbands alter the balance of power in the wife's direction. In those cases where the participation is equal or in which the husband is superior (by far the most frequent), the balance of power increases in the husband's direction (p. 39).

EDUCATION

Education was also influential in the distribution of power. The more education the husband has, the greater his power. High white-collar husbands continue to gain power if they exceed their wives' education (and chances are good that they do, in fact, exceed), and they lose it if they fall short of the wife. The same trend holds within the low white-collar and high blue-collar groups, leaving a low blue-collar reversal, i.e., low blue-collar husbands have more power even when their wives have superior educations (pp. 28, 38).

Mirra Komarovsky in Blue-collar marriage has drawn attention to the fact that education is a much more important variable when the husband's income and social status are relatively low. In working-class families, the less educated and unskilled husbands have more power than do those with higher incomes. She attempted to explain some of the causes of this power anomaly. First patriarchal attitudes are more prevalent among the less educated and hence, a source of power in some families. High school graduates, because of a social

milieu which does not sanction patriarchal authority (though it does sanction male privilege), tend to lose power. Second, among the less educated, the husband is more likely to excel in personal resources for the exercise of influence, and this margin of male superiority narrows among the high school graduates. Among the less educated, the husband has wider contacts in the community than his wife. He represents the world to his family, and he is the family's "secretary of state." In contrast, a few of the more educated wives enjoy wider contacts and higher status outside the home than their husbands. Third, the education of the spouses was found to affect their degrees of power because of mating patterns. The effect of educational inequality appears to explain the lower power of skilled workers in comparison with the semiskilled. The skilled worker is more likely than the semiskilled worker to marry a high school graduate. By virtue of their relatively high earnings, skilled workers may be able to marry better-educated women, but by marrying "upward" they lose the degree of power enjoyed by the semiskilled over their less-educated wives. Fourth, male prestige or social rank was a source of power in low blue-collar families(1967, pp. 226–229).

PHYSICAL COERCION

Komarovksy is one of the few sociologists who has mentioned physical coercion as a source of power in the family. In her discussion of the low blue-collar family, she found that the use of physical violence was a source of masculine power. However, not only the use of physical violence, but its threat can be an effective form of control. She reports that one woman said of her husband: "He is a big man and terribly strong. One time when he got sore at me, he pulled off the banister and he ripped up three steps." With the evidence of the damage in view, this woman realized, as she put it, what her husband could do to her if he should decide to strike her (1967, p. 227).

Lynn O'Connor has suggested that threats of violence (in gestures of dominance) are not limited to any particular class, but are a universal source of male power and control. After discussing dominance gestures in primates, she states (1970, p. 9):

Although there have been no systematic studies of the gestures of dominance and submission in human groups, the most casual observation will show their crucial role in the day-to-day mechanics of oppression. An example should clarify.

A husband and wife are at a party. The wife says something that the husband does not want her to say (perhaps it reveals something about him that might threaten his ranking with other men). He quickly tightens the muscles around his jaw and gives her a rapid but intense direct stare. Outsiders don't notice the interaction, though they may have a vaguely uncomfortable feeling that they are intruding on something private. The wife, who is acutely sensitive to the gesture of the man on whom she is dependent, immediately stops the conversation, lowers or turns her head slightly, averts her eyes, or gives off some other gestures of submission which communicate acquiescence to her husband and reduce his aggression. Peace is restored; the wife has been put in her place. If the wife does not respond with submission, she can expect to be punished. When gestures of dominance fail, the dominant animal usually resorts to violence. We all know stories about husbands beating up their wives after the party when they have reached the privacy of their home. Many of us have experienced at least a few blows from husbands or lovers when we refuse to submit to them. It is difficult to assess the frequency of physical attacks within so-called love relationships, because women rarely tell even one another when they have taken place. By developing a complicated ethic of loyalty (described above in terms of privacy), men have protected themselves from such reports leaking out and becoming public information. Having already been punished for stepping out of role, the woman is more than a little reluctant to tell anyone of the punishment because it would mean violating the loyalty code, which is an even worse infraction of the rules and most likely would result in further and perhaps more severe punishment.

That violence or the threat of violence may be more widespread than is currently admitted is also suggested by complaints made by wives in divorce. Goode in *Women in divorce* (1956, pp. 120, 123) found that almost one-third (32 percent) of the wives reported "authority-cruelty" as the reason for divorce. Authority problems are defined as being disagreements concerning permissible degree of dominance over wife and include cruelty, beating, jealousy, and "wanted to have own way." Since Goode did not code cruelty or beating separately, we have no definite evidence as to the frequency of such behavior, but there is evidence that problems with male dominance are widespread in the population. Goode (1956, p. 122) comments:

> . . . In different strata and groups, the husband may be permitted different control techniques. For example, the middle-class male will very likely be censured more if he uses force to control his wife than if he uses techniques of nagging, jealousy, or sulking. On the other hand, there is a strong reservoir of attitude on the part of the American male generally, that he has the *right* to tell his wife what to do. This attitude is given more overt expression, and is more frequently backed by force, in the lower strata. It is not so much that beating and cruelty are viewed as an obvious male right in marriage, but only that this is one of the techniques used from time to time, and with little or no subsequent guilt, for keeping control of the wife. . . . In our society, the husband who successfully asserts his dominance does enjoy some approval and even a modicum of envy from other males. Male dominance is to some extent actually approved.

SUBURBANIZATION

Blood and Wolfe also found that families living in the suburbs were more husband-dominant than those which live in the central city. This directly contradicts the popular image of suburban life as being dominated by women and therefore, oriented toward the satisfaction of women's needs. The data showed that suburban families were more husband-dominant at every status level than their urban peers (p. 36). They then speculated that suburban husbands were more powerful "because suburban wives feel more indebted to their husbands for providing them with a place to live which is more attractive than the industrial city of Detroit. If so, this fits the theory that power accrues to those husbands who are able to provide for their wives especially well" (p. 36).

In a recent study on the working class in suburbia, Tallman has suggested that other factors than the wife's gratitude might be working to build up the husband's power. He constructed a profile of the working-class marriage which indicated consistently that wives tend to maintain close ties with relatives and old girl friends while husbands continue their premarital peer group associations. Social and psychological support emanates, then, not from marriage partners, but from same-sex friends, and kin from long-standing and tight-knit social networks. As a consequence, there is a relatively high degree of conjugal role segmentation which is characterized in part by a lack of communication between the spouses. In general the experiences of working-class women are more localized and circumscribed than their male counterparts. Since their security and identity depend upon their position vis-à-vis a small group of intimates, their opinions and beliefs are both dependent upon and in accord with this group. Blue-collar women have minimal experience in the external world and tend to view it fearfully. Men, on the other hand, have more frequent social contacts, in part for occupational reasons, but also because they have been socialized into male roles which define them as family representatives to the outside world.

Tallman concluded that suburban women are more isolated because of disruptions in the primary group relations. The disruption of friendship and kinship ties are not only personally disintegrating for the wife but also demand fundamental changes in the role allocations in the family. Suburban wives are more dependent upon their husbands for a variety of services previously provided by members of tight-knit networks. In brief, he found that moving to the suburbs was experienced as a disintegrative force in the lives of many working-class women, leading to a greater isolation and dependence upon the husband (1969, pp. 66–69). This partial explanation of the husband's increased power in the suburbs as being due to the wife's in-creased isolation and dependence seems eminently more reasonable than Blood and Wolfe's explanation that it is due to gratitude on the part of the wife. Tallman's data also indicate that the wife frequently regrets the move to the suburbs, despite more pleasant living conditions, because of its disruption of the kinship and friendship network.

RACE

Blood and Wolfe report very little on black families, except to say that Negro husbands have unusually low power. Their data show that white husbands are always more powerful than their Negro status equals and that this is true within each occupational stratum, each income bracket, and each social level.[5] They concede that "the label 'black' is almost a synonym for low status in our society —and Detroit Negroes are no exception in having less education, lower incomes, inferior jobs, and lower prestige generally than whites. Since low status white husbands make relatively few decisions, we would expect Negro husbands to exercise little power, too" (p. 34).

What they fail to take into account (among other things) is that black women, too, are discriminated against in this society. They, too, have less education, lower incomes, inferior jobs, and lower prestige generally than whites. The fact that blacks are discriminated against does not explain power differentials within black families. To explain power differentials in black families, just as for white families, the sources of power for black men and black women must be examined and compared. Blood and Wolfe fail to do this.

Their primary purpose seems to be to demonstrate gross differences between black and white families, without bothering to report differences within black families. Andrew Billingsley in *Black families in white America* has criticized just this approach used in sociological studies. He draws attention to the fact that class variables are as important in black families as in white families. "Negro families are not only Negroes to be compared and contrasted with white families, they may also be upper-class (10 percent), middle-class (40 percent), or lower-class (50 percent), with urban or rural moorings, with southern or northern residence, and most importantly, they may be meaningfully compared and contrasted with each other" (1968, p. 8).

Billingsley accounts to some extent for what may be part of the white/black differentials in overall power. He notes that Negro samples are dominated by low-income families and points out that even where income levels between whites and blacks are similar, the groups are not truly comparable, for the Negro group reflects not only its income level but its experience with prejudice and subjugation as well.

Because both black husbands and black wives are discriminated against in this society, it is absurd to explain power differentials between them as being due to race (as Blood and Wolfe do), unless there are mitigating factors brought about by racial discrimination which operate in favor of one sex's access to sources of marital power. Since data on the black family are so sadly inadequate, I can at this point only examine some demographic data which have possible implications for power distributions in black families.

Black women comprised 40 percent of all black workers in 1960. They earned considerably less than black men. The median earnings of full-time year-round black women in 1959 was two-fifths that of black men.[6] (In 1964, it was 64.2 percent.)[7] The unemployment rate for black women is higher than for black men. In 1967, for Negro men aged 20–64, the unemployment rate was 3.7. For Negro women it was 6.0. The unemployment rates for black women under 20 were also higher than for Negro men.[8] Clearly, then, black women are not superior to black men in income.

In occupational status, we find that Negro women are most frequently in service jobs while Negro men are predominantly blue-collar workers. However, relatively more Negro women than men had professional or technical jobs, this being due primarily to their extensive employment as teachers and nurses. Of all full-time year-round Negro workers in 1960, Negro women constituted nearly all the private household workers. They were more than half the number of Negroes employed as professional workers (61 percent) and other service workers (51 percent). Except for the clerical group in which the numbers were about equal, the remaining occupational groups (sales, managers, oper-

atives, crafts, laborers, and farmers) had fewer Negro women than men.[9]

Negro women in general had a higher median education than Negro men. (This is also true in the white population.) The median educational level of nonwhite women was 8.5 years in 1960, but for men it was 7.9. However, at the top of the educational ladder, just as for the white population, men are more numerous.[10]

Though there are differences, we find that the relations *between the sexes* for both Negroes and whites are similar. Obviously, black men have suffered from discrimination in this society. This is evident in the figures of income, occupation, and education. However, it is also evident that Negro women have suffered discrimination, not only because of race, but also because of their sex. Thus, they are doubly oppressed. This, too, is evident in figures of income, occupation, and education.

Jesse Bernard in *Marriage and family among Negroes* has suggested still another variable which must be taken into account in Negro family patterns. She reports that there is an extraordinarily low sex ratio (number of males per 100 females) among urban Negroes as compared to whites. The ratio is especially low (88.4) in the critical years of marriageability. Bernard conjectures that the low sex ratio means that Negro women are competing for a relatively scarce "good" when they look forward to marriage, being buyers in a sellers' market (1966, p. 69). While this is certainly not the cause of power distributions in the black family, it does suggest a source of male power.[11] Delores Mack, in a study of black and white families, supports this contention (1969).

What these findings suggest is that researchers have not carefully evaluated the logic of the assumptions of their hypotheses. They have looked at the white community; there they have observed that education, occupation, and income are important sources of power.... They have ignored the possibility that the sources of power in the black community may be different from that in the white community. In fact, they have ignored one of the most potent forms of power in any marriage, but particularly sex power in black marriages. Certainly researchers have noted the preoccupation of the black male with sex. Some have viewed this preoccupation with sex as a form of escapism, failing to realize that this concentration on sexual activities may be a main source of power. The black male is well aware, as Eldridge Cleaver notes, that he is the desired sex object for both the white and the black female. He may use this power in his marriage, much as the white male uses his education and earning power as a lever in his marriage.

The threat or use of physical violence (as discussed above) is another factor which must be taken into account to explain power distributions in black as well as white families. Obviously, a great deal of research on the differences within black families is needed, as Billingsley has suggested.

LIFE CYCLE

The stages of the family life cycle also affect the marital power distribution. In the early (childless) stage of marriage, the wife is frequently working, but the pressure of social discrimination against women is already beginning to be exerted. Women are unable to procure anything but low-paying, low-status jobs as compared with their husbands. Already status background and autonomous experiences are being eroded. Though the married childless woman maintains some sort of independent social and economic status if she works, it is below that of her husband. During this period, the power of the husband is moderate.

With the birth of children, there is a substantial jump in power differentials, the husband universally gaining (Blood and Wolfe 1960, pp. 41–44). There is more than a little truth in the old saw that the best way to control a woman is to "keep her barefoot and pregnant," for there is evidence that the power of the wife declines as the number of children grows (Heer 1958, pp. 341–347). At this period after the first child is born, but before the oldest child is in school, the power of the husband reaches its maximum. Many women stop working during this stage and in doing so, become isolated and almost totally socially, economically, and emotionally dependent upon their husbands, further eroding any strength they may have gained

due to earning power or participation in organizations. She loses her position, cannot keep up with developments in her field, does not build up seniority. Further, she loses that precious "organizational" experience, the growth of competence and resources in the outside world, the community positions which contribute to power in the marriage. The boundaries of her world contract, the possibilities of growth diminish. If she returns to work, and most women do, she must begin again at a low-status job and she stays there—underemployed and underpaid. As her children grow up, she gradually regains some power in the family.

These data again call into question the theory of individual resources as the source of power in marriage. As David Heer pointed out, there is no reason, according to Blood and Wolfe's theory, for the power of the wife to be greater before she has borne children than when her children are preschool age. Surely the wife with preschool children is contributing more resources of the marriage than she did before their children were born (1963, p. 138). Power, then, is clearly not the result of individual contributions and resources in the marriage, but is related to questions of social worth; and the value of women and women's work, as viewed by society, is obviously very low. The contributions of women in the home are of little concern and are consequently little valued, as Margaret Benston explained in "The political economy of women's liberation" (1969, pp. 3–4).

> In sheer quantity, household labor, including child care, constitutes a huge amount of socially necessary production. Nevertheless, in a society based on commodity production, it is not usually considered "real work" since it is outside of trade and marketplace. It is precapitalist in a very real sense. The assignment of household work as the function of a special category "women" meant that this group *does* stand in a different relation to the production than the group "men." We will tentatively define women, then, as that group of people who are responsible for the production of simple use-values in those activities associated with the home and the family.
>
> Since men carry no responsibility for such production, the difference between the two

groups lies here. Notice that women are not excluded from commodity production. Their participation in wage labor occurs, but as a group, they have no structural responsibility in this area and such participation is ordinarily regarded as transient. Men, on the other hand, are responsible for commodity production; they are not, in principle, given any role in household labor.... The material basis for the inferior status of women is to be found in just this definition of women. In a society in which money determines value, women are a group who work outside the money economy. Their work is not worth money, is therefore valueless, is therefore not even real work. And women themselves, who do this valueless work, can hardly be expected to be worth as much as men, who work for money. In structural terms, the closest thing to the condition of women is the condition of others who are or were outside of commodity production, i.e., peasants or serfs.

THE HUSBAND: MOST LIKELY TO SUCCEED

Thus, it is clear that for a wife to gain even a modicum of power in the marital relationship, she must obtain it from external sources, i.e., she must participate in the work force, her education must be superior to that of her husband, and her participation in organizations must excel his. Equality of resources leaves the power in the hands of the husband. Access to these sources of power are structurally blocked for women, however.

In the general population, women are unable to procure anything but low-status, low-paying, dead-end jobs as compared with their husbands, be it factory or university.[12] Partly as a result of unequal pay for the same work, partly as a consequence of channeling women into low-paying jobs, the median income of women is far less than that of men workers. Black women tend to fare slightly better in relation to black men, but make only two-thirds as much as white women.

In higher socioeconomic classes, the husband is more likely to excel his wife in formal education than he is among blue-collar workers. Men pre-

Median income of year-round full-time workers by sex and color, 1964[13]

	Men	Women	Women as % of men
White	$6497	$3859	59.4
Nonwhite	4285	2674	62.2

dominate among college graduates, regardless of race, but adult women have a higher median of education (12.1 for women, 12.0 for men in 1964).[14] (We have already seen that the educational attainment of the nonwhite population is lower [8.5 for women, 7.9 for men], reflecting discrimination on the basis of race.)

All of these areas are sources of power in the marital relationship, and in all of these areas women are structurally blocked from realizing our capacities. It is not because of individual resources or personal competence, then, that husbands obtain power in marriage, but because of the discrimination against women in the larger society. Men gain resources as a class, not as individuals, and women are blocked as a class, not as individuals.

In our mutual mobility bet the woman (as a class) always loses in the fight for power within the marital relationship. We live in a system of institutionalized male supremacy, and the cards are systematically stacked against women in all areas—occupational, political, educational, legal, as well as within the institution of the family. As long as the structure of society remains the same, as long as categorical discrimination against women is carried out, there is relatively little chance for the woman to gain autonomy, regardless of how much goodwill there is on the part of her husband.

The equalitarian marriage as a norm is a myth. Under some conditions, women can gain power vis-à-vis their husbands, i.e., working women, women with higher educations than their husbands have more power than housewives or women with lesser or identical education as their husbands, but more power is not equal power. Equal power we do not have. Equal power we will never get so long as the present socioeconomic system remains.

NOTES

1. Blood and Wolfe's work plays a major part in this paper because it has been one of the most influential studies of marriage in the last ten years.

2. Goode, 1964, p. 87.

3. It should be made clear that legality is not necessarily a basis for decision making. It merely reflects the position of society as to how the power is to be distributed when such distributions are contested in the courts. This normally occurs upon dissolution of marriage and not in an ongoing relationship

4. Conversation with Ann Leffler, 1969.

5. Blood and Wolfe's report of the data is so skimpy that it makes interpretation difficult. For example, they say that the 35 high-income husbands (over $4000) have lower mean power (4.09) than their 68 less affluent colleagues (4.56). This is possibly analogous to the distribution in the white blue-collar class, where low blue-collar husbands have more power than the high blue-collar husbands. Comparisons are difficult because, for the general population, income was broken into five groups, while for black families they used only two—over $4000 and below $4000. They reported that "the generalization that the husband's power is correlated with occupational status also holds within the Negro race" (4.31, 4.60, no cases, and 5.00 respectively). The only mention of Negro husbands and social status was that the few white husbands in the lowest status groups differ sharply from their powerless Negro counterparts (no figures reported).

6. Negro women workers, Women's Bureau, Department of Labor, 1964: 23–25.

7. Fact Sheet on the Relative Position of Women and Men Workers in the Economy, U.S. Department of Labor, Women's Bureau, 1965, p. 3.

8. U.S. Department of Labor, Bureau of Labor Statistics, Employment and Earnings, Vol. 16, No 7, January 1970, Table A-1 (Data under Negro heading is for "Negro and other races").

9. Negro women workers, pp. 23–25.

10. Negro women workers, pp. 13–14.

11. This has also been suggested in several articles in *The black woman*, edited by Toni Cade (1970), particularly "Dear black man," Fran Sanders; "Who will revere the black woman?", Abbey Lincoln; "The black woman as woman," Kay Lindsey; "Double jeopardy: to be black and female," Frances Beale; "On the issue of roles," Toni Cade; "Black man, my man, listen!," Gail Stokes; "Is the black man castrated?," Jean Carey Bond and Pat Peery.

12. Handbook on women workers, U.S. Department of Labor, Women's Bureau, 1965, pp. 34–35.

13. Fact sheet on the relative position of women and men workers in the economy, U.S. Department of Labor, Women's Bureau, 1965, p. 3.

14. Handbook on women workers, 1965, p. 172.

REFERENCES

DE BEAUVOIR, SIMONE, 1968, *The second sex*. New York: Bantam Books.

BENSTON, MARGARET, 1969, The political economy of women's liberation, *Monthy Review*, September.

BERNARD, JESSE, 1966, *Marriage and family among Negroes*. Englewood Cliffs, N.J.: Prentice-Hall.

BILLINGSLEY, ANDREW, AND AMY TATE BILLINGSLEY, 1968, *Black families in white America*. Englewood Cliffs, N.J.: Prentice-Hall.

BLOOD, ROBERT O., JR., AND DONALD M. WOLFE, 1960, *Husbands and wives, the dynamics of married living*. New York: Free Press.

CADE, TONI, 1970, *The black woman, an anthology*. New York: New American Library.

CRONAN, SHEILA, 1969, Marriage. *The Feminist*. New York.

GALLEN, RICHARD T., 1967, *Wives' legal rights*. New York: Dell.

GOODE, WILLIAM, 1956, *Women in divorce*. New York: Free Press.

_____1963, *World revolution and family patterns*. New York: Free Press.

_____1964, *The family*. Englewood Cliffs, N.J.: Prentice-Hall.

HEER, DAVID M., 1958, Dominance and the working wife. *Social Forces* 36 (May):341–347.

_____1963, The measurement and bases of family power: an overview," *Marriage and Family Living* 25 (May):133–139.

KANOWITZ, LEO, 1969, *Women and the law, the unfinished revolution*. Albuquerque: The University of New Mexico Press.

KOMAROVSKY, MIRRA, 1967, *Blue-collar marriage.* New York: Vintage Books.

MACK, DELORES, 1969, *The husband-wife power relationship in black families and white families.* Ph.D. Dissertation, Stanford University.

O'CONNOR, LYNN, 1970, Male dominance, the nitty-gritty of oppression. *It Ain't Me, Babe* 1 (8) (June 11–July 1): 9–11.

PILPEL, HARRIET F., AND THEODORA ZAVIN, 1964, *Your marriage and the law.* New York: Collier Books.

SAFILIOS-ROTHSCHILD, CONSTANTIA, 1969, Family sociology or wives' family sociology? A cross-cultural examination of decision making. *Journal of Marriage and the Family* 31 (2) (May): 290–301.

TALLMAN, IRVING, 1969, Working class wives in suburbia: fulfillment or crisis?" *Journal of Marriage and the Family* 31 (1) (February):65–72.

WEISSTEIN, NAOMI, 1969, *Kinde, küche, kirche as scientific law: psychology constructs the female.* Boston: New England Free Press.

Government Publications

Fact sheet on the relative position of women and men workers in the economy, U. S. Department of Labor, Women's Bureau, 1965.

1965 Handbook on women workers, U.S. Department of Labor, Women's Bureau.

Negro women workers in 1960, U.S. Department of Labor, Women's Bureau.

U.S. Department of Labor, Bureau of Statistics, Employment and Earnings, Vol 16, No. 7, January 1970.

Know your rights: what a working wife should know about her legal rights, U.S. Department of Labor, Women's Bureau, 1965.

Chapter 6
Parenting

FROM THE TIME OF THEIR BIRTH AND FOR many years thereafter, human beings cannot survive on their own; rather, they require nurturance and care from others. This dependence is rooted in both biological and social conditions. Biologically, infants are dependent on others for their food, clothing, and shelter. Apart from these biological needs, young children also need aid in acquiring intellectual and social skills necessary for their future adult roles. In addition, human interaction is necessary for the fulfillment of psychological needs, such as the needs for security, self-esteem, and intimacy.

In American society, in contrast to some of the cultures mentioned in Chapter 2, parents are expected to fulfill the needs of children within the nuclear family. In the traditional nuclear family structure, the father role has largely centered on providing economically for the family, while the mother is expected to enact her role by participating full time in her children's care and socialization. In contrast to this traditional family structure, which has served as the normative model, other family forms have always existed. One consists of the dual career family, where both parents work, and also share in the different aspects of child-rearing. Another form is the single-parent family which currently constitutes over ten percent of all families. These last two family forms are most likely to need and utilize other institutions such as day care.

Social scientists at one time argued that the traditional family structure was the most advantageous for successful parenting. It was assumed that mothers were best suited to play the expressive, nurturing role. With the increase of women entering the labor force after World War II, and with the rebirth of feminism in the 1960s, the assumption that there was a biological need for child-care functions to be performed by women was questioned.

Empirical research comparing the children of employed women and housewives initially found few differences overall between the two groups of children when women were satisfied with their roles.[1] Most recent studies have shown that maternal employment has positive effects on children, particularly on girls. Children of employed mothers hold less stereotyped views of adult sex roles. Daughters were found to view women as competent and effective, while sons, mainly in the middle class, saw men as warm and expressive. Daughters of employed mothers generally have higher achievement aspirations.[2]

With the rising divorce rate, there has been an increase in single-parent families, in some cases for a temporary period. It was previously assumed that this family form had extremely negative consequences for the care and socialization of children. Though it is easier to care for children in two-parent families, given the greater resources, personal and economic, the clear-cut negative effects on children of single-parent families have not been found by researchers. In one study, the adjustment of children in unhappy intact homes was compared with the adjustment of children in broken one-parent homes and in homes where a remarriage had taken place. No differences were found.[3] At the same time, societal resources, such as adequate day-care facilities, are needed to make fulfillment of functions in single-parent families less difficult.[4]

In general, research suggests that children need consistent care, and sensitivity by caretakers in responding to their physical, intellectual, and psychological needs. However, there is no clear evidence that this caretaking role has to be performed by one person or has to take place in one type of setting.

Given the needs of children and these existing family structures, how successful are we in caring for and nurturing children? From the legal and clinical evidence of child abuse and parental neglect, it is clear that we are far from being totally successful. It has been estimated that 60,000 children are annually neglected or seriously abused by their mothers.[5] The articles in this section, dealing with structural and normative aspects of parental functioning, suggest sociological explanations for our successes and failures in this area.

According to Alice Rossi, we need to know more about the needs of parents, particularly mothers, in order to understand our inadequacies in child-rearing. She suggests that the traditional nuclear family structure "extracts too high a price of deprivation" for mothers to make it a satisfactory place for child care and child-rearing. In addition, the "transition to parenthood" for both sexes is abrupt, and characterized by inadequate training and lack of clear-cut guidelines.

The article by Jane Pearce relates the structure of the family to its capacity to fulfill the psychological-emotional needs of children. She suggests that the traditional, role-differentiated family does not allow either parent to fulfill all of his or her own needs. This is especially true for homebound mothers. In addition, if women's entire roles focus on their children, they are motivated to prolong their children's immaturity in order to maintain their own "employment." In the case of fathers, they are prevented from enjoying intimate contact with their children. Thus, parents (in particular, mothers) who are frustrated in the traditional nuclear family, transmit their own anger to their children.

In the article by R. D. Laing, an analysis is made of family communication patterns which have consequences for the satisfaction of needs of the different family members. Laing deals with the process of mystification, whereby one family member defines reality for another member to fit his or her own needs, while negating the other person's perception of reality. It is usually a child's needs that are negated.

To analyze the various dimensions of parenthood, students might utilize the symbolic interaction perspective to deal with the way the parent roles are learned at the different life-cycle stages. Given the limitations of parent-role learning dealt with by Rossi, how might men and women better prepare themselves for future parent roles?

From a functional perspective, students might assess the relative strengths and limitations of the different parental roles for the parents and the children. What are the different areas in which the lack of satisfying parental roles produce failure in child-rearing? What types of structural arrangements might improve the "transition to parenthood"?

A conflict perspective is illustrated by the Laing article. He shows how a definition of reality can be utilized to mask the manipulation of some family members by others. Using Laing's case studies, how does the family contribute to the creation of mental illness? What is the basis of the ability of some family members to manipulate other members?

NOTES

1. Marion Yarrow *et al.*, Child-rearing in families of working and nonworking mothers. *Sociometry* 25 (1962): 122–140.

2. Lois Wladis Hoffman, The effects of maternal employment on the child—a review of the research. *Developmental Psychology* 10 (2), 1974: 204–228.

3. Ivan Nye, Child adjustment in broken and in unhappy unbroken homes. *Marriage and Family Living* 19 (1957): 356-361.

4. Ruth Brandwein, Chris Brown, and Elizabeth Fox,

Women and children last. *Journal of Marriage and the Family* 36 (1974): 498-514.

5. Robert Bell, *Marriage and family interaction.* (3rd ed.) Homewood, Ill.: Dorsey, 1971 p. 435.

Transition to Parenthood

ALICE S. ROSSI

THE PROBLEM

THE CENTRAL CONCERN IN THIS SOCIO-logical analysis of parenthood will be with two closely related questions. (1) What is involved in the transition to parenthood: what must be learned and what readjustments of other role commitments must take place in order to move smoothly through the transition from a childless married state to parenthood? (2) What is the effect of parenthood on the adult: in what ways do parents, and in particular mothers, change as a result of their parental experiences?

To get a firmer conceptual handle on the problem, I shall first specify the stages in the development of the parental role and then explore several of the most salient features of the parental role by comparing it with the two other major adult social roles—the marital and work roles. Throughout the discussion, special attention will be given to the social changes that have taken place during the past few decades which facilitate or complicate the transition to and the experience of parenthood among young American adults.

FROM CHILD TO PARENT: AN EXAMPLE

What is unique about this perspective on parenthood is the focus on the adult parent rather than the child. Until quite recent years, concern in the behavioral sciences with the parent–child relationship has been confined almost exclusively to the child. Whether a psychological study such as Ferreira's on the influence of the pregnant woman's attitude to maternity upon postnatal behavior of the neonate,[1] Sears and Maccoby's survey of child-rearing practices,[2] or Brody's detailed observations of mothering,[3] the long tradition of studies of maternal deprivation[4] and more recently of maternal employment,[5] the child has been the center of attention. The design of such research has assumed that, if enough were known about what parents were like and what they in fact did in rearing their children, much of the variation among children could be accounted for.[6]

The very different order of questions which emerges when the parent replaces the child as the primary focus of analytic attention can best be shown with an illustration. Let us take, as our example, the point Benedek makes that the child's need for mothering is *absolute* while the need of an adult woman to mother is *relative*.[7] From a concern for the child, this discrepancy in need leads to an analysis of the impact on the child of separation from the mother or inadequacy of mothering. Family systems that provide numerous adults to care for the young child can make up for this discrepancy in need between mother and child, which may be why ethnographic accounts give little evidence of postpartum depression following childbirth in simpler societies. Yet our family system of isolated households, increasingly distant from kinswomen to assist in mothering, requires that new mothers shoulder total responsibility for the infant

Reprinted from *Journal of Marriage and the Family* 30, (1): 26-39, by permission of the author and the National Council on Family Relations.

precisely for that stage of the child's life when his need for mothering is far in excess of the mother's need for the child.

From the perspective of the mother, the question has therefore become: what does maternity deprive her of? Are the intrinsic gratifications of maternity sufficient to compensate for shelving or reducing a woman's involvement in nonfamily interests and social roles? The literature on maternal deprivation cannot answer such questions, because the concept, even in the careful specification Yarrow has given it,[8] has never meant anything but the effect on the child of various kinds of insufficient mothering. Yet what has been seen as a failure or inadequacy of individual women may in fact be a failure of the society to provide institutionalized substitutes for the extended kin to assist in the care of infants and young children. It may be that the role requirements of maternity in the American family system extract too high a price of deprivation for young adult women reared with highly diversified interests and social expectations concerning adult life. Here, as at several points in the course of this paper, familiar problems take on a new and suggestive research dimension when the focus is on the parent rather than the child.

BACKGROUND

Since it is a relatively recent development to focus on the parent side of the parent–child relationship, some preliminary attention to the emergence of this focus on parenthood is in order. Several developments in the behavioral sciences paved the way to this perspective. Of perhaps most importance have been the development of ego psychology and the problem of adaptation of Murray[9] and Hartmann,[10] the interpersonal focus of Sullivan's psychoanalytic theories,[11] and the life-cycle approach to identity of Erikson.[12] These have been fundamental to the growth of the human development perspective: that personality is not a stable given but a constantly changing phenomenon, that the individual changes along the life line as he lives through critical life experiences. The transition to parenthood, or the impact of parenthood upon the adult, is part of the heightened contemporary interest in adult socialization.

A second and related development has been the growing concern of behavioral scientists with crossing levels of analysis to adequately comprehend social and individual phenomena and to build theories appropriate to a complex social system. In the past, social anthropologists focused as purely on the level of prescriptive normative variables as psychologists had concentrated on intrapsychic processes at the individual level or sociologists on social-structural and institutional variables. These are adequate, perhaps, when societies are in a stable state of equilibrium and the social sciences were at early stages of conceptual development, but they become inadequate when the societies we study are undergoing rapid social change and we have an increasing amount of individual and subgroup variance to account for.

Psychology and anthropology were the first to join theoretical forces in their concern for the connections between culture and personality. The question of how culture is transmitted across the generations and finds its manifestations in the personality structure and social roles of the individual has brought renewed research attention to the primary institutions of the family and the schools, which provide the intermediary contexts through which culture is transmitted and built into personality structure.

It is no longer possible for a psychologist or a therapist to neglect the social environment of the individual subject or patient, nor is the "family" they are concerned with any longer confined to the family of origin, for current theory and therapy view the adult individual in the context of his current family of procreation. So too it is no longer possible for the sociologist to focus exclusively on the current family relationships of the individual. The incorporation of psychoanalytic theory into the informal, if not the formal, training of the sociologist has led to an increasing concern for the quality of relationships in the family of origin as determinants of the adult attitudes, values, and behavior which the sociologist studies.

Quite another tradition of research has led to the formulation of "normal crises of parenthood." "Crisis" research began with the studies of individuals undergoing traumatic experiences, such as that by Tyhurst on natural catastrophes,[13] Caplan on parental responses to premature births,[14] Lindemann on grief and bereavement,[15] and Janis on surgery.[16] In these studies attention was on differential response to stress—how and why individuals vary in the ease with which they coped with the stressful experience and achieved some reintegration. Sociological interest has been piqued as these studies were built upon by Rhona and Robert Rapoport's research on the honeymoon and the engagement as normal crises in the role transitions to marriage and their theoretical attempt to build a conceptual bridge between family and occupational research from a "transition task" perspective.[17] LeMasters, Dyer, and Hobbs have each conducted studies of parenthood precisely as a crisis or disruptive event in family life.[18]

I think, however, that the time is now ripe to drop the concept of "normal crises" and to speak directly, instead, of the transition to and impact of parenthood. There is an uncomfortable incongruity in speaking of any crisis as normal. If the transition is achieved and if a successful reintegration of personality or social roles occurs, then crisis is a misnomer. To confine attention to "normal crises" suggests, even if it is not logically implied, successful outcome, thus excluding from our analysis the deviant instances in which failure occurs.

Sociologists have been just as prone as psychologists to dichotomize normality and pathology. We have had one set of theories to deal with deviance, social problems, and conflict and quite another set in theoretical analyses of a normal system—whether a family or a society. In the latter case our theories seldom include categories to cover deviance, strain, dysfunction, or failure. Thus, Parsons and Bales's systems find "task leaders" oriented to problem solution, but not instrumental leaders attempting to undercut or destroy the goal of the group, and "sociometric stars" who play a positive integrative function in cementing ties among group members, but not negatively expressive persons with hostile aims of reducing or destroying such intragroup ties.[19]

Parsons's analysis of the experience of parenthood as a step in maturation and personality growth does not allow for negative outcome. In this view either parents show little or no positive impact upon themselves of their parental role experiences,

or they show a new level of maturity. Yet many women, whose interests and values made a congenial combination of wifehood and work role, may find that the addition of maternal responsibilities has the consequence of a fundamental and undesired change in both their relationships to their husbands and their involvements outside the family. Still other women, who might have kept a precarious hold on adequate functioning as adults had they *not* become parents, suffer severe retrogression with pregnancy and childbearing, because the reactivation of older unresolved conflicts with their own mothers is not favorably resolved but in fact leads to personality deterioration[20] and the transmission of pathology to their children.[21]

Where cultural pressure is very great to assume a particular adult role, as it is for American women to bear and rear children, latent desire and psychological readiness for parenthood may often be at odds with manifest desire and actual ability to perform adequately as parents. Clinicians and therapists are aware, as perhaps many sociologists are not, that failure, hostility, and destructiveness are as much a part of the family system and the relationships among family members as success, love, and solidarity are.[22]

A conceptual system which can deal with both successful and unsuccessful role transitions, or positive and negative impact of parenthood upon adult men and women, is thus more powerful than one built to handle success but not failure or vice versa. For these reasons I have concluded that it is misleading and restrictive to perpetuate the use of the concept of "normal crisis." A more fruitful point of departure is to build upon the stage-task concepts of Erikson, viewing parenthood as a developmental stage, as Benedek[23] and Hill[24] have done, a perspective carried into the research of Rausch, Goodrich, and Campbell[25] and of Rhona and Robert Rapoport[26] on adaptation to the early years of marriage and that of Cohen, Fearing *et al.*[27] on the adjustments involved in pregnancy.

ROLE CYCLE STAGES

A discussion of the impact of parenthood upon the parent will be assisted by two analytic devices. One is to follow a comparative approach, by asking in what basic structural ways the parental role differs from other primary adult roles. The marital and occupational roles will be used for this comparison. A second device is to specify the phases in the development of a social role. If the total life span may be said to have a cycle, each stage with its unique tasks, then by analogy a role may be said to have a cycle and each stage in that role cycle, to have its unique tasks and problems of adjustment. Four broad stages of a role cycle may be specified.

Anticipatory Stage

All major adult roles have a long history of anticipatory training for them, since parental and school socialization of children is dedicated precisely to this task of producing the kind of competent adult valued by the culture. For our present purposes, however, a narrower conception of the anticipatory stage is preferable: the engagement period in the case of the marital role, pregnancy in the case of the parental role, and the last stages of highly vocationally oriented schooling or on-the-job apprenticeship in the case of an occupational role.

Honeymoon Stage

This is the time period immediately following the full assumption of the adult role. The inception of this stage is more easily defined than its termination. In the case of the marital role, the honeymoon stage extends from the marriage ceremony itself through the literal honeymoon and on through an unspecified and individually varying period of time. Raush[28] has caught this stage of the marital role in his description of the "psychic honeymoon": that extended postmarital period when, through close intimacy and joint activity, the couple can explore each other's capacities and limitations. I shall arbitrarily consider the onset of pregnancy as marking the end of the honeymoon stage of the marital role. This stage of the parental role may involve an equivalent psychic honeymoon, that postchildbirth period during which, through intimacy and prolonged contact, an attachment between parent and child is laid down. There is a crucial difference, however, from the marital role in this stage. A woman knows her husband as a unique real person when

she enters the honeymoon stage of marriage. A good deal of preparatory adjustment on a firm reality-base is possible during the engagement period which is not possible in the equivalent pregnancy period. Fantasy is not corrected by the reality of a specific individual child until the birth of the child. The "quickening" is psychologically of special significance to women precisely because it marks the first evidence of a real baby rather than a purely fantasized one. On this basis alone there is greater interpersonal adjustment and learning during the honeymoon stage of the parental role than of the marital role.

Plateau Stage

This is the protracted middle period of a role cycle during which the role is fully exercised. Depending on the specific problem under analysis, one would obviously subdivide this large plateau stage further. For my present purposes it is not necessary to do so, since my focus is on the earlier anticipatory and honeymoon stages of the parental role and the overall impact of parenthood on adults.

Disengagement-Termination Stage

This period immediately precedes and includes the actual termination of the role. Marriage ends with the death of the spouse or, just as definitively, with separation and divorce. A unique characteristic of parental role termination is the fact that it is not clearly marked by any specific act but is an attenuated process of termination with little cultural prescription about when the authority and obligations of a parent end. Many parents, however, experience the marriage of the child as a psychological termination of the active parental role.

UNIQUE FEATURES OF PARENTAL ROLE

With this role cycle suggestion as a broader framework, we can narrow our focus to what are the unique and most salient features of the parental role. In doing so, special attention will be given to two further questions: (1) the impact of social changes over the past few decades in facilitating or complicating the transition to and experience of parenthood and (2) the new interpretations or new research suggested by the focus on the parent rather than the child.

Cultural Pressure to Assume the Role

On the level of cultural values, men have no freedom of choice where work is concerned: they must work to secure their status as adult men. The equivalent for women has been maternity. There is considerable pressure upon the growing girl and young woman to consider maternity necessary for a woman's fulfillment as an individual and to secure her status as an adult.[29]

This is not to say there are no fluctuations over time in the intensity of the cultural pressure to parenthood. During the depression years of the 1930s, there was more widespread awareness of the economic hardships parenthood can entail, and many demographic experts believe there was a great increase in illegal abortions during those years. Bird has discussed the dread with which a suspected pregnancy was viewed by many American women in the 1930s.[30] Quite a different set of pressures were at work during the 1950s, when the general societal tendency was toward withdrawal from active engagement with the issues of the larger society and a turning in to the gratifications of the private sphere of home and family life. Important in the background were the general affluence of the period and the expanded room and ease of child rearing that go with suburban living. For the past five years, there has been a drop in the birthrate in general, fourth and higher-order births in particular. During this same period there has been increased concern and debate about women's participation in politics and work, with more women now returning to work rather than conceiving the third or fourth child.[31]

Inception of the Parental Role

The decision to marry and the choice of a mate are voluntary acts of individuals in our family system. Engagements are therefore consciously considered, freely entered, and freely terminated if increased familiarity decreases, rather than increases, intimacy and commitment to the choice. The inception of a pregnancy, unlike the engagement, is not always a voluntary decision, for it may be the unintended consequence of a sexual act that was recreative in intent rather than procreative. Secondly, and again unlike the engagement, the termination of a pregnancy is not socially sanctioned, as shown by current resistance to abortion-law reform.

The implication of this difference is a much higher probability of unwanted pregnancies than of unwanted marriages in our family system. Coupled with the ample clinical evidence of parental rejection and sometimes cruelty to children, it is all the more surprising that there has not been more consistent research attention to the problem of *parental satisfaction*, as there has for long been on *marital satisfaction* or *work satisfaction*. Only the extreme iceberg tip of the parental satisfaction continuum is clearly demarcated and researched, as in the growing concern with "battered babies." Cultural and psychological resistance to the image of a nonnurturant woman may afflict social scientists as well as the American public.

The timing of a first pregnancy is critical to the manner in which parental responsibilities are joined to the marital relationship. The single most important change over the past few decades is extensive and efficient contraceptive usage, since this has meant for a growing proportion of new marriages, the possibility of and increasing preference for some postponement of childbearing after marriage. When pregnancy was likely to follow shortly after marriage, the major transition point in a woman's life was marriage itself. *This transition point is increasingly the first pregnancy rather than marriage.* It is accepted and increasingly expected that women will work after marriage, while household furnishings are acquired and spouses complete their advanced training or gain a foothold in their work.[32] This provides an early marriage period in which the fact of a wife's employment presses for a greater egalitarian relationship between husband and wife in decision making, commonality of experience, and sharing of household responsibilities.

The balance between individual autonomy and couple mutuality that develops during the honeymoon stage of such a marriage may be important in establishing a pattern that will later affect the quality of the parent–child relationship and the extent of sex-role segregation of duties between the parents. It is only in the context of a growing egalitarian base to the marital relationship that one could find, as Gavron has,[33] a tendency for parents to establish some barriers between themselves and their children, a marital defense against the institution of parenthood as she describes it. This may eventually replace the typical coalition in more traditional families of mother and children against husband–father. Parenthood will continue for some time to impose a degree of temporary segregation of primary responsibilities between husband and wife, but, when this takes place in the context of a previously established egalitarian relationship between the husband and wife, such role segregation may become blurred, with greater recognition of the wife's need for autonomy and the husband's role in the routines of home and child-rearing.[34]

There is one further significant social change that has important implications for the changed relationship between husband and wife: the increasing departure from an old pattern of role-inception phasing in which the young person first completed his schooling, then established himself in the world of work, then married and began his family. Marriage and parenthood are increasingly taking place *before* the schooling of the husband, and often of the wife, has been completed.[35] An important reason for this trend lies in the fact that, during the same decades in which the average age of physical-sexual maturation has dropped, the average amount of education which young people obtain has been on the increase. Particularly for the college and graduate or professional school population, family roles are often assumed before the degrees needed to enter careers have been obtained.

Just how long it now takes young people to complete their higher education has been investigated only recently in several longitudinal studies of college-graduate cohorts.[36] College is far less uniformly a four-year period than high school is. A full third of the college freshmen in one study had been out of high school a year or more before entering college.[37] In a large sample of college graduates in 1961, one in five were over 25 years of age at graduation.[38] Thus, financial difficulties, military service, change of career plans, and marriage itself

all tend to create interruptions in the college attendance of a significant proportion of college graduates. At the graduate and professional school level, this is even more marked: the mean age of men receiving the doctorate, for example, is 32, and of women, 36.[39] It is the exception rather than the rule for men and women who seek graduate degrees to go directly from college to graduate school and remain there until they secure their degrees.[40]

The major implication of this change is that more men and women are achieving full adult status in family roles while they are still less than fully adult in status terms in the occupational system. Graduate students are, increasingly, men and women with full family responsibilities. Within the family many more husbands and fathers are still students, often quite dependent on the earnings of their wives to see them through their advanced training.[41] No matter what the couple's desires and preferences are, this fact alone presses for more egalitarian relations between husband and wife, just as the adult family status of graduate students presses for more egalitarian relations between students and faculty.

Irrevocability

If marriages do not work out, there is now widespread acceptance of divorce and remarriage as a solution. The same point applies to the work world: we are free to leave an unsatisfactory job and seek another. But once a pregnancy occurs, there is little possibility of undoing the commitment to parenthood implicit in conception except in the rare instance of placing children for adoption. We can have ex-spouses and ex-jobs but not ex-children. This being so, it is scarcely surprising to find marked differences between the relationship of a parent and one child and the relationship of the same parent with another child. If the culture does not permit pregnancy termination, the equivalent to giving up a child is psychological withdrawal on the part of the parent.

This taps an important area in which a focus on the parent rather than the child may contribute a new interpretive dimension to an old problem: the long history of interest, in the social sciences, in differences among children associated with their sex-birth-order position in their sibling set. Research has largely been based on data gathered about and/or from the children, and interpretations make inferences back to the "probable" quality of the child's relation to a parent and how a parent might differ in relating to a first-born compared to a last-born child. The relevant research, directed at the parents (mothers in particular), remains to be done, but at least a few examples can be suggested of the different order of interpretation that flows from a focus on the parent.

Some birth-order research stresses the influence of sibs upon other sibs, as in Koch's finding that second-born boys with an older sister are more feminine than second-born boys with an older brother.[42] A similar sib-influence interpretation is offered in the major common finding of birth-order correlates, that sociability is greater among last-borns[43] and achievement among first-borns.[44] It has been suggested that last-borns use social skills to increase acceptance by their older sibs or are more peer-oriented because they receive less adult stimulation from parents. The tendency of first-borns to greater achievement has been interpreted in a corollary way, as a reflection of early assumption of responsibility for younger sibs, greater adult stimulation during the time the oldest was the only child in the family,[45] and the greater significance of the first-born for the larger kinship network of the family.[46]

Sociologists have shown increasing interest in structural family variables in recent years, a primary variable being family size. From Bossard's descriptive work on the large family[47] to more methodologically sophisticated work such as that by Rosen,[48] Elder and Bowerman,[49] Boocock,[50] and Nisbet,[51] the question posed is: what is the effect of growing up in a small family, compared with a large family, that is attributable to this group-size variable? Unfortunately, the theoretical point of departure for sociologists' expectations of the effect of the family-size variables is the Durkheim-Simmel tradition of the differential effect of group size or population density upon members or inhabitants.[52] In the case of the family, however, this overlooks the very important fact that family size is determined by the key figures *within* the group, i.e., the parents. To find that children in small families differ from children in large families is not simply due to the impact of group size upon individual members but to the very different involvement of the parent with the children and to relations between the parents themselves in small versus large families.

An important clue to a new interpretation can be gained by examining family size from the perspective of parental motivation toward having children. A small family is small for one of two primary reasons: either the parents wanted a small family and achieved their desired size, or they wanted a large family but were not able to attain it. In either case, there is a low probability of unwanted children. Indeed, in the latter eventuality they may take particularly great interest in the children they do have. Small families are therefore most likely to contain parents with a strong and positive orientation to each of the children they have. A large family, by contrast, is large either because the parents achieved the size they desired or because they have more children than they in fact wanted. Large families therefore have a higher probability than small families of including unwanted and unloved children. Consistent with this are Nye's finding that adolescents in small families have better relations with their parents than those in large families[53] and Sears and Maccoby's finding that mothers of large families are more restrictive toward their children than mothers of small families.[54]

This also means that last-born children are more likely to be unwanted than first- or middle-born children, particularly in large families. This is consistent with what is known of abortion patterns among married women, who typically resort to abortion only when they have achieved the number of children they want or feel they can afford to have. Only a small proportion of women faced with such unwanted pregnancies actually resort to abortion. *This suggests the possibility that the last-born child's reliance on social skills may be his device for securing the attention and loving involvement of a parent less positively predisposed to him than to his older siblings.*

In developing this interpretation, rather extreme cases have been stressed. Closer to the normal range, of families in which even the last-born child was desired and planned for, there is still another element which may contribute to the greater sociability of the last-born child. Most parents are themselves aware of the greater ease with which they face the care of a third fragile newborn than the first; clearly, parental skills and confidence are greater with last-born children than with first-born children. But this does not mean that the attitude of the parent is more positive toward the care of the third child than the first. There is no necessary correlation between skills in an area and enjoyment of that area. Searls[55] found that older homemakers are *more* skillful in domestic tasks but experience *less* enjoyment of them than younger homemakers, pointing to a declining euphoria for a particular role with the passage of time. In the same way, older people rate their marriages as "very happy" less often than younger people do.[56] It is perhaps culturally and psychologically more difficult to face the possibility that women may find less enjoyment of the maternal role with the passage of time, though women themselves know the difference between the romantic expectation concerning child care and the incorporation of the first baby into the household and the more realistic expectation and sharper assessment of their own abilities to do an adequate job of mothering as they face a third confinement. Last-born children may experience not only less verbal stimulation from their parents than first-born children but also less prompt and enthusiastic response to their demands—from feeding and diaper-change as infants to requests for stories read at three or a college education at eighteen—simply because the parents experience less intense gratification from the parent role with the third child than they did with the first. The child's response to this might well be to cultivate winning, pleasing manners in early childhood that blossom as charm and sociability in later life, showing both a greater need to be loved and greater pressure to seek approval.

One last point may be appropriately developed at this juncture. Mention was made earlier that for many women the personal outcome of experience in the parent role is not a higher level of maturation but the negative outcome of a depressed sense of self-worth, if not actual personality deterioration. There is considerable evidence that this is more prevalent than we recognize. On a qualitative level,

a close reading of the portrait of the working-class wife in Rainwater,[57] Newsom,[58] Komarovsky,[59] Gavron,[60] or Zweig[61] gives little suggestion that maternity has provided these women with opportunities for personal growth and development. So too, Cohen[62] notes with some surprise that in her sample of middle-class educated couples, as in Pavenstadt's study of lower-income women in Boston, there were more emotional difficulties and lower levels of maturation among multiparous women than primiparous women. On a more extensive sample basis, in Gurin's survey of Americans viewing their mental health,[63] as in Bradburn's reports on happiness,[64] single men are less happy and less active than single women, but among the married respondents the women are unhappier, have more problems, feel inadequate as parents, have a more negative and passive outlook on life, and show a more negative self-image. All of these characteristics increase with age among married women but show no relationship to age among men. While it may be true, as Gurin argues, that women are more introspective and hence more attuned to the psychological facets of experience than men are, this point does not account for the fact that the things which the women report are all on the negative side; few are on the positive side, indicative of euphoric sensitivity and pleasure. The possibility must be faced, and at some point researched, that women lose ground in personal development and self-esteem during the early and middle years of adulthood, whereas men gain ground in these respects during the same years. The retention of a high level of self-esteem may depend upon the adequacy of earlier preparation for major adult roles: men's training adequately prepares them for their primary adult roles in the occupational system, as it does for those women who opt to participate significantly in the work world. Training the qualities and skills needed for family roles in contemporary society may be inadequate for both sexes, but the lowering of self-esteem occurs only among women because their primary adult roles are within the family system.

Preparation for Parenthood

Four factors may be given special attention on the question of what preparation American couples bring to parenthood.

Paucity of preparation Our educational system is dedicated to the cognitive development of the young, and our primary teaching approach is the pragmatic one of learning by doing. How much one knows and how well he can apply what he knows are the standards by which the child is judged in school, as the employee is judged at work. The child can learn by doing in such subjects as science, mathematics, art work, or shop, but not in the subjects most relevant to successful family life: sex, home maintenance, child care, interpersonal competence, and empathy. If the home is deficient in training in these areas, the child is left with no preparation for a major segment of his adult life. A doctor facing his first patient in private practice has treated numerous patients under close supervision during his internship, but probably a majority of American mothers approach maternity with no previous child-care experience beyond sporadic baby-sitting, perhaps a course in child psychology, or occasional care of younger siblings.

Limited learning during pregnancy A second important point makes adjustment to parenthood potentially more stressful than marital adjustment. This is the lack of any realistic training for parenthood during the anticipatory stage of pregnancy. By contrast, during the engagement period preceding marriage, an individual has opportunities to develop the skills and make the adjustments which ease the transition to marriage. Through discussions of values and life goals, through sexual experimentation, shared social experiences as an engaged couple with friends and relatives, and planning and furnishing an apartment, the engaged couple can make considerable progress in developing mutuality in advance of the marriage itself.[65] No such headstart is possible in the case of pregnancy. What preparation exists is confined to reading, consultation with friends and parents, discussions between husband and wife, and a minor nesting phase in which a place and the equipment for a baby are prepared in the household.[66]

Abruptness of transition Thirdly, the birth of a child is not followed by any gradual taking on of responsibility, as in the case of a professional work role. It is as if the woman shifted from a graduate student to a full professor with little intervening apprenticeship experience of slowly increasing responsibility. The new mother starts out immediately on 24-hour duty, with responsibility for a fragile and mysterious infant totally dependent on her care.

If marital adjustment is more difficult for very young brides than more mature ones,[67] adjustment to motherhood may be even more difficult. A woman can adapt a passive dependence on a husband and still have a successful marriage, but a young mother with strong dependency needs is in for difficulty in maternal adjustment, because the role precludes such dependency. This situation was well described in Cohen's study[68] in a case of a young wife with a background of co-ed popularity and a passive dependent relationship to her admired and admiring husband, who collapsed into restricted incapacity when faced with the responsibilities of maintaining a home and caring for a child.

Lack of guidelines to successful parenthood If the central task of parenthood is the rearing of children to become the kind of competent adults valued by the society, then an important question facing any parent is what he or she specifically can do to create such a competent adult. This is where the parent is left with few or no guidelines from the expert. Parents can readily inform themselves concerning the young infant's nutritional, clothing, and medical needs and follow the general prescription that a child needs loving physical contact and emotional support. Such advice may be sufficient to produce a healthy, happy, and well-adjusted preschooler, but adult competency is quite another matter.

In fact, the adults who do "succeed" in American society show a complex of characteristics as children that current experts in child care would evaluate as "poor" to "bad." Biographies of leading authors and artists, as well as the more rigorous research inquiries of creativity among architects[69] or scientists,[70] do not portray childhoods with characteristics currently endorsed by mental health and child-care authorities. Indeed, there is often a predominance of tension in childhood family relations and traumatic loss rather than loving parental support, intense channeling of energy in one area of interest rather than an all-round profile of diverse interests, and social withdrawal and preference for loner activities rather than gregarious sociability.

Thus, the stress in current child-rearing advice on a high level of loving support but a low level of discipline or restriction on the behavior of the child—the "developmental" family type as Duvall calls it[71]—is a profile consistent with the focus on mental health, sociability, and adjustment. Yet the combination of both high support and high authority on the part of parents is most strongly related to the child's sense of responsibility, leadership quality, and achievement level, as found in Bronfenbrenner's studies[72] and that of Mussen and Distler.[73]

Brim points out[74] that we are a long way from being able to say just what parent role prescriptions have what effect on the adult characteristics of the child. We know even less about how such parental prescriptions should be changed to adapt to changed conceptions of competency in adulthood. In such an ambiguous context, the great interest parents take in school reports on their children or the pediatrician's assessment of the child's developmental progress should be seen as among the few indices parents have of how well *they* are doing as parents.

SYSTEM AND ROLE REQUIREMENTS INSTRUMENTALITY AND INTEGRATION

Typological dichotomies and unidimensional scales have loomed large in the search by social scientists for the most economical and general principles to account for some significant portion of the complex behavior or social organization they study. Thus, for example, the European dichotomy of *Gemeinschaft* and *Gesellschaft* became the American sociological distinction between rural and urban sociology, subfields that have outlasted their conceptual utility now that the rural environment has become urbanized and the interstices between country and city are swelling with suburban developments.

In recent years a new dichotomy has gained more acceptance in sociological circles—the Parsonian distinction between *instrumental* and *expressive*, an interesting dichotomy that is unfortunately applied in an indiscriminate way to all

manner of social phenomena including the analysis of teacher role conflict, occupational choice, the contrast between the family system and the occupational system, and the primary roles or personality tendencies of men compared to women.

On a system level, for example, the "instrumental" occupational system is characterized by rationality, efficiency, rejection of tradition, and depression of interpersonal loyalty, while the "expressive" family system is characterized by nurturance, integration, tension-management, ritual, and interpersonal solidarity. Applied to sex roles within the family, the husband–father emerges as the instrumental rational leader, a symbolic representative of the outside world, and the wife–mother emerges as the expressive, nurturant, affective center of the family. Such distinctions may be useful in the attempt to capture some general tendency of a system or a role, but they lead to more distortion than illumination when applied to the actual functioning of a specific system or social role or to the actual behavior of a given individual in a particular role.

Take, for example, the husband–father as the instrumental role within the family on the assumption that men are the major breadwinners and therefore carry the instrumentality associated with work into their roles within the family. To begin with, the family is not an experimental one-task small group but a complex, ongoing 24-hour entity with many tasks that must be performed. Secondly, we really know very little about how occupational roles affect the performance of family roles.[75] An aggressive courtroom lawyer or a shrewd business executive is not a lawyer or a businessman at home but a husband and a father. Unless shown to be in error, we should proceed on the assumption that behavior is role-specific. (Indeed, Brim[76] argues that even personality is role-specific.) A strict teacher may be an indulgent mother at home; a submissive wife may be a dominant mother; a dictatorial father may be an exploited and passive worker on the assembly line; or, as in some of Lidz's schizophrenic patients' families,[77] a passive dependent husband at home may be a successful dominant lawyer away from home.

There is, however, a more fundamental level to the criticism that the dichotomous usage of instrumentality and expressiveness, linked to sex and applied to intrafamily roles, leads to more distortion than illumination. The logic of my argument starts with the premise that every social system, group, or role has two primary, independent, structural axes. Whether these axes are called "authority and support," as in Straus's circumplex model,[78] or "instrumental and expressive" as by Parsons,[79] there are tasks to be performed and affective support to be given in all the cases cited. There must be discipline, rules, and division of labor in the nation–state as in the family or a business enterprise *and* there must be solidarity among the units comprising these same systems in order for the system to function adequately. *This means that the role of father, husband, wife, or mother each has these two independent dimensions of authority and support, instrumentality and expressiveness, work and love.* Little is gained by trying to stretch empirical results to fit the father role to the instrumental category, as Brim[80] has done, or the mother role to the expressive category, as Zelditch has done.[81]

In taking a next logical step from this premise, the critical issue, both theoretically and empirically, becomes gauging the *balance* between these two dimensions of the system or of the role. Roles or systems could be compared in terms of the average difference among them in the direction and extent of the discrepancy between authority and support; or individuals could be compared in terms of the variation among them in the discrepancy between the two dimensions in a given role.

An example may clarify these points. A teacher who is all loving, warm support to her students and plans many occasions to evoke integrative ties among them but who is incompetent in the exercise of authority or knowledge of the subjects she teaches would be judged by any school principal as an inadequate teacher. The same judgment of inadequacy would apply to a strict disciplinarian teacher, competent and informed about her subjects but totally lacking in any personal quality of warmth or ability to encourage integrative and cooperative responses among her students. Maximum adequacy of teacher performance requires a relatively high positive level on both of these two dimensions of the teacher role.

To claim that teachers have a basic conflict in approaching their role because they are required to be a "bisexual parent, permissive giver of love and harsh disciplinarian with a masculine intellectual grasp of the world," as Jackson and Moscovici[82] have argued, at least recognizes the two dimensions of the teacher role, though it shares the view of many sociologists that role *conflict* is inherent wherever these seeming polarities are required. Why conflict is predicted hinges on the assumed invariance of the linkage of the male to authority and the female to the expressive-integrative roles.

It is this latter assumed difference between the sexes that restricts theory-building in family sociology and produces so much puzzlement on the part of researchers into marriage and parenthood, sex-role socialization, or personality tendencies toward masculinity or femininity. Let me give one example of recent findings on this latter topic and then move on to apply the two-dimension concept to the parental role. Vincent[83] administered the Gough Femininity Scale along with several other scale batteries from the California Personality Inventory to several hundred college men and women. He found that women *low* on femininity were higher in the Class I scale which measures poise, ascendancy, and self-assurance, and men *high* in femininity were higher in dominance, capacity for status, and responsibility. Successful adult men in a technological society are rarely interested in racing cars, soldiering, or hunting; they are cautious, subtle, and psychologically attuned to others. So too, contemporary adult women who fear windstorms, the dark, strange places, automobile accidents, excitement, crowded parties, or practical jokes (and are therefore high on femininity in the Gough scale) will be inadequate for the task of managing an isolated household with neither men nor kinswomen close by to help them through daily crises, for the assumption of leadership roles in community organizations, or for holding down supplementary breadwinning or cakewinning jobs.

When Deutsch[84] and Escalona[85] point out that today's "neurotic" woman is not an assertive dominant person but a passive dependent one, the reason may be found in the social change in role expectations concerning competence among adult women, not that there has been a social change in the characteristics of neurotic women. In the past an assertive, dominant woman might have defined herself and been defined by her analyst as "neurotic" because she could not fill the expectations then held for adequacy among adult women. Today, it is the passive dependent woman who will be judged "neurotic" because she cannot fill adequately the expectations now set for and by her. What is really meant when we say that sex-role definitions have become increasingly blurred is that men are now required to show more integrative skills than in the past, and women more instrumental skills. This incurs potential sex-role "confusion" only by the standards of the past, not by the standards of what is required for contemporary adult competence in family and work roles.

Once freed from the assumption of a single bipolar continuum of masculinity–femininity,[86] authority-integration, or even independence-dependence,[87] one can observe increased instrumentality in a role with no implication of necessarily decreased integration, and vice versa. Thus, an increasing rationality in the care of children, the maintenance of a household, or meal planning for a family does not imply a decreasing level of integrative support associated with the wife–mother role. So, too, the increased involvement of a young father in playful encounters with his toddler carries no necessary implication of a change in the instrumental dimensions of his role.

The two-dimensional approach also frees our analyses of parenthood on two other important questions. Brim has reviewed much of the research on the parent-child relationship[88] and noted the necessity of specifying not only the sex of the parent but the sex of the child and whether a given parent–child dyad is a cross-sex or same-sex pair. It is clear from his review that fathers and mothers relate differently to their sons and daughters: fathers have been found to be stricter with their sons than with their daughters, and mothers stricter with their daughters than with their sons. Thus, a two-dimensional approach to the parent role is more appropriate to what is already empirically known about the parent–child relationship.

Secondly, only on a very general overview level does a parent maintain a particular level of support and of discipline toward a given child: situational variation is an important determinant of parental response to a child. A father with a general tendency toward relatively little emotional support of his son may offer a good deal of comfort if the child is hurt. An indulgent and loving mother may show an extreme degree of discipline when the same child misbehaves. Landreth found that her four-year-olds gave more mother responses on a care item concerning food than on bath-time or bedtime care and suggests, as Brim has,[89] that "any generalizations on parent roles should be made in terms of the role activities studied."[90]

Let me illustrate the utility of the two-dimensional concept by applying it to the parental role. Clearly there are a number of expressive requirements for adequate performance in this role: spontaneity and flexibility, the ability to be tender and loving and to respond to tenderness and love from a child, to take pleasure in tactile contact and in play, and to forget one's adultness and unself-consciously respond to the sensitivities and fantasies of a child. Equally important are the instrumental requirements for adequate performance in the parental role: firmness and consistency; the ability to manage time and energy; to plan and organize activities involving the child; to teach and to train the child in body controls, motor and language skills, and knowledge of the natural and social world; and interpersonal and value discriminations.

Assuming we had empirical measures of these two dimensions of the parental role, one could then compare individual women both by their levels on each of these dimensions and by the extent to which the discrepancy in level on the two dimensions was tipped toward a high expressive or instrumental dimension. This makes no assumptions about what the balance "should" be; that remains an empirical question awaiting a test in the form of output variables—the characteristics of children we deem to be critical for their competence as adults. Indeed, I would predict that an exhaustive count of the actual components of both the marital and parental roles would show a very high proportion of instrumental components in the parental role and a low proportion in the marital role and that this is an underlying reason why maternal role adjustment is more difficult for women than marital role adjustment. It also leaves as an open, empirical question what the variance is, among fathers, in the level of expressiveness and instrumentality in their paternal role performance and how the profile of fathers compares with that of mothers.

It would not surprise many of us, of course, if women scored higher than men on the expressive dimension and men scored higher on the instrumental dimension of the parental role. Yet quite the opposite might actually result. Men spend relatively little time with their children, and it is time of a particular kind: evenings, weekends, and vacations, when the activities and mood of the family are heavily on the expressive side. Women carry the major burden of the instrumental dimension of parenting. If, as Mabel Cohen[91] suggests, the rear-

ing of American boys is inadequate on the social and sexual dimension of development and the rearing of American girls is inadequate on the personal dimension of development, then from the perspective of adequate parenthood performance, we have indeed cause to reexamine the socialization of boys and girls in families and schools. Our current practices appear adequate as preparation for occupational life for men but not women, and inadequate as preparation for family life for both sexes.

However, this is to look too far ahead. At the present, this analysis of parenthood suggests we have much to rethink and much to research before we develop policy recommendations in this area.

NOTES

1. Antonio J. Ferreira, The pregnant woman's emotional attitude and its reflection on the newborn. *American Journal of Orthopsychiatry*, 1960, **30**: 553-561.

2. Robert Sears, E. Maccoby, and H. Levin, *Patterns of child-rearing*. Evanston, Illinois: Row, Peterson, 1957.

3. Sylvia Brody, *Patterns of mothering: maternal influences during infancy*. New York: International Universities Press, 1956.

4. Leon J. Yarrow, Maternal deprivation: toward an empirical and conceptual reevaluation. *Psychological Bulletin*, 1961, **58**: 6, 459-490.

5. F. Ivan Nye and L. W. Hoffman, *The employed mother in America*. Chicago: Rand McNally, 1963; Alice S. Rossi, Equality between the sexes: an immodest proposal, *Daedalus*, 1964, **93**: 2, 607-652.

6. The younger the child, the more was this the accepted view. It is only in recent years that research has paid any attention to the initiating role of the infant in the development of his attachment to maternal and other adult figures, as in Ainsworth's research which showed that infants become attached to the mother, not solely because she is instrumental in satisfying their primary visceral drives, but through a chain of behavioral interchange between the infant and the mother, thus supporting Bowlby's rejection of the secondary drive theory of the infant's ties to his mother. Mary D. Ainsworth, Patterns of attachment behavior shown by the infant in interaction with his mother. *Merrill-Palmer Quarterly*, 1964, **10**: 1: 51-58; John Bowlby, The nature of the child's tie to his mother. *International Journal of Psychoanalysis*, 1958, **39**: 1-34.

7. Therese Benedek, Parenthood as a developmental phase. *Journal of American Psychoanalytic Association*, 1959, **7**: 8: 389-417.

8. Yarrow, *op. cit.*

9. Henry A. Murray, *Explorations in personality*. New York: Oxford University Press, 1938.

10. Heinz Hartmann, *Ego psychology and the problem of adaptation*. New York: International Universities Press, Inc., 1958.

11. Patrick Mullahy (ed.), *The contributions of Harry Stack Sullivan*. New York: Hermitage House, 1952.

12. E. Erikson, Identity and the life cycle: selected papers. *Psychological Issues*, 1959, **1**: 1-171.

13. J. Tyhurst, Individual reactions to community disaster. *American Journal of Psychiatry*, 1951, **107**: 764-769.

14. G. Caplan, Patterns of parental response to the crisis of premature birth: a preliminary approach to modifying the mental health outcome. *Psychiatry*, 1960, **23**: 365-374.

15. E. Lindemann, Symptomatology and management of acute grief. *American Journal of Psychiatry*, 1944, **101**: 141-148.

16. Irving Janis, *Psychological stress*. New York: Wiley, 1958.

17. Rhona Rapoport, Normal crises, family structure, and mental health. *Family Process*, 1963, 2: 1: 68-80; Rhona Rapoport and Robert Rapoport, New light on the honeymoon. *Human Relations*, 1964, **17**: 1: 35-56; Rhona Rapoport, The transition from engagement to marriage, *Acta Sociologica*, 1964, 8, fasc.: 1-2, 36-55; and Robert Rapoport and Rhona

Rapoport, Work and family in contemporary society. *American Sociological Review*, 1965, **30**: 3: 381–394.

18. E. E. LeMasters, Parenthood as crisis. *Marriage and Family Living*, 1957, **19**, 352–355; Everett D. Dyer, Parenthood as crisis: A restudy. *Marriage and Family Living*, 1963, 25: 196–201; and Daniel F. Hobbs, Jr., Parenthood as crisis: a third study. *Journal of Marriage and the Family*, 1963, 27: 3: 367–372. LeMasters and Dyer both report the first experience of parenthood involves extensive to severe crises in the lives of their young parent respondents. Hobbs's study does not show first parenthood to be a crisis experience, but this may be due to the fact that his couples have very young (seven-week-old) first babies and are therefore still experiencing the euphoric honeymoon stage of parenthood.

19. Parsons's theoretical analysis of the family system builds directly on Bales's research on small groups. The latter are typically comprised of volunteers willing to attempt the single task put to the group. This positive orientation is most apt to yield the empirical discovery of "sociometric stars" and "task leaders," least apt to sensitize the researcher or theorist to the effect of hostile nonacceptance of the group task. Talcott Parsons and R. F. Bales, *Family, socialization and interaction process*. New York: Free Press, 1955.

   Yet the same limited definition of the key variables is found in the important attempts by Straus to develop the theory that every social system, as every personality, requires a circumplex model with two independent axes of authority and support. His discussion and examples indicate a variable definition with limited range: support is defined as High (+) or Low (−), but "low" covers both the absence of high support and the presence of negative support; there is love or neutrality in this system, but not hate. Applied to actual families, this groups destructive mothers with low-supportive mothers, much as the nonauthoritarian pole on the Authoritarian Personality Scale includes both mere nonauthoritarians and vigorously antiauthoritarian personalities. Murray A. Straus, Power and support structure of the family in relation to socialization. *Journal of Marriage and the Family*, 1964, **26**: 3: 318–326.

20. Mabel Blake Cohen, Personal identity and sexual identity. *Psychiatry*, 1966, **29**: 1: 1–14; Joseph C. Rheingold, *The fear of being a woman: a theory of maternal destructiveness*. New York: Grune and Stratton, 1964.

21. Theodore Lidz, S. Fleck, and A. Cornelison, *Schizophrenia and the family*. New York: International Universities Press, Inc., 1964; Rheingold, *op. cit.*

22. Cf. the long review of studies Rheingold covers in his book on maternal destructiveness, *op. cit.*

23. Benedek, *op. cit.*

24. Reuben Hill and D. A. Hansen, The identification of a conceptual framework utilized in family study. *Marriage and Family Living*, 1960, 22: 299–311.

25. Harold L. Raush, W. Goodrich, and J. D. Campbell. Adaptation to the first years of marriage. *Psychiatry*, 1963, 26: 4: 368–380.

26. Rapoport, *op. cit.*

27. Cohen, *op. cit.*

28. Raush *et al*, *op. cit.*

29. The greater the cultural pressure to assume a given adult social role, the greater will be the tendency for individual negative feelings toward that role to be expressed covertly. Men may complain about a given job but not about working per se, and hence their work dissatisfactions are often displaced to the non-work sphere, as psychosomatic complaints or irritation and dominance at home. An equivalent displacement for women of the ambivalence many may feel toward maternity is to dissatisfactions with the homemaker role.

30. Caroline Bird, *The invisible scar*. New York: David McKay, 1966.

31. When it is realized that a mean family size of 3.5 would double the population in 40 years, while a mean of 2.5 would yield a stable population in the same period, the social importance of withholding praise for procreative prowess is clear. At the same time, a drop in the birthrate may reduce the number of unwanted babies born, for such a drop would mean more efficient contraceptive usage and a closer correspondence between desired and attained family size.

32. James A. Davis, *Stipends and spouses: the finances of American arts and sciences graduate students*. Chicago: University of Chicago Press, 1962.

33. Hannah Gavron, *The captive wife*. London: Routledge and Kegan Paul, 1966.

34. The recent increase in natural childbirth, prenatal courses for expectant fathers, and greater participation of men during childbirth and postnatal care of the infant may therefore be a *consequence* of greater sharing between husband and wife when both work and jointly maintain their new households during the early months of marriage. Indeed, natural childbirth builds directly on this shifted base to the marital relationship. Goshen-Gottstein has found in an Israeli sample that women with a "traditional" orientation to marriage far exceed women with a "modern" orientation to marriage in menstrual difficulty, dislike of sexual intercourse, and pregnancy disorders and complaints such as vomiting. She argues that traditional women demand and expect little from their husbands and become demanding

and narcissistic by means of their children, as shown in pregnancy by an overexaggeration of symptoms and attention-seeking. Esther R. Goshen-Gottstein, *Marriage and first pregnancy: cultural influences on attitudes of Israeli women.* London: Tavistock Publications, 1966. A prolonged psychic honeymoon uncomplicated by an early pregnancy, and with the new acceptance of married women's employment, may help to cement the egalitarian relationship in the marriage and reduce both the tendency to pregnancy difficulties and the need for a narcissistic focus on the children. Such a background is fruitful ground for sympathy toward and acceptance of the natural childbirth ideology.

35. James A. Davis, *Stipends and spouses: the finances of American arts and sciences graduate students, op. cit.*; James A. Davis, *Great Aspirations.* Chicago: Aldine, 1964; Eli Ginsberg, *Life-styles of educated women.* New York: Columbia University Press, 1966; Ginsberg, *Educated American women: self-portraits.* New York: Columbia University Press, 1967; National Science Foundation, *Two years after the college degree—work and further study patterns.* Washington, D.C.: Government Printing Office, NSF 63-26, 1963.

36. Davis, *Great aspirations, op. cit.*; Laure Sharp, Graduate study and its relation to careers: the experience of a recent cohort of college graduates. *Journal of Human Resources,* 1966, 1: 2: 41-58.

37. James D. Cowhig and C. Nam, Educational status, college plans, and occupational status of farm and nonfarm youths, United States Bureau of the Census Series ERS (P-27). No. 30, 1961.

38. Davis, *Great aspirations, op. cit.*

39. Lindsey R. Harmon, *Profiles of Ph.D.s in the sciences: summary report on follow-up of doctorate cohorts, 1935-1960.* Washington, D.C.: National Research Council, Publication 1293, 1965.

40. Sharp, *op. cit.*

41. Davis, *Stipends and spouses, op. cit.*

42. Orville G. Brim, Family structure and sex-role learning by children. *Sociometry,* 1958, 21: 1-16; H. L. Koch, Sissiness and tomboyishness in relation to sibling characteristics. *Journal of Genetic Psychology,* 1956, 88: 231-244.

43. Charles MacArthur, Personalities of first and second children. *Psychiatry,* 1956, 19: 47-54; S. Schachter, Birth order and sociometric choice. *Journal of Abnormal and Social Psychology,* 1964, 68: 453-456.

44. Irving Harris, *The promised seed.* New York: Free Press, 1964; Bernard Rosen, Family structure and achievement motivation. *American Sociological Review,* 1961, 26: 574-585; Alice S. Rossi, Naming children in middle-class families. *American*

Sociological Review, 1965, **30**: 4: 499-513; Stanley Schachter, Birth order, eminence, and higher education. *American Sociological Review,* 1963, **28**: 757-768.

45. Harris, *op. cit.*

46. Rossi, Naming children in middle-class families, *op. cit.*

47. James H. Bossard, *Parent and child.* Philadelphia: University of Pennsylvania Press, 1953; James H. Bossard and E. Boll, *The large family system.* Philadelphia: University of Pennsylvania Press, 1956.

48. Rosen, *op. cit.*

49. Glen H. J. Elder and C. Bowerman, Family structure and child-rearing patterns: the effect of family size and sex composition on child-rearing practice. *American Sociological Review,* 1963, 28: 891-905.

50. Sarane S. Boocock, Toward a sociology of learning: a selective review of existing research. *Sociology of Education,* 1966, 39: 1: 1-45.

51. John Nisbet, Family environment and intelligence. In Halsey *et al.* (eds.), *Education, economy and society.* New York: Free Press, 1961.

52. Thus Rosen writes: "Considering the sociologist's traditional and continuing concern with group size as an independent variable (from Simmel and Durkheim to the recent experimental studies of small groups), there have been surprisingly few studies of the influence of group size upon the nature of interaction in the family," *op. cit.*, p. 576.

53. Ivan Nye, Adolescent-parent adjustment: age, sex, sibling, number, broken homes, and employed mothers as variables. *Marriage and Family Living,* 1952, 14: 327-332.

54. Sears *et al, op. cit.*

55. Laura G. Searls, Leisure role emphasis of college graduate homemakers. *Journal of Marriage and the Family,* 1966, 28: 1: 77-82.

56. Norman Bradburn and D. Caplovitz, *Reports on happiness.* Chicago: Aldine, 1965.

57. Lee Rainwater, R. Coleman, and G. Handel, *Workingman's wife.* New York: Oceana Publications, 1959.

58. John Newsom and E. Newsom, *Infant care in an urban community.* New York: International Universities Press, 1963.

59. Mirra Komarovsky, *Blue-collar marriage.* New York: Random House, Inc., 1962.

60. Gavron, *op. cit.*

61. Ferdinand Zweig, *Woman's life and labor.* London: Camelot Press, 1952.

62. Cohen, *op cit.*

63. Gerald Gurin, J. Veroff, and S. Feld, *Americans view their mental health*. New York: Basic Books, Monograph Series No. 4, Joint Commission on Mental Illness and Health, 1960.

64. Bradburn and Caplovitz, *op. cit.*

65. Rapoport, The transition from engagement to marriage, *op. cit.*; Raush *et al*, *op. cit.*

66. During the period when marriage was the critical transition in the adult woman's life rather than pregnancy, a good deal of anticipatory "nesting" behavior took place from the time of conception. Now more women work through a considerable portion of the first pregnancy, and such nesting behavior as exists may be confined to a few shopping expeditions or baby showers, thus adding to the abruptness of the transition and the difficulty of adjustment following the birth of a first child.

67. Lee G. Burchinal, Adolescent role deprivation and high school marriage. *Marriage and Family Living*, 1959, 21: 378-384; Floyd M. Martinson, Ego deficiency as a factor in marriage. *American Sociological Review*, 1955, 22: 161-164; J. Joel Moss and Ruby Gingles, The relationship of personality to the incidence of early marriage. *Marriage and Family Living*, 1959, 21: 373-377.

68. Cohen, *op. cit.*

69. Donald W. MacKinnon, Creativity and images of the self. In Robert W. White (ed.), *The study of lives*. New York: Atherton Press, 1963.

70. Anne Roe, *A psychological study of eminent biologists, psychological monographs*, 1951, 65: 14: 68 pages; Anne Roe, A psychological study of physical scientists. *Genetic Psychology Monographs*, 1951, 43: 121-239; Anne Roe, Crucial life experiences in the development of scientists. In E. P. Torrance (ed.), *Talent and education*. Minneapolis: University of Minnesota Press, 1960.

71. Evelyn M. Duvall, Conceptions of parenthood. *American Journal of Sociology*, 1946, 52: 193-203.

72. Urie Bronfenbrenner, Some familial antecedents of responsibility and leadership in adolescents. In L. Petrullo and B. Bass (eds.), *Studies in Leadership*. New York: Holt, Rinehart and Winston, 1960.

73. Paul Mussen and L. Distler, Masculinity, identification, and father-son relationships. *Journal of Abnormal and Social Psychology*, 1959, 59: 350-356.

74. Orville G. Brim, The parent-child relation as a social system: I. Parent and child roles. *Child Development*, 1952, 28: 3: 343-364.

75. Miller and Swanson have suggested a connection between the trend toward bureaucratic structure in the occupation world and the shift in child-rearing practices toward permissiveness and a greater stress on personal adjustment of children. Their findings are suggestive rather than definitive, however, and no hard research has subjected this question to empirical inquiry. Daniel R. Miller and G. Swanson, *The changing American parent*. New York: Wiley, 1958.

The same suggestive but nondefinitive clues are to be found in von Mering's study of the contrast between professional and nonprofessional women as mothers. She shows that the professionally active woman in her mother role tends toward a greater stress on discipline rather than indulgence and has a larger number of rules with fewer choices or suggestions to the child: the emphasis is in equipping the child to cope effectively with rules and techniques of his culture. The nonprofessional mother, by contrast, has a greater value stress on ensuring the child's emotional security, tending to take the role of the clinician in an attempt to diagnose the child's problems and behavior, Faye H. von Mering, Professional and nonprofessional women as mothers, *Journal of Social Psychology*, 1955, 42: 21-34.

76. Orville G. Brim, Personality development as role-learning. In Ira Iscoe and Harold Stevenson (eds.), *Personality development in children*. Austin, Tex.: University of Texas Press, 1960.

77. Lidz *et al*, *op. cit.*

78. Straus, *op. cit.*

79. Parsons and Bales, *op. cit.*

80. Brim, The parent-child relation as a social system: I. Parent and child roles, *op. cit.*

81. Parsons and Bales, *op. cit.*

82. Philip Jackson and F. Moscovici, The teacher-to-be: a study of embryonic identification with a professional role. *School Review*, 1963, 71: 41-65.

83. Clark E. Vincent, Implications of changes in male-female role expectations for interpreting m-f scores. *Journal of Marriage and the Family*, 1966, 28: 2: 196-199.

84. Helene Deutsch, *The psychology of women: a psychoanalytic interpretation*, 1: New York: Grune and Stratton, 1944.

85. Sibylle Escalona, The psychological situation of mother and child upon return from the hospital. In Milton Senn (ed.), *Problems of infancy and childhood: transactions of the third conference*, 1949.

86. Several authors have recently pointed out the inadequacy of social science usage of the masculinity-femininity concept. Landreth, in a study of parent-role appropriateness in giving physical care and companionship to the child, found her four-year-old subjects, particularly in New Zealand, made no simple linkage of activity to mother as opposed to father.

Catherine Landreth, Four-year-olds' notions about sex appropriateness of parental care and companionship activities, *Merrill-Palmer Quarterly*, 1963 **9**: 3: 175–182. She comments that in New Zealand "masculinity and femininity appear to be comfortably relegated to chromosome rather than to contrived activity" (p. 176). Lansky, in a study of the effect of the sex of the children upon the parents' own sex-identification, calls for devising tests which look at masculinity and femininity as two dimensions rather than a single continuum. Leonard M. Lansky, The family structure also affects the model: sex-role identification in parents of preschool children, *Merrill-Palmer Quarterly*, 1964, **10**: 1: 39–50.

87. Beller has already shown the value of such an approach, in a study that defined independence and dependence as two separate dimensions rather than the extremes of a bipolar continuum. He found, as hypothesized, a very *low* negative correlation between the two measures. E. K. Beller, Exploratory studies of dependency, (trans.). *N.Y. Academy of Science*, 1959, **21**: 414–426.

88. Brim, The parent–child relation, *op. cit.*

89. *Ibid.*

90. Landreth, *op. cit.*, 181.

91. Cohen, *op. cit.*

Marriage, Parenting, and Productivity

JANE PEARCE*

PARENTS ARE RESPONSIBLE FOR PREPARing the child for the society and the culture which he will enter as a young adult. This process of preparation has more to do with who the adults are, and what is going on in their lives, than with what they think they are setting out to do. Women who work, for example, have a better chance of raising children headed for maturity than do women who are supported and who devote themselves 168 hours a week to motherhood. No human being can hope to maintain emotional equilibrium with such a grueling assignment, no matter what the appearances are, or the good intentions.

Happy, productive parents raise children who can grow to be happy and productive. Parents oriented toward their own continued individual growth will best validate the lifetime growth process in the child. Such parents can appreciate both the rewards and the hazards of the child's attempt to organize his life to satisfy his real needs in the context of the world beyond the family. Since marriage is the contract by which men and women

undertake the responsibilities of parenthood, it is necessary to reevaluate the significance of marriage in the process of parenting, and the role of marriage in the preparation of citizens for our shifting social structure.

The child will develop the capacity to satisfy only those needs which have been responded to by the people involved in raising him. I refer here to real needs for registering one's own perceptions, for giving and receiving tenderness, for cooperation, creative contribution, and compassion; I do not refer to the substituted desires for power and prestige. Real needs are directed toward becoming more human, toward the capacity to give and receive tenderness, and to expand one's creativity beyond the restrictions of one's own particular subculture.

Tenderness can be defined as the satisfaction that one person gains in contributing to the other's

*Jane Pearce and Saul Newton are the coauthors of *The conditions of human growth*, Citadel Press, 1963, an expansion and elaboration of the work of Harry Stack Sullivan in *The interpersonal theory of psychiatry*.

growth, i.e., to the other's capacity to satisfy his own needs. Thus, it may begin with the mother's pleasure in helping the infant to relate to her nipple. Some years later, tenderness may be the mother's pleasure in validating her daughter's concern for a friend of the daughter's who the mother never especially liked.

Tenderness is basically gentle and includes a regret for the other's pain. Its forms may vary from a turn of the wrist, to a mutual glance, to a firm and direct confrontation. The gist of it is that it relates to the other's real need for growth and expansion with precision and accuracy as to the point at which the other's growth must take place. We are all in need of both giving and receiving tenderness. While it is a prerequisite for growth, satisfaction of the need for tenderness often runs counter to the organized restrictions of society. For this reason, real moves toward this satisfaction will, in all likelihood, produce anxiety.

Needs that are not responded to, and those that are met with anger or antagonism, go underground as forbidden, They remain frustrated unless brought to light in later expansive, validating relationships. If a particular need is difficult for the mothering one, if its satisfaction was never a real part of her life experience, her response to this need emerging in her child will be phobic and prohibiting.

Each person sets out, from infancy, to satisfy his own needs. Each move toward growth must be shared and enjoyed by another person in order to be successful. The encouragement implicit in this kind of pleasurable sharing is at the core of what we generally refer to as mothering. During the first year, the mother and other adults, by the mood of pleasure transmitted to the infant, promote the organization of his physiology, his mood range, his perceptions. When he learns to walk at about one year of age, his mastery of the physical world is expanded. Some parents are threatened by the necessity to validate the increased mobility and curiosity, and by their relative loss of control over the baby's actions. The emotional dominance of the parents at this age is absolute; but if they can, with good heart, take pleasure in the capacity of another adult to validate functions in the infant with which they have difficulty, the infant will develop these functions. He will also learn to seek out alternate validation for new experience. This learning is critical to the individual and to his capacity to incorporate new experience at any phase of life.

Other young ones are stimulating to a baby at any age. However, by two and a half he has learned to talk, and the need for access to people like himself becomes crucial. It is his first experience that he is like this other person whom he finds attractive. He is ready to reach beyond the role of being nurtured and to begin the process of learning to cope with people beyond the family. The longer the opportunity to find and to use such sources of alternate peer validation is denied, the more difficulty the child will have later in learning any new function or satisfying any new need beyond the limitations of the parents.

The child must develop his capacity to give and receive validation from others like himself. The parent's attitude toward his need for peers is of critical importance. The process begins with learning to feel comfortable in parallel play between children of nursery school age, in comfort with strangers, in excitement with acquaintances, and in a feeling of belonging with people.

He must go on from there to learn to compete, to compromise, and to cooperate with others of equivalent age and status, to give precedence to the group goal without losing his own. He needs ultimately to find the experience of love, of caring for the real needs of the other. This occurs first with someone of the same sex, perceived as similar, and later extends to more and more different people. Herein lies a base for a maturity that continues to grow throughout life.

The tradition has been that adults usually raise people who will be very much like themselves. Parents pass on to their children their own emotional limitations. These are imprinted during infancy and are reinforced by verbal and other prohibitions suited to the parents' values and convenience against free explorations with peers during the child's growing years. A static society can afford to perpetuate the restrictions on cooperation, compassion, and creativity which are thus handed down from generation to generation because the world is expected to function much the same for the grandchildren as it did for their grandparents. Our society can no longer afford this complacency because our world is changing at an unprecedented pace. The next generation must have more compassion, as well as the courage and imagination to overhaul thoroughly the economic and social structure.

The rare individual who continues to grow throughout his life—as a person and in his creative potential—is admired. All individuals are capable of this potential for continuing growth. This trait must now become available to the majority, since the world the majority will administer when they reach the ages of 40 to 60 cannot be run as if it were the same world it was when they reached 14 or 16.

Continued growth beyond the parents depends on a lifelong expansion of one's ability to make significant relationships with others whose inhibitions and restrictions are different from one's own. Conversely, the inability to grow is originally based on parental restrictions on interpersonal development. It is perpetuated subsequently by social, cultural, legal, and familial restrictions on adult interpersonal association.

The structure of the traditional marriage abruptly cuts off both partners from the urgent necessity of expanding their interpersonal milieu, and hence the opportunities for their own growth. Each partner enters marriage "programmed," since infancy, into rigidly separate sex-linked roles. The societally defined division of labor has traditionally dictated that the man supports the family while working outside the home while the woman keeps the house and raises the children. This means that within the framework of marriage, men may satisfy certain needs and women may satisfy others, but also that large fundamental needs of each partner are permanently frustrated.

The man anticipates the necessity for earning a living and searches for the most compatible and occasionally creative career he can look forward to. He usually enters the world outside his parents' home handicapped in using opportunities to make up antecedent experiential deficits. Nonetheless, the pressure of the necessity to cope with peers in his work pushes him to try to integrate missed experiences with parallel play in terms of its adult equivalent with strangers and acquaintances, and with group interaction. In other words, men are traditionally encouraged to aspire to some creative

self-expression, and interaction with colleagues. However, society continues to define fathering primarily in terms of economic support of the family, so that many men are denied the benefits of intimate contact with their children.

The women, while some new opportunities for working in the world may be offered, is still prepared for a life in which "femininity" means general incompetence. If she chooses to work before marriage, her career is supposed to be dull and uncreative, so that she will relinquish it without regret when the opportunity for motherhood is offered. The imperative for her to marry robs her of the anticipation, preparation, and motivation to move beyond minimal superficial relationships with acquaintances. Her manifest, traditional role is service—to her husband's career, and especially to her children. Within this role definition her needs for group interaction or for deep friendships have no legitimate room nor priority. Independence oriented to growth is downgraded; and creativity, in the serious sense, is excluded since competence is not "feminine."

The intimate, tender contact with her children offers a woman a second opportunity to integrate experiential deficits not orignially validated by her own parents. However, since within the framework of an isolated homebound existence such new learning has no future application, the mother can only transmit her despair about her own life to her children. Further, since the raising of children is her job, she must be oriented to prolonging their immaturity in order to justify her continued employment.

Women in this culture are expected to encourage their children's needs for growth while giving secondary priority to their own. This goes against the laws of human nature. Anyone who is not actively pursuing the satisfaction of his own real needs, expanding his own life in an appropriate direction, is actively fighting against growth. The denial of a specific need spreads to the denial of need in general, one's own, a spouse's, a friend's, or a child's need.

In fact, *neither* role in a traditionally defined marriage presses toward the experience of deep friendship with peers of the same sex. Such experience is a necessary base for the evolution of subsequent expansive maturity. Such maturity could lead to independence of particular values of society. Further, if these deep attachments are not pursued, the individual tends to lose the antecedent experiences of affectionate cooperation, or of enthusiastic casual interaction, and to retreat to the childhood battles with parents, using the marriage partner as a substitute for the original parents. The married couple's "freedom" from home becomes not very different from their life at home with their parents.

The traditional structure of marriage is one which demands the denial of certain needs in both partners and therefore enforces their restriction on the child's awareness of need and his search for satisfaction. Marriage as a business partnership is a contract for mutual exploitation in which each is trying to get more than he puts out and both lose. As a contract for the mutual restriction over each other's interpersonal relationships, it is a contract to halt real growth in either. As a partnership for raising children, it has a certain potential. This potential, however, depends entirely on the commitment of each adult involved to the expansion of his own life, and the filling in of areas of difficulty. Such expansion must involve the self-respect and economic independence of each, the productivity and creativity, and centrally, the evolution of interpersonal experience crucial to each. The agreement that the partner in parenting subjects himself to jurisdiction from the other in these crucial areas defeats both the adults and the project of raising children. The contract may work so smoothly that each partner seems to be oblivious to those changes he needs the most.

If anyone is not actively pursuing his own growth, expanding his own life in an appropriate direction, then he must be actively fighting it. Appropriate opportunities and stimuli impinge on him constantly. In the normal course of a day of living one runs into, or avoids, interesting strangers and potential friends. Not phoning a previous or a potential friend is an active decision. The denial of the specific need spreads to the denial of need and to a general, though sometimes subtle, contempt for the importance of satisfying needs, including those of the children.

The mother who is oriented to her own growth and creativity—with her child, with her peers, and with her work—can validate the need for open-ended growth in her evolving child. In her positive mood of optimism and challenge, and in her recognition of the possibility of satisfaction, she can be less respectful of class or family restrictions in her life. This will then be transmitted to the child, even if the amount of time spent with the child is greatly reduced.

A mother who is deeply involved in developing and using her own competence and who is herself learning through contact with other people is a real asset to the child. She can more readily accept the necessity for alternate validators, that is, other friendly, supportive adults who can confirm an additional range of perceptions and emotions in the growing child, and therefore make the child less totally dependent on the mood of the biological mother. As the infant moves towards relationships with his peers, both parent and nurse must encourage this move. The mother is still responsible both for direct contact with her child and for making arrangements for alternate contact. But if she is actively involved in meeting her own needs for growth, she will permit her child to grow equally.

For the child, the more people who are sincerely involved in a mutual growth project with him, the better. Anyone whose investment either in himself or in the child is hypocritical is a menace. The child urgently needs our enthusiasm for his connecting with his friends, as well as our enthusiasm for having friends ourselves. The rigidity of the old forms is thrown in perspective with the recognition of this need.

In accordance with tradition, the opportunity for alternate adult validation during infancy, if allowed at all by the emotional attitude of the parent, is by and large restricted to other adults with whom the parents can tolerate living. These include in-laws, siblings, both adult and child, other relatives, baby nurses, housekeepers, and very intimate friends.

As the child approaches 2½ there may be pressure from the clan, neighbors, or friends to "get your kids together with my kids." In both these circumstances the opportunities available are strictly circumscribed by the parents' personal choice of associates, by class, taste, and compatibility. As the issues of nursery school—or Head Start, kindergarten, and grade school—public or private—come up, there is a much wider field of peer associates. The parent, then, must exert more effort to program the child to select those the parent considers proper associates. "But her mother's house is dirty, dear." Or, to the older child she might say, "It was so kind of her to visit you. Are you sure she wanted to?" Every deviant validator can be eliminated in the pursuit of training the child for the role in society which the parent anticipates for him.

It often seems that all decisions about raising the children belong to the mother. In the evolution of the mechanisms of restriction of the child to "appropriate" class and social role, the mother is usually the overt implementator. However, the choice of adult associates is a mutual one; either marriage partner has a veto. Also, in general, the class position and mobility is somewhat more up to the man. Thus the apparent allocation of child-rearing to the mother is a thin disguise for a collaboration on the restriction of opportunities for the child. In society as currently structured, it is often true that the mother who works, by making a genuine economic contribution to her family, can remove some of the pressures her husband feels and enable him to be more available to the children. She will also be better able to understand his problems and experiences, since she too is involved in an active dialogue with the world. Yet this can only happen within the context of a life devoted to continued growth, for if a woman feels that this opportunity will lead nowhere, she will not capitalize on it. If, on the other hand, she can anticipate a productive, creative use of her potential, she can project this hopefulness to her children.

Motherhood is a temporary job. The goal of any responsible parent is that the children outgrow the parents. The mother who stares at a blank wall after her children leave home will telegraph her desperation to them throughout their growing

years, and will be more interested in prolonging their dependence upon her than in supporting their moves toward independent maturity. The mother dedicated to her own growth will transmit quite a different message, and her example will prepare her children to seek and find self-satisfaction in their own lives. The woman who has a lifework of her own has a base of self-esteem which runs counter to the flattery of the notion that her children (or spouse) need her; she therefore has no motivation to cherish their dependence and inadequacies. She also has no motivation to dramatize her own inadequacies in order to keep them taking care of her.

This is a statement about human needs in relation to the needs of a rapidly shifting civilization. It is also a statement about growth within the given society, and about the growth of society itself. A reorganization of family structure along less traditional and more expansive lines cannot be achieved with the framework of the status quo. It requires a social structure oriented to the legitimation of the parents' pursuit of their own growth. It also required extensive parallel reorganization of legal, cultural, and economic opportunities.

The present structure of marriage is both the result of the present structure of society, and a means to perpetuate it. The tendency to restrict tenderness to the nuclear family has the consequence of teaching the child the psychology of an economy of scarcity. The demands and prohibitions on his peer relationships as he negotiates the developmental eras are heavily overlaid by the class position of his family and their attitudes toward it. By styles of individual restrictiveness, the family produces individuals who are actively resistant to change and who, therefore, put a brake on social changes that are politically and economically inevitable.

The process of society's changing to forms that would catalyze and facilitate productive changes in family structure and child-rearing will, of necessity, involve breakdown of family, class, and distance as now structured. It is time to give up the fear of necessary change.

Mystification, Confusion, and Conflict

RONALD D. LAING

You can fool some of the people some of the time . . . .

MARX USED THE CONCEPT OF MYSTIFICA-tion to mean a plausible misrepresentation of what is going on (process) or what is being done (praxis) in the service of the interests of one socioeconomic class (the exploiters) over or against another class (the exploited). By representing forms of exploita-tion as forms of benevolence, the exploiters bemuse the exploited into feeling at one with their ex-ploiters, or into feeling gratitude for what (un-realized by them) is their exploitation, and, not least, into feeling bad or mad even to think of rebel-lion.

We can employ Marx's theoretical schema, not only to elucidate relations between classes of soci-ety but also in the field of the reciprocal interaction of person directly with person.

Every family has its differences (from mild dis-agreements to radically incompatible and contra-dictory interests or points of view), and every fam-ily has some means of handling them. Here one way of handling such contradictions is described under the rubric of *mystification*.

In this chapter I shall present in discursive form this and some related concepts currently being developed in research and therapy with families of schizophrenics, neurotics and normals at the Tavi-stock Clinic and Tavistock Institute of Human Relations, London.[1] I shall compare the concept of mystification to certain closely related concepts, and I shall give brief descriptions of certain aspects of some of the families investigated in order to demonstrate, it is hoped, the heuristic value of the theoretical discussion and its crucial import for therapy. This paper will not, however, discuss the practical aspects of therapy.

THE CONCEPT OF MYSTIFICATION

By mystification I mean both the *act* of mystifying and the *state* of being mystified. That is, I am using the term both in an active and in a passive sense.

To mystify, in the active sense, is to befuddle, cloud, obscure, mask whatever is going on, whether this be experience, action, or process, or whatever is "the issue." It induces confusion in the sense that there is failure to see what is "really" being experi-enced, or being done, or going on, and failure to dis-tinguish or discriminate the actual issues. This en-tails the substitution of false for true constructions of what is being experienced, being done (praxis), or going on (process), and the substitution of false issues for the actual issues.

The *state* of mystification, mystification in a passive sense, is possibly, though not necessarily, a *feeling* of being muddled or confused. The act of mystification, by definition, tends to induce, if not neutralized by counteraction, a state of mystifica-tion or confusion, not necessarily felt as such. It may or may not induce secondary conflicts, and these may or may not be recognized as such by the persons involved. The feeling of confusion and the experience of conflict have to be distinguished from mystification, either as act or state. Although one of the functions of mystification is to avoid authen-tic conflict, it is quite common for open conflict to

Part of the clinical material contained in this chapter also appeared in Laing and Esterson (1964). Re-printed from Boszormenyi-Nagy and Framo, *Inten-sive family therapy.* New York: Harper & Row, by permission.

occur in mystifying and mystified families. The masking effect of mystification may not avoid conflict, although it will cloud over what the conflict is about.

This effect may be enhanced if the seal is placed on mystification by mystifying the act of perceiving mystification for what it is, e.g., by turning the perception of mystification into the issue of this being a bad or a mad thing to do.

Thus, the mystified person (or persons) is by definition confused, but may or may not *feel* confused. If we detect mystification, we are alerted to the presence of a conflict of some kind that is being evaded. The mystified person, insofar as he has been mystified, is unable to see the authentic conflict, but may or may not experience intra- or interpersonal conflict of an inauthentic kind. He may experience false peace, false calm, or inauthentic conflict and confusion over false issues.

A certain amount of mystification occurs in everyday life. A common way to mystify one person about his or her experience is to confirm the content of an experience and to disconfirm its modality (regarding perception, imagination, fantasy, and dreaming as different modes of experience, a theory developed elsewhere (Laing 1962)).

Thus, if there is a contradiction between two persons' perceptions, the one person tells the other, "It is just your imagination"; that is, there is an attempt to forestall or resolve a contradiction, a clash, an incomparability by transposing one person's experiential modality from perception of imagination or from the memory of a perception to the memory of a dream ("You must have dreamt it").

Another form of mystification is when the one person disconfirms the content of the other's experience and replaces it by attributions of experience conjunctive with self's view of the other (cf. Brodey's (1959) concept of the "narcissistic relationship").

A child is playing noisily in the evening; his mother is tired and wants him to go to bed. A straight statement would be:

"I am tired, I want you to go to bed."

or

"Go to bed, because I say so."

or

"Go to bed, because it's your bedtime."

A mystifying way to induce the child to go to bed would be:

"I'm sure you feel tired, darling, and want to go to bed now, don't you?"

Mystification occurs here in different respects. What is ostensibly an attribution about how the child feels (you are tired) is "really" a command (go to bed). The child is told how he feels (he may or may not feel or be tired), and what he is told he feels is what mother feels herself (projective identification). If we suppose he does not *feel* tired, he may contradict his mother's statement. He may then become liable to a further mystifying ploy such as:

"Mother knows best."

or

"Don't be cheeky."

Mystification may be over issues to do with what *rights* and what *obligations* each person in the family has in respect of the others. For example, a boy of fourteen tells his parents he is unhappy, and they reply: "But you can't be unhappy. Haven't we given you everything you want? How can you be so ungrateful as to say you are unhappy after all that has been done for you, after all the sacrifices that have been made for you?"

Mystification is particularly potent when it involves this rights–obligations system in such a way that one person appears to have the *right* to determine the experience of another or, complementarily, when one person is under an *obligation* to the other(s) to experience, or not to experience, himself, them, his world, or any aspect of it, in a particular way. For instance, has the boy a right to be unhappy, or must he be happy because if he is not he is being ungrateful?

Implicit in Marx's formulation is that before enlightened action can be taken, the issues have to be demystified.

By issue we mean, as in law, "the point over which one affirms and another denies" (*Oxford English Dictionary*). The issue, in our material, frequently is how to define the "real" or "true" axis of orientation: the point at issue is what is to be the issue. Quarrels are often about what the quarrel is about: what is going on is a conflict, or a struggle, to agree to determine the "main issue." In the families of schizophrenics, one of the most fixed aspects of the extremely rigid family system is often a particular axis of orientation, which is the linchpin, so it seems, that keeps the whole family pattern in place.

In some families, every action of different members of the family is evaluated in terms of its particular axis or axes of orientation. An action of a family member thus plotted may become the issue, or the issue may be, as stated above, what is the valid axis of orientation to hold.

> Judith, aged 26, and her father frequently quarrel. He wishes to know where she goes when she leaves the house, who she is with, when she will be back. She says that he is interfering with her life. He says that he is simply doing his duty as a father. He says she is impudent because she does not obey him. She says he is being tyrannical. He says she is wrong to speak in that way to her father. She says she is entitled to express what views she likes. He says, provided that the views are correct and that they are not correct, etc.

Anyone, including the investigator, is free to make an issue out of any part of the interactivity of the family. The issue may be agreed upon among all the family members, but the investigators may not see the issue in the same terms as do the family members.

Our axis of orientation both as researchers and as therapists is to pick out what the axes of orientation and issues are for each member of the family in turn. These may be expressed explicitly or be implicit. Certain members of a family may conspicuously fail to recognize any axis of orientation or to pick up the existence of any issues other than their own.

In order to recognize persons and not simply objects, one must realize that the other human being is not only another object in space but another center of orientation to the objective world. It is just this recognition of each other as different centers of orientation, that is, as persons, which is in such short supply in the families of schizophrenics we have studied.

There are as many issues as people can invent, but we have come to regard the issue of person perception as central in all the families we have studied. Although this issue may be central as we perceive it, we have to recognize that it is not necessarily seen or accepted as such by the family members themselves.

If active mystification consists in disguising, masking, the praxes and/or processes of the family, in befogging the issues, and in attempting to deny that what is the issue for oneself may not be so for the other, we have to ask how we decide what to us is the central issue if our perception of the central issue is disjunctive with the perceptions of the family members themselves.

The only safeguard here is to present the perspectives of everyone in turn (including our own) on "the shared situation," and then to compare the evidence for the validity of different points of view. For instance, one can pick out certain axes of orientation in terms of which the actions of the family are evaluated by particular others:

> June's mother described the changes [top of page 243] in June's personality that came on (aged 15) six months before what to us were the first signs of psychosis. A change in her personality had occurred in the last six months after she had been to a holiday camp, and away from home, for the first time in her life.

In the six months between her first perception of such changes in June and the onset of what we recognized as a psychotic breakdown, June's mother had gone to two doctors complaining about these changes in June, which she regarded as expression of an "illness" and perhaps expressions of evil. "It's not June, you see. That's not my little girl." Neither doctor could see evidence of illness or evil in June. Her mother actively attributed these changes in June, that to us were normal maturational, culturally syntonic expressions of growing up and achieving greater autonomy, etc., to expressions of a more and more serious "illness" or of "evil." The girl was completely mystified, because although becoming more autonomous, she still trusted her mother. As her mother repeatedly told her that her developing autonomy and sexual

According to her mother, June:

Before	After
was boisterous	is quiet
told me everything	does not tell me what is going on inside her
went everywhere with me	wants to be by herself
was very happy and lively	often looks unhappy; is less lively
liked swimming and cycling	does not do this so much but reads more
was "sensible"	is "full of boys"
played dominoes, drafts, and cards at night with mother, father, and grandmother	is not interested in these games any more; prefers to sit in her room and read
was obedient	is disobedient and truculent
never thought of smoking	smokes one or two cigarettes a day without asking permission
used to believe in God	does not believe in God

maturation were expressions of either madness or badness, she began to *feel ill* and to *feel evil*. One can see this as *praxis* on her part to attempt to resolve the contradiction between the *processes* of her own maturation and her mother's barrage of negative attributions about them.

From our standpoint, June appears mystified. She feels she has a lovely mummy, she begs forgiveness for being such a bad daughter, she promises to get well. Although at this point she is complaining that "Hitler's soldiers are after her," not once in many interviews does her mother make any other complaints about June except to attack as bad or mad those processes of development that we regard as most normal about her.

That is, her mother's only axes of orientation, in terms of which she saw and evaluated the changes in June, were good–evil, sane–mad. As June began to recover from a psychotic breakdown, her mother became more and more alarmed that June was getting worse, seeing intensified evidence of evil in her concurrently with our evaluation that she was achieving greater ego strength and autonomy.

Mystification entails the action of one person *on the other*. It is *trans*personal. The *intra*personal defenses with which psychoanalysis has familiarized us, or the various forms of "bad faith" in

Sartre's sense, are best distinguished at present from ways of acting on the other. It in the nature of the mystifying action of persons on each other, rather than of each on himself or herself, that we wish particularly to consider in this paper.

The one person (*p*) seeks to induce in *the other* some change necessary for his (*p*'s) security. Mystification is one form of action on the other that serves the defenses, the security, of the own person. If the one person does not want to know something or to remember something, it is not enough to repress it (or otherwise "successfully" defend himself against it "in" himself); he must not be reminded of it by the other. The one person can deny something himself; he must next make the other deny it.

It is clear that not every action of the one person on another, in the service of the one person's security, peace of mind, self-interest, or whatever, is necessarily mystifying. There are many kinds of persuasion, coercion, deterrence, whereby the one person seeks to control, direct, exploit, manipulate the behavior of the other.

To say: "I can't stand you talking about that. Please be quiet," is an attempt to induce silence over this topic in the other, but no mystification is involved.

Similarly, no mystification is involved in such statements as:

"If you don't stop that I'll hit you."

or

"I think that is a horrible thing to say. I'm disgusted with you."

In the following instance, a threat of something very unpleasant induced the boy to deny his own memory. The tactic is not, however, one of mystification.

> A boy of four stuck a berry up his nose and could not get it out. He told his parents, who looked and could not see it. They were disinclined to believe that he had got a berry up his nose, but he complained of pain and so they called the doctor. He looked and could not see it. He said, showing the boy a long shining instrument, "I don't see anything, but if you say it's still there tomorrow, we shall have to take this to you." The boy was so terrified that he "confessed" that he had made up the whole story. It was not until twenty years later that he summoned up the courage to admit even to himself that he had actually put a berry up his nose.

By contrast, the following is an example of mystification.

MOTHER: I don't blame you for talking that way. I know you don't really mean it.
DAUGHTER: But I do mean it.
MOTHER: Now, dear, I know you don't. You can't help yourself.
DAUGHTER: I can help myself.
MOTHER: No, dear, I know you can't because you're ill. If I thought for a moment you weren't ill, I would be furious with you.

Here the mother is using quite naively a mystification which is at the very heart of much social theory. This is to convert praxis (what a person does) into process (an impersonal series of events of which no one is the author). This distinction between praxis and process has recently been drawn in an extremely lucid way by Sartre (1960).[2]

We unfortunately tend to perpetuate this particular mystification, I believe, when we employ the concept of family or group "pathology." Individual *psycho*pathology is a sufficiently problematic concept, since without splitting and reifying experience and behavior to invent "a psyche," one can attribute to this invention no pathology or physiology. But to speak of family "pathology" is even more problematic. The processes that occur in a group are generated by the praxis of its individual members. Mystification is a form of praxis; it is not a pathologic process.

The theoretically ultimate extreme of mystification is when the person (p) seeks to induce in the other (o) confusion (not necessarily recognized by o) as to o's whole experience (memory, perceptions, dreams, fantasy, imagination), processes, and actions. The mystified person is one who is given to understand that he feels happy or sad regardless of how he feels he feels, that he is responsible for this or not responsible for that regardless of what responsibility he has or has not taken upon himself. Capacities, or their lack, are attributed to him without reference to any shared empirical criteria of what these may or may not be. His own motives and intentions are discounted or minimized and replaced by others. His experience and actions generally are construed without reference to his own point of view. There is a radical failure to recognize his own self-perception and self-identity.[3] And, of course, when this is the case, not only his self-perceptions and self-identity are confused but his perceptions of others, of how they experience him and act toward him and of how he thinks they think he thinks, etc., are necessarily subjected to multiple mystifications at one and the same time.

THE FUNCTION OF MYSTIFICATION AND SOME RELATED CONCEPTS

The prime function of mystification appears to be to maintain the status quo. It is brought into play, or it is intensified, when one or more members of the family nexus (Laing 1962) threaten, or are felt to threaten, the status quo of the nexus by the way they are experiencing, and acting in, the situation they share with the other members of the family.

Mystification functions to maintain sterotyped roles (Ryckoff, Day, and Wynne 1959) and to fit other people into a preset mold, Procrustean fashion (Lidz, Cornelison, Terry, and Fleck 1958).

The parents struggle to preserve their own integration by maintaining their rigid preconceptions about who they are and who they ought to be, who their children are and ought to be, and the nature of the situation that characterizes family life. They are impervious (Lidz *et al.* 1958) to those emotional needs in their children that threaten to disrupt their preconceived schemata, and they mask or conceal disturbing situations in the family, acting as if they do not exist (Lidz *et al.*, 1958). Imperviousness and masking are very common concomitants of mystification in the present tense when, for instance, they are backed up by transpersonal action on the other person, when, for instance, attempts are made to induce the other to believe that his emotional needs are being satisfied when clearly they are not, or to represent such needs as unreasonable, greedy, or selfish because the parents are unable or unwilling to fulfil them, or to persuade the other that he just thinks he has needs but has not "really," and so on.

Needless to say, no mystifying-mystified relationship can be a reciprocally confirmatory one in a genuine sense. What may be confirmed by the one person is a false front put on by the other, a prefabricated schema on the one person's part that the other is induced more or less to embody. Elsewhere I have tried to describe the structure of certain forms of such unauthenic relationships (Laing 1960, 1961).

Such concepts are close to the concept of nonmutual complementarity developed by Wynne and his co-workers. The intense pseudomutuality described by these workers, "the predominant absorption in fitting together at the expense of the differentiation of the identities" (Wynne, Ryckoff, Day, and Hirsch 1958, p. 207) is very much in line with our findings.

Mystification appears to be one technique, highly developed in the families of schizophrenics, to maintain the rigid role structure in such pseudomutual nexuses. We are currently investigating the extent to which, and the manner in which, pseudomutuality and mystification occur in the families of nonschizophrenics. Lomas (1961), for instance, has described the family of a girl diagnosed as an hysteric in which unauthentic fitting together and rigidly maintained sterotyped roles of an engulfing nature were clearly in evidence.

Searles (1959) describes six modes of driving the other person crazy, or techniques that tend "to undermine the other person's confidence in his own emotional reactions and his own perception of reality." I have slightly recast Searle's six modes of schizogenesis into the following form.

1. *p* repeatedly calls attention to areas of the personality of which *o* is dimly aware, areas quite at variance with the kind of person *o* considers himself or herself to be.

2. *p* stimulates *o* sexually in a situation in which it would be disastrous for *o* to seek sexual gratification.

3. *p* simultaneously exposes *o* to stimulation and frustration or to rapidly alternating stimulation and frustration.

4. *p* relates to *o* at simultaneously unrelated levels (e.g., sexually and intellectually).

5. *p* switches from one emotional wavelength to another while on the same topic (being "serious" and then being "funny" about the same thing).

6. *p* switches from one topic to the next while maintaining the same emotional wavelength (e.g., a matter of life and death is discussed in the same manner as the most trivial happening (Laing, 1961, p. 131–132)).

Each of these modes of schizogenesis is liable to induce muddle in the victim, without the victim necessarily perceiving the muddle he is in. In this sense they are mystifying.

I have suggested (Laing 1961, pp. 132–136) that the schizogenic potential of such maneuvers lies not so much in the activation of various areas of the personality in opposition to one another, the activation, that is, of conflict, but in the generation of confusion or muddle or doubt, often unrecognized as such.

This emphasis on unconscious or unconscious confusion or doubt about one's self, the other(s), and the shared situation, this emphasis, that is, on a state of mystification, has much in common with Haley's (1959b) hypothesis that the control of the definition of relationships is a central problem in the origin of schizophrenia. The mystified person is operating in terms that have been misdefined for him. This definition is such that, without realizing it or without understanding why he may perhaps intensely but vaguely feel it to be so, he is in an untenable position (Laing 1961, p. 135). He may then attempt to escape from his untenable position in the mystified situation by in turn deepening the mystifications.

The concept of mystification overlaps, but is not synonymous with, the double-bind concept (Bateson, Jackson, Haley, and Weakland 1956). The double-bind would appear to be necessarily mystifying, but mystification need not be a complete double-bind. The essential distinction is that the mystified person, in contrast to the double-bind person, may be left with a relatively unequivocal "right" way to experience and to act. This right thing to experience or right way to act may entail, from our viewpoint as investigators and therapists, a betrayal of the person's potentialities for self-fulfillment, but this may by no means be felt by the person himself.

However, the right and wrong things to do in the mystified situation can be only *relatively* unequivocal. The tourniquet is always liable to be tightened by a further twist, and this is all that is necessary for the mystified situation to become a double-bind in the full sense.

In the example given earlier of the boy for whom happy equaled grateful and unhappy equaled selfish and ungrateful, the conflict and confusion would have been much intensified if strong prohibitions had been put on dishonesty. In such circumstances, to express unhappiness would be to be bad, since to be unhappy was to be selfish and ungrateful, while to put on an act of happiness would be equally bad because this would be dishonest.

In the case of the boy who put a berry up his nose, his parents could well be imagined saying: "But we *asked* you if your nose was all right and you told us it was and that you had made the whole thing up." This turns the situation into one that is at once double-binding and mystifying.

Case Descriptions

The following examples are from the families of three female schizophrenics, Maya, Ruby, and Ruth.[4]

MAYA

Maya (aged 28) thinks she started to imagine "sexual things" at about the age of 14 when she returned to live with her parents after a six-year separation during World War II. She would lie in her bedroom and wonder whether her parents had sexual intercourse. She began to get sexually excited, and at about that time she began to masturbate. She was very shy, however, and kept away from boys. She felt increasingly irritated at the physical presence of her father. She objected to him shaving in the same room while she had breakfast. She was frightened that her parents knew that she had sexual thoughts about them. She tried to tell them about this, but they told her *she did not have any thoughts of that kind.* She told them she masturbated *and they told her that she did not.* As for what happened in 1945 or 1946, we have, of course, only Maya's story to go on. However, when she told her parents in the presence of the interviewer that she still masturbated, her parents simply told her that she did not!

Maya's mother does not say: "How bad of you to masturbate," or "I can hardly believe that you could do *that.*" She does not tell Maya not to masturbate. She simply tells her that she does not.

Her mother repeatedly tried to induce Maya to forget various episodes that she (mother) did not want remembered. She did not, however, say: "I don't want you to mention this, much less remember it." She said, instead: "I want you to help the doctor by remembering, but of course you can't remember because you are ill."

Mrs. Abbott persistently questioned Maya about her memory in general, in order (one gathers, from the mother's point of view) to help her to get insight into the fact that she was ill by showing her either (1) that she was amnesic, or (2) that she had got some facts wrong, or (3) that she imagined she remembered because she had heard about it from her mother or father at a later date.

This "false" but "imaginary" memory was regarded by Mrs. Abbott with great concern. It was also a point on which Maya was most confused.

Mrs. Abbott finally told us (not in Maya's presence) that she prayed that Maya would never remember her "illness" because she (mother) thought it would upset her (daughter) to do so. In fact, she (mother) felt this so strongly that she said that it would be kindest even if it meant she had to remain in a hospital!

Both her parents thus not only contradicted Maya's memory, feelings, perceptions, motives, intentions, but their own attributions are curiously self-contradictory. And, further, while they spoke and acted as though they knew better than Maya what she remembered, what she did, what she imagined, what she wanted, what she felt, whether she was enjoying herself or whether she was tired, this "one-upmanship" was often maintained in a way which was further mystifying. For instance, on one occasion Maya said that she wanted to leave the hospital and that she thought her mother was trying to keep her in the hospital even though there was no need for her to be an in-patient any more. Her mother replied: "I think Maya is . . . I think Maya recognizes that whatever she wanted really for her good, I'd do. . . . wouldn't I. . . . Hmm? (no answer) No reservations in any way . . . I mean if there were any changes to be made I'd gladly make them . . . unless it was absolutely impossible." Nothing could have been further from what Maya recognized at that moment. But one notes the mystification in the statement. Whatever Maya wanted is qualified most decisively by "really" and "for her own good." Mrs. Abbott, of course, was arbiter (1) of what Maya "really" wanted, in contrast to what *she* might *think* she wanted, (2) of what was for her own good, (3) of what was possible.

Maya sometimes reacted to such mystifications by lucid perceptions of them. But this was much more difficult for her to achieve than for us. Her difficulty was that she could not herself tell when she could or could not trust her own memory, her mother and father, her own perspective and metaperspective, and her parents' statements of their perspective and metaperspectives.[5]

Close investigation of this family in fact revealed that her parents' statements to her about her, about themselves, about what they felt she felt they felt, etc., and even about what factually had happened could not be trusted. Maya *suspected* this, but she was told by her parents that such suspicions were her illness. She often therefore doubted the validity of her own suspicions; often

she denied what they said (delusionally) or invented some story that she clung to temporarily. For instance, she once insisted she had been in the hospital when she was eight, the occasion of her first separation from her parents.

This girl was an only child, born when her mother was 24, her father 30 years of age. Mother and father agreed that she had been her daddy's girl. She would wake him up at 4:30 in the morning when she was three to six, and they would go swimming together. She was always hand in hand with him. They sat close together at table, and he said prayers with her last thing at night. Until she was evacuated at the age of eight they went for frequent long walks together. Apart from brief visits home, she lived away from her parents until the age of 14.

Mrs. Abbott expressed nothing so simple as jealousy in and through her account of Maya's early intimacy with her father. She seemed to identify herself so much with Maya that she was living through her a re-vision of her relationship with her own father, which had been, according to her, one of rapid, unpredictable switches from acceptance to rejection and back.

When Maya at 14 came back to live permanently at home, she was changed. She wanted to study. She did not want to go swimming or for long walks with her father anymore. She no longer wanted to pray with him. She wanted to read the Bible by herself, for herself. She objected to her father expressing his affection for her by sitting close to her at meals. She wanted to sit farther away from him. Nor did she want to go to the cinema with her mother. She wanted to handle things in the house and wanted to do things for herself. For instance (mother's example), she washed a mirror without telling her mother she was going to do it. Her parents complained to us also that she did not want to understand her mother or father and that she could not tell them anything about herself.

Her parents' response to this changed state of affairs, which was evidently a great blow to them, was interesting. Both of them felt that Maya had exceptional mental powers, so much so that both the mother and the father became convinced *that she could read their thoughts.* Father attempted to confirm this by consulting a medium. They began to put this to the test in different ways.

FATHER: If I was downstairs and somebody came in and asked how Maya was, if I immediately went upstairs, Maya would say to me, "What have you been saying about me?" I said, "Nothing." She said, "Oh, yes, you have, I heard you." Now it was so extraordinary that unknown to Maya, I experimented with her, you see, and then when I'd proved it, I thought, "Well, I'll take Mrs. Abbott into my confidence," so I told her, and she said, "Oh, don't be silly, it's impossible." I said, 'All right, now when we take Maya in the car tonight, I'll sit beside her and I'll concentrate on her. I'll say something, and you watch what happens." When I was sitting down, she said, "Would you mind sitting at the other side of the car. I can't fathom Dad's thoughts." And that was true. Well, following that, one Sunday I said—it was winter—I said, "Now Maya will sit in the usual chair, and she'll be reading a book. Now you pick up a paper and I'll pick up a paper, and I'll give you the word and er . . . Maya was busy reading the paper and er. . . ." I nodded to my wife, then I concentrated on Maya behind the paper. She picked up the paper . . . her . . . em magazine or whatever it was and went to the front room. And her mother said, "Maya, where are you going? I haven't put the fire on." Maya said, "I can't understand. . . . No, I can't get to the depth of Dad's brain. Can't get to the depth of Dad's mind"!

Such mystifications have continued from before her first "illness" to the present, coming to light only after this investigation had been under way for over a year.

Maya's irritation, jumpiness, confusion, and occasional accusations that her mother and father were "influencing" her in some way had been, of course, completely "laughed off" by her father and mother in her presence for years, but in the course of the present investigation the father told Maya about this practice.

DAUGHTER: Well, I mean you shouldn't do it, it's not natural.

FATHER: I don't do it . . . I didn't do it . . . I thought . . . "Well, I'm doing the wrong thing, I won't do it."

DAUGHTER: I mean, the way I react would show you it's wrong.

FATHER: And there was a case in point a few weeks back, she fancied one of her mother's skirts.

DAUGHTER: I didn't. I tried it on and it fitted.

FATHER: Well, they had to go to a dressmaker . . . the dressmaker was recommended by someone. Mrs. Abbott went for it, and she said, "How much is that?" The woman said, "Four shillings." Mrs. Abbott said, "Oh, no, it must have cost you more than that," so she said, "Oh, well, your husband did me a good turn a few years back and I've never repaid him." I don't know what it was. Mrs. Abbott gave more, of course. So when Maya came home, she said, "Have you got the skirt, Mum?" She said, "Yes, and it cost a lot of money too, Maya." Maya said, "Oh, you can't kid me, they tell me it was four shillings."

DAUGHTER: No, seven I thought it was.

FATHER: No, it was four you said, exactly, and my wife looked at me and I looked at her. . . . So if you can account for that, I can't.

Another of Maya's "ideas of reference" was that something was going on between her parents that she could not fathom and that she thought was about her but she could not be sure.

Indeed there was. When mother, father and Maya were interviewed together, mother and father kept up a constant series of knowing smiles, winks, nods, gestures that were so "obvious" to the observer that he commented on them after about twenty minutes of the first triadic interview. From Maya's point of view, the mystification was that her mother and father neither acknowledged this remark from the researcher, nor had they ever, as far as we know, acknowledged the validity of similar perceptions and comments by Maya. As a result, so it seemed to us, she did not know when she was perceiving something to be going on and when she was imagining it. The open, yet secret, nonverbal exchanges between father and mother were in fact quite public and perfectly obvious. Her "paranoid" doubts about what was going on appeared, therefore, to be in part expressions of her lack of trust in the validity of her suspicions. She could not "really" believe that what she thought she saw to be going on was going on. Another consequence to Maya was that she could not discriminate between what (to the researchers) were not intended to be communicative actions (taking off spectacles, blinking, rubbing nose, frowning, and so on) of people generally and what were indeed signals between mother and father. The extraordinary thing was that some of these signals were partly "tests" to see if Maya would pick them up. An essential part of the game the parents played was, however, that if commented on, the rejoinder should be, "What do you mean, what wink?" and so on.

RUBY

When Ruby (aged 18) was admitted to the hospital, she was completely mute, in an inaccessible catatonic stupor. She at first refused to eat, but gradually she was coaxed to do so. After a few days she began to talk. She rambled in a vague way, and she often contradicted herself. At one moment, for instance, she said her mother loved her, and the next she said she was trying to poison her.

In clinical psychiatric terms, there was incongruity of thought and affect, e.g., she laughed when she spoke of her recent pregnancy and miscarriage. She complained of bangings in her head and of voices outside her head calling her "slut," "dirty," "prostitute." She thought that "people" were talking disparagingly about her. She said she was the Virgin Mary, and Elvis Presley's wife. She thought her family disliked her and wanted to get rid of her; she feared she would be abandoned in the hospital by them. "People" did not like her. She feared crowds and "people." When she was in a crowd, she felt the ground would open up under her feet. At night "people" were lying on top of her, having sexual intercourse with her; she had given birth to a rat after she was admitted to the hospital; she believed she saw herself on television.

It was clear that the fabric of this girl's sense of "reality," of what is the case and what is not the case, was in shreds.

The question is: Has what is usually called her "sense of reality" been torn in shreds by others?

Is the way this girl acts and are the things she says the intelligible effluxion of pathologic process?

This girl was confused particularly as to who she was—she oscillated between the Virgin Mary and Elvis Presley's wife—and she was confused as to whether or not her family and "people" in general loved her and in what sense—whether they liked the person she was or desired her sexually while despising her.

How socially intelligible are these areas of confusion?

In order to spare the reader the initial confusion of the investigators, not to say that of the girl, we tabulate her family nexus at the bottom of this page.

Simply, Ruby was an illegitimate child, reared by her mother, her mother's sister, and the sister's husband.

We shall refer to her biological relatives without inverted commas, and as she called them, and/or as they referred to themselves, with inverted commas.

Her mother and she lived with her mother's married sister, this sister's husband ('daddy' and 'uncle'), and their son (her cousin). Her father, who was married and had another family elsewhere, visited them occasionally. She referred to him as 'uncle.'

Her family violently disagreed in an initial interview with us about whether Ruby had grown up knowing "who she was." Her mother ('mummy') and her aunt ('mother') strongly maintained that she had no inkling of the real state of affairs, but her cousin (her 'brother') insisted that she must have known for years. They (mother, aunt, and uncle) argued also that no one in the district knew of this, but they admitted finally that of course everyone knew she was an illegitimate child, but no one would hold it against her. The most intricate splits

Biological status	*Titles Ruby was taught to use*
father	uncle
mother	mummy
aunt (mother's sister)	mother
uncle (mother's sister's husband)	daddy, later uncle
cousin	brother

and denials in her perception of herself and others were simultaneously expected of this girl and practiced by the others.

She got pregnant six months before admission to the hospital (miscarriage at four months).

Like so many of our families, this one was haunted by the specter of scandal and gossip, by the fear of what "people" were saying or thinking, etc. When Ruby was pregnant, all this became intensified. Ruby thought "people" were talking about her (they in fact were) and her family knew they were, but when she told them about this, they tried to reassure her by telling her not to be silly, not to imagine things, that of course no one was talking about her.

This was just one of the many mystifications to which this girl was subjected.

The following are a few of the others.

1) In her distracted, "paranoid" state, she said that she thought her mother, aunt, uncle, and cousin disliked her, picked on her, mocked her, despised her. As she got "well," she felt very remorseful about having thought such terrible things, and she said that her family had been "really good" to her and that she had a "lovely family."

Indeed, they gave her every reason to feel guilty for seeing them in this way, expressing dismay and horror that she should think that they did not love her.

In actuality, they told us that she was a slut and little better than a prostitute—and they told us this with vehemence and intensity.

They tried to make her feel bad or mad for perceiving their real feelings.

2) She guiltily suspected that they did not want her home from the hospital and accused them, in sudden outbursts, of wanting to get rid of her. They asked her how she could think such things, but in fact, they were extremely reluctant to have her at home.

They tried to make her think they wanted her home and to make her feel mad or bad if she perceived that they did not want her home, when, in fact, they did not want her home.

3) Extraordinarily confused attitudes were brought into play when she became pregnant.

As soon as they could after hearing about it from Ruby, 'mummy' and 'mother' got her on the sitting-room divan, and while trying to pump hot soapy water into her uterus, told her with tears, reproaches, sympathy, pityingly and vindictively at once, what a fool she was, what a slut she was, what a terrible plight she was in (just like her 'mummy'), what a bastard the boy was ("just like her father"), what a disgrace, history was repeating itself, how could one expect anything else . . . .

This was the first time her true parentage had ever been explicitly made known to her.

4) Subsequently, Ruby's feeling that people were talking about her began to develop in earnest. As we have noted, she was told this was nonsense, and her family told us that everyone was "very kind" to her "considering." Her cousin was the most honest. "Yes, most people are kind to her, just as if she were colored."

5) The whole family was choked with the sense of shame and scandal. While emphasizing this to Ruby again and again, they simultaneously told her that she was imagining things when she said she thought that people were talking about her.

6) Her family *accused* her of being spoiled and pampered, but when she tried to reject their pampering, they told her (1) she was ungrateful, and (2) she needed them, she was still a child, etc. (as though being spoiled was something *she* did).

The uncle was represented by the mother and aunt to the researchers also as a very good uncle who loved Ruby and who was like a father to her. They were assured that he was willing to do anything he could to help them elucidate Ruby's problem. Despite this, at no time was it possible to see him for a prearranged interview. Six mutually convenient appointments were made during the period of the investigation, and every one was broken, and broken either without any notice at all or with no more than twenty-four hours' notice. The uncle was seen eventually by the researchers, but only when they called at his house without notice.

According to the testimony of uncle, mother, and aunt to the researchers, this girl was repeatedly told by her uncle that if she did not "mend her ways" she would have to get out of the house. We know that on two occasions she was actually told by him to go and she did. But when she said to him that he had told her to get out, *he denied it to her* (though not to us)!

Her uncle told us tremblingly how she had pawed him, run her hands over his trousers, how he was sickened by it. His wife said rather coolly that he did not give the impression of having been sickened at the time.

Ruby, when questioned later, had apparently no conscious idea that her uncle did not like being cuddled and petted. She thought he liked it, she had done it to please him.

Not just in one area, but in every conceivable way—in respect of her clothes, her speech, her work, her friends—this girl was subject to mystifications, permeating all the interstices of her being.

The members of the families of the schizophrenic patients so far studied use mystification frequently as the preferred means of controlling the experience and action of the schizophrenic patient.

We have never yet seen a preschizophrenic who was not in a highly mystified state before his or her manifest psychotic breakdown.

This mystified state is, of course, unrecognized as such by the actively mystifying other family members, although it is frequently pointed out by a relatively detached member of the family circle (a "normal" sib, an aunt or uncle, a friend). The psychotic episode can sometimes be seen as an unsuccessful attempt to recognize the state of mystification the person is in. Each attempt at recognition is violently opposed by every conceivable mystification by the active mystifiers in the family.

RUTH

The following example of mystification again entails the confusion of praxis with process.

What to the investigators is an expression of the girl's real self, however disjunctive it is with her parents' model of what this is, her parents regard as mere process; that is, they ascribe no motive, agency, responsibility or intention, to such behavior. Behavior that to the investigators seems false and compliant, they regard as healthy, normal, and her true or real self. This paradoxical situation is a constantly repeated one in our data.

Ruth from time to time puts on colored woolen stockings and dresses generally in a way that is quite usual among certain sections of Londoners, but unusual in her parents' circle.

This is seen by her parents as a "symptom" of her illness. Her mother identified Ruth's act of putting on such stockings as the first sign of another "attack" coming on. That is, her mother (and father) convert her action (praxis) into a sign of a pathologic process. The same action is seen by the investigators as an assertion of a self that is disjunctive with her parents' rigidly held view of both of who Ruth is and what she ought to be.

These acts of self-assertion are met with tremendous violence both from Ruth herself and from her parents. The result is an ensuing period of disturbed experience and behavior that is clinically diagnosable as a "psychotic episode." It ends with a reconciliation on the basis that Ruth has been ill. While being ill she felt things, did things, said things, that she did not really mean, and which she could not help, because it was all due to her "illness." Now that she is better again she herself realizes this.

When Ruth puts on colored stockings at first, the issues for the parents are: what is making her disgrace us this way? She is a good girl. She is always so sensible and grateful. She is not usually stupid and inconsiderate. Even if she wants to wear stockings, etc., like that, she knows it upsets her father and she knows he has a bad heart. How can she upset him like that when she really loves him?

The difficulty in analyzing this girl in her nonpsychotic periods, as is not infrequently the case with schizophrenics in their "mute" phase, is that she completely sides with her parents in their view that she has "attacks" of her "illness" periodically. Only when she is "ill" does she repudiate (and then, of course, only with part of herself) her parents' "axis of orientation."

An approach to the logic of the mystification in this case might be attempted as follows.

X is good. All not-X is bad. Ruth is X. If Ruth were Y she would be bad. But Ruth appears to be Y.

Thus Y must be the equivalent to X, in which case Ruth is not really not-X, but is really X.

Moreover, if Ruth tries to be, or is, Y, she will be bad. But Ruth is person X, that is, she is good, so Ruth cannot be bad, so she must be mad.

Ruth wants to put on colored woolen stockings and go out with boys, but she does not want to be bad or mad. The mystification here is that without being bad or mad she cannot become anything except a dowdy aging spinster living at home with her aging parents. She is persecuted by the "voices" of her own unlived life if she is good and by the "voices" of her parents if she is bad. So she is maddened either way. She is thus in what I have called an *untenable position* (Laing 1961, p. 135).

The therapist's task is to help such a person to become *demystified*. The first phase of therapy, in such a case, consists largely in efforts at demystification, of untangling the knot that he or she is tied in, or raising issues that may never have been questioned or even thought of except when the person was "ill," namely, is it bad or is it a disgrace, or is it selfish, inconsiderate, ungrateful, etc., to be or to do not-X and is it necessarily good to be X, etc.?

But the *practice* of therapy is another story.

NOTES

1. Investigators: R. D. Laing (Chief Investigator), Dr. A. Esterson, Dr. A. Russell Lee (1959–1961), Dr. Peter Lomas, Miss Marion Bosanquet, P.S.W. Dr. Laing is a current Research Fellow of the Foundation's Fund for Research in Psychiatry. Dr. A. Russell Lee's participation was made possible by the National Institute of Mental Health, Bethesda, Md. (Grant No. MF-10, 579.)

2. For an exposition of this theory, see Laing and Cooper (1964).

3. In most forms of psychotherapy the therapist attributes motives and intentions to the patient which are not in accord with those the patient attributes to his own actions. But the therapist (one hopes) does not mystify the patient, in that he says implicitly or explicitly: You see yourself as motivated by A and intending B. I see you, however, as motivated by X and intending Y, and here is my evidence, drawn from my personal encounter with you.

4. For extended phenomenologic descriptions of these and other families of schizophrenics, see Laing and Esterson (1964).

5. By perspective is denoted p's point of view in a situation. By metaperspective is denoted p's viewpoint on o's point of view. (See Laing, 1961.)

REFERENCES

BATESON, G., D. D. JACKSON, J. HALEY, AND J. WEAKLAND 1956. Toward a theory of schizophrenia. *Behav. Sci.* 1: 251–264.

BRODEY, W. M. 1959. Some family operations and schizophrenia. *A.M.A. Arch. Gen. Psychiat.* 1: 379–402.

HALEY, J. 1959a. The family of the schizophrenic: a model system. *J. Nerv. Ment. Dis.* 129: 357–374.

———— 1959b. An interactional description of schizophrenia. *Psychiatry* 22: 321–332.

LAING, R. D. 1960. *The divided self.* London: Tavistock. Chicago: Quadrangle Press, 1961.

———— 1961. *The self and other.* London: Tavistock. Chicago: Quadrangle Press, 1962.

———— 1962. Series and nexus in the family. *New Left Rev.* 15, May–June.

————, AND R. D. COOPER 1964. *Reason and violence. a family,* vol. 1. *Families of schizophrenics.* London:

Tavistock. New York: Basic Books.

LIDZ, T., A. CORNELISON, D. TERRY, AND S. FLECK 1958. Intrafamilial environment of the schizophrenic patient: VI The transmission of irrationality. *A.M.A. Arch. Neurol. Psychiat.* 79: 305–316.

LOMAS, P. 1961. Family role and identity formation. *Int. J. Psycho-Anal.* 42, July–Oct.

RYCKOFF, I., J. DAY, AND L. C. WYNNE 1959. Maintenance of stereotyped roles in the families of schizophrenics. *A.M.A. Arch. Gen. Psychiat.* 1: 93–98.

SARTRE, J. P. 1960. *Critique de la raison dialectique.* Paris: Gallimard.

SEARLES, H. F. 1959. The effort to drive the other person crazy—an element in the etiology and psychotherapy of schizophrenia. *Brit. J. Med. Psychol.* 32: 1–18.

WYNNE, L. C., I. M. RYCKOFF, J. DAY, AND S. I. HIRSCH 1958. Pseudomutuality in the family relations of schizophrenics. *Psychiatry* 21: 205–220.

Chapter 7
Socialization

SOCIALIZATION IS A KEY SOCIOLOGICAL concept explaining how infants become functioning members of their society and members of their social groups. Socialization may be defined as the process whereby persons learn to behave in the manner expected by groups in which they are members. While socialization as a process of social learning occurs throughout life, the family is typically the unit in which most people receive their first and most intense socializing experiences. Our conception of who we are, of the self, emerges from contact and communication with others. Through socialization we learn about our social settings; we internalize the attitudes, values, and goals of others. In the experiences of the child, self and society develop at the same time. Social identity is socially bestowed, socially sustained, and socially transformed.[1] Among the factors that account for differences in socialization experiences are sex, social class, ethnicity, race, and religion.

The articles in this chapter represent a selected cross-section of socialization experiences. Sex role socialization starts at day one and persists throughout our lives. For example, children as young as three are aware of cultural definitions of masculinity and femininity.[2] By the fifth and sixth grade a majority of boys and girls have "been in love" and 84 percent of girls and 65 percent of boys expect that they will eventually marry. Girls more than boys fantasize about romance, dating, falling in love, and finding the appropriate person to marry.[3] Girls learn that in order to attract boys,

they should please them and not outdo them. Jo Freeman reports that although girls' grades continue to be better than boys' grades until late in high school, the girls' opinions of themselves "grow progressively worse with age and their opinions of boys and boys' abilities grow better."[4]

Sociologists have shown that while parents socialize their sons to mold their own world, girls are prepared to be molded by it. The goal of socialization for sons is to direct their impact onto the external world while for daughters the goal is protection from the impact of the external world.

Judith Bardwick and Elizabeth Douvan analyze the ways in which our society socializes boys and girls so that "most men and women come close to the society's ideal norms." Women learn that they are expected to be passive, dependent and compliant, while men learn that they should be task-oriented, assertive, self-disciplined, rational, and exercise emotional control. Girls learn to turn to others for acceptance and approval, while boys are taught to develop "a sense of self and criteria of worth which are relatively independent of others' responses." This has implications for how males and females fulfill their adult roles.

William Simon and John Gagnon deal with the development of sexual behavior and awareness of our own sexuality. These researchers suggest that sexual behavior is learned through social and cultural *scripting* and through our fantasy lives. We learn about sexual behavior as we learn other behavior, "through scripts, that in this case give the self, other persons, and situations erotic abilities or content."

The impact of social class location on parent–child relationships is analyzed by Melvin Kohn. Parent–child relationships are shaped by the different values in middle- and working-class families. For example, working-class parents tend to value conformity to external rules which lead them to emphasize greater constraints in the socialization process. Kohn connects differing value orientations in the middle and working classes to their differing life conditions.

From a symbolic interaction perspective the student might consider ways in which families train sons and daughters to be members of society. What sorts of roles are boys and girls expected to play in families? How do these expectations correspond to the roles men and women are expected to play once they leave their families? How do parents' relationships with their children affect children's views of themselves? How are gestures, words, tone of voice, and other forms of communication interpreted by members of families? How do children learn about sexuality in families?

From a structural functional perspective, readers might examine the effectiveness of socialization, as performed by the family, for the larger society. How effectively do families prepare boys and girls for the roles they assume later on? To what extent does socialization in the family prepare children for roles in the society?

From a conflict perspective, readers might evaluate the ways in which socialization patterns in the family reproduce the system of inequality in the society. How are inequalities perpetuated by families? How do the inequalities perpetuated by society affect the life chances and life-styles of children? How do families perpetuate sex-role stereotyping and discrimination against women? How do parents and children, exposed to different societal expectations and experiences, deal with each other in the family?

NOTES

1. Peter Berger analyzes the development of social identity in his *Invitation to sociology: a humanistic perspective*, Garden City: Long Island, Doubleday, 1963.

2. Jerome Kagan, Acquisition and significance of sex typing and sex-role identity. In M.L. Hoffman and L.W. Hoffman (eds.), *Review of child development research*. New York: Russell Sage Foundation, 1964, 1: 137–167.

3. Carlfred Broderick and George Rowe, A scale of preadolescent heterosexual development. *Journal of Marriage and the Family* 30, 1968: 97–101.

4. Jo Freeman (ed.), *Women: a feminist perspective*. Palo Alto, Calif.: Mayfield, 1975.

Ambivalence: The Socialization of Women

JUDITH M. BARDWICK AND
ELIZABETH DOUVAN

"WHAT ARE BIG BOYS MADE OF? WHAT are big boys made of?"

Independence, aggression, competitiveness, leadership, task orientation, outward orientation, assertiveness, innovation, self-discipline, stoicism, activity, analytic-mindedness, objectivity, courage, unsentimentality, rationality, confidence, and emotional control.

"What are big girls made of? What are big girls made of?"

From Chapter 9, "Ambivalence: The Socialization of Women," by Judith M. Bardwick and Elizabeth Douvan in *Woman in sexist society: studies in power and powerlessness*, edited by Vivian Gornick and Barbara K. Moran, © 1971 by Basic Books, New York.

Dependence, passivity, fragility, low pain tolerance, nonaggression, noncompetitiveness, inner orientation, interpersonal orientation, empathy, sensitivity, nurturance, subjectivity, intuitiveness, yieldingness, receptivity, inability to risk, emotional liability, supportiveness.[1]

These adjectives describe the idealized, simplified stereotypes of normal masculinity and femininity. They also describe real characteristics of boys and girls, men and women. While individual men and women may more resemble the stereotype of the opposite sex, group differences between the sexes bear out these stereotypic portraits. How does American society socialize its members so that most men and women come close to the society's ideal norms?

From infancy children have behavioral tendencies that evoke particular types of responses from parents, older siblings, and anyone else who interacts with the child. Such responses are a function of both individual values—whether the particular person values outgoing extroverted behavior, for example—and widespread social values of acceptable child behavior. Socialization refers to the pressures—rewarding, punishing, ignoring, and anticipating—that push the child toward evoking acceptable responses.

Comparisons between boys and girls in infancy and the earliest childhood years reveal modal differences between the sexes. Boys have higher activity levels, are more physically impulsive, are prone to act out aggression, are genitally sexual earlier, and appear to have cognitive and perceptual skills less well-developed than girls of the same age. Generally speaking, girls are less active physically, display less overt physical aggression, are more sensitive to physical pain, have significantly less genital sexuality, and display greater verbal, perceptual, and cognitive skills than boys.[2]

All impulsive, aggressive children are forced to restrain these tendencies since running away, biting, kicking, publicly masturbating, and other similar behaviors are injurious either to the child and his playmates or the pride of his parents. It is critically important to the development of sex differences that these tendencies are more typical of boys than of girls. In addition, girls' more mature skills enable

them to attend to stimuli, especially from other people, more swiftly and accurately than boys.[3] Girls are better at analyzing and anticipating environmental demands; in addition, they have greater verbal facility. Girls' characteristic behavior tends to disturb parents less than boys' characteristic behavior. The perceptual, cognitive, and verbal skills which for unknown reasons are more characteristic of girls enable them to analyze and anticipate adult demands and to conform their behavior to adult expectations.[4] This all means that if the socialization demands made upon boys and girls were actually the same, girls would be in a better position to cope with the world than are boys.

While these differences in response tendencies would be sufficient to result in group differences between boys and girls, another factor adds to the probability of sex differences. Many characteristic responses are acceptable in girls, ranging from the very feminine through the athletic tomboy. For boys, neither the passive sissy nor the aggressive and physical "bad boy" are acceptable. From around the age of two to two and a half, when children are no longer perceived as infants but as children, more boys than girls experience more prohibitions for a wider range of behavior. In addition, and of special importance, dependent behavior, normal to all young children, is permitted for girls and prohibited for boys. Thus, girls are not encouraged to give up old techniques of relating to adults and using others to define their identity, to manipulate the physical world, and to supply their emotional needs.[5]

When people find their ways of coping comfortable and gratifying, they are not motivated to develop new techniques which in the long run might be far more productive. All very young children are dependent on adults for their physical well-being and for the knowledge that they exist and have value. Girls' self-esteem remains dependent upon other people's acceptance and love; they continue to use the skills of others instead of evolving their own. The boys' impulsivity and sexuality are sources of enormous pleasure independent of anyone else's response; these pleasures are central to the early core-self. Negative sanctions from powerful adults against masturbation, exploration, and physical aggression threaten not only the obvious pleasures, but, at heart, self-integrity. Thus, boys are pressured by their own impulses and by society's demands to give up depending predominantly on the response of others for feelings of self-esteem. Adult responses are unpredictable and frequently threatening. Forced to affirm himself because of the loss of older, more stable sources of esteem, the boy begins, before the age of five, to develop a sense of self and criteria of worth which are relatively independent of others' responses. He turns to achievements in the outer and real world and begins to value himself for real achievements in terms of objective criteria.

On the other hand, neither the girl's characteristic responses nor widespread cultural values force her to give up older, more successful modes of relating and coping. Her sexuality is neither so genital nor so imperative[6] but, rather, an overall body sensuality, gratified by affection and cuddling. Since girls are less likely to masturbate, run away from home, or bite and draw blood, their lives are relatively free of crisis until puberty. Before that girls do not have to conform to threatening new criteria of acceptability to anywhere near the extent that boys do. When boys are pressured to give up their childish ways it is because those behaviors are perceived as feminine by parents. Boys have to earn their masculinity early. Until puberty, femininity is a verbal label, a given attribute—something that does not have to be earned. This results in a significant delay in the girl's search for identity, development of autonomy, and development of internal criteria for self-esteem. Because they continue to depend on others for self-definition and affirmation and are adept at anticipating other people's demands, girls are conformist. Girls are rewarded by good grades in school, parental love, teacher acceptance, and peer belonging. As a result, girls remain compliant and particularly amenable to molding by the culture.[7]

Longitudinal studies which measure the same people from earliest childhood through adulthood reveal that some characteristics remain stable over the life span in both sex groups, while other traits change.[8] While activity level and the tendency to be extroverted or introverted are rather stable in both sexes, other dimensions like passivity-dependence and aggression may remain stable or change

depending on sex. There are significant correlations over the life span for aggression in males and passivity and dependency in females; on the other hand, passivity and dependency in males and aggression in females show no consistency over the life span. These psychological dimensions change or remain constant depending on whether individual inclinations threaten idealized cultural concepts of masculinity and femininity.[9] Aggression in boys is permitted and encouraged and only the form is socialized; dependence and passivity in girls is permitted or encouraged, and only the form is altered. Sex differences in infancy and childhood are enlarged through socialization.

Schools are generally feminine places,[10] institutions where conformity is valued, taught largely by conformist women. The course content, the methods of assessing progress, and the personal conduct required create difficulties for boys who must inhibit impulsivity, curb aggression, and restrain deviance. The reward structure of the school system perpetuates the pattern set by relationships with the parents—boys are further pressured to turn to their peers for acceptance and to develop internal criteria and objective achievements; girls are further urged to continue the nondeviant noninnovative, conformist style of life.

Girls are rewarded with high grades in school, especially in the early years of grammar school. What do girls do especially well in? What are they being asked to master? Grammar, spelling, reading, arithmetic—tasks that depend a great deal upon memorization and demand little independence, assertiveness, analysis, innovativeness, creativity.[11] The dependent, passive girl, cued into the affirming responses of teachers, succeeds and is significantly rewarded in school for her "good" behavior and her competent memorizing skills.

It appears that until puberty academically successful girls evolve a "bisexual" or dual self-concept. Both sexes are rewarded for achievement, especially academic achievement. Girls, as well as boys, are permitted to compete in school or athletics without significant negative repercussions. The girl who is rewarded for these successes evolves a self-concept associated with being able to successfully cope and compete. While there are no negative repercussions and there is a high probability of rewards from parents and teachers as long as her friends are similarly achieving, this girl will also feel normally feminine (although questions of femininity are probably not critically important in self-evaluation of prepubertal girls unless they are markedly deviant). With the onset of the physical changes of puberty, definitions of normalcy and femininity change and come precipitately closer to the stereotype. Now behaviors and qualities that were rewarded, especially successful competing, may be perceived negatively.[12] Femininity also becomes an attribute that has to be earned—this task is made crucially difficult because of the girl's ambivalent feelings toward her body.[13]

The maturation of the girl's reproductive system brings joy and relief, feelings of normalcy, and the awareness of sexuality. Simultaneously, in normal girls the physical changes are accompanied by blood and pain, the expectation of body distortion in pregnancy, the threat of the trauma of birth, and the beginning of sexual desirability. In addition, the physical changes of menstruation are accompanied by significant and predictable emotional cycles sufficiently severe to alter the perception of her body as secure or stable.[14] Simultaneously joyful and fearful, the young adolescent girl must begin to evolve a feminine self-concept that accepts the functions and future responsibilities of her mature body; at the same time these physical changes are cues for alterations in the demands made upon her by the culture.[15] From the very beginning of adolescence, girls, as potential heterosexual partners, begin to be punished for conspicuous competing achievement and to be rewarded for heterosexual success. Socialization in adolescence emphasizes the use of the cosmetic exterior of the self to lure men, to secure affection, to succeed in the competition of dating. At the same time the girl is warned not to succeed too much: conspicuous success in competitive dating threatens her friendships with girls. She learns in puberty that she is likely to be punished for significant competition in either of her important spheres.

Thus, for a long time, even the girls who are competitive, verbally aggressive, and independent can feel normal, but with the onset of puberty girls are faced with their first major crises: they must come to terms with and find pleasure in their physi-

cal femininity and develop the proper psychological "femininity." Since they are still primarily cued to others for feelings of esteem, and largely defined by interpersonal relations, under the stress of their evolving incomplete feminine identity, most girls conform to the new socialization criteria. While girls characteristically achieved in grade school because of rewards for this "good" behavior from others (rather than for achievement's own sake), in adolescence the establishment of successful interpersonal relationships becomes the self-defining, most rewarding, achievement task.[16] When that change in priorities occurs—and it tends to be greatest in the later years of high school, and again in the later years of college—personal qualities, such as independence, aggression, and competitive achievement, that might threaten success in heterosexual relationships are largely given up.

While boys are often afraid of failing, girls are additionally afraid of succeeding.[17] The adolescent girl, her parents, her girl friends, and her boy friends perceive success, as measured by objective, visible achievement as antithetical to femininity. Some girls defer consciously, with tongue in cheek, but the majority, who were never significantly aggressive, active, or independent, internalize the norms and come to value themselves as they are desired by others. The only change from childhood is that the most important source of esteem is no longer the parents but the heterosexual partner.

The overwhelming majority of adolescent girls remain dependent upon others for feelings of affirmation. Unless in early life the girl exhibited the activity, aggression, or sexuality usually displayed by boys, and thereby experienced significant parental prohibitions, there is little likelihood that she will develop independent sources of esteem that refer back to herself. Instead, the loss of love remains for her the gravest source of injury to the self and, predictably, she will not gamble with that critical source of esteem.[18]

In the absence of independent and objective achievements, girls and women know their worth only from others' responses, know their identities only from their relationships as daughters, girl friends, wives, or mothers and, in a literal sense, personalize the world. When we ask female college students what would make them happy or unhappy, when would they consider themselves successful, both undergraduate and graduate students reply: "When I love and am loved; when I contribute to the welfare of others; when I have established a good family life and have happy, normal children; when I know I have created a good, rewarding stable relationship."[19] During adolescence as in childhood, females continue to esteem themselves insofar as they are esteemed by those with whom they have emotional relationships. For many women this never changes during their entire life-time.

Girls are socialized to use more oblique forms of aggression than boys, such as the deft use of verbal injury or interpersonal rejection. Their aggression is largely directed toward people whose return anger will not be catastrophic to self-esteem—that is, other females. In their relationships with their fathers and later with their boyfriends or husbands, girls do not threaten the important and frequently precarious heterosexual sources of love. Instead, aggression is more safely directed toward other women with whom they covertly compete for love. In relationships between men, aggression is overt and the power relationships are clear; female aggression is covert, the power relationships rarely admitted. With the denial and disguise of anger, a kind of dishonesty, a pervasive uncertainty, necessarily creeps into each of a woman's relationships, creating further anxiety and continued or increased efforts to secure affection.

The absence of objective success in work makes girls invest in, and be unendingly anxious about, their interpersonal worth. Women use interpersonal success as a route to self-esteem since that is how they have defined their major task. If they fail to establish a meaningful, rewarding, unambivalent love relationship, they remain cued into the response of others and suffer from a fragile or vulnerable sense of self. Those who are secure enough, who have evolved an identity and a feeling of worth in love relationships, may gamble and pursue atypical, nontraditional, competitive, masculine achievements.

According to Erik Erikson, the most important task in adolescence is the establishment of a sense of identity. This is more difficult for girls than for boys. Because her sexuality is internal, inaccessible,

and diffuse, because she feels ambivalent toward the functions of her mature reproductive system, because she is not punished for her impulsivity, because she is encouraged to remain dependent, a girl's search for her feminine identity is both complex and delayed. To add to her problems, she is aware both of the culture's preference for masculine achievements and of the fact that there is no longer a single certain route for achieving successful femininity. The problem grows even more complex, ever more subtle.

In these affluent times middle-class girls are apparently not punished simply for being girls. They are not prohibited from going to college, seeking school office, or achieving honors. Marriage and maternity are held out as wonderful goals, not necessarily as inhibiting dead ends. Although girls are rewarded for conformity, dependence, passivity, and competence, they are not clearly punished for the reverse. Until adolescence the idea of equal capacity, opportunity, and life-style is held out to them. But sometime in adolescence the message becomes clear that one had better not do too well, that competition is aggressive and unfeminine, that deviating threatens the heterosexual relationship.[20] Masculinity is clearly defined and earned through individual competitive achievement. For the girl overt freedoms, combined with cultural ambiguity, result in an unclear image of femininity. As a result of vagueness about how to become feminine or even what is feminine, the girl responds to the single clear directive—she withdraws from what is clearly masculine. In high school and increasingly in college, girls cease clearly masculine pursuits and perceive the establishment of interpersonal goals as the most salient route to identity.[21] This results in a maximization of interpersonal skills, an interpersonal view of the world, a withdrawal from the development of independence, activity, ability, and competition, and the absence of a professional work commitment.

The personality qualities that evolve as characteristic of the sexes function so as to enhance the probability of succeeding in the traditional sex roles. Whether you are male or female, if you have traditionally masculine personality qualities—objectivity rather than subjectivity, aggression rather than passivity, the motive to achieve rather than a fear of success, courage rather than conformity, and professional commitment, ambition, and drive[22]—you are more likely to succeed in masculine roles. Socialization enhances initial tendencies; consequently, relatively few women have these qualities.

Thus, the essence of the problem of role conflict lies in the fact that up until now very few women have succeeded in traditionally masculine roles, not only because of disparagement and prejudice, but largely because women have not been fundamentally equipped and determined to succeed. Some women's tragedy is their desire to succeed in competitive achievement and their contempt for the traditional role for which they are better equipped.

It is probably not accidental, therefore, that women dominate professions that utilize skills of nurturance, empathy, and competence, where aggressiveness and competitiveness are largely dysfunctional.[23] These professions, notably teaching, nursing, and secretarial work, are low in pay and status. The routes to occupational success for women are either atypical and hazardous or typical, safe, and low in the occupational hierarchy. (It is interesting to note that in the USSR, where over 70 percent of the physicians are women, medicine is a low-status occupation.)

In spite of an egalitarian ideal in which the roles and contributions of the sexes are declared to be equal and complementary, both men and women esteem masculine qualities and achievements. Too many women evaluate their bodies, personality qualities, and roles as second-rate. When male criteria are the norms against which female performance, qualities, or goals are measured, then women are not equal. It is not only that the culture values masculine productivity more than feminine productivity. The essence of the derogation lies in the evolution of the masculine as the yardstick against which everything is measured. Since the sexes are different, women are defined as not-men and that means not good, inferior. It is important to understand that women in this culture, as members of the culture, have internalized these self-destructive values.[24]

What we have described is ambivalence, not conflict. Conflict is the simultaneous desire to achieve a stable and rewarding heterosexual rela-tionship (and the rest of the female's traditional responsibilities and satisfactions) and to participate fully in competitive achievement and succeed. Conflict, in this sense, is understandable as a vying between traditional and nontraditional roles, between affiliative and achievement motives. (Most women resolve this potential difficulty by defining affiliation as achievement.) Ambivalence is clearly seen in the simultaneous enjoyment of one's feminine identity, qualities, goals, and achievements and the perception of them as less important, meaningful, or satisfying than those of men. Girls envy boys; boys do not envy girls.

The culture generally rewards masculine endeavors and those males who succeed—who acquire money, power, and status, who enjoy an easy and free sexuality, who acquire and produce things, who achieve in competition, who produce, who innovate and create. By these criteria, women have not produced equally. The contributions that most women make in the enhancement and stabilization of relationships, their competence and self-discipline, their creation of life are less esteemed by men and women alike. It is disturbing to review the extent to which women perceive their responsibilities, goals, their very capacities, as inferior to males; it is similarly distressing to perceive how widespread this self-destructive self-concept is. Society values masculinity; when it is achieved it is rewarded. Society does not value femininity as highly; when it is achieved it is not as highly rewarded.

Today we have a peculiar situation in which sex-role stereotypes persist and are internalized by adults and children, yet the labor force includes thirty-one million working women and the college population is almost half women.[25] The stereotype persists because there is always cultural lag, because few women achieve markedly responsible or powerful positions and because the overwhelming majority of working women perceive themselves as working in order to benefit the family.[26] In general, working women do not see work as an extension of egocentric interests or as the fulfillment of achievement ambitions, but as another place in which more traditional motives are gratified.

Perhaps the percentage of the female population who have had at least some college and who have achieved and been rewarded in the educational system face the most difficult problems.[27] Some part of this population has evolved—normally and not as a compensatory function—self-concepts and motives that take for granted the value of marriage and maternity, but also include individuality, creativity, independence, and successful competitive achievement. These characteristics become criteria by which the excellence of the self is measured. It is obvious that these characteristics are not highly functional within the traditional role, and moreover, cannot truly be achieved within the traditional female role. There would be no conflict if competitive achievement were the only aspect of these women's self-concept, but it is not. Characteristically, normal girls stimultaneously put priority upon successful heterosexual relationships, which lead to the establishment of the nuclear family and traditional responsibilities.[28] Most girls effect a compromise, recognizing the hierarchy of their motivations and the appropriateness of their heterosexual desires. They tend to marry, work for a few years, and then start having babies. Inexperienced and unprepared, they tell themselves that the traditional role is creative and fulfilling. But creativity and fulfillment are hard to distinguish under the unending and repetitive responsibilities of diapers, dishes, and dusting. They tell themselves that when the children enter school they will reenter the labor force or the university. For these women, who have internalized the unequal evaluation of roles, who have developed needs to achieve, who have been rewarded because of their achievements, the traditional role is inadequate because it cannot gratify those nonnurturant, nonsupportive, nondependent, nonpassive aspects of the self.

Very few young women understand the very real limits upon achieving imposed by maternity, because they traditionally have had little experience with traditional role responsibilities before they marry. Typically, girls do not ask why there are so few female role models around who succeed in work while they have young children. While children are a real achievement, a source of joy and fulfillment, they are also time-consuming and energy-depleting, a major source of responsibility and anxiety. In today's child-centered milieu, with the decline of the extended family and the dearth of adequate child-care facilities, the responsibility for child-rearing falls directly on the mother alone.

Success in the traditional tasks is the usual means by which girls achieve feelings of esteem about themselves, confidence, and identity.[29] In general they have continued, even as adults, to esteem themselves as they are valued by others; that source of esteem is interpersonal, best earned within the noncompetitive, nonaggressive traditional role. Without independent, objective competitive achievements, confidence is best secured within the traditional role—in spite of the priority given to masculine achievements. Whether or not the woman is achievement-oriented, her years of major child-rearing responsibiliites result in a decline in old work skills, a loss of confidence that she can work, a fear of failing within a competitive milieu that she has left. In other words, not only have specific techniques been lost or new data become unfamiliar, withdrawal from a competitive-achievement situation for a significant length of time creates the conviction that she is not able.

The very characteristics that make a woman most successful in family roles—the capacity to take pleasure in family-centered, repetitive activities, to sustain and support members of the family rather than pursuing her own goals, to enhance relationships through boundaryless empathy —these are all antithetical to success in the bounded, manipulative, competitive, rational, and egocentric world of work.[30] Because they are not highly motivated and because they are uncertain about what is normal or desirable, many women do not work. Even those who do continue to feel psychologically responsible for the maintenance of the family and are unwilling to jeopardize family relationships. Most work at jobs that contribute to family vacations, college fees, or the general family budget.[31] Even women who pursue a career or profession, rather than merely holding a meaningless job, assume the responsibility for two major, demanding roles. Rather than make this commitment, many women professionalize their voluntary or club activities, bringing qualities of aggression, competitiveness, and organizing skills to these "safer" activities.

Women tend not to participate in roles, or seek goals that threaten their important affiliative relationships because in those relationships they find most of their feelings of esteem and identity. This perpetuates psychological dependency which may be functional in the relationships but injurious to the self-concept of those who have internalized the values of the culture. Undeniably, it is destructive to feelings of esteem to know that you are capable and to be aware that you are not utilizing much of your potential.[32] The question of whether nontraditional success jeopardizes feelings of femininity has not yet been answered. Most women today would not be willing to achieve a greater success than their husbands. In this tradition-bound, sex-stereotyped culture, even though millions of women are employed, old values are internalized and serve as criteria for self-evaluation.

Neither men nor women entering marriage expect the sexes to share equally in privileges and responsibilities. Very few couples could honestly accept the wife's having the major economic responsibility for the family while the husband deferred to the demands of her work. Few individuals could reverse roles without feeling that he is not "masculine," and she is not "feminine."[33] Masculinity and femininity are aspects of the self that are clearly tied to roles—which role, how typical or deviant, how well accomplished, the extent of the commitment.

Yet a new reality is emerging today, for this is an era of changing norms. Although the unidimensional stereotype still persists and remains partially viable, it is also simplistic and inaccurate. Both men and women are rejecting the old role allocations which are exaggerated and costly because they push men and women into limited slots solely on the basis of sex. But an era of change results in new uncertainties and the need to evolve new clear criteria of masculinity and femininity, which can be earned and can offer feelings of self-esteem to both sexes.

The socialization model is no longer clear; in its pure form it exists primarily in media, less in life. Since almost half of American women work, the percentage rising with the rising level of education, it is clear that, at least for educated middle-class women, the simplistic stereotype is no longer valid. Similarly we find that more men are rejecting success as the sole source of esteem or masculinity.

The male turning toward his family reflects his need not to be bound or limited by a unidimensional role model. For both sexes this is a period of change in which both old and new values coexist, though the visible norms derive from the old model. Today's college students seem to be more aware than the generation that preceded them of the consequences of role choice; they seem to be evolving a goal in which men are more nurturant than they were, while females are freer to participate professionally without endangering the male's esteem.

Both the work and the housewife roles are romanticized, since romanticism is enhanced when reality does not intrude. Women glorify work when and because they do not participate in it. Role conflict for women is largely a feeling of having been arbitrarily shut out from where the action is—a reaction to a romanticized concept of work and a reaction against the reality of the repetitive world of child care. Frustration is freely available to today's woman: if she participates fully in some professional capacity she runs the risk of being atypical and nonfeminine. If she does not achieve the traditional role she is likely to feel unfulfilled as a person, as a woman. If she undertakes both roles, she is likely to be uncertain about whether she is doing either very well. If she undertakes only the traditional role she is likely to feel frustrated as an able individual. Most difficult of all, the norms of what is acceptable, desirable, or preferable are no longer clear. As a result, it is more difficult to achieve a feminine (or masculine) identity, to achieve self-esteem because one is not certain when one has succeeded. When norms are no longer clear, then not only the "masculine" achieving woman but also the nonworking traditionally "feminine" woman can feel anxious about her normalcy, her fulfillment. Many women try to cope with their anxiety by exaggerating, by conforming to stereotyped role images. When one is anxious or uncertain about one's femininity, a viable technique for quelling those anxious feelings is an exaggerated conformity, a larger-than-life commitment to *Kinder, Küche, Kirche*. In this way a woman creates images, sending out clarified and exaggerated cues to others. Thus, the message is clear and she can be more certain that the feedback will assure her of her femininity.

It is easy to be aware of the discrepancy between the stereotyped norm and the reality. People are not simple. Whenever one sees a total investment or role adoption in its stereotyped, unidimensional form, one suspects a flight from uncertainty about masculinity or femininity. During a period of transition one can expect to see increasing numbers of women quelling anxiety by fleeing into a unidimensional, stereotyped femininity. As new norms gain clarity and force, more flexible roles, personalities, and behaviors will evolve. Role freedom is a burden when choice is available but criteria are unclear; under these circumstances it is very difficult to know whether one has achieved womanhood or has dangerously jeopardized it.

NOTES

1. J. Silverman, Attentional styles and the study of sex differences. In D. Mostofsky (ed.), *Attention: contemporary studies and analysis.* New York: Appleton-Century-Crofts, 1970; H. A. Witkin *et al.*, *Personality through perception: an experimental and clinical study.* New York: Harper, 1954; J. Kagan, Acquisition and significance of sex typing and sex-role identity. In M. L. Hoffman and L. W. Hoffman (eds.), *Review of child development research.* New York: Russell Sage Foundation, 1964, 1: 137–167; L. M. Terman and L. E. Tyler, Psychological sex differences. In L. Carmichael (ed.), *A manual of child psychology,* (2nd ed.) New York: Wiley, 1954, Ch. 19; E. Douvan and J. Adelson, *The adolescent experience.* New York: Wiley, 1966.

2. Silverman, *op. cit.*; Terman and Tyler, *op. cit.*; R. Q. Bell and N. S. Costello, Three tests for sex differences in tactile sensitivity in the newborn. *Biologia Neonatorum* 7, 1964: 335–347; R. Q. Bell and J. F. Darling, The prone head reaction in the human neonate: relation with sex and tactile sensitivity. *Child Development* 36, 1965: 943–949; S. M. Garn, Roentgenogrammetric determinants of body composition. *Human Biology* 29, 1957: 337–353; J. Kagan and M. Lewis, Studies of attention in the human infant. *Merrill-Palmer Quarterly* 2, 1965: 95–127; M. Lewis, J. Kagan, and J. Kalafat, Patterns of fixation in the young infant. *Child Development* 37, 1966: 331–341; L. P. Lipsitt and N. Levy, Electrotactual threshold in the human neonate. *Child Development* 30, 1959: 547–554.

3. Kagan and Lewis, *op. cit.*; Lewis, Kagan, and Kalafat, *op. cit.* In spite of this initial advantage which might be thought to lead, logically and inevitably, to high-achievement investment, girls' socialization ends without realization of this early promise. J. Veroff, Social comparison and the development of achievement motivation. In C. Smith (ed.), *Achievement related motives in children,* New York: Russell-Sage Foundation, 1969: 46–101. Veroff suggests that the period of optimal generalization of the achievement motive is early, about the age of four or five. At this time girls are better at the truly critical tasks of speaking, comprehending, and remembering. But these accomplishments are taken

for granted by children, who strive rather to tie shoelaces, ride bicycles, climb trees, and jump rope—all physical accomplishments. In other words, at the time when the motive for achievement is learned and generalized, the children themselves define physical tasks as important. Girls' greater cognitive and verbal skills do not, therefore, contribute to the development of a higher achievement motivation.

4. E. Maccoby (ed.), *The development of sex differences.* Stanford: Stanford University Press, 1966.

5. J. M. Bardwick, *The psychology of women.* New York: Harper & Row, 1971.

6. Helene Deutsch, *Psychology of women.* New York: Grune & Stratton, 1944, vol. 1; K. Horney, On the genesis of the castration complex in women. *International Journal of Psychoanalysis* 5, 1924: 50–65.

7. Douvan and Adelson, *op. cit.*

8. N. Bayley, Consistency of maternal and child behaviors in the Berkeley growth study. *Vita Humana* 7, 1964: 73–95; M. P. Honzik and J. W. MacFarlane, Prediction of behavior and personality from 21 months to 30 years. Unpublished manuscript, 1963; J. Kagan and H. A. Moss, *Birth to maturity.* New York: Wiley, 1962; E. S. Schaefer and N. Bayley, Maternal behavior, child behavior, and inter-correlations from infancy through adolescence. *Monograph of the Society for Research on Child Development* 28, 1963, serial no. 87.

9. Kagan and Moss, *op. cit.*

10. H. S. Becker, Social class variations in one teacher-pupil relationship. *Journal of Educational Sociology* 25, 1952: 451–465.

11. Maccoby, *op. cit.*

12. M. S. Horner, Fail: bright women. *Psychology Today* 3, November, 1969: 36.

13. Bardwick, *op. cit.*; E. Douvan, New sources of conflict at adolescence and early adulthood. In Judith M. Bardwick *et al.*, *Feminine personality and conflict.* Belmont, Calif.: Brooks/Cole.

14. M. E. Ivey and J. M. Bardwick, Patterns of affective fluctuation in the menstrual cycle. *Psychosomatic Medicine* 30, 1968: 336–345.

15. Douvan, *op. cit.*

16. J. G. Coleman, *The adolescent society.* New York: Free Press, 1961.

17. Horner, *op. cit.*

18. Deutsch, *op. cit.*; Douvan and Adelson, *op. cit.*

19. J. Bardwick and J. Zweben, A predictive study of psychological and psychosomatic changes associated with oral contraceptives. Mimeograph, 1970.

20. M. Komarovsky, *Women in the modern world.* Boston: Little, Brown, 1953.

21. *Ibid.*; R. Goldsen, M. Rosenberg, R. Williams, E. A. Suchman, *What college students think.* Princeton, N.J.: Van Nostrand, 1961; Coleman *op. cit.*; N. Sanford, *The American college.* New York: Wiley, 1962.

22. T. Parsons, Age and sex in the social structure of the United States, *American Sociological Review* 7, 1942: 604-616.

23. M. Mead, *Male and female.*, New York: William Morrow, 1949.

24. Bardwick, *op. cit.*; Mead, *op. cit.*

25. R. E. Hartley, Children's concept of male and female roles, *Merrill-Palmer Quarterly* 6, 1960: 153-163.

26. F. I. Nye and L. W. Hoffman, *The employed mother in America.* Chicago: Rand McNally, 1963.

27. R. Baruch, The achievement motive in women: implications for career development. *Journal of Personality and Social Psychology* 5, 1967: 260-267.

28. Bardwick, *op. cit.*

29. Douvan and Adelson, *op. cit.*

30. D. L. Gutmann, Woman and their conception of ego strength. *Merrill-Palmer Quarterly* 11, 1965: 229-240.

31. Nye and Hoffman, *op. cit.*

32. G. Gurin, J. Veroff, and S. Feld, *Americans view their mental health.* New York: Basic Books, 1960.

33. D. J. Bem and S. L. Bem, Training the woman to know her place. Based on a lecture delivered at Carnegie Institute of Technology, October 21, 1966, revised 1967.

Psychosexual Development

WILLIAM SIMON AND JOHN H. GAGNON

ERIK ERIKSON HAS OBSERVED THAT, prior to Sigmund Freud, "sexologists" tended to believe that sexual capacities appeared suddenly with the onset of adolescence. Sexuality followed those external evidences of physiological change that occurred concurrent with or just after puberty. Psychoanalysis changed all that. In Freud's view, libido—the generation of psychosexual energies—should be viewed as a fundamental element of human experience at least beginning with birth, and possibly before that. Libido, therefore, is essential, a biological constant to be coped with at all levels of individual, social, and cultural development. The truth of this received wisdom, that is, that sexual development is a continuous contest between biological drive and cultural restraint, should be seriously questioned. Obviously sexuality has roots in biological processes, but so do many other capacities including many that involve physical and mental competence and vigor. There is, however, abundant evidence that the final states which these capacities attain escape the rigid impress of biology. This independence of biological constraint is rarely claimed for the area of sexuality, but we would like to argue that the sexual is precisely that realm where the sociocultural forms most completely dominate biological influences.

It is difficult to get data that might shed much light on the earliest aspects of these questions: Adults are hardly equipped with total recall and the preverbal or primitively verbal child does not have ability to report accurately on his own internal state. But it seems obvious—and it is a basic assumption of this paper—that with the beginnings of adolescence many new factors come into play, and to emphasize a straight-line developmental continuity with infant and childhood experiences may be seriously misleading. In particular, it is dangerous to assume that because some childhood behavior appears sexual to adults, it must be sexual.

An infant or a child engaged in genital play (even if orgasm is observed) can in no sense be seen as experiencing the complex set of feelings that accompanies adult or even adolescent masturbation.

Therefore, the authors reject the unproven assumption that "powerful" psychosexual drives are fixed biological attributes. More importantly, we reject the even more dubious assumption that sexual capacities or experiences tend to translate immediately into a kind of universal "knowing" or innate wisdom—that sexuality has a magical ability, possessed by no other capacity, that allows biological drives to be expressed directly in psychosocial and social behaviors.

The prevailing image of sexuality—particularly that of the Freudian tradition—is that of an intense, high-pressure drive that forces a person to seek physical sexual gratification, a drive that expresses itself indirectly if it cannot be expressed directly. The available data suggest to us a different picture—one that shows either lower levels of intensity, or, at least, greater variability. We find that there are many social situations or life-roles in which reduced sex activity or even deliberate celibacy is undertaken with little evidence that the libido has shifted in compensation to some other sphere.

A part of the legacy of Freud is that we have all become remarkably adept at discovering "sexual" elements in nonsexual behavior and symbolism. What we suggest instead (following Kenneth Burke's three-decade-old insight) is the reverse —that sexual behavior can often express and serve nonsexual motives.

We see sexual behavior therefore as *scripted* behavior, not the masked expression of a primordial drive. The individual can learn sexual behavior as he or she learns other behavior—through scripts that in this case give the self, other persons, and situations erotic abilities or content. Desire, privacy, opportunity, and propinquity with an attractive member of the opposite sex are not, in themselves, enough; in ordinary circumstances, nothing sexual will occur unless one or both actors organize these elements into an appropriate script. The very concern with foreplay in sex suggests this. From one point of view, foreplay may be defined as merely progressive physical excitement generated by touching naturally erogenous zones. The authors

have referred to this conception elsewhere as the "rubbing of two sticks together to make a fire" model. It would seem to be more valuable to see this activity as symbolically invested behavior through which the body is eroticized and through which mute, inarticulate motions and gestures are translated into a sociosexual drama.

A belief in the sociocultural dominance of sexual behavior finds support in cross-cultural research as well as in data restricted to the United States. Psychosexual development is universal—but it takes many forms and tempos. People in different cultures construct their scripts differently; and in our own society, different segments of the population act out different psychosexual dramas—something much less likely to occur if they were all reacting more or less blindly to the same superordinate urge. The most marked differences occur, of course, between male and female patterns of sexual behavior. Obviously, some of this is due to biological differences, including differences in hormonal functions at different ages. But the significance of social scripts predominates; the recent work of Masters and Johnson, for example, clearly points to far greater orgasmic capacities on the part of females than our culture would lead us to suspect. And within each sex—especially among men—different social and economic groups have different patterns.

Let us examine some of these variations, and see if we can decipher the scripts.

Whether one agrees with Freud or not, it is obvious that we do not become sexual all at once. There is continuity with the past. Even infant experiences can strongly influence later sexual development.

But continuity is not causality. Childhood experiences (even those that appear sexual) will in all likelihood be influential not because they are intrinsically sexual, but because they can affect a number of developmental trends, *including* the sexual. What situations in infancy—or even early childhood—can be called psychosexual in any sense other than that of creating potentials?

The key term, therefore, must remain potentiation. In infancy, we can locate some of the experiences (or sensations) that will bring about a sense of the body and its capacities for pleasure and discomfort and those that will influence the child's ability to relate to others. It is possible, of course, that through these primitive experiences, ranges are being established—but they are very broad and overlapping. Moreover, if these are profound experiences to the child—and they may well be that—they are not expressions of biological necessity, but of the earliest forms of social learning.

In childhood, after infancy there is what appears to be some real sex play. About half of all adults report that they did engage in some form of sex play as children; and the total who actually did may be half again as many. But, however the adult interprets it later, what did it mean to the child at the time? One suspects that, as in much of childhood role playing, their sense of the adult meanings attributed to the behavior is fragmentary and ill-formed. Many of the adults recall that, at the time, they were concerned with being found out. But here, too, were they concerned because of the real content of sex play, or because of the mystery and the lure of the forbidden that so often enchant the child? The child may be assimilating outside information about sex for which, at the time, he has no real internal correlate or understanding.

A small number of persons do have sociosexual activity during preadolescence—most of it initiated by adults. But for the majority of these, little apparently follows from it. Without appropriate sexual scripts, the experience remains unassimilated—at least in adult terms. For some, it is clear, a severe reaction may follow from falling "victim" to the sexuality of an adult—but, again, does this reaction come from the sexual act itself or from the social response, the strong reactions of others? (There is some evidence that early sexual activity of this sort is associated with deviant adjustments in later life. But this, too, may not be the result of sexual experiences in themselves so much as the consequence of having fallen out of the social main stream and, therefore, of running greater risks of isolation and alienation.)

In short, relatively few become truly active sexually before adolescence. And when they do (for girls more often than boys), it is seldom immediately related to sexual feelings or gratifications but is a use of sex for nonsexual goals and purposes. The "seductive" Lolita is rare; but she is significant: She illustrates a more general pattern of psychosexual development—a commitment to the

social relationships linked to sex before one can really grasp the social meaning of the physical relationships.

Of great importance are the values (or feelings, or images) that children pick up as being related to sex. Although we talk a lot about sexuality, as though trying to exorcise the demon of shame, learning about sex in our society is in large part learning about guilt; and learning how to manage sexuality commonly involves learning how to manage guilt. An important source of guilt in children comes from the imputation to them by adults of sexual appetites or abilities that they may not have, but that they learn, however imperfectly, to pretend they have. The gestural concomitants of sexual modesty are learned early. For instance, when do girls learn to sit or pick up objects with their knees together? When do they learn that the bust must be covered? However, since this behavior is learned unlinked to later adult sexual performances, what children must make of all this is very mysterious.

The learning of sex roles, or sex identities, involves many things that are remote from actual sexual experience, or that become involved with sexuality only after puberty. Masculinity or femininity, their meaning and postures, are rehearsed before adolescence in many nonsexual ways.

A number of scholars have pointed, for instance, to the importance of aggressive, deference, dependency, and dominance behavior in childhood. Jerome Kagan and Howard Moss have found that aggressive behavior in males and dependency in females are relatively stable aspects of development. But what is social role, and what is biology? They found that when aggressive behavior occurred among girls, it tended to appear most often among those from well-educated families that were more tolerant of deviation. Curiously, they also reported that "it was impossible to predict the character of adult sexuality in women from their preadolescent and early adolescent behavior," and that "erotic activity is more anxiety-arousing for females than for males," because "the traditional ego ideal for women dictates inhibition of sexual impulses."

The belief in the importance of early sex-role learning for boys can be viewed in two ways. First, it may directly indicate an early sexual capacity in male children. Or, second, early masculine identification may merely be an appropriate framework within which the sexual impulse (salient with puberty) and the socially available sexual scripts (or accepted patterns of sexual behavior) can most conveniently find expression. Our bias, of course, is toward the second.

But, as Kagan and Moss also noted, the sex role learned by the child does not reliably predict how he will act sexually as an adult. This finding also can be interpreted in the same two alternative ways. Where sexuality is viewed as a biological constant which struggles to express itself, the female sex role learning can be interpreted as the successful repression of sexual impulses. The other interpretation suggests that the difference lies not in learning how to handle a preexistent sexuality, but in learning how to *be* sexual. Differences between men and women, therefore, will have consequences both for *what* is done sexually, as well as *when*.

Once again, we prefer the latter interpretation, and some recent work that we have done with lesbians supports it. We observed that many of the major elements of their sex lives—the start of actual genital sexual behavior, the onset and frequency of masturbation, the time of entry in sociosexual patterns, the number of partners, and the reports of feelings of sexual deprivation—were for these homosexual women almost identical with those of ordinary women. Since sexuality would seem to be more important for lesbians—after all, they sacrifice much in order to follow their own sexual pathways—this is surprising. We concluded that the primary factor was something both categories of women share—the sex-role learning that occurs before sexuality itself becomes significant.

Social class also appears significant, more for boys than girls. Sex-role learning may vary by class; lower-class boys are supposed to be more aggressive and put much greater emphasis on early heterosexuality. The middle and upper classes tend to tolerate more deviance from traditional attitudes regarding appropriate male sex-role performances.

Given all these circumstances, it seems rather naive to think of sexuality as a constant pressure, with a peculiar necessity all its own. For us, the crucial period of childhood has significance not because of sexual occurrences, but because of nonsexual developments that will provide the names and judgments for later encounters with sexuality.

The actual beginnings and endings of adolescence are vague. Generally, the beginning marks the first time society, as such, acknowledges that the individual has sexual capacity. Training in the postures and rhetoric of the sexual experience is now accelerated. Most important, the adolescent begins to regard those about him (particularly his peers, but also adults) as sexual actors and finds confirmation from others for this view.

For some, as noted, adolescent sexual experience begins before they are considered adolescents. Kinsey reports that a tenth of his female sample and a fifth of his male sample had experienced orgasm through masturbation by age 12. But still, for the vast majority, despite some casual play and exploration that post-Freudians might view as masked sexuality, sexual experience begins with adolescence. Even those who have had prior experience find that it acquires new meanings with adolescence. They now relate such meanings to both larger spheres of social life and greater senses of self. For example, it is not uncommon during the transition between childhood and adolescence for boys and, more rarely, girls to report arousal and orgasm while doing things not manifestly sexual—climbing trees, sliding down bannisters, or other activities that involve genital contact—without defining them as sexual. Often they do not even take it seriously enough to try to explore or repeat what was, in all likelihood, a pleasurable experience.

Adolescent sexual development, therefore, really represents the beginning of adult sexuality. It marks a definite break with what went on before. Not only will future experiences occur in new and more complex contexts, but they will be conceived of as explicitly sexual and thereby begin to complicate social relationships. The need to manage sexuality will rise not only from physical needs and desires, but also from the new implications of personal relationships. Playing, or associating, with members of the opposite sex now acquires different meanings.

At adolescence, changes in the developments of boys and girls diverge and must be considered separately. The one thing both share at this point is a reinforcement of their new status by a dramatic biological event—for girls, menstruation, and for boys, the discovery of the ability to ejaculate. But here they part. For boys, the beginning of a commitment to sexuality is primarily genital; within two years of puberty all but a relatively few have had the experience of orgasm, almost universally brought about by masturbation. The corresponding organizing event for girls is not genitally sexual but social: they have arrived at an age where they will learn role performances linked with proximity to marriage. In contrast to boys, only two-thirds of girls will report every having masturbated (and, characteristically, the frequency is much less). For women, it is not until the late twenties that the incidence of orgasm from any source reaches that of boys at age 16. In fact, significantly, about half of the females who masturbate do so only after having experienced orgasm in some situation involving others. This contrast points to a basic distinction between the developmental processes for males and females: males move from privatized personal sexuality to sociosexuality; females do the reverse and at a later stage in the life cycle.

We have worked hard to demonstrate the dominance of social, psychological, and cultural influences over the biological; now, dealing with adolescent boys, we must briefly reverse course. There is much evidence that the early male sexual impulses—again, initially through masturbation—are linked to physiological changes, to high hormonal inputs during puberty. This produces an organism that, to put it simply, is more easily turned on. Male adolescents report frequent erections, often without apparent stimulation of any kind. Even so, though there is greater biological sensitization and hence masturbation is more likely, the meaning, organization, and continuance of this activity still tends to be subordinate to social and psychological factors.

Masturbation provides guilt and anxiety among most adolescent boys. This is not likely to change in spite of more "enlightened" rhetoric and discourse on the subject (generally, we have shifted from stark warnings of mental, moral, and physical damage to vague counsels against nonsocial or "inappropriate" behavior). However, it may be that this very guilt and anxiety gives the sexual experience an intensity of feeling that is often attributed to sex itself.

Such guilt and anxiety do not follow simply from social disapproval. Rather, they seem to come from several sources, including the difficulty the

boy has in presenting himself as a sexual being to his immediate family, particularly his parents. Another source is the fantasies or plans associated with masturbation—fantasies about doing sexual "things" to others or having others do sexual "things" to oneself; or having to learn and rehearse available but proscribed sexual scripts or patterns of behavior. And, of course, some guilt and anxiety center around the general disapproval of masturbation. After the early period of adolescence, in fact, most youths will not admit to their peers that they did or do it.

Nevertheless, masturbation is for most adolescent boys the major sexual activity, and they engage in it fairly frequently. It is an extremely positive and gratifying experience to them. Such an introduction to sexuality can lead to a capacity for detached sex activity—activity whose only sustaining motive is sexual. This may be the hallmark of male sexuality in our society.

Of the three sources of guilt and anxiety mentioned, the first—how to manage both sexuality and an attachment to family members—probably cuts across class lines. But the others should show remarkable class differences. The second one, how to manage a fairly elaborate and exotic fantasy life during masturbation, should be confined most typically to the higher classes, who are more experienced and adept at dealing with symbols. (It is possible, in fact, that this behavior, which girls rarely engage in, plays a role in the processes by which middle-class boys catch up with girls in measures of achievement and creativity and, by the end of adolescence, move out in front. However, this is only a hypothesis.)

The ability to fantasize during masturbation implies certain broad consequences. One is a tendency to see large parts of the environment in an erotic light, as well as the ability to respond, sexually and perhaps poetically, to many visual and auditory stimuli. We might also expect both a capacity and need for fairly elaborate forms of sexual activity. Further, since masturbatory fantasies generally deal with relationships and acts leading to coitus, they should also reinforce a developing capacity for heterosociality.

The third source of guilt and anxiety—the alleged "unmanliness" of masturbation—should more directly concern the lower-class male adolescent. ("Manliness" has always been an important value for lower-class males.) In these groups, social life is more often segregated by sex, and there are, generally, fewer rewarding social experiences from other sources. The adolescent therefore moves into heterosexual—if not heterosocial—relationships sooner than his middle-class counterparts. Sexual segregation makes it easier for him than for the middle-class boy to learn that he does not have to love everything he desires, and therefore to come more naturally to casual, if not exploitative, relationships. The second condition—fewer social rewards that his fellows would respect—should lead to an exaggerated concern for proving masculinity by direct displays of physical prowess, aggression, and visible sexual success. And these three, of course, may be mutually reinforcing.

In a sense, the lower-class male is the first to reach "sexual maturity" as defined by the Freudians. That is, he is generally the first to become aggressively heterosexual and exclusively genital. This characteristic, in fact, is a distinguishing difference between lower-class males and those above them socially.

But one consequence is that although their sex lives are almost exclusively heterosexual, they remain homosocial. They have intercourse with females, but the standards and the audience they refer to are those of their male fellows. Middle-class boys shift predominantly to coitus at a significantly later time. They, too, need and tend to have homosocial elements in their sexual lives. But their fantasies, their ability to symbolize, and their social training in a world in which distinctions between masculinity and femininity are less sharply drawn, allow them to withdraw more easily from an all-male world. This difference between social classes obviously has important consequences for stable adult relationships.

One thing common in male experience during adolescence is that while it provides much opportunity for sexual commitment, in one form or another, there is little training in how to handle emotional relations with girls. The imagery and rhetoric of romantic love is all around us; we are immersed in it. But whereas much is undoubtedly absorbed by the adolescent, he is not likely to tie it closely to his sexuality. In fact, such a connection

might be inhibiting, as indicated by the survival of the "bad-girl-who-does" and "good-girl-who-doesn't" distinction. This is important to keep in mind as we turn to the female side of the story.

In contrast to males, female sexual development during adolescence is so similar in all classes that it is easy to suspect that it is solely determined by biology. But, while girls do not have the same level of hormonal sensitization to sexuality at puberty as adolescent boys, there is little evidence of a biological or social inhibitor either. The "equipment" for sexual pleasure is clearly present by puberty, but tends not to be used by many females of any class. Masturbation rates are fairly low, and among those who do masturbate, fairly infrequent. Arousal from "sexual" materials or situations happens seldom, and exceedingly few girls report feeling sexually deprived during adolescence.

Basically, girls in our society are not encouraged to be sexual—and may be strongly discouraged from being so. Most of us accept the fact that while "bad boy" can mean many things, "bad girl" almost exclusively implies sexual delinquency. It is both difficult and dangerous for an adolescent girl to become too active sexually. As Joseph Rheingold puts it, where men need only fear sexual failure, women must fear both success and failure.

Does this long period of relative sexual inactivity among girls come from repression of an elemental drive, or merely from a failure to learn how to be sexual? The answers have important implications for their later sexual development. If it is repression, the path to a fuller sexuality must pass through processes of loss of inhibitions, during which the girl unlearns, in varying degrees, attitudes and values that block the expression of natural internal feelings. It also implies that the quest for ways to express directly sexual behavior and feelings that had been expressed nonsexually is secondary and of considerably less significance.

On the other hand, the "learning" answer suggests that women create or invent a capacity for sexual behavior, learning how and when to be aroused and how and when to respond. This approach implies greater flexibility; unlike the repression view, it makes sexuality both more and less than a basic force that may break loose at any time in strange or costly ways. The learning approach also lessens the power of sexuality altogether; all at once, particular kinds of sex activities need no longer be defined as either "healthy" or "sick." Lastly, subjectively, this approach appeals to the authors because it describes female sexuality in terms that seem less like a mere projection of male sexuality.

If sexual activity by adolescent girls assumes less specific forms than with boys, that does not mean that sexual learning and training do not occur. Curiously, though girls are, as a group, far less active sexually than boys, they receive far more training in self-consciously viewing themselves —and in viewing boys—as desirable mates. This is particularly true in recent years. Females begin early in adolescence to define attractiveness, at least partially, in sexual terms. We suspect that the use of sexual attractiveness for nonsexual purposes that marked our preadolescent "seductress" now begins to characterize many girls. Talcott Parsons' description of how the wife "uses" sex to bind the husband to the family, although harsh, may be quite accurate. More generally, in keeping with the childbearing and child-raising function of women, the development of a sexual role seems to involve a need to include in that role more than pleasure.

To round out the picture of the difference between the sexes, girls appear to be well-trained precisely in that area in which boys are poorly trained—that is, a belief in and a capacity for intense, emotionally charged relationships and the language of romantic love. When girls during this period describe having been aroused sexually, they more often report it as a response to romantic, rather than erotic, words and actions.

In later adolescence, as dates, parties, and other sociosexual activities increase, boys— committed to sexuality and relatively untrained in the language and actions of romantic love—interact with girls, committed to romantic love and relatively untrained in sexuality. Dating and courtship may well be considered processes in which each sex trains the other in what each wants and expects. What data are available suggest that this exchange system does not always work very smoothly. Thus, ironically, it is not uncommon to find that the boy becomes emotionally involved with his partner and therefore lets up on trying to seduce her, at the same time that the girl comes to feel that the boy's affection is genuine and therefore that sexual intimacy is more permissible.

In our recent study of college students, we found that boys typically had intercourse with their first coital partners one to three times, while with girls it was ten or more. Clearly, for the majority of females first intercourse becomes possible only in stable relationships or in those with strong bonds.

The male experience does conform to the general Freudian expectation that there is a developmental movement from a predominantly genital sexual commitment to a loving relationship with another person. But this movement is, in effect, reversed for females, with love or affection often a necessary precondition for intercourse. No wonder, therefore, that Freud had great difficulty understanding female sexuality—recall the concluding line in his great essay on women: "Woman, what does she want?" This "error"—the assumption that female sexuality is similar to or a mirror image of that of the male—may come from the fact that so many of those who constructed the theory were men. With Freud, in addition, we must remember the very concept of sexuality essential to most of 19th-century Europe—it was an elemental beast that had to be curbed.

It has been noted that there are very few class differences in sexuality among females, far fewer than among males. One difference, however, is very relevant to this discussion—the age of first intercourse. This varies inversely with social class—that is, the higher the class, the later the age of first intercourse—a relationship that is also true of first marriage. The correlation between these two ages suggests the necessary social and emotional linkage between courtship and the entrance into sexual activity on the part of women. A second difference, perhaps only indirectly related to social class, has to do with educational achievement: here, a sharp border line seems to separate from all other women those who have or have had graduate or professional work. If sexual success may be measured by the percentage of sex acts that culminate in orgasm, graduate and professional women are the most sexually successful women in the nation.

Why? One possible interpretation derives from the work of Abraham Maslow: Women who get so far in higher education are more likely to be more aggressive, perhaps to have strong needs to dominate; both these characteristics are associated with heightened sexuality. Another, more general interpretation would be that in a society in which girls are expected primarily to become wives and mothers, going on to graduate school represents a kind of deviancy—a failure of, or alienation from, normal female social adjustment. In effect, then, it would be this flawed socialization—not biology—that produced both commitment toward advanced training and toward heightened sexuality.

For both males and females, increasingly greater involvement in the social aspects of sexuality—"socializing" with the opposite sex —may be one factor that marks the end of adolescence. We know little about this transition, especially among noncollege boys and girls; but our present feeling is that sexuality plays an important role in it. First, sociosexuality is important in family formation and also in learning the roles and obligations involved in being an adult. Second, and more fundamental, late adolescence is when a youth is seeking, and experimenting toward finding, his identity—who and what he is and will be; and sociosexual activity is the one aspect of this exploration that we associate particularly with late adolescence.

Young people are particularly vulnerable at this time. This may be partly due to the fact that society has difficulty protecting the adolescent from the consequences of sexual behavior that it pretends he is not engaged in. But, more importantly, it may be because, at all ages, we all have great problems in discussing our sexual feelings and experiences in personal terms. These, in turn, make it extremely difficult to get support from others for an adolescent's experiments toward trying to invent his sexual self. We suspect that success or failure in the discovery or management of sexual identity may have consequences in personal development far beyond merely the sexual sphere—perhaps in confidence and feelings of self-worth, belonging, competence, guilt, force of personality, and so on.

In our society, all but a few ultimately marry. Handling sexual commitments inside marriage makes up the larger part of adult experience. Again, we have too little data for firm findings. The data we do have come largely from studies of broken and troubled marriages, and we do not know to what extent sexual problems in such marriages exceed those of intact marriages. It is possible that, because we have assumed that sex is important in most people's lives, we have exaggerated its importance in holding marriages together. Also, it is quite possible that, once people are married, sexuality declines relatively, becoming less important than other gratifications (such as domesticity or parenthood); or it may be that these other gratifications can minimize the effect of sexual dissatisfaction. Further, it may be possible that individuals learn to get sexual gratification, or an equivalent, from activities that are nonsexual, or only partially sexual.

The sexual desires and commitments of males are the main determinants of the rate of sexual activity in our society. Men are most interested in intercourse in the early years of marriage —woman's interest peaks much later; nonetheless, coital rates decline steadily throughout marriage. This decline derives from many things, only one of which is decline in biological capacity. With many men, it is more difficult to relate sexually to a wife who is pregnant or a mother. Lower-class adult men receive less support and plaudits from their male friends for married sexual performance than they did as single adolescents; and we might also add the lower-class disadvantage of less training in the use of auxiliary or symbolic sexually stimulating materials. For middle-class men, the decline is not as steep, owing perhaps to their greater ability to find stimulation from auxiliary sources, such as literature, movies, music, and romantic or erotic conversation. It should be further noted that for about 30 percent of college-educated men, masturbation continues regularly during marriage, even when the wife is available. An additional (if unknown) proportion do not physically masturbate, but derive additional excitement from the fantasies that accompany intercourse.

But even middle-class sexual activity declines more rapidly than bodily changes can account for. Perhaps the ways males learn to be sexual in our society make it very difficult to keep it up at a high level with the same woman for a long time. However, this may not be vital in maintaining the family, or even in the man's personal sense of well-being, because, as previously suggested, sexual dissatisfaction may become less important as other satisfactions increase. Therefore, it need seldom result in crisis.

About half of all married men and a quarter of all married women will have intercourse outside of marriage at one time or another. For women, infidelity seems to have been on the increase since the turn of the century—at the same time that their rates of orgasm have been increasing. It is possible that the very nature of female sexuality is changing. Work being done now may give us new light on this. For men, there are strong social-class differences—the lower class accounts for most extramarital activity, especially during the early years of marriage. We have observed that it is difficult for a lower-class man to acquire the appreciation of his fellows for married intercourse; extramarital sex, of course, is another matter.

In general, we feel that far from sexual needs affecting other adult concerns, the reverse may be true: adult sexual activity may become that aspect of a person's life most often used to act out other needs. There are some data that suggest this. Men who have trouble handling authority relationships at work more often have dreams about homosexuality; some others, under heavy stress on the job, have been shown to have more frequent episodic homosexual experiences. Such phenomena as the rise of sadomasochistic practices and experiments in group sex may also be tied to nonsexual tensions, the use of sex for nonsexual purposes.

It is only fairly recently in the history of man that he has been able to begin to understand that his own time and place do not embody some eternal principle or necessity, but are only dots on a continuum. It is difficult for many to believe that man can change, and is changing, in important ways. This conservative view is evident even in contemporary behavioral science; and a conception of man as having relatively constant sexual needs has become part of it. In an ever-changing world, it is perhaps comforting to think that man's sexuality does not change very much, and therefore is relatively easily explained. We cannot accept this. Instead, we have attempted to offer a description of sexual development as a variable social invention—an invention that in itself explains little, and require much continuing explanation.

Social Class and Parent–Child Relationships

MELVIN L. KOHN

THIS ESSAY IS AN ATTEMPT TO INTERpret, from a sociological perspective, the effects of social class upon parent–child relationships. Many past discussions of the problem seem somehow to lack this perspective, even though the problem is one of profound importance for sociology. Because most investigators have approached the problem from an interest in psychodynamics, rather than social structure, they have largely limited their attention to a few specific techniques used by mothers in the rearing of infants and very young children. They have discovered, *inter alia*, that social class has a decided bearing on which techniques parents use. But, since they have come at the problem from this perspective, their interest in social class has not gone beyond its effects for this very limited aspect of parent–child relationships.

Adapted from *American Journal of Sociology* **73**, 4 (January), 1963: 471–480. Copyright © 1963 by The University of Chicago Press.

The present analysis conceives the problem of social class and parent–child relationships as an instance of the more general problem of the effects of social structure upon behavior. It starts with the assumption that social class has proved to be so useful a concept because it refers to more than simply educational level, or occupation, or any of the large number of correlated variables. It is so useful because it captures the reality that the intricate interplay of all these variables creates different basic conditions of life at different levels of the social order. Members of different social classes, by virtue of enjoying (or suffering) different conditions of life, come to see the world differently—to develop different conceptions of social reality, different aspirations and hopes and fears, different conceptions of the desirable.

The last is particularly important for present purposes, for from people's conceptions of the desirable—and particularly from their conceptions of what characteristics are desirable in children—one can discern their objectives in child-rearing. Thus, conceptions of the desirable—that is, values[1]—become the key concept for this analysis, the bridge between position in the larger social structure and the behavior of the individual. The intent of the analysis is to trace the effects of social class position on parental values and the effects of values on behavior.

Since this approach differs from analyses focused on social class differences in the use of particular child-rearing techniques, it will be necessary to re-examine earlier formulations from the present perspective. Then three questions will be discussed, bringing into consideration the limited available data that are relevant: What differences are there in the values held by parents of different social classes? What is there about the conditions of life distinctive of these classes that might explain the differences in their values? What consequences do these differences in values have for parents' relationships with their children?

SOCIAL CLASS

Social classes will be defined as aggregates of individuals who occupy broadly similar positions in the scale of prestige.[2] In dealing with the research literature, we shall treat occupational position (or occupational position as weighted somewhat by education) as a serviceable index of social class for urban American society. And we shall adopt the model of social stratification implicit in most research, that of four relatively discrete classes: a "lower class" of unskilled manual workers, a "working class" of manual workers in semiskilled and skilled occupations, a "middle class" of white-collar workers and professionals, and an "elite," differentiated from the middle class not so much in terms of occupation as of wealth and lineage.

Almost all the empirical evidence, including that from our own research, stems from broad comparisons of the middle and working class. Thus we shall have little to say about the extremes of the class distribution. Furthermore, we shall have to act as if the middle and working classes were each homogeneous. They are not, even in terms of status considerations alone. There is evidence, for example, that within each broad social class, variations in parents' values quite regularly parallel gradations of social status. Moreover, the classes are heterogeneous with respect to other factors that affect parents' values, such as religion and ethnicity. But even when all such considerations are taken into account, the empirical evidence clearly shows that being on one side or the other of the line that divides manual from nonmanual workers has profound consequences for how one rears one's children.[3]

VALUES
OF MIDDLE- AND
WORKING-CLASS PARENTS

Of the entire range of values one might examine, it seems particularly strategic to focus on parents' conceptions of what characteristics would be most desirable for boys or girls the age of their own children. From this one can hope to discern the parents' goals in rearing their children. It must be assumed, however, that a parent will choose one characteristic as more desirable than another only if he considers it to be both important, in the sense that failure to develop this characteristic would affect the child adversely, and problematic, in the sense that it is neither to be taken for granted that the child will develop that characteristic not impossible for him to do so. In interpreting parents' value choices, we must keep in mind that their choices reflect not simply their goals but the goals whose achievement they regard as problematic.

Few studies, even in recent years, have directly investigated the relationship of social class to parental values. Fortunately, however, the results of these few are in essential agreement. The earliest study was Evelyn Millis Duvall's pioneering inquiry of 1946.[4] Duvall characterized working-class (and lower middle-class) parental values as "traditional"—they want their children to be neat and clean, to obey and respect adults, to please adults. In contrast to this emphasis on how the child comports himself, middle-class parental values are more "developmental"—they want their children to be eager to learn, to love and confide in the parents, to be happy, to share and cooperate, to be healthy and well.

Duvall's traditional-developmental dichotomy does not describe the difference between middle- and working-class parental values quite exactly, but it does point to the essence of the difference: working-class parents want the child to conform to externally imposed standards, while middle-class parents are far more attentive to his internal dynamics.

The few relevant findings of subsequent studies are entirely consistent with this basic point, especially in the repeated indications that working-class parents put far greater stress on obedience to parental commands than do middle-class parents.[5] Our own research, conducted in 1956–57, provides the evidence most directly comparable to Duvall's.[6] We, too, found that working-class parents value obedience, neatness, and cleanliness more highly than do middle-class parents, and that middle-class parents in turn value curiosity, happiness, consideration, and—most importantly—self-control more highly than do working-class parents. We further found that there are characteristic clusters of value choice in the two social classes: working-class parental values center on conformity to external proscriptions, middle-class parental values on *self*-direction. To working-class parents, it is the overt act that matters: the child should not transgress externally imposed rules; to middle-class parents, it is the child's motives and feelings that matter: the child should govern himself.

In fairness, it should be noted that middle- and working-class parents share many core values. Both, for example, value honesty very highly —although, characteristically, "honesty" has rather different connotations in the two social classes, implying "trustworthiness" for the working class and "truthfulness" for the middle class. The common theme, of course, is that parents of both social classes value a decent respect for the rights of others; middle- and working-class values are but variations on this common theme. The reason for emphasizing the variations rather than the common theme is that they seem to have far-ranging consequences for parents' relationships with their children and thus ought to be taken seriously.

It would be good if there were more evidence about parental values—data from other studies, in other locales, and especially, data derived from more than one mode of inquiry. But, what evidence we do have is consistent, so that there is at least some basis for believing it is reliable. Furthermore, there is evidence that the value choices made by parents in these inquiries are not simply a reflection of their assessments of their own children's deficiencies or excellences. Thus, we may take the findings of these studies as providing a limited, but probably valid, picture of the parents' generalized conceptions of what behavior would be desirable in their preadolescent children.

EXPLAINING CLASS DIFFERENCES IN PARENTAL VALUES

That middle-class parents are more likely to espouse some values, and working-class parents other values, must be a function of differences in their conditions of life. In the present state of our knowledge, it is difficult to disentangle the interacting variables with a sufficient degree of exactness to ascertain which conditions of life are crucial to the differences in values. Nevertheless, it is necessary to examine the principal components of class differences in life conditions to see what each may contribute.

The logical place to begin is with occupational differences, for these are certainly preeminently important, not only in defining social classes in urban, industrialized society, but also in determining much else about people's life conditions.[7] There are at last three respects in which middle-class occupations typically differ from working-class occupations, above and beyond their obvious status-linked differences in security, stability of income, and general social prestige. One is that middle-class occupations deal more with the manipulation of interpersonal relations, ideas, and symbols, while working-class occupations deal more with the manipulation of things. The second is that middle-class occupations are more subject to self-direction, while working-class occupations are more subject to standardization and direct supervision. The third is that getting ahead in middle-class occupations is more dependent upon one's own actions, while in working-class occupations it is more dependent upon collective action, particularly in unionized industries. From these differences, one can sketch differences in the characteristics that make for getting along, and getting ahead, in middle- and working-class occupations. Middle-class occupations require a greater degree of self-direction; working-class occupations, in larger measure, require that one follow explicit rules set down by someone in authority.

Obviously, these differences parallel the differences we have found between the two social classes in the characteristics valued by parents for children. At minimum, one can conclude that there is a congruence between occupational requirements and parental values. It is, moreover, a reasonable supposition, although not a necessary conclusion, that middle- and working-class parents value different characteristics in children *because* of these differences in their occupational circumstances. This supposition does not necessarily assume that parents consciously train their children to meet future occupational requirements; it may simply be that their own occupational experiences have significantly affected parents' conceptions of what is desirable behavior, on or off the job, for adults or for children.[8]

These differences in occupational circumstances are probably basic to the differences we have found between middle- and working-class parental values, but taken alone they do not sufficiently explain them. Parents need not accord preeminent importance to occupational requirements in their judgments of what is most desirable. For a sufficient explanation of class differences in values, it is necessary to recognize that other differences in middle- and working-class conditions of life reinforce the differences in occupational circumstances at every turn.

Educational differences, for example, above and beyond their importance as determinants of occupation, probably contribute independently to the differences in middle- and working-class parental values. At minimum, middle-class parents' greater attention to the child's internal dynamics is facilitated by their learned ability to deal with the subjective and the ideational. Furthermore, differences in levels and stability of income undoubtedly contribute to class differences in parental values. That middle-class parents still have somewhat higher levels of income, and much greater stability of income, makes them able to take for granted the respectability that is still problematic for working-class parents. They can afford to concentrate, instead, on motives and feelings—which, in the circumstances of their lives, are more important.

These considerations suggest that the differences between middle- and working-class parental values are probably a function of the entire complex of differences in life conditions characteristic of the two social classes. Consider, for example, the working-class situation. With the end of mass immigration, there has emerged a stable working class, largely derived from the manpower of rural areas, uninterested in mobility into the middle class, but very much interested in security, respectability, and the enjoyment of a decent standard of living.[9] This working class has come to enjoy a standard of living formerly reserved for the middle class, but has not chosen a middle-class style of life. In effect, the working class has striven for, and partially achieved, an American dream distinctly different from the dream of success and achievement. In an affluent society, it is possible for the worker to be the traditionalist—politically, economically, and, most relevant here, in his values for his children.[10] Working-class parents want their children to conform to external authority because the parents themselves are willing to accord respect to authority, in return for security and respectability. Their conservatism in child-rearing is part of a more general conservatism and traditionalism.

Middle-class parental values are a product of a quite different set of conditions. Much of what the working class values, they can take for granted. Instead, they can—and must—instill in their children a degree of self-direction that would be less appropriate to the conditions of life of the working class.[11] Certainly, there is substantial truth in the characterization of the middle-class way of life as one of great conformity. What must be noted here, however, is that *relative to* the working class, middle-class conditions of life require a more substantial degree of independence of action. Furthermore, the higher levels of education enjoyed by the middle class make possible a degree of internal scrutiny difficult to achieve without the skills in dealing with the abstract that college training sometimes provides. Finally, the economic security of most middle-class occupations, the level of income they provide, the status they confer, allow one to focus his attention on the subjective and the ideational. Middle-class conditions of life both allow and demand a greater degree of self-direction than do those of the working class.

CONSEQUENCES OF CLASS DIFFERENCES IN PARENTS' VALUES

What consequences do the differences between middle- and working-class parents' values have for the ways they raise their children?

Much of the research on techniques of infant- and child-training is of little relevance here. For example, with regard to parents' preferred techniques for disciplining children, a question of major interest to many investigators, Bronfenbrenner summarizes past studies as follows: "In matters of discipline, working-class parents are consistently more likely to employ physical punishment, while middle-class families rely more on reasoning, isolation, appeals to guilt, and other methods involving the threat of loss of love."[12] This, if still true,[13] is consistent with middle-class parents' greater atten-

tiveness to the child's internal dynamics, working-class parents' greater concern about the overt act. For present purposes, however, the crucial question is not *which* disciplinary method parents prefer, but when and why they use one or another method of discipline.

The most directly relevant available data are on the conditions under which middle- and working-class parents use physical punishment. Working-class parents are apt to resort to physical punishment when the direct and immediate consequences of their children's disobedient acts are most extreme, and to refrain from punishing when this might provoke an even greater disturbance.[14] Thus, they will punish a child for wild play when the furniture is damaged or the noise level becomes intolerable, but ignore the same actions when the direct and immediate consequences are not so extreme. Middle-class parents, on the other hand, seem to punish or refrain from punishing on the basis of their interpretation of the child's intent in acting as he does. Thus, they will punish a furious outburst when the context is such that they interpret it to be a loss of self-control, but will ignore an equally extreme outburst when the context is such that they interpret it to be merely an emotional release.

It is understandable that working-class parents react to the consequences rather than to the intent of their children's actions: the important thing is that the child not transgress externally imposed rules. Correspondingly, if middle-class parents are instead concerned about the child's motives and feelings, they can and must look beyond the overt act to why the child acts as he does. It would seem that middle- and working-class values direct parents to see their children's misbehavior in quite different ways, so that misbehavior which prompts middle-class parents to action does not seem as important to working-class parents, and vice versa.[15] Obviously, parents' values are not the only things that enter into their use of physical punishment. But unless one assumes a complete lack of goal-directedness in parental behavior, he would have to grant that parents' values direct their attention to some facets of their own and their children's behavior, and divert it from other facets.

The consequences of class differences in parental values extend far beyond differences in disciplinary practices. From a knowledge of their values for their children, one would expect middle-class parents to feel a greater obligation to be *supportive* of the children, if only because of their sensitivity to the children's internal dynamics. Working-class values, with their emphasis upon conformity to external rules, should lead to greater emphasis upon the parents' obligation to impose constraints.[16] And this, according to Bronfenbrenner, is precisely what has been shown in those few studies that have concerned themselves with the over-all relationship of parents to child: "Over the entire twenty-five year period studied, parent-child relationships in the middle class are consistently reported as more acceptant and equalitarian, while those in the working-class are oriented toward maintaining order and obedience."[17]

This conclusion is based primarily on studies of *mother*-child relationships in middle- and working-class families. Class differences in parental values have further ramifications for the father's role.[18] Mothers in each class would have their husbands play a role facilitative of the child's development of the characteristics valued in that class: Middle-class mothers want their husbands to be supportive of the children (especially of sons), with their responsibility for imposing constraints being of decidedly secondary importance; working-class mothers look to their husbands to be considerably more directive—support is accorded far less importance and constraint far more. Most middle-class fathers agree with their wives and play a role close to what their wives would have them play. Many working-class fathers, on the other hand, do not. It is not that they see the constraining role as less important than do their wives, but that many of them see no reason why they should have to shoulder the responsibility. From their point of view, the important thing is that the child be taught what limits he must not transgress. It does not much matter who does the teaching, and since mother has primary responsibility for child care, the job should be hers.

The net consequence is a quite different division of parental responsibilities in the two social classes. In middle-class families, mother's and father's roles usually are not sharply differentiated. What differentiation exists is largely a matter of each parent

taking special responsibility for being supportive of children of the parent's own sex. In working-class families, mother's and father's role are more sharply differentiated, with mother almost always being the more supportive parent. In some working-class families, mother specializes in support, father in constraint; in others, perhaps in most, mother raises the children, father provides the wherewithal.[19]

Thus, the differences in middle- and working-class parents' values have wide ramifications for their relationships with their children and with each other. Of course, many class differences in parent–child relationships are not directly attributable to differences in values; undoubtedly the very differences in their conditions of life that make for differences in parental values reinforce, at every juncture, parents' characteristic ways of relating to their children. But one could not account for these consistent differences in parent–child relationships in the two social classes without reference to the differences in parents' avowed values.

CONCLUSION

This paper serves to show how complex and demanding are the problems of interpreting the effects of social structure on behavior. Our inquiries habitually stop at the point of demonstrating that social position correlates with something, when we should want to pursue the question, "Why?" What are the processes by which position in social structure molds behavior? The present analysis has dealt with this question in one specific form: Why does social class matter for parents' relationships with their children? There is every reason to believe that the problems encountered in trying to deal with that question would recur in any analysis of the effects of social structure on behavior.

In this analysis, the concept of "values" has been used as the principal bridge from social position to behavior. The analysis has endeavored to show that middle-class parental values differ from those of working-class parents; that these differences are rooted in basic differences between middle- and working-class conditions of life; and that the differences between middle- and working-class parental values have important consequences for their relationships with their children. The interpretive model, in essence, is: social class—conditions of life—values—behavior.

The specifics of the present characterization of parental values may prove to be inexact; the discussion of the ways in which social class position affects values is undoubtedly partial; and the tracing of the consequences of differences in values for differences in parent–child relationships is certainly tentative and incomplete. I trust, however, that the perspective will prove to be valid and that this formulation will stimulate other investigators to deal more directly with the processes whereby social structure affects behavior.

NOTES

1. "A value is a conception, explicit or implicit, distinctive of an individual or characteristic of a group, of the desirable which influences the selection from available modes, means, and ends of action." Clyde Kluckhohn, Values and value orientations. In Talcott Parsons and Edward A. Shils (eds.), *Toward a general theory of action.* Cambridge, Mass.: Harvard University Press, 1951, p. 395. See also the discussion of values in Robin M. Williams, Jr., *American society: a sociological interpretation.* New York: Knopf, Inc., 1951, chap. xi, and his discussion of social class and culture on p. 101.

2. Williams, *op. cit.*, p. 89.

3. These, and other assertions of fact not referred to published sources, are based on research my colleagues and I have conducted. For the design of this research and the principal substantive findings see my Social class and parental values. *American Journal of Sociology* 64, January 1959: 337–351; my Social class and the exercise of parental authority. *American Sociological Review* 24, June 1959: 352–366; and with Eleanor E. Carroll, Social class and the allocation of parental responsibilities. *Sociometry* 23, December 1960: 372–392. I should like to express appreciation to my principal collaborators in this research, John A. Clausen and Eleanor E. Carroll.

4. Conceptions of parenthood. *American Journal of Sociology* 52, November 1946: 193–203.

5. Alex Inkeles has shown that this is true not only for the United States but for a number of other industrialized societies as well. Industrial man: the relation of status to experience, perception, and value. *American Journal of Sociology* 66, July 1960: 20–21 and Table 9.

6. Social class and parental values, *op. cit.*

7. For a thoughtful discussion of the influence of occupational role on parental values see David F. Aberle and Kaspar D. Naegele, Middle-class fathers' occupational role and attitudes toward children. *American Journal of Orthopsychiatry* 22, April 1952: 366–378.

8. Two objections might be raised here. (1) Occupational experiences may not be important for a mother's values, however crucial they are for her husband's, if she has had little or no work experience. But even those mothers who have had little or no occupational experience know something of occupational life from their husbands and others, and live in a culture in which occupation and career permeate all of life. (2) Parental values may be built not so much out of their own experiences as out of their expectations of the child's future experiences. This might seem particularly plausible in explaining working-class values, for their high valuation of such stereotypically *middle-class* characteristics as obedience, neatness, and cleanliness might imply that they are training their children for a middle-class life they expect the children to achieve. Few working-class parents, however, do expect (or even want) their children to go on to college and the middle-class jobs for which a college education is required. This is shown in Herbert H. Hyman, The value systems of different classes: a social psychological contribution to the analysis of stratification. In Reinhard Bendix and Seymour Martin Lipset (eds.), *Class, status and power: a reader in social stratification.* Glencoe, Ill.: Free Press, 1953, and confirmed in unpublished data from our own research.

9. See, e.g., S. M. Miller and Frank Riessman, The working-class subculture: a new view. *Social Problems* 9, Summer 1961: 86–97.

10. Relevant here is Seymour Martin Lipset's somewhat disillusioned Democracy and working-class authoritarianism. *American Sociological Review* 24, August 1959: 482–501.

11. It has been argued that as larger and larger proportions of the middle class have become imbedded in a bureaucratic way of life—in distinction to the entrepreneurial way of life of a bygone day—it has become more appropriate to raise children to be accommodative than to be self-reliant. But this point of view is a misreading of the conditions of life faced by the middle-class inhabitants of the bureaucratic world. Their jobs require at least as great a degree of self-reliance as do entrepreneurial enterprises. We tend to forget, nowadays, just how little the small- or medium-sized entrepreneur controlled the conditions of his own existence and just how much he was subjected to the petty authority of those on whose pleasure depended

the survival of his enterprise. And we fail to recognize the degree to which monolithic-seeming bureaucracies allow free play for—in fact, require—individual enterprise of new sorts: in the creation of ideas, the building of empires, the competition for advancement.

At any rate, our data show no substantial differences between the values of parents from bureaucratic and entrepreneurial occupational worlds, in either social class. But see Daniel R. Miller and Guy E. Swanson, *The changing American parent: a study in the Detroit area.* New York: Wiley, 1958.

12. Urie Bronfenbrenner, Socialization and social class through time and space. In Eleanor Maccoby, Theodore Newcomb, and Eugene L. Hartley (eds.), *Readings in social psychology.* New York: Holt, Rinehart and Winston, 1958, pp. 400–425.

13. Later studies, including our own, do not show this difference.

14. Social class and the exercise of parental authority, *op. cit.*

15. This is not to say that the methods used by parents of either social class are necessarily the most efficacious for achievement of their goals.

16. The justification for treating support and constraint as the two major dimensions of parent–child relationships lies in the theoretical argument of Talcott Parsons and Robert F. Bales, *Family, socialization, and interaction process.* Glencoe, Ill.: Free Press, 1955, esp. p. 45, and the empirical argument of Earl S. Schafer, A circumplex model for maternal behavior. *Journal of Abnormal and Social Psychology* 59, September 1959: 226–234.

17. Bronfenbrenner, *op. cit.*, p. 425.

18. From the very limited evidence available at the time of his review, Bronfenbrenner tentatively concluded: "though the middle-class father typically has a warmer relationship with the child, he is also likely to have more authority and status in family affairs" (*ibid.*, p. 422). The discussion here is based largely on subsequent research, esp. Social class and the allocation of parental responsibilities, *op. cit.*

19. Fragmentary data suggest sharp class differences in the husband-wife relationship that complement the differences in the division of parental responsibilities discussed above. For example, virtually no working-class wife reports that she and her husband ever go out on an evening or weekend without the children. And few working-class fathers do much to relieve their wives of the burden of caring for the children all the time. By and large, working-class fathers seem to lead a largely separate social life from that of their wives; the wife has full-time responsibility for the children, while the husband is free to go on his own way.

Chapter 8

The Later Years

THIS CHAPTER FOCUSES ON THE LATER years in the family's life cycle: the postparental stage and the aged family. The postparental stage of the family life cycle begins after the children leave home and the role of parent is no longer centrally salient for the husband and the wife. It is a 20th-century development stemming from shifts in fertility values, improved health and birth control technologies, that have resulted in smaller families, women completing their childbearing years earlier, and the increased life-expectancy of adults. There are two contradictory explanations as to the effects of this stage on the parents. On the one hand, the "empty-nest syndrome" sees the postparental stage as a lonely, depressing time, especially for the mother. On the other hand, it is felt that the postparental stage is a time for greater freedom and independence. Husband and wife, the original dyad, are together again, and they may enjoy a strong relationship without having to be concerned with the responsibilities for children.

Pauline Bart and Irwin Deutscher explore these contradictory explanations. Bart studied hospitalized depressed women between the ages of 40 and 59. She found that housewives who had overprotective relationships with their children are most likely to be depressed when their children leave home. Since the most salient role for the woman, that of mother, is no longer available nor important, the mother suffers both socially and psychologically. However, the woman who has prepared herself for this stage of the family life cycle by having an identity and self-image other than that of mother finds herself mentally healthier and better adjusted.

Deutscher suggests that some parents start learning the role behavior of the postparental stage while the children are still at home. This preparation for a forthcoming stage of the life cycle constitutes "anticipatory socialization," which later functions to help parents in their adjustment to the new stage. The adults Deutscher studied regard the postparental stage as "a time for new freedoms."

The reading on the aged family is aimed to dispel a myth surrounding the elderly. Ethel Shanas questions the myth that the elderly in our society are isolated. In a cross-cultural study analyzing the kin networks of the elderly, Shanas sees the family and kin networks as providing the primary psychological support for the elderly. Most are not shown to be isolated, and they have active contact with their family. However, we cannot assume that the quantity of interaction is positively related to its quality. In Chapter 11, Arlie Hochschild explains the emergence of old-age communes as a consequence of the inadequacy of the communication between the elderly and their families. Perhaps the best predictor of the quality of contact is the kind of contact between parents and children in earlier stages of the family life cycle.

There is general agreement that a major problem faced by the aged in the United States is a lack of resources, particularly economic ones. There has been little social planning with regard to the needs of the elderly. The elderly, most of whom live on fixed incomes, are particularly hard hit during times of rising living costs and rising prices (inflation) such as have been experienced in the United States in the years following the Vietnam War and into the present.

If youth is in many ways the most desirable age period in America, old age is generally the least desirable stage in the life cycle. A society which values new ideas, new products, new styles, and new ways of doing things and is suspicious of tradition and the past is not going to welcome old age nor accord high prestige to the elderly. With the exception of some older politicians and businessmen who retain high power and social prestige, most aged Americans have few important roles to play. While technology and medicine have prolonged life, our culture has failed to prepare persons for the transition from relatively productive middle-age years to the generally nonproductive retirement years. For many, old age "represents a devalued, unstructured role with sharp discontinuities from middle-age. Hence, the individual enters the situation with little incentive, role specification, or preparation."[1] Nor have we really questioned whether the later years need be nonproductive. Groups of senior citizens such as the Grey Panthers have called into question the concept of retirement

as a period of inactivity or second childhood. They call upon elderly persons to engage actively in political and social change work.

The articles can be approached through the three frameworks. A symbolic interactionist might be concerned with the following questions: How do the new role behavior stages come to be defined? How is the development of new role definitions impeded? What are the differential types of anticipatory socialization for the male and the female? How do the elderly define their roles in the kin network?

The structural functionalist would be concerned with the following: What are the consequences of anticipatory socialization for the postparental stage, and how may its absence lead to role strain? How are the aged integrated into the society? What functions does the extended family network have for the elderly?

The conflict theorist would be interested in studying how society's view of women may lead to the "empty nest" syndrome. How do behavior expectations for women as reproducers of labor lead to the problems women may exhibit in the postparental stage? What contradictions exist in the society so that the needs of many of the elderly, for example, those that do not have children, are not met?

NOTE

1. Leo Simmons, Social participation of the aged in different cultures. *Annals of the American Academy of Political and Social Science* **279**, 1952: 45.

The Loneliness
of the Long-distance Mother

PAULINE BART

*I don't want to be alone, and I'm going to be alone, and my
children will go their way and get married...of which I'm wishing
for it...and then I'll still be alone, and I got more and more alone,
and more and more alone.*

Sara

MIDDLE AGE, LIKE ADOLESCENCE, IS A
time of physiological as well as sociological
changes. At one time the stress often characterizing
both these ages was considered physiological in origin and therefore universal. In order to test the so-
called *Sturm und Drang* hypothesis concerning
adolescents, Margaret Mead went to Samoa where
she found adolescence not stressful at all. As there
seemed little reason to assume significant
physiological differences between Americans and
Samoans, she reasoned that adolescent stress in
Western nations had cultural origins. I went to
other cultures—unfortunately only through their
anthropological records—to learn whether the
changes of mid-life were psychologically stressful
for women, thus becoming, as it were, the Margaret
Mead of the menopause. I studied the roles available to women who were past childbearing and
whether women typically had problems with menopause.[1] I was particularly looking for an absence of
depression appearing for the first time in middle
age.

Unfortunately, data on the menopause were
scarce—available for only five out of the thirty
societies I studied. Clearly, anthropologists are
generally male and thus not interested in pursuing
such information—or unable to, for when the
anthropologists were female or when teams included females, information about menopause was
reported. Psychiatric data were also scarce, but
there was enough information on post-maternal
roles and on the relative status of women to allow
me to determine whether that status rose or fell in
middle age.

It appears that in each culture there is a
favored stage in the life cycle of women. For instance, if a woman has high status when she is
young, her power and prestige can be expected to
decline as she matures, and vice versa. Rather than
the usual image of society as a pyramid or ladder,
one can think of society as a social Ferris wheel.[2] I
attempted to correlate these age-related changes in
status with cultural and structural factors in the
society, paying special attention to roles for post-
menopausal women.

Most cultures had definite roles that women
were expected to fill after they were through with
childbearing and child-rearing, but these roles
varied from society to society. They included, in
addition to the wife role, the roles of grandmother,
economic producer, mother and mother-in-law,
participant in government, performer of magic and
ritual, and daughter of aged parents. The higher-
status roles on the list were those of grandmother,
mother-in-law and participator in government,
since the available economic role for women was
generally limited to performing hard work of little
prestige.

Using the following indices for higher status—more freedom (especially from taboos), more
respect, special privileges and more power and
influence—I found that in seventeen out of the
thirty cultures, women registered *higher* status

This article draws on data used in Pauline Bart,
Mother Portnoy's complaint, *Trans-Action* (Novem-
ber-December 1970). Reprinted by permission of the
author.

during middle age by at least one index. (Middle age will be defined here as the years from 40 to 65.) In twelve out of the thirty they had more respect, in eight they had more power and influence, in seven they had special privileges, and in four they had more freedom. In eleven cultures middle-aged women registered neither an increase nor a decrease in social status on any of these indices. In only two cultures, those of the Marquesans and the Trobrianders—cultures in a number of ways similar to our own—did women have less power and influence in middle age than they did when they were younger.

The cross-cultural study therefore indicated that middle age was not usually considered an especially stressful period for women. Consequently, purely biological explanations of the stress felt at this time by Western women can be rejected. Middle age need not be fraught with difficulty.

It needs to be noted, however, that a major buffer against problems facing women in mid-life has been the kinship group. The literature I surveyed showed that a strong tie to family and kin rather than a strong marital tie, an extended-family system rather than a nuclear-family system, an institutionalized grandmother role, a mother-in-law role rather than no role for a woman in relationship to her son- or daughter-in-law, plus residence patterns keeping one close to one's parents and siblings—all these factors strengthen kinship ties and tend to improve the woman's position in middle age. Thus, very clearly, a woman's status after she stops bearing children can be associated with the structural arrangements and cultural values of her society. Specifically, the associations which follow seem to hold true:

Raised status in middle age	*Lowered status in middle age*
Strong mother-child relationship reciprocal in later life	Weak maternal bond, adult-oriented culture
Institutionalized grandmother role	Noninstitutionalized grandmother role, grandmother role not important
Institutionalized mother-in-law role	Noninstitutionalized mother-in-law role, mother-in-law does not train daughter-in-law
Extensive menstrual taboos	Minimal menstrual taboos
Matrilocal, patrilocal, or duolocal residence pattern	Residence pattern that isolates women from kin and grown children, e.g. neolocal, avuncular
Age valued over youth	Youth valued over age

Turning to our own society with this chart in mind, we can begin to see why middle-aged women so often feel stress. In each instance, except for the mother–child bond, which in our society is strong but nonreciprocal, we fall on the right side, where the status of women drops in middle age. For women whose lives have not been child-centered and whose strong marital ties continue, or for those whose children set up residence near them, the transition to middle age may be buffered. But child-centered women note that the relationship with their children is nonreciprocal—that all they are entitled to is "respect." A child once reaching maturity in our culture need honor and look after her/his mother only on Mother's Day, unless she is widowed. And both for these women, and for those who have emphasized the maternal role or the glamour role, middle age may be a difficult stage in the life cycle. Our emphasis on youth and our stipulation that mothers-in-law should not interfere and grandmothers not meddle makes the middle years a time of stress for many thousands, if not millions, of American women.[3] But let one such woman, one of twenty I interviewed and tested in mental hospitals, speak for herself.

Raised status in middle age	*Lowered status in middle age*
Strong tie to parents, siblings, cousins and other kin	Marital tie stronger than tie to nuclear family
Extended-family system	Nuclear-family system
Reproduction important	Sex an end in itself

SARA: THE MARTYR MOTHER

This is Sara's second admission to a mental hospital. The first time, the diagnosis was "psychophysiological gastrointestinal reaction," but this time, knowing more about her, doctors have diagnosed "involutional depression."

Sara is Jewish. In her early sixties, she is divorced and in what has been called the "empty nest" stage. She represents an almost ideal type of all of the problems that beset an aging woman in our society, in addition to some that began in childhood. Not only did her mother reject her, not only did her husband reject her, but now her children and grandchildren are rejecting her, and she is unable to participate in work or voluntary activities that could give her life meaning because she is physically ill, and transportation is inaccessible. She needs to keep busy, and her activities are severely restricted. She must live alone, and she is phobic about being alone.

Sara has had many physical problems—arthritis, kidney trouble, and, at the time I saw her, severely swollen feet. She has had a hysterectomy and gall bladder surgery. According to her record, her frightened, depressed state was "induced by fear of living in an apartment in Las Vegas where she felt abandoned and unprotected." This feeling has been present "ever since she was asked to move out of her son's home in order to placate the anger of her daughter-in-law who felt she caused trouble by trying to absorb all of her son's time and sympathy." Her (male) psychiatrist characterizes Sara as hypochondriachal and self-pitying.

I asked Sara one question and she immediately launched into a long description of her troubles: her fears of being alone, the failure of medication to alleviate these fears, her physical illnesses, and more:

> I first of all have a lot of fears, and it isn't very easy I guess...to do something about it. And...these fears just follow me, and just push me in the wrong direction. I'm not really doing what I want to do. I want to go one way, but it just seems to take me the other way and I—can't control them.... The minute nobody's here, and those fears start working with me. Everything seems closed up, and everything looks dark.

Sara told me that as a child she felt she was "really nothing." Her Russian-born father died when she was about six, but she always felt close to him. Even now she believes that if he had lived,

> He would have always made me feel that I'm not alone, and that someone loves me. I am very strong for love.... This is a very big thing to me, and I wasn't very fortunate because Mother didn't give it to me, and I was hungry for it, and when I married I also thought it was going to be a wonderful thing because somebody is going to care, but my marriage never turned out good.

While Sara's first child, a son, was a baby, her husband started a produce store. Sara would go to the store four miles from their home at four o'clock in the morning in a horse and wagon holding the baby in her arms, feeding him.

> I worked hard my whole life and I thought that if I worked for him he would—he would be good to me, but he took all that good [I gave him] ...He didn't feel that I was human, too.

A daughter was born, but the marriage continued no better. Her husband was repeatedly unfaithful, and apparently contracted venereal disease. Since he needed to work during the night, he refused to let her have company during the day or evening so that he could rest and sleep. He was rude to her friends. And "even with sex he was very, very rude about it."

Me: How was he rude with sex?
Sara: Very much so. He was concerned ...about himself nothing about me. ...He had another woman that he took out, and I found out about it, but I didn't let on. I thought, well, if that's a weakness, maybe he'll overcome it. Let me try and, uh, cope with it enough to see if I couldn't get him to reason...maybe later I could. But I couldn't. He would always run away when I wanted to reason with him. He would slam the door and go away for a few days, come back and throw the dirty clothes into the bathroom hamper, and everything was coming to him, but nothing was coming to me.
Me: Were you ever able to have sex satisfactory for you?

Sara: I say no. He—he always felt that he was tired and it was "necessary" and it "wasn't necessary" when he thought it was. [What she apparently means is that he had sexual relations with her only when he wanted to.]

Years later, with her son in the army and her daughter still at home, Sara decided she could not "take" her marriage anymore. She divorced her husband. But after the divorce she became very frightened about having to be on her own. Although she had a job at the time, this did little to lessen her insecurity. In addition, she was "very hurt" at having had to get a divorce. This feeling was heightened whenever she sublet her apartment; her tenants made her feel it wasn't "nice" to divorce. It never occurred to her to consult a psychiatrist, either during her marriage or immediately after her divorce because "At those times if you went to a psychiatrist people thought you were insane."

She became physically ill immediately after the divorce. She had to have gall bladder surgery. Then she became anemic and had to be under a doctor's care. Then, nine years after the divorce, a hysterectomy was necessary. Ever since this operation she believes she has been "entirely different." "To me it feels like Sara died."

Sara has four grandchildren. When they were very small she took care of them, but now that they are older she is expected to leave them alone. Their lack of concern and respect hurts her, although she loves them "very dearly." Some years ago on the advice of her doctor and at the invitation of her daughter-in-law she left her home in New Jersey and went to Las Vegas to reap the benefits of the Nevada climate and to live with and help take care of her son's family. But when the grandchildren matured, Sara was no longer needed. Rather than tell her this, the daughter-in-law tried to drive Sara out with unkind treatment: "She just treated me so that—it just made me go. You know what I mean? You can treat a person enough to make them feel they want to go."

At that time her daughter in New Jersey was expecting a baby and so Sara seized the chance to go and help her. Before she left, her son told her that if she wanted to return to Las Vegas she would have to find another place to live. He pointed out

that perhaps she hadn't realized that living with them was a "temporary thing." Sara believes her daughter-in-law pressured him to do this. In New Jersey, she contacted friends to see whether she could remain in the East, but no one was willing to help her.

She returned to Las Vegas and tried to find work as a saleslady, but this was possible only during the Christmas rush.

It's very difficult in that town to get a job at my age, because it's considered as attraction and they—hire the young girls. . . . I couldn't get no work and I was pretty disappointed because I felt that there was nothing else in this Vegas that I could do.

She had belonged to the Sisterhood of the local temple and enjoyed attending services, being present at meetings and doing volunteer work. Now, living alone, she needed transportation so that she could participate in these activities. When her son did take her to services, he would rush her home as soon as possible after they were over, saying, "I'm not going to stay here all night, you know."

She asked her daughter-in-law, who was active in the Sisterhood, to inform the temple that she would be willing to help with any work that needed to be done. Her daughter-in-law said,

"They don't want people like you. Our organization wants young people. . .they want young blood that can do things. . . . What can you do?"

Not only was Sara unable to do volunteer work, she was no longer permitted to sing in the choir. When the synagogue had been small the cantor had asked her to sing. Then the Jewish community had built a larger temple and hired a new cantor who limited participation to people who could read music. Sara asked for a chance to learn how, but the cantor never offered to teach her or have anyone else teach her.

I asked Sara if she had been happier before her children left home, and she said, "Yes and no. Because my husband never let any of us enjoy it." When I asked specifically what changes in her own feelings of self-worth she had noticed since her children left, she replied: "I don't...I don't feel like...I don't feel at all that I'm wanted. I just feel like nothing."

Then I asked Sara what was the worst thing that had ever happened to her.

When I had to break up and be by myself, and be alone, and I'm just—I really feel that I'm not—not only not loved but not even liked sometimes by my own children.... They could respect me. If—they can't say good why should they...hurt my feelings and make me cry, and then call me a crybaby, or tell me that I ought to know better or something like that. My worst thing is that I'm alone, I'm not wanted, nobody interested themselves in me. Nobody cares.

Sara couldn't think of the best thing that had ever happened to her, but the best times of her life, she said, were when she was pregnant and when her children were babies.

I was glad that God gave me...the privilege of being a mother and—and I loved them. In fact, I wrapped my love so much around them.

She felt grateful to her husband, since "if it weren't for him it wouldn't be the children. *They were my whole life, that was it.*"

ROLE LOSS, RELIGION, AND DEPRESSION; OR WHY NOT TO BE A JEWISH MOTHER

Sara was typical in many ways of the twenty middle-aged women I interviewed in mental hospitals,[4] all but one of whom were or had been married and had children. All but two of these women were depressed, and eleven were Jewish. I had predicted that the Jewish mother, especially if she had limited herself to being a housewife, would be the one to find the departure of children most stressful, since this departure, according to my hypothesis, is most difficult for women whose primary role is that of mother. The devotion of the Jewish woman to her children is legendary, eulogized in songs and stories and more recently satirized by comedians and writers. From the widely selling books of such

prominent Jewish sons as Phillip Roth (*Portnoy's complaint*, 1967), Bruce J. Friedman (*A mother's kisses*, 1964), and Dan Greenburg (*How to be a Jewish mother*, 1965) we have been led to see that the other side of the coin of extreme devotion to children is overprotection, controlling behavior, and the development of a "martyr complex" by the mother.

When some crucial items in the interview protocols were analyzed, certain factors reminiscent of the cross-cultural survey began to emerge. These women did not have a kinship network to whom they could turn in times of trouble (here it should be noted that my data were gathered in Los Angeles, where this lack is probably more prevalent than in many other areas of the country). Though they did not believe that their children "owed" them anything, it was clear from the interviews that the Jewish women in particular had expectations of their children that were not being met. None of the women was spending time caring for grandchildren, but several had done so when the grandchildren were younger, and these women had had to cope with the loss of both mother and grandmother roles. When asked what they were most proud of, the women said their children. In general, they were least proud of their failure to have happy homes. Most of the women felt they were expected to keep busy and not "interfere" once their children were raised. They considered their lives lonelier now than when they were younger, and mentioned that they were less busy. This decline in activity, however, was not an asset, since it gave them more time to ruminate on their problems.

Perhaps the interview item most relevant for this essay was the one asking the women to rank in order of importance seven possible roles. These were: being a homemaker; taking part in church, club, and community activities; being a companion to my husband; helping my parents; being a sexual partner to my husband; my paying job; and helping my children.

Significantly, the mother role—"helping my children"—was most frequently ranked first or second. The role of homemaker was also ranked high. Roles such as "my paying job" and "taking part in church, club, and community activities" were considered unimportant. Thus, precisely those roles that become constricted with age were viewed as important, whereas the roles that could be expanded—the occupational and the organizational roles—were dismissed as unimportant.

All the Jewish women interviewed (but see below for epidemiological data), as expected, had had overprotective or overinvolved relationships with their children, and had experienced feelings of depression when the children left. My analysis of the interviews also showed that many of the women had severe physical illnesses before their hospitalization for depression and that in some cases the physical illness was associated with the failure of their marriages, since when ill they could not meet the expectations of their husbands. A strikingly high proportion of the women had lost their fathers at an early age. This loss deprived them of the opportunity to learn role relationships in an intact family, and therefore may have led to an overinvolvement in the maternal role and to depression when the role was lost.

The departure of their children seemed related to the depression of all of the empty-nest mothers, Jewish and non-Jewish alike. The major difference appeared to be that the non-Jewish mothers "keep a stiff upper lip"—they do not complain about their children, they do not express a desire to see them more often or state that they want to live with them—whereas two of the Jewish "empty-nest" mothers I interviewed said openly that they wanted to live with their children. They also talked about wanting a grandmother role.

The interview material lent support to the epidemiological data I had gathered earlier from the records of 533 women between the ages of 40 and 59, hospitalized for the first time for mental illness. The five hospitals varied from an upper-class private hospital to two state hospitals. Among these women, maternal role-loss seemed important only for those in the empty-nest stage. For women with some children still at home, depression seemed associated with other factors. On the basis of the epidemiological data the women with more than one role-loss—for example, both marital and maternal—did not have a higher rate of depression than the women with only one role-loss. However, these data showed only the presence or absence of depression, and nothing about the severity or intensity of the depression where present.[5] When the intensity

of depression could be observed, as in the interviews, those women with a multiple role-loss did appear to be in a worse situation than those with a single loss.

The epidemiological data did not support the hypothesis that maternal role loss would be especially stressful for Jewish women, primarily because the Jewish women in this group were found to be more likely to be depressed whatever their role state. Indeed, one of the most striking relationships to come to light is the high degree of association between being Jewish and being depressed. When ethnicity was cross-tabulated with depression, Jews had a higher rate than any other group—84 percent; Wasps had 47 percent and blacks 22 percent. In other words, whereas more than four out of every five of the Jewish women patients studied were diagnosed as depressed, less than half the non-Jewish sample had this diagnosis. If this high incidence of depression originates in the traditional Jewish socialization process, which makes aggression taboo and uses guilt as a means of social control, then depression should be less common among Jews from less traditional homes. Indeed, evidence to support this hypothesis was found, in the higher rate of depression among Jewish women with foreign-born mothers—only 67 percent of those with native-born mothers were depressed, as compared with 92 percent of those with foreign-born mothers (but the numbers were small).

All in all, however, the Jewish women were more depressed than the non-Jewish women for whatever category they were compared, although significantly, the difference in depression between Jews and non-Jews was markedly reduced when *only housewives with overprotective relationships with their children were studied.*[6] Non-Jews in this category also had an extremely high rate of depression. So you don't have to be Jewish to be a Jewish mother. The pathological effect of an overprotective mother on her children has been discussed by clinicians for many years. This investigation demonstrated that overprotection can be pathological for the mother. And Jews are more likely to have overinvolved relationships with their children than are non-Jews.

Contrary to my original hypothesis that women in high-status occupations would be relatively mildly affected by the loss of the maternal role, the epidemiological data showed that women with professional or managerial occupations had a high rate of depression. (The interview material bore less directly on this question, for the one woman among the twenty with role-loss who had had a job considered professional—she was a nurse—was not greatly involved in her profession. Far from considering it a "calling," she had become a nurse only after her first divorce and had stopped working outside the home during her first marriage.) The norms of our society are such that a woman is not expected to "fulfill" herself through an occupational role, but rather through the traditional feminine roles of housewife and mother. In addition, many women in high-status occupations suffer because of double messages about achievement, nonegalitarian marriages in which the wife's job is considered less important than the husband's and she is responsible for the housework, and the discrimination they experience at work. The fourteen women in the epidemiological sample with high-status occupations and maternal role-loss were also found to be either unhappily married or divorced. In view of a woman's cultural expectations and the considerable stresses and role contradictions she may face in a high-status occupation in a sexist society, it is not surprising that the occupational role could not be expanded to compensate for a lost maternal or marital role.

Nevertheless, my study did not support the theory advanced by a number of psychiatrists, most notably Helene Deutsch and Theresa Benedek,[7] that it is the so-called feminine and mothering woman who has the easiest time during the menopause and that it is the—in Deutsch's phrase—"masculine protester" who has the most difficulty. On the contrary, my findings indicate that it is the women who play the traditional feminine role—who are housewives, are not aggressive, are centered on their children, who in short, have "bought" the cultural proscriptions—who are most prone to depression when their children leave. The depressed women I studied, far from being masculine protesters, were half a standard deviation more "feminine" on the MMPI test than the mean for the criterion group.

This is not to say that all housewives who are overinvolved or overprotective with their children are hospitalized when their children leave home, or

that all housewives become depressed in middle age. Under the following conditions the women would continue to receive vicarious gratification:

1. Their husbands are financially successful
2. Their husbands do not become interested in other women, nor want a divorce, nor die
3. Their children fulfill their expectations, i.e.,
   a) The son obtains a good job
   b) The daughter makes a "good" marriage
   c) The mother–child relationship can continue through frequent phone calls and visits

If these conditions are met, then women of the type we have been discussing need not become depressed. But if any one of these conditions is not fulfilled, then such a woman may be in a dangerous situation. All of these cases depend on the actions of other people rather than the woman herself.

In *The revolution in psychiatry*, Ernest Becker says that it is the women who have been too closely integrated into the social structure who become depressed when they find that their "sacrifice," their exemplary behavior, has been in vain. They discover that it is the exploiters rather than the martyrs who are rewarded, contrary to what they have always believed. They were told that as women they should live for their children. They did so. Their husband became interested in other women or preoccupied with their jobs, or they died. Their children left home. Since their feelings of being useful stemmed primarily from husband and children, these losses left them with no sense of worth.[8]

Durkheim's work is also relevant to the stresses a mother may feel when her children leave, particularly his concepts of *egoistic* and *anomic* suicide. According to Durkheim it is not marriage that protects a woman from egoistic suicide, as it is for men. Rather it is the birth of children that reduces the suicide rate for women, and immunity to suicide increases with the "density" of the family. This density diminishes, needless to say, when the children mature and leave.

Durkheim focused on problems stemming from normlessness, from anomie. There are indeed few norms governing the relationship between an American woman and her adult children. When the children leave, the woman's situation is consequently normless. There would be, for example, no folkway, no pattern, no mores that could indicate to Sara just what she should expect from her children, just what their relationship should be with her.[9]

All the women I interviewed said their children "owed" them nothing. But there was an additional element of normative confusion faced by the Jewish women. The norms considered appropriate in parent–child relationships in traditional Jewish culture—and therefore adhered to by the women—may not have been completely internalized by their children. The children were also exposed to Anglo-Saxon parent–child relationships, which are more restrained and place more emphasis, at least on the verbal level, on the parent's desire for independence, both for her child and for herself.

INTEGRATION OF PSYCHIATRIC AND SOCIOLOGICAL THEORY

Both the psychodynamic and the existential theories of depression state that depression is a result of loss. Psychodynamically oriented psychiatrists consider the loss that of an ambivalently loved object, whereas existentialists, such as Ernest Becker, consider the loss to be a loss of meaning. In Freudian terms, depressives are understood as individuals who, instead of expressing anger toward the ambivalently loved lost object, turn the anger inward, against themselves. One possible way of combining the Freudian and existentialist views is as follows:

People who are intrapunitive, who do not express their anger, especially if they are women, are conforming to the cultural norms. Since they are "good," they expect to be rewarded. Should their husbands or children leave them, their life may seem meaningless; their world may no longer "make sense." Their introjected anger has led to "proper" behavior, which in turn has led to expectations of reward. If the reward does not materialize, but in fact tragedy strikes, they will suffer from a loss of meaning and become depressed.

The loss that was the independent variable for this study was role-loss, especially the loss of the maternal role for middle-aged women who had over-involved or overprotective relationships with their children. There is no direct evidence that the "lost" children were ambivalently loved, although some of the interviews I held might suggest that ambivalence was present. It was, however, quite clear that both the interviewees and the epidemiological sample were made up of "norm-following" women.

WHAT NEEDS TO BE DONE

The cross-cultural study, showing the multiplicity of possible roles for middle-aged women, made it clear that not only need status not drop in mid-life but in most cultures it actually rises. That fact, however, would be cold comfort to the American women we have studied who are already depressed. It is unreasonable to expect them to change their value systems or personality structures or characteristic patterns of interaction at this stage of the game. These women are not psychotic, if by psychotic we mean the patient does not know what reality is. They know exactly what their reality is: that is why they are depressed. We must change society so that these tragedies will not be repeated. More basic changes are required than the "band-aid" reforms making it easier for older women to re-enter the labor force. The entire system of sex roles should be changed so that women could, if they chose, remain in the labor force after childbearing. (This is particularly important for professional women and those whose occupations have changing skills.) Not only should there be adequate 24-hour-a-day, parent-controlled day-care centers, but men should share the child-care and housekeeping responsibilities. The value system should change so that a man's "masculinity" will not be measured by his occupational achievement, freeing him then to devote more time and energy to his family; and a woman's sense of adequacy should not be dependent on her fulfilling the traditional female roles of wife and mother in the traditional manner. She should have other options, such as not being considered a failure if she does not marry, and deciding not to have children even if she does marry. There are many industrialized societies—such as the Soviet Union, Poland, Sweden, and Finland—where women play a vital part in the economy. Our record on the participation of women in the professions is shameful when we look at that of these other countries. It is interesting to note, however, that even there, when professions (e.g., medicine or pharmacy) have changed from primarily masculine to primarily feminine, they are redefined so as to require "naturally feminine" qualities and skills.

Age discrimination as well as sex discrimination and sexism should be overcome. Although both older men and older women are discriminated against, such discrimination hurts women earlier because of the double standard in aging. A woman's physical attractiveness is one of her assets and a requirement for certain jobs, such as receptionist, hostess, waitress.

The increasing participation of women in the labor force (if not prevented by a decreased demand for workers in the 1970s), declining desired and actual fecundity, the power of the women's movement in fighting sex discrimination and loosening sex role stereotypes, and the increasing self-esteem and self-confidence of women in general should improve the situation of middle-aged women.

Most imperative of all, we must nurture a new sense of worth in the girls of our society, to ensure that as women they will not feel useless when their children or their husbands leave them. If one's satisfaction, one's sense of value, comes from other people rather than from one's own accomplishments, it follows that when these people depart, one is left with an empty shell in place of self. On the other hand, if one's sense of self comes from her own accomplishments, one is not so vulnerable to breakdown when significant others leave.

The woman's liberation movement, by pointing out alternative life styles, by providing the emotional support necessary for deviating from the conventional sex roles, and by emphasizing the importance of women actualizing their own selves, fulfilling their own potentials, can aid in the development of personhood for both men and women.

NOTES

1. The cultures and peoples studied were all preliterate, peasant or traditional: the Andaman Islanders, Serbs, Toda, Twi, Nupe, Tiv, Yoruba, Azande, Bushmen, Lovedu, Bedouin, Wolof, Aleuts, Comanche, Yurok, Navajo, Zuni, Ifugao, Aranda, Trobrianders, Samoans, Marquesans, Pukapukans, Jivaro; and peasant or traditional cultures in Burma, China, rural Ireland, Poland, India, the Soviet Union, and the Philippines. The following aspects of all these cultures were studied: ontogeny, social personality, personality traits, and personality disorders, division of labor by sex, age stratification, sex status, celibacy, family relationships, grandparents and grandchildren, dependency, old-age dependency, adulthood, senescence, and the activities, status, and treatment of the aged.

2. Pauline Bart, Why women's status changes in middle age: the turns of the social Ferris wheel. *Sociological Symposium*, Fall 1969: 1.

3. See, however, Neugarten's work on healthy middle-aged women: Bernice Neugarten (ed.), *Middle-aged and aging: a reader in social psychology*. University of Chicago Press, 1968.

4. Of the women interviewed eleven were married, one separated, six divorced, one widowed and one single. Of the eight women whose children had all departed (the empty-nest women), four were married, and four were divorced, widowed, or separated. Of those who had at least one child out of the home but at least one child still at home (partially empty-nest) three were married and none were divorced, widowed, or separated. Four women had marital but not maternal role loss, one had partial marital role loss but not maternal role loss, and four had no role loss. Eighteen of the twenty were diagnosed depressed. Eleven women were Jewish and nine women were housewives.

5. I did not find that women diagnosed as psychotic had more severe symptoms than those with "neurotic" depression. Diagnosis depended primarily on hospital.

6. But in this comparison 80 percent of the Jewish women had such a relationship while only 48 percent of the non-Jewish women did.

7. Helene Deutsch, *The psychology of women: a psychoanalytic interpretation*. New York: Grune and Stratton, 1945, vol. 2; Theresa Benedek and Boris Rubenstein, *Psychosexual functions in women*. New York: Ronald, 1952, pp. 1–11.

8. Ernest Becker, *The revolution in psychiatry*. Glencoe, Ill.: Free Press, 1964.

9. Emile Durkheim, *Suicide*. John A. Spaulding and George Simpson (trans.). Glencoe, Ill.: Free Press, 1951.

Socialization
for Postparental Life

IRWIN DEUTSCHER

THE NOTION OF LIFE CAREERS—OF a developmental process—as a perspective for viewing the etiology of individual or institutional behavior is not new (Hughes 1959). The word "career" itself carries the connotation of a progressively developing sequence of *work* experiences. It need not, however, be restricted to the experiences of individuals. The "natural history" approach to institutional development employs an identical perspective (House 1936, pp. 141–157). In attempting to understand and describe the family career, or stages in the development of the American family, the concept of the "family cycle" has been frequently, although not intensively, employed (Cavan 1960, Ch. 2; Hiltner 1953; Waller and Hill 1951, Ch. 20). Perhaps more than any other analyst, Paul C. Glick (1955, 1947) has consistently exploited this concept in an effort to direct his analysis of demographic shifts in family structure. In this paper some of the social-psychological problems of transition from one phase of the family cycle to another will be examined.[1]

THE POSTPARENTAL PHASE OF THE FAMILY CYCLE

The span of time from the beginning of a family with the marriage of a young couple, the bearing, rearing, and marrying of their children, through the time when they are again alone together, until the ultimate death of one or both of them, is referred to as the family cycle. Cavan (1953, pp. 262–263; 1960, pp. 28–38) has described, as thoroughly as anyone, variations in family organization through the family circle. She sees the cycle as "significant in that with each stage, changes occur in the family membership and consequently in family organization, roles, and interpersonal relationships." This paper focuses on the transition from the phase during which children are being launched into the adult world to the phase Cavan (1953, p. 573) calls postparental: "The postparental couple are the husband and wife usually...in their forties and fifties....The most obvious change is the withdrawal of adolescent and young children from the family, leaving husband and wife as the family unit."

In the family career pattern of a large segment of our adult urban population, this appears to be emerging as a new phase of the family cycle, largely as a result of two demographic shifts: the fact that these people can expect to live considerably longer than their parents or grandparents and the fact that they averaged fewer children over a shorter span of years than their parents or grandparents.[2] The typical couple of two generations ago had a life expectancy which enabled them to survive together for 31 years after marriage, two years short of the time when their *fifth* child was expected to marry. But, "the decline in size of family and the improved survival prospects of the population since 1890 not only have assured the average parents of our day that they will live to see their children married but also have made it probable that they will have one-fourth of their married life still to come when their last child leaves the parental home" (Glick 1947).

THE PROBLEM OF TRANSITION

In her classic formulation of "Continuities and discontinuities in cultural conditioning," Ruth Benedict highlighted the problem of socially structured impediments to continuous socialization through the life cycle. She begins with the observation that there are certain discontinuities in the life

This selection is reprinted from Irwin Deutscher, Socialization for postparental life. In Arnold Rose (ed.), *Human behavior and social processes.* Boston: Houghton Mifflin Company, 1962: 506–525.

cycle which are facts of nature and inescapable; thus, "Every man who rounds out his human potentialities must have been a son first and a father later and the two roles are physiologically in great contrast" (Benedict 1938). The important point, however, is that there is a great deal of variability in the way in which the transition is effected in different societies. Moving from Benedict's focus on the transition between childhood and adulthood to a focus on the transition from the launching to the postparental stage of the family cycle, and shifting from the concepts of "culture" and "conditioning" to the concepts of "role" and "socialization," we have a perspective within which to view the problems of transition and the modes of adaptation to postparental life.

Theoretically, it might be expected that the transition to postparental life would be a difficult one for the middle-aged spouses to make. Since this is an emerging phase of the family cycle, few of those entering it can find role models: in most cases one of their own parents was dead before the last of their own siblings was launched. This lack of anticipatory socialization—the absence of an opportunity to take the role of a postparental spouse, to rehearse the part before having to play the role themselves—ought theoretically to make for an extremely difficult situation after the children leave home. Much of the descriptive literature indicates that this, indeed, is a dangerous time of life (Burgess 1945, p. 626; Christensen 1950, p. 409; Duvall and Hill 1948, p. 3; Kinsey *et al.* 1953, pp. 353–354; Lowery 1943; Pollack 1948, p. 79; Tibbitts 1951, p. 7; Waller and Hill 1951, p. 43). *Nevertheless, despite expectations based on both theory and clinical experience, when urban middle-class postparental couples describe their life, the hurdle does not appear to have been insurmountable and the adaptations are seldom pathological.*[3]

In discussing postparental life, middle-aged spouses clearly reveal that it is not sound to assume that anticipatory socialization is absent because this is a new stage of the family cycle—that is, because middle-aged couples of today have not had the experience of observing their parents make such a transition. In spite of the fact that the identical situation could not be observed and rehearsed —that there was no opportunity to learn to take the role of the other by observing others—*analogous* situations exist in one's own life. Sussman (1953) recognizes this when he suggests that "most parents are gradually prepared to some degree for the day when their children marry and leave home by their periodic absences away at school or elsewhere."[4] Such periodic absences do not, however, represent the full extent to which such socialization by analogy can occur.

Situations such as these provide an opportunity for the parent to rehearse in his own mind what life will be like when his children are gone. Anomalously, he himself becomes the "other" whose role he has an opportunity to take. Even though these practice situations may not be considered as permanent, important, or serious (they are more nearly instances of "playing-at-roles" than "role-playing") it will be seen that they provide the continuity in role conditioning—the socializing opportunity—that is needed. The word "opportunity" is used advisedly. Individuals react to the socialization process in different ways; on some it "takes" and on others it doesn't. The simple fact that an individual is provided with a potentially socializing experience does not necessarily result in his defining it as such or in his being socialized as a result of the experience. The remainder of this paper will be devoted to an examination of what these socializing opportunities are and the manner in which they appear to facilitate the transition to postparental life.

OPPORTUNITIES FOR ANTICIPATORY SOCIALIZATION

Change as a Cultural Value

One of the underlying cultural values of our contemporary society is the focus on change for its own sake. In a sense all Americans are socialized from early childhood to believe that change is both inevitable and good. The notion that things will not remain the same—politically, economically, or socially—is an integral part of our national ethos. Otherwise there could be no Horatio Alger myth. Otherwise the political slogan, "It's time for a change," could not have been so effective as it obviously was in 1952. Otherwise Southern segregationists would not concede that the best they can do is fight a *delaying* action against integration. Change apparently is accepted as something both natural and inevitable by the vast majority of the members of our society. Such a value provides a general conditioning for the acceptance of new and different situations regardless of their specific nature.

In our interviews, we find evidence that middle-class urban Americans have internalized this value and are able logically to relate it to the family cycle. One mother observes philosophically that "it seems like life spaces itself. You look forward to finishing up one space but then another space always pops up. When this is accomplished, something else comes along." The clearest statements, however, come from two of the fathers. One of them, when asked how it felt to become a grandfather responded that "like most things in my life, it's just a matter of course. Things can be expected, like you expect changes in jobs and expect children to be married. Natural events come afterward and you take those things as a matter of course." This process, felt to be "natural" in our society, is described in full detail by the other father:

> Of course you hate to give up your daughter, but I think we all understand that is the way of life; you can't stand still; you can't be the same forever. Life moves on and that is the most natural thing. You see them grow. You see them graduate from high school. Then you see them graduate from college—you follow along. It is changing all the time. First it is childhood. You hold them on your lap, then you go walking with them. Then you see them through high school. I was her chauffeur, all the time taking her to social functions. She went through music school, then she got a bachelor of arts, then we sent her for four years to Juilliard and she got her bachelor's and master's there. Then she comes out and teaches in college for one year and then she gets married and settles down.

It is clear that at least some people are aware of a life cycle and a family cycle and are resigned (if

not committed) to a philosophy of change. Whether or not one is willing to accept the conditioning effect of a basic cultural emphasis on change per se, there remain several more specific types of experiences which provide parents with an opportunity for anticipatory socialization.

The Temporary Departure of Children

Opportunities for middle-class parents at least to play at a postparental role frequently occur when the children leave home for college. However, such opportunities are exploited to varying degrees or, to put it another way, the experience is defined differently by different couples. Some parents make no mention of the possibility of college as a socializing experience for themselves. Presumably many of these do not see that possibility. On the other hand, there are others who see clearly what is happening. A mother claims that, "The breaking point is when your children go away to college. After that you grow used to it. By the time they get married you're used to the idea of their being away and adjust to it."

The question, "Do you think your child was ready to marry when he did?" brought out the functionality of the college experience. One father responded, "Yes, I thought she was. She had already gone through college—those five years of college and two years working. She was ready to get married." More important is that the college experience meant that he was now ready for her to get married. This kind of projection—the notion that college is training for the child to get away rather than training for the parent to release him—is expressed most clearly by a mother:

> It's only natural, when you have a family of three without any relatives near by, to notice a gap when she gets married. Of course, the first adjustment is when they go away to school; that's the first break. It's healthy for an only child to go far away to school. It makes them more self-sufficient. She had been in school away from home since she was 16 and I think she was very well adjusted. Being away like that she learned to be independent, and make

her own decisions and take responsibilities on her own. It was a sort of training period which prepared her [sic, "us"?] for leaving us [sic, "her"?].

Another mother says of her recently married son, "We had gotten used to just being by ourselves while he was in the Navy and away at college." This brings us to another frequently occurring opportunity for parents to play at the postparental role: the departure of children for military service. Life experiences tend to be evaluated in comparison with other experiences. They are not just good or bad; they are better or worse. Apparently it is better to lose a child through marriage than through war: "My most unhappy time was around the war years when my boy was in service. I worried over him coming back; he was missing several times." This is the kind of socialization that gives a parent a sense of relief to have a child home and married. We learn from another mother that, "When he was sent overseas, I was so worried about him over there that it was a relief when he got married and settled down." The importance of this as a learning experience is illustrated by the mother whose three children are now married, but who says of the time when her son went into service and she still had two others at home, "I think that the lonesomest part of my life I ever had was when my son was in service. We missed our boy." Her husband, interestingly enough, explicitly states that the Army experience serves as preparation for marriage. When asked if he thought his children were mature enough to get married, he responded: "Well, I thought more so about the boy because he was in the Army, but I did think that she (the daughter) should have waited."

Being in the armed forces serves both to wean the parents away from the children and the children away from the parents. Still another mother reports that:

After he came out of the service he had aged a lot. He used to confide in us about life and to tell us about everything that was happening in school. But after he went into service he changed. We always spent our afternoons together—both the children. We'd go out for

drives for picnics or something like that. But after he came home from service he didn't do that anymore. He wasn't contented to be at home.

But then, after the anguish of wartime separation, another woman implies that it is good just to know that the child is safe and is in this country:

He was in the Second World War and he was overseas. And after having been so far away from home he feels like he's practically right here, because we can telephone and it's just 50 miles. After having been in Europe a couple of years, you know 50 miles away is "at home."

There are other experiences which, like college or service in the armed forces, give parents an opportunity to practice living without their children. Nearly a quarter of the families interviewed had parted with their children for extended periods of time while they were still in their teens. For example, there is the son who couldn't get along with his father: "My son used to say that as much as he would like to stay here, he couldn't take things off of his dad any longer. So I never insisted on him staying. He left a couple of times and would come back."

Then there is the child with the wanderlust: "That boy wasn't interested in anything except to hitchhike—just to get as far as he could and to see what he could see. He was walking when he was eight months old and has been walking ever since." More common than either of these two experiences is the departure of children prior to marriage in search of work. Although this sometimes occurs with daughters, it is more frequently the sons who leave for this reason:

(Do you remember how you felt when you first found out he was going to get married?) Yes, he was the first one. Both of them are married now. It was all right. He was able to take care of himself. He was away from home a lot. He and the oldest boy were up in Detroit on defense work. They have really been away from home a long time—ever since 1940.

(How did you find it when the children left? Did you have a lot of time on your hands?) Well, that came gradually. The war had something to do with that. They were both in the war before they got married and we were alone then. And the youngest one went to aviation school. He was just barely 18 when he got his first job in Texas. Then he went to Phoenix and then he came home and then he went into service. And the other boy was at home for awhile and then he had to go. So with their coming and going it kinda eased off gradually.

Finally, in connection with these temporary departures of children prior to marriage, a word should be said about the modern middle-class urban high school complex. In some cases it results in the home being little more than a place to sleep and certainly in infrequent contacts with the parents. This reaction was obtained only from fathers. Possibly mothers maintain closer contacts with their children—especially with daughters—during the high school years. Be this as it may, one father reports that:

There is a difference when they grow older —particularly when they went to high school. Naturally they got their own friends and you saw less of them than you did before. They'd come home from school late and then they'd have a game or maybe the girl would have a date and you might see them at dinner time but you probably wouldn't see them until breakfast—or maybe after the game or date.

Another father stated that the "best years" were when his boys were around nine or ten: "(When they started to grow up did you feel that they were growing away from you?) No, but when they go to high school they have different ideas and interests than the people at home have." There is, however, another side to this coin. The proud father of a high school athlete was asked when was the happiest time of his life: "Oh—that kid of mine—the things he did when he was in high school. It was like living your life over again. I guess I really enjoyed that period."

On the basis of such observations, there is reason to believe that there are bridges—transitional learning experiences which aid parents in adapting themselves to postparental life. These appear to provide continuity in role conditioning. Such "rehearsals" are not as difficult as "opening night," the real and permanent departure of the children which will come later. They are defined as temporary and are broken by regular visits home or the expectation that the children will at some time again return to live at home. But the "temporary" can gradually shift into the permanent without any traumatic transition: "My daughter went to California, to Berkeley, to go to school. Then she decided to work there a while and then she got married out there and she has lived there ever since." The fact that these socializing experiences occur at a time when the parents are still extremely active with their own affairs should not be ignored. It is probably easier to prepare for and accept such a transition in early middle age than in later years when it will actually occur. When one mother was asked how she made out at home with the children all off to college, she shrugged off the question with, "Oh, I don't know. I was just too busy to be bothered about anything."

Life without Father

If there are temporary departures of the children which provide parents with an opportunity to practice the postparental role, there is also a combination of recent historical events and cultural expectations which have provided middle-class fathers with an additional opportunity to practice this role. The historical events are the Great Depression and the Second World War; the cultural expectations are those related to the middle-class notion of "work." Unlike some of the temporary departures of children mentioned in the preceding section, a temporary shattering of the family constellation due to the exigencies of war, work, or economic depression can be rationalized as beyond the control of those involved—attributed to immitigable external forces. Such rationalization is not always possible when the family breakup results from a unilateral decision on the part of a child to leave home for reasons related to education or work. When opportunities to engage in these pursuits are locally available, the parents may view the child's decision as a rejection of themselves. Such a definition of the situation (whether accurate or inaccurate) is hardly conducive to promoting a smooth transition into postparental life.

Some fathers, owing to the press of circumstances, have lived for extended periods of time away from their wives and children.

> I was having a rough time. I was six months or a year on WPA and when I got off that I couldn't find anything. But I had a brother in Portland, Oregon, so I went out there and it seems I was away from mother (wife) and the kids for close to a year and a half.

> During the war my husband was on a swing-shift and worked nights and then he was in the Hawaiian Islands for a year working for the Navy.

> Let me tell you how it was. On a certain day I had $50,000 in the bank and a $25,000 home paid for and all the trimmings to go with it. Three months later I borrowed $25 to send my wife and children up to Kansas City (from Oklahoma). It was months before I got things straightened out enough to join them.

> My husband was 38 and the company sent us to Ottawa (Kansas). The draft board there just had a high quota and they scraped the bottom of the barrel. That's how they got him.

Nearly one in every five of the families interviewed was broken for extended periods of time under circumstances similar to those described above. It is relevant that these experiences most often were narrated in response to questions about how close the father was to the children when they were growing up.

A somewhat more common experience (also usually discussed in relation to that same line of questioning) is the detachment of the father from his growing children and his lack of involvement in their activities as a result of his being "on the road." One third of these middle-class fathers found it necessary to travel regularly during some phase of their work career, and in all but one case this was defined as alienating the father from the children. When asked if she felt that she was closer to her children than her husband, one wife answered, "I think I was, definitely, because my husband is a traveling man. I really reared the children; most of the time he was only home Saturdays and Sundays." Other wives of traveling men tend to respond in like manner:

> He travels from Monday to Thursday and he's in Thursday evening until Monday morning. (Do you think this had anything to do with his relationship with the children when they were growing up?) Yes, quite a bit! They didn't have the companionship with their dad that I thought they should have had.

This is not a one-sided "mama's" point of view. As the following couplets excerpted from husband and wife interviews reveal, the husbands are in essential agreement on this matter:

> (1) *Wife:* (Do you think your husband's occupation kept him away from the boys?) Very definitely! It was unfortunate too. He felt he was just not able to devote the time to them and it was not up to me to say what he should and should not do. (He was out of town a good part of the time?) Yes, when they were young he was gone a great deal. Then later on he had so much responsibility in the office. He was the kind that went early and stayed late. You see he had had considerable trouble when he was younger, seeing his mother working and slaving while his father was ill and he didn't want me to have to do the same thing. *That* result has been fine. But as for the boys, he never did have much time for them.

> *Husband:* (Did you feel that your job kept you away from your children—that you didn't have enough time to spend with them?) I didn't have enough time to spend with them. When I was traveling I was away a great deal, and then when I went into the office my job there kept me on the job from early in the morning until dinner time and then I worked a good many nights at home. So I didn't have too much time with them.

> (2) *Wife:* (Which one of you was closer to the children when they were younger?) I would say I was. For one thing, he was gone so much. He would only see them on weekends. So I would

definitely say they were closer to me. They respect their father and think a lot of him, but they wouldn't bring their problems to him as much as they would to me.

Husband: (Tell me how your work affects your family life?) Well, like the average man gets up and goes to work every morning, I am out for a week! Now that we have better highways and faster cars you can make most all your territory in a week's time. I used to make a lot of two and three weeks' trips because we had slower cars and not very good highways and it took just that much longer.

Although improvements in transportation may have reduced the periods of absence, they still exist. However, simply because a man travels does not mean that he has become detached from his children and family. A railroader and his wife demonstrate how a family can be tightly knit because his absence for short periods results in his being home for five or six day "weekends." This traveling man had the opportunity to be closer to his family than most who do not travel:

(Do you think it took away from your family too much to be on the road?) Well, I was away from the family. Like a trip from here to Omaha and Colorado it was two nights and one day away and come in and sleep a day and then go right back out again when I had to make two round trips. So I was four nights off on the road, but then I'd come in and I'd have five days off one time and six the next.

And from his wife:

Yes, he was on the road a lot. He was on the Super Chief on the Santa Fe Main Line. He was on that train for 11 years. (Would you rather he worked at something that kept him home?) Oh my no! He liked his work. He was on the railroad for 44 years. (Do you think his being away from home affected his relationship with the children?) No, no; they were always regular companions—all of them. He knew the children as well as I did.

As has been indicated in some of the passages cited, even when father is at home, he may be so in body only, being engrossed in his work day and night whether on the road or in town. When this kind of commitment to work evolves, men whose work never takes them out of town may see less of their families than some who, like the railroader, travel a great deal. One mother generalizes: "I think most men are so occupied with their work that they sort of leave that (rearing of children) to the mother." A father whose work has never taken him out of town concurs: "I'm afraid I left most of bringing him up to his mother. Lots of times when he was growing up I had to work late. I wouldn't get home till 9:30 or 10:00 at night and I'd be out to the office at 5:00 in the morning."

It is important, however, that this parental detachment not be overemphasized. Not all middle-class fathers orient themselves to the work role so strongly. There are certainly some who leave their work at the office: "I have no night work. My work is at the office and when I leave the office I'm through until the next day, regardless of what I've got. I've never made a practice of bringing work home." There are others who emphasize that, in spite of many temptations, they have steadfastly refused to take their work out of the office.

It would seem that there are a good many cases among urban middle-class families where life goes on without father during the years when the child is growing up. As dysfunctional as this may be to the family at that stage, it does provide the fathers with continuity in role conditioning which can stand them in good stead at the later postparental stage when the time comes for the children to depart permanently.

The Mother-in-law Myth as a Conditioning Device

If the work role helps to condition fathers for the departure of their children, at least some mothers appear to be provided with a conditioning device which is the distinctive property of their sex. That device is the cultural myth of the mother-in-law: "As soon as my youngsters were born I made up my mind that I was not going to be a mother-in-law like you read about." Such a resolution, if intended seriously, could go far in preparing a mother to accept the departure of her children. In addition to the folklore on the mother-in-law, there is the reality of experience.

My son got married before he even finished his education. He was only 17 years old, but I did not say a word! I don't think it's good policy. That can be a very tender spot. I know because I went through it. I had a mother-in-law—well, she was just butting into everything all the time. I just resolved never to act like that myself. The Bible says something about to hold your peace. And that's not prose. That's just the way it should be. People when they get married should get away from relatives. Far enough away so that it takes three days for a postcard to get to them and three more for it to get back.

The following mother expresses the same opinion even more vehemently:

I'll go to the county home before I'll live with any of my children. I have very definite ideas on that. Because I had his mother with us every winter for 20 years whether I had room for her or not and it *doesn't* work and I very *definitely* will *not* do a thing like that! If I have to take a dose of strychnine first, I won't!

Humor is, of course, an effective form of social control—especially in an increasingly other-directed society. Mothers, like everyone else, are sensitive to the pleas of the mass media for conformity. They want to be "good" mothers-in-law and Evelyn Duvall's study (1954) indicates that they are—that the mother-in-law is not nearly the center of conflict in America that she is often thought to be. It is very possible that a more accurate statement would be that the mother-in-law is not nearly the center of conflict that she *used* to be. The pressures of experience and folklore as indicated in the passages cited above may have brought about a shift in the self-conception of mothers-in-law and in the role which they play. In any event, at least in some cases, these myths and experiences provide an opportunity for mothers to anticipate and prepare themselves for postparental life—a socializing opportunity.

Survivals of an Older Family Pattern

The postparental phase of the family cycle was described earlier as a newly emerging phenomenon resulting from increasing longevity and decreasing fertility. No longer is it true, as it was at the turn of the century, that both parents will have died before the last of their children was launched. However, as with any emerging phenomenon, fragmentary survivals of the earlier pattern remain. In such cases, there is, in effect, no transition to make —these people have no postparental period. Take, for example, the couple with six children ranging in age from 31 to 44, with three of them married and residing in the metropolitan area and a fourth divorced and living at home. Their daily life remains essentially the same as it has always been, although the work is somewhat lighter and the economic situation somewhat more secure:

(Tell me just how you spend a typical day nowadays?) Well, I do my housework in the morning and then I get meals again, and the children will come in once in a while and sometimes I go down to one of my daughters'. That is all I do. I have a fine family. They are all good Christian children and I am just as proud of them as I can be.

Life has changed so little for this couple that they even argue about the same kinds of trivialities they did 30 years ago:

...take that rug there in the dining room. I didn't like the color but he bought it anyway because it was a good buy. It was a remnant. But it seemed to me that a rug is something that you have to live with for a long time and it ought to satisfy you. But he said that I had had my way with the wallpaper so he went ahead and bought it.

An extended family need not be one of procreation; even with few children, postparental couples may refer themselves to a large family of orientation. This older pattern manifests itself in the case of a couple one of whose two married children is now living in Minneapolis. In spite of this, there is a plethora of parental siblings, in-laws, nephews, nieces, and grandchildren—all part of a second- and third-generation Irish clan residing in the Kansas City area:

(Tell me what you do with your time these days?) Well, we are quite home people, that is, with the grandchildren, the daughter, and his (husband's) people. He has seven brothers and they are all living in Kansas City, and we are very close to one another—the husbands and wives. We have picnics, and we go from home to home for little parties and then I have my sisters too and they live here. You know, we just enjoy family. I have brothers and sisters and he has all brothers. So that gives me a lot of sister-in-laws too. So we are very family people—very home people.

This kind of extended family support appears to lessen the trauma of the disintegration of the family of procreation. Most families, however, find themselves far more isolated from "kinfolk" in the modern American city.

SUMMARY AND CONCLUSIONS

We have seen that several conditioning situations present themselves as potential aids in the socialization of parents for postparental life. These situations provide an opportunity to anticipate postparental roles, not by taking the role of the other in the usual sense, but by experiencing analogous situations which are quasi-postparental and which enable the parents to play at anticipated roles. There is the underlying value in our society on change for its sake—a value which can be applied to the particular case of change in the family structure; there are the temporary departures of children during the adolescent years for college, service in the armed forces, and a variety of other reasons; there is the modern complex of urban high school life, which can move the children into a world which is foreign to their parents; there are the exigencies of the work situation which often remove the middle-class father from the family during the years when the children are growing up; there is the myth and the reality of the mother-in-law which some mothers internalize as lessons for themselves. In addition, remnants of the older extended family

pattern which tend to reduce the impact of the transition cannot be ignored.

It was stated earlier that *theoretically* this could be assumed to be a difficult transition to make, largely because of the absence of role models—the absence of socialization to play postparental roles. However, the middle-aged couples whose children have left home indicate that there are opportunities for them to learn these new roles before they are thrust upon them.

It was also stated earlier that much of the descriptive literature indicates that this is a difficult period of life. By and large such observations are based on clinical experiences with persons who have so much difficulty in making the transition that they must seek outside help. The small group of postparental spouses interviewed by the present writer represent a random sample of such people who discussed their lives in their own living room. Although definite conclusions cannot be drawn from the responses of this small fragment of the population, they have managed to provide us with some notion of the variety of alternative modes of anticipatory socialization available to their ilk. It would appear from their comments that it is reasonable to assume that people do have opportunities to prepare for postparental life and, in addition, that most of them take advantage of these opportunities.

This phase of the family cycle is seen by the majority of middle-aged spouses as a time of new freedoms: freedom from the economic responsibilities of children; freedom to be mobile (geographically); freedom from housework and other chores. And, finally, freedom to be one's self for the first time since the children came along. No longer do the parents need to live the self-consciously restricted existence of models for their own children: "We just take life easy now that the children are grown. We even serve dinner right from the stove when we're alone. It's hotter that way, but you just couldn't let down like that when your children are still at home."

NOTES

1. This paper is based on a part of the author's doctoral dissertation (Deutscher 1968). The research was facilitated by a predoctoral research training fellowship from the Social Science Research Council and a grant from Community Studies, Inc., of Kansas City, Missouri.

2. Although it may appear that, in terms of average number of children, the offspring of the current crop of postparental couples are reverting to the patterns of older generations, this reversion is more apparent than real: "The fact that the crude birth rate has been higher in the postwar period than in the 1930s is due primarily to the operation of two factors: a larger proportion of women have been marrying at younger ages, and more of those marrying have started their families relatively soon after marriage. These factors may have only a minor effect on the final average

number of children that women will have borne by the end of the childbearing period . . ."(Freedman *et al.* 1959, p. 215).

3. Observations made and materials cited below are derived from intensive interviews with 49 urban middle-class postparental spouses. The investigator gathered sufficient data on family characteristics from approximately 540 middle-class households to determine whether or not they met his criteria of postparental. Those selected were between 40 and 65 years of age, had from one to four children all of whom had been launched, and both parents were alive and living together. Self-selection occurred in only two cases where the family refused to be interviewed.

4. A similar perspective can be found in John Sirjamaki (1953, p. 135).

REFERENCES

BENEDICT, RUTH. Continuities and discontinuities in cultural conditioning. *Psychiatry*, 1938, **1**: 161–167.

BURGESS, ERNEST W., AND H. LOCKE. *The family: from institution to companionship.* New York: American Book, 1945.

CAVAN, RUTH S. *The American family.* New York: Thomas Y. Crowell, 1953.

————. *Marriage and family in the modern world.* New York: Thomas Y. Crowell, 1960.

CHRISTENSEN, HAROLD. *Marriage analysis.* New York: Ronald, 1950.

DEUTSCHER, IRWIN. Married life in the middle years: a study of the middle-class urban postparental couple. Ph.D. dissertation, Department of Sociology, University of Missouri, 1958.

DUVALL, EVELYN M. *In-laws: pro and con.* New York: Association Press, 1954.

————. Implications for education through the family life cycle. *Marriage and Family Living*, November 1958, **20**: 334–342.

————, AND R. HILL. *The dynamics of family interaction.* National Conference on Family Life, Inc., 1948 (mimeographed).

FREEDMAN, RONALD, P. K. WHELPTON, AND A. A. CAMPBELL. *Family planning, sterility, and population growth.* New York: McGraw-Hill, 1959.

GLICK, PAUL C. The family cycle. *American Sociological Review*, April 1947, **12**: 164–169.

————. The cycle of the family. *Marriage and Family Living*, February 1955, **17**.

HILTNER, HELEN J. Changing family tasks of adults. *Marriage and Family Living*, May 1953, **15**: 110–113.

HOUSE, FLOYD N. The natural history of institutions. In Floyd N. House (ed.), *The development of sociology.* New York: McGraw-Hill, 1936, pp. 141–157.

HUGHES, EVERETT C. *Men and their work.* New York: Free Press, 1959.

KINSEY, ALFRED, W. B. POMEROY, C. E. MARTIN, AND P. H. GEBHARD. *Sexual behavior in the human female.* Philadelphia: W. B. Saunders, 1953.

LOWREY, LAWSON G. Adjustment over the life span. In George Lawton (ed.), *New goals for old age.* New York: Columbia University Press, 1943, pp. 8–9.

POLLAK, OTTO. *Social adjustment in old age.* New York: Social Science Research Council, Bulletin 59, 1948.

SIRJAMAKI, JOHN. *The American family in the twentieth century.* Cambridge, Mass.: Harvard University Press, 1953.

SUSSMAN, MARVIN B. Parental participation in mate selection and its effect upon family continuity. *Social Forces*, October 1953, **32**: 76–77.

TIBBITTS, CLARK. National aspects of an aging population. In Clark Tibbitts and Wilma Donahue (eds.), *Growing in the older years.* Ann Arbor, Mich.: The University of Michigan Press, 1951.

WALLER, WILLARD, AND R. HILL. *The family: a dynamic interpretation.* New York: Dryden, 1951.

Family-Kin Networks and Aging in Cross-cultural Perspective

ETHEL SHANAS

SOCIAL MYTHS ARE THOSE BELIEFS THAT everyone in a society takes for granted. An American myth, widely held, is that old people are isolated from their families. In the mass media—in newspapers, magazines, and television—when the aged are considered at all the prototype old person is usually an old lady, physically decrepit, living in a single room surrounded by filth and squalor. Such old ladies are always reported as completely alone, without relatives, without anyone who cares. These accounts tend to peak at the Christmas–New Year season, and at times of national concern.

The mass media can scarcely be censured for the dissemination of what is essentially a myth about the elderly. In restating this myth they share the position of the United Nations which in a background document on the elderly circulated to the General Assembly states categorically that the extended family breaks down in developed countries (United Nations, 1971, p. 9). After all, for many years, family sociologists have stated that with industrialization and urbanization old people become physically and socially isolated from their children and other relatives.

The facts are quite different. Old people in the United States are not physically and socially isolated from their children and relatives. Instead they form part of a kin network of three and four generations, and interact with children, grandchildren, and other relatives. Marvin Sussman, a leader in empirical family research, has summarized numerous studies of the relationships of adult children and their parents in the United States. Sussman (1965) says:

> The extended kin network is the basic social system in American urban society within which parent–adult child relationships are identified, described and analyzed. . . . The evidence also refutes the notion that nuclear family units are isolated and dependent upon the activities of other institutions and social systems.

The evidence is pervasive that the extended kin network, defined as a social system of grandparents, adult children, grandchildren, and other relatives is widespread in the United States and that help patterns among kin are common. Even Professor Talcott Parsons, a foremost exponent in the 1940s of the position that the isolated nuclear family was the usual American family, now believes that in the normal American family ". . . extended kin, especially members of the family of orientation but not only they, serve as a 'reserve' of expectations of solidarity, and willingness to implement them, which can be mobilized in case of need" (1965).

Even if there is agreement that kin networks do exist in the United States (Adams 1968, 1970; Shanas 1967; Shanas and Streib 1965), the argument is still advanced that somehow old people in the United States are less likely to see their children than old people in other countries, that their relatives are more likely to abandon them, etc. Empirical evidence is now available which enables us to compare the situation of old people in this country with that of old people in other Western

A revised version of a paper given at the meetings of the American Association of the Advancement of Science, Philadelphia, 1971. The critical comments of Professors Betty E. Cogswell, Jacquelyne J. Jackson, Gordon F. Streib, and Marvin B. Sussman are gratefully acknowledged.

The Danish, British, and American data were collected in 1962 as part of an international research program funded by the United States Public Health Service. The Polish, Yugoslav, and Israeli data were collected on research projects sponsored by the Social and Rehabilitation Service of the United States Department of Health, Education, and Welfare (1967, 1969) and have been made available through the cooperation of that agency and the investigators in the respective countries, Professor Jerzy Piotrowski, Dr. Yves Nedeljkovic, and Dr. Uri Avner, Mrs. Thea Nathan, and Miss Hanna Weihl.

industrialized countries and in the developing countries of eastern Europe and the Near East.

In the present paper I shall compare the family situation of old people in the United States with the family situation of old people in two other Western industrialized countries, Denmark and Great Britain, and with the family situation of old people in two Eastern European countries, Poland and Yugoslavia, and in Israel. Data will be presented on the composition of the families of old people in these six countries, on the living arrangements of old people, on the proximity of old people to their children, and on their contacts with the children, brothers and sisters, and other relatives. The data show clearly that irrespective of country old people who have children are not isolated from their children, either physically or socially, and that contacts with brothers and sisters are maintained in old age. These findings are general for the United States, the other Western industrialized countries, and the developing countries of Eastern Europe. There are some differences, however, between old people in the industrial and developing countries in their extended family contacts. The reasons for these similarities and differences will be discussed below.

METHODS

The data for the six countries reported here are from an extensive cross-national collaborative research program on the social and economic circumstances of persons aged 65 and over. The criticism has been made that "Much of the literature on interaction between related households is confused in its conceptualization, inaccurate in its operationalization and unrepresentative in its sampling" (Gibson 1972, p. 4). The present data, on the contrary, come from nationwide area probability samples of approximately 2500 persons living outside of institutions in Denmark, Britain, the United States, Poland, and Yugoslavia and from a probability sample of 1142 older Jewish residents of Israel living in towns and cities. The data are based on reports of old people themselves. It is well known that different interpretations of questions by respondents in different countries may affect their answers but whether or not one has children or

siblings and when one last saw children or siblings is a relatively straightforward factual phenomenon.

In sample surveys such as these, every eligible respondent (in this instance, every person aged 65 and over outside of an institution) has an equal chance of being located and interviewed. Further, it is possible to generalize from these samples to the total population which the sample represents.

The data were collected in 1962 in Denmark, Britain, and the United States (Shanas et al. 1968), in 1966 and 1967 in Poland and Israel, and in 1969 in Yugoslavia. The research was limited to old people living outside of institutions and therefore excludes from four to five percent of the elderly in each country. This four to five percent includes a disproportionate number of the oldest people in the population, and those most likely to have no children. Comparisons of each of the study samples with independent estimates of the elderly population, however, show generally good agreement.

FINDINGS

Family Composition

Adult children are the major social and psychological support of the elderly. The old man who responded to the question "Did you do anything when you were younger to take care of yourself in your old age?" by saying "Yes, I had children," assessed accurately and with psychological insight the relationships of old parents and adult children.

Four of every five old people in the United States have at least one living child. This is roughly the same proportion as in Denmark, Yugoslavia, Poland, and among Jews of Western origin (born in Europe, America, Australia, South Africa) in Israel. A somewhat lower proportion of old people in Britain have living children, a function of the high proportion of single women in the older British population, a demographic phenomenon which has been traced to Britain's manpower loss in the first World War. At the other extreme, almost all older Israeli Jews of oriental origin (born in North Africa and Asia) have living children. See Table 1.

Old persons with only one or two children are especially dependent upon these children. Those with three or more living children have a family "reserve." In the United States, Denmark, Britain,

Table 1 The proportion of persons aged 65 and over in six countries who have living children and/or siblings

Percentage of persons with:	Denmark	Britain	United States	Poland	Yugoslavia	Israel	
						Western	Oriental
Living children	82	76	82	86	86	84	92
Three or more children	51	48	57	56	49	35	75
Siblings	79	77	79	67	72	65	
(Number of persons in sample)	(2446)	(2500)	(2442)	(2693)	(2645)	(793)	(349)

NOTE: Data are for the noninstitutional population only.
SOURCE: Denmark, Britain and the United States: Ethel Shanas, Peter Townsend, Dorothy Wedderburn, Henning Friis, Poul Milhøj, Jan Stehouwer. *Old people in three industrial societies.* New York: Atherton, 1968; Poland: Jerzy Piotrowski. *Requirements for aged people and the related need for developing social welfare facilities.* Warsaw, 1968; Yugoslavia: Yves Nedeljkovic. *Old people in Yugoslavia.* Belgrade: Institute of Social Policy, 1970. Israel: Jan Stehouwer. The role of the family and the community in the care of the elderly, in U. N. European Social Development Programme. *Symposium on Research and Welfare Policies for the Elderly.* New York: United Nations, 1970.

Yugoslavia, and Poland about half of all old people have three or more children. In Israel only a third of those of Western origin have three or more children, and among oriental Jews with a large family tradition three-fourths have this many children. See Table 2.

Brothers and sisters also are important social and psychological supports in old age. Often when people have no children or have never married their siblings provide them with the kinds of supports that others get from children. Those now numbered among the old are the survivors of large families and most of them have living brothers and sisters. In the Western industrialized countries roughly eight of every ten old persons have such relatives. Even in Poland, Yugoslavia, and Israel where the elderly lost numerous relatives in the second World War about seven of every ten still report living brothers and sisters.

Most old people, then, whether in the industrial Western countries or in Eastern Europe or Israel have children and/or brothers and sisters still alive. It is not enough to have children or relatives, however. For them to function as social supports for the old person they must be physically close to him and see him often.

The Living Arrangements of Old People

The living arrangements of old people reflect a variety of factors: whether the person is married or unmarried, whether or not he has children, whether his children are married or unmarried, what his income level is, his state of health, the supply of housing available to him, etc.

In the United States and in other Western industrial countries most married old people live apart from their children and relatives. This is also the case for Israelis of Western origins. In Western cultures this is what old people want—to live independently in their own homes as long as possible. They want to be near children but not with them. As the Austrian sociologists Rosenmayr and Köckeis put it (1963; 1965), old people want "intimacy at a distance." In Eastern Europe while roughly half of all married couples live apart from their children and relatives, substantial proportions share a house with married children. Among married oriental Jews in Israel while half live apart from their children large families result in numbers of unmarried children still remaining in the household of aged parents.

Table 2 The living arrangements of persons aged 65 and over in six countries by marital status

Household composition*	Marital status and country						
	Married persons						
Percentage of persons living with:	Denmark	Britain	United States	Poland	Yugoslavia	Israel	
						Western	Oriental
Spouse only	82	68	79	50	49	82	47
Plus married child	1	5	2	22	33	4	10
Plus unmarried child	14	23	15	19	11	12	41
Plus other relative	—	3	3	3	5		
Plus others	3	1	1	6	2	2	2
(Number of persons)	(1399)	(1211)	(1335)	(1263)	(1392)	(508)	(204)
	Unmarried persons						
Percentage of persons:							
Living alone	61	43	48	30	32	50	23
With married child	7	19	14	38	44	35	47
With unmarried child	15	18	20	16	8	9	21
With other relatives	7	13	12	9	8	—	
With others	10	6	6	7	8	6	9
(Number of persons)	(1107)	(1289)	(1107)	(1451)	(1192)	(285)	(145)

SOURCE: See Table 1. Percentages in this table based on all persons whether or not they have children.
*This is a priority code, *i.e.*, households with married children may also include unmarried children, etc.

Similar findings are reported for unmarried old people, that is the widowed, separated, divorced, and single. In Western countries about half live alone. In Eastern Europe and among oriental Jews in Israel, however, lesser proportions live alone and many unmarried persons share homes with their married children.

The main reasons for the differences in living arrangements between the aged in Western countries and in the Eastern European countries would appear to be twofold: the still relatively large agricultural populations of Eastern Europe compared with the Western countries, with families sharing a common household (Halpern 1958), and the tremendous housing shortages which followed the devastation of the second World War and the succeeding rapid urbanization of the Eastern European countries. Acute housing shortages appear to make shared living arrangements among old people

and their children inevitable. This can be seen in Israel where Israelis of Western origins, who as married couples live apart from children, as widows or widowers are as likely to share homes with their children as are the Eastern Europeans.

Whether in the United States, in the other Western industrialized countries, or in Eastern Europe or Israel, roughly one unmarried old person in ten lives with a relative. These relatives usually are brothers and sisters, sometimes married, but more often themselves single or widowed.

The fact that old people do not live with their children does not mean that they are physically isolated from their children. Living apart from children is compensated for by having at least one child in the immediate vicinity, often next door or only a short distance away. Table 3 gives the proportion of old people with children who have at least one child either in the same household or within ten

Table 3 The proportion of elderly persons in six countries whose nearest child lives either in the same household or within ten minutes distance

Country		Percent
Denmark		52
Britain		66
United States		61
Poland		70
Yugoslavia		73
Israel*	Western origin	55
	Oriental origin	84

SOURCE: See Table 1. Percentages in this table based on number of persons with children. Data for Israel from H. Weihl *et al.*, *Investigation of the family life, living conditions and needs of the noninstitutionalized urban Jewish aged 65 plus in Israel.* Jerusalem: Ministry of Social Welfare, n.d.

*Excludes seven percent of the sample (largely Jews of Western origin) all of those children live abroad.

minutes distance from them. These proportions range from 52 percent in Denmark to 73 percent in Yugoslavia. "Distance" is defined by the older respondents themselves who were asked, "How close is your nearest child, by the usual methods of transport?" In most cases, persons whose nearest child was said to be within ten minutes' distance were reporting a child within ten minutes' walk from them. From one-half to three-fourths of all old people with children, then, either live with a child or within ten minutes of a child. Neither the long-time industrialization in the three Western countries nor the rapid urbanization of Poland and Yugoslavia has physically removed old people from their children. Where an old person has several children there seems to be one among them, sometimes the oldest, sometimes the youngest, often a daughter, but in agricultural settings more likely a son, who remains in close residential proximity to the old person.

Family Contacts

Kin networks in industrialized and urbanized societies are not dependent on common households or even on physical proximity. As David Schneider (1971) has said: "The number of hours it takes to go from one place to another are not in themselves matters of kinship." What is important in kin relationships is the socioemotional distance between kin which makes them turn to one another in case of need. One measure of socioemotional distance is the frequency with which kin see one another. Do children and other relatives of old people see them often? Table 4 gives the proportion of old people, living apart from their children, irrespective of distance, who saw at least one child within 24 hours of their interview. The table also shows the proportion of these persons who saw at least one of their children within the preceding week.

In every country at least half of all people living apart from children had seen one of their children either the day they were interviewed or the day before that. In Poland, the proportion of such contacts between old people and their children reached 64 percent. In every country the proportion of old people living apart from children who had seen a child within the last week was between 70 and 80 percent. The elderly in Denmark who were least likely to live within ten minutes distance of a child led all other countries in the proportion seeing children within the preceding week. The evidence is very clear. In the industrial Western countries, in the countries of Eastern Europe, and in Israel old people who live apart from their children continue to see at least one of their children regularly. While some children in the family may live at great

Table 4 The proportion of elderly persons in six countries not living with a child who saw a child within the last 24 hours and within the last week

Country	Saw child within last 24 hours	Saw child within last week
	%	%
Denmark	53	80
Britain	47	77
United States	52	78
Poland	64	77
Yugoslavia	51	71
Israel	48	76

SOURCE: See Table 1. Percentages in this table based on number of persons with children.

distances, others are close enough for daily or at least weekly visiting. See Table 5.

Contacts with siblings are less frequent than contact with children. Nonetheless from three to four of every ten old people with siblings saw at least one during the preceding week. The magnitude of sibling contact in the later decades of life has been noted by Elaine Cumming and David Schneider in the United States (1961), and by Peter Townsend in his studies in Britain and in the cross-national studies of which these data are a part (Shanas *et al.*, 1968). In every country but Yugoslavia, women are more likely to see their siblings than are men. This reflects the higher proportions of widowed and single persons among women than among men. These women may need various kinds of services and family support from brothers and sisters, and brothers and sisters are expected to make such support available.

Table 6 summarizes the family contacts during a week of all old persons except those who live with children. This table includes the "isolated aged" who are supposed to be so common in the United States. Four of every five old persons in the United States, excluding those who live with children, had some contact with a family member during the week before they were interviewed. The American aged are seen as often by their family members as the aged in Denmark or Britain. The Polish aged have the highest proportion of family contacts, largely because of their continuous contact with their children whether or not these are in the same household. Yugoslavia and Britain emerge as the

two countries most likely to have really isolated aged persons since in both countries about one in every ten persons not living with children is without children or other relatives.

SUMMARY

The data presented in this paper compare the American elderly with old people in other Western industrialized countries, in eastern Europe, and in Israel. Four of every five old people in the United States, roughly the same proportion as in Denmark, Yugoslavia, Poland and among Western Jews in Israel have at least one living child. Being a parent of an adult child does not mean that an old person lives with a child. In all of the countries studied, with the exception among oriental Jews in Israel, the right of married couples to live in a separate household is recognized. That right is granted to both the elderly and the young. Wherever possible, widowed old persons continue to live apart from their children.

The fact that old people live separately from their adult children does not mean that the generations do not see one another. At least one child is likely to be physically close to the old person and at least one child sees the old person often. Where there are no children, siblings and other relatives, the so-called extended kin, often take the place of children in helping old people remain integrated within the society.

As one compares the United States and the Western urbanized countries with the eastern European countries it is apparent that with urbanization contacts of the elderly with their kin become somewhat fewer. They do not vanish, however (see Greenfield 1961). Family and kin remain important to the elderly irrespective of country. To quote Professor Talcott Parsons (1965):

> The family can thus be seen to have two primary functions, not one. On the one hand it is the primary agent of socialization for the child, while on the other it is the primary basis of security for the normal adult.

The mass media and some sociologists to the contrary, the family and the kin network remain the major social and psychological support of the American elderly.

Table 5 The proportion of elderly men and women in six countries who saw a sibling within the last week

Country	Men	Women
	%	%
Denmark	32	37
Britain	28	41 .
United States	34	43
Poland	33	38
Yugoslavia	48	40
Israel	28	28

SOURCE: See Table 1. Percentages in this table based on number of persons with siblings.

Table 6 Family contacts of men and women, aged 65 and over, in five countries excluding those who share a home with children

Percentage distribution

Family contacts	Denmark			Britain			United States			Poland			Yugoslavia		
	Men	Women	All	Men	Women	All	Men	Women	All	Men	Women	All	Men	Women	All
Saw child during previous week	63	63	63	52	49	50	60	59	59	89	79	84	67	67	67
No contact with child but saw sibling or relative	5	5	5	7	5	6	7	9	8	3	3	3	7	3	5
Have no children, saw sibling or relative	6	10	9	15	25	21	12	17	14	5	11	8	8	11	10
Have no children, no family contact	24	21	22	19	13	15	21	14	18	2	6	4	9	7	8
Have neither children, sibling or relative	2	1	2	7	8	8	–	1	1	1	1	1	9	12	10
Total	100	100	100	100	100	100	100	100	100	100	100	100	100	100	100
(Number of persons)	(935)	(1086)	(2021)	(692)	(1006)	(1698)	(878)	(1008)	(1886)	(576)	(845)	(1421)	(584)	(645)	(1229)

Source: See Table 1. Percentages in this table based on all persons not living with children, irrespective of whether they have children. Israeli data not available.

REFERENCES

ADAMS, BERT N. 1968. *Kinship in an urban setting.* Chicago: Markham Publishing Company.

——— 1970. Isolation, function and beyond: American kinship in the 1960s. *Journal of Marriage and the Family* 32 (November): 575–598.

CUMMING, ELAINE, AND DAVID M. SCHNEIDER 1961. Sibling solidarity: a property of American kinship. *American Anthropologist* 63 (June): 498–507.

GIBSON, GEOFFREY 1972. Kin family network: overheralded structure in past conceptualizations of family functioning. *Journal of Marriage and the Family* 34 (February): 13–23.

GREENFIELD, SIDNEY M. 1961. Industrialization and the family in sociological theory. *American Journal of Sociology* 67 (November): 312–322.

HALPERN, JOEL M. 1958. *A Serbian village.* New York: Columbia University Press.

NEDELJKOVIC, Y. *Old people in Yugoslavia. Analytical tables.* Belgrade: Institute of Social Policy.

PARSONS, TALCOTT 1965. The normal American family. In Seymour Farber, Piero Mustacchi, and Roger H. Wilson (eds.), *Man and civilization: the family's search for survival.* New York: McGraw-Hill.

PIOTROWSKI, J. 1968. *Requirements for aged people and the related needs for developing social welfare facilities.* Warsaw.

ROSENMAYR, LEOPOLD, AND EVA KÖCKEIS 1963. Propositions for a sociological theory of aging and the family. *International Social Science Journal* 15: 418.

——— 1965. Umwelt und Familie Alter Menschen. Neuwied and Berlin: Luchterhand.

SCHNEIDER, DAVID 1971. A relative is a person. In B. N. Adams and T. Weirath (eds.), *Readings on the sociology of the family.* Chicago: Markham Publishing Company.

SHANAS, ETHEL 1967. Family help patterns and social class in three countries. *Journal of Marriage and the Family* 29: 257–266.

———, AND GORDON F. STREIB (eds.) 1965. *Social structure and the family: generational relations.* Englewood Cliffs, N.J.: Prentice-Hall.

———, AND P. TOWNSEND, D. WEDDERBURN, H. FRIIS, P. MILHØJ, AND J. STEHOUWER 1968. *Old people in three industrial societies.* New York and London: Atherton and Routledge and Kegan Paul.

STEHOUWER, JAN 1970. The role of the family and the community in the care of the elderly. In *United Nations European Social Development Programme.* Symposium on Research and Social Welfare Policies for the Elderly. New York: United Nations.

SUSSMAN, MARVIN B. 1965. Relationships of adult children and their parents in the United States. In E. Shanas and G. F. Streib (eds.), *Social structure and the family: generational relations.* Englewood Cliffs, N.J.: Prentice-Hall.

UNITED NATIONS 1971. *Questions of the elderly and the aged.* General Assembly. A/8364. August 31, 1971. New York: United Nations.

WEIHL, HANNAH, THEA NATHAN, AND URI AVNER 1970. *Investigation of the family life, living conditions and needs of the noninstitutionalized urban Jewish aged 65+ in Israel.* Jerusalem: State of Israel. Ministry of Social Welfare.

Chapter 9

Dissolution

DISSOLUTION OF THE FAMILY COMES about through desertion, separation, divorce, and death. Divorce has become a major factor in the termination of marriage relationships. In 1910, one out of every 100 marriages ended in divorce. Today, it is expected that one out of every three marriages will probably end up in divorce. Although there is a tendency in our society to blame the parties involved if the marriage fails, Ray Birdwhistell, Janet Kohen, and Roslyn Feldberg see the explanation for divorce as stemming from the larger society: Birdwhistell in the ideologies of society concerning the family; and Kohen and Feldberg in the structure of the family and its relationship to the economic system.

Ray Birdwhistell, while not explicitly discussing divorce, presents an analysis of the ideologies surrounding the contemporary American family. There is a great emphasis on romantic love within marriage which leads to the isolation of the dyad. Personal relationships outside the family are limited. Furthermore, parents are given total responsibility for the personality development of the children. Hence, the family is a closed unit with too many idealized objectives to pursue. Because of this, the high divorce rate may be inevitable.

Janet Kohen and Roslyn Feldberg are concerned with locating the reasons for divorce within the structure of the society rather than in the individual. They see the high divorce rate as related to the corporate order. The family is supposed to meet all of the emotional needs of the individual so that the corporate order need not be concerned with this.

Perhaps this is why the ideology of romantic love (as discussed by Birdwhistell) exists within marriage. This idealized version of marriage developed with the beginning of industrialization. However, the demands of the corporate order exacerbate the family's function of meeting the individual's psychological needs. For example, the corporate order demands that the worker spend a minimum of eight hours per day away from the family.

The second set of articles is concerned with the dissolution of marriage through death. There is a much greater number of widows than widowers because (1) men have a shorter life expectancy than women, (2) men marry younger women, and (3) widowers tend to remarry faster then widows do. Once a marriage is terminated through death, the surviving widow or widower must begin to learn new roles, since they are no longer part of a dyad. The problems may be exacerbated by the age of the individuals involved. Helena Lopata presents an overview of the demography of American widows: their age, living arrangements, educational levels, and other social factors affecting widowhood. The status of a widow tends to be lower than that of a wife, since the woman's status in our society has been derived from her husband's occupational position. She is also single in a couple-oriented society.

The problems of the widower, as analyzed by Irwin Gerber, are related to his sex role. Males are not supposed to be emotional; they are not supposed to have difficulties coping. Gerber shows how

309

males do in fact have emotional problems connected to widowerhood. While Lopata shows how widows may have difficulties in fulfilling instrumental tasks, Gerber discusses how widowers may have problems with the expressive roles. This stems from the sexual differentiation within marriage which exists prior to the death of a spouse.

The symbolic interactionist would be interested in how divorced people come to define themselves as successes or failures if they get divorced. One would examine how the widow and widower define their new roles and how they cope with the difficulties posed by these roles. The symbolic interactionist might also be concerned with how widows and widowers determine when they are no longer bereaved.

A structural functionalist might ask: How does role strain lead to divorce? How are the bereaved integrated into society? How explicit are the norms governing the widow and widower roles?

Using the Kohen and Feldberg article, a conflict theorist would ask: How is our economic structure related to our high divorce rate? How are conflicts in the family derived from demands of the corporate order? While studying bereavement a question from the conflict perspective would be: How do sexual and age inequalities existing in the society compound the difficulties of the bereaved?

The Idealized Model of the American Family

RAY L. BIRDWHISTELL

OUTSIDE OF *GOVERNMENT*, PERHAPS NO social form has been so broadly discussed, so idealized, so reviled, and so little understood as is *the family* and, particularly *the American family*. Perhaps this is because it is so difficult to see in perspective a new form whose novelty is masked by the fact that its function is so ancient. Accumulating evidence indicates that social organisms from fish to man, in order to survive, have found it necessary to order certain aspects of their lives around courtship, mating, reproduction, and care of the young. The locale of such functioning has been determined by, and has, in turn, conditioned the territorial organization of the group. Yet, notwithstanding this long and multivariant history, and however inventive man himself has been over the ages, in the past century we may have developed a new type of organization in the so-called American family. The self-centered husband-wife, parent–child unit, so idealized in Western European and American society today may be not only a novel way of organizing familial functioning, but it may also be a temporary and ultimately nonviable social form.

In another article, I discussed the fact that a unit restricted to a husband and a wife and their offspring was a useful form for a pioneering or exploration group before settlement.[1] There seems to be ample evidence that this limited unit functioned well to permit individuals quick social mobility (up and down), in that, in the absence of extended loyalties, it allowed the individuals to leave homelands and traditional values with minimal strain. However, this "segmental" family could seldom become a secure base for socialization, maturation, and long-term satisfactory social living if its strength depended upon the exclusion or the secularization of loyalties to individuals or groups outside the husband–wife, parent–child range. Obviously, such a tight and limited form of family organization permits great flexibility as new territories are opened up or as the loosening of class barriers within societies permits individual men and women and their

Reprinted by permission of the author, from *Social casework* (April 1970) pp. 195-198, Family Service Association of America.

spouses and children easier passage from one social class to another. If, however, in order to permit mobility, the unit is so organized as to resist all interpersonal relationships with other than immediate family members, such a unit (except perhaps in societies far simpler than any we have yet discovered) lacks lateral supports. It must derive all its support from the impersonal structures of the society, the formalized governmental, educational, economic, and religious institutions. In other words, if the only legitimate personal relationships must come from *within* the unit, and if the young, as they mature, must leave the unit to set up another such unit, such an organization is, by necessity, short-lived and self-destructive, the elderly are left lonely and isolated, and the maturing young are guilty of destroying the unit by the act of maturation.

Although this husband-wife, parent-child family type has been seen as *the* American family and as such has been idealized by the press and has been overvalued by both moralists and social scientists of the last half century, it is a relatively recent development as far as actual and extensive operation is concerned. Sometime following the Civil War, two social inventions, which seemed to be the result of the emergent awareness of man's capacity to learn and to influence and be influenced by other men, changed the direction of both marital arrangements and child care. For a variety of reasons—and these reasons range all the way from the development of machine manufacture, the wide distribution of population, the development of mobility through education, and the changing role and expectations of women with the consequent change (although not nearly so recognized) in the role of men—there emerged a new concept of the ideal relationship between marriage partners: romantic marriage and the romanticized conjugal unit increasingly became the American ideal.

ROMANTICIZED RELATIONSHIPS

Romantic love is a concept that idealizes the feelings between a male and a female. It is not particularly new; a number of societies across the world have idealized this relationship and, at least since the time of the Greeks, there have been periods of varied emphasis upon this ideal in Western society. Traditionally, romantic love has been seen, however, as a premarital or an extramarital situation apart from the everyday, sustaining aspects of social living. As sociologists viewed it during the first quarter of this century, the trouble with romantic love was that it had lost its romantic function whereby men and women could escape in fantasy from everyday life. Romantic love became vulgarized and regarded as the justification or the necessary precondition for marriage.

Toward the end of the last century and during the first quarter of this century, romantic love was domesticated and extended in scope. There emerged the ideal of the romantic marriage in which one male and one female meet and fall in love and that love should be sufficient to sustain their relationship "until death do them part." This was a new development in that not only did the mating involve exclusive sexual rights and duties but all emotional response became included and negotiated under the compact. In short, the ideal stated and still states that one man and one woman should marry one another and contract to satisfy *all* of the other's emotional and physical needs. Concepts of sexual infidelity were unconsciously extended to include all the personal feelings of the two individuals involving outsiders. Not only does this involve a secularization of all nonfamilial associations but it illegitimizes all those associations outside the marriage which threaten to become personal. If all personal attachments, to be legitimate, must be intrafamilial, the outside must be depersonalized. This situation is not an optimal one for the development of mutual understanding and conventions of fidelity. Counter-infidelity operations preclude the growth of fidelity operations. Loyalty becomes little more than an antidote to disloyalty and there is an accelerating isolation both inside and outside the family.

The concept of romantic marriage idealized the closed, exclusive, and isolating dyad. As such it must be threatened by the appearance of outsiders, including the children born to it. To include "parenting" as the natural extension of being a husband or wife does not reduce the strain upon the pair, particularly if the couple is caught in a system of values in which their love is finally proved by the personalities of their maturing children. As if this romanticized and overdemanding ideal of the dyad were not enough to impose upon man, a second invention just before the turn of the century completed the nonsense. This was the invention of defining parents not only as legally, morally, religiously, and economically responsible for their children but also as finally responsible for the personalities of their children. As personality became seen as a result of "proper" child care and child care as the final responsibility of the parents, the parents (particularly the mother) were regarded as the cause of "bad" personalities.

IDEALIZED MODEL
OF FAMILY LIFE

It is difficult to know just what proportion of the American population lives in these exclusive, self-concerned, segmentalized, husband–wife, parent–child units. It is even more difficult to know how many Americans use the ideal as a way of measuring their marriages, their parenthood, or their relationships to their spouses or children. It is, however, perfectly obvious that this is the model presented to the public by science, in art, and by the mass communication facilities. More seriously, it is the model used by our legal, social, psychiatric, and clerical experts. When all agencies designed to assist men and women and children in trouble accept as ideal the condition which occasioned the difficulty, the very devices for ameliorating social pathology contribute to it instead.

It requires but little reflection to see that the American family, as idealized, is an overloaded institution. It is easy to see, too, that the goals set by the concept are unattainable and leave people failing both as spouses and as parents. This can have even more tragic results if the people who find it impossible to live in such a situation, because they are human and have human needs, seek help to escape and are directed back into the pathological situation. The counselor, the therapist, or the legal adviser who accepts the ideal becomes the reinforcer of the pathology.

The ideal has far-reaching results and breeds its own mythologies. We have described our culture as child-centered and we have felt the children to be unappreciative of the attention given them. I am not at all sure this is true. Perhaps it would be better to say that we have become a "marriage and parenting-centered" society, with the children not the center of the attention but rather a necessary component of it. The behavior of the child is given attention not because of himself but as a measurement of the marriage or of the parents as parents. At least this is the way it appears to many of the young. The child says, "You don't care about me; you are only thinking of yourself." This makes little sense to the anxious parent who is constantly concerned with whether he or she is "doing the right thing with the child." Neither does the parent who tells the child, "Everything we do is for you and we want you to make us proud," make much sense to the child. Such statements as these delight the "expert" who sees the parent-child difficulty as a consequence of the failure of parents and children to communicate. In my opinion, we miss the point when we focus upon the ploys, the recurrent tactics of action and reaction *within* the family. Such a view obscures the more salient fact that the institution itself is distorted and must be reorganized; these small events are but symptoms of the larger pathology. Unless the family unit can be expanded and its members supported in larger social relationships, we can give little more than first aid to its members.

DETRIMENTAL EFFECTS
OF THE IDEALIZED MODEL

I cannot pretend to be objective about my personal dismay at the mischief occasioned by the acceptance of this American family ideal. One aspect of the present conflict in America is the so-called generation gap. This concept is useful for pointing out the recent extraordinary acceleration of social time and for directing our energies toward the revision of increasingly outmoded legal, economic, educational, and religious formulations and structures. Unfortunately, for many adhering to the romanticized American family concept, *generation* translates *parent* and *child*, and as the adult deals with or reads about the young, he does so as a guilty or insufficiently appreciated parent; as the young attempt to deal with the adult world, they tend to operate by the same logic. Necessary social changes become points of nonproductive, intergenerational conflict when the adversary method is reduced to an extended family squabble. Creative energies are easily dissipated when the angry child tries to engage with the guilty adult in a way directly related to the idealized family sphere. The child has been instructed by the parent that his (the child's) personality success or failure can be directly related to the acts of commission or omission on the part of the parents. When the child angrily accuses, the parent accepts the charge in submissive impotence or is resentful because the child is insufficiently grateful for what the parent has been able to do. The fact that all adults become the "establishment" makes negotiation outside the family difficult too. Social change becomes inhibited or distorted by temper tantrums, sullenness, or whining on the part of the child. Angry, reactive government officials can confirm the adolescent conception of the outside world (as well as acting out the exasperation of the guilty parent); the equally reactive adolescent rebel leader often fulfills in his actions the projections of the guilty parent. It is not surprising that both the self-designated representatives of the adult establishment and the self-selected spokesmen of the disappointed adolescents disdain education, social science, and psychiatry and scorn those moderates and liberals who see choices other than those of armed rebellion or armed suppression.

It is not difficult to be critical or horrified at the effects of this impossibly overloaded and guilt-creating social unit, the family. There seems no reason to be amazed that even as an ideal the family has occasioned anger, hostility, disappointment, and guilt, all of which contribute to neurosis if not to psychosis and social pathology. It is amazing that so many people have withstood the force of such a patently pathogenic institution and have achieved a reasonable adaptation to living with other people. The number of reasonably well-adjusted human beings in American society is indeed a testament to

NOTE

1. Ray L. Birdwhistell. The American family: some perspectives. *Psychiatry* 29: 203–212 (August 1966).

man's flexibility, his ability
tive environment, and his c
impossible idealizations.

CONCLUSION

It would be naive to believe that the present turmoil in America and throughout the world is a *result* of "bad families," "bad mental health," or the failure of communication between the generations. Such reductionism is obscure and exhausting at a time when we must direct our energies to the solution of critical domestic and international problems. Constructive, even revolutionary, energies are all too easily dissipated by pseudo-familial hyperbole, temper tantrums, and pout. These confrontations are effective, however, because many Americans are so miserable in their limited and emotionally depriving domestic existence. The idealized family with its concentration upon intrafamilial matters is an aspect—and perhaps a critical one—both of the organized immature anger that precludes effective negotiation and of the weary isolationism of many who constitute the so-called silent majority and whose painful preoccupation with unsatisfactory marriages and stressful parent–child relationships saps their few energies.

We would not have a healthy society simply if husbands and wives understood each other better, or if parents and children could be directed toward less destructive interaction. If, however, we could reduce the pathology inherent in the present family ideal by unmasking its impossible goals, we might have better access to the talent and energy now so wastefully employed by so many unhappy and dissatisfied people.

The problem is how to open up these closed families and how to permit the flow of energy and information to and from them. It is clear that that problem cannot be solved as long as our lawmakers, clinicians, and moralists accept impossible ideals and operate in terms of them.

Isolation and Invasion: The Conditions of Marriage and Divorce

JANET KOHEN AND ROSLYN L. FELDBERG

THE UNITED STATES HAS AMONG THE highest divorce rates of all industrialized countries, but it also has among the highest marriage and remarriage rates (Carter and Glick 1970). This pattern is perhaps best explained by noting the lack of any popular understanding of the structural conditions which underlie the organization of family life. The rates, which might appear paradoxical at first glance, are not independent—all are consequences of the same structure. The ideology of marriage provides the motive to marry, the contradictions between that ideology and the realities of married life lead to divorce and the absence of alternative structures and ideologies lead to remarriage.

The American ideology of the family emphasizes personal fulfillment as the reason for maintaining family relationships and love as the basis for marriage (Theodorson 1965). Most people in our society do marry, probably expecting what that ideology promises, but they find themselves pressured into organizing their family life along other dimensions. Internal family responsibilities, demands of formal organizations, the problems of financing a family, sex-role stereotypes, and sex discrimination limit couples' choices in the way they organize their family life. The resulting family structure may complicate, if not preclude, finding personal satisfaction within the family (Yorburg 1973).

Divorce is often the consequence but people do not view their divorces in these terms. Structural problems are largely invisible to people who must cope with the personal consequences of these problems on a daily basis: the spouse who is always tired, always irritable, or always away from the family. Having learned that marriage results from being in love with the right person, they feel that they or their partners are responsible for their disappointments. Divorce comes to be viewed as a matter of mistaken choice, as a personal, not an organizational, failure. The community and some academics (Glick 1975) view divorce similarly and encourage divorced persons to embark on a more thorough search for new, more compatible partners. The cycle continues.

This cycle embodies the contradictory relationship between the family and the corporate, capitalist order (Smith 1973; Vogel 1973). The contradictions are two-fold. First, as an institution which reinforces the standards of the corporate order, the family is involved in creating the frustrations and problems which it is later expected to solve or, at least, contain. Parents produce the next generation of workers, teaching them to value themselves as workers or, at least, to accept the necessity of disciplined employment. Husbands' and wives' joint commitment to provide for their children and each other strengthens their attachment to the work which supports all of them. At the same time, both spouses look to each other to provide the emotional fulfillment that makes it easier to withstand the strains of the unrewarding work they actually experience. Second, the family unit's dependence on the corporate order for daily necessities forces family members to organize their relationships around the demands of that order creating a family structure which is poorly suited to meeting emotional needs. The family becomes the haven-that-isn't, regardless of the sources of members' emotional needs. Through sex-determined family division of labor, the woman, as the overseer of family emotional life, becomes responsible for the consequences of this contradiction. Our analysis centers on the second contradiction.[1]

The remainder of this paper focuses on the consequences and implications of this contradiction for the adult members of the family. Unless specified otherwise, the term family will be used interchangeably with married couple. While the ideology and structure of the family have important implications for children, the arguments raised here deal with the effects of this contradiction on adult choices to enter, maintain, or leave a marital relationship.

IDEOLOGY OF THE FAMILY

Sociologists and other students of family change have emphasized the shift in responsibilities of the family from preindustrial to industrial societies. As societies industrialized, many of the traditional family functions were transferred to external organizations. Although the contemporary family still shares responsibility for these functions (Vincent 1966), only in the area of emotional-nurturant needs does the family retain its dominant position. Most people view the family primarily as an emotional unit, oriented to individual well-being, and expect it to be the one group in which they will find stable interpersonal relationships which offer support, sharing and intimate communication (Burgess and Locke 1953; Baum 1971).

Love has become the most important basis for marriage and public control over the choice of marriage partners has been minimized. In preindustrial times, people viewed the family as a central political, religious and economic unit (Bremner 1970; Hunt 1970). Members also received their education and met their emotional needs within the family but these were secondary concerns (Burgess and Locke 1953; Aries 1962; Goode 1963). As long as the family was the primary social unit, marriages were the subject of family negotiations. Affection might develop later but the marriage itself was based on satisfactory economic arrangements between the families of the "to-be-married" couple, as well as religious and legal considerations (Bremner 1970; Hunt 1970). Today spouses are expected to find each other and decide to marry as a consequence of love. While parents still "interfere" their right to do

so is no longer publicly supported since love is a matter between the individuals involved.

Within the family, the allocation of responsibilities reflects societal beliefs about the innate, complementary attributes assumed to define the sexes. This division of labor prescribes a role for males that makes them marginal to the central function of the family, the emotional-nurturant one. Men are believed to be best at instrumental tasks and consequently have major responsibility for the family's relationship to external organizations. In contrast, women are believed to be specifically gifted in understanding and ministering to emotional needs. They are thought to achieve their fulfillment through bearing and caring for children and nurturing others (Parsons 1965). The female's presumed superiority is translated into responsibility.

Assumptions about the family are integral to the cultural ideology which affects all organizations in the society. The ramifications of this relationship appear in many areas. For example, managers of formal organizations often assume that people's family roles determine their degree of commitment to the organization. Married men are expected to be deeply involved in formal organizations because of their economic and political responsibility for their families, and may be preferred employees on those grounds. Married women who participate in extrafamilial organizations are assumed to be engaged in activities of secondary importance to their family role (Bart 1972; Siegal and Haas 1963). They can be hired on temporary or part-time bases, paid low wages, or treated as hobbyists, do-gooders, or volunteers.

Each of the ideological components which defines the family is part of the heritage people learn and come to expect from family relationships. This heritage is both academically and popularly expressed in images and media. Guides to child-rearing prescribed parent–child interaction to foster the emotional growth of children; divorce laws legitimate mental cruelty and emotional incompatibility as reasons for divorce; writers argue for the elimination of the family because it has failed as a unit to provide for the emotional well-being of its members; child development experts caution mothers that their every response to the child during "the first five years" can leave indelible scars or create a genius; and television programs, women's pages and movies thrive on the resolution of family emotional problems or the search to find a romantic marital partner.

FAMILY STRUCTURE

Although people's beliefs affect the way they organize their activities, family structure is not a summary of personal choices. Variations in family structure by culture, pattern of economic organization, and social class have been repeatedly described in published research (Goode 1963; Bott 1971; Komarovsky 1967). The effects of these variables are evident in the routine life of the household. For example, cultural differences determine the style of meals, economic organization determines the place they are eaten—at home or in the factory—and the amount of time devoted to them and social class determines whether there will be anything to eat and if so, the quality of the basic ingredients.

Although social class is fundamental, circumscribing the effect of the other variables on personal choices for the organization of family life, these choices are further limited by the family's dependence on resources obtained from external organizations. The effect of family dependence on these organizations is inescapable because family activities cannot be performed without resources obtained from them. These resources are available according to the hiring practices, business hours and other demands of these organizations, not according to family members' choices of what would be best for them. The consequences of this dependence are far-reaching. Even tasks such as child-rearing which appear to be purely internal family matters are affected by it. This section will analyze the structure of the family by specifying the activities performed and the allocation of responsibility for these activities among adult family members.

Theoretically the activities which must be performed can be separated from the people who are assigned responsibility for them, but it is almost impossible to discuss family responsibilities without implicitly assigning them to husband or wife.

Our discussion follows these conventions, not to reinforce them but to point out how they create tensions in the structure of the family

Family life is based on paid work which is done outside the family, generally by the husband/father. The paycheck is a double link. It connects the family to external organizations and the man to the family. Through the paycheck the goods and services of other units are purchased. By providing the financial basis for these purchases, the man contributes to the family and secures his place in it. However, compromises as well as cash are transferred through this link. The organizations which control the paycheck determine who will work, at what hours, and for what pay—indirectly they control the basic arrangements of family life and the standard at which the family lives. The assignment of paid work to the man supports the sex-based division of labor within the family. Although there is evidence that the role of the man in the family has widened to include an emerging responsibility for his wife's sexual satisfaction and some obligation for arranging family recreation (Nye 1974), these contributions to the internal functioning of the family are still severely limited when the 24-hour needs of family members are taken as the base for evaluating his contributions. Overall, the man meets his major family obligations through his job outside the home. Most of his participation in the internal life of the family is treated as voluntary, varying according to his preferences, the marital relationship, and the amount of satisfaction he derives from family life.

Partly because it is performed outside the family in the man's world and partly because it is paid, outside "work" is highly valued and visible. The home-centered work of the family is much less visible, hidden by walls and by the absence of pay. When these tasks are discussed, housework and child care are the centers of attention. Housework makes a vital contribution to the family and to external organizations, but the work and its true importance are rarely recognized (Benston 1969; Oakley 1974; Engels 1972). Commercials glorify the housewife and the care she lavishes on her family but depict the content of her work as trivial, requiring little time and few skills, particularly if she uses the right consumer goods. Nevertheless family and labor force survival depend on this work. Cleaning, washing, cooking and diaper-changing have to be done to maintain those who work in the labor force, to supply basics for children being trained as members of the society and to maintain the housewife herself as the supplier of these services (Vogel 1973). The estimates of time needed to do housework range from 30–90 hours per week (Bernard 1971a) and the 16 or so different occupations involved require considerable organizational skill on the part of the housewife (Pyun 1969).

While housework is often underplayed and trivialized, child care is dramatized as the essence of the family and particularly as the most meaningful activity of the woman (Mitchell 1971). Here again the ideology of the family conflicts with reality. Child care cannot be separated from housework because both are done simultaneously. Much of child care becomes listening for trouble or preventing the child from undoing the cleaning up that is in process. In addition, child care is not solely the mother's prerogative. For children over the age of five, school teachers routinely share child care responsibilities with the family. Of women with children under the age of five, the one-third who do paid work supplement their own child-care activities with those of a relative, baby-sitter, or child-care center. While the value of school has been accepted for children five and over, the ideology of maternal child care extracts a psychological price from women with younger children and for those with older children whose work hours do not correspond to school hours. Both the women and the community often view shared child care as a failure of the woman to meet her responsibility and as detrimental to the child (Centers 1948; Komarovsky 1973; Wortis 1971). Whether the mother does all or shares part of the child care, she remains responsible for routine physical care, training, discipline and play as well as supervision and arrangements for the child's contacts outside the home: social life, skills training, formal schooling and baby-sitting (Nye and Hoffman 1965).

Neither housework nor child care is consistent with the beliefs which justify its place in the sex-based division of labor. Both are assigned to the woman because of her supposed superiority in emotional and nurturant skills and her "internal,"

domestic orientation; but success in either depends on her ability to deal with "external" organizations and her cognitive, physical, and organizational skills.

While family activities are often shaped by demands which conflict with family ideology, the division of labor obscures the conflict. The sexual division of labor gives substance to the internal/external dichotomy, masking the way that household patterns are shaped by "external" pressures and the fact that the energies of family members are devoted largely to organizational, not family, tasks. The image of the woman's work as home-centered and responsive to the needs of family members is perpetuated by the contrast to the highly visible, external work of the man. If his work is so clearly tied to external organizations, her complementary tasks must be family-determined. As long as someone negotiates the conflicts between family needs and extrafamilial organizations, the sexual division of labor enables spouses to maintain their belief in the autonomy and "privateness" of the family and to view its structure as a consequence of their personal choices.

THE FAMILY AS AN EMOTIONAL UNIT

If people believe that the family is an expression of personal choices, then it is reasonable for them to seek personal fulfillment in the family. Doing so highlights the conflict between what is satisfying for each spouse and what is required for family maintenance. Work which provides routine necessities takes priority; emotional well-being must be continually compromised. Interpersonal relationships and concerns are either fitted in around these constants or ignored.

Most couples expect to spend some time together. How much depends on class, occupation, or the peculiarities of individual struggles to earn a living (Kahl 1962; Komarovsky 1967). At most, families can spend dinner time and the hours outside paid work in the same setting. But time spent together is not necessarily time shared. The sex-based division of labor can foster conflict rather than harmony even in activities meant to be relaxing. What creates leisure often creates housework. Wives are usually expected to plan, prepare, serve, and clean up whether it's dinner, a party or just beer and popcorn in front of the TV. A night out must be preceded by arrangements for the children, their meal, their bath, their baby-sitter.

Merely communicating emotional concerns or discussing the difficulties which create stress is problematic. Family division of labor means that most couples spend their days apart, in different settings, doing work which makes different types of demands. This creates different concerns and provides each of them with different experiences (Baum 1971). Since responding to emotional needs requires some time and understanding of the situations and experiences which produce and reproduce those needs, the divergent daily lives of spouses make them unlikely supporters or even companions of each other (Lynd and Lynd 1929).

The conventional division of labor creates other problems too. Responsibility for resolving tension and creating emotional harmony is assigned to women on the basis of sex-role stereotypes. Since men must adapt to external organizations which generally ignore emotional needs, they often have relatively little experience, skill, or commitment in providing psychological support.[2] The man's relationship to the family is expressed mainly through his job. Most men don't particularly like what they are doing but they must work to provide money for their families. The cost of devoting their time to employment is that men have little opportunity to develop other aspects of themselves (Gintis 1972). Ironically the alienation of men from their major daily activity propels them to a greater dependency on their families for support and comfort, at the same time that it may reduce their ability to reciprocate.

The husband's one-sided contribution not only results in direct clashes but also reinforces the traditional role allocation, leaving the woman with almost total responsibility for the stability of the family and the emotional well-being of its members (Bott 1971). For example, the presence of emotional problems in the child or his/her maladjustment in school is often attributed to the mother's mistakes or neglect in caring for the child's emotional growth (Ilg and Ames 1966; Spock 1967). Clearly with such a division of roles the woman is expected to

minister to everyone, and be ministered to by no one (Bernard 1971b).

Maintaining family harmony and stability is only a part of her responsibilities. Satisfactory family life is premised on housework and child care being done. These responsibilities often conflict with her nurturant ones. If she fails to iron shirts, wash clothes, prepare dinner or clean, she disrupts the routine grounds of everyday life and can prompt a good deal of stress among family members. But doing the work can create stress as well. Obtaining resources from external organizations means she must meet their schedules even when she knows that this activity interferes with what is best for someone in the family. For example, she must get to the grocery store before it closes even if it means breaking up the children's play group. Home-centered work requires additional compromises. Any job requires some concentration and attention to work means family members must wait. When she does have time to attend to emotional needs, she may have to make choices between her spouse and her children (Rossi 1968). In such cases, whatever the choice, it will be "wrong" for at least one family member. Under such circumstances, it is not surprising to find that the number of women dissatisfied with their marriages is greatest when there are dependent children in the family (Rollins and Feldman 1970).

The allocation of emotional work to the woman has implications for her self-concept. Since family structure is not conducive to meeting emotional demands as they arise, the woman is structurally positioned to fail. When emotional needs and crises go unresolved in the home, the woman, as the adult primarily responsible for this area of family life, may question her self-worth. At the very least, she is unlikely to find the fulfillment she sought in family life (Gurin, Veroff and Feld 1960; Bradburn and Caplovitz 1965).

NONFAMILIAL EMOTIONAL RESOURCES

When family relationships either provide limited personal satisfactions or become the context in which tensions and conflicts are expressed, family members may seek relationships outside the immediate family. These may be formal services or informal and even illicit relationships. Access to them, type, and extent of use vary on the basis of sex, class, and the peculiarities of people's daily activities. Regardless of the relationships found or used, people will discover them to be limited by the same dynamics which create internal family difficulties.

Given the societal belief that the family is the primary unit providing for people's long-term emotional needs, structural arrangements outside of the family are rarely set up to secure people's emotional well-being. This is immediately apparent to the runaway child or the spouse who remains as a result of death, illness, desertion or divorce. Outside of the often tenuous connections with kin, the resources one can "count on" are emergency, situationally specific, and often expensive formal resources. Informal resources such as friendships and acquaintances, as well as kin, are often restricted by their involvements within formal organizations. Formal organizations encourage supportive relationships only when they facilitate the goals of the organization. Accessibility revolves around organizational needs. Furthermore, these relationships are tolerated by the family only as long as they don't interfere with the routine family activities of either party to a relationship.

Professional services and kin groups are generally viewed as "available" to most people. Whether they can or do use them for either routine support or in crisis is another question. Counselors, psychiatrists, and social workers are formally trained to deal with people's emotional problems. These professionals are available to those who are defined as having serious problems but often only if there is money to pay for them. They do not usually deal with routine structural problems of most families nor, for that matter, do they have much impact on the more serious conflicts which result in divorce (Goode 1956). They are a very limited resource. Professional–client relationships are neither long-term nor reciprocal; they are focused on working through problems with termination as one of the initial goals.

Parents, sisters, brothers, cousins, and the rest of the extended family of in-laws created by marriage make an important and, in most cases, long-term contribution to the members of the nuclear family (Bott 1971; Komarovsky 1967) although there is some evidence indicating a decline in felt responsibility toward kin (Nye 1974). Many family studies emphasize the close relationships between mothers and married daughters or sons but even here there are limits on the extent to which these relationships can provide emotional support (Komarovsky 1967). The tension from overstepping these limits is symbolized in the popular culture by the interminable phone call between the wife and her mother. Extended family members are expected to respond to needs of their kin but not at the expense of meeting the needs and demands of their own families.

Outside of professional services and kin, other relationships are not available to people on a regular basis. Old classmates, acquaintances, or members of a peer group, neighborhood clique, or hobby and special interest groups may become the basis for personal gratification by chance or through conscious determination and effort to seek them out. Contact with these individuals provides the opportunities for "friendship" but friendship is normally a voluntary and noncontractual relationship. It is viewed as "secondary" and subject to change due to the vagaries of either the family or other formal organizations. Long-standing friendships may have to be broken if there is a company transfer or layoff. A night of bridge or poker may be preempted by child-care responsibilities or overtime work. Any friendship may be terminated if it threatens other family members by the intensity of a member's involvement.

For most people, friendships and alternative sources of gratifications are often developed within the boundaries of formal organizations because most of a person's life outside of the family is spent there. These relationships carry with them the special problems created by the demands and pressures of the organization as well as the usual demands from the family. They are particularly tenuous and complicated. Formal organizations do not negate the possibility of friendships or personal satisfactions among their members. Such personal involvements are often allowed or even fostered, not for the intrinsic worth they have for the member's well-being but because they further the specific goals of the organization. For example, in work organizations efficiency is usually measured in terms of cost and productivity. Under some circumstances job satisfaction and morale can increase efficiency (Gintis 1972) and work is structured to foster these worker responses as long as they do not threaten managerial control. So too, management's concern with a proper corporate image is revealed in its monitoring of the "private" lives of middle managers. Company resources are used to encourage these employees to have stable, personal/family relationships which conform to the norms of corporate respectability (Smith 1973). Because the manager's personal life is considered part of the corporate image, life-styles which deviate from the accepted patterns may severely limit the individual's career in the company.

In order to contain work related relationships and gratifications which might interfere with company interests, the managers of organizations often develop mechanisms which limit or restrict their workers. There are "no talking" rules in some offices and factories; coffee breaks are taken according to section rather than personal preference; transfers ignore long-standing relationships; promotions for lower level managers often depend on the image they present when entertaining customers or participating in civic organizations. Such practices preclude the development of stable alternative relationships or life-styles just as rules against nepotism prevented stable relationships from being introduced into the organization.

Involvements in external sources of gratification create a double bind for the family members. On the one hand, since people form families for emotional reasons, external involvements may threaten the family. On the other hand, when these involvements result in benefits (money, knowledge, "connections") which facilitate family survival they may be tolerated or even encouraged. Long hours and frequent absences resulting from these involvements become more acceptable when they are interpreted as obligatory for the job which is essential for the family's survival or the basis of its future economic security. Some involvements support the family both emotionally and economically. A mother who derives satisfaction from paid work not only contributes money but also may be warmer

and more supportive in the family than one who seeks, but does not find, personal fulfillment exclusively within the family. However, none of these benefits is secure because none is taken into account when the structures of organizations are changed.

In all of these relationships, marital status as distinct from family membership, is a structured interference. Being married creates a barrier to developing alternative sources of satisfaction even when the couple recognizes the need for such sources and willingly accommodates to their use. Since most people view the married couple as a unit, they respond to each spouse as a member of a couple and expect each to participate in social activities as a member of the marital pair. Even when participating alone, each is treated as a representative of the interests of the other, regardless of what those interests are. A married person is seen as part of a unit, not as an individual in it. (The single person encounters problems from the same ideology. He or she is often excluded or treated as a less than equal participant).

In general, the type of relationship which is developed varies in the extent to which it is perceived as threatening by the members of the family. Involvements with work mates and same-sex friendships are viewed as appropriate as long as they do not become extreme. The most "dangerous" relationships are extramarital sexual ones: adultery, homosexuality, and, to a lesser degree, prostitution (Hunt 1969). Not only do these relationships create stress by taking a family member away during "family time," but they also compete directly with the central emotional relationships in that family member's life. As with other, less threatening extrafamilial resources, these relationships are most likely to be tolerated when they infringe least on the family's ability to carry out its survival and emotional activities.

Without long-term structured alternatives for satisfying emotional needs, people are left with groups and friendships which are tenuous, unpredictable, and secondary to organizational goals and family activities. These relationships are difficult to develop. Even when they are cultivated they must be compromised by organizational and family priorities. Ironically, the family member must turn back to the family for his/her emotional needs to be satisfied even though its inability to provide such satisfaction generates a search for alternatives.

THE MOVE TO DIVORCE

With limited alternative relationships, the strains produced by the contradictions between family life and the external order lead many people to divorce. The pattern of their marital breakups is determined by the structure of relationships within the family. For the man the major gain from the family is an emotional one. He contributes the money essential for family survival and expects services and emotional gratification in return. When he is unsatisfied with the exchange, he can either seek a divorce or begin to develop alternative relationships. For the woman the emotional tie is strengthened by the economic security she obtains for herself and her children through marriage. The breakup of the marriage means the loss of both. If she begins to develop alternative relationships, she jeopardizes her material survival as well as her marriage. Thus, the woman may be more likely to remain in a marriage which no longer offers her emotional satisfaction, as long as her husband is a "good provider."

When the man fails to be a good provider or the woman is employed in economically viable work, her relationship to the family is structurally changed.[3] She finds herself taking care of housework and children, although she is no longer dependent on her spouse's job. Her double tie to marriage is reduced to a single, emotional one. Now she too may remain committed to the marriage only as long as it provides emotional satisfaction. When that satisfaction is gone, the extra work of caring for and supporting her spouse becomes a liability. In this instance marital breakup can be an advantage. It means less housework and an end to the strains of an unsatisfying relationship. When the major bond between spouses is an emotional one, the continuity of the marriage depends on the very satisfactions which are most readily jeopardized by the external order's demands on family life.

The societal response to divorce remains consistent with the ideology of the family. It explains divorce as a consequence of failure ignoring the realities of family life (Goode 1956; Marsden 1969; Glasser and Navarre 1965). As a result structural problems are rarely taken into account by couples, the courts or the community. Couples seek divorces for a wide variety of "personal" reasons and judges grant them according to a list of legally acceptable grounds for divorce (Goode 1956). The grounds for divorce are gradually being extended to recognize the psychological consequences of unsatisfactory marriages (mental cruelty, incompatibility, and "no fault") while continuing to ignore their structural basis.

Services available to troubled spouses also reflect this perspective. Psychotherapy, a service sought out by spouses or offered in connection with the divorce court, concentrates on the personalities of the husband and wife and the tensions resulting from their interaction. Various forms of family counseling exist to help the couple learn to communicate better, express their conflicts and rehabilitate their marriage. Sensitivity training and T-groups also exist, at a price, to help spouses express their emotions. None of these varieties of personal and family counseling gives priority to the structural impediments of family life such as disruptive work hours, the eventlessness of housewifery, too little money, or a location which creates continual scheduling difficulties. Where these problems are acknowledged, they are treated as the inevitable parameters of existence. The couple either adapts to them together or separates to adapt to them singly.

If structural problems are so important, why do they remain obscure? Why do couples view their family difficulties or their own divorces as a result of personal failure or wrong choices? Because people believe the prevailing ideology of the family; an ideology in which the family is simply a private structure based on love. This ideology obscures the relationship between the family and the public arena, reducing the problems of family life to the formula of "not enough love." The inevitable conflicts which derive from responding to the imperatives of external organizations are experienced within the supposedly private territory of the family as personal conflicts of husband and wife and become evidence that they cannot provide the necessary love for each other.

The basis of these conflicts is further obscured by the sex-based division of labor in the family. The man is insulated from awareness of the internal work of the family by the wife/mother who arranges family activities around the demands of his schedule, particularly his employment, and creates the illusion that his activities dovetail with her own and those of the children. Since they both accept the demands of certain external institutions as legitimate, maneuverings around these demands take place with little discussion of the problems involved. The consequences of these maneuverings remain and are experienced directly as personal conflicts.

For the woman the relationship between structural problems and personal ones is even more complex because love mystifies her work. Arranging schedules and juggling conflicting demands are jobs imposed on her by the organizational involvements of her husband and children. Attending to these jobs is not viewed as her work for those organizations; it is an expression of her love for her family. The better she manages, the less visible her work is and the more loving she is thought to be. The difficulties she experiences in this work become part of her relationships to the members of the family and surface as interpersonal failings.

For both spouses marital and individual problems are easily identified, particularly when expressed in anger, drinking, physical abuse, or mental illness, and they become the focus of attention. While the family deals with its immediate situation, the problems remain personal and their social bases are not explored (Mills 1959).

Locating the source of problems within the couple reinforces the myth that marriage to the "right" person will result in a happy family life. Thousands of people explain their marital difficulties by appealing to this rationale—that they made a "poor choice" and should "try again" in another marriage (Goode 1956; Carter and Glick 1970). The alternatives for divorced people encourage changing themselves to be more desirable marriage partners or finding new, more compatible partners. The high rates of marriage and remarriage can be viewed as indicators not of the success of the family but of the strength of the ideology and of the desire to get what that ideology promises.

CONCLUSIONS

Without wishing to deny personal differences, we have argued that many so-called personal problems arise from the family's relationship to powerful organizations which force husbands and wives to compromise their personal commitments in order to maintain and educate their families. For many, these compromises are translated into family disharmony and marital breakup. Recognizing this link is a way of understanding the conditions of family life. In real families some people do find joy, love, and companionship, even if they eventually divorce. However, individual triumphs over the conditions of family life are not the answer to problems involved.

Many people have outlined ways of changing the family to increase its effectiveness as an emotional unit. Their proposals have generally fallen in two categories: those which treat family difficulties as a result of the personalities of those involved and those which treat such difficulties as the result of the internal structure of the family. Those that isolate immaturity or neurosis (Bergler 1948; Rheinstein 1972) as "the problem" accept the ideology of love as the *raison d'être* for family, and neglect both the internal structure of family life and the link of the family to the larger society. Those that propose changes in the internal structure of the family point to features which are essential for redefining men's and women's positions within the family but they do not go far enough (Holmstrom 1972; Wortis 1971). Shared housework and child care by both sexes would eliminate the strains of the internal, sex-based division of labor but the conflict between maintenance and nurturance tasks would remain. Now both husband and wife would express that conflict. The establishment of high quality child-care facilities outside the home would reduce some of the moment-to-moment pressures that result from schedule juggling, but would tie the family to the calendar of yet another external organization.

The marriage relationship will continue to be difficult whatever alternatives are invented to improve it, for it cannot be separated or insulated from the pressures of the rest of the society. The problem with most existing proposals for change is that they treat the family as if it were what the dominant cultural ideology says it is—a separate, independent institution for personal life. But the family and marital relationships cannot be private—they are social relationships linked to the wider society and structured by it.

Our analysis of the conditions of family life in this society implies two general areas for change. First, the ideology of the family must be questioned. People need to assess the potential and the limitations of family life as an emotional resource, a process which involves questioning a complex of related beliefs surrounding sex roles, motherhood, and the privacy of the family. Such questioning has already begun, spurred on by the women's movement and the growth of an alternative vision of personal satisfaction for women. The consequences have been dramatic. New structures, compatible with the emerging feminist ideologies, are being developed. However, the success of achieving emotional support and meeting personal needs in any structure is dependent on another change—a change in the corporate order.

In essence the conditions of family life and the conditions of production and consumption are bound together. The time, energy, and personal strength people can offer to each other in the family are determined by their daily encounters with the organizations in which they work, shop, and obtain services and vice versa. Doing difficult tasks is not the issue. The issue is the conditions under which tasks are performed and the experiences people have in doing them. When these experiences are empty, frustrating, or demeaning, people are poorly equipped to provide emotional support for others. By concentrating on the technical bases of efficiency, managers have structured organizations which create new blockages in the activities of people who staff and use them. While large businesses come immediately to mind as examples of this phenomenon, other organizations are equally representative. Day-care centers which reduce child-care responsibilities may increase family strain on other levels. Setting hours at which children must be at the center, requiring a minimal number of days enrolled, restricting parents from coming and children from leaving are usually technical decisions producing more efficient use of staff time even when they are justified by an ideology of nurturance.

Regardless of the organizations involved, the family cannot be a corrective for them. It is part of them. Only when the organizations are formed in ways which offer new possibilities for personal development and satisfaction can the potential for various forms of family relationships be realized. In practical terms, this means that family members must have decision-making power over the resources which they need to maintain the family. We are talking of nothing less than eliminating the tension between nurturance and maintenance. Such a radical change in social structure involves redefining the entire corporate order so that human needs, not profitability or efficiency, become the ultimate criterion for the activities and goals of organizations.

NOTES

1. We do not discuss the evolution of the ideology which emphasizes the expressive function of the family. However, we would argue that the nuclear family is an integral economic unit and that the emphasis on its expressive character is consistent with and reinforces capitalistic economies. Thus the family promotes excessive consumerism in its attempt to satisfy its members' needs within the family unit; it isolates people in the home, preventing the development of collective responsibility; it legitimizes the subordinate status of women, keeping them a special labor force which can be used to hold wages down and retard unionization; it represses spontaneity and ad hoc organization, making joint responses more difficult and it perpetuates the beliefs which support capitalism. To emphasize the family's isolation within the corporate order, we use an "internal/external" dichotomy, although the family's connection with and participation in that external order are assumed throughout.

2. Although particular men may provide psychological support for others, their ability to do so is seen as a product of their individual personality development. One of the current concerns with the American male is precisely that his socialization excludes initiation into an expressive or nurturant role (Brenton 1966; Balswick and Peek 1971).

3. Greater employment opportunities do make divorce a more readily available option for women, but as yet few of them have the job skills or receive the wages that would make their work the basis of family sup-

port. In fact, the relative wages of women have declined over the past two decades (Women's Bureau 1969).

REFERENCES

ARIES, PHILLIPPE 1962. *Centuries of childhood: a social history of family life.* New York: Vintage Books.

BALSWICK, J., AND C. PEEK 1971. The inexpressive male: a tragedy of American society. *Family Coordinator* 20:363–368.

BART, PAULINE 1972. Are you a housewife or do you work?: women in traditional roles. Presented for Women: Resources for a Changing World. Radcliffe Institute, Radcliffe College, Cambridge.

BAUM, MARTHA 1971. Love, marriage, and the division of labor. *Sociological Inquiry* 41 (Winter):107–117.

BENSTON, MARGARET 1969. The political economy of women's liberation. *Monthly Review* 24 (September):13–27.

BERGLER, EDMUND 1948. *Divorce won't help.* New York: Harper & Row.

BERNARD, JESSIE 1971a. *Women and the public interest.* Chicago: Aldine-Atherton.

———, 1971b. No news, but new ideas. In Paul Bohannan (ed.), *Divorce and after.* Garden City, New York: Anchor Books, pp. 3–29.

BLOOD, ROBERT O., JR., AND DONALD M. WOLFE 1960. *Husbands and wives.* New York: Free Press.

BOTT, ELIZABETH 1971. *Family and social network.* (2nd ed.) New York: Macmillan-Free Press.

BRADBURN, ROBERT, AND DAVID CAPLOVITZ 1965. *Reports on happiness.* Chicago: Aldine.

BREMNER, ROBERT H. 1970. *Children and youth in America: a documentary history.* Cambridge, Mass.: Harvard University Press.

BRENTON, MYRON 1966. *The American male.* Greenwich, Conn.: Fawcett.

BURGESS, E., AND M. LOCKE 1953. *The family: from institution to companionship.* New York: American Book.

CARTER, HUGH, AND PAUL C. GLICK 1970. *Marriage and divorce: a social and economic study.* Cambridge, Mass.: Harvard University Press.

CENTERS, RICHARD 1948. Attitude and belief in relation to occupational stratification. *Journal of Social Psychology* 27 (May):159–185.

ENGELS, FRIEDRICH 1972. *The origin of the family, private property, and the state.* New York: International Publishers.

GINTIS, HERBERT 1972. Alienation in capitalist society. In R. Edwards, M. Reich and T. Weisskopf (eds.), *The capitalist system.* Englewood Cliffs, N.J.: Prentice-Hall, pp. 274–284.

GLASSER, PAUL, AND ELIZABETH NAVARRE 1965. The problems of families in the AFDC Program. *Children* 12 (July-August):151–157.

GLICK, PAUL C. 1975. A demographer looks at American families. *Journal of Marriage and the Family* 37 (February):15–26.

GOODE, WILLIAM J. 1956. *Women in divorce.* Glencoe, Illinois: Free Press.

——— 1963. *World revolution and family patterns.* New York: Free Press.

GURIN, G., J. VEROFF, AND S. FELD 1960. *Americans view their mental health.* New York: Basic Books.

HOLMSTROM, L. 1972. *The two-career family.* Cambridge, Mass.: Schenkman.

HUNT, DAVID 1970. *Parents and children in history.* New York: Basic Books.

HUNT, MORTON 1969. *The affair.* Cleveland: World.

ILG, FRANCIS, AND LOUISE BATES AMES 1966. *Child behavior.* New York: Harper & Row.

KAHL, JOSEPH A. 1962. *The American class structure.* New York: Holt, Rinehart and Winston.

KOMAROVSKY, MIRRA 1967. *Blue-collar marriage.* New York: Random House.

——— 1973. Cultural contradictions and sex roles: the masculine case. *American Journal of Sociology* 78 (January):873–884.

LYND, ROBERT S., AND HELEN MERRILL LYND 1929. *Middletown: a study in American culture.* New York: Harcourt Brace and World.

MARSDEN, DENNIS 1969. *Mothers alone: poverty and the fatherless family.* London: Allen Lane, the Penguin Press.

MILLS, C. WRIGHT 1959. *The sociological imagination.* New York: Oxford University Press.

MITCHELL, JULIET 1971. *Woman's estate.* New York: Pantheon.

NYE, F. IVAN 1974. Emerging and declining family roles. *Journal of Marriage and the Family* 33 (May):238–245.

NYE, F.I., AND L. W. HOFFMAN (eds.) 1965. *The employed mother in America.* Chicago: Rand McNally.

OAKLEY, ANN 1974. *Woman's work.* New York: Pantheon.

PARSONS, TALCOTT 1965. The normal American family. In S. M. Farber, P. Mustacchi, and R. H. L. Wilson (eds.), *Man and civilization: the family's search for survival.* New York: McGraw-Hill, pp. 31–50.

PYUN, CHONG SOO 1969. The monetary value of a housewife: an economic analysis for use in litigation. *American Journal of Economics and Sociology* 28 (July):271–284.

RHEINSTEIN, MAX 1972. *Marriage stability, divorce, and the law.* Chicago: University of Chicago Press.

ROLLINS, BOYD C., AND HAROLD FELDMAN 1970. Marital satisfaction over the family life cycle. *Journal of Marriage and the Family* 32 (February):20–27.

ROSSI, ALICE 1968. Transition to parenthood. *Journal of Marriage and the Family* 30 (February):26–39.

SIEGAL, A. E., AND M. B. HAAS 1963. The working mother: a review of research. *Child Development* 34: 513–542.

SMITH, DOROTHY 1973. Women, the family, and corporate capitalism. In M.L. Stephenson (ed.), *Women in Canada.* Toronto: New Press, pp. 2–35.

SPOCK, BENJAMIN 1967. *Baby and child care.* New York: Pocket Books.

THEODORSON, GEORGE A. 1965. Romanticism and motivation to marry in the United States, Singapore, Burma and India. *Social Forces* 44 (September):17–27.

VINCENT, CLARK 1966. Familia spongia: the adaptive function. *Journal of Marriage and the Family* 28 (February):29–36.

VOGEL, LISE 1973. The earthly family. *Radical America* 7 (Fall):9–50.

WOMEN'S BUREAU 1969. *Handbook on women workers,* Bulletin 294. United States Department of Labor, Washington, D.C.

WORTIS, ROCHELLE PAUL 1971. The acceptance of the concept of the maternal role by behavioral scientists: its effects on women. *American Journal of Orthopsychiatry* 41 (October):733–746.

YORBURG, BETTY 1973. *The changing family.* New York: Columbia University Press.

Widowhood in America

HELENA Z. LOPATA

FACTORS AFFECTING WIDOWHOOD

AS AMERICAN SOCIETY BECOMES MORE urbanized and industrialized, its major institutions and their numerous subinstitutions continue to become more complex and more segregated from each other. They are operated by large complicated organizations, participation in which requires voluntary entrance, with specified qualifications and through bureaucratic procedures. Only the family, the local parish, and the informal peer group of neighbors still offer relatively automatic entrance to individuals. Such small and stable social groups in which people have traditionally been able to immerse their activities and identities are insufficient for maintaining urban life. They are being supplemented, and sometimes replaced, by formal groups whose formally educated members have the ability to enter and withdraw from a variety of social relations. Although the growing urban centers may make difficult the maintenance of life around a secure small group, the city and its environs can provide its residents with a great range of activities and encounters, developing and utilizing their potentials. Urbanites can have a multidimensional and institutionally rich social life space, involving a number of different roles entirely absent in a village or small town. They can carry on diverse activities and relate to a great diversity of people in primary and intimate, or in secondary and even fleeting interaction.

The changes in rapidly urbanizing and industrializing societies such as America are not, however, experienced evenly by their members. Many people lead very restricted or isolated lives even within the wealth of opportunities technically available to them. The social life space of each person is dependent upon his or her location in the social system and his ability to utilize the resources offered by the

Reprinted by permission of author and publisher, Schankman.

society. This ability includes understanding of the social system and knowledge of how to mobilize the environment to meet needs. In our heterogeneous society, many members are restricted in the lifestyles available to them. This is particularly true of older widows, socialized into traditional roles, encouraged into passive stances vis-à-vis the world and with limited skills because of age and sex.

The factors constricting the choices of lifestyles available to older widows include their ethnic group affiliation. Ethnic cultures, based upon past heritage and present conditions in the adopted land, stipulate the proper living arrangements for widows, as well as for the other members of the group. Those in marginal positions may build combined patterns, with the help of varying degrees of cooperation from the two groups between which they are located, but the gradual dissolution of the ethnic community has left many of them socially isolated and restricted.

The location of the widow in the social class system also affects her life-style. The older woman is apt to have obtained no, or minimal, training in roles providing a source of livelihood in an urban setting. She is likely to have depended upon her husband as the main breadwinner of the family. His income was generally not high enough for them to save much money, nor did he invest heavily in insurance, so they did not build an estate sufficient to maintain the widow above the poverty line once he died. At the same time the traditional attitude of rejecting financial help from the society and even from families prevents the older woman from increasing her income this way. She holds dilemma-producing attitudes, not wanting to take "charity" from the government, yet being unwilling to become dependent on married offspring by moving in with them or even exchanging services. Traditional means of self-support are becoming less available for the elderly in modern society, due to their movement off the land, their consumption-oriented spending habits, and the inflation which drastically reduces the purchasing power of past savings. Many are home owners, particularly in the latter part of life, but the sale of these structures does not bring enough to cover rent for more than a very limited time. Income from lodgers has decreased as

an easily available source of livelihood for older women, since immigration laws and the high American marital rate make boarders a rarity. Technological change makes past skills outdated and new ones hard to learn. Job placement is becoming more and more formally organized, with intermediary agencies not known to older people who have been trained for a more direct system. Thus, for the older widow especially, the increasing openness of the economic sphere of life has simply increased the gap between the opportunities to live a desired life at any social level and the ability of the woman to take advantage of them.

The decline of the community and the extended family as protective systems ensuring that financially uneducated women would not be cheated by nonaltruistically inclined petty and major criminals has resulted in a loss of millions of dollars by widows who suddenly acquired even a small inheritance or life insurance payment. Many widows are not so old as to desire disengagement from society at the time of their husband's death. Women are living much longer than in traditional America, while men have not expanded their life expectancy in equal proportion.

Since women marry men older than themselves, they have a very high probability of becoming widows, their average age when that event occurs being 56 years. Despite this statistical fact, lifestyles for American widows are generally built upon the assumption either that they are young and can soon remarry or that they are very old and removed from the realm of active involvement. The trouble is that most widows are neither, but the society has not taken sufficient cognizance of this fact to modify the facilities and roles available to them. As a result, their potential for action is lost to the community, leaving many widows idly to perform tasks in functionally insignificant social roles. There are three widows to every widower aged sixty-five and over in America. The widowers have a wider range of choice for a second wife, especially since they can go out of their age group in a relatively open way, which the older widows cannot do (Leslie 1967, pp. 632-636; Metropolitan Life Insurance Company 1945, pp. 1-3). Although widowers have less of a problem with remarriage, they, too, usually lack appropriate living facilities, as Felix Berardo (1967, 1968), Pihlblad and Rosencranz (1968), and Adams (1969) have recognized.

The status of the widow tends to be peripheral in other aspects of society's life. In general, her status is not as high as that of wife, since women have traditionally derived most of their social position from that of their husband. Only in cases where the husband had been an outstanding public figure may the wife retain special status after his death. Some women have professions or are involved in respected volunteer work to the extent that their status undergoes no change in the transition from wife to widow, but they are rare. Because American society is increasingly leisure-oriented, the prestige of the nonworking woman may become higher than it has been in the past. But the advantages brought about by a decrease in the puritanical work-orientation may not always be enjoyed by a widow if her single status excludes her from much of the leisure activity in a couple-companionate environment.

Even the religious institution has changed sufficiently to make strong involvement in its groups difficult for the widow. The value system has become increasingly secular and, as Geoffrey Gorer (1965) concluded, even the rituals, such as those of mourning and bereavement, have become deinstitutionalized in the Western world. Religion is tending to become bureaucratically rational, making older people uncomfortable in the changing churches. Many of the activities are directed toward young families and those who are older feel left out of the social life.

One of the most difficult changes in the lives of older widows has been their decreasing functionality in the family institution. Particularly in the wide belt of its middle classes, the American society is developing a neolocal, bilateral, and egalitarian family. Each family unit is small, increasingly independent and isolated from the others. In spite of the occasional service interchange observed by Sussman, Litwak, and Shanas and Streib (contained in Shanas and Streib 1965), each unit of husband, wife, and small children is based separately, often in relatively far time–distance locations from kin members. This means that the daily life of each family has become the sole responsibility of the adults managing each household, making it less likely that the widow can fill her life with interaction from her own household. Within each homestead of even married children, let alone siblings, there is no central role available to her. The widow herself does not wish to relinquish her own independent position for the periphery of someone else's life. Most older people in America, as in the European countries of England and Denmark, do not wish to live with their married children; they define the ideal situation as what is called in Austria, "Intimacy at a distance" (Rosenmayr and Köckeis 1963). Other assessments of the ideal situation are not so rosy. Reports of contacts are not necessarily reports of intimacy, as Irving Rosow (1967) has pointed out. The American family system involves interaction from separate households, which is not guaranteed to provide intimacy.

Mate selection in this society is based increasingly on "love" developed during a dating and courtship period of the teen years. Self-selection of the mate and the fundamental isolation of the married unit have placed a heavy burden of affective, economic, and child-rearing functions upon the couple. In the middle classes, and on up from there, the wife is expected to be a companion and major assistant to her husband. The burden has produced a variety of "solutions," as reflected by the whole range of marital relational styles, from divorce and desertion to close companionate ties. Widowhood affects women differently, depending on the location of their marriage along the continuum of closeness.

The marriage contract varies from state to state as to inheritance rights, but in general, the American widow may inherit all or a sizable segment of the estate. If no formal will is registered, she is apt simply to take over the management of the property after her husband's death. She is usually the guardian or at least one of the guardians of goods held in trust for the children. No system of levirate or widow inheritance operates in this society, although cases of voluntary marriage by the deceased husband's brother are occasionally reported. The *in genetricem* rights of the male kin group are no longer viable in any but the upper class and, as we shall see later, most widows do not continue a close relation with that group once the connecting link is gone. Even the children's obligation to retain the family name of their late father is regarded more as a duty to him than to his kin. Small children may even take the last name of the mother's new husband, if she remarries, for the responsibility of making them feel part of the new unit may outweigh loyalty to the former husband.

The life-styles of American widows vary so greatly that it is impossible to define "the American widow" beyond the simple statement that she is a woman whose husband has died. Her style varies not only by her location in the social system, be it an upper-class suburb, the slum or the "gold coast" of a city, an ethnic community, a small town, or a farm, but by her own combination of characteristics. Patterns emerge when such factors as the educational achievement of the woman is compared to her social life space so that we find that the more training she has, the more social roles and social relations she is able to enter and maintain. At the other side of the picture, we find widows immersed in kin relations who infrequently see anyone else. Old neighborhoods still exist in urban centers, where the elderly continue to live near people they have known all their lives. Public housing high-rises bring together people in similar circumstances, creating opportunities for the new friendships found by Rosow (1967) to be facilitated by high density situations in Cleveland. Small towns in Missouri (Pihlblad and Rosencranz 1968), Wisconsin (Bultena and Marshall 1969), and other Middle West states attract the widows of farmers from nearby areas and often have as much as a 150 percent proportion of the "normal" number of aged. Specially developed "leisure world" (*Practical Builder* 1966) communities of same age peers guarantee carefree and nonlonely living (Bultena and Wood 1969). Other towns have become focal points of seasonal migration for the "snow birds" who live in age-segregated environments for only part of the year. Widows with sufficient money travel a good deal and often comprise a major segment of the passengers on tours or cruises.

Younger widows face problems of child-rearing, returning to work, and reestablishing themselves as eligibles in the marriage market. Older widows may also hold jobs, full- or part-time, and join voluntary associations. Some combine these with an active family interaction, others with a clique activity with women in the same circumstances. Some widows remarry. Since the years of widowhood are often long, involvement in one set of roles can shift into another as life circumstances change. The degree of flexibility in life-styles varies considerably. Some women become "perpetual widows"; others move from work roles to an increased involvement in the lives of their grandchildren.

DEMOGRAPHIC FACTS

At the time this book went to print the detailed characteristics of the American population of 1970 had not become publicly available, and it will be another year or so before more complicated calculations concerning any category of member are worked out. The figures which are now available show that 12.5 percent of all women aged 14 and over were widows in 1970, 22.1 percent being single, 58.4 percent being married with the spouse present, 3.5 percent being married with the spouse absent and 3.5 being divorced. Forty-three percent of the households headed by women are minus a male head because of death. The latter figure is a drop from 50.9 percent of female heads of households who were widows in 1960, due to an increase in the proportion of divorced and married women with spouse absent from the home (United States Bureau of the Census 1971, p. 29).

The detailed demographic characteristics of widows in America have been most effectively summarized as of 1960 by the Statistical Bulletin of the Metropolitan Life Insurance Company:

> During the past two decades the number of widows in the United States has been growing by more than 100,000 a year, compared with an annual increase of about 80,000 in the 1920's and of about 50,000 at the turn of the century. In March 1961, there were approximately 8¼ million widows in the country, and it is expected that their total will continue to rise rapidly.
>
> Widows in the population have been outnumbering widowers by a steadily widening margin—a consequence of the higher mortality among men than women, and also of the higher

remarriage rate among widowers. Currently the ratio of widows to widowers is 4 to 1; about 50 years ago, it was little more than 2 to 1.

In 1961, almost three-fifths of the widows in the United States were 65 years of age or older. One in every 4 widows was in the age group 55–64 years, and only one in every 17 was under age 45.

It should be noted, however, that a large number of newly widowed women are still in their middle years. Of the 550,000 women widowed in 1961, about 90,000 were under age 45; somewhat over half of the total were under 60 years of age.

At all but the oldest ages, widows constitute a smaller proportion of the women residing in farm areas than those living in our cities and small towns. At ages 75 and over, the percentage widowed is practically the same in both groups.

Three-fourths of the women who become widows at age 45 can expect to live an additional 25 years. The same number of years remain to 9 out of every 10 women widowed at ages 35 or earlier. Of the widows bereft of their spouse at age 65, somewhat more than half can expect to live 15 years longer and about a third still have 20 years of life before them. (Metropolitan Life Insurance Company 1962, pp. 1–4).

The greater the age gap between husband and wife (with the husband being the older, as is traditional in America), the greater the probability that the woman will become a widow. For a woman aged 55 or younger the odds are approximately 54 out of 100 that she will be left a widow if she is married to a man five years her junior; 64 out of 100 if he is five years her senior; and 80 out of 100 if he is ten years older (Metropolitan Life Insurance Company 1969, pp. 10–11).

The United States is not the only country facing an increase of the proportion of widows over widowers. An American government report on "Changes in mortality trends in England and Wales, 1931–1961" concludes that "One feature of the mortality rates throughout the whole period 1931–1961 is the widening gap between the sexes. This has occurred at every age from one to 84, and

for almost every disease which has been considered; evidently there are some factors in modern society which are inimical to the survival of the male but are beneficial to the female" (National Center for Health Statistics 1965, p. 35). This trend is most obvious among older people. "For elderly persons, 65–84 years of age, the male death rate in 1931 was about 31 percent higher than the female rate, whereas in 1961 it was 60 percent higher" (National Center for Health Statistics 1965, p. 36).

By percentage of total and by race, the detailed distribution in the United States of females aged 50 and over indicates a slight increase, parallel with age increase, of the proportion who never married (see Table 1). A simultaneous decrease in the proportion of older women who have been divorced is indicative of the national trends, for it is only in recent years that marital dissolution has increased in popularity. The figures do not indicate who among the currently married had been in the divorce category in prior years. The proportions in the single and divorced columns are relatively small however, and have not changed as dramatically as those for the married and widowed American females. With each decade of life the proportion of women who are married decreases as the proportion of widows increases so that in fact three-fourths of the women in their early eighties are widowed. The table also indicates the inequality of widowhood rates between white and nonwhite members of our society. In all age decades, the nonwhite woman has a much smaller chance of remaining married and a much greater chance of being widowed than the white woman. The largest gap between whites and nonwhites, one of fourteen percent, is in the age group of the sixties. The difference in the proportion of white to nonwhite widows decreases in the very latest decades of life, but at no time is the nonwhite rate lower than that of the whites.

The distribution of the widowed in the population of American females has changed since 1890, the year for which we have the first set of even partial census statistics.

A comparison of Table 1 and Table 2 shows that in the years between 1950 and 1960 there is a decrease in the proportion of widows to the total number of American women in every age decade of life. The same tendency can be observed for 1930 and for

Table 1 Marital status of white (W) and nonwhite (NW) American women aged 50 and over* (1960)

Age	% of Total	Single W	Single NW	% of Total	Married W	Married NW	% of Total	Widowed W	Widowed NW	% of Total	Divorced W	Divorced NW
50–54	7.6	7.8	6.1	77.0	77.9	68.9	11.1	10.2	19.8	4.2	4.1	5.2
55–59	8.2	8.4	6.9	69.9	70.9	60.7	17.9	16.8	28.2	3.9	3.9	5.2
60–64	7.7	7.9	4.7	61.4	62.3	52.0	27.6	26.5	39.9	3.3	3.3	3.3
65–69	7.9	8.2	4.3	51.6	52.4	42.5	37.9	36.7	50.6	2.7	2.7	2.5
70–74	8.4	8.7	4.4	39.1	39.6	32.4	50.4	49.6	61.2	2.1	2.1	2.0
75–79	8.8	9.1	4.4	27.4	27.8	22.9	62.2	61.6	71.3	1.5	1.5	1.4
80–84	9.5	9.9	4.5	16.2	16.3	14.8	73.1	72.7	79.6	1.1	1.1	1.1
85–86 +	9.6	10.0	4.3	8.2	8.1	9.3	81.4	81.0	85.4	0.8	0.8	1.0

*Source: The United States Census of Population, 1960 United States Summary, Detailed Characteristics, segments of Table 176, pp. 1–427, 435.

Table 2 Percentage of American women who are widowed, 1890–1950, by white (W) and nonwhite (NW)*

Decade Age	1950 Total	1950 W	1950 NW	1940 Total	1940 W	1940 NW	1930 Total
45–49	8.6	7.4	19.1	10.7	9.4	24.0	11.6
50–54	13.9	12.6	27.4	15.9	14.6	31.5	16.9
55–59	20.5	19.3	35.1	22.4	21.3	37.9	23.4
60–64	29.7	28.6	44.9	31.3	30.3	46.8	33.1
65–69	41.1	39.7	56.7	43.1	41.8	58.8	44.1
70–74	53.3	52.3	68.0	55.5	54.5	70.0	55.9
75–79	65.1	64.6	74.6	67.3	66.8	76.9	73.9 (75 and
80–84	75.9	75.5	82.9	77.1	76.7	84.2	over)
85 and over	82.9	82.9	83.4	85.1	84.7	89.1	

Decade Age	1920 Total	1910 Total	1900 Total	1890 Total
45–54	15.3	15.7	17.6	18.4
55–64	29.5	30.0	32.3	33.3
65 and over	58.4	58.1	59.3	58.6
Age not reported	14.6	16.5	15.7	17.3

*United States Census of Population, 1960 United States Summary, Detailed Characteristics, PC (I)-1D Table 177, pp. 146–148.

1940, which is the iast year for which we have the same statistical categories. In other words, the proportion of women who are widows has decreased since at least 1930 and probably since 1890 (it definitely has decreased, if comparisons are made between 1890 and 1930, but the figures for the years of 1920 and 1910 are harder to categorize). However, the percentage of widows in the American population has increased, with one exception, from a low of 10.3 in 1910 to 10.8 in 1920 and in 1930, 11.8 in 1940, 11.0 in 1950, and 12.2 in 1960.

The discrepancy between the rates of widowhood of whites and blacks is a continuous one with a long history (see Table 2). Black women have also experienced a drop in the proportion who are widowed at about the same rate as white women. Unfortunately, before 1940 the data were not broken down by color. A more detailed comparison between the two groups in the decades contained in the two tables shows that the gap between rates of widowhood has decreased steadily in all but the eldest group. The amount of decrease is less as the widows grow older, leaving minute figures of change, particularly in the 1940–1950 period, for women who are over 60 years of age. Even within this group, the black rates dropped between 1950 and 1960. Black women aged 50 to 54 had a 16.9 percent higher rate of widowhood than white women in 1940, a 14.8 percent higher rate in 1950, and a 9.6 percent higher rate in 1960. This indicates a higher death rate on their part, a lower death frequency on the part of the male, or marriage to younger men.

Facts concerning the women 14 years of age or older who were analyzed in the 1960 Census Summary indicate some factors that contribute to marital differences in this country. The median age of the American woman above the childhood years (up to fourteen) is 40.8; that of the man is 40.0 (see Table 3).

The rural farm and the rural nonfarm girls get married and fall out of the single category at the earliest ages. Next come the nonwhites. The urban women are the slowest to marry. The youngest divorced group is composed of nonwhite females, who are also the youngest to be widowed. The rural women on or off the farm are the oldest widows,

Table 3 The median age of American women who are 14 years old or over in different marital situations by race and urban-rural residence*

Category of women	Median age by marital status				
	Total	Single	Married	Widowed	Divorced
Total	40.8	19.0	40.7	67.8	44.9
White	41.3	19.0	41.0	68.4	45.0
Non-white	37.2	18.9	38.1	62.2	41.5
Urban	41.0	19.8	40.5	67.4	44.9
Rural, nonfarm	39.6	17.7	39.8	68.7	44.9
Rural farm	42.9	17.8	45.1	69.7	44.6

*United States Census of Population, 1960 United States Summary, Detailed Characteristics, PC (I)-iD, Table 176, pp. 1–427, 435.

which indicates mobility of the younger women from rural areas to cities, or a longer life span of males. Younger widows seem to gravitate to urban areas, which means that the older women who remain form a disproportionate part of the rural population.

The highest proportion of American widows lives alone or with unmarried children. The older the woman (up until the last stages of life when physical health problems make maintenance of self and house impossible), the more likely she is not to have anyone else in the household (see Table 4). This table also indicates the widow's dependence upon unmarried offspring or other young people.

A recent cross-cultural study of people aged 65 and over in America, England, and Denmark has produced some interesting results. "In all three countries, it is unusual for three successive generations to share a common household. In Denmark, approximately five percent, in the United States eight percent, and in Britain thirteen percent of the respective samples live in such households" (Stehouwer 1968). About a quarter of the aged population in Denmark (28 percent), in Britain (22

Table 4 Living arrangements of widows in the United States, March 1961 (numbers in thousands)

Living arrangement	Total	Urban and rural nonfarm	Rural-farm
Total	8,217	7,770	447
Head of household	5,639	5,367	272
With relative in household	2,336	2,161	175
With no relative in household	3,303	3,206	97
Living in household of others			
Relatives	2,111	1,942	169
Together with own children under age 18	47	37	10
Without own children under age 18	2,064	1,905	159
Nonrelatives	287	281	6
Together with relatives	13	13	0
Without relatives	274	268	6
Inmate of institution*	145	145	0
Living in hotel, dormitory, etc.	35	35	0

*Estimated by the Statistical Bureau of the Metropolitan Life Insurance Company.
SOURCE: Bureau of the Census, Current Population Report, Series P-20, Nos. 114 and 116.

percent), and in the United States (22 percent) live alone. One third of the elderly population in Britain, and slightly less than half in Denmark and in the United States, live as married couples, in a household of their own, without other members. The remaining of the elderly, 27 percent in Denmark, 45 percent in Britain, and 35 percent in the United States live in households which have a more differentiated structure. Most of these households include an adult child, especially an unmarried or previously married child" (Stehouwer 1968, p. 184).

An interesting comment made by Jan Stehouwer (1968, p. 185), the author of the above quotation, is of significance for the study with which this book is concerned:

> For the generation of older people represented in the three national samples, the last child normally would have left the parental home as the parents approached their late 50s. Nevertheless, approximately 14 percent of all married elderly couples in Denmark and in the United States and 23 percent of those in Britain, live with an unmarried child. Among those who are widowed and divorced, 15 percent in Denmark, 11 percent in Britain and 20 percent in the United States live with an unmarried child.

Only seven percent of the Danish unmarried women (meaning single, widowed, and divorced, most of whom at the age of sixty-five and over are widowed) live with siblings or other relatives, but the proportion is as high as thirteen percent in Britain and twelve percent in the United States. In the case of Americans, these relatives may be a parent, niece or nephew, or grandchild. Nine percent of the Danes who fall in this category, five percent of the Britishers, and five percent of the Americans live with other people who are not relatives. Five percent of the Danish unmarried women, 17 percent of the British, and 15 percent of the Americans live with married children, which means that they share a residence with more than one person (Stehouwer 1968, p. 208). The explanation of the residential pattern differentiating Denmark from the other two societies rests upon a tradition of independence in all spheres of life and on the help given by the country through "public care for the aged and a general pension system" (Stehouwer 1968, p. 224). Each generation is financially independent of the other, and cooperative movements, as well as voluntary associations, attract the active participation of the elderly. Despite such differences and despite the fact that Americans are more likely to live with others than Danes are, the figures also show a strong tendency for older members of this society to reject residence with others. In fact, the household "consisting of a widowed (sometimes a divorced or separated) parent living alone" is one of the major five categories of households which the authors of that study distinguish: "About twenty-two to twenty-eight percent of those aged sixty-five and over" are in this type of household. A second category is that of "households consisting of a widowed (or divorced or separated) parent and married or unmarried children." About nine to twenty percent of those aged 65 and over were placed there (Stehouwer 1968, p. 218).

Independence from adult married offspring does not necessarily imply economic affluence. In fact, the widow who is 65 years or older is very likely to be living on an income which puts her below most criteria for the poverty level. Various estimates have concluded recently that "The likelihood of poverty is greater among families headed by a woman than among families headed by a man. The likelihood is even greater if the families headed by a woman are nonwhite. In 1964, 63 percent of the nonwhite and 29 percent of the white families headed by a woman were poor. The comparable proportions for nonwhite and white husband–wife families were 32 and 10 percent, respectively" (Department of Administration on Aging 1968, pp. 1–3). Older people living alone or with nonrelatives showed an even poorer income picture. Half of them had 1965 incomes of less than $1348. This median was only 40.6 percent of the median for people under 65 who are not living in families. Those who are old and living in such arrangements include one-third with incomes of less than $1000 and almost three out of five with incomes of less than $1500 (Brotman 1968). Part of the reason for such a meagerness of income is the fact that many of the older widows had never received significant incomes or worked in occupations covered by Social Security at that time. Many of the husbands had not obtained the education or achieved the occupational level which would guarantee income-producing investments or a high return rate on some other policy. Many recently widowed and younger persons had work experience producing relatively good incomes, insurance, and some sort of union or work policy which assists survivors, but the older population is often left with no means of support, let alone a comfortable life. A domestic worker married to a chauffeur is not likely to receive much inheritance at his death

nor to have other sources of income, if she is physically incapacitated or otherwise unable to keep on doing housecleaning.

Two problems prevent the widowed woman from obtaining a job which offers an above-poverty income. One is her age; the second is her educational background. More younger widows try to work, but this does not guarantee them high incomes. According to statistics of the United States Department of Labor, 23 percent of all families headed by a woman who was employed in March 1965 had an income below the poverty level in 1964 (1966, p. 1). The Department of Labor also reported that widowed, divorced, or separated women formed 41 percent of the working population in 1966. These women, however, are not distributed evenly by age, as indicated by the statistics on percentages of previously married women who obtained jobs: 59 percent of those between 16 and 24 years of age; 67 percent of those between 25 and 44; 63 percent of those between 45 and 64; and only 10 percent of those 65 and over (United States Department of Labor 1966). There are social as well as financial difficulties for the previously married older woman who does not work; employment provides not only income, but (except for domestics and those in similarly isolating occupations) also a guaranteed source of social interaction. Most older widows find employment in jobs which do not pay great wages, because few have reached high levels of formal education. Almost six percent of the persons aged 65 and over (or a million) never went to school at all, and 11 percent (or two million) had less than five years of elementary school. This makes a total of 17 percent of the aged, or three million people, who are at least functionally illiterate. By comparison, only five percent of the 25 to 64 age group falls into this category. At the other end of the educational ladder, only about five percent of the older group are college graduates, as compared with 11 percent of the younger segment of the population (Brotman 1968, p. 3).

The education of the aged population, most of whom are women and a high proportion of whom are widowed, is not evenly distributed in the 65 and over group. Whites and urbanites (that is, people who in their youth attended schools in the city) tend to have completed more years of schooling than nonwhites and nonmetropolitan residents. See Table 5.

All in all, the national figures describing America's older women show them to be relatively uneducated and marginal to the labor force.

Table 5 Median number of years of schooling completed by persons aged 65+, by white (W) and nonwhite (NW), and residence, March 1966*

Class	All	Male	Female
Total	8.5	8.4	8.6
W	8.6	8.5	8.7
NW	5.2	4.7	5.6
Metropolitan	8.7	8.6	8.7
W	8.7	8.6	8.8
NW	6.0	6.0	6.1
Nonmetropolitan	8.4	8.3	8.5
W	8.5	8.4	8.6
NW	4.0	3.4	4.7

*SOURCE: Herman B. Brotman, "Educational attainment of the older population," Administration on Aging, *Useful Facts* No. 28, September 11, 1967, p. 4.

REFERENCES

ADAMS, DAVID, 1969. Adjustment to widowhood. Columbia, Missouri: University of Missouri. (Mimeographed.)

BERARDO, FELIX, 1967. Social adaptation to widowhood among a rural-urban aged population. Agricultural Experiment Station Bulletin 689 (December). Washington State University.

_____, 1968. Widowhood status in the United States: perspective on a neglected aspect of the family life-cycle. *The Family Coordinator* 17 (July): 191–203.

_____. Survivorship and social isolation: the case of the aged widower. (Mimeographed.)

BULTENA, GORDON, AND D. MARSHALL, 1969. Family patterns of migrant and nonmigrant retirees. Department of Rural Sociology, University of Wisconsin. (Mimeographed.)

GORER, GEOFFREY, 1965. *Death, grief and mourning.* New York: Doubleday.

LESLIE, GERALD, 1967. *The family in social context.* New York: Oxford University Press.

METROPOLITAN LIFE INSURANCE CO., 1945. The chances of remarriage for the widowed and divorced. *Statistical Bulletin* 26 (May): 1–3.

_____, 1962. The American widow. *Statistical Bulletin* 43 (November): 1–4.

_____, 1969. Chances of dependency. *Statistical Bulletin* 50 (January): 10–11.

NATIONAL CENTER FOR HEALTH STATISTICS, 1965. Changes in mortality trends: England and Wales, 1931–1961. *Vital and Health Statistics* 3 (November): 35.

PIHLBLAD, TERENCE, AND HOWARD ROSENCRANZ, 1968. *Old people in the small town.* Columbia, Missouri: University of Missouri.

PRACTICAL BUILDER, 1966. What makes Ross W. Cortese the world's largest home builder? *Practical Builder* (May): 82–92.

ROSENMAYR, LEOPOLD, AND E. KÖCKEIS, 1963. Propositions for a sociological theory of aging and the family. *International Social Science Journal* 15: 410–426.

ROSOW, IRVING, 1967. *The social integration of the aged.* New York: The Free Press of Macmillan.

SHANAS, ETHEL, AND GORDON R. STREIB (eds.), 1965. *Social structure and the family: generational relations.* Englewood Cliffs, N.J.: Prentice-Hall.

STEHOUWER, JAN, 1968. The household and family relations of old people. In Ethel Shanas (ed.), *Old people in three industrial societies.* New York: Atherton.

UNITED STATES BUREAU OF THE CENSUS, 1971. *Current Population Reports.* Series P-23, No. 37, "Social and economic characteristics of the population in metropolitan and nonmetropolitan areas: 1970 and 1960. United States Government Printing Office, Washington, D.C.

The Widower and the Family

IRWIN GERBER

IN ORDER TO SET THE TONE FOR THIS paper, let us state a general empirical fact: one way or another women usually come out of bereavement *worse* than men. Based on this general observation, there is one challenging point for discussion:

> Does the above mean that widowers have *no* bereavement problems worthy of support and assistance, or are we being influenced by our societal image of the male as primarily a wage earner, emotionally strong, more stoic and less dependent than the female?

We note that while there is a popular book entitled *Widow* (Cain 1974), as far as we are aware there is no complementary book called *Widower*. Very little journalistic and professional writing is available for the widower. Even with the extraordinary interest in thanatology during the past decade, we see almost no interest in the male surviving spouse. The only concentrated work has been completed by Felix Berardo (1970).

There are two possible reasons for this hiatus in research on the widower. First, the sex-role position of the male in our society includes the characteristics of independence, inner strength, and self-care. The male is assumed to be less vulnerable to life-stress than the female, and more self-sufficient when problems do arise. Based on this image of the male, it is understandable why there has been less concern for the widower. A look at the latest census data for widows and widowers offers the second reason for the lack of interest in the widower. Males die faster and earlier than females. The result is a larger percentage of widows than widowers. Therefore, it can be suggested that widowers, in comparison to their female counterparts, are a minority within the bereaved population. This is particularly true for the older widower, aged 65 and older. Like other minority groups, widowers hold a low priority position within society. Of the two reasons discussed above for the almost total lack of interest in

the male surviving spouse, we have selected the first—the male sex role—as the focal concern of this paper.

Is there a lack of interest in the male survivor because the widower goes through bereavement with *no* problems? We have to answer *no*. The widower certainly does experience his share of medical, emotional, and social adjustment problems. Our contention is that the widower, young and old, has received little attention from researchers because of his sex-role position in our society. This unique set of expectations, although changing because of the women's movement, explains why the widower is given less societal support. The male in our society is considered an instrumental leader whose major role is to be a producer, a wage-earner in an economy limiting his sphere of other than work activity. In addition, the male is supposed to withdraw from those daily activities and responses to those activities society has defined as "women's work." The male is therefore supposed to be an unemotional (no crying in public) individual who is tough-skinned to the point of being independent from others to satisfy his needs. In general, the married male is relatively unaware of his childrens' daily activities; has little responsibility for maintaining extended family ties such as contacting close family members for a family gathering; and the male is in general considered an object to cater to because of his crucial position in establishing the family's economic position.

We are proposing that this picture of the self-sufficient, comparatively unemotional male is the basic reason why there has been less interest in the widower than in the widow who is considered to be more vulnerable. And it is *exactly* for these reasons that the widower has certain unique socioemotional problems in adjusting to the loss of a spouse. A sample of these problems and suggested causes will be briefly discussed.

Reprinted by permission of the author.

YOUNGER WIDOWER WITH CHILDREN

The younger widower with children faces a number of problems. The major ones are elaborated upon below:

1. The sociocultural prescription of not crying or showing deep emotion in the presence of others can create stress and also guilt for the widower.

2. His awareness of how dependent he was on his spouse for maintaining the emotional level of the family is obvious after her death.

3. Not every widower can afford a domestic helper to take care of the children, to prepare meals, to shop for food, and to clean the house. Most widowers have to handle these tasks themselves or with some help from relatives. The younger the children, the more difficult are the daily family chores and needs.

4. The younger widower has to assume a new role obligation he has not previously handled. Not only are we talking about the time involved in taking care of these chores, while holding down a job, but of equal importance we must consider the emotional pressures when the widower, for example, realizes that he knows very little about the needs of his children. How many fathers have sufficient knowledge about their son's friends to help make a decision as to whom should be invited to a birthday party?

5. Because of the male's withdrawal from initiating contact with family members, widowers, over time, may still continue this socially acceptable pattern to the point of isolating themselves from potentially important sources of support. In addition, the image of the male spouse as strong and independent may further reduce his opportunity for family support. Society is more likely to expect the widower to fend for himself, an expectation society does not hold for the widow.

OLDER WIDOWER

Here we are referring to the *retired* widower whose children have long since moved out of the house to establish their own life-styles. The problems of the older widower are somewhat different from those of the younger widower, but are nevertheless the result of the same sex-role position our society has given to all males.

1. For the retired elderly widower, bereavement adjustment is compounded by the fact that he, in contrast to the younger widower, is *no longer* functioning in the main role of wage-earner. In general, a retired widower with fairly good health must prepare meals, take care of the home, and provide himself with activities to occupy his time. The older widower is generally unprepared to do these activities and finds little enjoyment in them. Most older widowers cannot afford to employ a home aide. We must remember, the female spouse carries into her widowed role activities she has been doing throughout her married life. The elderly widower is confronted with a host of *practical* problems resulting from the death of his wife.

2. Because of his nonproducing and noncontributing role in society, the elderly retired widower finds it difficult to occupy his time. This is particularly crucial when the older widower has poor health (something that most younger widowers do not have to worry about). If the retired widower is under seventy years of age, he will find that most of his friends in their 60s are still around and probably married. This makes it more difficult for him to maintain his friendship patterns.

3. The fact that the elderly widower does not occupy his traditional role of wage-earner means that if he lives with his children he is likely to be seen as a burden. The widowed mother can prepare meals, clean the house, and sew. The father, most likely, will not be able to contribute to the household in the same fashion.

4. For the widower who remarries these problems do not exist. Presently, there is a five-to-one ratio of widows to widowers. Therefore, it is easier for the widower to remarry or find someone to live with. However, we cannot assume that all retired widowers remarry, particularly those who have major medical problems.

In conclusion, our society's image and approach to the male sets the stage for some of the socioemotional problems he encounters when his spouse dies. Whether or not these problems are worse than those experienced by the widow is *not* the critical point for discussion. It is our opinion that we must be more alert to the needs of the widower than we have been. We must convince the widower and society that to seek assistance is not a sign of "manly weakness" and we must also attempt to set up more assistance groups to attract the widower in order to meet his daily needs. How- ever, if we are sincerely concerned about the fate of the widower our expectations of the male role before widowhood must be changed. Hopefully, some of the sex-role changes resulting from the women's liberation movement will produce a future genera- tion of males who will be less restrictive in family activities than the males of present and past generations.

REFERENCES

CAIN, L. *Widow.* New York: William Morrow, 1974.

BERARDO, F.M. Survivorship and social isolation: the case of the aged widower. *Family Coordinator*, 1970, 19:11-25.

Part Three

Social Change and the Nuclear Family

Chapter 10

Alternatives within the Nuclear Family

TRADITIONALLY, SOCIOLOGISTS HAVE regarded the family as providing a structure in which personal needs are expected to be met. Within the division of labor characterizing industrial society, major functions of the nuclear family are to meet individuals' emotional and sexual needs. Yet, many people are questioning the traditional nuclear family's ability to fulfill these functions. Is it possible for one key relationship to meet all of the sexual and psychological needs of the individual? Are husbands and wives emotionally and intellectually satisfied with differentiated roles within the family? Must all women engage in the reproductive function of the family? Within this chapter, we see responses to disaffection with the traditional role definitions regarding expressive and instrumental behaviors of men and women within the family structure. The nuclear family form remains, while the norms with regard to family behavior are changing.

The idea of "Open Marriage" as proposed by the O'Neills[1] posits complete independence and equality between husband and wife: intellectual, occupational, and sexual equality. Both husband and wife are to be considered independent partners within the marriage relationship. R.N. Whitehurst deals with the societal factors that have led to sexually "open marriages," such as affluence, decreasing religious influence, and anonymity in urban areas. These factors have lessened the social controls over marriage and produced greater opportunity for personal autonomy and experimentation.

From a study of 35 couples living in open marriages, Whitehurst analyzes the problems concerning social networks, the division of labor, and feelings related to honesty and jealousy. He views the individuals who choose open marriage as "active seekers of some more or less utopian ideal who are willing to pay the price in uncertainty, anxiety, and to commit themselves to high levels of interaction to attempt to accommodate problems."

Anne Marie Ambert studies marital decision making about swinging. Swinging is defined as "the pursuit of sexual activities with extramarital partners by both spouses at the same time and usually in the same place." Hence, swinging is an alternative to the traditional monogamous norm of the nuclear family. Ambert found that the husband tends to have greater influence in the decision to swing. He is the one who is most likely to initiate a discussion about swinging, and to make the final decision to participate in swinging. Hence, although the traditional sexual norms are not followed, the traditional inequality within the family vis-à-vis decision making still remains.

Naomi Gerstel deals with the changing role definitions of men and women in terms of their task orientations. She studied commuter marriages, which are those marriages in which "the spouses live in separate residences for varying lengths of time," so that each may pursue occupations which are in different locations. Partners in commuter marriages define the occupational careers of both the husband and wife as equally important. This is in contrast to the traditional role definition of wife, which defines her most salient role as being within the family.

Another alternative within the nuclear family, the alternative of the voluntarily childless wife, is analyzed by J. E. Veevers. Again, role redefinition is involved, particularly for the woman. Veevers discusses how voluntarily childless wives protect themselves from the societal pressures to have children, and the mechanisms they use to support their positive definitions of childlessness.

Hence, the alternatives within the family do not envision a change within the structure of the nuclear family, but of its norms. The family still consists of one man and one woman, and possibly children, but the norms attached to the roles of husbands and wives are being changed, particularly the norms concerning sexual behavior, and those norms concerned with wives' statuses.

Utilizing a symbolic interaction analysis, the following questions may be asked: How do new meanings become attached to roles, and how do these new meanings get perpetuated? Specifically,

how is swinging initiated in marriage? How do voluntarily childless women maintain their positive feelings toward remaining childless? What is the process by which couples in open marriages periodically renegotiate their relationship? How does our socialization process hinder sexual independence and experimentation?

From a structural functional perspective, the reader might ask: What are the structural changes in American society which have brought about alterations within the family? Which family patterns have changed? What are the positive and negative consequences of these changes for different family members? How are men and women differentially affected by open marriage, swinging, and commuter marriages?

From a conflict perspective, readers might focus on power differentials and inequalities in the traditional nuclear family and larger society which have produced conflict and change. To what degree do the changes discussed in this chapter produce greater equality within the family?

NOTE

1. Nena O'Neill and George O'Neill, *Open marriage*, New York: M. Evans, 1972.

Open Marriage: Problems and Prospects

R. N. WHITEHURST

THE INCREASED OPENNESS OF THE LATE 60s coupled with radical activities, media coverage of the so-called death of the family and increasing divorce, desertion, and liberation, child-battering, and assorted family problems have created an atmosphere favorable to experimentation with marriage forms as a basis for renewal. Increasingly,

many people appear to be seeking new life-styles as well as alternatives to divorce; among these can be found a variety of forms of open marriage, popularized by the O'Neills' best-seller of 1972. The following can be seen as an interpretation of the

Reprinted by permission of the author.

social factors relating to creation of the potential for open marriages, a discussion of problems and solutions found in this form, and finally an evaluation of the potential for the futures of marriage in terms of increased sexual openness.

Throughout this paper, a distinction will be made between role-open marriage (ROM) and sexually open marriage (SOM). Although SOM most usually includes aspects of ROM, ROM of itself never includes a provision for outside sexuality. The O'Neills are advocates of ROM; this paper essentially deals with SOM.

FACTORS RELATED TO OPEN MARRIAGE

In the course of this century family ties in the context of social controls have weakened considerably. High mobility rates, decreasing religious influence, and anonymity in urban areas have all been associated with increased potential for marital variation. This relative absence of effective social controls over marriage coupled with more openness in the media about sexual matters, open talk of swinging, communes, trial marriages, homosexuality, and other variant life-styles has given larger numbers of people opportunities to experiment. In addition, economic status of the comfortable middle classes has provided leisure and means to effect new adaptations of life-styles. It is also probably true that affluence lends itself to a vague uneasiness about the self—and that this in turn may lead to experimentation with new life-styles.

All this when understood in the time-context of rapid changes in the entire societal outlook in the past generation has created a large range of open choices to fill needs that were once squarely met by clear answers to life's pressing questions. Religion is no longer insistent on (nor can it secure by threats of hell-fire and brimstone) a lifelong monogamous, heterosexual relationship. The community no longer has clear and unequivocal answers to its deviants, nor has it the collective sanctioning power over neighbors as it once did.

We are in a period when people are faced with more options and fewer rules as to how to behave; this means there will be, especially in the absence of strong sanctions, more people opting for life-styles at variance with the standard marital form.

THE NORMATIVE VACUUM

Students of collective behavior suggest that fads, crazes, emotional contagion, and social movements are enhanced in their potential development by absence or weakness of social forms, ambiguous and open decisions, and changed perspectives and values (Broom and Selznick 1963, p. 256). These characteristics are indisputably with us and contribute to the large normative vacuum which must be filled by those entering marriage. No firm set of guidelines suffices for everyone these days. It is probably a safe generalization to suggest that young people entering marriage today (given the ordinary urban, nonreligious, and isolated noncommunity setting) will have more complex problems, less certainty in their relationships, fewer social supports in event of troubles and thus become even more divorce-prone than now. (Serious inflation, depressions, or other economic upheavals and crisis situations may alter this as they have in the past.) Our current conception of the "one-and-only" theory of love tends likewise to promote divorce and serial marriages.

Some young and not so young people have begun to realize that divorce is not an instant solution to the problem of relationships; rather, they are seeking to open up marriages on at least a trial basis. It should be noted that SOM, however, does not often resolve an already bad marital situation; this probably rarely works. Opening up the possibility, however, does provide at least some means to discuss potentials rationally and to eyeball with a partner with respect to where each stands on such an issue. Partner variability in basic life philosophies with respect to open marriages creates underlying value problems which sometimes cannot be resolved short of divorce.

SAMPLE AND PROFILE OF SUBJECTS

This study is a beginning and tentative summary of data secured from 35 pairs living in open marriages or nonmarital relationships similar to marriage. The sample is nonrandom, accumulated by reference from those in or having knowledge of open marriages. This paper is conceived as a first effort in the basic description and analysis of entry, development, and demise of open marriages and is general in nature.

The age of respondents in the current sample ranged from 20 to 62. The concept of "openness" with respect to the relationship is variously defined. All but one of the couples, however, understood an open marriage as SOM or to be working toward that goal. Outside dating was done on an individual basis with females appearing to have the most frequent occurrence of outside dating experiences.

Most SOM people are professionals or career types, and have been influenced toward open marriage by the O'Neills' book *Open marriage* and Robert Rimmer's novels as well as by friends, media discussions, therapy groups, and by general dissatisfactions with isolation of urban life and conventional marriage.

Males have more often made radical alterations in their philosophies of life than females. Men seem to have been serious as youths, often overprotected, deeply religious, and conventional. This may merely be a matter of degree only as varied from female experience. Several of the couples have had limited group marriage experience or desire to try such an arrangement. These have not been notably satisfactory for most and have not lasted long periods of time. There are severe logistics living problems apparent for open marriage types who desire more of a communal or group living style. Some respondents are active in humanist associations or may be involved in Unitarian churches; most are not active in any church and consider themselves either agnostics or atheists; they often express ideas about the sacredness of life and living it to the full as a sacred obligation. The woman's movement is an important impetus for both men and women to evaluate sex roles and the nature of equality in open marriages.

There seem to be many routes by which people come into open marriage and a number of diverse ways of conceptualizing its basic nature. Many commonalities also exist, such as the existence of pain and complexity of relationship, feelings of great personal worth in the growth experiences, and an overall positive interpretation of the ultimate meanings of open marriage.

The sample included people from both coasts, from urban areas or suburban ones as diverse as Vancouver and Toronto, Seattle and New York and even the deep south. Personal desires for growth, autonomy and freedom seem to characterize the respondents.

The question has often been raised of late as to why people who want an SOM want a marriage at all. The answer probably lies in understanding some people as seekers of variety, complexity, romance, and even problems. The tensions set up by SOM tend to be seen as not undesirable and do hold the promise of greater personal fulfillment on one hand while satisfying some of the remaining needs for a core of tolerably solid stability on the other.

SOME MALE-FEMALE DIFFERENCES

The most common complaint women register about their men centers on their men's inability to maintain good communications when the emotional chips are down.[1] Men have a large array of defensive and escape mechanisms well institutionalized in the culture which allows them escape into work, sports, or all-male activities when too much is demanded at home. Women, on the other hand, have little training in the realities they ordinarily are required to cope with in marriage; rather, their idealized version of reality sold by bride's magazines and the happy-homemaker stereotype tends to become tarnished by what may be called the "Betty Friedan" syndrome.[2] Men, in contrast to women, are rarely socialized to view women as persons worthy of the full-human involvement required, for example, by men's jobs—when in reality a good relationship requires much much more than this. These themes have been elaborated elsewhere, but it is crucial to note socialization differences between the sexes as a starting point for marital problems (Lewis 1972; Slater 1974).

OPEN VERSUS CLOSED MARRIAGE

Among the rationales for consideration of opening up marriages are a few prominent items: many people who are prone to try this adaptation have come to feel in recent times that the restrictiveness of a conventionally monogamous life has some serious drawbacks. Probably most conventional people feel these at times (and perhaps some of them all the time) but are unwilling to risk the danger of confrontation, accommodation, and the pain that may be involved in opening up a relationship. As a result of this built-in problem of conventional marriages, most of them tend to have areas of uncommunicated needs and at least some doubts about the nature of the commitment. The ways in which conventional marriages become so circumscribed have not been the target of research, but could well be. Since all relationships involve trade-offs, the normal trade-off is to give up novelty, the thrill of the promise of further romantic or sensuous or emotional involvement with another for the sake of stability and security. Although flirting with adultery, the conventional society provides a series of morals and rationales to support the normal adaptation.[3]

Open marriage is, however, one potential response to the perceived tension between wanting to maintain a secure primary-bonded relationship and the temptations of clandestine adultery. As an intervening marriage type, some couples consider what Myers (1974) has called the "Fourth Compartment" in marriage as a more reasonable substitute for divorce.[4]

Although ultimately the "fourth compartment" idea is much less threatening than open marriage (for it does not necessarily involve telling all to the partner), it has less appeal to many who insist on an open relationship as a part of their primary setting. Setting up rules for either can be complex, challenging, and create problems which may be too difficult for most people conventionally reared in this competitive, jealousy-producing, and self-oriented, possessive culture. Culturally, however, we have created a setting of freedom—for both males and females—in ways which heretofore have been unattainable. We have set aside most of the social controls over traditional marriage or seriously weakened them. We have learned to question authority and absolutes; we are becoming a nation of relativists. In such a setting, strains are created within marriage as they are created by stepping outside it. Although it would be an error to think great numbers of people are attempting open marriages, it may be crucial to note that nearly all of the participants in the presently reported study show little inclination to return to conventional life-styles.

ADAPTATION IN OPEN MARRIAGES

Although there are a great number of problems in both open and conventional marriages, open marriages are characterized by some specific and recurring problems unique to that situation. Among the difficult problems in adapting to open marriage is the necessity to recognize and deal with the social network of the couple in some ways changed by the new type of marital interaction. Given the current cultural normative sense about what is proper in relationships, most open marriage couples find it is either difficult or impossible to anticipate acceptance of their arrangement on the part of many friends and relatives. Most clearly, though, it is friends and co-workers who have a very difficult time grasping the nature of openness and relating to it. Thus, open marriages seem to develop more closeness as a boundary-maintaining device, thereby increasing the potential solidarity of the pair as a bulwark against the great portions of the outside world which do not understand or condone the life-style they live. This limited sociability potential for open marriage necessitates careful selection of friends and acquaintances. SOM couples therefore are more or less constantly scrutinizing others in a social context to ascertain who may be a supportive friend as contrasted to all others. This problem of resolving the social nature of friend networks is a common one that SOM couples seem to face. The remainder of the problems necessitating adaptation are more variable and often experientially different for males and females. Most of the problems discussed below, however, are not unique to SOM, but tend to take on an exaggerated form since they are thrown in bold relief in SOM in ways not likely to occur in conventional marriages.

The problems of honesty coupled with a desired degree of openness are major issues in SOM. How to establish a degree of honesty and still maintain the pair bond with a strong sense of togetherness is difficult—especially for people conventionally reared to hide many feelings and values. Facing openness is a threat not many can work through with great success, although those who manage it express a real sense of growth and accomplishment. There is great variability in the degree of openness desired; thus SOM requires rather lengthy and sometimes constant renegotiation and accommodation in the relationship. This can be wearing both emotionally and physically and be time consuming as well.

In the interest of peace (although in most marriages this is an artifact of developing a less than desired working consensus) and "efficiency" of getting on with other aspects of life, most conventional marriages shun such a demanding prospect.

Problems of controlling the partner (developing a consensus) and working out an amicable household division of labor are also often important. Control problems run the gamut of human interaction but at times they are crucial in SOM situations. In part this is probably due to the fact that the double-standard is squarely faced in SOM and men are often poorly equipped to enlarge their share of task takeover in the house. Intellectually, they are often willing to try, but either the quality of effort is seen as puny and the frequency of work, or lack of perseverance over time, seems to be more usual. There are many patterns, however, and there is no simple answer to the question of the ways in which SOM couples adapt.

Time together (or time away from home, with or without others), jealousy and sex problems also seem to be deeply involved in control problems. Most couples in the present study have worked out what they feel is an amicable, workable solution but not one that is perfect. The continuance of SOM should be understood as predicated on the sense of positive growth and rewards experienced by the participants and not evaluated in terms of the relationship problems it seems to create. Most suggest

that the rewards from working together on problems openly has added materially to their own growth enhancement and increased potential as persons. There are diverse ways the time problem has been attacked by SOM partners and there seems to be no standard solution. Among those used by the subjects, some system that more or less guarantees equality to both parties is the goal. The problem of course lies in the differential commitment to SOM and to outside partners. There are studied attempts to avoid time-discrimination between partners, but this kind of parity is almost impossible to achieve; thus, one partner or other (usually the least involved outside—and not always the woman) has to cope with some kind of feelings of being "left out." Whether the partners consider this as a problem for the alone person to cope with or a problem to be worked at together (the usual approach) it is difficult to create an atmosphere wherein both are always content with the situation.

One salvation in these marriages with respect to this problem inheres in the nature of SOM people; they are most often individuals with careers of their own and who have outside interests and contacts, making it likely they will not suffer so much from aloneness since they are seldom without either things to do or people of significance in their lives. This is presumably why SOM will not work for large numbers of people as both partners benefit when there are strong individual lives and interests as well as commitment to the primary partnership.

Sexual problems per se seem relatively rare, as SOM people seem committed to the notion that sexuality and sensuality are fun and vital life-giving elements of relationships; they thus approach this area of life in a more naturalistic, less rigid way than do many conventionals. There are, however, some sex-related problems, notably relating to fear of loss of a partner, time jealousy, and some hangover feelings of possessiveness of partners. This should not be news to people reared in such a restrictive culture that imparts such feelings about the privacy and possessiveness of sex as we learn.

There were few evidences of any double standards, even though some anxieties were expressed about sexual sharing. One case of a reversed double standard was reported by one couple: the wife had been sexually active with more than one partner before the recent marriage (about two years ago) as had the husband. The husband was very willing to continue this pattern of outside involvements, but the wife's insecurities about her husband being with someone else sexually created so much anxiety in her that he agreed to sexual exclusiveness with her alone. The upshot is that she is working out her own feelings with him about this, while in the meantime she still has outside sex with other men. He is permitted to have relationships so long as they are not fully sexual. The wife is presuming that she will learn to cope with this eventually; in the meantime, however, she is continuing the present pattern. She is well aware of her inconsistent approach at this time but feels as yet she cannot cope with her husband's outside sexual affairs. The husband in the meantime values the primary relationship so much that he is willing to keep things this way for the present. By and large for most SOM people, sexuality and sex are not big problems; this is probably in part due to rather complete commitments to the notion of SOM and ease with partners' own sexuality in general.

There is sometimes contention and accommodation called for in terms of the ways in which openness is used by partners. One person reported she felt that her impending divorce was in part due to the misuse of the freedoms she and her partner had developed. When it was used for relaxed good times, fun and ego-enhancement, it seemed to work fine. When it came to be used as an escape from the other partner, it became destructive of the relationship. This may be a valuable insight which may have broader application to arrangements other than the open marriage type of relationship.

The SOM arrangement does not always lend tranquility and event-free living to the lives of those who partake. In fact, there are real limiting potentials to the selectivity of people for SOM in that they appear to be active seekers of some more or less utopian ideal and willing to pay the price in uncertainty and anxiety, and to commit themselves to high levels of interaction to attempt to accommodate problems. On balance then, we can guess that open marriage is usually a success in terms of certain personal benefits, but sometimes falls short of enabling people to find stability and permanence in their lives. People in SOM have thus more or less

consciously opted for a pleasure-pain formula for their lives that they calculate will have enhanced payoff in areas other than tranquility and possibly even stability. Although all seem to want the best of both worlds, stability of a primary relationship and ego-enhancement from outside relations as well, few achieve these as full successes. It is fair to note, however, that no regrets were expressed by respondents since all placed an extremely high value on the growth experience and were unwilling to give up on the notion of SOM. Its viability as a mode of life was not seriously questioned by those who had tried it. A not uncommon comment however was something like "It hurts" when generalizing about the SOM experience. There seems to be a rather universal feeling though that there is no growth without pain; thus pain is often understood as a part of the growth process—not necessarily desired but simply existentially there as an inevitable part of the life-style of SOM.

SEX DIFFERENCES IN SOM EXPERIENCE

From the limited sample data available, there seems to be no real discernible pattern of difference by sex with respect to most SOM behaviors. Knapp (1974) has reported that women seem to initiate the major proportion of outside sexual contacts, however, and this seems supported by the implications of the present study. Women feel they have an easier time of making contacts which may eventuate in an outside sexual partnership and emotional fulfillment of their needs than do men. In part this may be a function of the personality types selected for SOM or it may be that women who get into SOM develop a style which is uncharacteristic of most other women—namely, the ability in interacting with men to ask for and seek out what they want instead of playing the passive stereotypical female role. At any rate, no couples expressed the feeling that there was any real male advantage in pursuing outside relationships in SOM. The only place women still seem to lose in this type of setting is in terms of inequality in household division of labor. Although men in SOM appear to be willing (at least intellectually) to share household duties, they, either by dint of nontraining or undiligence, seem to do what women often consider inferior work in the house. There may be subtleties of male reluctance to learn to do adequate housework, there may be power plays involved, but basically it seems to be a problem of differential male-female conceptions of when a house is "clean enough." Most men's view of this is at variance with their wives, although this is sometimes reversed as well. There are probably no safe generalizations which can be made about male–female differences at this time as sex affects SOM.

USES AND MISUSES OF OPEN MARRIAGE

Open marriage appears to have many benefits and many hazards; among the most clear benefits are the ways in which the process helps people to open up their lives to new experiences, people, and awareness of themselves in the world, enabling them to function as more complete, fulfilled, and adequately functioning humans. When SOM works toward goals such as these (without undue problems which the participants cannot handle) it seems to be optimized as an experience.

When SOM adds to the zest of life more than it adds complexities and problems which are unmanageable, it is seen as a good thing. Thus, some people have set criteria, some more or less consciously, that lend themselves to evaluation of the changes in their relationship on this basis: does it add more zest, more life, more fun? Is life more interesting now, more worthwhile? If these questions are not asked explicitly, they seem to be the criteria of judgment used implicitly by many. If, however, people tend to use the SOM experience for some less healthy reasons, it often seems doomed to failure. For example, most subjects recommended that the relationship be solidly bound as a pair unit before trying to open it to outsiders. If SOM is seen as a "band-aid" or some kind of repair kit for a faulty relationship, it seems foredoomed to failure.[5] If it is used as a means of escaping an unhappy spousal tie or to seek an ally against a hurtful spouse, or to simply act out vengeful or other neurotic reactions with a spouse, failure is likely. Many people come into SOM by routes associated with group dynam-

ics, therapy sessions, and other related means and are thus open to suggestions about growth and change and are thus likely to be (perhaps) aware of selves (and expanded marital potential) in ways that conventionals may not.

In the cases examined for this study, there is no indication of formal contract negotiations for either entry into or maintenance of SOM. There is a tremendous variety of more or less explicit verbal contracting done, most of it subject to change and accommodation as time goes by. There is thus set up a large area of interaction which does not occur in conventional marriages. Only a selected minority of pairs are able to face the difficulties and complexities of rather continuing negotiations required by SOM. Although formal contracts are shunned as mechanistic and rigid, there are many rules which are imposed on partners. One couple holds an annual reevaluation and renegotiation session, another holds to a rule (or tries to) which is a credo: "Do nothing of which your spouse will disapprove; disapprove of nothing your spouse does."[6]

The basic contractual nature of SOM appears to involve the commitment to openness, at least with respect to the range and numbers of options available to partners; this is a significant variation when contrasted to the average conventional marriage in that most aspects are set and only a narrow range of minor adaptations are negotiable. Therefore, the implicit contract of SOM involves the idea that "we will contract to contract items as these come up and need accommodation and negotiation."

OPEN MARRIAGE AS PARADOX

Sometimes seen as a paradox of SOM is what appears to often be the case, the primary bond becomes at once both more and less important. Western minds are unused generally to thinking in terms of the simultaneous occurrence in one experience of polarities, such as the concurrent development of closeness and apartness in a marital relationship; this is, however, precisely what happens in a number of SOM situations. The experience of going into the world of others outside the marriage seems to enhance and make more intense the primary bond. Whether this is an outcome of a folknorm of open marriage—a self-fulfilling prophecy—is unknown. One might well suggest that the origins of this reality for SOM participants are less important than the consequences for the lives of people who share this belief. If the consequences of such a belief tend to make people in SOM feel closer to each other, then this is a reality in their lives and cannot be questioned as to its validity. Most North Americans, however, would be reluctant to adopt such a belief system readily as this involves a fairly straightforward rejection of one of our most cherished folk beliefs about love—that it can be good only with one person at a time. A number of other folk beliefs tend to support the persistence of the monogamous ideal as well—one conclusion to be drawn is that SOM types are either not subject to folklore in the same ways as others or that they have become somehow inured to this body of folklore and possibly subject to another. To the average mind in the West, the SOM marriage system appears as paradoxical, for it seems to give people what our common wisdom says is impossible, simultaneously a more intense and important pair-bond with the primary partner as well as more independence, freedom and autonomy to interact with significant others.

DEALING WITH COMPLEXITY, JEALOUSY, AND POSSESSIVENESS

All respondents claimed to have experienced problems in adapting to SOM, but there was likewise wide consensus about the positive elements related to both personal growth and relationship changes. Pain and pleasure seem to be well mixed in the polarities of SOM. There seems to be no way rather severe pains can be avoided in the SOM setting, but since it is closely associated with growth, it seems acceptable if not desired. People in SOM in fact can probably be characterized as seekers of complexity at a price. The gains made in openness, newly discovered self-feelings, and enhanced self-esteem are clearly associated with development of SOM styles. Unequivocally, the subjects stressed that they felt the direction of their lives was toward something better with respect to feelings about themselves in

relation to the outside world. This was not always reflected from harmony in the primary relationship; rather it seems to be an outgrowth of the pain and struggle within it—and this certainly does not imply that all SOM experiences are successful, at least if "success" as a criterion is seen in terms of pair stability and lack of confrontation and argument, strain and pain. People in SOM are independent and often find themselves handling the tensions between possessiveness and belonging on the one hand and autonomy and loneliness on the other. The dynamic tensions set up in these pairs are clear to see; SOM is therefore contraindicated for large numbers of people who do not feel so ambivalent toward their freedoms and who do not know how to handle as much autonomy and alone time as SOM people sometimes face in their lives.[7] Since many SOM people are professionals, they spend varying periods of time apart from each other, thus facilitating this kind of adaptation to life. It is presumptuous at this point to suggest that SOM is responsible for or in some way "causes" people to become more open to new worlds of experience; in fact, one respondent suggested that it was her burgeoning awareness of the world and herself in it that created the potential for open marriage.

FIDELITY AND LOYALTY

The kinds of changes defined by SOM relationships necessarily create an obsolescence of the older meaning of fidelity. Exactly what this is replaced by in SOM is a bit variable at the moment and is subject to negotiation and redefinition. In such a normative vacuum as occurs in this kind of setting, people must of necessity create new rules and definitions. The tendency seems to be for SOM relationships to define loyalty and fidelity in new terms that do not imply ownership, possessiveness, or exclusivity, but rather involve the notion of primariness of the pair. It is as though SOM people define their relationship in a hierarchy of significant others as being "the most significant other." A priority is thus established which does not preclude other relationships but attempts to keep the primary bond intact. This of course creates the nexus of debate and complexity in SOM as there are many ways of defining the "correctness" of the nature of the primary bond. Exactly how norms develop and diffuse among couples who practice SOM is poorly understood; in part, this is due to books, media coverage, etc., but principally it seems to be a matter of people with similar life-styles and ideologies sharing ideas and information with each other. A network of latest happenings in the counterculture of SOM appears to operate at some level. There is thus a series of emergent conceptions about changes in the definition of the nature of loyalty and fidelity, not clearly enough set forth so that any picture emerges at the moment.[8]

FUTURES OF OPEN MARRIAGES

As a life-style, SOM is not likely to fade into obscurity, due to the continued influence of urbanism, secularism, anonymity, and larger spheres of personal freedom for many people today. Probably many more variations and forms of SOM will appear through time.

The basic problem of the stability (or instability) of SOM inheres in the same set of social conditions that creates strains for conventional marriages. The relative failure of networks to support the novel forms of SOM must be seen as a major factor in the instability of this life-style. Much the same can be said of conventional marriages, but at least these have the weight of law and custom as well as some remaining community positive sanctions for their perseverance.[9]

Among the comments made about the regrets of those in SOM situations was one woman who said she was truly sorry she could not share her life-style (information about it) with her mother and other relatives. Friends and acquaintances must be chosen with care to avoid the disapproval of being tagged a wild deviant. This wariness produces a kind of strain which people in SOM must cope with and attempt to relieve by increased pair solidarity and choosing friends that fit their life-style philosophy.

Given some means to support SOM by outside agencies, easing of the negative sanctions imposed by middle-class morality today and a general awareness of its workability, it is likely that a greater seg-

ment of people, most likely from the upper middle classes, will begin to make this form more stable and more functional. For great numbers, however, it is doomed to failure for the reasons mentioned above plus the fact that our conception of privatized monogamy is deeply entrenched by early socialization and custom. Given some successful examples of SOM, these barriers may begin to crumble; in fact, this has already begun to happen in large cities in North America. It is unlikely, however, that SOM will come close to replacing the old standby—the clandestine affair, unsavory as certain aspects of it seem to be to middle-Americans.

SUMMARY AND CONCLUSIONS

Open marriage is a response to a variety of changing social conditions involving urbanism, anonymity, freedoms and emphasis on expressive sexuality. As well, it reflects the decreasingly effective social controls such as family, religion, and community. These no longer combine to force people into preordained life-styles, set by outside authority and sanctioned clearly by these agencies. A normative vacuum tends to have resulted from all this, eventuating in experimentation and variety-filled life-styles. Among this variety can be found many people attempting variations of open marriage. Male–female socialization patterns in America make perfect or good adaptation to SOM problematic; people continue to attempt, some successfully, this adaptation. The circumscribed nature of conventional marriages creates tensions for some that make a trial at open marriages seem a plausible alternative to divorce or separation. Although it is likely that clandestine adultery will continue as the dominant pattern of extramarital sexuality, increasing numbers appear to be attempting open marriages or "fourth compartment" type relationships.

Adaptation to SOM is never smooth and problem-free and is characterized by complexities, pain, and multiple accommodations by both partners. Handling friend networks, making an equal sex-role division of labor, allocating time together and separately, and avoiding feelings of aloneness are among major problems SOM people must work out. Some feelings of jealousy and possessiveness seem to persist but are not insurmountable. There seem to be few sex differences in the problems and pains of SOM, and on occasion both men and women tend to misuse relationships and to create hurts for partners and themselves. The apparent paradox in SOM involves what seems to be a contradiction in this culture; as open marriages become more solidly pair-bound they also become looser in terms of autonomy of partners and time spent together. Only a selected minority at present can probably develop or sustain long-term open marriages and can handle the problems attendant. Finally, it appears that SOM might be evaluated from the insider's view, that is, not in terms of rates of success as seen in pair longevity but rather in terms of personal growth and enhanced self-feelings.[10] There are necessarily some emergent patterns which newly define fidelity and loyalty; these are not well understood at this time and they are somewhat variable. Making the pair-bond central, however, is a theme for most SOM people; consensus as to how to achieve this and how much openness constitutes "open" is variable, both between and among partners. Open marriages are not likely to go away as an unconventional adaptation to marriage even though only a small minority of people seem to practice it now. Given social supports and increased general acceptance, it may become a more prevalent form, but cannot at present be seen as anything other than a ripple on the current scene of marriage adaptations. Its implications however may be far-reaching, especially with increased success rates or with economic situations requiring sharing of households. This could lead to SOM and may well prove to be a stimulator of such activities in the near future.

NOTES

1. Jacquelyn Knapp in her thesis found a similar complaint of women to be that men were not demonstrative enough, and did not give enough affection. This is not materially different from standard marriages; one may wonder, however, about this question; that is, if women do not get enough affection from one man (husband) and the husband is giving at least some to other women, what is the solution? Obviously this problem has implications for all types of marriage.

2. This refers to the section in *The feminine mystique* by Friedan in which the woman married for several years asks, after pondering her supposedly life-fulfilling package of husband, children, house, and other elements presumed to bring satisfaction, "Is this all?" This is also called by some feminists as "The problem with no name."

3. For example, the moral of the recent popular film "A Touch of Class." In this film, the errant male in a loving affair finally got his comeuppance (losing the girl) and right prevailed as once more the goodness of monogamous marriage shone through as the one right way to live. Although this film obviously showed the pains and pleasures of adultery, it was obvious that the moral of "right-living" (monogamy) won out. The irony of these kinds of films seems to be that North Americans viewing these films can in a sense have their cake and eat it too—vicariously at least. While witnessing the fun and games of adultery, they are finally and absolutely told that it is a bad game. The ultimate impressions created by the media, however, are poorly understood as to their impact on moral behavior.

4. Lonny Myers suggests that each partner in a marriage is entitled to a sphere of privacy for her or his own-style activity, regardless of the kind of activity. This comes only after working out the couple, children, and job-and-community relations for the pair.

5. This may not be true in all cases, however. Knapp reports knowing of cases that violate the apparently general rule.

6. One may note that if the last part of this credo is obeyed, it nullifies and makes redundant the first half (and vice versa)!

7. An interesting note was one woman's typo error, when she described herself as "somewhat independent" and her husband as somewhat of a "loaner." (It is unknown if this spelling was accidental or intended.)

8. There is no reason to believe that the pace of social change affecting such life-styles is slowing. The kinds of changes occurring in the counterculture in the past several years make normative consensus and language describing change problematic. Everyone knows of the need for clarity in reconceptualization of these changing behaviors, but no one seems to know how to achieve the goal.

9. These factors, coupled with the economic salience of marriage (primarily for women), keep most marriages intact. It is less likely that marriages remain intact out of positive elements than the fear of the

unknown world (beyond marriage), fears of isolation, ridicule, feelings of failure, and existentially living with a known situation as a preferable choice to an unknown one. Economics certainly plays a very large part in preservation of the marital status quo for many. The suggestion is that it is negative factors which keep many marriages together and not primarily positive ones.

10. Marital longevity is still a much-used yardstick of goodness of a relationship. Some couples insist that "it's not how long you make it, but *how you make it* (together) long or short."

REFERENCES

BROOM, LEONARD, AND PHILIP SELZNICK. *Sociology.* (3rd ed.) New York: Harper & Row, 1963.

KNAPP, JACQUELYN J. Comarital sex and marriage counseling: sexually open marriage and related attitudes and practices of marriage counselors. Unpublished Ph.D. thesis. Gainesville: University of Florida, 1974.

LEWIS, MICHAEL. There's no unisex in the nursery. *Psychology Today* 5, 12 (May)1972: 54-57.

MYERS, LONNY. Marriage, honesty, and personal growth. In Robert N. Whitehurst and Roger W. Libby (eds.), *Renovating marriage.* Danville, Calif.: Consensus Publishers, 1973, pp. 345-359. Also, the "4th compartment" notion is dealt with more extensively by Myers in her forthcoming book on the topic.

O'NEILL, NENA, AND GEORGE O'NEILL. *Open marriage: a new life-style for couples.* New York: M. Evans, 1972.

RIMMER, ROBERT. *Thursday my love, Proposition 31, You and I searching for tomorrow, The Harrad experiment, The rebellion of Yale Marrat.* These novels are among Rimmer's collection of topics dealing with life in the near future as potential life-styles. He has been influential as an ideological leader for those in avant-garde marriages.

SLATER, PHILIP, note on a commentary from Slater's newest book titled *Earthwalk.* This commentary in Harper's Magazine, "Wraparound" section, May, 1974, pp. 102-105.

Swinging: A Study of Decision Making in Marriage[1]

ANNE-MARIE (HENSHEL) AMBERT

ONE VERY IMPORTANT ASPECT OF THE life of married couples, sex, has been generally omitted in studies of decision-making patterns among married couples. Swinging, defined as the pursuit of sexual activities with extramarital partners by both spouses at the same time and usually in the same place (Walshok 1971), can, because of its nonspontaneous character, lend itself to research from the decision-making perspective. While studies of marital decision-making patterns became prevalent more than a decade ago, only in the late 1960s did researchers direct their attention to swinging as a social phenomenon. This new research trend partakes of a more general cultural impetus leading to experimentation with alternate

life styles and follows the windfall of the "sexual revolution" of the past decades, a revolution characterized by a diminution of the double standard (Reiss 1967), a wider acceptance of premarital coitus among women, the pill, and a growing interest in sex as a form of leisure and of achievement (Gagnon and Simon 1970).

Measurements of marital decision-making patterns have traditionally involved the eight areas included in Blood and Wolfe's now classic study (1960, p. 19): the choice of husband's job, car, life

Reprinted from *American Journal of Sociology* 78, 4 (January 1973): 885–887 by permission of the author and the University of Chicago Press.

insurance, vacation, housing, wife's working, physician, and food budget. Other researchers have added items regarding child rearing (Smith 1969), family planning (Dyer and Urban 1958), relations with relatives, and choice of friends (Safilios-Rothschild 1969). Most studies on middle-class couples point to a certain equalization of decision making (e.g., Kandel and Lesser 1972; Smith 1969; Blood and Wolfe 1960). However, certain researchers have questioned these conclusions. The possible advantage the male retains in this process is being reviewed in light of various structural factors (Gillespie 1971). In addition, methodological shortcomings have been pinpointed in the reappraisal of past studies. Most important for our purposes is the criticism that, in the overall decision-making score, all decisions are given equal weight regardless of their importance for the entire family. It is also pointed out that since some decisions are made less frequently than others, they may alter the absolute power of either spouse. Depending on which decisions a researcher chooses to include, "one could get a completely different picture of the over-all power structure" (Safilios-Rothschild 1969, pp. 297–98).

Swinging has been described as "an outgrowth of the dramatic changes that have taken place in this century in the position of women in American society and, more crucially, changes that have taken place in the conception of female sexuality and female sexual rights" (Denfeld and Gordon 1970, p. 89). Bell (1972) points out that "swinging represents a single standard of sex—that what is right for the man is also right for the woman." Swinging is also seen as benefiting wives as much as and, in certain respects, more than their husbands (Bartell 1971; Smith and Smith 1970). Yet, in spite of these equalitarian trends, researchers note passim that husbands are the usual instigators in the initial involvement in swinging (Palson and Palson 1972; Bell 1972, 1971; Bartell 1971; Smith and Smith 1970). However, a systematic decision-making approach has yet to be applied; the present article is a modest attempt in this direction.

THREE QUESTIONS

Three questions related to the preinvolvement stage of swinging are explored in this pilot study, with the ultimate aim of relating swinging to a more general discussion of marital power. (1) Which of the two spouses first becomes aware of swinging as an activity engaged in by people similar to them? (2) Which of the two spouses first suggests swinging as a likely alternative? (3) Who makes the final decision to swing? In each instance, there are three possible outcomes: the husband, the wife, or the two jointly.

The inclusion of the first question deserves additional explanation. It is very important that swinging be perceived by either or both spouses as an activity accessible to them rather than as an activity restricted to a particular, perhaps deviant, group. The first question, like the second and third, pertains to the relative position of the spouses in society. The spouse who has more access to certain information may have a double advantage; not only will he or she be able to act as the informant to the other and thereby acquire a measure of power but also, in the context of swinging, he or she may distort the information to induce the other into this activity or to avoid involvement.

METHOD AND SAMPLE

This research was designed as a pilot study to explore the attitudes and decision-making behavior of women who swing, using a nonstructured, open-end questionnaire. The sample was purposely limited to women. While husband-wife response discrepancies have occurred whenever both spouses have been studied regarding decision making (Safilios-Rothschild 1970, 1969), the answers the women in this sample gave are largely validated by other researchers' work on swinging where both partners had been interviewed and/or observed (Palson and Palson 1972; Bell 1971; Smith and Smith 1970).

The first contact was made through a personal referral; additional names were solicited from each interviewee. Thirty-two names were gathered; three could not be reached and four refused. The final sample of 25 is not random, and, at this point, it is difficult to imagine how randomness could be achieved with swingers. A preset sampling condition was that all the women had to be currently living with the husband they were swinging with. Two exceptions occurred: one couple had ceased swinging two months earlier; and another woman was swinging as a single, with married couples but as the extra female, while the husband was unaware of her activities.

All the women lived in the Toronto metropolitan area. The median and average age was 30, with a range from 23 to 40. Fifteen were full-time housekeepers, nine were employed—four of these part-time only—and one was a student. Occupations included nursing, teaching, and secretarial work. Five had attended only high school, eight had additional training such as nursing, another five had some college, and seven had a baccalaureate. Five couples had no children; the median number for the others was two (average 2.2). The husbands were close to their wives in age, had more education (10 had graduate training), and tended to be semi-professionals, professionals, and executives.

I made initial contact when I arrived at the homes of respondents unannounced. I immediately told them how I obtained their names and emphasized the confidentiality of the study. I saw the women alone; the usual length of the interview was 2–2.5 hours. While some subjects' answers were probably influenced by their perception of the interview situation, there is ample evidence that the women confided in me as frankly as possible. For instance, while social conventions usually preclude such admissions (Laws 1971, p. 485), most discussed their marital problems. Then, all volunteered unsolicited information, and practically all

said that they had enjoyed the interview. Finally at least half switched roles with me at some point during the encounter.

RESULTS

The responses to the three questions are summarized in Table 1. The husband is shown to have a definite advantage over his wife by being the first to become aware of swinging as an accessible activity. This advantage is structural; occupational circumstances were the main source of their information. As we proceed through the decision-making process, the wife as the sole or joint initiator plays an ever lesser role. Only three women, including the "lone" swinger, were the first to suggest swinging as a possibility, and five others went through this process jointly with their husbands.[2] Seventeen husbands (68%) made the initial suggestion. Finally, only two women, again including the "lone" swinger, reported having been the one who had made the decision that led to involvement, and seven other wives reported a joint decision. The husbands alone therefore made 59% of *all* the initial decisions, 28% were joint decisions, while only 12% were made by the women.[3]

It appears that there was a lapse between the time the couples learned of swinging and the time when they considered it seriously. More time elapsed before the final decision was reached,

Table 1 Initiating agent(s) toward involvement in swinging: incidence by stage

Initiating agent(s)	First to learn of swinging (1)	First suggested it (2)	Reached final decision (3)	Total
Husband	11	17	16*	44
Wife	4	3	2	9
Both spouses together	9	5	7	21
No data	1	0	0	1
Totals	25	25	25	75

*One of these 16 cases is not clear-cut. Although the scale seemed tipped in favor of the husband, the spouses could have actually reached the decision jointly.

indicating that decision making as discussed here is multiphasic (Safilios-Rothschild 1970). A third lapse occurred between the decision to swing and the involvement. Unfortunately, while the respondents could not recall the threefold decision-making process, they could not recall well enough the duration of various time spans involved. It would be interesting to know whether the process proceeds more quickly when the husband initiates the idea and makes the final decision as, for instance, Goode found for the decision to divorce (1965, p. 145). That husbands have an advantage in decisions about swinging is usually mentioned only casually by researchers; rather, there is a tendency to emphasize that women tend to adapt better to the new sexual freedom than their husbands, that they may obtain more sexual gratification than their husbands, and that swinging may be a more important channel of socialization toward true sexual freedom for them. These advantages are not shrugged off here but are viewed within the implicit and probably unconscious value context in which they were presented. For instance, if sexual freedom and equality is seen as an improvement over the double standard, one may be tempted to conclude that it is "good"; and, if it is such a great improvement for women that it offsets their decision-making disadvantage, we may thereby have an indication that the sexual freedom advantage may be more highly valued than the possible advantage the women could have were they the decision makers (jointly or singly).

Unlike studies of swinging, studies of marital decision making have tended to emphasize who made the decision rather than the comparative advantages to either spouse once the decision had been implemented. For example, if the husband decides to buy a car, the subsequent advantages arising from this decision for the wife are not discussed. It is pertinent that we adopt the same approach here for comparative purposes. Neverthe-

less, it should be added that, in this study, when the advantages the wives reported having gained from swinging were compared to the disadvantages similarly reported, the latter outweighed the former in 11 cases.[4]

Our data, as well as those mentioned by other researchers, seem to indicate that when we can obtain a measure of decision making with regard to nonspontaneous sex—and sex in general is an important correlate of marital happiness (Burgess and Wallin 1953; Locke 1951)—the egalitarian model does not hold in its entirety.

In spite of expectations of change in the sex structure, males still have a higher status than females; by the same token, they are the ones to confer status on women, both professionally and globally, the latter through marriage.[5] There are also indications that marriage is more important for women's happiness than for men's in our society (Bernard 1971, p. 87). Therefore, applying principles of lesser commitment (e.g., Blau 1964) or of least interest (Waller and Hill 1951, p. 191) for the males, it is not surprising that wives tend to do more of the adjusting in marriage (Blood and Wolfe 1960, p. 23; Rainwater and Weinstein 1960, pp. 68–69; Burgess and Wallin 1953, p. 618). Our data support these related points. In terms of exchange, the wife usually has less power (and decision making is one indicator power) for she has fewer alternatives outside marriage;[6] she has fewer "commodities" of high *social* value to offer, and she has a higher need for the husband's *social* commodities than he has for hers. Her contributions to the marital relationship are of lower social value (Pitts 1964), thereby requiring that she increase them even if there already was imbalance (Blau 1964). Again, our data substantiate this perspective. In the context of decision making, swinging can be viewed as a male institution, and confirmations of the advent of a "sexual revolution" and of the abolition of the double standard should be reconsidered.

NOTES

1. Paper read at the annual meeting of the Canadian Sociological Association, Montreal, June 1972. I am grateful to Frederick Elkin for his most helpful comments on an earlier draft of this article.

2. A joint suggestion means that the matter was discussed jointly even though, in terms of seconds, one of the two spouses may have said it first. This is in contrast to the other cases when one spouse leaps

ahead, brings up the suggestion, and there is an obvious psychological discrepancy between the two partners at that time.

3. As the spouses' relative resources have been a topic of importance in discussions on decision making (e.g., Rodman 1967; Heer 1963; Blood and Wolfe 1960), the wife's employment status was taken into consideration and found to be unrelated to the phenomenon under study.

4. The interviewees were asked (1) what they thought swinging had added to their lives and to their marital relationships, (2) to evaluate the problems involved,

and (3) to weigh the advantages against the disadvantages.

5. In another study, 30 percent of 113 Toronto students agreed with the statement that they tended to take unmarried women above 35 less seriously than unmarried men of the same age. This finding surfaced in spite of the fact that many students had tried to adopt a "liberal" attitude. Subsequent classroom discussions more than amply validated the trend.

6. Thibaut and Kelley's (1959) treatment of power in the dyad is highly relevant here.

REFERENCES

BARTELL, GILBERT D. 1971. *Group sex.* New York: Wyden.

BELL, ROBERT R. 1971. *Social deviance.* Homewood, Ill.: Dorsey.

———— 1972. Review of *Group sex*, by Gilbert D. Bartell. *Journal of Marriage and the Family* 34 (February): 193-194.

BERNARD, JESSIE 1971. The paradox of the happy marriage. In Vivan Gornick and Barbara K. Moran (eds.), *Women in sexist society.* New York: Basic.

BLAU, PETER M. 1964. *Exchange and power in social life.* New York: Wiley.

BLOOD, ROBERT O., JR., AND DONALD M. WOLFE 1960. *Husbands and wives: the dynamics of married living.* New York: Free Press.

BURGESS, ERNEST W., AND PAUL WALLIN 1953. *Engagement and marriage.* Philadelphia: Lippincott.

DENFELD, DUANE, AND MICHAEL GORDON 1970. The sociology of mate swapping: or the family that swings together clings together. *Journal of Sex Research* 6 (May): 85-100.

DYER, WILLIAM G., AND DICK URBAN 1958. The institutionalization of equalitarian family norms. *Marriage and Family Living* 20 (February): 53-58.

GAGNON, JOHN H., AND WILLIAM SIMON (eds.) 1970. *The sexual scene.* Chicago: Transaction.

GILLESPIE, DAIR L. 1971. Who has the power? The marital struggle. *Journal of Marriage and the Family* 33 (August): 445-458.

GOODE, WILLIAM J. 1965. *Women in divorce.* New York: Free Press.

HEER, DAVID M. 1963. The measurement and bases of family power: an overview. *Journal of Marriage and the Family* 25 (May): 133-139.

KANDEL, DENISE B., AND GERALD S. LESSER 1972. Marital decision-making in American and Danish urban families: a research note. *Journal of Marriage and the Family* 34 (February): 134-138.

LAWS, JUDITH LONG 1971. A feminist review of marital adjustment literature: the rape of the locke. *Journal of Marriage and the Family* 33 (August): 483-516.

LOCKE, HARVEY J. 1951. *Predicting adjustment in marriage: a comparison of a divorced and a happily married group.* New York: Holt.

PALSON, CHARLES, AND REBECCA PALSON 1972. Swinging in wedlock. *Society* 9 (February): 28-37.

PITTS, JESSE R. 1964. The structural-functional approach. In Harold T. Christensen (ed.), *Handbook of marriage and the family.* Chicago: Rand McNally.

RAINWATER, LEE, AND KAROL K. WEINSTEIN 1960. *And the poor get children.* Chicago: Quadrangle.

REISS, IRA L. 1967. *The social context of premarital sexual permissiveness.* New York: Holt, Rinehart and Winston.

RODMAN, HYMAN 1967. Marital power in France, Greece, Yugoslavia, and the United States. *Journal of Marriage and the Family* 29 (May): 320-324.

SAFILIOS-ROTHSCHILD, CONSTANTINA 1969. Family sociology or wives' family sociology? A cross-cultural examination of decision making. *Journal of Marriage and the Family* 31 (May): 290-301.

———— 1970. The study of family power structure: a review 1960-1969. *Journal of Marriage and the Family* 32 (May): 539-552.

SMITH, HERBERT L. 1969. Husband-wife task performance and decision-making patterns. In J. Ross Eshleman (ed.), *Perspectives in marriage and the family.* Boston: Allyn & Bacon.

SMITH, JAMES R., AND LYNN G. SMITH 1970. Co-marital sex and the sexual freedom movement. *Journal of Sex Research* 6 (May): 131-142.

THIBAUT, JOHN W., AND HAROLD H. KELLEY 1959. *The social psychology of groups.* New York: Wiley.

WALLER, W. W., AND R. HILL 1951. *Family.* (Rev. ed.) New York: Holt, Rinehart and Winston.

WALSHOK, MARY LINDENSTEIN 1971. The emergence of middle-class deviant subcultures: the case of swingers. *Social Problems* 18 (Spring): 488-495.

The Feasibility of Commuter Marriage

NAOMI R. GERSTEL

INTRODUCTION

THE ALTERNATIVE FORMS OF MARRIAGE —communes, swinging, group sex, group marriage—which seem to have captured the imagination of sociologists, psychologists, and journalists are all designed to strengthen the linkages between the couple and some larger community. There is, however, both in society as a whole and in the family in particular, a secular trend working in the opposite direction, toward greater individuation, privatization, and isolation. (See for example Goode 1963; Laslett 1974; Young and Wilmott 1973.) The communal alternatives are reactions or compensations rather than a realization of the dominant trend itself.

This paper will deal with "commuter marriage," a family type which has received very little attention. It is a marital form in which the spouses live in separate residences for varying lengths of time. Commuter marriage is in striking contrast to most other alternative forms. Rather than a movement toward communalism, it is part of a movement toward individualism. The spouses chose a degree of spatial isolation from one another in order to gain increased individual satisfaction. This marital form is quite consistent with the historical trends in the organization of the family which have involved such changes as a movement from an ideal of an extended family to an ideal of a conjugal or modified extended family, an increase in women working outside the home, and increased equality between spouses. Furthermore, it is in accord with more recent ideological trends. The women's liberation movement makes it increasingly acceptable for women to be dedicated to their careers and legitimizes the demand by women for individual freedom and personal growth.

Attempts to resolve the strain between individualism and communalism have frequently failed. This is particularly clear in communes where the assertion of individual freedom has caused major difficulty (Berger 1974; Zablocki 1971). This same conflict is apparent on the level of the individual in the conjugal family. One specific aspect of this strain can be seen in dual career families. Because of the simultaneous participation in both an occupational and familial system, conflicts occur over where to live. In a recent empirical examination of dual career families, Holmstrom (1972) found that 75 percent of the couples faced the issue of geographic separation due to career commitment. Commuter marriage is a mechanism of individuation which is an attempt to deal with this strain. This marital form is certainly not the only alternative of the future. Perhaps only a small number of people will ever engage in it. But rather, in a pluralistic system, it is one alternative, which, as this paper will show, is appropriate only in certain stages of the marital and occupational life cycle. Here, I will deal with the question of its potential for success in contemporary American society by presenting preliminary analysis of data drawn from ongoing research.

DEFINITION

Commuter marriage is a marital form in which members of a couple spend at least two nights in a week in separate residences and yet are still married and intend to remain so. The separation is a result of both the husband's and wife's participation in demanding careers that require commitments in different locations.

Superficially, other patterns of marital separation may seem identical to commuter marriage. Immigrant workers, traveling salesmen, prisoners, and military personnel undergo familial separation.

Research reported here was funded by a fellowship to the author from the Business and Professional Women's Foundation and by a traineeship to the author from the National Institute of Mental Health.

These examples appear structurally similar, but in a number of essential ways they differ from the type of separation I am examining. First, commuter marriage is limited to dual career families, and the traveling spouse is often the woman, rather than the man, who typically travels in the cases mentioned above. Traditionally, women have been excluded from tasks involving mobility (Murdock 1949). In my sample, 32 percent of the women and 52 percent of the men did all of the traveling between homes, and the spouses alternated in 16 percent of the cases. Second, in the case of soldiers and prisoners, separation is obligatory. For the commuting couples in this study, separation is voluntary. The individuals involved may subjectively define it as necessary, as when one cannot get any job requiring his or her skills in the same locale as his or her spouse. However, either they could survive on one salary, or one spouse could lower his or her job aspirations and take a position not demanding full use of acquired skills. Third, for emigrants and traveling salesmen, the primary motivation for commuting is increased earning ability. However, for dual career families, commuting may actually have a net financial cost. (See below.) Their primary motivation tends to be increased personal satisfaction which follows increased career involvement. Finally, in some of the cases above, a separate home is not extablished. Among the dual career commuters, the commuting is patterned; that is, they always commute to the same geographic location and thus have a "secondary home." For all of these reasons, commuter marriage is a genuinely distinct phenomenon, though analysis of it may aid in the understanding of other structurally similar familial types.

METHODOLOGY

I gathered an extensive list of commuters through three sources: news media, personal contact, and commuters themselves. My final sample includes 94 individuals, almost all of whom are married to another person in the sample. The majority of these ($n=54$) were those who were commuting at the time of the interview. A second smaller group consisted of those who had commuted in the recent past but no longer did so ($n=10$). This group allows consideration of long-term effects and post-commuting adjustment. A third group consisted of those who divorced while in the process of commuting ($n=10$). This group aids in the analysis of the ways in which commuting is a source of strain in marriage. Finally, I included a group ($n=20$) who were members of dual career noncommuting couples in order to distinguish what is specific to commuting from what is general to dual career families. As the necessary population parameters are not available, I was not able to obtain a random sample of commuting couples. Thus, I cannot generalize with assurance to the total commuting population. However, as I did find patterns, I believe the data are suggestive if not definitive.

With those I included in my final sample, I carried out intensive interviews. As these commuters are by definition living in separate locations, and geographic distribution was desired, they were interviewed in 14 different states. Each interview lasted from two to four hours and was carried on with the spouses separately so they could talk freely and independently of their mates. I used an open-ended, discursive interviewing technique.

CAN IT WORK?
LIMITING CONDITIONS
OF THE FEASIBILITY
OF COMMUTING

The viability of commuter marriage hinges on both the articulation of this marital form with the social structure as well as its potential for satisfying individual needs. In order to evaluate its place in the familial system in future decades, it would be necessary to consider such issues as the future of women's liberation, the future of the job market, and the possibilities for technological developments in transportation and communication. Only knowledge of these factors could provide an answer to the question of whether or not commuter marriage is built into and compatible with the social structure in a way which makes it something more than a transitory phenomenon. In this paper, I will not attempt to deal with the structural issues mentioned above. I will deal only with the question of its potential for the satisfaction of individual needs.

While individual satisfaction is not a sufficient condition to explain the staying power of a marital form, it is nonetheless a necessary condition for its survival. This paper deals with the conditions which aid or hinder an individual's willingness to engage in commuter marriage and the costs and benefits which are the results of such a marital organization.

To approach this, I suggest that there are conditions under which commuter marriage is extremely difficult. These fall into three categories: conditions of the commute itself, working conditions of the commuter, and familial conditions of the commuter.

Conditions of the Commute Itself

The length of the distance that must be traveled is the primary limiting condition of the commute. In my sample, the distance varied greatly: from as little as 40 to as many as 2650 miles apart. The greater the distance traveled, the more burdensome and stressful the partners find the commute.

There are two factors which underly the greater difficulty of increased distance: increased cost, both for travel and phone, and increased time and energy output. And most importantly, this increased cost and increased energy required for greater distances mean the spouses spend more time apart. In my sample, the median consecutive time apart is five days a week. However, there was a wide range: from three days to two months. As with distance, when the time apart increases, the dissatisfactions and strains increase. When the couple is separated for long periods, the commuter marriage begins to look like a nonmarriage, especially if the commute is not perceived as temporary. Completely separate lives begin to be established. The spouses feel as though they are losing touch with one another; the level of shared reality declines to a minute proportion. As one woman expressed it:

> There was an awful period when we didn't see each other for a month. That's too long. By the end of the month, your patterns of not seeing each other are too well established.

The opposite point of view is stated by a women who was separated from her husband for only three days a week:

> Commuting isn't that big a deal. When we lived together, we spent an awful lot of time apart anyway because we both do so much work.

Conditions of Work

First, a low income severely limits the possibility of commuting. In my sample, the median income for women was $19,000 and for men was $24,000. The median combined family income was $39,000. This marital form is a class-linked phenomenon; some families simply do not have an adequate income. There is the expense of both travel and long-distance telephone calls. Financial needs are increased by the added expense of a second home, and often, especially if there are children, hired help is seen as necessary.

Another factor which acts as a limitation is the inflexibility of some working schedules. An academic faculty job is much more appropriate for commuting than that of an administrator in an organization.[1] Academics have much greater discretion in time and place of their work as well as more and longer vacations. Thus, the amount of time that must be spent apart is reduced. In my sample, 64 percent of the women and 52 percent of the men were academics.

Finally, a third work-related factor that acts as a limit on commuting is the immobility of work-related materials. For example, a laboratory researcher must stay much closer to a specific location than must someone doing a piece of library research, where the required sources may be carried with him or her, located in another library, or partially stored in two locations.

Family Conditions

The primary familial property which may act as a limit is the presence of children. In my sample, 50 percent of the respondents either did not have children or had grown children no longer living at home. Of the remaining half, only 25 percent had children under 12 years, and none had children under four. I propose that for the general population of commuters, commuter marriage takes a curvilinear form over the marriage cycle. Those with no children[2] or grown children commute most frequently. As evidence, I point to the contrasting responses of those with and without children. Those without children most often said they would not commute with children, especially young children at home. And often, those with children found it more stressful. Though they did frequently delegate the task of child care to a housekeeper, they were still left with a sense of guilt that they were not acting as responsible parents. In addition, the domestic work load was increased for the individuals left with the children. This was most often the mother, though many fathers, over 33 percent of my sample, did keep the children. The younger the child, the greater the sense of guilt, dissatisfaction, and domestic work load became. Older children, on the other hand, often helped the parent in the primary home, both in performing household tasks and alleviating loneliness.

Second, if the couple was not married for more than a few years, the experience of commuting was especially stressful. As one commuter, who had been married twenty years, said:

> Time means a lot to me...partly a clue to my attitude to my wife. I don't understand how someone at age 50 can pick up and go off and make a relationship with another person. I mean you can get to know them. But time is a tremendous advantage.

McCubin *et al.* (1975), in a study of prisoners of war and their families, found that the longer a couple was married before separation, the greater the likelihood of reintegration of the marriage when the couple was reunited. This was interpreted as an indication of the evolution of stable family units over time. It appears that a basis of trust, shared history, and stability must be established or separation becomes destructive. Time devoted to an activity or relationship is one component of an individual's commitment to it (Becker 1960; Hess 1971). In my sample, the mean number of years married was 15, though the range was one year to 26 years. One woman, who had been married for only one year, illustrates the problem:

> I think it is especially dangerous to commute when you have been married as short a time as we have. We haven't even gotten used to living together yet.

DISADVANTAGES OF THE COMMUTER MARRIAGE

I have considered conditions which make commuting extremely difficult as an alternative marital style. But what if one has the best possible conditions? There are a number of disadvantages inherent in commuting. I will focus on three aspects of marriage: sex, communication, and social network. These are inherently shared activities, and cannot be done alone. They clearly involve some loss, but how much?

Sex

Most commuters stated that the frequency of intercourse went down somewhat; the amount of decrease for the most part depended upon the length of time apart. If there was any change at all in the intensity of the sexual relationship, it was only slight in either direction. The most frequent reported change was: yes, it increased in intensity and passion for the first night together. But the commuters became habituated to one another very quickly. There were a few people who experienced the opposite effect. As one woman said:

> The bad thing about commuting is that it has got to be good because you don't have very much time. And he arrives and wants to make love that night. And I don't because every time he goes away and comes back, it takes me about 24 hours or so to recognize him or something.

This woman, like a few others, felt that a period of transition was necessary before she felt comfortable with sexuality.

Communication

Recent trends have emphasized the need for open, frank communication. This is not only a reference to the need for people to talk, but to the need for certain kinds of talk, that which is sensitive, supportive, and revealing. In effect, a distinction can be made between conversation and "real" communication. However, in light of the commuter's experience, it appears that it is not solely intense personal communication which is required for sustaining an intimate relationship. Though commuters did not feel they were less open with their spouses when they came together, they certainly felt a reduction in the amount of conversation. This was not only true of sustained, focused discussion, but the everyday informal interaction which typically goes on in families. And because of this loss, the lives of the commuters become less intertwined. Generally, women seemed to feel this more severely as a loss.[3] As they expressed a greater need for talking with their husbands, they also expressed an experience of greater dissatisfaction in its absence.

However, in contemporary American society, face-to-face interaction is not a prerequisite for conversation. There is a mechanism to maintain ties across distance. This is the telephone which as the ad says is "the next best thing to being there."[4] However, telephonic communication is only verbal. Facial expressions are unavailable for interpretation. Touching, as an expression of affection, is impossible. Conversations must be planned and require full participation of the members. And given the expense of long-distance telephone calls, talkers summarize and delete "unessential" information. As one man said:

> Sometimes we talk at the table over coffee. Something occurs to me and may occur after a lengthy silence. And a lengthy silence for us can be ten minutes. Well, a lengthy silence over the phone is impossible. So, I think a lot of our daily experiences are lost.

Other Social Relationships

Sex and communication cannot be done alone. But in addition to these activities, one of the greatest costs of commuting involves activity which could be done separately. This is the socializing by commuters with others.

Commuters compartmentalize their lives into two areas: work and marriage. Though it has been argued that professionals give higher priority to work than marriage (Young and Wilmott 1973), marriage is still the foremost intimate relationship for these people. Family demands have higher priority than other, less intimate, personal relationships (Maissonneuve 1966). As commuters are restricted in the time they have with one another, they chose to be together as much and as intensely as possible. And when others are included, the intensity of their own interaction is reduced. Thus, commuters voluntarily eliminate social interactions with others for the period of time they are in the same residence. As one woman said:

> We really don't have time to have fun with friends a lot which we had been used to. Like we used to be very groupie people and spent a lot of time with our friends. Now we have only weekends together, and if we are lucky, three nights. We get kind of selfish with our time and spend at most one evening with other people. That's kind of hard on us because we used to enjoy spending evenings with others.

Though the choice is voluntarily made to eliminate others, the loss is still felt as a real loss.[5]

The social world is structured to induce loneliness for these people even when they are apart. After a certain age, generally the late teens or early twenties, shared recreation is carried on among couples (Babchuk 1965). As a result, the invitations commuters receive when they are apart are reduced in number. As one man expressed a sentiment that most commuters share:

> You would be amazed at how little I have been asked out this year. I think people have not asked me out being single. A couple might have been invited.

Of course, commuters do meet some individuals who are single. But the commuter is in an ambivalent status. He or she is neither married nor single in terms of the social environment. As Merton (1957) argued, social interaction is experienced as rewarding when the participants share statuses and values. One's marital status has implications for his or her potential to share experiences. Stein (1975), in a study of singles, documented the separation of singles and marrieds. Thus, commuters are limited in developing friendships with unmarried individuals. But even if they do share other central statuses and values, such as occupation, with an unmarried person, their potential friendship pool is further delimited by social norms. Cross sex relationships are potentially sexual and subject to negative social sanctions. One man expressed it in the following words.

If I have a close friend, a single woman, and I invite her in many times, there is an artificiality of that relationship that even the greatest honesty in the world can't erase... especially if it is really close....June (*a pseudonym for his wife*) and I developed some close single women friends when she was here. Friends so close I am sure they wouldn't want to put pressure on the marriage. I just don't see that much of them anymore. That's sad. Sexual faithfulness is not a big thing on my scale of priorities. But that doesn't remove the problem at all.

This limitation on married friends may be especially problematic for professional women, at this point in time, as they are in environments dominated by men.

There are even more extreme losses for the spouse who does the traveling. They are more likely to be leaving close friends behind. The secondary home is likely to be smaller and lack resources for entertainment. The holding of social events is felt to be appropriate, and required, only when both husband and wife are present. And as the social world is one of exchange, and they do not reciprocate, this adds to the diminution of invitations. This becomes particularly problematic if the commuters are apart on weekends. As the social world is temporally structured around the unit of the weekend, the time spent alone increases.

Responses of outsiders to the commuters often involve images of sexual freedom and a mate in every port. Quite a few of these people engage in extramarital affairs. But so do quite a few people in the general noncommuting population (Hunt 1974). The surprise finding is that commuting is not the cause of these affairs. This can be shown by dividing commuters into two categories. The first group exhibited no change in extramarital behavior after commuting began; 81 percent of the population exhibited this stable behavior. These are both the people who did not have affairs before commuting and continued not to as well as the people who had affairs before commuting and continued to do so. First, 48 percent of the total sample never had an affair. Some were simply opposed to such behavior. As one man of this type said:

It depends on your attitude. Obviously you can have other sexual partners, theoretically. But my notion of marriage precludes that. So, it didn't make any difference. My attitude is quite stable.

Second, there were those who engaged in extramarital affairs before commuting and continued to do so (33 percent of the total sample). It was easier when they were apart as it did not involve any deception (if they kept these affairs from their spouse), and they could spend more time with the other person, but they had already, before commuting, been predisposed to extramarital relationships.

In the second category, there was a change in the extramarital behavior after commuting (19 percent of the total sample). The smallness of this group already suggests that commuting is likely to have relatively little effect on outside relationships. But there is striking evidence when we look at those who did undergo change. Of those who did change, 70 percent changed in the direction of not having affairs. A larger proportion of the total sample had affairs before commuting than did so after commuting (46 percent versus 39 percent). As one woman gave expression to this surprise finding:

We decided before marriage that marriage shouldn't interfere with that kind of thing. He had some and I had some in the first couple of years we were married. And I figure I am getting terribly old because I haven't met anybody in the last few years that I find interesting.

Perhaps one is more likely to engage in other sexual relationships when living with his or her spouse as the fear of affairs developing into an alternative relationship is lessened. Individuals often talked about the satisfaction gained from casual affairs, but the reluctance to engage in serious ones. One is a threat to marriage; the other is not. In any case, opportunity, in terms of time and space apart from the mate, is not the determinant of extramarital relationships.

ADVANTAGES OF THE COMMUTER MARRIAGE

As my research indicates, there are difficulties involved in commuter marriage that would not be present in a single residence marriage. However, some people do not perceive these as an unreasonable trade for greater career opportunities. In addition, the commuter marriage involves advantages which can be understood by examining the dyad as a constraint or mechanism of social control. Commuting is essentially a form of individuation or partial liberation from these controls.

Advantages to the Individual

Increased autonomy is one of the benefits commuters are quick to discern. They discover they can do many things they were not aware of previously. This is especially the case in activities which are traditionally defined as sex-linked. A woman finds she can mow the lawn or take care of the car; a man discovers he can cook a good meal or sew on a button. A sense of self-effectiveness is established.[6]

There are also changes in the structure of the individual's everyday lives. Dual career families generally have quite complex, routinized existences (Rapaport and Rapaport 1971; Holmstrom 1972). However, when these people are apart, their lives change shape, become deroutinized and simplified. As one woman expressed this benefit quite emphatically:

> I was really unprepared for the fierce joy I have felt at being my own woman, being able to concentrate on my own activities, my own thoughts, and my own desires. It's a completely selfish, self-centered existence.

People talked about being able to eat when and what they wanted to eat, clean the house when they wanted to clean the house, relax in front of the TV when they wanted to and work hard when they felt like it. They needed to fit no demands but their own into a daily schedule.

For these committed career people, this deroutinization and simplification often had as its consequence an increase in the amount and intensity of work during the time the two spouses were apart. They often found that with time completely their own, their work dominated their lives. As one woman said:

> I have gotten tons more done without him. Because when I am living here alone, I can get

up at 7:00 or 7:30 A.M. and be out the door just like that. And I come home at night and I don't have to go through the rigamarole of fixing dinner just for myself. I throw tacos together and I am happy. As soon as dinner and the news are over, I go right back to work. So just taking everything into account, I must get twice the work done.

Or as another woman put it:

> Because for the first time since I was in graduate school, the full 24 hours is really my own to decide what to do with. And so, well, for instance, last night, I walked out of my office at 1:15 in the morning and that is not a typical. I think it has been in the sense that maybe I am burning the midnight oil a little bit more than I used to.

As these women's remarks illustrate, work does not need to be fitted into the intricacies of familial life. Rather, if an individual gains satisfaction from intensive work, he or she can schedule his or her life around it. No guilt about overworking is felt since it is an individual choice without consequences for anyone else.

Finally, some commuters pointed to enjoying a sense of private space. As one woman said, when I asked her about loneliness:

> No. In fact, I would say that one of the problems with being married is that you don't have enough chance to be on your own. And I think that is something I have always felt a little bit, partly because when I work, not in the office, but at home, you don't have the same kind of privacy. And commuting has certainly changed that. You call it loneliness, and I call it privacy. And I see it positively rather than negatively.

A delicate balance between freedom and involvement is sought. Many of the commuters suggested that there were limits to the separation beyond which benefits were lost. If the limits were overextended, the benefits became costs and independence loneliness. Perhaps the very existence of contrasting experiences enhanced the enjoyment of both.[7]

Advantages for the Marital Couple

Commuters found that when they came together, it was not all cost, but that there was some gain for them as an interacting unit. They invest themselves heavily in their marital relationships when they are together, and often regard this shared time as special, important time to concentrate on the relationship. There is less trivial conflict. As one women said:

> We relate to each other more agreeably because we have missed each other and we are always glad to see each other and the little daily picky things that may lead to squabbles don't come up when you are concentrating on each other and the major issues. So, it is sort of fun.

In addition, there are more diverse experiences to share which can be stimulating to the other. As one women said:

> The main advantage that I see in commuting is that it resolves the problems that most long-term marriages have of at some point being a little bored with one another. And because of the fact that you are in some way leading a much more independent life, you have different things to bring back to the relationship between you. You also, in a sense, stop taking things for granted that you might do otherwise.

For some, the change is translated into increased romance. Some even turned it into a celebration, giving each other presents and doing one another special favors. So, though there are losses in communication, there can be upturns in feelings, though this is rarely translated into sexual intensity. Rather, there is a sense of warmth and affection with which many couples in one residence marriages lose touch (Pineo 1961).

CONCLUSION

Now that I have considered the conditions which either prohibit or facilitate commuter marriage, as well as considered some of the costs and benefits, I can answer the question I posed earlier: can it work? Yes, it seems to be a viable pattern under certain conditions. Though there are costs for the couples involved, there are also benefits. However, commuters feel that aside from the career opportunities it provides, the costs outweigh the benefits. They got married to live together and would prefer to continue to do so. Furthermore, almost all commuters conceived of their situation as temporary whether they had plans for reuniting or not. The very anticipation of change alleviated the stress. As one man said:

> There is something schizo about the whole thing. But as I look at it as something temporary, it doesn't bother me that much.

I would like to suggest that understanding commuter marriage as a temporary adaptation leads us to a more general approach for understanding the family in contemporary society. Two methods of analysis, which are usually done separately, should be combined. First, many analysts discuss the family, and its future, in terms of a classification of forms within a pluralistic system. (For example, see Ramey 1972; Otto 1970.) One couple is on a commune; another is in a conjugal family. This notion of pluralism involves various structures coexisting at *one point in time* for *different individuals*. Second, other analysts (Hill and Rodgers 1964; Rollins and Cannon 1974) examine the life cycle of the "normal" family and suggest that the marital unit for any given family is not static. It is constantly undergoing change as it adapts to changes in the life cycle of the family. When these two approaches are combined, there is another means for understanding the family: pluralism of *family structures in any one individual's life history*. That is, at one point in time, an individual may have a commuter marriage, and at another in a conjugal, single residence, family. This second conception of pluralism can be specified by examining not only the stages of a marital life cycle but also the stages of a career sequence, and then specifying the family structure which best fits the combination of both. This is especially relevant to an analysis of committed professional couples with a highly structured career line.

For the purposes of this paper, the family cycle can be divided into five stages.

1. *Early marriage:* the first one or two years of marriage, often referred to as the "honeymoon period" (Hill and Rodgers 1964)

2. *Transition period:* between the honeymoon and reproduction of children

3. *Childbearing years:* when children are around the house

4. *Family middle years:* when children have left home, often referred to as the "empty-nest" period

5. *Retirement years:* when both spouses stop working and are more likely to be around the home

If one looks at the "fit" between these familial stages and stages in the occupational sequence, a commuter marriage articulates most appropriately with the second and fourth stage. In the second stage of the family life cycle, children are not yet born, but a level of trust and intimacy has been established. As for the occupational cycle, individuals have generally not yet established their reputations in their careers (Clausen 1971). At this occupational stage, positions are harder to find than they will be later. And good first jobs often affect the possibility of good second jobs. Thus, it is useful as well as possible for an individual to optimize her or his career placement in this familial stage by commuting. At the fourth familial stage, children have gone and more energy can be redirected to careers. This is the time when many women go back to work (Smuts 1972). Reputations of those with steady careers are established. This is the final point at which one can choose to optimize his or her career involvement. Both spouses may not be able to find jobs in the same locale, especially those they evaluate most positively. Thus, commuting may again be most appropriate. An indivi-

dual's reasons for choosing to commute at these two points are likely to be different. In the second stage, it is more likely that jobs are not available in the desired location. In the fourth stage, a job may be available but if the individual has accumulated a reputation and wants finally to optimize his or her rewards, the best job may not be locally available. So, in the first stage, any job is sought; in the last stage, the optimal job is sought.

Commuting is least appropriate in stages 1, 3, and 5. In the first stage, a couple must first establish a baseline of intimacy and affection. This is the period when companionship is at its highest for most couples (Blood and Wolfe 1966). Perhaps a nuclear family is most effective at this stage. In the third stage, when children arrive, it is both easier to provide care and probably better for the child when there is more than one adult present. There is, however, a problem in both the commuter and noncommuter nuclear families in this stage. With the arrival of children, demand for income and job security increases. Though few people are presently likely to take this choice, a communal arrangement may be the most appropriate at this stage. And in the final stage, retirement, there is no job to follow.[8] Again, perhaps some type of extended family or collective living arrangement would be most fitting here. Thus different forms will be more or less appropriate at different periods.

Stresses and strains are not associated exclusively with a particular family structure. Rather, these conflicts can be best understood when the relationship between familial structure, family life cycle, and occupational life cycle are considered together. If sociologists of the family are attempting to analyze the flexibility of the family, as I am here, the specific points of elasticity must be investigated.

NOTES

1. This is applicable even if only one of the spouses is an academic and he or she can do all of the traveling.

2. Childlessness is still a relatively rare choice in our society, though it is increasing (Sklar and Berkov, 1974). Professional women, the group most pertinent to this study, are more likely to be childless, have smaller families, and start childbearing later (Astin 1969; Holmstrom 1972).

3. Other research has found that women find communication a more important aspect of marriage (Bernard 1973) and that it is more highly related to general marital satisfaction for wives than for husbands (Thorp 1963).

4. Technological developments such as the phone and, in fact, the jet plane, which allow for fast contact across distance have made commuter marriage a

feasible marital form in this century. Litwak (1970) has suggested that these same mechanisms allow for the persistence of the modified extended family in contemporary society.

5. This may actually have the unintended consequence of easing commuting. Friends act as social integrators (Hess 1971). Given their deviant status, commuters, by eliminating friends, also eliminate negative social pressures which could occur because of the course they have chosen to pursue.

6. This is not to suggest one individual can get as much done as two, nor as quickly. Many commuters did

remark upon lowered efficiency and standards in domestic tasks.

7. These benefits did not obtain to the same degree for those who had children staying with them while their partner was away. Thus, if one of the commuters had a child at home, the benefits were asymmetrical.

8. Commuter marriage may articulate with the retirement stage for those who are forced to retire from a particular institution, which is close to their spouse, but who still desire to work and must go elsewhere to do it.

REFERENCES

ASTIN, HELEN S. 1969. *The woman doctorate in America.* New York: Free Press.

BABCHUK, NICHOLAS 1965. The primary friends and kin: a study of the associations of middle-class couples. *Social Forces* 43 (May):483–493.

BECKER, HOWARD S. 1960. Notes on the concept of commitment. *American Journal of Sociology* 66 (July):32–40.

BERGER, BENNETT M., BRUCE M. HACKETT, AND R. M. MILLAR 1974. Childbearing practices in the communal family. In Arlene Skolnick and Jerome H. Skolnick (eds.), *Intimacy, family and society.* Boston: Little, Brown, pp. 441–463.

BERGER, PETER, AND HANSFRIED KELLNER 1974. Marriage and the construction of reality. In Rose L. Coser (ed.), *The family: its structure and function.* New York: St. Martin's Press, pp. 157–174.

BERNARD, JESSIE 1973. *The sex game.* New York: Atheneum.

BLOOD, ROBERT O., AND DONALD M. WOLFE 1960. *Husbands and wives.* New York: Free Press.

CONSTANTINE, LARRY L., AND JOAN M. CONSTANTINE 1973. *Group marriage.* New York: Collier Books.

CLAUSEN, JOHN A. 1972. The life course of individuals. In Matilda Riley, Marilyn Johnson, and Anne Foder (eds.), *Aging and society, a sociology of age stratification.* (Vol. 3.) New York: Russell Sage Foundation, pp. 457–513.

GOODE, WILLIAM 1963. *World revolution and family patterns.* New York: Free Press.

HESS, BETH 1972. Friendship. In Matilda Riley, Marilyn Johnson, and Ann Foder (eds.), *Aging and society, a sociology of age stratification.* (Vol. 3.) New York: Russell Sage Foundation, pp. 357–393.

HILL, REUBEN, AND ROY H. ROGERS 1964. The developmental approach. In Harold T. Christenson (ed.), *Handbook of marriage and the family.* Chicago: Rand McNally, pp. 171–211.

HOLMSTROM, LYNDA LYTLE 1972. *The two-career family.* Cambridge, Mass.: Schenkman.

HUNT, MORTON 1974. Sexual behavior in the '70s. Chicago, Ill.: Playboy Press.

LASLETT, BARBARA 1974. The family as public and private institution: an historical perspective. In Arlene Skolnick and Jerome Skolnick (eds.), *Intimacy, family, and society.* Boston: Little, Brown, pp. 94–113.

LITWAK, EUGENE 1960a. Occupational mobility and extended family cohesion. *American Sociological Review* 25 (June):9–21.

———— 1960b. Geographic mobility and extended family cohesion. *American Sociological Review* 25 (June): 385–394.

———— 1970. Technological innovation and ideal forms of family structure in an industrial democratic society. In Reuben Hill and Rene Konig (eds.), *Families in east and west.* Paris: Mouton, pp. 348–396.

MAISSONNEUVE, JEAN 1966. *Psycho-sociologie des affinities.* Paris: Presses Universitaires de France.

MCCUBIN, HAMILTON, BARBARA B. DAHL, AND BEVERLEY A. ROSS 1974. The returned prisoner of war: factors in family reintegration. *Journal of Marriage and Family* 37 (August):471–478.

MERTON, ROBERT K., AND PAUL LAZARSFELD 1954. Friendship as a social process: a substantive and methodological analysis. In M. Berger, T. Abel. and C. H. Page (eds.), *Freedom and control in modern society.* Princeton N.J.: Van Nostrand, pp. 18–66.

MURDOCK, GEORGE PETER 1949. *Social structure.* New York: Free Press.

OTTO, HERBERT A. 1970. Introduction. In Herbert Otto (ed.), *The family in search of a future.* New York: Appleton-Century-Crofts, pp. 1–9.

PARSONS, TALCOTT 1949. The social structure of the family. In Ruth Anshen (ed.), *The family: its structure and function.* New York: Harper & Row, pp. 173–301.

PINEO, PETER C. 1961. Disenchantment in the later years of marriage. *Marriage and Family Living* 23 (June): 3–11.

RAMEY, JAMES 1974. Emerging patterns of innovative behavior in marriage. In Marvin B. Sussman (ed.), *Sourcebook in marriage and the family*. Boston: Houghton Mifflin, pp. 43-60.

RAPAPORT, RHONA, AND ROBERT R. RAPAPORT 1971. *Dual career families*. Middlesex, England: Penguin.

ROLLINS, BOYD C., AND KENNETH L. CANNON 1974. Marital satisfaction over the family life cycle: a reexamination. *Journal of Marriage and Family* 36 (May): 271-282.

SKLAR, J., AND B. BERKOV 1974. Abortion, illegitimacy, and the American birthrate. *Science* 185: 909-915.

STEIN, PETER 1975. Singlehood: an alternative to marriage. *Family Coordinator* 24 (October):489-502.

SMUTS, ROBERT W. 1971. *Women and work in America*. New York: Schocken.

THARP, RONALD G. 1963. Dimensions of marriage role. *Journal of Marriage and Family* 25 (November): 389-404.

YOUNG, MICHAEL, AND PETER WILMOTT 1973. *The symmetrical family*. New York: Pantheon.

ZABLOCKI, BENJAMIN 1971. *The joyful community*. Baltimore: Penguin.

The Moral Careers of Voluntarily Childless Wives: Notes on the Defense of a Variant World View

J. E. VEEVERS

THE DOMINANT CULTURAL DEFINITIONS of parenthood indicate that wanting and having children are natural and normal behaviors, which constitute religious and civic moral responsibilities, and which reflect sexual competence. Children are defined as the meaning of marriage, and as sources of intrinsic satisfaction which are necessary for the achievement of social maturity and for the maintenance of stable and adjusted personalities (Veevers 1973a). The voluntarily childless therefore constitute a deviant category: statistically, socially, ethically, and perhaps even psychologically (Veevers 1972a).[1] For decades, social scientists have been aware of numerous societal mechanisms which directly or indirectly encourage reproduction (Hollingworth 1916). It is therefore not surprising that those few couples who deliberately choose not to become parents are viewed unfavorably and are subjected to a variety of pronatalist pressures. However, given the pervasiveness of the cultural press to parenthood, it is surprising that some couples appear not to be significantly affected by the social sanctions they experience. Paradoxically, although aware of extensive and intensive social pressures to have children, their reaction is more one of indifference than of concern. The present paper is concerned with only one aspect of voluntary childlessness, namely the extent to which some childless women are virtually impervious to pronatalist propaganda, and the mechanisms which support their variant values and which render nugatory concerted social efforts to persuade married women to become mothers.

A preliminary version of this paper was presented to the Eastern Sociological Association at their annual meeting in Philadelphia, PA, April, 1974. The author is deeply indebted to Professor Norman W. Bell, Department of Sociology, The University of Toronto, for his guidance at all stages of research and to Professor Douglas F. Cousineau, Department of Sociology, Glendon College, York University, for his critical evaluation of the manuscript.

Over the past several years, an ongoing research project has been devoted to the study of childlessness, and has collected data from a group of deliberately childless wives (Veevers 1973b, 1973c, 1975). Intensive in-depth interviews were conducted with a nonrandom, self-selected group of eighty-one wives who had been married for at least five years and who were living with their husbands. Respondents were predominantly white, middle-class, well-educated, working women in urban areas. About one-third of the women decided before marriage never to have children; the other two-thirds remained childless as a results of a series of postponements of childbearing. About a quarter of the couples had been surgically sterilized, and another quarter were seriously considering sterilizing operations.[2]

The behaviors involved in questioning the inevitability of procreation, in debating the pros and cons of motherhood, and in ultimately deciding not to have children are socially unacceptable, with varying degrees of reprehensibleness depending upon the particular situation. Early in their marriages, it becomes necessary for voluntarily childless women to confront the fact of their deviance from conventional social expectations, to evaluate it in terms of the belief systems and values of others, and to come to terms with the observed contradictions. All of the wives interviewed reported that virtually everyone disapproved of their rejection of motherhood. Moreover, such disapproval was perceived as the basis for a number of implicit and explicit social sanctions, some of which were intended as purely expressive behaviors on the part of others, and some of which were designed to make them change their minds about the desirability of motherhood. The women reported social pressure from their parents, in-laws, siblings, work associates, friends, and doctors—from almost everywhere except their husbands.[3] However, most also reported that they were not significantly affected by the social sanctions they experienced. Although many reported that in the past various punishments and pressures had left them feeling uncomfortable and upset, very few reported that they were still distressed by them. Rather, they seemed to be generally unperturbed by social disapproval.

Over a decade ago, Nettler (1961, p. 281) pointed out that moral and conforming people tend to perceive the world differently than immoral and deviant ones.

There is little doubt that bad people see the world differently from good. Many studies tell us so. Part of this perception involves preferences, tastes, self-conceptions and attitudes, but part of the difference in perception concerns how the world really is. . . .

Voluntarily childless wives, who according to conventional definitions have opted for an immoral and nonconforming kind of married life, tend to hold a number of unusual beliefs concerning both the consequences of parenting and the attributes of the kinds of persons who elect to become parents. Almost all of the women interviewed had husbands who wholeheartedly concurred with their opinions on the nondesirability of child rearing. At least under the conditions of a stable marriage to a sympathetic and like-minded mate, it appears that many voluntarily childless wives are able to resolve adequately the real or perceived conflicts between their own world views and those of most women.[4] The minimization or elimination of the potential stress associated with an immoral and variant belief system can be usefully conceptualized in terms of their utilization of two general alternatives: the strategy of "rejection of difference" and the strategy of "acceptance of difference" (Kirk 1964).

Wives who employ the first alternative seek to minimize the discrepancy between themselves and mothers, and to deny the stereotypic traits associated with childlessness. The major mechanism involved in the "rejection of difference" strategy is the reliance on the possibility of adopting a child at some future date. Although plans for adoption remain purely hypothetical, they are of considerable symbolic importance as a means of reaffirming psychological normalcy and of avoiding the ambivalence which may be associated with irreversible decisions. Consideration of adoption, no matter how remote the possibility, maintains the definition of oneself as a normal person who is merely postponing parenthood rather than avoiding it (Veevers 1973b).

The wives who employ the second strategy of "acceptance of difference" believe that they are in fact essentially unlike wives who are mothers but interpret these differences as evidence of desirable and/or superior personal attributes. Together with their husbands, wives who opt for this strategy evolve a deviant belief system in which motherhood is defined in negative rather than in positive terms and which therefore enables them to disregard most of the social pressures toward parenthood. Their constructed reality is most readily understood as being almost the complete inversion of the motherhood mystique.[5] The existence of a maternal instinct is denied, and the accusation that childlessness is abnormal is thereby dismissed.[6] The experiences of pregnancy and childbirth are perceived to be at best unpleasant and at worst difficult and dangerous, and pregnancy is defined as an occasion for the sick role (Rosengren 1962). Child care is seen as excessively burdensome and unrewarding. Motherhood is not defined as necessary for fulfillment (much less sufficient), and in many cases it is perceived as having a directly deleterious effect on a woman's life chances. If motherhood does not actually preclude the achievement of self-actualization, marital happiness, and career success, it makes the achievement of these goals much more problematic. Parenthood is defined as a "trap," which directly and indirectly interferes with personal happiness and the maximization of one's potential by dramatically reducing one's freedom, options, and resources. Although some advantages of having children may be reluctantly acknowledged, there is no question that in the overall balancing of pros and cons, childlessness is clearly to be preferred to parenthood. The defense of such a belief system, which is intrinsically at odds with so much of the folk wisdom, is continually problematic. The remainder of the present paper will be concerned with the processes whereby voluntarily childless wives protect a belief system which renders them virtually impervious to the demands of persons who advocate motherhood.

At least four mechanisms facilitate the maintenance of variant belief systems. First, selective perception can allow one to give special attention to those perceptions which are congruent with one's beliefs; to ignore those perceptions which suggest contradictory conclusions; and to interpret ambiguous evidence as confirming one's beliefs. Second, differential association and identification can lead to interaction with those who share one's beliefs, coupled with disparagement of those whose beliefs differ, and relative physical and/or psychological isolation from them. Third, social situations can be actively structured so that their outcomes support one's beliefs. Fourth, one can capitalize on the ambivalence of the divergent larger culture toward one's beliefs.[7] Although more than one of these mechanisms may be employed simultaneously by the voluntarily childless, for convenience in analysis they will be discussed separately.

SELECTIVE PERCEPTION OF THE CONSEQUENCES OF PARENTHOOD

The world view of the voluntarily childless can be readily formulated, maintained, and bolstered by the careful selection of supporting "evidence" and the equally careful denial of contradictory data. If one starts with the premise that "most people who have children think it was a good decision," one can select from an endless array of testimonials on the joys of parenthood. Any selection of women's magazines, like *Good Housekeeping, Redbook, McCall's,* or *Woman's Day*, would produce a dozen articles and stories to that effect (Friedan 1963, pp. 28–61). Conversely, if one starts with the premise that "If people really admitted the truth, they would agree that children are more often a nuisance than a pleasure to their parents" (Nettler 1957), one can also select equally convincing evidence. There are a minority of women whose "murmur of maternal lamentation" is public and continuous. For every poetic Mother's Day-type tribute to the sustaining influence of the "hand that rocks the cradle," there is a lament on the number of frustrated and frustrating rejecting mothers, whose indifference and unhappiness leave lifelong scars on their unfortunate offspring. All the voluntarily childless wife has to do is to concentrate on the evidence concerning rejecting mothers who are unloving and unloved. By tending to ignore the testimony of satisfied parents, she is free to emphasize the testimony of those disgruntled parents who neither planned nor wanted their progeny.

Selective perception is also useful in the interpretation of the "real" meaning of comments made by parents about their children. Even the most devoted and enthusiastic parent occasionally gets tired or resentful or angry. The task of child rearing is difficult. Wanting to do it may make it easier, but positive attitudes alone cannot make it easy.

It is inevitable that the child will be viewed with some degree of ambivalence by both father and mother, for he represents a degree of direct interference with most of the dominant values and compulsions of the modern middle class: career, social and economic success, hedonistic enjoyment (Green 1946, 37).

When the childless observe parents being hostile towards their children or expressing the anger and resentment they inevitably feel occasionally, they conclude that, just as they suspected all along, parents do not "really" want or love their children. Rather, in response to social pressures to act respectably and responsibly, they are making the best of a bad situation. One of the ways to sanction the voluntarily childless is to deny the integrity of their belief system and to assume that no matter what the couple says or does, deep down they "really" want to be parents like everyone else. The childless use the same kind of reasoning in denying the rewarding aspects of parenthood, and in assuming that parents had children first and learned to put up with them second, and that deep down they "really" would prefer to be childless. In either case, the processes of selective perception can operate independently of conclusive evidence, since virtually nothing is known of the relative satisfactions and dissatisfactions of different kinds of parental and childless couples under different circumstances.

The processes of selective perception are aptly illustrated with an extreme example. During the past decade, there has been increasing publicity and concern with the battered-child syndrome, often with the implication that the occurrence of child abuse is quite widespread. Some voluntarily childless women, aware of this phenomenon, interpret it as meaning that there are many women who did not

want children but who were forced by social pressure to have them anyway. Child beating is an unfortunate but a predictable result. In their opinion, for every woman who actually beats her child seriously enough to make the newspapers, there are a number of others who abuse them in less serious ways and many others who feel like beating them. Evidence concerning child beating is noted and is interpreted as justifying childlessness in two ways. First, it implies that the dislike of children is more common than is usually supposed, and that the preference for childlessness is not really deviant. Second, it implies that although childlessness may have some undesirable consequences, these are not nearly as undesirable as forcing women to have children whom they can abuse.

DIFFERENTIAL ASSOCIATION: PLURALISTIC IGNORANCE AND SOCIAL ISOLATION

Many deviant constructions of reality, even those which are endorsed by only a small proportion of the population, still find a considerable amount of group support. The legitimacy of the behaviors involved is defended by what Buckner (1971) has termed "counter-institutions." Under certain conditions, many people find that they have similar conflicts between the accepted institutional version of social reality and their own reality construction and attempt to resolve these contradictions by uniting to form new institutional alternatives. "The final step in the career of a deviant is movement into an organized deviant group" (Becker 1963, p. 37). Counter-institutions are extremely important in coping with negative social pressure, in that they provide a working philosophy for the deviant: "...explaining to him and to others why he is that way, that other people have also been that way, and why it is all right for him to be that way" (Becker 1963, p. 38). In other words, they provide ready-made explanations and accounts.[8]

Voluntary childlessness is not yet considered an acceptable alternative to conventional family life. To the extent that the avoidance of motherhood is atypical in our society and the childless are stigmatized and defined as abnormal, it might be expected that childless women would tend to select other childless women as friends. By seeking appropriate kinds of interaction, the childless might be protected from negative self-definitions and/or unfavorable social reactions. In fact, however, voluntary childlessness appears to be a marked example of pluralistic ignorance. The women interviewed were largely unaware of the existence of others in the society who also reject the motherhood mystique. Unlike other deviant groups, they do not have any subcultural support in the sense of being a recognized minority with a distinct point of view; in most cases, neither do they have an immediate group of childless friends who support their decision. The absence of a well-developed counter-institution means that the childless wife is not supplied with reasons which explain and justify her behavior. Consequently, the process of accounting for childlessness may be a difficult one and, at least during the early stages of her career, her verbalizations and insights may be far from adequate.

How does the childless wife maintain her variant world view in spite of the absence of supportive counter-institutions? Data from the present study suggest that the husband is the main source of psychological and social support. Berger and Kellner (1970) argue convincingly that, at least in our society, one's spouse constitutes the main significant other in the construction of social reality. Although the couple begin their relationship as separate individuals with separate and largely unknown biographies, during the development of the marriage they begin to construct a third reality, incorporating both of their world views with modifications and adding a third perspective which is new and which is developed during the course of the marital dialogue. The construction of a social reality within marriage involves: "the reconstruction of the two biographies in terms of a cohesive and mutually correlated common memory" (Berger and Kellner 1970, p. 67). In the absence of a known peer group, childless wives may still have the minimal requirements for the maintenance of a comfortable world view, namely a reference-group-of-one which, under intimate conditions, may serve the function as well as a larger unit. It has often been noted that married couples tend to form a subculture of their own; among the voluntarily childless wives studied,

the husbands provided the main—if not the only—source of consensual validation.

Even the childless couple who concur on the desirability of maintaining their child-free state are still faced with the problem of maintaining their stance in the absence of a supportive counter-institution. One of the mechanisms useful in protecting deviant belief systems involves relative isolation from those whose beliefs differ. Many childless wives report that they gradually loose touch with their friends who have children, especially if those friends take their child-care responsibilities and privileges too seriously. Those friends who have opted for motherhood are gradually replaced by persons who are more likely to provide consensual validation for the rejection of the motherhood mystique. One strategy is to surround yourself with other people who could not reasonably be expected to have children, namely single people. Alternatively, one may seek out the companionship of others who, although not childless, share similar attitudes toward children.[9] Some parents openly acknowledge that they would have preferred to be childless had not fate intervened in the form of accidental pregnancies. Other parents may also make suitable companions if they have not allowed the mere fact of procreation to make a dramatic difference to their marriage and consider children to be only one minor facet of complex lives. In the rhetoric of the childless, they are "sensible" about their children, meaning that their involvement with them is minimal and that almost all of their energies and interests are devoted to adult as opposed to childish concerns. Although such couples are rare, they are not as rare as other voluntarily childless couples and they do increase the pool of potential friends.

Even without physical isolation, the voluntarily childless may manage to protect their belief system by remaining psychologically isolated. After several years of marriage, the childless may learn to protect their belief system by becoming very selective in the persons to whom they choose to reveal their true feelings. Weinberg reports that nudists managed the problem of societal disapproval by only telling those from whom they expected a favorable response. Thus, one nudist comments: "Everyone we talked to reacted favorably" but goes on to quality his observation with the explanation: "If we didn't anticipate a favorable reaction, we wouldn't have talked with them" (Weinberg, 1970, p. 397). In the same way, voluntarily childless couples avoid expressing their views on children except to those people they can expect to approve and, if they are skillful in their judgments, they may experience little direct disapproval. Demands that the childless account for their world view may be deftly turned aside with pat and stereotypic answers, which do not inform the inquirer, but which do serve to satisfy his or her curiosity, and thereby protect the childless from involved, and potentially disruptive, conversations.[10] The ability to maintain social relationships while avoiding accounting requires considerable skill and experience, and is usually achieved only after several years of marriage.

Psychological isolation is facilitated not only by avoidance of communication but also by the disparagement of out-group members. This is the process of the "condemnation of the condemners" (Skyes and Matza 1957, p. 668) or of the "rejection of the rejectors." To maintain in-group/out-group boundaries, and to reaffirm the rightness of their own position, the childless use a number of unique terms to describe parenthood. Although frequently their terms are technically correct, their usage is distinctly different, and their connotation is distinctly more negative than the meanings usually associated with something as sacred as motherhood. The most common form of disparagement is to refer to mothers exclusively in terms of their reproductive functions, as for example the frequent reference to mothers of large families as "breeders." There is a heavy emphasis on qualifying terms, as for example the expressed reluctance to be "*just* an incubator" or disdain for women who are "*merely* baby machines." An original description of pregnancy is as a "festering uterus." One woman characterizes the psychological satisfactions of pregnancy as just so much "bovine belly watching." There are many references to the accidental nature of pregnancies which occur to "fertile Myrtles," and to the involuntary nature of motherhood for "planned parenthood flunk-outs." The use of terms usually employed with reference to animals is intended to be degrading. For example, the childless

may refer to the process of giving birth as "whelping" or "hatching" or "folding." If a woman is indiscreet enough to have more than one child, her offspring may be referred to as a "litter" or a "brood." The women who become special targets for disdain are those who elect to stay home and to become full-time mothers, in which case they may be called "frustrated hausfrau" or "the diaper set," and be assumed to be concerned only with "prams, pabulum, and poopoo." Almost any housewife, but especially anyone who takes her occupation seriously, is designated as a "typical Susy Homemaker." If women are preoccupied with child care, and worse discuss it and debate the advantages of different methods, they are in danger of being considered "militant mamas," and their children are facetiously referred to as "prodigies." If, as has been suggested, people tend to stereotype the childless (Veevers 1972a), there can be little doubt that the childless also stereotype housewives and mothers. Their expressions of superiority involve two related themes; one, that the fact of motherhood per se does not reflect any special talent, skill, or ability; and two, that the act of mothering is of minimal significance for society. They express, in one way or another, the considered opinion that "all it takes to be a mother is lying on your back."

THE BORROWED BABY: TOWARD TRIAL PARENTHOOD

In many ways, the decision to have children is more taxing than the decision to get married. When an individual is contemplating matrimony, there is ample opportunity to assess the characteristics of the prospective mate and to evaluate their desirability. However, in deciding to become a parent, there is no opportunity to assess the characteristics of the prospective child. With the possible exception of privately arranged adoptions, the parent must be reconciled to whatever kind of child fate sends. In addition, the decision to get married is not an irrevocable one. Divorce, although perhaps not to be preferred, is always a possible alternative for all but the very devout. However, with parenthood the decision once made is essentially irreversible.

One may be an ex-mate, but never an ex-parent. To pursue the comparison, an individual considering whether or not to get married has an opportunity to rehearse the roles to be performed. A number of forms of trial marriage, of "playing house," are available for the couple who are attracted toward each other but who are hesitant about making a definite commitment. However, for the individual considering whether or not to have a child there are not comparable forms of trial reproduction, of "playing parent." The only situation which even begins to approximate a trial period is the waiting time legally required before adoptions can be finalized.

Most couples who follow the normal career of parenthood cope with these issues in part by keeping them below the level of awareness. They do not have to decide to become parents because they have never questioned the inevitability of parenthood, or if they have questioned it, they have remained committed to idealized and romanticized notions of what it would be like. Some voluntarily childless couples occasionally try to test the accuracy of their perceptions of children, and the strength of their convictions about parenthood roles. From time to time, such wives and husbands may deliberately seek out opportunities to interact with children, or to watch parents in the performance of their duties. However, most of these encounters do little to persuade them from their initial commitment to childlessness. Intentionally or not, when the childless do seek experience with parental roles they tend to structure the social situation in such a way as to almost ensure that the experience will be a negative one and will therefore support their beliefs. A common strategy is to "borrow" other people's children for the evening or the weekend and see how one feels when responsible for their care. These experiments, which many couples have tried at one time or another, very seldom produce positive results. Friends and relatives of childless couples usually assume that if the childless could only have more experience interacting with children, and through greater exposure learn what children are really like, they would change their minds and decide to become parents after all. In fact, often the direct confrontation with real children leads to more negative

evaluations than the consideration of children as an abstract possibility. Several factors contribute to such conclusions.

First, a major impediment to the successful evaluation of trial parenting is the simple factor of time. From what little we know of "parenthood as crisis," it is apparent that for most couples it is a transitory crisis, and that after a period of time the adjustment of the husband and wife to the child, and to their new relationship to each other, improves (LeMasters 1957; Rossi 1968; Jacoby 1969). However, when childless couples borrow a baby for an evening or for a weekend, they are trying in the space of a few hours or days to make a complex adjustment which, among parental couples, may take weeks or even months to achieve.

Second, when childless couples literally borrow a child for a weekend, they often move him or her into their own home while the parents are out of town. In this situation, the child is taken out of its familiar surroundings and placed in a new and hence often threatening environment—a situation which does not increase its lovability. Often, the new environment is the home of the childless couple which, being designed for the comfort of adults, is not particularly suitable for the comfort of children. Nor, in many cases, has it been "child-proofed." The surfaces are not stain-proof and washable, the scattered objects are not either unbreakable or out of reach, and the areas of seclusion in the home (such as the master bedroom or the study) have not been adequately closed off from childish interference. Usually, parents child-proof their home gradually over a period of several years, in stages roughly concomitant with the growing child's increasing proclivity for exploration and destruction. If the childless try to child-proof their home at all, they do so only in a cursory manner over a few hours. Consequently, the child is much more "trouble" and "bother" than he is in a home which over several years has been gradually redesigned and rearranged to facilitate child care.

Third, when the childless try to test their attitudes towards children, they often select a situation wherein child care is likely to be especially difficult or demanding. They may elect to help a friend during a time of crisis and disruption, such as a move to a new home, or an illness or death in the family. Although the child may be very well adjusted and easy to care for under most circumstances, to the extent that the child is aware of the crisis and fearful of the real or imagined disruptions associated with it, he or she is prone to unusual behavior problems. Alternatively the childless may elect to care for children who are atypical, and who are in some way less desirable than other children. For example, one wife deliberately sought to test her attitudes toward children by doing volunteer work in a hospital for sick children. It apparently did not occur to her that even the most lovable and appealing children might be somewhat unappealing under the dual stress of being sick and being in an alien and threatening hospital environment. Similarly, another wife was influenced by her husband's reported experiences with children in a guidance clinic. It apparently did not occur either to her or to her husband that the clinic children with whom he had interacted briefly were not typical children at all, but those who for some reason had been defined by their parents and by professionals as being emotionally disturbed, or at least as having behavior problems beyond the "normal" range.

SOCIETAL AMBIVALENCE TOWARD PARENTHOOD

Although our culture might plausibly be characterized as child-centered and pronatalist, there does exist some ambivalence concerning at least two issues relating to reproduction: it is recognized that children are very demanding of time, attention, energy, money, and other scarce resources; and it is therefore recognized that completely unlimited reproduction is not desirable. In creating and defending the construction of reality which defines nonparenthood in positive rather than in negative terms, the voluntarily childless effectively capitalize on these two cultural ambivalences. The essence of the mechanism supporting their deviant belief system is redefinition. The expressed disapproval of childless persons is redefined as unexpressed envy of them. Simultaneously, the orientation that procreation is an obligation, or at least a God-given right, is redefined as a privilege.

Rejecting the Rejectors: The Interpretation of Disapproval as Envy

Very little work, theoretical or otherwise, has been done concerning the related phenomena of envy and jealousy.[11] One exception to this is work of Ranulf (1964), who provides a brief theory of resentment. Ranulf notes that for the middle class, commitment to a middle-class morality of hard work and restraint is in fact necessary for the maintenance of a middle-class way of life. He then suggests that resentment, and the disinterested punitiveness associated with it, are most likely to occur when individuals are: "forced, either by the material conditions or by the moral rigorists among whom they are living" to follow the traditional morality, and where they: "have generally felt their lives to be unsatisfactory or even miserable" (Ranulf 1964, p. 43).

> The disinterested tendency to inflict punishment is a distinctive characteristic of . . . a social class living under conditions which force its members to an extraordinary high degree of self-restraint and subject them to frustration of natural desires (Ranulf 1964, p. 198).

Ranulf is concerned with the resentment of the middle class of others in different strata of society, but his analysis is equally applicable to any group who is forced to follow a moralistic position and who observe other less moral groups reaping a disproportionate amount of social gains. Such an extreme description does not usually apply to voluntary parents who chose to have children and who are gratified by them, but it does apply to those who became parents against their own wishes or their better judgment, and who are now constrained by their parental obligations to sacrifice many of their "natural desires" for the sake of supporting, supervising, and guiding their offspring.

Childless wives often believe that most mothers had little choice about having children, in that they either conceived accidentally, or succumbed reluctantly to the general cultural press to parenthood. Moreover, they tend to perceive that whether or not parents initially wanted children, they tend to obtain very little gratification from them. LeMasters (1970, p. 19) draws an analogy between the institution of the family and the institution of the military and suggests that parents sometimes view nonparents as draft-dodgers. To pursue the analogy, the childless tend to believe that most parents are draftees or even conscripts who did not volunteer for parental duty but who were pressed into service just the same. They see themselves not as draft-dodgers but as a special kind of conscientious objectors.

The childless believe that many persons who react to them with apparent scorn, hostility, or pity are in fact secretly jealous of the freedom and other advantages which the childless enjoy. Any recommendations regarding the desirability of adopting parental roles can therefore be construed as not necessarily motivated by an unselfish concern for the best interest of the childless. The redefinition of disapproval into envy allows the childless to disregard the advice offered to them by parents on the ground that such ostensibly benevolent advisors are motivated by a sense of disinterested punitiveness rather than by a sincere desire to guide the childless to a more fulfilling life-style. The limited evidence available supports the conjecture that many parents may in fact envy childless couples or at least envy their opportunity to participate in the child-free life-style. Be that as it may, in maintaining the construction of reality supporting deliberate childlessness, it is important that the childless *believe* this to be the case. By impugning the motives of persons advocating parenthood, the childless are able to discredit the validity of pronatalist propaganda and reject the persons who are rejecting them.

Parenthood:
Obligation, Right, or Privilege?

In the traditional world view, which perceived the family primarily as an institution which existed for the purpose of fulfilling essential societal functions, parenthood was defined in terms of a civic obligation to bear children. Married couples were felt to have a duty to produce children for the benefit of their extended families and ultimately for the benefit of the state. The more children they produced, the more responsible and commendable they were. With the decline of the traditional world view, and

with the concomitant rapid population growth, the dominant definitions of parenthood shifted from being an obligation to being a right. Married couples were no longer required to produce unlimited numbers of children but they were entitled to produce as many as they wanted and/or as they could afford. The expressed concern of the planned parenthood movement regarding the "right of every child to be wanted" also implies the "right to every child you want."

Recently, a third definition of parenthood is being advocated, in which having children is considered to be neither an obligation nor a right but a privilege. Beginning with the premise that the world is already overpopulated and in acute danger of becoming more so, unlimited procreation must be viewed with alarm. The case for compulsory birth control, although not yet acceptable, is gaining more publicity and credibility as population pressures become more acute (Harper 1959; Chasteen 1972).

In the construction and maintenance of a world view supporting voluntary childlessness, the definition of parenthood as a privilege rather than a right or an obligation is of immense value. Rather than beginning with the assumption that society needs children and placing the burden of proof on a couple to show valid reasons why they should be exempt from contributing, this viewpoint begins with the assertion that society has too many people already and places the burden of proof on a couple to show valid reasons why they should be allowed to aggravate existing "people pollution" (Veevers 1975). If parenthood is a privilege, then one is entirely justified in choosing not to take advantage of it. It is even possible for the voluntarily childless to interpret their disinclination to parenthood as a virtue to be rewarded in that by unselfishly choosing to "sacrifice" the privilege of parenthood, they make it possible for others to enjoy it more often.[12]

VOLUNTARY CHILDLESSNESS AS A VIABLE OPTION

Although the present research is limited in scope and is based on a purposive sample, it does suggest that for some persons, under some conditions, the child-free alternative may be a viable family form, conducive to both personal and marital satisfaction and adjustment. The translation of this general conclusion into social policy would require extensive additional data concerning controlled comparisons of the probable effects of having or not having children, in response to a variety of motivations and under a variety of circumstances. Data from the present study suggest a number of hypotheses concerning the kinds of persons who, under specific conditions, are most likely to find voluntary childlessness an acceptable option. These hypotheses are offered in summary form not as a guide to social policy, which would be premature, but as a guide to the formulation of focus points for future research. For voluntary childlessness to constitute a viable family form, it first seems necessary that there be a genuine agreement of husband and wife on the undesirability of child rearing, an agreement which may be most likely among nonconventional persons from conventional but not especially happy families of origin. Second, it seems necessary that there be both an awareness of the advantages of the child-free life-style and an ability to utilize these advantages in the development of sustaining interests outside the home. Third, it seems necessary for the persons involved to evolve an adequate defense of their variant world view, using some or all of the strategies suggested in the preceding discussion.

Given the cultural saliency of childbearing norms in our society and the absence of a developed subculture for the support of antinatalist views, it would seem essential that successful voluntary childless couples be in complete accord with each other regarding their fertility decisions. Obviously, becoming or not becoming parents is not an issue open to compromise in the way that other potential conflicts, such as those regarding the optimal number of children, might be partly resolved by compromise. Persons who adopt the conventional orientations towards parenthood as a natural and essential part of marriage are going to feel exceedingly martyred if they are denied this right; conversely, persons who do not want children are going to feel exceedingly martyred if a responsibility of this magnitude is foisted upon them against their will. In terms of the adjustment of childless couples, as long as both persons are ultimately willing to forgo having children and feel that they have made that decision without undue pressure, it does not seem to matter if husband and wife reached their decisions independently or if the couple gradually evolved an antinatalist stance over the course of the early years of marriage or if one partner became disenchanted with the prospect of parenthood and then converted his or her mate to his or her point of view. The kinds of persons most likely to come to such conclusions would seem to be the kinds of persons who also tend to be unconventional in other ways, as, for example, persons who are essentially nonreligious in their orientation to the world, whether or not they actually style themselves as atheists or agnostics. The challenge to the motherhood mystique may be most prevalent among those persons who come from stable but unhappy homes and who therefore have had firsthand experience with the possibility that adherence to the conventional norms is no guarantee of satisfaction (Veevers 1973c). It also seems probable that the childless are more likely than parents to be only children or firstborn children from very large families, where the role of "little mother" has been imposed from an early age.

The manifold reasons for questioning the inevitability of motherhood and for assessing the disadvantages of having children are probably not in and of themselves sufficient for successful adjustment to the status of voluntary childlessness. In addition to negative factors for not having children, it is important that there also be positive factors for being child-free. Although the opportunities open to those without children are clearly different from those open to those who are mothers, it is also necessary that the childless women recognize the existence of such opportunities and take advantage of them. The time, energy, emotion, and future-orientation which are often preempted by children may be directed, with considerable satisfaction, toward other goals. The dominant themes of the child-free life-style are beyond the scope of this paper and are discussed in detail elsewhere (Veevers 1975), but in general they include commitment to careers, the quest for experience, the absence of generativity, and the idealization of the husband–wife relationship. In addition, an important factor may be the quest for gender–role identity. Even for the most emancipated couples, it is difficult to escape the implicit cultural restraints imposed by existing sex roles. It seems probable that many couples who can begin to approximate gender–role equality on a one-to-one basis may find it difficult, if not impossible, to continue that equality in a triad and may revert to more conventional definitions. Although the women's liberation movement is not explicitly directed towards the advancement of voluntary childlessness, it is clear that many of its goals may be more readily achieved by childless women than by mothers and that its endorsement of life satisfactions outside of the conventional wife-mother role may greatly enhance the probability that a voluntarily childless woman may both participate in the child-free life-style and feel fulfilled doing so. It seems probable that one condition for successful adjustment to the role of voluntarily childless wife is involvement in some meaningful activity outside the home and outside the bounds of the man–woman relationship. As one moves towards gender equality, it seems more and more likely that such an activity would involve participation in the work force and that virtually all childless women would be gainfully employed. However, it is also possible that comparable satisfactions might be found in activities which do not necessarily have a commercial value, such as writing, painting, dancing, and other expressive activities, especially if some means were evolved whereby childless men would also have comparable time and resources to indulge in nonwork-oriented activities.

Although successful adjustment to voluntary childlessness seems to require the perception of free choice in selecting the role, the consent and support of one's spouse, and the involvement in the positive aspects of the child-free life-style, these conditions are not in and of themselves sufficient for personal or marital happiness. Voluntarily childless wives are acutely aware of the fact that almost all people strongly disagree with their views on the value of motherhood and strongly disapprove of them for endorsing an antinatalist position. In addition, voluntarily childless wives feel subjected to a variety of direct and indirect social sanctions apparently intended to punish them for their immoral attitudes and/or to induce them to conform to the dominant fertility norms. Paradoxically, in spite of an awareness of the constancy and magnitude of adverse social reactions to the deliberate avoidance of the motherhood role, many childless wives are relatively unperturbed. Data from the present study suggest that, at least for those wives who are in stable marriages and who have the support of their husbands, it is quite possible to develop and to maintain a comfortable and integrated world view justifying the variant preference for a child-free existence. The essence of this alternative construction of reality is the discrediting of one's discreditors. The voluntarily childless are able to redefine the conventional meanings of parenthood by cynically and skeptically questioning romantic beliefs which are generally thought to be unquestionable. They cast aspersions on the attributes of the kinds of persons who elect to become parents; they impugn the motivations involved both in having children oneself and recommending that others do likewise; and they disparge the consequences of having children. The extent to which the world view of the voluntarily childless is or is not an accurate one is, for the purposes of the present discussion, irrelevant. Regardless of the facts of the consequences of procreation (if, indeed, these could be objectively ascertained), the world view of the voluntarily childless provides an integrated and apparently adequate basis for the maintenance of self-esteem and psychological stability in the face of massive social disapproval.

The primary unit for the construction and defense of the alternative social reality shared by voluntarily childless couples appears to be the husband–wife dyad. The conclusions of the dyad are then maintained and defended through several basic strategies. *Selective perception* allows the couple to concentrate on the disadvantages of having children and the advantages of remaining child-free while remaining impervious to the compensatory aspects of parenthood. The *structuring of social situations* associated with trial parenthood is such that, intentionally or not, experiences with borrowed children are unlikely to be very rewarding. *Differential association* with persons who either are childless, or who would like to be, reinforces the commitment to the belief system and minimizes the danger of conversion to competing ideologies. Although the childless do not have a well-developed subculture, a counter-institution is beginning to emerge spearheaded by the National Organization For Non-Parents (NON) founded in 1971.[13] Finally, the fact of *social ambivalence* towards parenthood allows the childless to reinterpret disapproval as envy. The accelerating impact of population pressures has begun to shift the burden of proof away from questioning the rights of persons to remain childless to questioning the rights of persons to procreate. Increased media awareness of the desirability, but also of the difficulty, of achieving gender-role equality has made manifest many of the undesirable aspects of the motherhood role. Since it seems probable that male–female equality is more readily and quickly achieved focusing only on husband–wife roles, without the added complications of father–mother roles,

part of the attributed envy of the childless woman may be due to her apparent liberation from the constraints of the traditional female stereotype.

Although voluntary childlessness will never be a viable option for a large proportion of families, it is quite possible that it might be the best life-style for more than five percent of all couples. If we wish to encourage a plurality of life-styles, in order to maximize the probability of an individual finding one to which he or she is uniquely suited, it would seem desirable to consider voluntary childlessness as one possible variation of the conventional family model, a variation which may be expected to be generally satisfactory providing there is genuine husband–wife consensus as to its desirability, providing there is an awareness and a utilization of the manifold advantages of the child-free life-style, and providing there is an adequate development of strategies for the defense of such a variant world view.

NOTES

1. The term deviant is used here in a descriptive sense, with the connotation of variant, rather than in the pejorative sense with a connotation of pathological. Thus, the childless are clearly a statistically deviant category, in that they constitute only about five percent of the population (Veevers 1972b).

2. Parents and would-be parents are often surprised and even appalled when some childless couples are willing to be sterilized and hence to make an essentially irreversible commitment to permanent childlessness. The response to the question of sterilization is especially intense if the vasectomy or tubal ligation is sought by couples who have been married for only a short time and/or who are still very young. Given this perspective, it is noteworthy that the same parents and would-be parents seldom consider that having a child is also an irreversible decision, with the possible but unlikely exception of a couple committing infanticide. In spite of this obvious fact, they do not consider it at all remarkable when the irreversible decision to *stop* being childless is made by very young persons, including teenagers who have been married only several months.

3. It must be remembered that no direct data are available on the ways which are employed to punish the childless and to persuade them to become parents. Rather, what are available are the reports of childless wives of the sanctions which they have perceived. While such reports are of crucial importance in exam-

ining the processes whereby the voluntarily childless construct their atypical version of social reality, it is possible that the women themselves are not accurate informants on social dynamics. Definitive conclusions about sanctions per se must await further research. It is, for example, possible that some wives are very sensitive and perceive sanctions where none are intended. Conversely, some wives may be relatively insensitive and fail to recognize punishments and indications of disapproval when others are expressly trying to sanction them. It is also possible that wives may accurately perceive disapproval by others, but that the source of that disapproval is not related to their childlessness per se, but to some other devalued trait.

4. It is important to emphasize that this conclusion does not necessarily imply that social pressures towards maternity are ineffectual. The selection of respondents systematically precludes attention to women who were differently affected by social pressure. For example, it may be assumed that some women who initially did not want children eventually succumbed to social sanctions and reluctantly decided to opt for motherhood as a means of avoiding stigmatization and of gaining social approval. Also, in some cases, women who rejected motherhood may not have had the approval and support of their husbands, and the resulting conflict may have been so disruptive that the marriages did not remain intact for a period of five years or more.

5. The world view of the voluntarily childless has been expressed in considerable detail in two books: Ellen Peck's *The baby trap* (1971) and Anna and Arnold Silverman's *The case against having children* (1971).

6. One example of the kind of logic involved in the redefinition of the maternal mystique is one childless wife's unique and original reinterpretation of the issue of a maternal instinct. Commenting that she is often considered "unnatural," she elaborated: "What are intelligence and technology for if not to improve on nature? I read somewhere a phrase that struck me as right on—'Nature isn't interested in individuals: nature is only interested in species.' And to me that's the answer."

7. Simmons (1964) was concerned with the belief system of the Espers, a group of religious mystics. Other authors have referred to similar kinds of processes. For an example of the application of the same approach to the study of juvenile delinquency, see Sykes and Matza (1957). A similar analysis is offered by Weinberg (1966) concerning the process of becoming a nudist.

8. For example, although male homosexuality is characteristic of only a small proportion of all men in our society, there is a well developed counterculture concerning it. When the homosexual is troubled by not knowing the reasons for his sexual preferences, he can readily find a proliferation of materials which explain his homosexuality to him, and can select from a smorgasbord of explanations the one which is most comforting for his own case. When parents or friends or lovers demand to know why he is the way he is, he can refer them to a bibliography of materials. When his life-style is questioned, he can select from a well-developed array of excuses and justifications which legitimate it and which define homosexuality as an acceptable or even a superior life-style, complete with accounts, excuses, and justifications (Scott and Lyman 1968).

9. The idea of differential association and of its importance in the development of deviant behavior is borrowed from criminology, specifically from the work of Sutherland and Cressey (1972) and of Glaser (1962).

10. For example, one wife reported that when asked why she has no children, she simply counters with a rhetorical question: "How do you know we can have children?" thereby implicitly conveying the suggestion of involuntary childlessness. Another wife explains matter-of-factly that she is childless because her husband is sterile. While this is perfectly true, she neglects to elaborate that the reason he is sterile is that he had a vasectomy during the second year of their marriage, an operation to which she gave her full consent.

11. One exception to this generalization is Schoeck's *Envy: a theory of social behaviour* (1966), which includes a review of the treatment of the topic in the social sciences as well as numerous other approaches. Schoeck (1966, 23) notes that: "Nowadays we are generally reticient and inhibited when it comes to the imputation of envious motives. Sociological and political publications of the period from about 1800 to 1920 investigated the effects and nature of envy far more freely and thoroughly than is done today."

12. Within the same perspective, the childless may counter the often repeated accusation that they are selfish with the observation that many parents have children for essentially selfish reasons relating not to what they can do for children but to what children can do for them. Thus, parents who seek to live vicariously through their children, or who regard their children as status-props or consumer durables, are defined as selfish rather than generous in their motivations, and the childless quite accurately observe that an altruistic desire to fulfill the needs of society was probably not the chief consideration in the decision to become parents.

13. The National Organization for Non-Parents was founded by Ellen Peck and has its headquarters at 8 Sudbrook Lane, Baltimore, Maryland 21208.

REFERENCES

BECKER, HOWARD S. *Outsiders: studies in the sociology of deviance.* New York: Free Press, 1963.

BERGER, PETER, AND HANSFRIED KELLNER. Marriage and the construction of reality. In H. Q. Drietzel (ed.), *Recent Sociology* 2: 50–73. London: Macmillan, 1970.

BUCKNER, H. TAYLOR. *Deviance, reality, and change.* New York: Random House, 1971.

CHASTEEN, EDGAR. *The case for compulsory birth control.* Englewood Cliffs, N.J.: Prentice-Hall, 1972.

FRIEDAN, BETTY. *The feminine mystique.* New York: Dell Publishing, 1963.

GLASER, DANIEL. The differential association theory of crime. In Arnold Rose (ed.), *Human behavior and social processes*, pp. 425–443. Boston: Houghton Mifflin, 1962.

GREEN, ARNOLD. The middle-class male child and neurosis. *American Sociological Review*, 1946, 11: 31–41.

HARPER, ROBERT A. The responsibilities of parenthood: a marriage counsellor's view. *Eugenics Quarterly*, 1959, 6: 8–13.

HOLLINGWORTH, LETA S. Social devices for impelling women to bear and rear children. *American Journal of Sociology*, 1916, 22: 19–29.

JACOBY, ARTHUR P. Transition to parenthood: a reassessment. *Journal of Marriage and the Family*, 1969, **31**: 720-727.

KIRK, DAVID. *Shared fate.* New York: Free Press, 1964.

LEMASTERS, E. E. Parenthood as crisis. *Marriage and Family Living*, 1957, **19**: 352-355.

————. *Parents in modern America.* Homewood, Ill.: Dorsey Press, 1970.

NETTLER, GWYNN. A measure of alienation. *American Sociological Review*, 1957, **22**: 670-677.

————. Good men, bad men, and the perception of reality. *Sociometry*, 1961, **24**: 279-293.

PECK, ELLEN. *The baby trap.* New York: Bernard Geis Associates, 1971.

RANULF, SVEND. *Moral indignation and middle-class psychology: a sociological study.* New York: Schocken, 1964.

ROSENGREN, WILLIAM R. Social instability and attitudes toward pregnancy as a social role. *Social Problems*, 1962, **9**: 371-378.

ROSSI, ALICE S. Transition to parenthood. *Journal of Marriage and the Family*, 1968, **30**: 26-39.

SCHOECK, HELMUT. *Envy: a theory of social behaviour.* London: Secker and Warburg, 1966.

SCOTT, MARVIN B., AND STANFORD M. LYMAN. Accounts. *American Sociological Review*, 1968, **33**: 46-62.

SILVERMAN, ANNA, AND ARNOLD SILVERMAN. *The case against having children.* New York: David McKay, 1971.

SIMMONS, J.L. On maintaining deviant belief systems: a case study. *Social Problems*, 1964, **11**: 250-256.

SUTHERLAND, EDWIN H., AND DONALD R. CRESSEY. *Principles of criminology.* New York: J. B. Lippincott, 1972.

SYKES, GRESHAM M., AND DAVID MATZA. Techniques of neutralization: a theory of delinquency. *American Sociological Review*, 1957, **22**: 664-670.

VEEVERS, J. E. The violation of fertility mores: voluntary childlessness as deviant behaviour. In C. Boydell *et al.* (eds.), *Deviant behaviour and societal reaction*, pp. 571-592. Toronto: Holt, Rinehart and Winston, 1972a.

————. Factors in the incidence of childlessness in Canada: an analysis of census data. *Social Biology*, 1972b, **19**: 266-274.

————. The social meanings of parenthood. *Psychiatry: Journal for the Study of Interpersonal Processes*, 1973a, **36**: 291-310.

————. Voluntarily childless wives: an exploratory study. *Sociology and Social Research: An International Quarterly*, 1973b, **57**: 356-366.

————. The child-free alternative: rejection of the motherhood mystique. In Marylee Stephenson (ed.), *Women in Canada*, pp. 183-199. Toronto: New Press, 1973c.

————. The life-style of voluntarily childless couples. In Lyle Larson (ed.), *The Canadian family in comparative perspective.* Toronto: Prentice-Hall, 1975.

WEINBERG, M. S. Becoming a nudist. *Psychiatry: Journal for the Study of Interpersonal Processes*, 1966, **29**: 15-24.

————. The nudist management of respectability: strategy for and consequences of the construction of a situated morality. In Jack D. Douglas (ed.), *Deviance and respectability: the social construction of moral meanings*, pp. 375-403. New York: Basic Books, 1970.

Chapter 11

Alternatives to the Nuclear Family

IN CONTRAST TO THE PREVIOUS CHAPTER which considered family variations which essentially maintained the basic structure of the nuclear family, this chapter deals with alternatives to the nuclear family. The four alternative structures considered here arise out of the need for integration and involvement in a community different from the traditional nuclear family. Various needs—emotional, intellectual, and spiritual—are not satisfied for some individuals within the nuclear family. These individuals may embrace various alternatives to the family.

The specific needs for expanded involvement by each group are quite disparate, however: singlehood arises out of needs marriage does not meet; old age communes arise out of needs created by the loss through death of a marital partner; lesbianism involves the desire to enlarge and/or alter the pool of potential lovers; and urban religious communes involve transcendence of marital dynamics for the purpose of sharing a higher consciousness with a community of believers.

Peter Stein views singlehood as arising out of the needs for autonomy, personal growth, and involvements in friendships and a variety of relationships to a greater degree than is often experienced in the marital context. He suggests that singlehood is a viable alternative to marriage for certain individuals if alternative social supports are available. In addition, Stein suggests that singlehood as an alternative could be further strengthened if societal discrimination and bias against single men and women were eliminated.

Ann Koedt views lesbianism, or sexual-love relationships between two women, as arising out of various needs or experiences: (1) falling in love with an individual who happens to be of the same sex (and thus defined by conventional society as an ineligible marital partner), (2) as one means to avoid male chauvinism, (3) as a means to overcome passivity and submissiveness experienced by women in male–female relationships, and (4) as the consequence of being socialized into a certain role during childhood. She compares the ideology of the organized gay movement, which focuses on the right to have sex with a person of one's own sex, with the radical feminist movement, which advocates the total elimination of sex roles.

Arlie Hochschild views communes for the older population as a response to loneliness and isolation experienced by the older segment of the population, particularly widows and widowers. Hochschild analyzes the ambiguous status of the aged and the stigma attached to them. These social processes suggest that age-segregated communities may fulfill greater needs for the aged than other kinds of social arrangements.

In a study of communes, Jane Ferrar focuses on a particular communal form which supports and maintains the existing marital structure, but at the same time transcends it. She suggests that the nuclear family is more likely to remain intact in religious communes than in communes held together by ideologies involving personal growth or political beliefs. This is the case because, in religious communes, transcendent goals take precedence over marital interests and thus negate, or diffuse, marital conflict.

Readers might assess these four articles by considering, from a functionalist perspective, the different needs fulfilled by these structures for their members in contrast to the needs fulfilled by the nuclear family. What are the gains and losses of membership in each structure? Why does the larger society stigmatize these alternate structures, particularly those of singlehood, lesbianism, and communes? Does society, or particular groups in it, have a vested interest in maintaining the nuclear family as at least the model form, if not the form experienced by all societal members?

Utilizing a conflict perspective, students might analyze the relationship between power in the larger society and the impetus to participate in variant family forms. How is the differential distribution of material resources, status, and power with respect to sex and age related to the motivation to form lesbian relationships and old-age communes?

From a symbolic interaction perspective, readers might consider the relationship between particular values and the maintenance, destruction, or alteration of family forms. How do the different ideological bases for the urban communities discussed by Ferrar differentially affect the viability of the nuclear families within them?

Singlehood: An Alternative to Marriage

PETER J. STEIN

Well, today I think I'll stay single forever. It's a hell of a lot more freedom than it would be either in a marriage or an exclusive relationship....This affords the opportunity of getting to know well and be friends with a lot of different people. No restrictions except the restrictions that I happen to choose.

Joan M., 31, college instructor

SERIOUS RESEARCH ABOUT SINGLES IS notably missing from the field of family sociology. "To date there has been very little empirical research on the state of singleness, and virtually none on single men. Sociologists are as human and as culture-bound as anyone else and thus tend to ignore those elements of society that do not conform to our cultural norms...the neglect reflects our adherence to the ideal that everyone should marry...."(Duberman 1974). There are a few valuable studies of those previously married, such as Helena Lopata's study of widowhood (1973),

William Goode's study of divorced women (1956), Jessie Bernard's study of second marriages (1956), and Lucile Duberman's study of reconstituted families (1975). However, an examination of twelve leading texts in family sociology revealed that only three dealt with singles, and, even then, rather briefly. When not completely ignored by most of the writers on the family, single people are defined in terms of their relationship to marriage. In our

Reprinted by permission of the author and the National Council of Family Relations.

society, adulthood has been synonymous with marriage and parenthood, to the extent that "the good life is defined as marriage...any living arrangement is wrong that may make any marriageable individual forego marriage" (Mead 1967). Hence, the prevailing attitude that those who remain single are seen as deviant or in some way inadequate for normal adult roles.

There is, however, an emergent new style of singlehood that opposes the generally held view that single people are not single by right or by choice; rather, that single people do indeed have a choice and a growing number of them are exercising that choice consciously and voluntarily, in order to pursue life-styles that will meet their needs for human growth and supportive interpersonal relationships. The emergence of singlehood as a life-style is seen as a developmental phenomenon in response to the dissatisfaction with traditional marriage. As such, it represents a significant change in the cultural expectations underlying many of our social values.

An inquiry to determine the extent to which singlehood provides a viable alternative to marriage and family life is particularly urgent in view of the increasing number of single persons in American society. Paul C. Glick, a prominent demographer who has studied the fluctuations in marriage patterns since the Depression, notes the movement away from conformity to the marriage and family norm, "especially as such conformity comes in conflict with the development of the full potentiality of each member of the family" (1975). The demographic trends are most striking in the recent delay in marriage among the young and growing divorce rates.

Summarizing 1960 census data Glick (1969) predicted that "of all the young in 1960, probably all but 3 or 4 percent will eventually marry." Recent demographic data, however, indicates a dramatic shift in patterns that suggest the percentage of persons opting against marriage is rising rapidly. In March 1974 there were 16,817,300 single men eighteen years and older in the United States and 16,476,000 single women. Thus there was a total of 33,293,300 never married, separated, and divorced men and women eighteen years and older. Of the never married, 12.7 million were between the ages of

20 and 34; this represents a 50 percent increase for that age group since 1960. The rate of marriage among single persons under 45 is as low now as it had been at the end of the Depression in the mid-1930s. "For the first time since soon after World War II the marriage total for a 12-month period was significantly smaller (by 68,000) than it had been in the preceding year. However, the divorce total for the 12 months ending in August 1974 had continued to rise (by 56,000) above the level for the preceding 12 months" (Glick 1975). This amounts to a divorce rate of 4.5 per 1000, the highest in the world. The 1.3 million persons under 34 years of age who are divorced but have not remarried is more than double the 1960 figure. Thus, the growing divorce rate has also increased the number of singles, most of whom now stay unmarried for a longer period of time than did their counterparts a decade earlier.

Some supporting evidence for the decreasing attraction of marriage comes from attitudinal studies. In a 1962 study of unmarried college women, Bell found that "only 2 percent of them had little or no interest in future marriage" (Bell 1971). In a panel study conducted a decade later, in which unmarried college women were queried in their freshman and senior years, Stein found significant shifts in attitudes. As first-year students, only 2.7 percent of the sample did not expect to marry, while as seniors 7.7 percent did not expect to marry. In 1973, as seniors, a startling 40 percent of the women said they did not know whether or not they would marry (Stein 1973).

The panel study by Stein also showed that 39 percent of seniors felt that traditional marriage is becoming obsolete, and 25 percent agreed with the statement that the traditional family structure of mother, father, and children living under one roof no longer works. This parallels national trends in student values as cited in the Yankelovitch survey of *The changing values on campus* (1972), which reports that the number of students who believe that the present institution of marriage is becoming obsolete has increased from 24 percent in 1969 to 28 percent in 1970, to 34 percent in 1971. In 1971 (these questions were not asked earlier), 32 percent of students did not look forward to being married, or were not sure about it, and 29 percent either agreed or were not sure that traditional family structure works.

These attitude changes are also reflected in the nationwide data collected by the Census Bureau. The median age at first marriage for women increased from 20.3 in 1960 to 21.0 in 1973. The corresponding increase for men was from 22.8 in 1960 to 23.2 in 1973. The proportion of singles in the 20–24 age group increased by ten percent for women and four percent for men. Within this age group, 57 percent of men and 38 percent of women are single. While in Glick's words, "it is too early to predict with confidence that the increase in single-ness among the young will lead to an eventual decline in lifetime marriage...just as cohorts of young women who have postponed childbearing for an unusually long time seldom make up for the child deficit as they grow older, so also young people who are delaying marriage may never make up for the marriage deficit later on. They may try alternatives to marriage and they may like them" (Glick 1975, p. 18).

The trend toward the erosion of the ideological and economic bases for traditional marriage is such that "men no longer (have) to marry to get sex and women no longer (have) to marry to get financial support" (Bird 1972), and given the development of the women's liberation movement and its stress u̲p̲o̲n̲ self-fulfillment through means other than wifehood and motherhood, as well as the impact of other social movements such as communal living, open marriage, and gay liberation, there is clear evidence that "conventional marriage is no longer inevitable or even necessarily desirable. People can choose relationships that emphasize companion-ship, rather than children and family, and their relations need not be heterosexual, exclusive, or permanent" (Passin 1973). More and more people are postponing or rejecting marriage in favor of independence.

In an attempt to identify the major aspects of the emerging life-styles of singlehood the author conducted 20 in-depth interviews with single persons who have intentionally made the choice to stay single.[1] The focus here is an exploration of the reasons people choose to remain single and some of their experiences in being single.[2] For the purposes of the following   analysis we included only those

men and women who responded negatively to the following three questions: (1) Is there one person of the opposite sex or the same sex you now see exclusively? (2) Do you plan to marry in the near future? (3) Do you hope to live with one person in a sexually exclusive relationship in the near future? When asked how long they plan to stay single, respondents' answers ranged from a minimum of five years to the rest of their lives. Although most did not categorically discount marriage, it was a low priority concern for all of them.

This exploratory study represents 20 adults, ten men and ten women. The median age for men is 34.6 and their ages range from a low of 27 to a high of 45. The median age for women is 28.7 and their ages range from 22 to 33 years of age. Women respondents included two psychiatric social workers, an interior designer, a grammar school teacher, a college instructor, an educational test designer, a statistician, a programmer, an editorial assistant for a major publishing firm, and a high school teacher. The men included a lawyer, two writers, a furniture salesman, two college profes-sors, a systems analyst, a programmer, a health administrator, and a legal secretary.

Four of the women have been married, one of them twice. Six of the women have lived with men in sexually exclusive relationships for periods ranging from six months to three years. Seven of the men have been married and six, including four of those who have also been married, have lived in sexually exclusive relationships with women. None is currently involved in a sexually exclusive relationship.

The selection of respondents deliberately favored persons who at some time in their lives have been involved in exclusive relationships, in or out of marriage. (Only one woman and one man have never been.) For the purpose of this study we are combining those who have been legally married with those who have cohabited without the legal sanction since their experiences were very similar.[3] Such respondents, it was felt, would be able to assess their preference for singlehood on the basis of comparative experience. Having tried both singlehood and nonsinglehood, they are in a better position to make decisions than the less experienced singles, particularly those who are just leaving families. The men and women we interviewed have clearly chosen, at least for the forseeable future, the single state as the more viable life-style for the fulfillment of their needs.

THE DECISION TO REMAIN SINGLE

Marriage is a purposeless institution. Everything that marriage provides—tenderness, love, sex, warmth—you don't have to sign a lifetime contract for.

Gary M., 35, hospital administrator

Of the men and women who are members of our sample, nine have never been married, eleven have been married, and twelve have lived with a member of the opposite sex in a mutually exclusive monogamous relationship. None is currently seeking mates, and though some may well marry eventually, most feel they will not.

The positive choice of singlehood over marriage contrasts our respondents with those interviewed by Kuhn in the fifties. Kuhn, in his analysis of those who fail to marry, concluded that failure to marry reflected a high rate of personal and social problems; there is little suggestion in his findings that such people might be making a conscious, positive decision not to marry. Kuhn cites a number of reasons why individuals never marry: (1) hostility toward marriage or toward members of the opposite sex; (2) homosexuality; (3) emotional fixation on one or both parents causing an inability to love someone else; (4) poor health or deviant physical characteristics; (5) unattractiveness; (6) unwillingness to assume responsibility; (7) inability to find "the one," the true love based on romantic expectations; (8) social inadequacy in the dating-mating game; (9) marriage perceived as a threat to career goals; (10) economic factors precluding the financial responsibilities of marriage; (11) geographical, educational, or occupational isolation such that the chance of meeting an eligible mate is drastically limited.

The main thrust of Kuhn's findings is that never to marry is a failure which reflects an individual's shortcomings and inadequacies. Singles are expected to adapt to a social context that rewards marriage and wherein "almost all major roles and related values are based on assumption of marital experience" (Kuhn 1955). Bell (1975), in a discussion of Kuhn's work, suggests that certain characteristics, such as unattractiveness, are "a factor in *not being selected,* whereas hostile marriage attitudes refer to *not actively selecting.*"

Bell further states that "a person who is not actively seeking a mate has . . . withdrawn from the mate selection process." This description also applies to our respondents, who are not actively selecting a mate. They have exercised the choice not to do so. However, in contrast to Kuhn's findings, most of our respondents offered positive reasons for remaining single. Such factors as homosexuality, parent fixation, physical or health problems, unattractiveness, unrealistic romantic expectations, economic problems, conflict between marriage and career desires, and isolation from the dating market did not characterize any of our respondents. There did not appear to be a lack of proficiency in dealing with the dating-mating game, but rather a rejection of it as competitive, outmoded, and exploitative.

Negative attitudes toward marriage and its implied roles and responsibilities may be termed "pushes" away from marriage toward singlehood insofar as dissatisfaction motivates the search for an alternative. Our respondents reflected a spectrum of negative attitudes, mostly based on their own experience in a marriage or coresidential exclusive relationship. While most did not question the validity of marriage as an institution, the majority were quite certain that they would not choose to marry in the future. Several persons indicated that although they felt some guilt about not being married because of pressures from family or married friends, they rejected marriage as a choice. The idea of a nonmarital exclusive relationship elicited more ambivalent feelings. A number of the respondents stated that they were open about this as an option for some future time, on a strictly tentative and experimental basis, however. All respondents emphasized that exclusivity at this time in their lives would constitute a critical limitation on their freedom and growth.

Indeed, the theme of marriage as a restriction and obstacle to human growth showed up as the strongest push in our study. It was often based on the attitude that one central relationship as an exclusive source of emotional support and social identity was both unrealistic and confining. In response to the question of why he chose to remain single, Tom said:

When I was in an unofficial marriage with a woman, I would see only her and would be totally focused on her as the deciding factor of how my mood would be. It was a way of keeping myself out of having anything for myself and depriving myself of friends.

With the nuclear family marriage has come to mean a closed, often mechanical interaction of two. Respondents emphasized that such dependency on one's mate cannot satisfy the multiple demands of self-development. Garry, divorced three years ago after a ten-year marriage, stated:

It's simplistic to think that one person is always going to fill all my needs and that I'm not going to change and she's not going to change.

Correlative with the lack of self-development is the sense of isolation often felt in an exclusive relationship. This was cited as a second major push. A number of respondents pointed out that marriage, rather than singlehood, paradoxically creates conditions of loneliness they did not want to experience. Marilyn, discussing her marriage, exemplifies this problem:

The marriage lasted about five years....I didn't know what I was missing, but I knew I was missing something. I felt a tremendous isolation....

Loneliness may occur because of inability to share experience meaningfully with one's mate. Many respondents described a feeling of disconnectedness and resultant frustration, both psychological and sexual, within the marital relationship that we may identify as a push. Steve noted how the failure to communicate with his wife, while he was involved in graduate school and she with their infant, drew him apart, creating anger and temporary impotence. Driven to seek relation-

ships with other women, he experienced guilt and further estrangement which subsequently led to his divorce.

Several respondents mentioned the tendency in marriage to associate only with mutually satisfying friends as a push toward the single state. Joan remarked that "While I was married I was really upset at how limited the ability to have other friends was." In fact, Tom suggested, it is the fear of involvement with people that brings about the overinvolvement with a mate:

I find that it is easier for single people to have friends than married people because I think the reason why people get married is to cut down on the amount of friends they have. Marriage is a protective thing....

As Pearce and Newton (1969) have observed, "the early marriage can constitute a flight from experience," and friendships normally make up an important part of one's experience. An individual may recognize this pattern, however, and come to desire more interpersonal involvement. Since for many of our interviewees marriage has functioned to avoid friendships, loneliness tends to be associated with marriage and accordingly serves as a push away from it.

A final push brought out by a majority of the men and women we interviewed was the idea that marriage restricts opportunities. The dominant view was that marriage is an entrapment, requiring constant accommodation and compromise and cutting off variety of experience. In stating his reasons for singlehood, Steve implied these objections to marriage:

There aren't any conditions under which I would consider getting married...I want freedom of choice, freedom to do what I want instead of being tied to living with just one person and doing the same, mutually satisfying, things over and over.

Most respondents concluded that the security and interdependence of marriage inhibits independence, experimentation, and learning. They rejected what they saw as a stalemated, boring situation.

Members of our study offered many positive reasons for remaining single. They spoke of freedom, enjoyment, opportunities to meet people and develop friendships, economic independence, more and better sexual experiences, and personal development. These values may be termed "pulls" toward singlehood insofar as they are positive inducements. Margaret Adams (1971), in a discussion of some of the problems faced by single women, suggests three factors that can make being single pleasurable: economic independence, social and psychological autonomy, and a clear intent to remain single by preference. Adams notes that "the unmarried woman has greater freedom to take advantage of the exceptional opportunities for new experiences offered by today's rapidly changing world." These women who remain unmarried past thirty "are beginning to build up economic independence, an investment in work, and a viable value system that allows them to identify and exploit major sources of personal and social satisfaction in other areas than marriage and family."

Adams' observations are reflected in the responses of the women in our study. Lilith spoke of the abundant opportunities she has available to her with attainment of economic self-sufficiency:

> There are so many things I want to do. Now that I've completed school and am making a good living, there is fun to be had. I've started a dance class, learned pottery, and joined a women's group.

The satisfaction of economic independence and the options it presents constitutes a strong pull toward singlehood. Most of the other female respondents corroborated Lilith's experience of finding her time and energies fully taken up in a meaningful lifestyle. The consensus was that marriage or an exclusive relationship would only impinge on the freedom to pursue their personal development.

The pull of psychological autonomy was emphatically brought out by most women respondents, who stated that while theoretically women can be both married and active in a career or involved in stimulating relationships, this is very hard to realize. Most testified to a feeling of being secondary to the male in an exclusive relationship and a tendency to put his needs ahead of their own. Susan, for example, who had lived with a man for about a year, found herself focusing on her partner's activities and discounting hers. With singlehood came greater self-assurance and motivation. A

psychiatric social worker, Susan has become involved in several professional activities, particularly in helping to organize a regional conference dealing with health care issues. She reported enjoying her newly felt freedom and feeling better about her professional development.

Alice's experiences underscored the pull of social autonomy in particular. Her three-year monogamous relationship, in which she tried to be all things to her mate—"friend, lover, mother, shrink"—culminated in her feeling like a "victim," isolated from her own needs. Through a women's group

> I started to feel like I really could have other people available to me and . . . it was really possible to get together with other people.

Alice's single life-style today emphasizes growth through multiple friendships and sexual freedom. Instead of modeling her life on a mate, she is moving outward, enjoying a diversity of human contacts that she is convinced have helped her attain a stronger and clearer sense of selfhood.

Male respondents often cited the pull of a loosely structured life. Rather than being bound into the roles of husband, father, and breadwinner, they felt free as singles to try out a plurality of roles, through which they could seek elements of their own identity. Roger mused on some of the options:

> clown, promoter, radical, friend, playboy, priest . . . you name it, the possibilities are there. I'm in a situation to discover my potentials and act on them. It's an exciting process, sometimes frightening, but I like having alternatives to choose from.

Married six years, Roger, a writer, prefers the "more existential" situation of a single. He enjoys making day-to-day decisions, decisions that are individual instead of joint, and often spontaneous, based on a changing assessment of his needs. Flexibility in schedule and greater mobility have helped him create a freeflowing, integrated life, as opposed to the "disjunctive" pattern of his marriage. He writes, studies, travels, and relaxes without the guilt and constraints associated with his former life.

Singlehood can create the conditions through which an individual attains self-respect and confidence. This emerged as a major pull, related closely to the psychological autonomy already discussed in relation to women. Although marriage is associated with responsibility, many of the single men interviewed believed that being on their own gave them a stronger sense of their capacities by eliminating both pressures and excuses. Jim, who has been married twice, but has lived as a single for five years, noted:

> I am having an experience I never had before since I was always answerable to someone—my family or wife. I never had the experience of being completely self-motivated, having to consider someone else's reaction to what I do—approval, disapproval, does the job pay enough. It makes me feel potent...and very responsible for what I do. Productive, capable of dealing with life's exigencies, and capable even of seeking friendly help when I need it. Whether you are self-realized or not cannot be blamed or credited to someone else.

Both men and women mentioned sexual availability as an important motivation, or pull, for remaining single. They enjoyed the stimulation and variety of an open dating pattern and tended to see their cross-sex relationships in terms of friendship rather than romance. Many respondents testified to the difficulty of achieving a fully open and relaxed accommodation to people of the opposite sex, however. They felt a measure of distance due to their social conditioning, specifically the norms of the double standard, the attitude that sexual intercourse must be condoned by marriage, and the learning of steroptyped sex roles. Monogamy as a social ideal further perpetuates the distancing of the sexes since it requires guarding against extramarital liaison. "I think," Marion commented:

> my upbringing, everybody's upbringing, tended to dichotomize sexual relationships and friendships. With a person of the opposite sex you are either in a sexual relationship or you are not...but it is the sexual nature of the relationship that determines the relationship and not the friendly nature of it. That has tended to make enemies out of us.

Still, respondents emphatically chose to work at overcoming their acquired fears and reserves rather than accent the lack of human interaction seemingly imposed by society. Furthermore, many respondents had discovered that the attempt to develop friendly cross-sex relationships was linked to the process of growing closer to members of their own sex. Steve observed that:

> my wife would be threatened by having another woman over to talk about a project or work together, whereas being single I can have multiple nonsexual relationships with men and women as well as sexual relationships.

Others spoke of the increase in same-sex friendships they had experienced once they left a sexually exclusive situation and removed much of the motivation for possessiveness and jealousy.

Our respondents, then, indicated that singlehood provides a situation conducive to human growth and self-fulfillment, and that the framework of marriage is no longer necessary in order to find emotional support, sex, and an active social life. Unencumbered by the constraints of marriage, there is, among the members of our sample, a redirection of social energies and social interaction through which singlehood by choice may be seen as a positive alternative to marriage.

THE SOCIAL CONTEXT OF BEING SINGLE

> *This society has not yet learned to accept singles. Marriage is still sold to us, but the sales pitch is breaking down. Most of my friends are pretty skeptical about it. Yet if you look at the tax structures, the banks, the mass media, the churches— they all want us to marry.*
>
> Dan, 36, systems analyst

The dominant value system in American society upholds the importance of marriage in such a way that singlehood is devalued and derogated by an array of social sanctions. Adams (1971) speaks of "the severe psychological and social devaluation that has settled like an accretion around the concept of singleness...this attitude is a societal product capable of being changed once its destructive potential is understood." This social bias results in overt and subtle pressures to conform to the marital norm, in discrimination by certain institutions, and in commercial exploitation. The social context is weighted against singlehood despite the growing numbers of singles and their emergent ideology. That the case for singlehood has not been presented to society is underscored by the stereotyping of singles, when, in fact, "the diversity of single life...contradicts both the old fashioned image of unmarried people as lonely losers and the current media picture of 'swingles' who cavort through an endless round of bars, parties, and no-strings-attached sexual adventures" (Jacoby 1974).

The prevailing attitudes which maintain that the most desirable and acceptable adult life condition lies within marriage generate pushes in the socialization process. For many, the pushes have been so well internalized that they appear as pulls in the outlook and behavior of young men and women. Marriage seems to them not only a desirable state but also the only natural one. All of our interviewees, indeed most Americans, have been socialized according to the values of previous generations, wherein one's social status, sex-role, and self-image are embedded in marital status. Among the respondents, five have been married once, one twice, seven have lived in an exclusive relationship, and five have done both. Thus for 17 for the 20 we spoke to, the pushes and pulls toward marriage or marriage-like living arrangements were strong enough to have convinced them at an earlier time in their lives that this was desirable. It was only after the marital situation was in effect that its underlying assumptions were questioned and largely rejected. Because of the social context, however, single persons continue to experience the contradictions stemming from a clash between the older values stressing marriage and parenthood, and the newer values stressing the choice to marry or remain single, the modification of traditional sex-roles, equalitarianism, individual freedom, and self-actualization.

This often creates for singles an uncertainty about their own social indentity. This is heightened by a continuing push toward marriage in the form of pressure from parents, relatives, colleagues, and married friends. Such pressures were felt by many of our respondents. Jim, a writer, said that he felt:

a nonspecific pressure, a sort of wonderment that at 35 I can be alone. I sometimes feel pressure from my own confusion of how come I don't conform to the patterns of people who are in the same situation as I am in terms of career and age.

Brenda, who at 28 has never been married, sometimes feels that she should be. She feels her parents pressuring her to marry, and, although she does not plan to marry in the near future, she is concerned about what others think of her:

When I tell people I'm 28 and not married, they look at me like there's something wrong with me—they think I'm a lesbian. Some just feel sorry for me. What a drag.

A more subtle form of social pressure is illustrated by Phil, an assistant professor at a major university:

It was hard being the only single person in the department. I would be invited to social gatherings and would get pretty nervous about who my date should be. The men would get into shop talk and the women, in some other part of the house, would talk about their families, the school system, and summer vacations. My date and I would usually feel uneasy, not quite fitting in and yet feeling a bit guilty about not fitting in.

Lucile Duberman (1974) states that "unattached people, especially women, are considered a threat to married people." Most of our respondents corroborated this by indicating flatly that they "were not friendly with" or "avoided" married couples. Joan, one of the few who elaborated, speaking of the relationship with married couples whom she knows, said:

They're looking for a nice doctor for me to marry. I also found that when I'm friends with married people, I have to be very careful in how I act around husbands. Either one or both might think I'm coming on to the husband, when I'm really not.

A further example of the confusion and emotional frustration generated by singles' lower status may be seen in Ellen's statement.

What does it mean for me to be single? There is a whole part of me that sees as freedom the possibilities of meeting different people and having different kinds of relationships, which is the exciting part. And then, there is the part of me that looks at where I'm not doing what I'm supposed to be doing, where I'll ultimately end up lonely, where something is the matter with me because I'm not in love with somebody, whatever that means.

Respondents in this study testified to the strength of the pushes brought to bear in a marriage-oriented society. For some this amounts to an assault on their identity. "Not being married seemed abnormal," commented Mike, a 45-year old lawyer. While they may find some recourse in associating with others who share their life-style, they must contend with misunderstanding and condemnation from the society at large. Natalie, who, as a programmer, works in a predominantly male occupation, reported a "depressing" conversation she'd had with several of her male colleagues, all of whom were married:

My boss couldn't, or didn't want to, understand why I was not married. He imagines all sorts of orgies going on. Two of the younger guys said they felt sorry for me, that I was missing out on a lot of fun. When I told them I was happy and that I neither wanted to marry nor be a mother, they looked upset...they couldn't understand my position and I think they didn't believe me. I was pretty upset by it.

As Natalie reflected further, she began to feel that her own certainty about remaining single had threatened her colleagues. Instead of dealing with and accepting her values, they challenged her perception of her needs and tried to convince her that she was wrong.

Lack of tolerance and perpetuation of sterotypes extends from attempts to dissuade singles to outright discrimination, as seen, for instance, in the job market. In a survey of 50 major corporations, it was found that 80 percent of the responding companies asserted that marriage was not essential to upward mobility; however, a majority indicated that only two percent of their executives, including junior management, were single. Over 60 percent reported that single executives tend to make snap judgments, and 25 percent believed singles to be "less stable" than married people (Jacoby 1974).

Without cultural support structures for remaining single, those who are not married are highly susceptible to commercial exploitation and mass misrepresentation. Singles are subjected to commercialized approaches and appeals that play up the ways and means of finding a mate. Whether the item being sold is an alluring cologne or a "singles weekend," the approach is essentially the same. Entrepreneurs have become skilled in exploiting the needs of single people for self-worth and meaningful relationships through the merchandising of images of glamour and adventure.[4]

Singles bars serve as a prominent example. In an interesting ethnographic study, Allon and Fischel (1973) examine the social motivations of patrons. They report that men and women frequent singles bars in search of companionship, affection, excitement, and social acceptance. Using Seeman's discussion of alienation, they identify the singles' attempted moves from various degrees of powerlessness, isolation, normlessness, and self-estrangement in the direction of intimacy, social integration, opportunity for nurturant behavior, and reassurance of worth. Though some are successful in their search and make contact with others who can meet some of their needs, for most the singles bar scene is a disappointment. The amount of role-playing required severely limits the quality of interaction.

A number of respondents in our sample had experienced the exploitation of the "singles scene." One of the men, who used to frequent various singles clubs on the east side of Manhattan, talked about his degrading and depressing experiences:

I went into one place and I was ready to check the women over, but when they started checking me back, I panicked. Those questions about what I did, which meant like how much money I make and what I would be worth ten years from now, really threw me. I felt like I should carry a vita around and just hand it over.

Paul, corroborating the findings of Allon and Fischel, related one episode with a real sense of sadness.

She was standing next to me . . . and I asked her if she'd ever been to this place before. Of course, we'd both been here before. We had a drink, exchanged lots of small talk bullshit, and eventually split for her place. She kept saying that she didn't like New York and the scene, and I kept thinking about her large breasts and how much longer it would be before we got into bed. . . . The next morning I lied about having an early appointment somewhere. . . . When I got home, my stomach started hurting and I had a bad headache. It's not what I wanted.

As Allon and Fischel report, "the goal of all these establishments is not to provide an adequate alternative to marriage, but to provide places where . . . singles can meet, have fun, and contemplate marriage." Certainly, the social settings provided by singles bars are not conducive to the development of meaningful relationships between men and women. They epitomize the commercial exploitation to which singles are subject in their search for "eligible" single members of the opposite sex. In the absence of places designed to meet the human needs of single people, in the absence of an ideology that makes singlehood a viable alternative, and in the absence of control by singles over their own lives and environments, the conditions of exploitation thus continue to flourish.

The consequences of exploitation, discrimination, and the misrepresented stereotypical image of singles are to be seen in a recent study of single men (Gilder 1974). Statistics indicate that single men, as opposed to married counterparts, are more prone to mental and physical problems, suicide, crime, and lower income status. In some cases the existence of such problems undoubtedly predates and accounts for the individuals' failure to marry. The probability, however, given the disproportion in statistics, is that the experiences of the two groups are sharply differentiated: it is harder to be single in American society. Although Gilder uses these data to support the necessity of traditional marriage, it is here suggested that these statistics result not from failure to marry, in itself, but rather may represent in part the high cost of rigid social attitudes in a society that regards singles as deviants and as categorically unstable and incomplete.[5]

These data reflect the "destructive potential" inherent in the "severe psychological and social devaluation . . . of singleness," to reiterate the words of Margaret Adams. These negative social forces reflect the lack of a positive ideology of singlehood and a lack of supportive values.

TOWARD AN IDEOLOGY OF SINGLEHOOD

Why shouldn't I stay single? I'm enjoying it and not feeling guilty about it any more.

Frank, 37, writer

We have examined some of the dynamics in the choice of singlehood by 20 respondents and viewed their situation in a marriage-oriented society. The material collected in this exploratory study provides a tentative profile on an emerging group. Women and men who remain single by choice are subject to self-doubt and to economic and social discrimination, but they are developing an ideology which enables them to articulate and support their alternative life-style. The growing number of singles in America implies that the values represented by this challenge to traditional marriage hold validity for many people at the present time.

It is instructive to chart the movement from marriage to singlehood suggested by the respondents' experiences as a series of pushes and pulls. (See Table 1.) Typically, they were propelled by the factors cited into a marriage or marriage-like situation; subsequently their motivations for marriage were overcome by their dissatisfactions and the attractions of singlehood were found more compelling.

The strength of these pushes and pulls is highly relative. There is, for example, considerable difference between the experience of a person legally married for ten years and that of a person involved in an exclusive relationship for six months. Since the research on singles is just beginning, there are currently more questions to be asked than there are available answers. More data is required for identification on the points in people's lives when the decisions to remain single or to marry, cohabit, or separate are made. We need to differentiate segments of the singles population in terms of their life

Table 1

Toward being married

Pushes	*Pulls*
Economic security	Influence of parents
Influence from mass media	Desire for family
Pressure from parents	Example of peers
Need to leave home	Romanticization of marriage
Interpersonal and personal reasons	Love
Fear of independence	Physical attraction
Loneliness	Emotional attachment
Alternatives did not seem feasible	Security, social status, prestige
Cultural expectations, socialization	
Regular sex	
Guilt over singlehood	

Toward being single

Pushes	*Pulls*
Restrictions	Career opportunities
Suffocating one-to-one relationships,	Variety of experiences
feeling trapped	Self-sufficiency
Obstacles to self-development	Sexual availability
Boredom, unhappiness, and anger	Exciting life-style
Role playing and conformity to expectations	Freedom to change and experiment
Poor communication with mate	Mobility
Sexual frustration	Sustaining friendships
Lack of friends, isolation, loneliness	Supportive groups
Limitations on mobility and available experience	Men's and women's groups
Influence of and participation in the	Group living arrangements
women's movement	Specialized groups

histories and commitments. What sorts of men and women choose singlehood from the start? How many people are pushed to become single as a reaction against marriage? Which singles regard their situation as temporary and which as permanent? What are the social correlates of various sorts of decisions?

The life history may be the best source for such data. Kimball Young (1952) has devised a comprehensive guideline for this approach. The life history provides data on all members of the family, on the individual's developmental history and subjective experiences, sense of self, power operations, satisfactions and frustrations, dating and sexual experi-ences. Viewed in light of the social and economic background, including demographic, ethnic, religious, educational, and occupational patterns, life histories could reveal specific causal factors linked to the choice of singlehood. Panel studies, which yield data from a sample of respondents questioned at different intervals, may also prove a fruitful approach to the study of singlehood, since they allow a close charting and comparison of individuals' developments.

National studies to date reveal a pattern of discontent with traditional marriage. Longitudinal studies systematically report that disenchantment, disengagement, and corrosion mark the developmental course of marriage. Skolnick summarizes a number of them, including a national study in which researchers interviewed couples during their engagement period, again after five years of marriage, and a third time after they had been married 18 to 20 years. "They found a decline over time in the following areas: companionship, demonstration of affection including both kissing and intercourse, common interests, common beliefs and values, beliefs in the permanence of marriage, and marital adjustment. Feelings of loneliness increased." She concludes that "The pushes and pulls generated by contemporary social life strain the best of marriages and, at the same time, hold together couples whose marriages are only 'empty shells.' " Hicks and Platt concur. There is an increasing realization on the part of counselors and social scientists that, contrary to conventional wisdom, marital stability does not necessarily indicate marital satisfaction.[6]

Active experimentation with alternatives to the nuclear family underscores the discontent with marriage as a norm. There has been a growth in the number and types of nontraditional family forms in the late 1960s and 1970s. Cogswell and Sussman (1972) discuss these variant family forms, including open marriage, group and multilateral marriages, communal families, cohabiting couples, one-parent families, "swinging," and other experimental forms. Singlehood represents one of the most significant alternatives in terms of the numbers of people who have chosen to stay single and the shift in public opinion from a negative to a more positive image of the single state. Our contention is that the visibility of singlehood will increase with the development of a positive ideology that in turn will attract more adherents.

Evidence exists that singlehood is emerging as a social movement, overlapping with other liberation movements, but in the process of establishing a distinctive body of ideas. Lewis Killian (1973) identifies three elements of a social movement; it begins in response to sources of discontent; it has a set of goals and subsequently evolves a program to implement the goals. The ideas supporting the goals and program constitute the ideology of the movement. Using Killian's criteria, singlehood may be considered at present a potential social movement. As evidenced by our respondents' comments, many people choose to be single in part because they are pushed by the restrictions of marriage. Their goals are variously cited as self-development, change, interaction, freedom of choice, and more varied opportunities. Their program, so far tentative, centers on the development of social and personal support structures, and additionally, the elimination of social biases and discrimination.

The heterogeneity of the singles population makes the development of a cohesive ideology, with its body of shared meanings, somewhat difficult. However, the ideology and goals of women's, men's, and gay liberation movements are helping to lay the groundwork. Their common critique of conventional marriage and sex-role stereotyping has served to articulate and direct the general discontent of people who have felt "trapped" in marriage. The format of rap sessions, or consciousness raising, provides in itself a model of people relating intimately outside the context of a one-to-one relationship. This example of a supportive group conveys the implicit message that dependence on a marital partner may be both limiting and unnecessary for the satisfaction of interpersonal needs. The extensive publicity given these movements by the mass media, furthermore, has added coherence to their major shared concepts of self-actualization, freedom in life-style, and the importance of open-ended human relationships.

Other groups and organizations have also emerged as social support structures for the development of a singles ideology, particularly in regard to the decision about parenthood. Zero Population Growth provides a rationale for persons wishing to limit or avoid having children. The National Organization of Non-Parents, additionally, in Veevers' words (1973) functions as a "truly supportive social movement" for married and nonmarried people who seek adult status without having children. Parents-Without-Partners, designed to help single parents, also heightens awareness that there are viable options outside marriage.

The greatest need single people feel, in their departure from traditional family structure, is for substitute networks of human relationships that provide the basic satisfactions of intimacy, sharing, and continuity. This theme emerged in all the interviews through the emphasis respondents placed on their friendships and interpersonal (bonding) activities. The feeling of support from like-minded people appears to be an essential psychological condition for the choice of singlehood. While individuals may be driven into singlehood through a negative reaction to marriage, they cannot sustain it for long without validation from people they respect. The single people we spoke to are very much rooted in a web of social interactions which they have joined by their own volition. This context of friendly relationships, as reported by our respondents, differs from the family environment in being more open, more subject to change, and based more on a sense of choice and free exchange that on an accident of birth, blood ties, conventionality, and reciprocal role-obligations. However, although respondents emphasized the importance of variety and change, they were virtually unanimous in upholding the value of close, caring friendships that last over a period of time.

Certain more formal structures are emerging to provide intimacy and continuity among adults. They frequently take the form of group living arrangements, illustrating one type of what Cogswell and Sussman call the experimental family. While communal homes might include the socialization of children, they "focus on the needs for identity, intimacy, and interaction of adult members." Other structures include women's and men's groups, therapy and encounter groups, and organizations centered around specialized interests. Although not restricted to singles, they are particularly well adapted to meet the needs of single people, and they were cited by respondents as illustrations of the positive content of their lives. Such group interactions foster friendship and spur growth by providing a supportive context. The interactions may be painful, as in the feedback given in a group living situation or therapy session, for example, but the sense of mutual concern was felt to be dominant. Respondents spoke about the relief they had found in discovering other people shared similar feelings and experiences. Through day-to-day living or in regular rap sessions they reported achieving close peer relationships that enabled them to overcome the role-playing, competitiveness, and reserve that had characterized their interactions in the past.

As Caroline Bird (1972, p. 348) has written, the satisfactions of caring and daily involvement are being provided by a variety of groups in ways that are frequently more successful than traditional marriage:

> not the least of these is the frankly experimental and informal character of the group which encourages exploration of the psyche of the other and dispenses with sanctions that shrivel mutuality.

Singlehood for our respondents would clearly not be a desirable choice without the existence of sometimes frightening yet basically joyful human involvement.

The collective portrait that emerges is one of single persons who are trying to forge a meaningful life in a society that, though changing, continues to uphold marriage and the family as the model for interpersonal bonding. While the experience of being single is beset by problems and pressures created by restrictive social attitudes, singlehood as an alternative life-style is in the process of cultural emergence.

As it has with other minority groups, the social credence of singlehood will grow as its supportive ideology develops, and, as our interviews suggest, it will then be recognized as an acceptable and viable choice.

NOTES

1. For a more extensive analysis of single men and women see Peter J. Stein, *Single.* Englewood Cliffs, N.J.: Prentice-Hall, 1976.

2. Some of the problems faced by singles are paralleled in the experiences of married women who decide to be childless. Veevers shows how the voluntarily childless constitute a deviant category: statistically, socially, ethically, and psychologically. For example,

Veevers reports that "all of the wives interviewed reported that virtually everyone disapproved of their rejection of motherhood...everyone except their husbands." Her article examines four mechanisms employed by childless wives to justify their deviant life-style: selective perception of the experience of parenthood, association with advocates of childlessness (and psychological isolation from detractors), structuring of social situations to reinforce the variant view (as in "borrowing" children under adverse circumstances), and reinterpretation of societal ambivalence toward parenthood as envy of a superior life-style. Similar mechanisms are no doubt used by singles, whose way of life also runs counter to the norm. While the present study focuses on reasons given by respondents for their choice, our data reveals a reliance on support structures parallel to those described by Veevers. Further study of the psychological mechanisms of singles is presented in Stein's book *Single* (Prentice-Hall, 1976). J. E. Veevers, The moral careers of voluntarily childless wives, *Marriage and the family in Canada: a reader* (Toronto, 1975).

3. The interviews, although not focused primarily on the interaction between partners, did not reveal any important differences in the mode of interaction or the experiences of married and cohabiting couples. Marriages did last longer on the average: cohabiting couples stayed together from six months to three years; marriages lasted from a low of three years to a high of eleven years. The average cohabiting couple stayed together for sixteen months; the average married couple stayed together for six years and three months.

4. The increased number of single people has spurred various business enterprises to supply the services singles are willing to buy and consume. *Newsweek* estimates that the unmarried population spends some $40 billion annually. Chateau D'Vie, a year-round country club designed for single people, opened in a New York City suburb and promptly signed up one thousand members at an annual cost of $550 per person. In July of 1973, a new monthly magazine called *Single* had its initial press run of 750,000 copies.

The large cities, like New York, San Francisco, Chicago, etc. have always catered to single people. Clubs for single people—there are more than 40 such clubs in New York City alone—are only one index of such commercial interest in singles. Bars, resort areas, special tours, summer communities, dances, etc., all reflect commercial interest in single persons. Housing units for single people are booming in 1972, about 100,000 singles-only units were built throughout the United States.

5. The major methodological problem with Gilder's data is his indiscriminate use of correlational techniques. He relies on cross-sectional studies and does not search out longitudinal or panel studies, nor has he conducted any original researchof his own. As we suggest in the last section of this paper there is a need for longitudinal data supplemented by the life history method. For a more extensive analysis and comparison of cross-sectional and longitudinal data see Peter Stein. The impact of the family, education and the social-historical context on the values of college students, unpublished Ph.D. dissertation, Princeton University, 1969.

6. Arlene Skolnick, *The intimate environment* (1973, pp. 218, 230–31). She cites Mary W. Hicks and Marilyn Platt, Marital happiness and stability. *Journal of Marriage and the Family*. 1970, **32**: 553–574.

REFERENCES

ADAMS, MARGARET. The single women in today's society. *The American Journal of Orthopsychiatry*, 1971, **41**: 776–786.

ALLON, NATALIE, AND DIANE FISHEL. Urban courting patterns: singles' bars. Paper presented at the annual meeting of the American Sociological Association in New York City, August 1973.

BELL, ROBERT. *Marriage and family interaction.* Homewood, Ill.: Dorsey, 1971.

BERNARD, JESSIE. *Remarriage.* New York: Dryden Press, 1956.

BIRD, CAROLINE. The case against marriage. In Louise Kapp Howe (ed.), *The future of the family.* New York: Simon and Schuster, 1972.

COGSWELL, BETTY E., AND MARVIN B. SUSSMAN. Changing family and marriage forms: complications for human service systems. *The Family Coordinator*, 1972, **21**: 505–516.

DUBERMAN, LUCILE. *The reconstituted family.* Chicago: Nelson-Hall, 1975.

————. *Marriage and its alternatives.* New York: Praeger, 1974.

GILDER, GEORGE. *Naked nomads.* New York: Quadrangle, 1974.

GLICK, PAUL C. A demographer looks at American families. *Journal of Marriage and the Family*, 1975, **37**: 15–26.

————. Bachelors and spinsters. In Jeffrey Hadden and Marie Borgatta (eds.), *Marriage and the family.* Itasca, Ill.: Peacock, 1969.

GOODE, WILLIAM. *Women in divorce.* New York: Free Press, 1965.

HICKS, MARY W., AND MARILYN PLATT. Marital happiness and stability. *Journal of Marriage and the Family*, 1970, **32**: 553–574.

JACOBY, SUSAN. 49 million singles can't be all right. *New York Times Magazine*, February 17, 1974.

KILLIAN, LEWIS. Social movements. In *Society today*. (2nd ed.) Del Mar, Calif.: CRM Books, 1973.

KUHN, MANFRED. How mates are sorted. In Howard

Becker and Rueben Hill (eds.), *Family, marriage and parenthood.* Boston: Heath, 1955.

LOPATA, HELENA ZNANIECKI. *Widowhood in an American city.* Cambridge, Mass.: Schenkman, 1973.

MEAD, MARGARET. *Male and female.* New York: W. Morrow, 1967.

PASSIN, HERBERT. The single past imperfect. *Single* 1, August 1973.

PEARCE, JANE, AND SAUL NEWTON. *The conditions of human growth.* New York: Citadel, 1969.

SKOLNICK, ARLENE. *The intimate environment.* Boston: Little, Brown, 1973.

STEIN, PETER. *Single.* Englewood Cliffs, N.J.: Prentice-Hall, 1976.

————. Changing attitudes of college students. Unpublished manuscript, Rutgers University, 1973.

VEEVERS, J. E. The moral careers of voluntarily childless wives: notes on the defence of a variant world view. *Marriage and the family in Canada: a reader.* Toronto: Copp-Clark, 1975.

————. Voluntary childless wives: an exploratory study. *Sociology and Social Research,* 1973, 57: 356–365.

YANKELOVICH, DANIEL. *The changing values on campus.* New York: Washington Square Press, 1972.

YOUNG, KIMBALL. *Personality and problems of adjustment.* New York: Appleton-Century-Crofts, 1952.

Lesbianism and Feminism

ANNE KOEDT

*Female homosexuality is becoming an increasingly important prob-
lem. It is believed by some that women are becoming rapidly
defeminized as a result of their overt desire for emancipation, and
that this "psychic masculinization" of modern women contributes
to frigidity....Some sexologists fear that this defeminization
trend may seriously affect the sexual happiness of modern women.
They claim it will more than likely influence the susceptibility of
many to a homosexual way of thinking and living.*

Frank S. Caprio, M.D.
Variations in sexual behavior

Feminism is the theory; lesbianism is the practice.

Attributed to Ti-Grace Atkinson

*When Gertrude Stein entertained friends, she conversed only with
the men and left Alice Toklas the duty of talking with the ladies.*

Simone de Beauvoir
The second sex

*Only women can give each other a new sense of self....We must
be available and supportive to one another, [and] give our commitment and our love....*

Radicalesbians
"Woman identified woman"

I like her breasts and don't understand her legs.

Jill Johnston

LESBIAN BAITING

FEMINISTS HAVE BEEN CALLED "LES-
bian" long before they may have, in fact, considered
its application in their personal lives; it has been an
insult directed at them with escalated regularity
ever since they began working politically for
women's liberation. Their reaction to lesbian baiting has been mixed. On the one hand it was clear
that feminism was threatening to men, and that
men were retaliating with whatever verbal weapons
were at hand. But the threat of being called lesbian
touched real fears; to the extent that a woman was
involved with a man, she feared being considered
Unfeminine and Unwomanly, and thus being rejected. There was also the larger threat: the fear of
male rejection in general. Since it is through husbands that women gain economic and social

security, through male employers that they earn a
living, and in general through male power that they
survive, to incur the wrath of men is no small
matter. Women knew this long before they put it in
feminist terms. Thus it is not just vanity and personal idiosyncrasy for women to wish to remain in
the good graces of men. It is a practical reflection of
reality.

For feminists the main educational value of
lesbian baiting has been its exposure of the very

clear connection in men's minds between being "unfeminine" and being independent. Being called unfeminine is a comparatively gentle threat informing you that you are beginning to waver, whereas being called a lesbian is the danger signal—the final warning that you are about to leave the Territory of Womanhood altogether.

Acts of feminine transgression may take different forms. A woman may appear too self-reliant and assertive; she may work politically for women's rights; she may be too smart for her colleagues; or she may have important close friends who are women. Often women have been called "lesbian" by complete strangers simply because they were sitting in a cafe obviously engrossed in their own conversation and not interested in the men around them. (Curiously enough it is precisely on the most seemingly "feminine" women that men will frequent this kind of abuse, since the purpose is more to scare the women back into "place" than to pinpoint any actual lesbianism.)

The consideration of lesbianism as a personal option grew out of very different reasons. For many feminists there had always been a logical, theoretical connection between the elimination of sex roles and the possibility of loving other women. With some this became a reality when they met a woman they were attracted to. For others lesbianism has meant a freedom from male relationships in general, a release from the task of looking for that elusive "special" man who wasn't a male chauvinist. Other feminists saw a love relationship with a woman as a positive thing because they felt other women would not encourage the passivity and submissiveness that they had previously found themselves falling into with men. Most important of all, perhaps, women found that there were other women to love in their own right as persons.

DEFINITIONS

With the increased interaction between the gay and women's liberation movements, a heightened consciousness about lesbianism has evolved among feminists—and along with it a corresponding disagreement and confusion as to what exactly it means to be a lesbian. It is clear that more is being implied than the straight dictionary definition of women sleeping with members of their own sex. Some women define it as meaning having sex *exclusively* with women, a more rigid definition than the one commonly used. Other gay women see lesbianism as much more than a defining term for the sex of your bed partner; to them it is a "total life commitment to a life with women" and "an entire system of world view and life living."[1] Indeed, some gay women seek to equate their lesbianism with vanguard radical feminism since, as some of them say, "we rejected men and sex roles long before there even *was* a women's liberation movement." For the purposes of this discussion the meaning of the word lesbianism is restricted to its simplest definition of "women having sexual relations with women," so that the various "life-style" arguments which are sometimes added to the basic definition can be looked at separately.

I think that the first thing to do is to define radical feminism: To me it means the advocacy of the total elimination of sex roles. A radical feminist, then, is one who believes in this and works politically toward that end.[2] Basic to the position of radical feminism is the concept that biology is not destiny, and that male and female roles are learned—indeed that they are male political constructs that serve to ensure power and superior status for men. Thus the biological male is the oppressor not by virtue of his male biology, but by virtue of his *rationalizing* his *supremacy* on the basis of that biological difference. The argument that "man is the enemy" is then true only insofar as the man adopts the male supremacy role.

What then is the relationship between lesbianism and radical feminism? Taking even the most minimal definitions of lesbianism and feminism, you can find one major point of agreement: biology does not determine sex roles. Thus, since roles are learned there is nothing inherently "masculine" or "feminine" in behavior.

Beyond these basic assumptions, however, there are important differences. Radical feminism naturally incorporates the notion of lesbianism[3] —but with strict reservations. Mainly I think that many radical feminists have resented the whole baggage of assumed implications that some gay women have tagged onto lesbianism. It has been presented too often as a package deal where if you accepted the idea of lesbianism, you would necessarily also have to accept a whole gay position which frequently runs contrary to radical feminism.

The following are some of the points of disagreement.

HOMOSEXUALITY AS "SICK" OR "HEALTHY"

The agreement that there is nothing innately sick about persons having sex with someone of their own sex does not mean that therefore all gay behavior is healthy in feminist terms. A lesbian acting like a man or a gay man acting like a woman is not necessarily sicker than heterosexuals acting out the same roles; but it is not healthy. *All role playing is sick*, be it "simulated" or "authentic" according to society's terms.

The fact that there has occurred a role transfer, and that now it is being acted out by the "wrong" sex, does not change the nature of *what* is being acted out. A male homosexual who dresses up with make-up, makes catty remarks about other women, worries excessively about boy friend approval, and in general displays the insecurity and helplessness that have been the symptoms of women's oppression, is as far away from being the full person he could be as the woman acting out that same role. The point is that they are, in a sense, both in drag.

On the other hand, two lesbians who have chosen not to fall into imitative roles, but are instead exploring the positive aspects of both "masculine" and "feminine" behavior beyond roles —forming something new and equal in the process—would in my opinion probably be healthy.

GAY AS RADICAL FEMINIST VANGUARD

One position advanced by some lesbians is the idea that lesbians are the vanguard of the women's movement because (1) they broke with sex roles before there even was a feminist movement, and (2) they have no need for men at all. (Somehow they are the revolution.) The following is one example of this position:

Feel the real glow that comes from "our" sisterhood. We can teach you something about being gentle and kind for we never felt competitive. Remember WE long before YOU have known discontent with male society and WE long before YOU knew and appreciated the full potential of everything female.... It is WE who say welcome to you, long blind and oppressed sisters, we have been fighting against male supremacy for a long time, join US! We are not intimidated by relational differences, for we have never felt mortgaged by society.[4]

Several points seem to be ignored with this kind of argument. For one, there is a confusion of a personal with a political solution. Sex roles and male supremacy will not go away simply by women becoming lesbians. It will take a great deal of sophisticated political muscle and collective energy for women to eliminate sexism. So at best a lesbian relationship can give a woman more happiness and freedom in her private life (assuming both women are not playing roles). But a radical feminist is not just one who tries to live the good nonsexist life at home; she is one who is working politically in society to destroy the institutions of sexism.

Another assumption implicit in the argument of "lesbian-as-the-vanguard-feminist" is that having balked at one aspect of sexism—namely, exclusive heterosexuality—they are therefore radical feminists. *Any* woman who defies her role—be it refusing to be a mother, wanting to be a biochemist, or simply refusing to cater to a man's ego—is defying the sex-role system. It is an act of rebellion. In the case of lesbianism, the act of rebellion often has earned the woman severe social ostracism. However, it becomes radical only if it is then placed in the context of wanting to destroy the system as a whole, that is, destroying the sex-role system as opposed to just rejecting men. Indeed, there can be reformism within lesbianism too; when a lesbian says "I have nothing against men; I just don't want to be involved with them," she is really describing an accommodation within the sexist system even though she has performed the rebellious act of violating that system by being a lesbian. It is also in this context that a statement like "feminism is the theory; lesbianism is the practice" is erroneous.

For not only is the sex of a woman's lover insufficient information to infer radical feminism, but there is also the false implication that to have no men in your personal life means you are therefore living the life of fighting for radical feminist change.

The notion that lesbians have no need for men at all also needs clarification. First of all, since we are all women living in a male society, we do in fact depend regularly upon men for many crucial things, even if we do not choose to have men in our personal relationships. It is for this reason that one woman alone will not be fully liberated until all women are liberated. However, taking the statement to mean having no need for men in *personal relationships* (which can be an important achievement for women, since one should obviously want the person, not the man), one must still ask the question: has the male role been discarded? Thus again the crucial point is not the sex of your bed partner but the sex role of your bed partner.

GAY MOVEMENT AS A CIVIL RIGHTS MOVEMENT

The organized gay movement seeks to protect the freedom of any homosexual, no matter what her or his individual style of homosexuality may be. This means protection of the transvestite, the queen, the "butch" lesbian, the couple that wants a marriage license, or the homosexual who may prefer no particular role. They are all united on one thing: the right to have sex with someone of one's own sex (i.e., "freedom of sexual preference").

As is clear from the wide range of homosexual behavior, not all modes necessarily reflect a dislike for sex roles per se. Nor was the choice necessarily made deliberately. The boy who grew up trained as a girl, or the girl who was somehow socialized more toward the male role, did not in their childhood choose to reverse sex roles. Each was saddled with a role (as were we all) and had to make the best of it in a society that scorned such an occurrence. Merle Miller in an article in the *New York Times* (January 17, 1971), where he "came out" as a homosexual, said: "Gay is good, Gay is proud. Well, yes, I suppose. If I had been given a choice (but who is?), I would prefer to be straight." His point was not that

gay is sick but rather that he did not choose his gayness. And, furthermore, had he been trained heterosexually, society would have been a great deal easier on him. Which is a very understandable sentiment given the cruelty and discrimination that is practiced against homosexuals. In such cases the bravery and rebelliousness is to be found rather in the ability to act out homosexuality in spite of social abuse.

In uniting to change oppressive laws, electing officials who will work toward these ends, and changing social attitudes which are discriminatory against homosexuals, the gay movement is addressing itself to its civil rights. It is my feeling that the gay liberation issue is in fact a civil rights issue (as opposed to a radical issue) because it is united around the secondary issue of "freedom of sexual preference." Whereas in fact the real root of antihomosexuality is sexism. That is, the *radical* gay person would have to be a feminist. This tracing of the roots of gay oppression to sexism is also expressed in Radicalesbian's "Woman identified woman":

> It should first be understood that lesbianism, like male homosexuality, is a category of behavior possible only in a sexist society characterized by rigid sex roles and dominated by male supremacy.... In a society in which men do not oppress women, and sexual expression is allowed to follow feelings, the categories of homosexuality and heterosexuality would disappear.

BISEXUALITY

One position taken by some lesbians is that bisexuality is a copout. This is usually argued in terms like "until all heterosexuals go gay, we are going to remain homosexual," or "lesbianism is more than having sex with women; it is a whole lifestyle and commitment to women. Bisexuality is a sign of not being able to leave men and be free. We are *women-* (not men-) identified women."

The first position mentioned is an apparently tactical argument (though it has also been used by some, I think, to dismiss the discussion of bisexuality altogether by safely pushing it off into the

Millennium), and makes the case for politically identifying yourself with the most discriminated against elements—even though you might really believe in bisexuality.[5]

Taking that argument at face value (and I don't completely), I think it is a dangerous thing to advocate politically. For by, in effect, promoting exclusive homosexuality, they lend political support to the notion that it *does* matter what the sex of your partner may be. While I recognize the absolute necessity for the gay movement to concentrate on the freedom of people to sleep with members of their own sex (since it is here that discrimination exists), it must at the same time always be referred back to its larger, radical perspective: that it is oppressive for that very question even to be asked. As a matter of fact, if "freedom of sexual preference" is the demand, the solution obviously must be a bisexuality where the question becomes irrelevant.

I think in fact that the reason why bisexuality has been considered such an unpopular word by most gays is not to be found primarily in the arguments just discussed, but rather in gay adherence to a kind of fierce homosexual counter-definition which has developed. That is, a counter identity—a "life-style" and "world view"—has been created around the fact of their homosexuality. This identity is so strong sometimes that to even advocate or predict bisexuality is considered "genocide." The following is an example: In a response to a statement by Dotson Rader that "as bisexuality is increasingly accepted as the norm, the position of the homosexual *qua* homosexual will fade," one gay response was that "The homosexual, like the Jew, is offered the choice between integration or the gas chamber."[6]

It is not with the actual gay counterculture that I want to quarrel; I think it is a very understandable reaction to an intolerable exclusion of homosexuals from society. To be denied the ordinary benefits and interaction of other people, to be stripped of your identity by a society that recognizes you as valid only if your role and your biology are "properly" matched—to be thus denied must of course result in a new resolution of identity. Since gays have been rejected on the basis of their homosexuality, it is not surprising that homosexuality has become the core of the new identity.

The disagreement with feminism comes rather in an attempt to make a revolutionary political position out of this adjustment. The often heard complaint from feminists that "we are being defined once again by whom we sleep with" is correct, I think. The lesson to be learned from a feminist analysis of sex roles is that there is no behavior implied from our biology beyond, as Wilma Scott Heide has noted, the role of sperm donor and wet nurse.[7] A woman has historically been defined, on the basis of biology, as incomplete without a man. Feminists have rejected this notion, and must equally reject any new definition which offers a woman her identity by virtue of the fact that she may love or sleep with other women.

It is for this reason, also, that I disagree with the Radicalesbian concept of the "woman-identified-woman." For we ought not to be "identified" on the basis of whom we have relationships with. And there is a confusion in such a term; it seems to mix up the biological woman with the political woman. I think the often used feminist definition of "woman-identified" as meaning having identified with the female *role* in society is more useful; it refers to a specific political phenomenon of internalization. So far as finding a term which describes women's solidarity or sisterhood on the basis of our common oppression, the term is feminism. Beyond that, what is left is the biological female—an autonomous being who gains her identity by virtue of her own achievements and characteristics, not by virtue of whom she has a love relationship with.

Once we begin to discuss persons as *persons* (a word which doesn't ask the sex of an individual), even the word "bisexuality" may eventually be dropped, since implicit in its use is still an eagerness to inform you that it is *both* sexes. Perhaps we will finally return to a simpler word like "sexuality," where the relevant information is simply "sex among persons."

If you don't sleep with women . . . .

If you are a feminist who is not sleeping with a woman, you may risk hearing any of the following accusations: "You're oppressing me if you don't sleep with women"; "You're not a radical feminist if you don't sleep with women"; or "You don't love women if you don't sleep with them." I have even seen a woman's argument about an entirely different aspect of feminism be dismissed by some lesbians because she was not having sexual relations with women. Leaving aside for a minute the motives for making such accusations, there is an outrageous thing going on here strictly in terms of pressuring women about their personal lives.

This perversion of "the personal is the political" argument, it must be noted, was not invented by those gay women who may be using it now; the women's movement has had sporadic waves of personal attacks on women—always in the guise of radicalism (and usually by a very small minority of women). I have seen women being told they could not be trusted as feminists because they wore miniskirts, because they were married (in one group quotas were set lest the group's quality be lowered by "unliberated women"), or because they wanted to have children. This rejection of women who are not living the "liberated life" has predictably now come to include rejection on the basis of the "unliberated" sex life.

The original genius of the phrase "the personal is political" was that it opened up the area of women's private lives to political analysis. Before that, the isolation of women from each other had been accomplished by labeling a woman's experience "personal." Women had thus been kept from seeing their common condition as women and their common oppression by men.

However, opening up women's experience to political analysis has also resulted in a misuse of the phrase. While it is true that there are political implications in everything a woman *qua* woman experiences, it is not therefore true that a woman's life is the political property of the women's movement. And it seems to me to show a disrespect for another woman to presume that it is any group's (or individual's) prerogative to pass revolutionary judgment on the progress of her life.

There is a further point: Even the most radical feminist is not the liberated woman. We are all crawling out of femininity into a new sense of personhood. Only a woman herself may decide what her next step is going to be. I do not think women have a political obligation to the movement to change; they should do so only if they see it in their own self-interest. If the women's movement believes that feminism *is* in women's self-interest, then the task at hand is to make it understood through shared insights, analysis, and experience. That is, feminism is an offering, not a directive, and one therefore enters a woman's private life at her invitation only. Thus a statement like "you don't love women if you don't sleep with them" must above all be dismissed on the grounds that it is confusing the right to discuss feminism with the right to, uninvited, discuss a woman's private life and make political judgments about it.

However, taking the issue presented in the above accusation (outside of its guilt-provoking personal context),[8] there are several points to consider. One element of truth is that some women are unable to relate sexually to other women because of a strong self-hatred for themselves as women (and therefore all women). But there may also be many other reasons. A woman may not be interested in sleeping with anyone—a freedom women are granted even less often than the right to sleep with other women. She may not have met a woman she's attracted to. Or she may be involved with a man whom she likes as a person, without this necessarily being a rejection of women. It should also be noted that the women who suffer from strong self-hatred may not necessarily find it impossible to relate sexually to women. They may instead find that taking the male part in a lesbian relationship will symbolically remove them from their feminine role. Such a woman then may become one who "balls" women so as not to be one.

All in all, as has been noted earlier, there is no magic that makes lesbianism proof positive of any high feminist motives. Rather, what the woman brings to her relationship as far as relinquishing sex roles will, I think, determine her ultimate attitude about really loving other women.

CONCLUSION

Homosexuality, with its obvious scorn for the "rules" of biology, challenges a cornerstone of sexist ideology and consequently makes most men nervous. There is at this time less fear of female homosexuality than of male homosexuality, possibly because men still feel secure that isolated lesbian examples will not tempt most women away from their prescribed feminine roles, and perhaps also because lesbianism is frequently seen by men as something erotic (it seems, alas, we can still remain sex objects in men's eyes even when making love to each other).

With male homosexuality, however, men (and thus male society) are more personally threatened. The precise irony of male supremacy is that it is a system rationalized on the basis of biology but actualized through socialization. Deviants who inadvertently were socialized differently, or who chose differently, are thus a threat to the *premise* that biology is destiny. Thus, to have another man break rank is to threaten all men's group-supremacy status. Also, for a man to leave the "superior" group is to go down—that is, become "inferior" or "feminine." Frequently male homosexuals may touch on the unspoken fears in many men that they are not powerful and "manly" enough to fulfill their supremacy destiny, and the gay male thus becomes the symbol of total male "failure." Still other men display a robust camaraderie (à la Mailer) where "buggering" a fellow male obviously means that one would have to play woman, and good fellowship wouldn't allow another man such degradation.

To understand men's fear of homosexuality, then, is above all to understand men's fear of losing their place of power in society with women. And to hold that power, men must preserve both the "absoluteness" of their ideology and the group unity of their members.

It must be kept in mind that while homosexuality does contain an implicit threat to sexist ideology, it is, at best, only a small part of the whole fight to bring down the sex-role system. (Indeed, if the gay movement were to be seen as only the demand for the right of making role transfers within society, for example, it would work against feminism by supporting a reformed version of the sex-role system.)

Thus it is only in the most radical interpretation that lesbianism becomes an organic part of the larger feminist fight. In this context it joins the multitude of other rebellions women have been making against their prescribed role—be it in work, in law, or in personal relationships. As with all such rebellions, they are only personal accommodations to living in a sexist society unless they are understood politically and fought for collectively. The larger political truth is still that we are women living in a male society where men have the power and we don't; that our "female role" is a creation that is nothing more than a male political expediency for maintaining that power; and that until the women's movement alters these ancient political facts we cannot speak of being free collectively or individually.

NOTES

1. Anon., *Vortex*, Lawrence, Kansas.

2. She does not by this definition live a life untouched by sex roles; there are no "liberated" women in that sense.

3. Reform feminism which envisions *only* an "equal partnership with men" clearly has in mind improved male-female relationships, not new possibilities for loving and relating sexually to women as well.

4. T. B., letter, *Everywoman*, March 26, 1971.

5. See for example *A gay manifesto* by Carl Wittman (Gay Flames Pamphlet No. 9).

6. Letter to the Editor, *Evergreen*, May, 1971.

7. Judith Hole and Ellen Levine, *Rebirth of feminism*. Chicago: Quadrangle, 1971, p. 76.

8. Regarding motives: provoking guilt is a tactic not so much for informing as it is for controlling others.

Communal Living in Old Age

ARLIE HOCHSCHILD

ALONG WITH BLACKS, WOMEN, AND adolescents, the old have emerged as a "social problem"—a label usually given to people who lack power. There is not one social problem, but rather many. There is the problem of poverty, of poor health, and of loneliness. Underlying all three is a condition that is hard to isolate as a "problem," a condition that cannot be changed without radically altering the entire society. Namely this: apart from a privileged elite for whom old age is a harvest of honor and riches, the old in America are not needed by society.

And despite what some of us hope, there is no sign that old people will regain power and many signs that they will continue to lose it. There is no sign that the retirement age will go up and many signs that it will continue to drop. There is no sign that more old people will find work and many signs that young people also will have a hard time finding it. In 1900 two out of three men over 65 were working, while today less than a third are.

As work becomes less important as a source of friendships for the old, neighborhoods tend to become more important, especially for the working and lower classes. The old in the United States today either live together with young people (in the same family or neighborhood) or separate from them (alone or with other old people.) I will discuss why the first, more common and accepted setting often leads to isolation and why the second, newer and less approved, generally does not. I will also try to show how a new and increasingly common alternative to isolation is communities of old people. Ironically the conservative, fundamentalist widows from Oklahoma and Texas whom I studied are among the least likely to talk about "communal living" and "alternatives to the nuclear family" even while they have improvised something of the sort.

INTEGRATION

When one searches for an example of án old person living with his children, grandchildren, and assorted relatives, the mind moves to other times and places—to the grandfather in Thomas Mann's novel *Buddenbrooks*, for example, set in 19th-century Germany. The grandfather lived, worked, commanded, protected, bequeathed, and finally died in the heart of the Buddenbrook family. He was a powerful man, not a social problem. It was by virtue of him that cousins and aunts and uncles were tied together. For him, biological death and social retirement more or less coincided, so that his old age merely continued the life he knew in what is now called "middle" age. But social conditions were different there and then.

In the United States today only about 8 percent of people over 65 live with their children and grandchildren, and probably no more than this ever did in the past. About a fourth to a third of old people now live with an adult child (but not with a grandchild). A widowed grandmother may move in with her daughter and son-in-law, or a divorced man may live on with his mother and father. But it has been rare to see two generations of *intact* marriages living together, and since World War II it has become even more rare.

More often, old people live alone or with friends who are not related. This does not mean that the old are cut off from their children: 84 percent of American old people live less than an hour away from a child. But typically they do not live together.

And, more important, most old people do not *want* to live with their children. Many who do live with them do so because it saves money, not because it's a good social arrangement. Less than 10 percent of a recent national sample of old people said they wanted to live with a child or relative. Only 17 percent recommended it to other old people able to care for themselves. Even for ill or disabled old people, more (39 percent) recommended going to a nursing home or getting nursing care than recommended moving in with children (23 percent).

Reprinted by permission of the author. From Louise Knapp Howe (ed.), *The future of the family*.

Many young people feel the same way. According to a survey I did of students in two sociology classes at the University of California at Berkeley in 1968, only a small proportion (7 percent) expected their aged parents to live with them, and only 4 percent expected to live with their own adult children. (Even in the counterculture, communes are usually composed of people the same age, generally under thirty.)

Moreover, when the old live near young people outside the family, they usually do not make friends with them. In fact, the old person with young neighbors is often more isolated than his peer who lives near other old people. In a very important and excellent study of Cleveland residents, the sociologist Irving Rosow compared 1200 old people living in three kinds of housing: one with a mix of ages ("normal"), one with quite a few old people ("age concentrated"), and one with almost all old people ("age dense"). Those living with many other old people made the most friends. But even in the normal neighborhoods (with about 12 percent old people), most befriended not young people but others their own age. Finally, a study of five hundred old people in Elmira, New York, showed that the older a widow, the less isolated she was, since she was less likely to be the only widow on the block and more likely to have (other widow) friends.

This means that the more "segregated" the neighborhood itself, the more integrated the old person is *within* it. One survey of older clients of five social agencies in Schenectady, New York, showed that of those needing rehousing, 60 percent did not want to live in a neighborhood with small children. In another case, a retirement public apartment building reserved a third of its units for younger families in order to stimulate friendships across the age barrier. Out of 88 friendships reported, only one old person made friends with a young person. A more recent study sampling the old in the same housing checked this point again and found that of all the old people's neighbor friends, only 4 percent were young.

A mutual disinterest between young and old can, in varying degree, isolate the old. Not all old people are like the widow in the British film *The Whisperers*, living alone in a musty flat with the radio and cat for company. More typical perhaps is the "emancipated" older couple living on their own,

separate from their children, in neighborhoods with young working neighbors.

But this situation too can easily dissolve into isolation. Each member of the couple has a fair chance of living alone within a few years. At age 65 already 55 percent are widowed or single—30 percent of the men and 70 percent of the women. Poor health and death gradually steal away those special friendships with long histories, and retirement narrows the circle of acquaintances which, on hindsight, rested on having work in common.

It has become a sad commonplace to associate being old with being alone. We call isolation a punishment for the prisoner, but perhaps a majority of American old people are in some degree isolated or soon will be. It has gradually come to seem "natural," and ironically age-integrated settings make it seem more so.

SEPARATION

Old people live together in a number of places: private retirement villages for the well-to-do, public housing projects and rundown hotels for the poor. While most of the 9 percent of the United States population over 65 live in independent housing in age-integrated neighborhoods, they are only 3 percent of the population in some new suburbs and 30 percent in cities such as St. Petersburg, Florida. Since World War II, there has been a mushroom growth of old-age housing, drop-in centers, and retirement settlements such as Ryderwood in Washington, Moosehaven in Florida, Sun City (which has over twelve thousand residents) in Arizona, and the Rossmoor Leisure Worlds in California.

Contrasted to the image of Buddenbrook in his family or the widow alone is the new archetype: the sociable, tanned older couple given to organized shuffleboard tournaments, bingo parties, and a life of busy leisure. Here the old person is not integrated with the young, but neither is he isolated. He may even find a new mate. One study found that almost a third of the married couples in a retirement community had met and married there.

Many outsiders feel ambivalent toward these new old-age subcultures, partly because they are based on leisure and partly because they separate old people from young people. But according to virtually all the reported research, the old people who live in them like the life and choose it freely.

A CASE IN POINT

I recently worked and observed life in Merrill Court (this is not its real name), a California public housing project for poor people over 62. Initially, I should confess, I felt that there was something sad about a group of old people living together, something artificial, maybe even depressing. But it soon became clear to me that they themselves were not depressed. They saw nothing sad about living together and felt a shade of pity for those who had to live alone. They felt they *had* problems, but they did not feel they *were* one.

The findings of this and other research suggest that the kind of communal life I found at Merrill Court was due more to the setting than to the particular characteristics of the people who happened to live there. Although the residents are not part of a random sample, their characteristics do not distinguish them so very much from this generation of American old people as a whole. Most of the residents were poor, rural-born Anglo-Saxon Protestant widowed females in their late sixties. And most Americans over 65 are poor. (The 1962 average income for couples was about $2800 and for singles less than $1400.) Thirteen percent of the population in 1960 was over sixty, and of that strata roughly 60 percent were in their sixties. Most old people today were born in rural areas, although most (70 percent) now live in urban areas. Nationwide, 45 percent of old people are male and 55 percent female; in Merrill Court all but 5 out of 43 were women. The residents were probably no more sociable than other old people, since the housing office picked them as their names came up on waiting lists, and they picked the housing not for its social life but because it was cheap.

I should say what the apartment building itself looked like, since the way it was built allowed certain social patterns that might not have emerged otherwise. It had five floors: a ground floor with one apartment and a large recreation room for common use, and four other floors with ten apartments each. On each floor there was an elevator midway between the apartments and a long porch extending

the length of all the apartments. It was nearly impossible to walk from any apartment to the elevator without being watched from the series of living-room windows that looked out onto the porch. This was because the chairs inside each living room were arranged so as to face the window and the television at the same time. A woman who was sewing or watching television in her apartment could easily glance up through the window and see or wave to a passerby. Those in the apartments closest to the elevator saw the most passersby and were the "informants" about the whereabouts of people on their floor. I saw more people by simply sitting in one apartment's "television chair" than I ever did knocking on doors.

The residents slept in separate apartments, but they did not live alone. Most waking hours were spent in each other's company, either over the telephone or over a cup of coffee. As a result, they kept an eye on each other and usually noted when someone was deviating from a routine. One day, when I knocked on the door of a resident, her neighbor came out and said, "I don't know where she is, it couldn't be the doctor's. She goes to the doctor's on Tuesday, it couldn't be shopping, she shopped yesterday with her daughter. I don't think she's downstairs, she says she's worked enough today. Maybe she's visiting Abbie. They neighbor a lot. Try the second floor."

Neighboring was also a way to spot sickness or death. As one resident noted, "This morning I looked to see if Judson's curtains were open. That's how we do on this floor, when we get up we open our curtains just a bit, so others walking by outside know that everything's all right. If the curtains aren't drawn by midmorning, we knock to see." (The residents of many midcity hotels make similar arrangements with each other, and in St. Petersburg, Florida, an old person can arrange to be called by a volunteer several times a day.) Some residents also shopped or laundered clothes for other residents, and on several floors they habitually cooked for each other by turn.

In addition to the private apartments, there was a large recreation room downstairs where one came to attend the Monday-morning service-club meetings. If someone stayed up in her apartment during the club meeting on Monday morning it was more often out of spite than indifference. For down-stairs was a hub of activity: there people were weav-ing rugs, knitting clothes, sewing aprons, cooking pies or practicing music—a five-piece band, includ-ing washtub bass, played in nursing homes for the "old folks" there. As people worked, they joked and gossiped and, if the mood was right, sang ballads. The activities changed from month to month, but the work, the gossip and the arranging did not. One widow compared the work downstairs to an old-fashioned "workin' in," as she put it: "Neighbors would come in and help out if you were takin' in a harvest or doin' some cannin'. One time our barn burned down and we had another one up in two days. Doin' it together, we got more done, see?"

LIBERATION BY SEPARATION

The similarity of the residents liberated them and liberated their topics of conversation. In a society that raises an eyebrow at those who do not "act their age," the old-age subculture of Merrill Court freed the old to dance a jig, to tell an off-color joke and to flirt without worrying about letting grand-motherly decorum slip. Among themselves, they developed a backstage talk about playing the role of old person. Just as one plays the role of woman to man and black person to white, so one plays the role of old person to young people. Thus, on occasions protected from the young, the old are able to drop the role. Outside such a community old people often try, with powder and wig, to "pass" as younger, but within such a community they don't need to.

To bring old people together is not to free them from all social constraint but to substitute old-age constraints for age-integrated ones. A typical morn-ing's talk in the recreation room might move from what Molly had on today when she went shopping to what Mrs. Barber eats for dinner to whether it is appropriate to wear hats to church or curlers to the doctor's office. If a resident broke the rules by wear-ing a hat to church, she normally felt it necessary to explain why. On the other hand, there was much they could do and say together that they could not—or would not—with young people.

One reason they talked differently among them-selves was simply that some topics were more rele-vant to them than to their younger families or friends—for example, whether or not Medicare pays for chiropractors, visiting hours at various hospi-tals, the merits of different kinds of dentures, yarn prices, and the latest episode in daytime TV serials. When daughters dropped in downstairs, the topic generally shifted to something of more mutual con-cern, such as whether Jackie had gone downhill since marrying Onassis.

LIFTING THE TABOO ON DEATH

The residents talked with each other about other people's deaths and the prospect of their own quite freely, in straightforward, noneuphemistic lan-guage. Death was a fact of life in the community: six residents died in the course of my three years of field work there. There was a collective concern with, as they put it, "being ready," facing up, and each death taught the residents something about it. They felt there was a "good" way and a "bad" way to die. One woman's death especially was the com-munity's example of "the right way to die"—to face death rather than turn one's back on it, all the while living fully to the end. She was praised as much for remaining active as for having her will and burial arranged and being on good terms with her family.

They could not, in the same way, share these concerns with their young family and friends. In fact, it was from the young that they more often heard comments of denial such as "You don't look a day over fifty" or "You get younger every day."

Geoffrey Gorer, in his essay "The Pornography of Death," suggests part of the problem when he notes that death is replacing sex as the new "unmentionable." Compared to those in the 19th century, we are more prudish about death, whereas sex, another natural process, is now more open to frank discussion. Death and decay are considered as "disgusting" as birth and copulation were a cen-tury ago—a new "not before the children" sort of thing.

However, just as the former taboo on sex tended to be lifted in sex-segregated company, so too perhaps the taboo on death is lifted in age-segre-gated company. Men alone together and women alone together, even in the Victorian age, may have talked about sex more freely. In the same way, the old among the old feel freer to talk about death.

The age solidarity in Merrill Court tends to liberate the topic of death and the unembarrassed expression of grief. Only a small proportion of old people live in such old-age communities, but it is probably true that in general the old among the old feel less constrained to deny death or to observe the taboo on talk related to it.

STATUS AMONG THE OLD: THE "POOR DEAR" HIERARCHY

Old age has been called a "normal stigma." But while young people may think of the old categorically, the old, especially when they get together, measure small differences between each other, especially differences in luck.

In fact, "luck" is not entirely luck. Health and life expectancy, for example, are often considered luck, but an upper-class person can expect to live ten years longer than a lower-class person. Among the residents of Merrill Court, he who maintained good health, friends in good health, and good relations with children ranked high. Those who fell short on any of these criteria were often referred to as "poor dears."

The "poor dear" system operated like a set of valves through which a sense of superiority ran in only one direction. The hierarchy honored those at the top and pitied (or scorned) those at the bottom, creating status distinctions among those who, in the eyes of the outside society, were social equals. Someone who was unlucky (a "poor dear") did not blame herself for bad luck, nor did she accept the stigmatized status imposed from above by the lucky, and especially the *relatively* lucky. Rather, the "poor dear" would turn to someone she thought still less fortunate to whom she offered solicitude.

This luck hierarchy is only part of a larger old-age status hierarchy which is based on attributes other than luck. For example, at the countywide Senior Citizens Forum, the term "poor dear" often arose with reference to other old people. Senior citizens who are politically active referred to those "poor dears" who are active in recreation. Old people with passive life-styles in good health referred to those in poor health as "poor dears," and those in poor health but living in independent housing referred to those in nursing homes as "poor dears." Within the nursing home there was a distinction between those who were ambulatory and those who were not. Among those who were not ambulatory there was a distinction between those who could enjoy food and those who could not. Almost everyone, it seems, had a "poor dear."

The way in which the old look for luck differences among themselves parallels the pattern found at the bottom of other class, racial, and sexual hierarchies as well. To find oneself lucky within a generally stigmatized category is to gain the semblance of high status when society withholds it from others in the category. The way in which old people "feel above" and condescend to other old people may be linked to the fact that the young feel above and condescend to them.

CONCLUSION

Deprived of function and power, old people have few clearly defined roles. The former roles that applied to a wife, a worker, or a parent have faded with time. But the resulting ambiguity does not obtain in a community of old people such as this. If one is no longer a mother to a brood of small children, or a wife or a provider, one can be the club treasurer, a bowling partner, a volunteer worker in a nursing home, or a neighbor's caretaker.

For friends lost through death there are replacements; at Merrill Court whenever an apartment is vacated, it is immediately filled by the first on a long list of applicants at the housing agency. If there is no longer work that "has to be done," something like it is there. With each new role come new customs and new notions of the right and wrong of it. The residents have built themselves an order out of ambiguity, a set of obligations to the outside world and to each other where few had existed before. Lacking responsibilities to the young, they take on responsibilities to each other, and if the outside world watches them less for being old, they watch each other more. They have renewed their social contract with life, on the basis of a new sibling solidarity.

Young people are not alone in their search for "relevant models." Since the parents of today's old people usually died earlier, in the social prime of middle age, an individual does not know what to expect of himself if he lives in pretty good health to a time when he is no longer needed and when he is isolated from others faced with the same dilemma. A community of peers in old life provides models for how to age, when, in this respect, the last generation of old people as well as the young are no help.

Communities of old people need not substitute for warm ties with young family and friends. But the decline of the extended family creates the need for a new social shelter, another pool of friendships, another bond with society apart from family. Old-fashioned values may fade, but the communal experiments of this generation of old people may forecast new social networks for the next.

Marriages in Urban Communal Households: Comparing the Spiritual and the Secular

JANE W. FERRAR

ALTHOUGH COMMUNES ARE OFTEN billed as alternative family forms (and are yoked indiscriminately with two-career families, open marriages, group marriages, and the like) they are, more precisely, alternative household structures. As Jessie Bernard (1972, pp. 193–194) puts it: "the term commune applies to a life-style, not to a form of marriage...a commune is merely a pattern of living, a life-style, a household." Rosabeth Kanter (1973, p. 279), who has studied both 19th-century and contemporary communes, agrees:

> Do communes themselves constitute "families," or do communes contain families in their midst? My answer is that communes are a larger, blanket social order that contain or potentially contain smaller family units, but in many cases smaller families have given up their autonomy and separation and have merged with the community.

While communes vary dramatically along every conceivable dimension of structure and content (and are, therefore, bound to be experienced by *some* as alternative families) they are most accurately regarded not as experimental family forms but as experimental household contexts in which the business (and pleasures and strains) of marriage and family life may be carried out. Nonetheless, since "the nature of the household in which a marriage functions is a powerful determinant of the nature of the relationship itself" (Bernard 1972, p. vii) communal households, like all other households, can come to influence the style, quality and fate of family interactions conducted within their boundaries. And yet, the communal contextual influence on family life has rarely been granted systematic attention.[1]

The present study, which is an attempt to explore some of the relationships between urban communal contexts and family experiences, assumes that innovative household and family forms are increasing rapidly in the United States (Zablocki and Kanter, 1976) and that urban communal households

This is a revised version of a paper prepared for presentation at the Annual Meetings of the Midwest Sociological Society, April 21–24, 1976 (St. Louis, Missouri).

Portions of the research reported here were funded by a grant from the National Institute of Mental Health (#MH 2525-02) to Benjamin Zablocki, Columbia University, and portions were funded by fellowships to the author from the Danforth Foundation and the American Association of University Women. The author wishes to thank her colleagues on the Urban Communes Project, Columbia University, and the members of the New York Chapter of Sociologists for Women in Society for their help and suggestions.

will emerge as significant contributors to these innovations.

URBAN COMMUNES

Although communes have been a peripheral part of American social life since the 17th century (Zablocki 1971; Kanter 1972), only within the last ten years have substantial numbers of communal households begun to appear in metropolitan areas. While it is virtually impossible to estimate the actual numbers of urban communal households in the United States, there is uniform agreement among contemporary communal observers that the numbers of urban communal households are steadily growing and, in all likelihood, are growing at a substantially faster rate than are their rural counterparts.[2] These urban communes, however, have attracted scant sociological attention. They have been hard to find, their communities are astonishingly fragile and transient, the groups often lack names and other trappings of institutionalization and, unlike many rural groups, urban communes have inspired very little self-descriptive literature.

Despite their limited investigative lure, however, urban communes present a unique structural setting for communal household life: they provide opportunities for community while at the same time allowing for commitments of limited ability. As Rosabeth Kanter (1973, p. 6) puts it:

> The contemporary urban commune is an entirely new development...for the most part merely providing an alternate way for people to share a more meaningful, intimate household in the city while they continue to participate in the mainstream culture for the rest of their lives.

Although Kanter's "contemporary urban commune" refers specifically to noncreedal groups —groups which require neither wholesale renunciations of existing institutions nor total affirmations of alternative realities, the "limited liability" aspect of urban communes applies in part also to the more purposive creedal communities. Because of the urban commune's functional interdependence with the institutions of the larger society (particularly when contrasted with the potential for self-

sufficiency among rural groups) and because of the high permeability of urban communes' boundaries, members of both creedal and noncreedal groups may readily cross over into the mainstream society to maintain access to conventional urban jobs for which they may have been trained and educated and to pursue noncommune-oriented interests, activities, and relationships.

Despite their broad structural similarities, however, urban communes differ widely from one another as household contexts for intimate relationships. Some groups, for instance, insist on monogamy in marriage and celibacy for all nonmarrieds, while other groups promote nonattachment and nonexclusivity in all romantic and sexual allegiances. Some groups view marriage as an ongoing battle of the sexes for power and control, and others view marriage as a vehicle for greater unity with a higher consciousness. Some devote a great deal of energy to ego-building and personal change through innovative growth experiences, while others attempt to follow ancient teachings and prescribed rituals in the search to lose the self. Thus, while objective criteria may select out certain households as communes, contextual variations may vastly alter the experiences of actual residents.

The present report, part of ongoing research on family life in urban communes, explores the effects on marital relationships of one contextual variable: unity of purpose among household members.

Data Sources

The data from which the present findings are extracted come from two waves of ethnographic and survey research conducted in 65 separate urban communal households located in six major cities throughout the United States. Fieldwork for the study began in five of the cities (Atlanta, Houston, Twin Cities, Los Angeles, and New York) during the summer of 1974. The sixth city (Boston) was kept six months out of phase in order to control both for seasonal effects and for the effects of specific historical events which might influence changes observed between the 1974 and 1975 waves of data collection. A second panel of data was collected during the summer of 1975, with Boston again following six months out of phase.

Selection of communes and data collection During the first month of fieldwork in each city, fieldworkers spent full time compiling a comprehensive census of communities which appeared to satisfy the following definition of commune:

> A group of five or more adults (plus possible children) most of whom are unrelated by marriage or blood, who have decided to live together, without compulsion, primarily for the sake of the pursuit of some ideological or personal goals for which a collective household is deemed essential (Urban Communes Project 1976, p. 3).

The month-long census netted well over 400 communes. From the full census list, a representative sample of ten communes was drawn for indepth study in each city.[3] The criteria for selection were designed to be both representative and to accommodate cross-city comparisons.[4]

Data collection methods were of two varieties: ethnographic and survey research. Ethnographic data was gathered by fieldworkers who spent long periods observing each household's daily life and who maintained daily field notes. In addition, fieldworkers conducted extensive (1–3 hour), loosely structured taped interviews with between two and five members of each group (some of these interviews were conducted on a group basis and some were private). Additional ethnographic data reside in the often copious marginalia of the survey instruments. Survey research data was gathered through the administration of six survey instruments which were developed specifically for the study and which variously employed the commune, the individual and dyadic relationships as units of analysis. Data for the present study of family life draw upon all available sources.

Classifying the communes Since all communes share certain structural features (e.g., common residence, economic interdependence, primary group interactions with several people), all communes must also face certain problems which arise from these structural features. Thus, for example, each group must be concerned with issues of interpersonal awareness and organizational division of labor and must, therefore, to a greater or lesser de-

gree, devote communal energies to these issues. Despite some similarities in structures (and resulting exigencies), however, the communal groups in the sample lend themselves to differential classification on a variety of dimensions (e.g., population size, longevity, leadership structure). For the present study, the communal groups have been classified according to their ideological types, that is, the primary motivation for the group's collective existence. This mode of classification was expected to yield substantial variability among the groups in terms of members' marriage and family experiences, since the attitudes, values and behaviors stemming from primary motivations are likely to include expectations concerning the nature of members' interactions and therefore, of course, the interactions of married members.

Commune ideologies Primary motivation assignments were derived from a variety of sources: communal statements of purpose, individual members' statements of private motives and goals, criteria for acceptance of new members, and day-to-day group activities and behaviors. Although some groups presented "borderline" classification dilemmas (for example, the politically leftist group whose members were strongly motivated by political concerns but whose criterion for membership was, primarily, family status [i.e., were applicants married or single, did they have children or not?]) and, although some groups have gone through dramatic motivational shifts (for example, the group in Los Angeles which started as an SDS activist collective, became a full-blown teenage crash pad, which turned into a collective food program and then moved into a period of radical therapies involvement and has now emerged as a cooperative household with a central family and fairly stable membership), the great majority of the communes fell comfortably into the following seven categories:

1. *Eastern religious* Households of individuals who were living together for the express purpose of increasing collective and individual spiritual awareness through the discipline and practices of an Eastern religion.

2. *Christian religious* Households of individuals who were living together to increase their individual

and collective devotion to Christ and to Christian practices.

3. *Family life* Households of individuals who were primarily concerned (although rarely *uniquely* concerned) with creating an alternative household style to the isolated nuclear family residence.

4. *Cooperative* Collective households whose members were together primarily for convenience (particularly the sharing of chores), economy, pleasure, and experimentation, but who were not strongly committed to communal life as an alternative household style.

5. *Political* Households of individuals who were living together in order to further political activity or to elevate political consciousness in a supportive environment, or who were living together expressly for the creation of a noncapitalistic political model. Membership in such groups always entails some consideration of individuals' political orientation.

6. *Personal growth* Households of individuals who were living together for the express purpose of increasing individual personal awareness through institutionalized therapeutic activities.

7. *Rehabilitative* Communities of individuals, together through assignment or choice, for the express purpose of remedying a perceived personal malfunctioning (drug abuse, mental health). These groups are included in the sample for their general historical and sociological interest of community re-

habilitation programs but are excluded from the present analysis.

The distribution of the 65 households in the entire sample is given in Table 1.

As is clear from Table 1, the largest category of sampled households are those classified as either Eastern or Christian religious (35 percent of households; 36 percent of communes). While this distribution may, in part, be an artifact of the sample design (deliberate selection of federated religious households), the sample design itself reflects the fieldwork census data and confirms fieldworker observations concerning the rapid proliferation of religious communal households in the United States. Since the current research represents the first attempt to observe systematically the urban communal movement on a national level, and since other observers of contemporary communal life have, with almost conspiratorial regularity, excluded from their observations those communal groups which are informed by transcending ideologies (see, for instance, Berger *et al.* 1971; Kanter and Halter 1975; Jaffe 1975) the best evidence we have concerning the national distribution of urban communal household types is this study's census results which are reflected roughly in the current sample distribution.

Married couple population Of the 40 legally married, cohabitating couples who appeared in the original sample, ten couples were living in Eastern religious households; five couples were living in Chris-

Table 1 Distribution of entire sample by ideological type

Household type	No. residential households		No. communal groups		Population	
Eastern religious	15	(23%)	14	(23%)	178	(27%)
Christian religious	8	(12%)	8	(13%)	61	(9%)
Family life	5	(8%)	5	(8%)	43	(7%)
Cooperative	18	(28%)	18	(30%)	134	(20%)
Political	7	(11%)	7	(12%)	48	(7%)
Personal growth	9	(14%)	5	(8%)	102	(15%)
Rehabilitative	3	(5%)	3	(5%)	101	(15%)
Totals	65	(101%)	60	(99%)	667	(100%)

**Table 2 Distribution of married couples
by household type***

Household type	No. couples		Total population	
Eastern religious	10	(25%)	178	(31%)
Christian religious	5	(13%)	61	(11%)
Family life	11	(28%)	43	(8%)
Cooperative	9	(23%)	134	(24%)
Political	2	(5%)	48	(9%)
Personal growth	3	(8%)	102	(18%)
Totals	40		566	

*Distribution excludes rehabilitative population
(101 individuals; no couples)

tian religious households; eleven couples were living in family life households; nine couples were in cooperative households; three couples were in personal growth households; and two couples were in political households. There were no couples in the rehabilitative households since the rules in all three groups forbade cohabitation of spouses. (See Table 2.)

HOW THEY FARED

Marital Stability

Communal living has received overwhelmingly bad press in terms of its effects on marital stability. Both sociological theory (Slater 1963; Kanter 1972; Coser 1974) and available data (Zablocki 1974; Jaffe 1975) support one communalist's observation that "something very subtle happens to the average marriage when one undertakes to live communally. Perhaps the first thing that happens is that it is gravely endangered" (quoted in Muncy 1973, p. 12). Or, as one recently separated communal mother put it to me: "Your study should be very interesting *if* you can find anyone who's still married."

While marital intactness is scarcely a sufficient measure of marital contentedness, marital dissolution can certainly be taken as a gross measure of marital discontent. And, on this measure, urban communal life seems not to have "gravely endan-

gered" the marriages of most of the couples in the sample. Of the 40 married couples surveyed in the first wave of data collection, 35 couples (87.5 percent) were still together in the summer of 1975. This unexpectedly high rate of marital intactness contradicts both lay mythology concerning the causes (marital discontent) and the consequences (marital dissolution) of communal living for married pairs and contradicts also previous findings based on more limited samples (see, for instance, Jaffe, 1975.)

Several factors must be taken into account, however, in interpreting the relevance of this marital intactness statistic. To begin with, the returns on marital intactness are by no means fully in. Each of these couples has several decades more of marriage to weather either in or out of communal households. And yet, what little data we have concerning marital fates in communal households suggests that the first year or two of communal living is the most difficult for married couples (Zablocki 1974; Kanter *et al.* 1975; Jaffe 1975). In addition, the wide variation in the sample of personal background factors which relate to marital break-up (age, years of marriage, age at marriage, number of children, socioeconomic background, religion) makes it extremely difficult to estimate meaningfully some "expected" rate of marital dissolution for this population. Whether these couples will, over the course of their marital lifetimes, exceed or fall short of their "expected" marital stability rates (based on national averages) is, of course, a question that cannot be answered here.

A third consideration which complicates the interpretation of the intactness statistic is that while 35 of the 40 couples were still married, not all of the 35 intact couples were still living communally (or in the same communal household) and it may be that those couples who left the communal household did so, in part, to preserve their marriages from the marriage-dissolving effects of communal life. This suggestion, that the high rate of marital intactness is connected, at least in part, with high rates of communal defection, is given preliminary credence by the finding that 16 of the 35 intact marriages are being conducted outside of the original communal context. This could suggest that for more than 50 percent of the intact couples, marital intactness is somehow related to communal defection. However, a case by case exploration reveals the spuriousness of the connection between intactness and defection since eight of the sixteen couples are still living communally but in different households connected with their original communal federations and only four of the couples left their original communal households for reasons even remotely connected with tensions between communal and family commitments. Therefore, we have no reason to believe that the marital intactness rate is in any way attributable to the commune defection rate.

Household Contexts

It is proposed here instead that the high rate of marital intactness in the present sample is due, in large part, to the high percentage of couples (38 percent) who are living in households designed primarily for the pursuit of spiritual and religious goals and activities. This suggestion arises from the empirical finding that 100 percent of the 15 religious household couples are still intact (as compared with 80 percent of the 25 secular household couples) and from the theoretical understanding that both the nature of the communal purpose in religious households and the extent of unity concerning commitment to that purpose provide a household context which is both marriage protective and marriage stabilizing.

Nature of the Communal Purpose

For both married and single members of religious households, the stated goal of communal living is the same: mutual spiritual enlightenment through community life. The goal in these religious households, be they Eastern or Christian oriented, is one of de-egoization, of submission of the self and personality to a larger consciousness. In this context, marital unity is part of the larger unification process, and all members, married or single, may be part of and share equally in the larger process.[6] Unity in marriage is subsumed under unity of higher consciousness. In this context, also, the marital relationship necessarily assumes less importance as a source of individual satisfaction than it does in most secular households where the primary source of satisfaction is, precisely, interpersonal

relationships. As a result, harmonious marriages belong to the communal purpose and process, they are part of the larger unification process which is under way and marriage is not ordinarily regarded (or experienced) as a competitor or usurper of group energies and strength. If, then, the unified marriage is viewed as a contributor to group energies, there is more likely to be group support for marital relationships, and this support should feed into the relationships themselves, encouraging them to even greater unity.

In secular households, both the purpose of communal life and the unity of commitment to that purpose are generally different from the purpose and commitment in religious households. For married members of secular households there are often disparate goals for the male and female partners (e.g., more economic sharing for him, more sex-role equality for her) (see Ramey 1972 and Bernard 1972 for a discussion of different communal goals for men and women). In addition, there are often disparate goals for married and single members (more variety for the marrieds, more stability for the singles). (Dennis Jaffe (1975) has convincingly documented the marriage-negating properties of many secular communes which promote individual autonomy and expression). Since there is extensive contextual support for these individualistic goals, married members pursuing individual destinies are not encouraged to forgo those destinies for some higher purpose. In addition, in a household setting where members are attempting to forge a group out of disparate, individualistic visions, mating and coupling are certain to interfere (at least on occasion) with the sense of "we" (and therefore to be viewed or treated less supportively than they are in religious households where marital strength may belong to the larger purpose).

When we examine responses by religious and secular householders to the question: "why did you finally come and live in this household?" the differences in purpose between the two types come clear.

Christian religious, wife: I went through a whole lot of different thoughts, wondering what commitment to Jesus is. I realized I couldn't do it alone, I needed other brothers and sisters. That search, the desire to know Him more led me to think about community.

The Lord finally gave me to realize that the best way to come close to Him was to live in community.

Christian religious, husband: It was hard to live the kind of Christian life I was called to when I was living alone with my family. I needed a more intense Christian life. I felt a call to give my entire being to live in a total Christian environment, one which would not distract me from my total commitment to Jesus.

Eastern religious, wife: I realized that living in a community of seekers was part of the path. Everyone doing the same thing, everyone believing the same thing would make it all so much easier. And it has.

Eastern religious, husband: The way is with others. The (*guru*) encourages us to live together to follow his teachings and to help each other in right understanding. I joined because I knew he was right.

Family life, wife: Before we moved here I was struggling in terms of a new identity, from a dependent person to developing more individuality. We were seeking new directions, that's why we moved. We felt a need to start a whole new structure. Since I've moved here I've discovered that I'm a person who is worth getting to know in my own right, independently of my husband. This was one of the important reasons, I now realize, that I wanted to live with other people in a community.

Cooperative, husband: I wanted to live in a commune so that I could be both at home and with my clique of friends. Before, when we lived as a nuclear family, I'd be at home a lot and want to be with my friends, or if I'd been with them I'd feel I should be at home. Things are a lot less strained now than they were then.

Family life, husband: As I became more humanistic in my profession (*clinical psychology*) I developed new relationships with my colleagues. Then I went to a three-week seminar in growth and human potential. I became aware of the desolation and barrenness of the suburbs where we were living.... For two years I was searching for a way to get into communal living

so I could practice more what I was feeling about my own potential, but I couldn't find anyone to do it with. There was no one we knew or met who we felt we could live with at all. We figured the people we lived with would be crucial for fulfilling our own potential.

As these quotes suggest, many members of religious groups are working toward a single, collective goal along a prescribed path or discipline, while many members of secular groups are seeking individual goals or, perhaps, similar goals to be reached via widely differing paths. In addition, the secular householders express interest in personalities and relationships while the religious householders are more involved with the goals regardless of the personalities involved in attaining them (as long as the unity of purpose is present).

The differences between the ego-repressing and ego-enhancing orientations of religious and secular households are particularly evident in the relationship (sociometric choice) questionnaires in which each member was asked to characterize all other members and to comment on certain features of their relationships with others. Religious householders expressed a great deal of difficulty in answering these questions and filled the margins with such comments as: "Question has no meaning," "There are no differences among members," "Characteristic applies to everyone," "We are all the same here." As one woman from an Eastern religious group explained in the margin:

> The questionnaire about the relationships I felt was really on a level of consciousness that I am no longer actively into. I am more into relating to people through the meditation and seeing people as love and going through life together, than who is more jealous, etc. Our commune is built around the knowledge revealed by (*the guru*). This knowledge allows us to open up and realize our true nature. When we do this, things flow. Life flows in this household.

Such responses of nondifferentiation were extremely rare in the secular groups, where individual differences were clearly recognized and freely acknowledged.

What effects might household contexts of normative de-individualization and group unity of purpose have on marital relationships? When transcendent goals take precedence over marital interactions and satisfactions, personality differences and tensions are likely to be trivialized and suppressed so that the collective goal of higher consciousness may be achieved. Both married and unmarried members are likely to work for the repression and trivialization of tensions and conflicts so that personality vagaries will not interfere with collective goals. This orientation toward conflict is often reversed in secular groups where the expression of anger is frequently valued (and, in fact, is often facilitated by a paid outsider who helps the group members "get out their anger"). As one woman in a family life household put it:

> It was during our encounter group sessions with Ed (*professional group "facilitator"*) that I began to realize how really angry I was with Barry (*her husband of six years*). I realized that when I argued with him or yelled at him he would just withdraw behind a wall of indifference and that made me all the angrier. I learned through the group how to express my anger productively and to recognize that Barry's withdrawal is defense and that I am really hurting him when I mean to be.

In religious households, therefore, where angry interpersonal feelings are expected to be worked out through self-examination, prayer, meditation, consultation of scriptures, and appeals to higher authorities and purposes, and where there is normative disapproval of the expression of unexamined anger, interpersonal tensions are likely to be minimized, suppressed, and, ultimately, trivialized, so that married individuals (like everyone else) are discouraged from finding fault with others, including their spouses. In secular households, however, where anger tends to be legitimized and validated, and where spontaneous expressions of angry feelings often gain support and approval, the inherent strains in the marital relationship often attract the energies of the group and the strains are escalated into unendurable (marriage-dissolving) conflicts.

In the religious households, therefore, which are dedicated to a purpose beyond the present, interpersonal relations are simply not the most important factor of communal life and, as a result, marriages (and all other intimate relationships) are not made to carry the full freight of human needs, expectations, and desires.

SOME PRELIMINARY FINDINGS

In order to investigate the empirical support for these theoretical speculations, data concerning observations about couples' behaviors were explored to discover whether religious and secular households reported different types of couple behavior. In every commune, every participating member of every household was asked to contribute observations about the couples in his or her household. One

Table 3 For each couple, to what extent do you feel they are part of the commune as a unit, or as individual members (or as either)?*

Type	No. votes	% as unit	% as individuals	% either	No. couples	No. communes
Christian religious	25	56	0	44	5	3
Eastern religious	82	42	23	35	10	5
Cooperative	42	14	31	55	9	6
Family	26	8	54	39	6	4
Personal growth	9	0	44	56	3	1
Political	7	0	57	43	2	2
Totals	191				35	21

*Frequencies exclude five couples in one family/political household for which information is not available.

Table 4 Does each pair tend to agree (or at least not disagree openly) on most commune issues?*

Type	No. votes	% disagree frequently	% disagree sometimes	% disagree rarely	No. couples	No. communes
Christian religious	24	0	8	92	5	3
Eastern religious	79	4	17	80	10	5
Cooperative	42	17	21	62	9	6
Family	27	33	48	19	6	4
Personal growth†	9	0	33	67	3	1
Political	7	14	71	14	2	2
Totals	188				35	21

*Frequencies exclude five couples in one family/political household for which information is not available.

† The personal growth commune included here has a strong spiritual orientation with a carefully documented ideology and set of practices. The ideological cohesiveness of this group probably affects rates of agreement concerning communal issues.

question asked: "For each couple, to what extent do you feel they are part of the commune as a unit or as individual members, or as neither?" And another question asked: "Does each pair tend to agree (or at least not disagree openly) on most commune issues?" These questions were expected to elucidate the differences between the two types of households in regard to couple behavior: whether unity or individualism seemed to prevail among married householders. The responses to these questions for communes in which there were married couples are given in Tables 3 and 4.

As is clear from these two tables, couples in religious households are far more likely to be seen as a unit than as individuals, and are perceived as agreeing on commune issues much more frequently than are secular couples. Although it is entirely possible that the ideology of unity in the religious communes blinds household respondents to actual dissension among married couples, this very ideological support of nonconflict provides a context of expectations which, it would seem, reinforces the partners' goals of unity. (It is this very expectation of no conflict, of course, which is at work in traditional societies where the good of the community, kin, or tribe is placed before marital considerations and where, throughout history, rates of marital intactness have been generally high).

A second test of the "unified household" notion involved analysis of attitude questionnaire items. For the present study, only one item was analyzed:

"With respect to relations between husband and wife these days, there are no clear guidelines to tell us what is right and what is wrong." See Table 5.

**Table 5 Marital anomie
"With respect to relations between husband and wife these days there are no clear guidelines to tell us what is right and wrong"***

Type	Weighted mean	No. votes	No. communes
Christian religious	4.63	49	7
Eastern religious	4.09	108	15
Family life	2.84	25	4
Cooperative	2.74	94	18
Political	2.37	30	6
Personal growth	2.02	44	4
Totals		350	54†

* 1 = agree strongly
  2 = agree slightly
  3 = no opinion
  4 = disagree slightly
  5 = disagree strongly

† This total excludes: 3 rehabilitative communes
                       1 family/political commune
                       1 political commune
                       1 personal growth commune

which did not participate in the attitude questionnaires part of the study.

The expectation was that religious householders would disagree more strongly with this statement than would secular householders because the higher principles which govern all human interactions for religious householders would also, of course, govern interactions for married persons and therefore guidelines for married people would, in fact, be quite clear. The results of the analysis strongly confirm this expectation. Religious householders disagree firmly with the statement (with a weighted mean of 4.3 on a five-point scale); while secular householders agree unanimously with the statement (with a weighted mean of 2.5). Since all of the religious households yielded a score above 4.1 and all the secular households yielded a score below 2.8, the secular households would seem to be significantly more anomic with respect to marriage, at least as measured by this one item.

The connection, then, between marital experiences and household contexts (particularly those concerned with purpose and commitment to purpose) appears to be quite strong. In secular households, the uniqueness of the individual personality and pursuit of personal goals will often be given precedence and support by the group and, as a result, marital relationships may falter. In religious households, the goals of one are the goals of all (at least ideally), and the unification of a married couple is seen as a manifestation of and a contributor to the general unified spirit.

What we learn from this is that communal living, in and of itself, does not necessarily endanger marriage. Despite the much discussed strains of commitment between family roles and community roles, when the individual, the family unit and the community are all oriented toward one transcending purpose the communal context may be highly marriage supportive and marriage compatible.

In some ways, of course, the differences between secular and religious communal households reflect directly the differences between modern and traditional marital relationships. Although in both communal cases the marriage is embedded in a community (a traditional structure), in the religious instances, the entire community aspires to be in unity with the relationship (and the relationship to be in unity with the group) and both individuals and couples consider the community and its goals to be indistinguishable from private aspirations. In secular communes, on the other hand, individual goals often take precedence over both community and, in many cases, marital goals. That is why, of course, religious communes have tended to be more stable over time than have secular communes (Kanter 1972), and it is also why marriages conducted in religious household contexts appear to be more stable and unified than those conducted in secular households.

NOTES

1. The very recent exception to this analytic neglect is the research conducted in Boston and New Haven on middle-class urban communes. See Jaffe 1975; Kanter and Halter 1975; Kanter, Jaffe, and Weisberg 1975; Jaffe and Kanter 1975.

2. The difficulties involved in estimating the number of urban communes will be somewhat alleviated in 1980 when the Census Bureau will begin to enumerate communal households in its decennial survey.

3. Although ten communal groups were selected in each of the six cities, two of these communal groups were comprised of tightly interdependent (though geographically separated) households (in one case five households, in one case two households). Thus, the final sample consisted of 60 communal groups located in 65 residential communal households.

4. There was, however, one significant deviation from representativeness. Early in the fieldwork a number of nationwide federations of communal households (whose members move freely among households in different states) was located. In fact, close to a dozen such federations were identified during the 1974 fieldwork. Households belonging to a few of these federations were deliberately selected to facilitate cross-regional comparisons and to provide information on this important new household phenomenon. For further information on sampling and data collection procedures, see Ferrar 1976 and Zablocki, forthcoming.

5. Of the four intact couples who left their original communal households for "family" reasons, two couples were the only parents in their respective households

and therefore were subject to the strains of child-rearing responsibilities in nonchild-oriented houses. As a result, only two couples of the 35 intact couples appear to have left their original communal households in order to facilitate their marital relationships through nuclear family living.

6. In many religious communities, of course, celibacy is the rule. I am talking here only about religious communities which condone and support married life.

REFERENCES

BERGER, BENNET, B. M. HACKETT, AND R. M. MILLER 1970. *Progress report to NIMH.* Washington, D.C., (mimeographed).

BERNARD, JESSIE 1972. *The future of marriage.* New York: World Publishing.

COSER, LEWIS A. 1974. Greedy organizations. New York: Free Press.

FERRAR, JANE W. 1976. Urban communal households: a new context for marriages. Paper prepared for presentation at the Annual Meetings of the Midwest Sociological Society, (St. Louis) April 21–24, 1976.

HERSHBERGER, ANN 1973. The transiency of urban communes. In Rosabeth M. Kanter (ed.), *Communes: creating and managing the collective life.* New York: Harper & Row.

JAFFE, DENNIS 1975. *Couples in communes.* Unpublished Ph.D dissertation, Yale University: New Haven.

————, AND ROSABETH M. KANTER 1975. Couple strains in communal households: a four-factor model of the separation process. *Journal of Social Issues* 31.

KANTER, ROSABETH M. AND MARILYN HALTER 1975. De-house-wifing women, domesticating men: equality between the sexes in urban communes. In J. Heiss (ed.), *Marriage and family interaction.* (2nd ed.) Chicago: Rand McNally.

KANTER, ROSABETH M. (ed.) 1973. Communes: creating and managing the collective life. New York: Harper & Row.

KANTER, ROSABETH M. 1972. Commitment and community: communes and utopias in sociological perspective. Cambridge: Harvard University Press.

————, DENNIS JAFFE, AND D. K. WEISBERG 1975. Coupling, parenting and the presence of others: intimate relationships in communal households. *Family Coordinator* 24 (October): 365–382.

MUNCY, RAYMOND LEE 1974. Sex and marriage in utopian communities. Baltimore: Penguin.

RAMEY, JAMES 1972. Communes, group marriage, and the upper middle class. *Journal of Marriage and the Family* 34: 647–655.

SLATER, PHILIP E. 1963. On social regression. *American Sociological Review* 28 (June): 339–364.

URBAN COMMUNES PROJECT 1976. *Second report to participants.* New York: Columbia University, (mimeographed).

ZABLOCKI, BENJAMIN 1971. *The joyful community.* Baltimore: Penguin Books.

————, 1973. *Communes and the future of community in America.* Paper delivered at the annual meetings of the American Sociological Association, New York (August 27–30).

————, 1974. Alienation and the investment of self in the urban commune. (Xeroxed research proposal.)

————, forthcoming. *Alienation and charisma: American communitarian experiments 1965–1975.* New York: Free Press.

————, AND ROSABETH M. KANTER 1976. The differentiation of life-styles. *Annual Review of Sociology.* Palo Alto: Annual Reviews.

Chapter 12

The Future of the Family

IN THIS BOOK, WE HAVE DEALT WITH THE traditional nuclear family by viewing it in a broader societal context, as well as examining its internal structure through the life cycle stages. In addition, alternatives to the traditional nuclear family which have proliferated and become popularized in the media in recent years such as communes, open marriage, commuter marriage and childless marriage have been presented. The key questions to be addressed in this chapter are: (1) overall, what have been the key dimensions of family change? and (2) are these changes likely to be of a transitory or permanent nature? To answer these questions, several factors must be considered. First, what societal forces brought these variant family forces into existence? Second, how powerful are the sources of resistance to these changes? And third, what is the viability of the alternative structures in terms of personal and societal needs?

Suzanne Keller surveys structural changes in the recent past that have given rise to the alternative forms of the family. First, the traditional marriage form is imbued with contradictions involving the structural instability of dyads and the primary goal of happiness which is vague and difficult to sustain. Second, occupational and educational trends have altered the traditional relationships between the sexes. And third, biological and technological changes such as the prolongation of life and the future possibilities of frozen sperm banks and the separation of conception from gesta-

tion affect the family and the position of women in it. On the basis of these trends, she predicts future family patterns involving greater variety in sexual and marital experiences, decreases in exclusiveness and possessiveness, more room for personal choice, communal living and multistage marriages.

Teresa Marciano also deals with structural and ideological bases for alternative family forms. She sees the lessening of female dependence on males, the decreasing social stigmatizing of sexual experimentation, and increasing personal affluence as leading to choices in favor of alternative structures. These alternative choices are labeled as "variant" rather than as "deviant" due to the middle- and upper middle-class bias of researchers reacting to behavior of their own social class. Marciano locates these new family forms within the context of a world economic system dominated by multinational corporations and a worldwide mass media structure. Two particular forms of "variant" families. child-free life-styles and communes, are analyzed with respect to their viability and permanence.

Judith Lorber deals with family changes with respect to the needs of children for stable parenting. She suggests that alternative structural mechanisms that guarantee the procreation and socialization of children need to replace the traditional sexual division of labor which ties women to procreation and child rearing. Various potential alternative structures are suggested such as parenting by select groups, professional breeders and child rearers, and child–adult pairing. The potential benefits and losses from each are analyzed with respect to various social needs.

In hypothesizing about the future of the family, the articles in this chapter focus on the social forces creating alternative family forms and the viability of these forms with respect to personal and societal needs. It is also important to consider social institutions and forces which have resisted these changes and have perpetuated traditional family forms. For example, Pauline Bart[1] has contrasted the structural changes that have given rise to the alternative family forms with the lack of change in the socialization of children in schools and in the educational media. For example, children's picture books illustrate traditional sex-linked roles of men and women. These books present obsolete information about society and present role models that ignore sex-role changes in the larger society. The educational system thus represents a source of resistance to family change.

From a functionalist perspective, students might assess the consequences that the different family alternatives have for different social groups —the two sexes, the different classes, the different age groups, including children—and for the society as a whole. Who benefits and who loses from each alternative structure? How do the alternative structures fulfill necessary social functions previously fulfilled by the traditional nuclear family?

From a conflict perspective, readers might assess the interrelationship between the economy and the variant family forms. What do the world economic system and international control by elites described by Marciano suggest for future cross-cultural family forms? How will changing sex roles of women alter an economy that according to Marxist analyses presented in the articles has depended on flexible labor pools to complement fluctuations in the business cycle, and on female consumerism?

Finally, utilizing a symbolic interaction perspective, readers might consider the various societal sources and processes for the creation of identities congruent with the variant family forms in the same way that Bart analyzed the contribution of the educational system. How do the identities of children formed by interaction in their families of origin, religious institutions, or exposure to various media sources prepare them for future family roles?

NOTE

1. Pauline Bart, 1974. Why women see the future differently from men. In Alvin Toffler (ed.), *Learning for tomorrow*. New York: Vintage.

Does the Family Have a Future?

SUZANNE KELLER

SOME THIRTY-FIVE YEARS AGO, TWO venerable students of human behavior engaged in a six-session debate on marriage and the family over the B.B.C. Their names were Bronislaw Malinowski and Robert Briffault, the one a world-famous anthropologist best known for his studies of the Trobriand Islands, the other a social historian devoted to resurrecting the matriarchies of prehistory. Of the two, paradoxically, it was Briffault, the self-trained historian, who turned out to be the cultural relativist whereas Malinowski, a pioneer in cross-cultural research, exhibited the very ethnocentrism his studies were designed to dispel.

Reprinted from the *Journal of Comparative Family Studies* (Spring 1971) by permission of author and publisher.

Both men noted that the family was in trouble in their day. Both were distressed by this and sought to discover remedies if not solutions. Despite their common concern, however, they were soon embroiled in vivid and vociferous controversy about the nature of the crisis and its cure. (*Marriage: past and present*, ed. M. F. Ashley-Montagu, Boston, Porter Sargent, 1956.)

Briffault concluded from his reading of the evidence that the family rests on sentiments rooted in culture and social tradition rather than in human nature. Unless one grasps these social and cultural essentials, one cannot hope to understand, much less cure, what ails it. No recourse to natural instinct or to the "dictatorship of tradition or moral coercion" could save the modern family from its destined decline.

Malinowski disagreed. The family, he admitted, might be passing through a grave crisis but the illness was not fatal. Marriage and the family, "the foundation of human society," and a key source of spiritual and material progress, were here to stay, though not without some needed improvements. Among these were the establishment of a single standard of morality, greater legal and economic equality between husband and wife, and greater freedom in parent–child relations.

The disagreement of these two men stemmed, as it so often does, not from different diagnoses but from different definitions of the phenomenon. Malinowski defined the family as a legal union of one man and one woman, together with their offspring, bound by reciprocal rights and duties, and cooperating for the sake of economic and moral survival. Briffault defined the family much more broadly as any association involving economic production and sexual procreation. In his sense, the clan was a family.

The two agreed on only one point: parenthood and above all maternity are the pivots in the anatomy of marriage and the family. If these change, so must the familial organization that contained them. Thus if one can identify such pivotal changes, their difficulties are overcome while ours may be said to be just beginning.

There is good reason to suppose that such changes are now upon us. The malaise of our time reflects not simply a temporary disenchantment with an ancient institution but a profound convulsion of the social order. The family is indeed suffering a sea change.

It is curious to note how much more quickly the popular press, including the so-called women's magazines, have caught on to changing marital, sexual, and parental styles. While many of the experts are still serving up conventional and tradition-bound idols—the hard-working, responsible, breadwinner husband–father, the self-effacing, ministering, wife–mother, the grateful, respectful children—these magazines tempt the contemporary reader with less standard and more challenging fare. Whether in New York or in Athens, the newsstands flaunt their provocative titles—"Is This the Last Marrying Generation?", "Alimony for Ex-Husbands," "Why We Don't Want to Have Children," "Are Husbands Superfluous?"—in nonchalant profusion. These and other assaults on our sexual and moral codes in the shape of the new theater, the new woman, the new youth and TV soap operas akin to a psychiatrist's case files, persuade us that something seems to be afoot in the whole sphere of marriage and family relations which many had thought immune to change. In point of fact the question is not *whether* the family is changing but how and how much; how important are these changes, how permanent, how salutary? The answers depend largely on the way we ask our questions and define our terms.

The family means many things to many people but in its essence it refers to those socially patterned ideals and practices concerned with biological and cultural survival of the species. When we speak of the family we are using a kind of shorthand, a label for a social invention not very different, in essence, from other social inventions, let us say the Corporation or the University, and no more permanent than these. This label designates a particular set of social practices concerned with procreation and child rearing; with the heterosexual partnerships that make this possible and the parent–child relations that make it enduring. As is true of all collective habits, once established, such practices are exceedingly resistant to change, in part because they evoke strong sentiments and in part because no acceptable alternatives are offered. Since most individuals are unable to step outside of their cultures, they are unable to note the arbitrary and variable nature of their conventions. Accordingly, they ascribe to their folkways and creeds an antiquity, an inevitability, and a universality these do not possess.

The idea that the family is universal is highly misleading despite its popularity. All surviving societies have indeed found ways to stabilize the processes of reproduction and child care else they would not have survived to tell their tale. But since they differ greatly in how they arrange these matters (and since they are willing to engage in Hot and Cold Wars to defend such differences) the generalization does not help us explain the phenomenon but more nearly explains it away.

In truth there are as many forms of the family as there are forms of society, some so different from ours that we consider them unnatural and incomprehensible. There are, for example, societies in which couples do not share a household and do not have sole responsibility for their offspring; others in which our domestic unit of husband and wife is divided into two separate units, a conjugal one of biological parents and a brother-sister unit for economic sustenance. There are societies in which children virtually rear each other and societies in which the wise father does not know his own child. All of these are clearly very different from our 20th century, industrial-urban conception of the family as a legally united couple, sharing bed and board, jointly responsible for bearing and rearing their children, and formally isolated from their next of kin in all but a sentimental sense. This product of a long and complicated evolutionary development from prehistoric times is no simple replica of the ancient productive and reproductive institutions from which it derives its name and some of its characteristic features. The contemporary family really has little in common with its historic Hebrew, Greek, and Roman ancestors.

The family of these great civilizations of the West was a household community of hundreds, and sometimes thousands, of members ("familia" is the Latin term for household). Only some of the members were related by blood and by far the larger part were servants and slaves, artisans, friends, and distant relations. In its patriarchal form (again culturally variable), this large community was

formally held together by the role of eldest male who more nearly resembled the general of an army than a modern husband-father. In its prime, this household community constituted a miniature society, a decentralized version of a social organization that had grown too large and unwieldy for effective management. In this it resembles the giant bureaucracies of our own day, and their proposed decentralization into locally based, locally staffed subsystems, designed to offset the evils of remote control while nevertheless maintaining their connection with it. Far from having been universal, this ancient family type, with its gods and shrines, schools and handicrafts, was not even widely prevalent within its own social borders. Confined to the landed and propertied upper classes, it remained an unattainable ideal for the bulk of common men who made up the society.

The fallacy of universality has done students of human behavior a great disservice. By leading us to seek and hence to find a single pattern, it has blinded us to historical precedents for multiple legitimate family arrangements. As a result we have been rather impoverished in our speculations and proposals about alternative future arrangements in the family sphere.

A second common fallacy asserts that the family is *the* basic institution of society, hereby revealing a misunderstanding of how a society works. For as a social institution, the family is by definition a specialized element which provides society with certain needed services and depends on it for others. This means that you cannot tamper with a society without expecting the family to be affected in some way and vice versa. In the contemporary jargon, we are in the presence of a feedback system. Whatever social changes we anticipate, therefore, the family cannot be kept immune from them.

A final fallacy concerns the presumed naturalness of the family in proof of which a motley and ill-assorted grab bag of anecdotal evidence from the animal kingdom is adduced. But careful perusal of ethological accounts suggests that animals vary as greatly as we do, their mating and parental groupings including such novelties as the love death, males who bear children, total and guilt-free "promiscuity," and other "abnormal" features. The range of variation is so wide, in fact, that virtually any human arrangement can be justified by recourse to the habits of some animal species.

In sum, if we wish to understand what is happening to the family—to our family—in our own day, we must examine and observe it in the here and now. In so doing it would be well to keep in mind that the family is an abstraction at best, serving as guide and image of what a particular society considers desirable and appropriate in family relations, not what takes place in actual fact. In reality there are always a number of empirical family types at variance with this, though they usually pay lip service to the overarching cultural ideal.

CHALLENGES TO THE CONTEMPORARY INDUSTRIAL FAMILY

In the United States, as in other industrial societies, the ideal family consists of a legally constituted husband–wife team, their young, dependent children, living in a household of their own, provided for by the husband's earnings as main breadwinner, and emotionally united by the wife's exclusive concentration on the home. Probably no more than one-third of all families at a particular moment in time, and chiefly in the middle and would-be middle classes, actually live up to this image. The remaining majority all lack one or more of the essential attributes—in lacking a natural parent, or in not being economically self-sufficient, or in having made other necessary modifications.

One contrasting form is the extended family in which the couple share household arrangements and expenses with parents, siblings, or other close relatives. The children are then reared by several generations and have a choice of models on which to pattern their behavior. This type, frequent in working class and immigrant milieus, may be as cohesive and effective as the ideal type but it lacks the cultural legitimacy and desirability of the latter.

A third family type, prevalent among the poor of all ethnic and racial backgrounds, is the mother–child family. Contrary to our prejudices, this need not be a deviant or distorted family form, for it may be the only viable and appropriate one in its particular setting. Its defects may stem more from adverse social judgments than from intrinsic failings. Deficient in cultural resources and status, it may nevertheless provide a humane and spirited setting for its members, particularly if some sense of stability and continuity has been achieved. Less fortunate are the numerous nonfamilies, ex-families, and nonintact families such as the divorced, the widowed, the unmarriageables, and many other fragmented social forms, who have no recognized social place. None of these, however, threaten the existing order since they are seen and see themselves as involuntarily different, imperfect, or unfortunate. As such, they do not challenge the ideals of family and marital relations but simply suggest how difficult it is to live up to them. When we talk of family change or decline, however, it is precisely the ideal standards which we have in mind. A challenge to them cannot be met by simple reaffirmations of old truths, disapproval, shock, or ridicule of the challengers, or feigned indifference. Such challenges must be met head on.

Today the family and its social and psychological underpinnings are being fundamentally challenged from at least three sources: (1) from accumulated failures and contradictions in marriage; (2) from pervasive occupational and educational trends including the changing relations between the sexes, the spread of birth control, and the changing nature of work; and (3) from novel developments in biology. Let me briefly examine each.

It is generally agreed that even in its ideal form, the industrial–urban family makes great, some would say excessive, demands on its members. For one thing it rests on the dyadic principle or pair relationship which, as Georg Simmel observed long ago, is inherently tragic and unstable. Whether in chess, tennis, or marriage, two are required to start and continue the game but only one can destroy it. In this instance, moreover, the two are expected to retain their separate identities as male and female and yet be one in flesh and spirit. No wonder that the image of the couple, a major source of fusion and of schism in our society, is highly contradictory according to whether we think of the sexes as locked in love or in combat. Nor do children, the symbols of their union, necessarily unify them.

Their own growing pains and cultural demands force them into mutually exclusive sociosexual identities, thereby increasing the intimate polarity. In fact, children arouse parental ambivalence in a number of ways, not the least of which is that they demand all but give back all too little. And yet their upbringing and sustenance, the moral and emotional climate, as well as the accumulation of economic and educational resources needed for survival, all rest on this small, fragile, essential but very limited unit. Held together by sentimental rather than by corporate bonds, the happiness of the partners is a primary goal although no one is very sure what happiness means nor how it may be achieved and sustained.

To these potentials for stress and strain must be added the loss of many erstwhile functions to school, state, and society, and with it something of the glamour and challenge of family commitments. Few today expect the family to be employment agency, welfare state, old age insurance, or school for life. Yet once upon a time, not too long ago at that, it was all that and more. At the same time, however, with fewer resources, some new burdens have been added stemming from rising standards of child health, education, and welfare. This makes parents even more crucially responsible for the potential fate of their children over whom they have increasingly less exclusive control.

Like most social institutions in the throes of change, moreover, the modern family is also beset by numerous internal contradictions engendered by the conflict between traditional patterns of authority and a new egalitarianism between husbands and wives and parents and children. The equality of the spouses, for example, collides with the continuing greater economic responsibilities, hence authority, of the husband. The voluntary harness of love chafes under the constraint of numerous obligations and duties imposed by marriage, and dominance patterns by sex or age clash with new demands for mutuality, reciprocity, equity, and individualism. These, together with some unavoidable disillusionments and disappointments in marriage, set the stage for the influence of broader and less subjective social trends.

One such trend, demographic in nature but bound to have profound social implications, concerns the lengthened life expectancy and the shortened reproductive span for women. Earlier ages at marriage, fewer children per couple, and closer spacing of children means: the girl who marries at 20 will have all her children by age 26, have all her children in school by her early thirties, have the first child leave home for job, schooling, or marriage in her late thirties, and have all her children out of the home by her early forties. This leaves some thirty to forty years to do with as personal pleasure or social need dictate. The contrast with her grandmother is striking: later marriage, and more children spaced farther apart, meant all the children in school no earlier than her middle or late thirties and the last to leave home (if he or she ever did) not before her early fifties. At which time grandmother was probably a widow and close to the end of her own lifespan. The empty nest thus not only occurs earlier today but it lasts longer, affecting not this or that unfortunate individual woman but many if not most women. Hence what may in the past have been an individual misfortune has turned into a social emergency of major proportions. More unexpected free time, more time without a socially recognized or appreciated function, more premature retirements surely puts the conventional modern wife, geared to the domestic welfare of husband, home, and children, at a singular disadvantage relative to the never-married career woman. Destined to outlive her husband, stripped of major domestic responsibilities in her prime years, what is she to do with this windfall of extra hours and years? Surely we must expect and prepare for a major cultural shift in the education and upbringing of female children. If women cannot afford to make motherhood and domestic concerns the sole foci of their identities, they must be encouraged, early in life, to prepare themselves for some occupation or profession not as an adjunct or as a last resort in case of economic need but as an equally legitimate pursuit. The child rearing of girls must increasingly be geared to developing a feminine identity that stresses autonomy, nondependency, and self-assertion in work and in life.

Some adjunct trends are indirectly stimulating just such a reorientation. When women are compelled, as they often are, to earn their own living or to supplement inadequate family resources necessitated by the high emphasis on personal consumption and the high cost of services increasingly deemed essential as national standards rise, conventional work-dependency patterns are shattered. For, since the male breadwinner is already fully occupied, often with two jobs, or if he cannot or will not work, his wife is forced to step in. Thus there is generated internal family pressure—arising from a concern for family welfare but ultimately not confined to it—for wives to be gainfully employed outside of the home. And fully three-fourths in the post-childbearing ages already are, albeit under far from ideal conditions. Torn between home and job, between the precepts of early childhood with its promise of permanent security at the side of a strong male and the pressures of a later reality, unaided by a society unaware or indifferent to her problems, the double-duty wife must manage as best she can.

That this need not be so is demonstrated by a number of modern societies whose public policies are far better meshed with changing social realities. Surely one of our more neglected institutions—the single-family household which, despite all the appliances, remains essentially backward and primitive in its conditions of work—will need some revamping and modernizing. More household appliances, more and more attractive alternatives to the individually run household, more nursery schools, and a total overhaul of work schedules not now geared to a woman's life and interests cannot be long in coming. While these will help women in all of their multiple tasks they may also of course further challenge the presumed joys of exclusive domesticity.

All in all, it would appear that the social importance of the family relative to other significant social arenas will, as Briffault among others correctly anticipated, decline. Even today when the family still exerts a strong emotional and sentimental hold its social weight is not what it once was. All of us ideally are still born in intact families but not all of us need to establish families to survive. Marriage and children continue to be extolled as supreme social and personal goals but they are no longer—especially for men—indispensable for a meaningful existence. As individual self-sufficiency, fed by economic affluence or economic self-restraint, increases, so does one's exemption from unwanted economic as well as kinship responsibilities. Today the important frontiers seem to lie else-

where, in science, politics, and outer space. This must affect the attractions of family life for both men and women. For men, because they will see less and less reason to assume full economic and social responsibilities for four to five human beings in addition to themselves as it becomes more difficult and less necessary to do so. This, together with the continued decline of patriarchal authority and male dominance—even in the illusory forms in which they have managed to hang on—will remove some of the psychic rewards which prompted many men to marry, while the disappearance of lineage as mainstays of the social and class order will deprive paternity of its social justification. For women, the household may soon prove too small for the scope of their ambitions and power drives. Until recently these were directed first of all to their children, secondarily to their mates. But with the decline of parental control over children a major erstwhile source of challenge and creativity is removed from the family sphere. This must weaken the mother-wife complex, historically sustained by the necessity and exaltation of motherhood and the taboo on illegitimacy.

Above all, the move towards worldwide population and birth control must affect the salience of parenthood for men and women, as a shift of cultural emphasis and individual priorities deflates maternity as woman's chief social purpose and paternity as the prod to male exertions in the world of work. Very soon, I suspect, the cultural presses of the world will slant their messages against the bearing and rearing of children. Maternity, far from being a duty, not even a right, will then become a rare privilege to be granted to a select and qualified few. Perhaps the day is not far off when reproduction will be confined to a fraction of the population, and what was once inescapable necessity may become voluntary, planned, choice. Just as agricultural societies in which everyone had to produce food were once superseded by industrial societies in which a scant six percent now produce food for all, so one day the few may produce children for the many.

This along with changing attitudes towards sex, abortion, adoption, illegitimacy, the spread of the pill, better knowledge of human behavior, and a growing skepticism that the family is the only proper crucible for child rearing, creates a powerful recipe for change. Worldwide demands for greater and better opportunities for self-development, and a growing awareness that these opportunities are inextricably enhanced or curtailed by the family as a prime determinant of life-chances, will play a major role in this change. Equal opportunity, it is now clear, cannot stop at the crib but must start there. "It is idle," commented Dr. Robert S. Morrison, a Cornell biologist, "to talk of a society of equal opportunity as long as that society abandons its newcomers solely to their families for their most impressionable years." (*New York Times*, October 30, 1966) One of the great, still largely un-' challenged, injustices may well be that one cannot choose one's parents.

The trends that I have sketched would affect marriage, male–female, and parent–child relations even if no other developments were on the horizon. But there are. As yet barely discernible and still far from being applicable to human beings, recent breakthroughs in biology—with their promise of a greatly extended life span, novel modes of reproduction, and dramatic possibilities for genetic intervention—cannot be ignored in a discussion devoted to the future of the family.

REVOLUTION IN BIOLOGY

If the early part of this century belonged to physics and the middle period to exploratory ventures into outer space, the next few decades belong to biology. The prolongation of life to double or triple its current span seems virtually assured, the extension of female fertility into the sixties is more than a distinct possibility, and novel ways of reproducing the human species have moved from science fiction to the laboratory. The question then arises, What will happen when biological reproduction will not only be inadvisable for the sake of collective well-being but superseded by new forms and eventually by nonhuman forms of reproduction?

A number of already existing possibilities may give us a foretaste of what is to come. For example, the separation of conception from gestation means that motherhood can become specialized, permitting some women to conceive and rear many children and others to bear them without having to

provide for them. Frozen sperm banks (of known donors) are envisioned from which prospective mothers could choose the fathers of their children on the basis of particularly admired or desired qualities, thereby advancing an age-old dream of selecting a distinguished paternity for their children based on demonstrated rather than potential male achievement. And it would grant men a sort of immortality to sire offspring long after their biological deaths as well as challenge the implicit equation now made between fathers and husbands. Finally, the as yet remote possibility to reproduce the human species without sexual intercourse, by permanently separating sex from procreation, would permit unmarried women (and men) to have children without being married, reduces a prime motive for marriage and may well dethrone—inconceivable as this may seem—the heterosexual couple. All of these pose questions of legal and social policy to plague the most subtle Solon. Who is the father of a child—the progenitor or the provider where these have become legitimately distinct roles? Who is the mother—the woman who conceives the child or the one who carries it to term? Who will decide on sex ratios once sex determination becomes routine? Along with such challenges and redefinitions of human responsibility, some see the fate of heterosexuality itself to lie in the balance. In part of course this rests on one's assumptions about the nature of sexuality and sexual identity.

Anatomy alone has never been sufficient for the classification of human beings into male and female which each society labors to develop and then calls natural. Anatomy is but one—and by no means always a reliable—identifying characteristic. Despite our beliefs, sex identification, even in the strictest physical sense, is by no means clear-cut. Various endeavors to find foolproof methods of classification—for example, for participation in the Olympics—have been unsuccessful, as at least nine separate and often uncorrelated components of sexual phenotype have been identified. But if we cannot count on absolute physical differentiations between the sexes, we do even less well when it comes to their social and psychological attributes. Several decades of research have shown beyond doubt that most of what we mean by the difference between the sexes is a blend of cultural myth and social necessity, which must be learned, painstakingly and imperfectly, from birth on. Once acquired, sexual identity is not fixed but needs to be reinforced and propped up in a myriad of ways of which we are quite unaware.

In the past this complicated learning process was guided by what we may call the categorical reproductive imperative which proclaimed procreation as an unquestioned social goal and which steered the procreative and sexual capacities and aspirations of men and women toward appropriate channels virtually from birth on. Many other features strengthened these tendencies—symbolism and sentiment, work patterns and friendships, all kinds of subtle and not so subtle rewards and punishments for being a "real" man, a real woman. But once the reproductive imperative is transformed into a reproductive ban what will be the rationale for the continuance of the exclusive heterosexual polarity in the future? If we keep in mind that only two out of our forty-six chromosomes are sex-carrying, perhaps these two will disappear as their utility subsides. Even without such dramatic changes, already there is speculation that heterosexuality will become but one among several forms of sexuality, these having previously been suppressed by strong social sanctions against sexual deviation as well as their inability to reproduce themselves in standard fashion. More than three decades ago, Olaf Stapleton, one of the most imaginative science fiction writers of the century, postulated the emergence of at least six subsexes out of the familiar ancient polarity. At about the same time, Margaret Mead, in the brilliant epilogue to her book on sex and temperament (*Sex and Temperament in Three Primitive Societies,* William Morrow and Co., New York, 1935), suggested a reorganization and recategorization of human identity not along but across traditional sex lines so as to produce a better alignment between individual capacity and social necessity. In our time we have witnessed the emergence of Unisex (the term is McLuhan's) and predictions which range from the disappearance of sex to its manifold elaboration.

Some are speculating about a future in which only one of the current sexes will survive, the other having become superfluous or obsolescent. Depending on the taste, temperament—and sex—of the

particular writer, women and men have alternately been so honored (or cursed). It is not always easy to tell which aspect of sex—the anatomical, psychological, or cultural—the writer has in mind but as the following comment suggests, much more than anatomy is at stake.

> Does the man and woman thing have a future? The question may not be hypothetical much longer. Within 10 years . . . we may be able to choose the sex of our offspring; and later to reproduce without mating male and female cells. This means it will someday be possible to have a world with only one sex, woman, and thereby avoid the squabbles, confusions, and headaches that have dogged this whole business of sex down the centuries. A manless world suggests several scientific scenarios. The most pessimistic would have society changing not at all, but continuing on its manly ways of eager acquisition, hot competition, and mindless aggression. In which case, half the women would become "men" and go right on getting ulcers, shouting "charge," and pinning medals on each other. (George B. Leonard, "The Man and Woman Thing," *Look*, December 25, 1968)

Long before the demise of heterosexuality as a mainstay of the social order, however, we will have to come to terms with changing sexual attitudes and mores ushered in by what has been called the sexual revolution. This liberalization, this rejection of old taboos, half-truths, and hypocrisies, also means a crisis of identity as men and women, programmed for more traditional roles, search for the boundaries of their sexual selves in an attempt to establish a territoriality of the soul.

Confusion is hardly, of course, a novel aspect of the human condition. Not knowing where we have come from, why we are here, nor where we are headed, it could hardly be otherwise. There have always been dissatisfied men and women rejecting the roles their cultures have assigned them or the responsibilities attached to these. But these are the stuff of poetry and drama, grist for the analyst's couch or the priest's confessional, in other words private torments and agonies kept concealed from an unsympathetic world. It is only when such torments become transmuted into public grievance and so become publicly heard and acknowledged that we can be said to be undergoing profound changes akin to what we are experiencing today.

Returning now to our main question—Does the family have a future?—it should be apparent that I expect some basic and irreversible changes in the decades ahead and the emergence of some novel forms of human togetherness. Not that the current scene does not already offer some provocative variations on ancient themes, but most of these gain little public attention, still less approval, and so they are unable to alter professed beliefs and standards. Moreover, every culture has its own forms of self-justification and self-righteousness and in our eagerness to affirm the intrinsic superiority of our ways, we neglect to note the magnitude of variations and deviations from the ideals we espouse. What are we to make, for example, of such dubious allegiance to the monogamous ideal as serial marriages or secret adulteries? Or, less morally questionable, what of the quasi-organized part-time family arrangements necessitated by extreme occupational and geographic mobility? Consider for a moment the millions of families of salesmen, pilots, seacaptains, soldiers, sailors, and junior executives where the man of the house is not often *in* the house. These absentee husbands–fathers who magically reenter the family circle just long enough to be appreciated, leaving their wives in charge of the homes they pay for and of the children they sired, are surely no more than part-time mates. If we know little about the adjustments they have had to make or their children's responses, this is because they clearly do not fit in with our somewhat outmoded stereotyped notions of what family relations ought to be. Or consider another homegrown example, the institution of governesses and boarding schools to rear upper-class children. Where is the upper-class mother and how does she spend her time between vacations and homecoming weekends? Then there are of course many countries around the world —Israel, Sweden, the socialist countries, some of the African societies—where all or nearly all women, most of them mothers, work outside of the home as a matter of course. And because these societies are free from guilt and ambivalence about the working mother, they have managed to incorporate these realities

more gracefully into their scheme of things, developing a number of useful innovations along the way. Thus even in our own day, adaptations and modifications exist and have not destroyed all notions of family loyalty, responsibility, and commitment.

In fact, people may be more ready for change than official pronouncements and expert opinions assume. The spread of contraceptive information and the acceptance of full birth control have been remarkable. The relaxation of many erstwhile taboos has proceeded at breakneck speed, and the use of public forums to discuss such vital but previously forbidden topics as abortion, homosexuality, or illegitimacy is dramatic and startling in a society rooted in Puritanism. A number of studies, moreover, show that the better educated are more open to reexamination and change in all spheres, including the family. Since these groups are on the increase, we may expect greater receptivity to such changes in the future. Even such startling proposed innovations as egg transplants, test-tube babies, and cloning are not rejected out of hand if they would help achieve the family goals most Americans prize. (See "The Second Genesis" by Albert Rosenfeld, and the Louis Harris Poll, *Life*, June 1969, pp. 31–46.)

Public response to a changing moral and social climate is of course hard to predict. In particular, as regards family concerns, the reactions of women, so crucially bound up with motherhood and child rearing in their self-definitions, are of especial interest. In this connection one study of more than 15,000 women college students attending four-year liberal arts colleges in the United States is relevant for its findings on how such a nationwide sample of young coeds, a group of great future significance, feels about marriage, motherhood, and career. (Charles F. Westoff and Raymond H. Potvin, *College Women and Fertility Values*, Princeton University Press, 1967) Selecting only those items on which there was wide consensus and omitting details of interest to the specialist, the general pattern of answers was unmistakable. The large majority of these would-be wives and mothers disapproved of large families (three or more children), did not consider children to be the most important reason for marriage, favored birth control and birth planning, and thought it possible for a woman to pursue family and career simultaneously. They split evenly on the matter of whether a woman's main satisfaction should come from family rather than career, or community activities, and they were virtually united in thinking that mothers with very young children should not work. The latter strongly identifies them as Americans, I think, where nursery schools and other aids to working mothers—including moral support—are not only lacking but still largely disapproved of.

Thus if we dare to speculate further about the future of the family we will be on safe ground with the following anticipations: (1) a trend towards greater, legitimate variety in sexual and marital experience; (2) a decrease in the negative emotions—exclusiveness, possessiveness, fear and jealousy—associated with these; (3) greater room for personal choice in the kind, extent, and duration of intimate relationships, which may greatly improve their quality as people will both give and demand more of them; (4) entirely new forms of communal living arrangements in which several couples will share the tasks of child rearing and economic support as well as the pleasures of relaxation; (5) multistage marriages geared to the changing life cycle and the presence or absence of dependent children. Of these proposals, some, such as Margaret Mead's, would have the young and the immature of any age test themselves and their capacities to relate to others in an individual form of marriage which would last only so long as it fulfilled both partners. In contrast to this, older, more experienced, and more mature couples who were ready to take on the burdens of parenthood would make a deeper and longer lasting commitment. Other proposals would reverse this sequence and have couples assume parental commitments when young and, having discharged their debt to society, be then free to explore more personal, individualistic partnerships. Neither of these seems as yet to be particularly appealing to the readers who responded to Mead's proposal as set forth in *Redbook Magazine*. (Margaret Mead, "Marriage in Two Steps," *Redbook Magazine*, July 1966; "The Life Cycle and Its Variation: The Division of Roles," *Daedalus*, Summer 1967; "A Continuing Dialogue on Marriage: Why Just Living Together Won't Work," *Redbook Magazine*, April 1968)

For the immediate future, it appears that most Americans opt for and anticipate their participation in durable, intimate, heterosexual partnerships as anchors and pivots of their adult lives. They expect these to be freer and more flexible than was true in the past, however, and less bound to duty and involuntary personal restrictions. They cannot imagine and do not wish a life without them.

Speculating for the long-range future, we cannot ignore the potential implications of the emerging cultural taboo on unrestricted reproduction and the shift in public concern away from the family as the central preoccupation of one's life. Hard as it may seem, perhaps some day we will cease to relate to families just as we no longer relate ourselves to clans, and instead be bound up with some new, as yet unnamed, principle of human association. If and when this happens, we may also see a world of Unisex, Multisex, or Nonsex. None of this can happen, however, if we refuse to shed some of our most cherished preconceptions, such as that monogamy is superior to other forms of marriage or that women naturally make the best mothers. Much as we may be convinced of these now, time may reveal them as yet another illusion, another example of made-to-order truths.

Ultimately all social change involves moral doubt and moral reassessment. If we refuse to consider change while there still is time, time will pass us by. Only by examining and taking stock of what is can we hope to affect what will be. This is our chance to invent and thus to humanize the future.

Variant Family Forms in a World Perspective

TERESA DONATI MARCIANO

VARIANT FAMILY FORMS[1] HAVE RECEIVED increasing attention in sociological literature (Libby and Whitehurst 1973; Sussman 1972, 1974; Skolnick and Skolnick 1971, 1974). The nature of the phenomena examined, their increased visibility, the discipline itself, and the location of these in time invite two speculations: first, the question of what makes these phenomena "variant" (and positively evaluated by researchers) when in another time they might have been viewed as "aberrant" or "deviant" (and negatively evaluated, overtly or implicitly); and second, a wider theoretical framework for these studies—which Moore (1966a, 1966b) and more recently Wallerstein (1974) propose—a global or world-system perspective. The two speculations converge in that, treating the labeling process which creates the term "variant," the world view emphasizes that those who make the labels do so in particular social and historical contexts.

The nuclear model of the family, where "deviance" is any nonnuclear form, has been under attack (Skolnick and Skolnick 1971); old notions of "deviance" have also been heavily criticized (Rock 1973; Rawls 1971). Criticisms of the functional perspective have also influenced these authors despite new insights into that perspective (Davis 1959; Goode 1971). And greater visibility of variant forms has further cast doubt upon the nuclear model. This visibility in turn stimulates further personal experimentation and sociological research.

Variant family forms become more visible partly as a result of new "self-revelation," the emphasis upon "open" relationships. As the sexes move toward equality, there are concomitant advantages and strains in restructured sex roles. The advantage in terms of openness is that with equality, the formerly subordinate sex has less to lose by self-revelation and articulated demands upon the other. Concealment of one's real pref-

erences and deference to the desires of one partner in order to conform to modal expectations are more likely under conditions of economic dependence and social stigmatizing of sexual experimentation.

There is also heightened strain partly from greater tensions among various roles for both men and women; the strains which men are in fact facing constitute a relatively neglected area of research. Strains in women's roles have received more attention for a much longer time (Komarovsky 1946). With the Liberation, women have moved from the sense that strains were resolvable by conforming, to the present sense that strains are symptoms of structural oppression and resolvable by alternative modes of male–female relationships. The endless self-fascination of academics has increased the numbers of books and articles devoted to the unfolding restructuring of these relationships as academics attempt to define the patterns that have affected their own lives.

These strains, which produce internal and interpersonal conflicts, require some form of accommodation. Repression and anxiety are unpalatable alternatives to talking-and-restructuring processes in the resolution of conflicts. Visibility increases as more and more people are caught in the transitional states between traditional/prior roles that have ceased to satisfy, and those still evolving, restructured roles that institutionalize self-expression, continued openness, and presumably more satisfying life-styles. In these cases, the search for value-priorities and less oppressive structures often leads to a closer examination of variant family forms.

The media enter at various levels to legitimate the process by giving it salience as a widely shared problem. Magazines, radio, and television, in dis-

Reprinted from the *Family Coordinator*, October 1975, by permission of the author and publisher.

cussing new norms, serve also to diffuse them. The media become channels not only of information but also of communication among those sharing certain kinds of problems and resolutions. Specialized media (*Communities*, Synergy *Newsletter*, or the older *Village Voice*) grow in number and audience to provide "marketplaces" or "clearinghouses" for the exchange of ideas and the meeting of those interested in experimentation with others.

Personal affuence or the availability of welfare payment support, the institutionalized patterns of mobility in which the young depart from nuclear family settings to live on college campuses or travel or simply to establish their own households, and the resultant access to alternative forms of living and alternative value systems additionally enter the high-visibility equation of variant family forms today.

Finally, the new experimental forms are becoming "respectable rebellions" as the shock potential or different sexual practices and living arrangements recedes, accompanied by a questioning in all age groups of the values of monogamy exclusivity, lifelong marriage, and sexual divisions of labor. In this sense, countercultural movements of the past decade have "stretched" the range of permissive norms by posing life-style alternatives so "radical" as to decrease the sanctions on relatively milder variations—e.g., unmarried cohabitation as a less "radical" option than the same situation in which children are born to that union (Marciano 1975).

Linked to self-revelation and visibility is the question of why elites, those favored in the rewards system, should have come to this point of risk-taking and experimentation. Explanations of the apparent dissatisfaction, boredom, and restlessness have been attempted by numerous writers (Roszak 1969, 1973; Reich 1970; Slater 1970; Harrington 1965; King 1972). Perhaps most basically, the problem of *meaning* has assumed a new importance in technologically developed areas of the modern world. The transition from subsistence to affluence gave control through science over the physical environment. The values of nonempirical, institutional beliefs—religion, patriotism, mythology —were concurrently placed in doubt. Over time,

however, tangible rewards came to be taken for granted and ceased to satisfy. New avenues for the pursuit of happiness were sought. Goods, things, objects—possessed in abundance—represented neither spirit nor enduring benefit.

Durkheim had long ago perceived this (1915, 1933, 1952). Time and again he returned to the absence of intrinsic meaning in objects, the social character of "meaning," and the limited capacity for human happiness (1933, p. 325). No direct or necessary correlate existed "between the variations of happiness and the advances of the division of labor" (1933, p. 250). Dissatisfactions with life-style-meanings are not, furthermore, confined to capitalist countries if these dissatisfactions do spring from the insufficiency of tangible goods to provide meaning. Industrial system hierarchies do not vary in any significant way across national boundaries, even where ideologies among nations appear antithetical (Inkeles and Rossi 1956). A *world* elite is therefore subject to these questions of meaning and to the search for values.

If older values have been found wanting —thrift, reverence, self-control—as irrelevant to the good *physical* life, their corollaries (sexual repression, monogamy, exclusivity) have also lost relevance. The mores cannot lose power in one area of life without being seriously weakened in their hold over other areas. If deferred gratification of physical wants becomes outmoded in conditions of affluence, family systems and sexual practices associated with it also become outmoded.

The resulting experimentation with life-style thus invites questioning of *all* the old assumptions about the good, the moral, the proper, and the most meaningful. Variant family forms become one avenue for the pursuit of anwers to questions of meaning.

Variant family forms have already been legitimated or "professionalized" through organizations that promote and defend nonmodal alternative values and life-styles—as with Parents Without Partners or the National Organization for Non-Parents. In both cases also, redefinition of nuclear units has occured.

The nuclear unit itself may be considered "variant" in many parts of the world, vis-à-vis modal types of family structure, as for example where joint family (Pakistan) predominates. Whether in fact this is simply a case of how nuclear families relate, and whether the nuclear family is actually more prevalent than has been assumed in pre-industrial societies, has provided an interesting area of research also needing further study. Wozniak (1972), for example, questions the assumed relation between industrialization, the breakdown of extended families, and the presence of nuclear families as "new" modal types.

In this paper however it is assumed that on a world scale, families will come to and move through a nuclear structure; that attitudes toward that movement are defined and labeled in particular ways as a result of world processes; and that there is some historical basis for predicting the future direction and place of variant forms in world lifestyles.

"VARIANT" AND "DEVIANT"

The major difference between "variant" and "deviant" family forms appears to be the voluntary or involuntary character of their origins and the subjective sense of freedom or victimization associated with participants in those forms.

In terms of the larger social structure, they are similar in that both are nonmodal forms in a presumed modality which is nuclear, though the nuclear form may undergo re-formation with divorce and remarriage. Both "deviant" and "variant" forms do, however, tend to affront the values embodied in the prevailing mores. "Deviant" forms (consensual unions, female-headed households resulting from illegitimacy and desertion, child-abusers, alcoholic parents) in the context of the mores have "variant" counterparts, such as cohabitation, serial monogamy, and voluntary single parenthood. There are also communes in which children are allowed access to the sexual and drug-taking practices of their parents and which might be viewed as "abuse" in other contexts. (See Berger et al. 1973.) It is hardly accidental that these counterparts should exist. More privileged classes have begun to preempt forms of life-style which often were first found at less privileged class levels (Bernard 1972, p. 91 and passim).

"Deviant" forms, then, are so labeled in cases where suffering and deprivation occur, while "variant" forms are so labeled where they involve voluntary participation and a sense of self-actualization. The labeling of "deviant" forms has been done by professionals who tend to identify with middle- or upper middle-class values, and who regard lower-class variations as results of mental or physical pathology. In this sense, pathology equates with involuntary action, whether structurally induced or not. "Variant" forms thus are treated in the literature as voluntary or intentional formations created with relatively high degrees of consciousness of their unusual character. "Deviant" forms are involuntary, unintentional results of inability to conform to modal expectations. Those living in variant forms typically are able, outwardly, to conform easily to modal structural demands (education, work)—but a higher consciousness and sense of personal competence exacerbate dissatisfaction and impel the search for alternatives. In "deviant" forms, people have lost control over their lives, at least temporarily. In "variant" forms control over one's life has pursued with new determination. These contrasts are definitional; they are assumptions that underlie positive or negative evaluations by researchers. Also, one or more of the following tends to be assumed about deviant families: malintegration to the disadvantage of the larger society (Merton 1971); low degrees of self-esteem and mental health among participants in these structures (Liebow 1967); linkages to criminality where socialization and/or physical maintenance supports types of behavior which victimize the larger society economically and/or physically (Cohen 1955). Implicit notions of respectability also operate here: the middle-class women's choice of single parenthood is "liberation," while the same choice by a poor woman is assumed to involve ignorance of contraception and transience in the consensual union. The intentional quality of the form is thus at issue, with respectability affixing to variant intent rather than to deviant accident, as researchers perceive it.

Dissenters in the deviance area of sociological research have been notable for their attempts to link class structure to these biases in definition and labeling. Societal power arrangements—class systems and unequal distributions of opportunities, rewards, and penalities—structure the capacity of any group to gain legitimacy for its existence, especially where that existence lies outside the normative modality. Paul Rock's *Deviant Behavior* (1973) and its philosophical counterpart, John Rawl's *A Theory of Justice* (1971) are notable contributions to this evolving view of deviance. The term "variant family form," with its sense of harbinger-of-the-future, its avant garde air, is so labeled because the classes (middle and upper-middle) which predominate in reported research are the classes which have access to or control of reportage in the media and scholarly journals. They are the classes as well from which researchers are drawn, so that the experimenters share many problems and values with those who study them. The positive research orientation to "variant" family forms is thus in part a result of experimenters' apparently having solved problems confronted by the researchers as well. These classes, moreover, know how to exert political and legal pressure to protect themselves from repression and harassment. "Variant" as opposed to "deviant" is a definition, then, which is the outcome of a world process where definitional capacity has been placed in the hands of a favored class segment of the world-system. That favored segment, redefining its own needs and explorations, supplying the personnel of the research enterprise, reflects and projects its own adaptive-evolutionary movement into the research endeavor.

The rapidity with which this has occurred can be demonstrated by a hypothetical backward movement in time from 1974 to 1924 to consider, say, the idea of homosexual marriage. Fifty years ago such a marriage would be viewed as a pathological flaunting of perversion. As recently in fact as 1958 (and maintained without revision in 1968) Vidich and Bensman include as "pathological behavior disorders" alcoholism (which is currently more strongly defined as a physical disease than a social pathology), and "sexual perverts," a term so wide-ranging as to make no distinctions between gay lifestyles, exhibitionism, voyeurism, and so on (1968, p. 228).

Or again, in demonstration: the "Beats" of the 1950s living in "variant forms": they cohabited, they practiced "open marriage" in a number of forms. But they had little money, having opted out of the rewards system, and lived as role models for extremely few. They were *not* optimists about their nonconformity; they were "beat"—beaten down, beat out, as opposed to "self-actualizing" or "open"—terms to which variant form participants lay claim (Family Synergy *Newsletter*).

Participation in variant family forms by more privileged classes occurs as a result of processes in which (a) they can take risks as such risks show promise of meeting new needs and alleviating strains or boredom in older forms; (b) where worldwide media and multinational corporations extend questions of values and the class system profile beyond the "developed" areas of the world; and (c) where this risk-taking does not compromise the benefits or privileges derived from elite positions in the world class structure. Just as the label of "deviance" and its policy results are one mode of control over the experimentation of nonelites, "variant" definitions become justifications for similar experiments in elite contexts.

Given the ideological power of variant forms among participants, the variants may in fact constitute types of adaptive interphase between current modal norm sets, or modal structures, and modalities of the future. Using a bell curve diagram for convenience, change can be illustrated by juxtaposed curves: [See Fig. 1.]

Variant family forms are voluntary experiments of a wider variety and often higher consciousness than has been the case with interphase phenomena in the past. Oneida, Hutterites, and Bruderhof (the latter two persisting today) are exceptions partly because they locate in a world-setting vis-à-vis a cosmos of transcendent meaning (Zablocki 1971; Carden 1969; Swan 1972). Their "interphase" has been, subjectively, between this world and the next rather than a this-worldly future.

That part of the curve which reads "deviant" has also received a variety of treatments including the conflict perspective, as with the female-headed household in the culture of poverty which has been regarded as a dialectical-evolutionary phenomenon in an exploitative class structure (Rodman 1964; Ladner 1971). That classes below the middle class

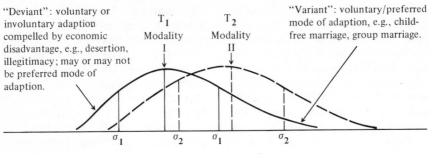

"Deviant": voluntary or involuntary adaption compelled by economic disadvantage, e.g., desertion, illegitimacy; may or may not be preferred mode of adaption.

T_1 Modality I

T_2 Modality II

"Variant": voluntary/preferred mode of adaption, e.g., child-free marriage, group marriage.

σ_1 σ_2 σ_1 σ_2

Figure 1

may consciously prefer modes of behavior labeled as "deviant" (such as "desertion," so labeled by researchers) or that these might be personally and/or economically rational adaptations has been given little credence. The capacity for conscious experimentation likewise has been overlooked, for those classes are too often stereotyped as unimaginative, uncreative, and anti-intraceptive.

But views of variant family forms that stem from a perceived rejection of monogamy and exclusivity also contain conflict elements. For example, as relative status positions of men, women, and children change, conflicting normative orientations must be anticipated in the mate selection and marital processes (Ramey 1972b). Not only are intergenerational norm changes built into a rapid-change social structure (Davis 1940), but there are also potential sources of conflict in the continual resocialization of spouses, so that homogamy at the outset of marriage no longer necessarily indicates the continued sharing of values through the marriage cycle (Toffler 1970). As increasing numbers of achieved statuses become available to both sexes of all ages, and as liberation movements proceed, the varieties of conflict possibilities increase simply in terms of individual status sets, let alone the concurrent status sets occupied by various members of a given family.[2] Forces external to the family also introduce normative legitimation or strain, so that an internal family dynamic is paralleled by a family-culture dynamic. Variant family forms as conflict adaptations would thus appear more likely as strains increase.

Both of these have been treated in the literature, but with limitations on the scale and historical scope of the phenomena. Moore's call for a "global

sociology" (1966a) and Wallerstein's "world-system" conceptualization are instances of attempts to treat the *world* as the social system and the scale appropriate to sociological study. (See Appendix pp. 441–442 for an elaboration of this perspective.)

In part, our current mode of family sociology has been influenced by its traditions starting with Ernest Burgess and the Chicago School. Family sociology began as a problem-solving enterprise, which examined the consequences for family systems of immediate, microlevel social forces. In later times, even where cross-national research has been attempted, there has been enormous difficulty in testing macrolevel propositions. Some of these can hold at a commonsense level alone—such as the change, with industrialization, from consanguineal to conjugal patterns as a modal type of change. Already, however, its common sense derives from an understanding of history and economics—so that these, elaborated in their world-scale interactive process, can be viewed as good steps forward in global understandings (Sussman 1974b).

The traditional change perspective in the study of family has tended to concentrate upon intra-institutional change. An alternative view might be to treat family as *process:* on a world-scale, it would be a study of multilevel varying-rate sets of concurrent forces moving in time, at a scale larger than that of one culture or any nationally bounded set of cultures and subcultures. An historical-evolutionary (adaptive) world view would serve as a framework against which current developments in the family could be set. It would incorporate the enlarged scale of world social forces as they act and react, including political and economic changes, and taking account of the world-scale arena of change.

Family as process would reflect the impact of the world-scale as life decisions are made in family settings. Economic decisions in the family, for example, are less and less likely to escape what economists have called "international demonstration effect," a shorthand term for the impetus to consumerism in nations with low levels of technological development.[3] In turn, there are consequences for family mobility, and indeed, fertility and mortality, in the drive for employment in cash economies; and where this drive is frustrated, political consequences are likely to include unrest, disruption, and even revolution.

As another example, courtship patterns on a world-scale are tied to economic and political forces in that nature of "homogamy" changes as social characteristics of a population (education, religion, et cetera) change; these changes in turn may be supported or resisted by political ideologies that defend particular systems of distributions of rights and privileges. Those ideologies may provide further leverage for younger age groups to assert their choices in courtship against their elders.

Although a world approach does not, by virtue of its assumptions, solve theoretical problems of deviance (definitions in a class-struggle framework still pose problems of values and socialization), it does provide two major advantages.

First, it lengthens the time perspective on social phenomena. Even Merton (1971) was compelled to distinguish types of deviance as those which are currently "destructive" and those which foreshadow wider acceptance when he separated "aberrant" from "nonconforming" behavior. What he described is more likely class process in time than a value process in limited temporal contexts. He contrasts the nonconformer with the aberrant: the nonconformer, for "disinterested purposes," denies in public the legitimacy of social norms, appealing "to an allegedly higher morality" (1971, pp. 830–831). Nonconformity is therefore knowledge and self-confidence, and an historical perspective that immediately bespeaks education and, therefore, class. It is a *post hoc* distinction between deviance which succeeds over time and that which fails.

A second advantage of world perspectives is the idea of *process* as the appropriate level for study

(Hopkins, 1974). Variants or deviations in this context become part of the range of components of a total phenomenon, rather than aberrations on modality. Multiple values and change-rate disparities could thus presumably be more effectively understood for policy uses than has been the case in the past.

"VARIANT" FORMS AND WORLD CLASS PROCESS

The links between the world class process as the outcome of the world division of labor and the visibility of variant family forms can be established through the answers to three questions: (1) What is making social experimentation so much more—and more consciously—possible among world elites? (2) Why is it visible on a world-scale, with potential for effect at that scale? (3) How does it affect world normative modalities? The answers to the first two involve education, income, the media, multinational (global) corporations, and the effect of visible countercultures through the media. The third question involves projections, and will be treated in the final section of this paper.

In terms of variant family forms, the relation between available income and the freedom to specify one's own areas of conformity or variation (which in a sense is Durkheim's organic solidarity carried to a very high degree of the freedom he saw inherent in it) is the capacity to draw on the rewards system at a high level. Scientists, academics, and supranational personnel of global corporations all operate in frameworks that transcend national boundaries and are instrumental in nature. All emphasize the demonstrable—whether in terms of evidence, argument, or profit—so that questions of meaning must be met. All these statuses at the same time encourage their occupants to use knowledge as a resource in examining options; those statuses likewise enable individuals and groups to buy certain kinds of immunity from the sanctioning-repression forces of their surrounding cultures. This involves the ability to take advantage of whatever protective legislation is available (e.g., using the courts to enforce rights of privacy; private property, even where held communally, establishing physical barriers against unfriendly surveillance; the ability to transfer from one geographical area to another, doing the same work but in less repressive settings); and they encourage a capacity to draw self-definition from the longer world view and higher sense of personal efficacy which accompany higher education and income.

To change this system of goods-and-rewards distribution yet maintain high productivity levels, there is Wallerstein's proposal of a socialist world government as an alternative, in which there would be a "reintegration of the levels of political and economic decision making" (1974, p. 348). Such a system would presumably open negotiated options which are presently available mainly to those who "opt out" completely or to the privileged groups just described who continue to obtain rewards of the current system while acting dialectically as potential forces in systemic change. The dialectic resides in the fact that those who benefit most are most likely to live in contradiction to modal norms within the prevailing system.

In this sense, the degree to which change at higher levels of the world class process presages change for all class levels may well depend on the continuing expansion of elite groupings throughout the world, or on a revolution which alters the nature of class process on a world scale. A "revolution" assumes that values change with a concomitant reduction of the threat of repression for all members of society. Until that time, visible adaptations and ideological views defending them are most likely of success where economic and knowledge power are available, and thus far it has centered in elites, especially those residing in more privileged parts of the world. Nonelites in such areas are more readily able to emulate—but not challenge too much—these apparently contracultural experiments. In less privileged areas those who wish to experiment may be less capable of open defense and consequently more likely to suffer penalties as negative influences or deviants.

Perhaps the single most important change in the world division of labor is the rise of the global corporation which, through the concentration of economic power on a world-scale, tends to produce more cohesive elites and their greater ability to control the diffusion of information about consumption and living styles (Barnet and Muller, 1975). The control of media above all is a control of visible aspirations, and although commentators have concentrated on the American dominance of communications or the decline of specifically American control, the pattern is one of promulgating values associated with the advance of technology. Schiller (1970), for example, though attacking the exploitative aspects of the American media empire, is actually speaking of world-system effects of media. Even a self-deluding book such as Lerner and Schramm's *Communication and Change in Developing Countries* (1967), where national culture is believed capable of prevailing against the impact of external values, must concede that same influence. Lerner (1967, p. 122–125), for example, speaks of empathy (the capacity to identify with strange situations) induced by the media, and that people are thereby encouraged to try new ways. "Empathy" as defined can only lead to changes in the norms, and norms can hardly be ignored as major components of any culture.

If programming and advertising—integral parts of the media package, especially in low-literacy countries where television is most useful for distributing entertainment-sales messages—are conveying values, they do so in a world of multiple and contradictory value processes. How these will continue and trigger a new chain-reaction effect, e.g., the decline of female chastity norms, marital options for both sexes (including built-in extramarital contact), the decline of institutional–religious control and the class/race/sex/liberations, need to be studied in a global perspective.

PROJECTIONS ON VARIANT FAMILY FORMS: CHILD-FREE LIFE-STYLES AND COMMUNAL FAMILIES

The global or world view of family process, then, stresses the linkage between family (and other institutional processes) and the world division of labor. As the global impact of media is felt cumulatively, and as control centers of production come to transcend national boundaries, reference groups also globalize. "Other families" whose forms of adaptation may be emulated with variations may reside in a different part of the planet. The capacity to identify with others, and the experience of strain and adaptation, are increasingly effects that operate simultaneously throughout the world on groups similarly located in the production-distribution process. Workers everywhere, for example, experience the urbanizing, standardizing conditions of work and share similar strains and felt grievances in the system of wages, distributions of goods and services, and aspirations for a better life. The more privileged in this system will also want "more" of what is perceived to be available and desirable. Because they are more favored in the distribution of system rewards, including leisure and education, those factors operate partly dialectically to question the system that provides them, and to question the meaning of possessing them. Wanting "more" then tends to entail finding more meaning, more freedom to work out problems of use and meaning, and more "rights" to protect their experimentation.

Some experiments such as swinging, group marriage, open marriage, and homosexual/lesbian marriage show promise of persisting as trial forms at least of variant life-styles. Specific projections, however, now seem most solid for child-free and communal families as two adaptations on a global scale. However long-term in effect the growing number and consciousness of child-free couples may actually be, their existence and increase appear solidly based in family trends of the next 30 to 50 years. And however transient the phenomenon of any given commune, including apparently long-term experiments such as Twin Oaks, the communal style of family living also has indications of persistence as a special form of option for individuals and families in the future. While the projections for these two may be generalizable to other types of variant family forms, the treatment limited here to these two constitutes: (a) a starting attempt which hopefully will be enlarged and expanded in scope and research by future efforts; and (b) a set of linked phenomena in which segmental and diffuse roles operate at different life points.

Child-free Life-styles

The expansion of achieved statuses available to both sexes correlates with the increasing division of labor and industrialization. Social definition by ascriptive characteristics tends to decline. In societies where increasingly segmental roles also make possible a wider capacity to establish friendship independent of kin networks (shifting the value –sanction systems) and where employment structures move individuals from subsistence to "maintenance," a term of convenience denoting a point where the daily struggle to exist is replaced by fairly steady income and opportunity; and where secularization reduces religio-familial control over the young while political processes legitimate their independence and economic processes implement it, questions of meaning and creative capacity tend to become more prominent. As maintenance advances to relative affluence ("relative" as a sense of enlarged freedom and options), personal creativity becomes a more significant value, while kin-group duties (e.g., having children) become less significant. "Creativity" denotes self-actualizing activities, those which locate the individual in expressive forms, in the sense of Lynd's (1939) "rhythms," the freed ebbs and flows of human energies. If at one time in extended or nuclear structures the major opportunities for creativity for women and men centered in the bearing and socialization of children, expansion of life opportunities beyond the confines of family and the technical capacity to avoid pregnancy also expand opportunities for creativity.

Such alternative opportunities reduce the allure of having children at all, or move the creative aspects of child rearing into even greater salience as they compete with other forms of creativity. In the latter case, where questions of meaning and values of "self-actualization" become more important, the creativity aspects of child rearing lose more to competing avenues of self-expression. "Drag" in the normative process, i.e., the persistence of norms under conditions which make conformity nonimperative, such as valuing having children to carry on family name or to maintain population levels, serves to introduce areas of conflict and strain into the decisional process over whether or not to have children. Segmental role structures and independence of kin networks serve to reduce strain by reducing required physical contact with older kin, and thereby, the contact with values which have ceased to constitute "imperatives."[4]

As both sexes have educational opportunities of wider scope and greater parity, the cost to females of having children becomes relatively greater than the status rewards of motherhood, where the trade-off is motherhood for career. While for many families the career and child rearing structures may combine, they remain essentially contradictory sets of obligations under modern work conditions. The articulation of these strains, in demands for day care and in divorce rates which rise despite the presence of young children of divorcing parents, represent justifications for those who resolve potential strain by opting out of parenting roles. The media make these life-styles more visible, so that the child-free become potential models which others may follow, while the capacity of children to bond a married pair more tightly visibly declines. Age segregation, enhanced by educational and residential patterns, further reduces a sense of generational continuity; and immediate gratification of needs defined by age peers add to psychic costs of child rearing as opposed to child-free life-styles. Where population pressure is already great, and where productivity bases can be maintained by substituting machinery for people (automation), political pressures which encourage or discourage child-free life-styles become policies which are outgrowths of technological capacities to plan for and support aging populations, and perceived military threat of lack of it. Either would impel a use of fiscal and legislative measures to increase or decrease the number of children people have. As the number of child-free couples increases in classes which have definitional and policy capacity, or where those couples can effectively defend their options against redefinitions by other groups in the population, child-free life-styles may persist as permanent options among increasing numbers of couples, or as long-term options in which the choice of having a child is longer and longer delayed in the marriage cycle. The global media may accelerate this process in areas where religious and kin networks still maintain relatively high degrees of control over the young, so that the media accelerate the rate of socialization to normative options which first evolve out of more advanced conditions of economy and technology.

The freedom exercised in conditions of high segmentation will not necessarily suffice to express a full range of life choices. The option for more diffuse life-styles may also be desired, in the search for values and meaning, and here is where the future role of the communal family seems greatest.

Communal Family Structures

The communal experience shows promise of becoming at least a temporary option for an increasing number of individuals and families. The very reason advanced to explain the transience of the communal option—individualism as an intensified value in postindustrial society, and use of group experience to enhance insight into self (Veysey 1974)—would justify a projected continuation and expansion of that experience in population where the division of labor had advanced to maintenance and beyond. In exploring avenues of creativity and meaning, a variety of options will be tested and they are related to the evolution of status and role sequence in the world process over time.[5] For those who enter and leave communal settings, that experience constitutes part of the total sequential role patterns of their lives. Some enter and remain in communal settings. For others, just as expanded educational and work opportunities have expanded the total number of status and role sequences (e.g., for women, from high school-to-marriage, to high school—college—work—marriage), so communal living may become an additional, optional gradient on a global scale.

In fact, variant family forms such as communes may serve in the role sequence as future equivalents of monastic retreat houses in the middle ages. They become a place in which to live intensely a certain value-style, and to explore one's relation to the universe in a communal framework. As then, so in the future, communes may constitute places of renewal, self-integration, and alternative experience. As extended kin networks and joint households offer reduced attractions for or contradict such experiences, intentional families tend to serve as way stations to self-knowledge, where that knowledge becomes counterpoise to the scientific advances which structure the technological society. Communal families moreover easily fit the modular conception of industrialized societies; ongoing communes, like the monasteries or Twin Oaks, can absorb and send forth members without internal disruption.

A world perspective on these, then, would look across cultures to the spectrum of options available in different world areas at the same time, with an eye to the enlargement of the spectrum in any given place, the global causes, and the consequent effects of that enlargement.

APPENDIX: THE "GLOBAL" OR "WORLD-SYSTEM" VIEW

Work in sociology toward understanding the intimate connection between changing economic mode, world scale, its political and necessarily familial consequences, has treated the nation-state as the major boundary between cultures (e.g., Goode 1963; Blisten 1963; Nimkoff 1965).

In 1966 Wilbert Moore counseled social scientists that the nation-state has ceased to demarcate major cultural influences (1966a, p. 480). "Global Sociology" would treat the *world* as a system, in no small part due to increasing similarities bred by the world division of labor. Immanuel Wallerstein in *The Modern World System* (1974; first of a projected four volumes) has most recently called for a world-system approach, and provides the following framework for that perspective:

A. The only social system is world-system; social change can be discussed only in that context. (Note: See Moore, 1966a, who makes a similar point.) That world system has persisted for 500 years with no sign of its disappearing.

B. The premise of world-system is that the world division of labor has underpinned every other world process in the past 500 years. Change is accounted for by an internal conflict dynamic moving through time, within the self-contained organism that is the world-system.

C. The conflict dynamic is embodied in world-system class processes. Differing relations to the division of labor (the organization of production) and the rewards obtained from it, delineate classes and status groups. These are key elements in the world-system which are analyzed in turn by their self-consciousness and the geographical scope of their self-definition (1974, p. 351).

D. The world view incorporates multiple value systems juxtaposed at any given time in the modern world (1974, p. 356). This assumes rates of change within the world-system which vary among world social pressures and which vary in time and duration.

E. Quantification is now impossible with the historical data and methodological sophistication available; in fact, the methodological questions are continuingly the object of attention from those who use world-system perspective to illuminate world social processes. Wallerstein's stated method is to describe the world-system at the level of "the evolutions of structures of the whole system," while particular events are described "only insofar as they threw light upon the system as typical instances of some mechanism, or as they were crucial turning points in institutional change" (1974, p. 8). Microlevel data, while not sufficient to describe world processes, are useful to provide and study indicators of what are in fact macrolevel changes.

F. In order to elucidate the character of world-system, there is need for a "unidisciplinary approach" in which anthropology, economics, political science, sociology and history cease to demarcate limited areas of study, or even to constitute a multidisciplinary approach, but rather are interwoven to provide concurrent treatment of the processes in world-system change (1974, p. 11).

World-scale has not been ignored outside sociology: Margaret Mead (1970) set it as her framework to explain the simultaneous change which affects youth irrespective of their national locations. In fact, world-scale as the necessary framework for research and speculation was anticipated by Adam Smith in 1776 and received much attention earlier in this century from Graham Wallas (1914) and his student, Walter Lippmann (1936). All three perceived a world process which was the outgrowth of the division of labor and consequent increased interdependence of nations, so that nations would cease to constitute organic and self-contained entities, but would become part of the international division of labor which would result in a world-entity. They viewed the world system as a reflection of the rise of capitalism. Even the socialist world view, crystallized in Marx's work and continued since, assumes world commonalities. Marx abhorred the division of labor and its consequences; he viewed class rather than nation as the moving force in history, and class struggle as its dynamic. But he above all envisaged a Utopia in which work would be "life's prime want" (1875) so

that the Calvinist-Capitalist connections made by Weber can be ultimately embodied in Marx. The irony, of course, was that Weber's *Protestant Ethic* was an attempt to counter the Communist Manifesto's philosophy that social being—class —alone determines consciousness. But modern technology *without* a division of labor appears more than utopian; it would be, within our current social-organization capacities, a speculation on the order of science fiction.

Latter-day thinkers who prefer the socialist alternative do not envisage the utopian communist state which Marx saw, but rather assume a continued division of labor though without its exploitative aspects in the class system. Even those advocating visionary answers to the modern technocracy's impact on human lives assume both world-scale and adaptation to the division of labor (Roszak 1973).

NOTES

1. For the purposes of this paper, the term "variant family forms" subsumes "variant marital forms." This author's research among childless couples, for example, indicates that such spouses consider their dyad a family. Moreover, "variant family form" as the generic term, implies marital adaptations. In the case of married couples swinging, where children are typically excluded from involvement, the family form (swinging spouses, "normal" child-rearing patterns) as a *whole* is variant, the marital arrangements constituting a variant subsystem in a nuclear family. Even here, however, effects on the family in terms of how children will be socialized hardly seem avoidable.

2. This terminology follows Merton (1957, pp. 369–370) wherein role set is defined as "that *complement of role relationships which persons have by virtue of occupying a particular social status*" (empasis in original). At a given time, a person's full complement of statuses constitutes the status set.

3. In such cases, investment in development tends to be hampered by an unwillingness to save and a preference to spend, because consumer goods are visible through international media which advertise lifestyles and possessions available to developed areas in which savings for and resultant industrial development already occurred. If a country moves to close its borders against consumer-oriented influences, it is likely to open or intensify contact with world areas that have faced similar problems, and adopt ideologies to support closure which are likely to have consequences for the relative statuses of family members.

Cuba and China are nations that come to mind as examples of this; they have not extricated themselves from world influences but have chosen to emphasize and exlude different types of orientation available in the world political context. Over time, there has been "re-entry" into contact with world areas of different orientation, but in each case only after a strong ideological program has fixed the directions of economic preference. Although they once again open themselves to international demonstration effect, with pressures from their people to spend rather than invest, the status changes that occurred tend to persist and evolve on egalitarian lines rather than traditional-consumer ones, and this in turn reflects in male-female patternings. Problems in estimating such effects were noted by Liberson and Hansen (1974) though they focused on linguistic diversity.

4. Options may be secured by marital contracts. There is an apparent contradiction between self-revelation/openness and the use of written contracts for the household or marital bond. Yet where economic survival and clan alliances recede as powerful motives for marriage, and love advances as the only reasonable ground on which dyads form, contracts may reflect the normative lag (or "drag") upon new life-styles. In macrosociological terms, as roles grow more segmental, contractual specificity in a diffuse (love) relationship reflects the voluntaristic nature of marital or dyadic bonds. Contractual arrangements need not be made for norms so generally internalized

as to constitute modal forms of everyday behavior; such arrangements tend rather to reflect juxtaposed and conflicting value systems. Traditional values antithetical to freely formed, androgynous dyads might erode relationships embodying new values. Contracts may attempt to avoid this erosion.

5. Again, the terminology follows Merton: "the succession of statuses occurring with sufficient frequency as to be socially patterned will be designated as *status sequence*" (1957, p. 370, emphasis in original). And: "Conducing to this function of anticipatory socialization is the structural circumstance of what can be called 'role gradations.'" The individual moves more or less continuously through a sequence of statuses and associated roles, each phase of which does not differ greatly from the one that has gone before" (1957, p. 385).

REFERENCES

BARNET, RICHARD, AND RONALD MULLER. *Global reach: the power of the multinational corporations.* New York: Simon and Schuster. 1975. Originally appearing in the *New Yorker*, December 2 and December 9, 1974.

BERGER, BENNET M., BRUCE M. HACKETT, AND MERVYN R. MILLER. *Child-rearing practices in the communal family.* Progress report to the National Institute of Mental Health, Grant No. 1-RO1-MH 16570-01A1SP to Scientific Analysis Corporation, San Francisco, 1973.

BERNARD, JESSIE. *The future of marriage.* New York: Bantam, 1972.

BLISTEN, DOROTHY R. *The world of the family: a comparative study of family organizations in their social and cultural settings.* New York: Random House, 1963.

CARDEN, MAREN LOCKWOOD. *Oneida: utopian community to modern corporation.* Baltimore: The Johns Hopkins Press, 1969.

COHEN, ALBERT. *Delinquent boys: the culture of the gang.* New York: Free Press, 1955.

Communities: A journal of cooperative living. Twin Oaks Community, Rt. 4, Louisa, Va. 23093.

DAVIS, KINGSLEY. The sociology of parent-youth conflict. *American Sociological Review,* 1940, 5: 523-534.

————. The myth of functional analysis as a special method in sociology and anthropology. *American Sociological Review,* 1959, 24: 757-773.

DURKHEIM, EMILE. *The elementary forms of the religious life.* New York: Free Press, (1965), 1915.

————. *The division of labor in society.* Glencoe: Free Press, 1933.

————. *Suicide: a study in sociology.* London: Routledge and Kegan Paul, Ltd., 1952.

Family synergy. *Newsletter,* P.O. Box 30103 Terminal Annex, Los Angeles, 1970-1974.

GOODE, WILLIAM J. *World revolution and family patterns.* New York: Free Press-Macmillan, 1963.

————. Introduction. In William J. Goode, Elizabeth Hopkins, and Helen McClure (eds.), *Social systems and family patterns: a propositional inventory.* New York: Bobbs-Merrill, 1971.

HARRINGTON, MICHAEL. *The accidental century.* New York: Macmillan, 1965.

HOPKINS, TERENCE K. Presentation at ASA annual meetings, Montreal, Canada, 1974.

INKELES, ALEX, AND PETER N. ROSSI. National comparisons of occupational prestige. *American Journal of Sociology,* 1956, 61: 329-339.

KOMAROVSKY, MIRRA. Cultural contradictions and sex roles. *American Journal of Sociology,* 1946, 52: 184-189.

LADNER, JOYCE. *Tomorrow's tomorrow: the black woman.* Garden City, N.Y.: Doubleday, 1971.

LERNER, DANIEL, AND WILBUR SCHRAMM (eds.). *Communication and change in developing countries.* Honolulu: East-West Center Press, 1967.

LIBBY, ROGER W., AND ROBERT N. WHITEHURST (eds.). *Renovating marriage: toward new sexual life-styles.* Danville, Calif.: Consensus Publishers, 1973.

LIEBERSON, STANLEY, AND LYNN K. HANSEN. National development, mother tongue, and the comparative study of nations. *American Sociological Review,* 1974, 39: 523-541.

LIEBOW, ELLIOT. *Tally's corner.* Boston: Little, Brown, 1967.

LIPPMANN, WALTER. *The good society.* New York: Grosset and Dunlap University Library, 1936.

LYND, ROBERT S. *Knowledge for what? The place of social science in American culture.* New York: Grove Press Evergreen, (1946), 1939.

MARCIANO, TERESA D. Suburban physical and social structures. *Growth and Change,* 1975, 6, (2): 9-13.

MARX, KARL. Critique of the Gotha program. Reprinted in Lewis S. Fleur (ed.), *Marx and Engels: basic writings on politics and philosophy.* Garden City: Doubleday, 1975.

MEAD, MARGARET. *Culture and commitment.* New York: Natural History Press, 1970.

MERTON, ROBERT K. *Social theory and social structure.* (Rev. ed.) Glencoe, Ill.: Free Press, 1957.

_____. Social problems and sociological theory. In Robert K. Merton and Robert Nisbet (eds.), *Contemporary social problems.* (3rd ed.) New York: Harcourt, Brace, Jovanovich, 1971.

MOORE, WILBERT E. Global sociology: the world as a singular system. *American Journal of Sociology,* 1966a, **71**: 475–482.

_____. The utility of Utopias. *American Sociological Review,* 1966b, **31**: 765–772.

NIMKOFF, M. F. (ed.). *Comparative family systems.* Boston: Houghton Mifflin, 1965.

RAMEY, JAMES W. Emerging patterns of innovative behavior in marriage. *Family Coordinator,* 1972a, **21**: 435–456.

_____. Communes, group marriage, and the upper-middle class. *Journal of Marriage and the Family,* 1972b, **34**: 647–655.

RAWLS, JOHN. *A theory of justice.* Cambridge: Harvard University Press, 1971.

REICH, CHARLES A. *The greening of America.* New York: Random House, 1970.

ROCK, PAUL. *Deviant behavior.* London: Hutchinson, 1973.

RODMAN, HYMAN. Middle-class misconceptions about lower-class families. In Arthur B. Shostak and William Gomberg (eds.), *Blue-collar world.* Englewood Cliffs, N.J.: Prentice-Hall, 1964.

ROSZAK, THEODORE. *The Making of a counterculture: reflections and transcendence in postindustrial society.* Garden City: Doubleday, 1969.

_____. *Where the wasteland ends.* New York: Doubleday Anchor, 1973.

SCHILLER, HERBERT I. *Mass communications and American empire.* New York: Augustus Kelley, 1970.

SKOLNICK, ARLENE, AND JEROME H. SKOLNICK. *Family in transition: rethinking marriage, sexuality, child rearing, and family organization.* Boston: Little, Brown, 1971.

_____. *Intimacy, family, and society.* Boston: Little, Brown, 1974.

SLATER, PHILIP. *The pursuit of loneliness.* Boston: Beacon Press, 1970.

SMITH, ADAM. *An inquiry into the nature and causes of the wealth of nations.* London: Dent (1962), 1776.

SUSSMAN, MARVIN (ed.) Variant marriage styles and family forms. *Family Coordinator,* 1972, **21**: Entire Issue.

_____. *Sourcebook in marriage and the family,* 4th ed. Boston: Houghton-Mifflin, 1974a.

_____. Cross-national research: an impossible dream? Paper presented to the World Congress of Sociology, Toronto, Canada, August, 1974b.

SWAN, JON. The 400-year-old-commune. *Atlantic,* 1972, **230**, (5), 90–100.

TOFFLER, ALVIN. *Future shock.* New York: Random House, 1970.

VEYSEY, LAURENCE. Communal sex and communal survival: Individualism busts the commune boom. *Psychology Today,* 1974, 8, (7), 73–79.

VIDICH, ARTHUR J., AND JOSEPH BENSMAN. *Small town in mass society: class, power, and religion in a rural community.* (Rev. ed.) Princeton, N.J.: Princeton University Press, 1968.

WALLAS, GRAHAM. *The great society: a psychological analysis.* Lincoln: University of Nebraska Press, (1967), 1914.

WALLERSTEIN, IMMANUEL. *The modern world-systems: capitalist agriculture and the origins of the European world economy in the sixteenth century.* New York: Academic Press, 1974.

WOZNIAK, PETER. *Family systems, industrialization, and demographic factors: an appraisal of the arguments and evidence.* Paper presented at ASA, New Orleans, 1972.

ZABLOCKI, BENJAMIN. *The joyful community: an account of Bruderhof, a communal movement now in its third generation.* Baltimore: Pelican, 1971.

Beyond Equality of the Sexes: The Question of the Children[1]

JUDITH LORBER

THE CURRENT CALLS FOR REFORM OR revolution in sex roles, family structure, and child-rearing patterns have neglected to tackle the enormous question of what will happen when women's liberation succeeds in achieving all its goals. Since these goals are nothing less than the removal of the structural mechanisms that in the past have guaranteed the production and socialization of children, it is extremely important that we all be prepared with alternatives to the system currently being breached.

One feminist goal—legalized abortion on demand —has now totally separated sexual activity from procreation in the United States, and *Newsweek* reported on July 16, 1973 that 12.7 million single people in this country are between the ages 20 and 34, the prime childbearing years. If the United States Congress passes the Equal Rights Amendment, husbands and fathers will no longer be legally responsible for the support of their wives and children, and we will have attained a second feminist goal—removal of the legal underpinnings of the sexual division of labor. Women, whether they like it or not, will have to support themselves and their share of their children. They are then sure to insist on equal opportunities for gainful employment throughout their lifetimes, and in order to take advantage of these opportunities, quite likely to restrict their production of children, especially if adequate and affordable child-care services are not available.[2]

Another feminist goal is total freedom of choice of sex partners throughout one's life. The effect of a lifelong sexual market has been predicted to be compatible with monogamatic marriage provided there is openness, swinging, multilaterality, or serialness (see Sussman 1972). But the result seems to be a divorce epidemic, with almost 900,000 divorces in 1973 (Roberts 1974).

If we remove the structural underpinnings of marriage and the family that have supported these systems in the past—sexual division of labor, economic dependence on males of women and children, and the combination of procreation with sex —can we still achieve an orderly system of coupling and child rearing? If the structural mechanisms which guaranteed a replacement level of fertility and relatively stable parenting in the past are eroded, what new structural mechanisms can take their place?

PAST STRUCTURAL SUPPORTS TO STABLE PARENTING

Levi-Strauss (1973, p. 30) argues that:

> . . . when the family is given a small functional value, it tends to disappear even below the level of the conjugal type. . . . Our would-be universal conjugal family, then, corresponds more to an unstable equilibrium between extremes than to a permanent and everlasting need coming from the deepest requirements of human nature.

His contention is that an artificial division of labor between the sexes is socially necessary if heterosexual coupling of any continuity is to take place, and that need for heterosexual coupling is not to provide sexual satisfaction or emotional intimacy but to guarantee the production of children. (Also see Murdock 1965, pp. 7–10.) Similarly, the artificial division of a social group into those who can marry each other and those who cannot marry each other ensures the affiliation of groups larger than nuclear families. We have reduced, in Western

Reprinted from the *Family Coordinator* (Oct., 1975) by permission of the author and publisher.

society, the bonds of kinship affiliation. If we remove the sexual division of labor, we may have destroyed the basic structural mechanisms for long-term heterosexual coupling. As Sidney M. Greenfield pointed out in 1965 (p. 374):

> ...in this affluent, market-oriented society all basic needs can be satisfied in the market. That is, there is no fundamental sexual division of labor that leads men and women to marry because they cannot survive without the services of a mate. Everything from food and clothing to sexual gratification can be purchased in the market.

One thing, however, is not very well provided in the market, and that is love. Greenfield argued that there was still a structural mechanism encouraging marriage in the Western world—the force of romantic love. For Americans, the expected climax of falling in love has been marriage. Thus, "...the romantic love complex in middle-class America serves as the reward-motive that induces individuals to occupy the structurally essential positions of husband–father and wife–mother" (Greenfield 1965, p. 375). But if romantic love can strike once, it can strike twice, three times, who knows how many times in a lifetime if there are no restrictions. As long as the choices remain open, you have, in Juliet Mitchell's wry words, "that absurdity—a *free* choice for *life*" (1971, p. 114, italics in original). As she puts it:

> There is a formal contradiction between the voluntary contractual character of "marriage" and the spontaneous uncontrollable character of "love"—the passion that is celebrated precisely for its involuntary force. The notion that it occurs only once in every life and can therefore be integrated into a voluntary contract, becomes decreasingly plausible in the light of everyday experience—once sexual repression as a psychoideological system becomes at all relaxed.

Certainly, the use of the motive—"I've fallen in love with someone else," or "I'm not in love with you any more"—as a reason to divorce is a case in point.

If, then, we do not have a sexual division of labor or the need for long-term emotional intimacy to ensure fairly long-term heterosexual coupling, what is to guarantee the continued production and socialization of children in postindustrial Western societies? So far, childhood socialization of girls for future motherhood and later social pressure, particularly from potential grandparents, have ensured at least one marriage and the bearing of one or two children. However, with the increasing divorce rate, the consequent need for gainful employment among mothers, and the lack of adequate professional child care, women are growing increasingly disenchanted with the idea of having children, and the current population rate in the United States is for the first time below replacement level. Because of overpopulation, restriction on the birthrate has had moral support. But suppose current trends continue? Experience in the Soviet Union after the first World War and the early days of the Israeli kibbutzes shows that without social encouragement to have children, and with the attraction of equal opportunities for work, woman can reduce their birthrate to the point where the adult labor supply is drastically curtailed. In both historical instances, a return to conventional family patterns ensured an adequate birthrate. It may be increasingly difficult, however, for governments to return to pronatalist policies once women have a taste of the freedom that comes from antinatalism, productive careers, and sexual openness. Why should they go back to being submissive wives and self-sacrificing mothers?

The more radical feminists, such as Mitchell (1971) and Firestone (1971), advocate nonbiological reproduction of children as the cornerstone for the complete liberation of women, but so far *in utero* pregnancy has not been technologically replaced. However, the actual production of children is not the problem so much as what seems to be their need for stable parenting during the greater part of childhood if they are going to be able to develop into responsible adulthood (cf. Goldstein *et al.* 1973). Less radical advocates of reform see the solution in shared parental and work roles plus good professional child care (Rossi 1964; Bernard 1972, pp. 248–66). But how are parental and work roles to be shared if the parents do not stay married, and the typical pattern after divorce is for fathers to be economic supports and weekend playmates for their children? In her *Redbook* article, "Marriage in Two Steps," Margaret Mead (1966) advocated long-term marital contracts if there are children. Firestone, who feels with Mitchell that diversified households are just as good for children as two heterosexual parents, argues for groups of ten adults and three to four children to contract to live together for ten-to-twelve-year periods (1971, pp. 229–234). Given the current trends, couples or diversified households would probably choose not to be responsible for children rather than have their options for individual freedom so curtailed. The members of some religious communes have made such commitments, but they have sacrificed individual goals for those of the group (see Kanter 1972; Zablocki 1971).

The basic sociological question that has so far gone unanswered is—what structural arrangements can be devised to ensure the stable socialization of children in postindustrial societies and at the same time maximize individual freedom for both women and men?[3] By structural arrangements is meant institutionalized rewards, either monetary or psychological, and legal or strong societal enforcements for approved behavior. It is impractical to assume that children will be conceived, carried to term, birthed, and raised for fifteen to twenty years without strong and well-enforced social pressures. As Davis and Blake (1956) have shown, fertility rates do not happen accidentally, but are the result of the push and pull of pronatalist or antinatalist structural arrangements. Some alternative structural arrangements already exist as variant family forms in our society. Each has its advantages and disadvantages. An examination of several structural arrangements and their social implications may lead to a better sense of what deliberate child-rearing policies we want to encourage for the future.

PARENTING BY SELECTED GROUPS

One possible child-rearing arrangement is to produce and raise all the children by a few selected parents, using a combination of sociopsychological and monetary rewards and elevating parenthood to the status of a religious vocation. Family-focused, geographically stable, close-knit communities with

maximum fertility and life-long monogamy do exist at present. And interestingly, the tie that binds them and infuses their desire to have many children is their religion. These high-fertility groups are the Amish, the Hutterites, the Mormons, fundamentalist Protestants, Orthodox Jews, and traditional Catholics.

If, however, such a system were to put the socialization of children first, and religious persuasion second, rather than having people born in a family-oriented group produce many children, future parents could be selected at an early age by test, personality, and "call." They could then be separated from the nonparentally minded children for training in special schools for their main future roles as the producers and socializers of the country's children. They would have to vow to live with one mate and their children for life. They would also have to bear and rear the maximum number of children humans can produce during the fertility bearing period. Both parents should be paid for their parenting work out of the taxes of the nonparents, although the families could work at farming, handcrafts, or cottage industries.

It would probably be a good idea for the families to live in communities separate from the singles, who would be encouraged not to have children, although they could, of course, mate as they pleased. Extensive use of contraception and abortions would keep the singles' fertility rate to a minimum. The few children they had should, for the child's welfare, be given to a family to be raised properly.

The disadvantage of such a system of socialization is that, if all family life were relegated to a select group, a deep social division between the family-oriented and the individually oriented would soon emerge because of the different social values of each group. The family-oriented, even today, value monogamy, kinship, geographical stability, and their supportive religious beliefs, and disapprove of free sexuality, divorce, contraception, and abortion on demand. In contrast, the individually oriented value flexible mating rules, efficient contraception, and abortion on demand in order to pursue their individual goals, be they travel, job hopping, creative work, or polymorphous sexuality. Encouraging the production and rearing of children only by those with a family-oriented calling, while the nonfamily-oriented are left free to follow their individual pursuits, is probably not compatible with a unified society.

However, if the world's countries are divided into the child-oriented and the nonchild-oriented, the world's population needs could adequately be met in the near future by just the currently over-populated, underdeveloped countries. If we envisage a world-system of child-exchange, those in nations with surplus wealth could be taxed to support the poor parents and children, and the parents could then ship their children to the low-fertility countries to supply their needs for labor. Such a system of emigration is actually happening today, but by adults, mostly males, whose affectional ties are still with their countries of origin. A common occurrence is then a value conflict between the traditionally minded immigrant laborers and the modern importers of that labor.

A simpler arrangement could be devised by which the underpopulated industrialized nations bought the surplus children of the overpopulated nations at an early age. But if such a system is not to end up in exploitation and indentured labor, then the qualified imported children must have an opportunity to be educated for administrative and professional positions. A system of removing children from their parents and educating them for future occupations is still another kind of child-rearing arrangement to be considered.

PROFESSIONAL BREEDERS AND CHILD-REARERS

In addition to or in place of importing children, a system of completely professional breeders and child rearers could be developed. Childbearing could be a profession and could be conducted with the best of modern technology—fertility drugs for multiple births, sperm banks, embryo transfers, and uterine implants to expand the gene pool, and so on (cf. Keller 1971). Professional breeders could be paid top salaries, like today's athletes, for the 15–20 years of their prime childbearing time. Those who were impregnated could live in well-run dormitories, with excellent physical care, food, and entertainment.

The children born of these professional breeders could be reared by well-trained professional parent-teachers in age-graded peer groups. They could live in small cottages with attached schools. The professional parent-teachers could specialize in age groups, as in the Israeli kibbutz, or as our school-teachers do. In order to foster primary group relationships, the children's peer groups could remain the same until they were ready for the adult world.

But could they function on their own adult-hood? In *Children of the Dream*, Bettelheim notes the group conformity, the severe reduction in a sense of individuality, and the repression of feelings among kibbutz-raised children, which he attributes to their communal upbringing (1969, pp. 223–319). Certainly, bureaucratic, state-run institutions would have enormous possibilities for totalitarianism and limitation of choices of occupation and living arrangements. Professionalism means standards, and who is to set the standards where there are no interested parents to exert some pressure? The probable outcome might be the nightmare envisaged by old and new science-fiction writers, with children specifically bred and trained for certain roles (see Huxley 1939, Berger 1973). Of course, other writers, notably Skinner (1962, 1971) take a positive view of scientific socialization.

Even without the science-fiction aspects, the question of professionalism in child rearing raises serious questions for the immediate future. Currently, parenting in America is an amateur enterprise, and inherited and self-developed concepts and techniques of child rearing prevail. The dominance of the lay person is not really jeopardized by the existence of professionals, such as pediatricians, child psychologists and psychiatrists, and school teachers. The books of pediatricians and child psychologists and psychiatrists offer advice that may or may not be followed by the parents of well, normal children. When professionals must be turned to for help with a medical or emotional problem, their expertise is deferred to because of the parents' limited knowledge, but only with reference to that problem.

Schoolteachers, despite mass education legally imposed from the ages of six to sixteen, have never dominated the child-rearing process. First, they get a child already socialized at home and do not ever have the child anywhere near full time. Second, they do not have the prestige, autonomy, or full authority of true professionals; in their social status, organizational position, and control over their work, they are semiprofessionals (see Lortie 1969; Simpson and Simpson 1969; Leggatt 1970). Third, they too are frequently mothers, and so they and the lay people primarily responsible for child rearing share many of the same values when they are of the same social class. Consequently, the socialization of American children has, to date, been dominated by untrained female amateurs and trained female semiprofessionals.

If child rearing should become fully professionalized, so that children are put in the care of professional child rearers at an early age and for most of their waking lives, then the values of the professionals will prevail, and these may not necessarily reflect the values of the parents. In countries where the professional child rearers invoke governmental values, as in Communist China, and these are also subscribed to by the parents, there is little conflict or dissatisfaction (Sidel 1972). Should, however, the parents' values differ from professional values, then, given the professionals' authority, which will be derived from their technical expertise and will be backed by social prestige, professional values will supersede those of the parents. Unless there is a system of alternative services available to parents, child rearing could become a monopoly dominated by the knowledge, concepts, and values of one type of professional, who, by virtue of their control of recruitment and training and autonomy over their work, would allow for only one system of childhood socialization. (For an account of this process in medicine, see Freidson 1970a, 1970b.)

A second major danger in the total professionalization of child rearing is that women may end up, not the pragmatically trained lay experts they are today, but simply the passive consumers of male-dominated services. Such masculinization occurred in American gynecology and obstetrics at the beginning of this century, when experienced female midwives were legally driven from practice by university trained, mostly male, obstetricians (Kobrin 1966). The replacement for normal childbirth of lay experts by professionals has resulted in

an impersonal, overly technical, male-dominated service which is now, in a kind of pendulum swing, being challenged by feminist self-help health groups.

Can, then, professional experts in child rearing be used to provide widely available services to relieve individual parents of the total burden of child rearing without having the professionals dominate the process? They could—if parents were a large, vocal, highly involved, and prestigious group.

CHILD SERVICE OR PAIRING

There is a possible system that could combine professional expertise and services with individual, emotionally intimate child rearing, and also not interfere with anyone's free sexual and occupational choices. The system I would like to suggest is one which pairs one child to one adult in a kind of national "child-service." In such a system every able-bodied adult would be encouraged, if not required, to be fully responsible for the rearing of one child. Whether anyone could raise more than one child would depend on population needs. There could be exemptions from child service on the grounds of some kind of conscientious objection, but the social values should be such as to make child rearing a highly approved activity. There must be a good state-supported system of a variety of professional child-care services and schools, so that every parent could work or go to school or play part of the day and be parent part of the day. It would also be useful to have child allowances to even out economic inequities and allow greater choice of alternative child-care services.

The child one reared could be one's biological child or an adopted child. The sexes of parents and children could be mixed, as there would be no sexual division of labor. Each adult could give his/her child his/her name, and be legally responsible for financial support, emotional sustenance, and upbringing. Parent and child could live with each other, with another parent and child of the same or opposite sex, in larger households, or in communes. Adults would be free to choose sexual partners of either sex, to form long- or short-term relationships, or none at all. If a couple had two biological children, one could be assigned to him and one to her, thus obviating a custody fight should the couple decide to separate and live with others.

Such a system of child service could first, spread the burden of child rearing among all able-bodied adults; second, permit freedom of sexual choice and living arrangements among adults without disturbing children's identification and emotional stability; third, give adults kin they can call their own no matter how they choose to mate sexually; and finally, legally assign social responsibility for every child in the society. If adults received their children at about the ages of 18 to 20, given a lifespan of about 70 years, you could have three-to-four generation families. With the unilineal descent system of parent–child, such families would consist legally of three to four people with the same name, which is about the size of many intact nuclear families today. The addition of friends, lovers, colleagues, and house-mates could of course expand one's intimate network, but even without nonfamily others, there would always be at least *one* person everyone could call his or her own. (In case of death, another parent or child could be paired up.) Such a kinship system would spread not only the work of child rearing, but the joys, too. As Margaret Drabble said in an article entitled "With All My Love, (Signed) Mama" (1973):

> If I had written a piece a few years ago declaring that children were my greatest pleasure, many people would have assumed that I was simply being polite, dutiful, womanly, and deceitful. Now, thank goodness, I may well be considered grossly irresponsible and wicked, and may therefore be believed.

The beginnings of such a system of parent–child pairing can be seen in the single-parent movement, where single people, male and female, are becoming parents by birth or adoption without having been or planning to be married (cf. Klein 1973). Many of the features of pairing could be instituted today by married or cohabiting couples who want to have children but are realistic about the possibilities of a split. Men could refuse to support anyone but themselves and one-half of any children shared with a woman. Since judges

still automatically award custody to the mother if she wants the children and an unmarried father has no rights over his children if a mother will not accept child support, if men do not want to be deprived of their children in case of a split-up, they should insist on two children and a written guarantee that one of them will be permanently theirs without a custody fight.

Women could also support themselves and contribute half the support of any children they share with a man. They could decide not to take on a man's name and insist that one of their children have their own name. In the case of a split-up, if there are two children, they should agree to take only one to live with them.

The children in turn would know from birth which adult they belonged to and would have no doubts about that adult leaving them or of having to live separately from that adult. Parents would have to learn to temper authority with love, and to moderate their emotional ties with day care, schools, and other adults. Everyone would have to learn to parent well, but with early training, shared experiences, and the guidance and services of professionals, parenting would not be difficult to learn and practice.

THE QUESTION OF THE CHILDREN NOW

Described above are three broad alternatives to the traditional pattern of child rearing—that is, to the sexual division of labor whereby most women have prime responsibility for the socialization of the children and are economically dependent on their husbands, and most men are responsible for the financial support of their wives and children. These alternatives were the training of selected men and women to be paid parents for large families, professional rearing of children in age-graded groups, and single parenting of one child.

Obviously, none of these alternative arrangements is likely to be adopted or imposed nationwide, nor are married couples likely to stop trying to develop more equalitarian sex roles within the traditional family pattern. Indeed, many of the problems and inequities of the current system could be eased considerably without drastic restructuring of family life on a large scale, but in order to do so we would need genuine national recognition that parenting is not an individual concern alone, but a governmental one too. Two measures which would demonstrate true national concern for children are tax-supported child allowances beyond meager standard tax deductions, and the development and staffing of expanded day-care centers, both free and private. Our present system of free public and paid private-school education would ideally be extended to service the "whole child," with day-long educational and recreational programs, overnight and weekend accommodations, nursing care during routine illness, and psychological help.

With such national support for children, adults could be freer to choose a compatible life-style. Child allowances and professional care-cum-education could be variously used by parents who favor bringing up many or a few children the traditional way, by working couples who want to share or minimize child-care duties, and by single parents.

That is, a system of child allowances could be used by full-time mothers to pay for their children's schooling and recreation. It could pay for more extended services to cover for working married or single parents whose children live at home, but must be looked after during the working day, and when parents have to go on trips. And it could also pay for the boarding of children with professional "parents" when they cannot be adequately cared for at home or need specialized help. For older children, child allowances could even be paid directly to those who want to live in children's "communes" under minimal adult supervision.

In sum, if both men and women are to be able to move away from traditional parenting arrangements, structural provision must be made for supplemental economic support of children and for complementary parental services. The result could be true sexual equality and greater individual choices in all areas of life without the sacrifice of the joys of parenting and the emotional security of children.

NOTES

1. An earlier version of this paper was presented at the Annual Meeting of Sociologists for Women in Society, New York, New York, August, 1973. I have benefited from the comments of so many people who heard or read this paper that I cannot thank each individually.

2. Low fertility rates (one to two children) are the norm in Eastern Europe, where the nonworking woman is a deviant, but where the governments have failed to provide nurseries (Fogarty *et al.* 1971, pp. 47–98).

3. Mitchell says, "The explosive possibilities of sexual freedom and the more lax attitudes to marriage which *could* undermine the family are made never to do so—at least for the woman, who is nearly always left holding the baby" (1971, p. 174, italics in the original).

REFERENCES

BERGER, THOMAS. *Regiment of women*. New York: Simon and Schuster, 1973.

BERNARD, JESSIE. *The future of marriage*. New York: World, 1972.

BETTELHEIM, BRUNO. *Children of the dream*. New York: Avon, 1969.

DAVIS, KINGSLEY, AND JUDITH BLAKE. Social structure and fertility: an analytic framework. *Economic Development and Cultural Change*, 1956, 4: 211–214.

DRABBLE, MARGARET. With all my love, (signed) mama. *New York Times*, August 4, 1973.

FIRESTONE, SHULAMITH. *The dialectic of sex*. New York: Bantam, 1971.

FOGARTY, MICHAEL. P., RHONA RAPOPORT, AND ROBERT N. RAPOPORT. *Sex, career, and family*. Beverley Hills, Calif.: Sage Publications, 1971.

FREIDSON, ELIOT. *Profession of medicine*. New York: Dodd, Mead, 1970a.

———. *Professional dominance*. New York: Atherton, 1970b.

GOLDSTEIN, JOSEPH, ANNA FREUD, AND ALBERT J. SOLNIT. *Beyond the best interests of the child*. New York: Free Press, 1973.

GREENFIELD, SIDNEY M. Love and marriage in modern America: a functional analysis. *Sociological Quarterly*, 1965, 6: 361–377.

HUXLEY, ALDOUS. *Brave new world*. New York: Harper, 1939.

KANTER, ROSABETH MOSS. *Commitment and community*. Cambridge: Harvard University Press, 1972.

KELLER, SUZANNE. Does the family have a future? *Journal of Comparative Family Studies*, 1971, 2: 1–14.

KLEIN, CAROLE. *The single-parent experience*. New York: Walker, 1973.

KOBRIN, FRANCES E. The American midwife controversy: a crisis of professionalization. *Bulletin of the History of Medicine*, 1966, **40**: 350–363.

LEGGATT, T. Teaching as a profession. In John A. Jackson (ed.), *Professions and professionalization*. Cambridge: Cambridge University Press, 1970, pp. 153–177.

LEVI-STRAUSS, CLAUDE. The family. In David A. Schultz and Robert A. Wilson (eds.), *Readings on the changing family*. Englewood Cliffs, N.J.: Prentice-Hall, 1973, pp. 20–40.

LORTIE, DAN C. The balance of control and autonomy in elementary school teaching. In Amitai Etzioni (ed.), *The semiprofessions and their organization*. New York: Free Press, 1969, pp. 1–53.

MEAD, MARGARET. Marriage in two steps. *Redbook Magazine*, July, 1966.

MITCHELL, JULIET. *Woman's estate*. New York: Vintage, 1971.

MURDOCK, GEORGE PETER. *Social structure*. New York: Free Press, 1965.

ROBERTS, STEVEN V. But why the epidemic? It could be as simple as "making do won't do." *New York Times*, January 5, 1974.

ROSSI, ALICE. Equality between the sexes: an immodest proposal. *Daedalus*, 1964, **93**: 607–652.

SKINNER, B. F. *Walden two*. New York: Macmillan, 1962.

————. *Beyond freedom and dignity*. New York: Knopf, 1971.

SIDEL, RUTH. *Women and child care in China*. New York: Hill and Wang, 1972.

SIMPSON, RICHARD L., AND IDA HARPER SIMPSON. Women and bureaucracy in the semiprofessions. In Amitai Etzioni (ed.), *The semiprofessions and their organization*. New York: Free Press, 1969, pp. 196–265.

SUSSMAN, MARVIN (ed.). *Nontraditional family forms in the 1970s*. Minneapolis: National Council on Family Relations, 1972.

ZABLOCKI, BENJAMIN. *The joyful community*. Baltimore: Penguin, 1971.